PSYCHOLOGY OF EMOTIONS, MOTIVATIONS AND ACTIONS

BIO-PSYCHO-SOCIAL PERSPECTIVES ON INTERPERSONAL VIOLENCE

PSYCHOLOGY OF EMOTIONS, MOTIVATIONS AND ACTIONS

Psychology of Aggression
James P. Morgan (Editor)
2004. ISBN 1-59454-136-1

New Research on the Psychology of Fear
Paul L. Gower (Editor)
2005. ISBN: 1-59454-334-8

Impulsivity: Causes, Control and Disorders
George H. Lassiter (Editor)
2009. ISBN: 978-60741-951-8

Handbook of Stress: Causes, Effects and Control
Pascal Heidenreich and Isidor Prüter (Editors)
2009. ISBN: 978-1-60741-858-0

Handbook of Aggressive Behavior Research
Caitriona Quin and Scott Tawse (Editors)
2009. ISBN: 978-1-60741-583-1

Handbook of Aggressive Behavior Research
Caitriona Quin and Scott Tawse (Editors)
2009. ISBN: 978-1-61668-572-0 (E-book)

The Psychology of Pessimism
Daniel X. Choi; Ravi B. DeSilva and John R. T. Monson
2010. ISBN: 978-1-60876-802-8

Psychological Well-Being
Ingrid E. Wells (Editor)
2010. ISBN: 978-1-61668-180-7

Psychological Well-Being
Ingrid E. Wells (Editor)
2010. ISBN: 978-1-61668-804-2 (E-book)

Psychology of Denial
Sofia K. Ogden and Ashley D. Biebers (Editors)
2010. ISBN: 978-1-61668-094-7

Psychology of Neuroticism and Shame
Raymond G. Jackson (Editor)
2010. ISBN: 978-1-60876-870-7

Psychology of Hate
Carol T. Lockhardt (Editor)
2010. ISBN: 978-1-61668-050-3

Bio-Psycho-Social Perspectives on Interpersonal Violence
Martha Frías-Armenta and Victor Corral-Verdigp (Editors)
2010. ISBN: 978-1-61668-159-3

Psychology of Risk Perception
Joana G. Lavino and Rasmus B. Neumann (Editors)
2010. ISBN: 978-1-60876-960-5

Psychology of Persuasion
Janos Csapó and Andor Magyar (Editors)
2010. ISBN: 978-1-60876-590-4

Psychology of Happiness
Anna Mäkinen and Paul Hájek (Editors)
2010. ISBN: 978-1-60876-555-3

Personal Strivings as a Predictor of Emotional Intelligence
Ferenc Margitics and Zsuzsa Pauwlik
2010. ISBN: 978-1-60876-620-8

Psychology of Thinking
David A. Contreras (Editor)
2010. ISBN: 978-1-61668-934-6

Psychology of Thinking
David A. Contreras (Editor)
2010. ISBN: 978-1-61728-029-0 (E-book)

Psychology of Expectations
Pablo León and Nino Tamez (Editors)
2010. ISBN: 978-1-60876-832-5

**Cognitive and Neuroscientific Aspects of Human Love:
A Guide for Marriage and Couples Counseling**
Wiiliam A. Lambos and William G. Emener
2010. ISBN: 978-1-61668-281-1

Psychology of Intuition
Bartoli Ruelas and Vanessa Briseño (Editors)
2010. ISBN: 978-1-60876-899-8

**Extraverted and Energized:
Review and Tests of Stress Moderation and Mediation**
Dave Korotkov
2010. ISBN: 978-1-61668-325-2

**Extraverted and Energized:
Review and Tests of Stress Moderation and Mediation**
Dave Korotkov
2010. ISBN: 978-1-61668-703-8 (E-book)

**Emotion's Effects on Attention and Memory:
Relevance to Posttraumatic Stress Disorder**
Katherine Mickley Steinmetz and Elizabeth Kensinger
2010. ISBN: 978-1-61668-239-2

**Emotion's Effects on Attention and Memory:
Relevance to Posttraumatic Stress Disorder**
Katherine Mickley Steinmetz and Elizabeth Kensinger
2010. ISBN: 978-1-61668-532-4 (E-book)

**Friendships: Types, Cultural,
Psychological and Social Aspects**
Joan C. Tolle (Editor)
2010. ISBN: 978-1-61668-008-4

**Friendships: Types, Cultural,
Psychological and Social Aspects**
Joan C. Toller (Editor)
2010. ISBN: 978-1-61668-386-3 (E-book)

Reputation and the Evolution of Generous Behavior
Pat Barclay
2010. ISBN: 978-1-61668-153-1

Reputation and the Evolution of Generous Behavior
Pat Barclay
2010. ISBN: 978-1-61668-402-0 (E-book)

Smoking as a Risk Factor for Suicide
Maurizio Pompili
2010. ISBN: 978-1-61668-507-2

Smoking as a Risk Factor for Suicide
Maurizio Pompili
2010. ISBN: 978-1-61668-817-2 (E-book)

Creativity: Fostering, Measuring and Contexts
Alessandra M. Corrigan (Editor)
2010. ISBN: 978-1-61668-807-3

Creativity: Fostering, Measuring and Contexts
Alessandra M. Corrigan (Editor)
2010. ISBN: 978-1-61728-067-2 (E-book)

Personality Traits: Classifications, Effects and Changes
John Paul Villanueva (Editor)
2010. ISBN: 978-1-61668-619-2

PSYCHOLOGY OF EMOTIONS, MOTIVATIONS AND ACTIONS

BIO-PSYCHO-SOCIAL PERSPECTIVES ON INTERPERSONAL VIOLENCE

MARTHA FRÍAS-ARMENTA
AND
VICTOR CORRAL-VERDUGO
EDITORS

Nova Science Publishers, Inc.
New York

Copyright © 2010 by Nova Science Publishers, Inc.

All rights reserved. No part of this book may be reproduced, stored in a retrieval system or transmitted in any form or by any means: electronic, electrostatic, magnetic, tape, mechanical photocopying, recording or otherwise without the written permission of the Publisher.

For permission to use material from this book please contact us:
Telephone 631-231-7269; Fax 631-231-8175
Web Site: http://www.novapublishers.com

NOTICE TO THE READER

The Publisher has taken reasonable care in the preparation of this book, but makes no expressed or implied warranty of any kind and assumes no responsibility for any errors or omissions. No liability is assumed for incidental or consequential damages in connection with or arising out of information contained in this book. The Publisher shall not be liable for any special, consequential, or exemplary damages resulting, in whole or in part, from the readers' use of, or reliance upon, this material.

Independent verification should be sought for any data, advice or recommendations contained in this book. In addition, no responsibility is assumed by the publisher for any injury and/or damage to persons or property arising from any methods, products, instructions, ideas or otherwise contained in this publication.

This publication is designed to provide accurate and authoritative information with regard to the subject matter covered herein. It is sold with the clear understanding that the Publisher is not engaged in rendering legal or any other professional services. If legal or any other expert assistance is required, the services of a competent person should be sought. FROM A DECLARATION OF PARTICIPANTS JOINTLY ADOPTED BY A COMMITTEE OF THE AMERICAN BAR ASSOCIATION AND A COMMITTEE OF PUBLISHERS.

LIBRARY OF CONGRESS CATALOGING-IN-PUBLICATION DATA

Library of Congress Cataloging-in-Publication Data

Bio-psycho-social perspectives on interpersonal violence / editors, Martha
Frias-Armenta and Victor Corral-Verdigp.
   p. cm.
 Includes index.
 ISBN 978-1-61668-159-3 (hardcover)
 1. Violence--Psychological aspects. 2. Violence--Social aspects. I.
Frmas Armenta, Martha. II. Corral-Verdigp, Victor.
 BF575.A3B566 2010
 303.6--dc22
                         2010001158

Published by Nova Science Publishers, Inc. ✚ *New York*

CONTENTS

Preface		xi
Part One: Aquaintance and Stranger Violence. A) Personal Variables		1
Chapter 1	Aggression, Risk-Taking, and Alternative Life History Strategies: The Behavioral Ecology of Social Deviance *Aurelio José Figueredo and W. Jake Jacobs*	3
Chapter 2	Executive Functions, Attention and Juvenile Delinquency *Martha Frías-Armenta, Pablo Valdez-Ramírez, Guadalupe Nava-Cruz, Aurelio J. Figueredo and Victor Corral-Verdugo*	29
Chapter 3	A Study of Personality Traits in Undergraduates: Alexithymia and Its Relationship to the Psychopathic Deviate *José Moral de la Rubia*	51
Chapter 4	Self-Control, Self-Regulation, and Juvenile Delinquency *Martha Frías-Armenta, Jorge Borrani, Pablo Valdez, Hugo Tirado and Xochitl Ortiz Jiménez*	79
Chapter 5	Child Maltreatment, Self Regulation, and Parenting *José Concepción Gaxiola Romero and Martha Frías Armenta*	101
Part One B): Contextual Variables		123
Chapter 6	Environmental Factors in Housing Habitability as Determinants of Family Violence *Victor Corral-Verdugo, Martha Frías-Armenta and Daniel González-Lomelí*	125
Chapter 7	The Role of Family Communication and School Adjustment in Adolescents' Violent Behavior *María Elena Villarreal-González, Juan Carlos Sánchez-Sosa and Gonzalo Musitu-Ochoa*	143

Chapter 8	Violent Offenders: A Qualitative Study of Murderous Violence in Venezuela *Alejandro Moreno*	167
Part Two:	**Institutional Violence**	191
Chapter 9	Environmental and Personal Variables Predicting School Bullying: A Study with Mexican Adolescents *Victor Corral Verdugo, Blanca Fraijo-Sing, Martha Frías-Armenta and César Tapia–Fonllem*	193
Chapter 10	Violence in Prison: Institutional Constraints and Inmate's Agressiveness *Rui Abrunhosa Gonçalves*	217
Chapter 11	Media Effects on Antisocial Behavior in Children and Adolescents *Pablo Espinosa and Miguel Clemente*	233
Chapter 12	Witnesses to Bullying: Voices for Prevention and Intervention in Schools *Marcela López, María José Aguilar and Josefina Rubiales*	259
Part Three:	**Interventions, Methods and Evaluation in Interpersonal Violence**	279
Chapter 13	Methods in Psychology & Law and Criminological Research. The Assessment of Interventions for Prevention of Crime *Eugenio De Gregorio*	281
Chapter 14	The Impact of the PPS-VCJ on Attitudes and Behavior of Juveniles Placed in Centers as a Result of Judicial Measures *Ana M. Martín, Cristina Ruiz, Estefanía Hernández-Fernaud, José Luis Arregui and Bernardo Hernández*	311
Chapter 15	Juvenile Offenders' Recidivism in Spain: A Quantitative Revision *Juan García-García, Elena Ortega-Campos and Leticia de la Fuente-Sánchez*	333
Index		355

PREFACE

Nowadays, violence is one of the most important problems faced by humanity. Millions are victims of interpersonal and collective aggression, whose impacts on people's lives are devastating, and the topic is one of the most challenging and sensitive to address in most nations of the world. Violence is defined by the World Health Organization as "The intentional use of physical force or power, threatened or actual, against oneself, another person or against a group or community that either results in or has a high likelihood of resulting in injury, death, psychological harm, maldevelopment or deprivation." It includes a broad range of manifestations: psychological harm, deprivation and maldevelopment, among others (Krug, Dahlberg, Mercy, Zwi, and Lozano, 2002). Violence is also defined as any act carried out with the intention to physically hurt another person (Straus & Gelles, 1999).

The World Health Organization (2002) characterizes violence in three types: self-directed, interpersonal and collective. Self-directed violence is divided into suicidal and self-abuse. Interpersonal violence, in turn, includes family & intimate partner and community violence. Collective violence is classified as social, political and economic.

In particular, *interpersonal violence* –aggression against another individuals, including partners, family and community members- causes thousands of deaths, and results in enormous personal, social and economic costs. In addition, interpersonal violence seems to be at the base of the most collective manifestations of social violence.

The argument of this book is that interpersonal violence can be prevented and its impact reduced; the study of its causes could help to reach this objective. Once that its factors are identified they could be changed through effective interventions. The purpose of the present volume is to analyze interpersonal violence from an international, multi-thematic and theoretically-diverse perspective. An international team of scholars offers theoretical explanations and research results related to this insidious manifestation of aggressive behavior. They also discuss the effectiveness of interventional programs and their evaluations. The text includes a wide range of topics on interpersonal violence, unveiling its multi-factorial nature. The resulting explanatory models involve situational and personal variables explaining this instance of violence, including the analysis of complex relations among those factors. Neuropsychological variables, for instance, are studied as risk factors for antisocial behavior; authors in this book show that delay in neuropsychological development makes juveniles more vulnerable and prone to criminal acts. Impulsivity and lack of self-control are also related to criminal behavior, according to more classical theories of crime. In turn, evolutionary psychology authors explain violence as produced by a strategy for survival, or for genes reproduction. Moreover, environmental psychology researchers show that environmental settings contain conditions for violence, such as housing habitability characteristics, which result in family violence. In addition, school's social and physical disorganization could promote bullying. Mass media exposition is another risk factor for interpersonal violence that is analyzed in this text. Violence in prison is also studied: inmates have to deal with different risk factors; one related to the pain resulting for imprisonment and another caused by interpersonal interactions with authorities and peers; a discussion of possible interventions to reduce such consequences is conducted. Community intervention is one of the most effective treatments for juvenile delinquency; one of such programs is presented and discussed. Last but not least, the book analyzes methodological issues related to criminological research, including program evaluation approaches and a meta-analysis of factors explaining and predicting redicivism in juvenile delinquents. Since interpersonal violence is a complex problem that needs a multi dimensional perspective this book concludes that methods approaching it have to offer a global perspective in terms of theories, research designs, measures, and evaluations.

The book contains three main sections. Part one deals with acquaintance and stranger violence and is divided in a sub-section A, addressing personal variables, and a sub-section B, discussing contextual factors. Part two is about institutional violence, which includes interpersonal violence occurring at schools and prisons and the effects of the media on violent behavior. Finally, part three presents interventions, methods and evaluations utilized in the field of interpersonal violence.

In chapter 1, Figueredo and Jacobs propose a *strategic* model of social deviance in considering that interpersonal aggression implies an overall adaptive strategy for survival and reproduction that may have an attendant effect of producing collateral harm to others. By departing from an evolutionary psychology perspective, the authors discuss the impact that an enhanced executive functioning might play in social functioning as well as the fundamental role of rule governance in social deviance, as mediated by executive functions.

In chapter 2, Frías-Armenta, Valdez, Nava, Figueredo and Corral-Verdugo elucidate whether juvenile delinquents have poorer executive functioning in inhibition, flexibility, and attention, than control adolescents. They administered a series of measures assessing these neuropsychological variables to three groups of juveniles. Their findings revealed some differences between institutionalized adolescents and a control group as well as significant differences in inhibitory tasks between juveniles with serious and statutory offenses. The authors conclude that minors' inability to respond adequately to the social environment is at least partially a result from neuropsychological impairment.

Moral de la Rubia, in chapter 3, analyzes the relation between alexithymia and psychopathy deviation in young people, trying to clarify the role that depression plays in this association. He also investigates gender differences in alexithymia and psychopathy deviation. The study's findings made the author conclude that alexithymia and psychopathic deviation are two different concepts, weakly related, and mediated by depression. These findings also suggest that males tend, more than females, to psychopathic deviation and to an externally oriented thinking.

Chapter 4, written by Frías-Armenta, Borrani, Valdez, Tirado and Ortiz tests a model of self-control and self-regulation, as predictors of antisocial behavior, with juvenile delinquents internalized in an institution and adolescents from the general community in a Mexican city. They found that all the participants in their study reported some kind of antisocial behavior. They also found that, both self-regulation and self-control produced a negative influence on antisocial behavior and conclude that lack of self-control is an important factor in the prediction of deviate behavior.

In chapter 5, Gaxiola-Romero and Frías-Armenta try to identify the protective function of social support and the effects of dispositional resilience and self-regulatory skills on the intergenerational transmission of child abuse in Mexican mothers. The authors tested a model whose results confirm a negative relation between lack of self-regulation and resilience, so that the lower the mother's self-regulation the lower her resilience. They also found that mothers' history of child abuse was positively related to a negative parenting style.

Corral-Verdugo, Frías-Armenta and González-Lomelí, in chapter 6, address the importance of the physical design and functionality of households (housing habitability) in explaining family violence. Their study shows that negative habitability conditions (poor illumination, lack of privacy, lack of depth, noise, and extreme temperatures) significantly and positively affect child abuse and interpartner violence. The authors discuss their findings in terms of the need of paying attention to the physical housing design as a promoter of family positive functioning.

Chapter 7, written by Villarreal-González, Sánchez-Sosa and Musitu-Ochoa elaborate on the role of family communication and school adjustment in the prevention of adolescents' violent behavior. Their study analyzed the relation between familial (functioning, communication), school (academic expectations and performance) and social (integration and participation) factors and adolescents' violent behavior mediated by social self-esteem and psychological disorders (depressive symptomatology and perceived stress). The authors found an indirect effect of familial, school and community variables on adolescents' violent behavior mediated through social self-esteem and psychological disorder.

In turn, Moreno, in chapter 8, after reviewing quantitative aspects of interpersonal violence in Venezuela, studies in depth the qualitative dimension of this phenomenon, approaching violent individuals' motivations. Once he rules out easy causal interpretations, and detects the well founded personal/social origins of that violence, the author suggests some possible corrective interventions. He also explains the role played by the Catholic Church and a number of private institutions in facing such a problem; as well as the attitudes of several organizations, which contrast with the government response that, according to the author, seems not to be taking care of their citizens at all.

In chapter 9, Corral-Verdugo, Fraijo-Sing, Frías-Armenta and Tapia-Fonllem attempt to elucidate some of the factors that predict bullying at Mexican schools. According to results of the empirical study they present, the context of abuse had a direct effect on children's perception of bullying, action taken and time of abuse, and these variables produced a direct effect on bullying. The authors discuss the effect of context on bullying and also the reactions of teachers. Their data reveal that some places, school time and actions taken by teachers could create or facilitate opportunities for bullying.

Gonçalves, in chapter 10, illustrates two different instances of violence within prisons. One is performed by the institution and is directly linked with the pains of imprisonment, while the other relates to the interactions that prisoners establish with the institution, staff and among themselves. The authors describe some common prison stressors, their effects on inmates, and their ability to cope with them. Then, he describes the violent (physical, sexual, psychological, economical and social) interactions that occur between inmates. Finally, the author addresses prison-staff problems and how they affect the relationship with prisoners and the institutional climate.

Espinoza and Clemente, in chapter 11, review current research on the topic of the effects of media on antisocial and aggressive behaviour, which has focused on how media violence effects on arousal, affect, cognition and behavior. According to this review, the effects of media violence relate to the development, over-learning and reinforcement of aggression-related knowledge structures, including hostile attribution bias, aggressive actions against others, expectations of violence, positive attitudes towards violence, the belief that violence is acceptable and appropriate to solve problems, and desensitization.

Chapter 12 was written by López, Aguilar and Rubiales. It describes the bullying situation in an Argentinian Junior–Senior High School, exploring its impact and manifestations. The authors were aimed at assessing the attitude shown by bystanders towards bullying, hypothesising that witnesses' attitude favors the bullying situation, and therefore does not benefit their report and intervention. They constructed, validated and administered an instrument to students whose results confirm the stated hypothesis and allow the analysis of possible reasons preventing the report and intervention of the witnesses.

In chapter 13, de Gregorio analyzes themes of research in psychology & law and criminology that deal with evaluation of interventions for the prevention of crime. The author describes classical methodological themes, as well as historical phases, epistemological issues and debates between quantitative and qualitative approaches. He addresses the basic assumptions for evaluation research and provides examples of effective projects. He finally reviews criteria and indicators to consider in evaluating the effectiveness of interventions.

Martín, Ruiz, Hernández-Fernaud, Arreguín and Hernández, in chapter 14, analyze the impact of services provided by an educational tutorial program on the attitudes and behaviors of juveniles interned at treatment centers as a result of judicial measures. The program focused on basic education, work skills training, training in cross-curricular contents and the implementation of the Spanish short version for juveniles of the R&R program The authors found that all or most sessions of the program resulted in changes in participants' attitudes and behaviors. The staff in charge of delivering the PPS-VCJ was satisfied with the experience; however, they also identified several difficulties that might be solved if larger numbers of juveniles received all sessions in the program.

Finally, García-García, Ortega-Campos and la Fuente-Sánchez, in chapter 15 present a meta-analysis of variables explaining and predicting recidivism in juvenile offenders. They used a collection of studies conducted in Spain on juvenile offender recidivism. The bibliographic search selected a total of 22 papers including 26 independent studies which data from 22,484 adolescents. The most mentioned factors found in the analysis included demographic variables, family factors, use of substances, child abuse, and relation with dissocial peer-groups among others.

This book was edited as a result of a sabbatical year spent at the Autonomous University of Nuevo Leon, Mexico during 2008-2009. The support we received from this institution and from our own -The University of Sonora- is greatly acknowledged. The Mexican Council of Science and Technology (CONACyT) funded a project on juvenile delinquency, which resulted in some of the chapters of this book. We wish to express our gratitude to these three wonderful institutions. Most importantly, we recognize and appreciate the important contribution of this book's authors. We hope the readers will find the contents of this text interesting and –especially- useful, as we did.

Martha Frías-Armenta, Víctor Corral-Verdugo

PART ONE:
AQUAINTANCE AND STRANGER VIOLENCE

A) PERSONAL VARIABLES

Chapter 1

AGGRESSION, RISK-TAKING, AND ALTERNATIVE LIFE HISTORY STRATEGIES: THE BEHAVIORAL ECOLOGY OF SOCIAL DEVIANCE

Aurelio José Figueredo and W. Jake Jacobs
Ethology and Evolutionary Psychology, University of Arizona

ABSTRACT

We consider the major characteristics of what has been called *social deviance*, particularly in relation to aggressive behavior that may occasion harm to other members of society, and how social deviance and aggression relate to critical individual differences in reproductive life history strategy. We conclude that social deviance is not as pathological as traditionally supposed and propose a *strategic*, rather than *hydraulic*, model of aggressive motivation. We start by considering the role of intraspecific aggression within an overall adaptive strategy of survival and reproduction that may have an attendant effect of producing collateral harm to others, and then proceed to a theoretical analysis of risk-taking behavior as potentially producing harm to the self in certain environments. We then develop an integrative theory by which life history evolution will connect these two conceptualizations of social deviance into a unified framework involving the behavioral ecology of risk-taking behavior and the strategic implications of synchronies and asynchronies of the costs and benefits of risk-taking in relation to life history strategy. Central to this framework is the evidently enhanced executive functioning of slow life history strategists, and more specifically, a superior capacity for rule governance - the control of behavior through verbal statements rather than through the direct experience of specific environmental contingencies. Executive functions include abilities to plan, inhibit or delay responding, initiate behavior, and shift between activities flexibly. These abilities all involve rule governance, which permits individuals to respond adaptively in a variety of different contexts without requiring previous experience with every possible set of circumstances. The fundamental role of rule governance in social deviance, as mediated by executive functions, is discussed. Finally, we consider the implications of this unified framework for the evolution and development of convergent interests (*mutualistic*) and divergent interests (*antagonistic*) social strategies, which constitute the fundamental cognitive schemata underlying social deviance.

The Concept of Social Deviance

The distinction between normal and abnormal behaviors, or *social deviance*, has been debated as far back as the critique by Benedict (1934):

> Each of these traits, in proportion as it reinforces the chosen behavior patterns of that culture, is for that culture normal. Those individuals to whom it is congenial, either congenitally or as the result of childhood sets, are accorded prestige in that culture and are not visited with the social contempt or disapproval which their traits would call down upon them in a society that was differently organized. On the other hand, those individuals whose characteristics are not congenial to the selected type of human behavior in that community are the deviants, no matter how valued their personality traits may be in a contrasted civilization....

In the spirit of Cultural Relativism that prevailed within Boasian Cultural Anthropology, Benedict viewed deviance as relative to the prevailing social norms, and insisted that the concept of social deviance not be used in a pejorative manner.

Modern Evolutionary Psychology takes a similar view in understanding deviant social behavior. In this case, it is not only the general cultural environment to be considered, but the various alternative life history strategies available within any given society that must be considered. The adaptive value of any given trait, viewed as a behavioral *tactic*, must be considered in the light of the overall, presumably adaptive, reproductive *strategy* in which it is embedded. Recognizing the existence of alternative life history strategies is thus essential to an understanding of what traditional social science refers to as social deviance.

In the present chapter, we will consider the major characteristics of what has been called social deviance, particularly in relation to aggressive behavior that may occasion harm to other members of society, and how they relate to critical individual differences in reproductive life history strategy that might not be as pathological as traditionally supposed. We start with a consideration of the role of intraspecific aggression within an overall adaptive strategy of survival and reproduction that may have the incidental effect of producing collateral harm to others and then proceed with a theoretical analysis of risk-taking behavior as potentially producing harm to the self in certain environments. Afterwards, we will develop an integrative theory by which life history evolution will connect these two conceptualizations of social deviance into a unified framework.

The Hydraulic and Strategic Models of Aggressive Motivation

Historically, there have been two major classes of conceptual model for aggressive motivation in the behavioral sciences. These two classes of conceptual model can be distinguished by their implicit or explicit utilization of either *hydraulic* or *strategic* metaphors. Although the choice of figurative imagery does not fully specify any of the various models that have been proposed, that rhetorical choice either constrains *a priori* or delimits *a posteriori* certain important parameters of these models. Thus, the metaphors that we adopt may either shape our thinking from the outset, or be found instead to be well-suited to ideas that conform to their general pattern, albeit after the fact. We therefore consider it productive to explore the heuristic value of examining the defining parameters of these two powerful metaphors and what they call tell us about the commonalities among our theories of aggression.

Hydraulic models are often referred to as "energy" models. The figurative use of the concept of motivational (or in some cases "psychic") energy, however, has been criticized as confusing the question when the literal physical energies of neural transmission and physiological metabolism are so often also intimately involved in the discussion (*cf.,* Hinde, 1960). Furthermore, it can also be observed, without any *ad hominem* maliciousness, that the dynamics of actual physical energy were not particularly familiar to most "energy" theorists. This can be discerned from the fact that numerous descriptions (*cf.,* Lorenz, 1966; Freud 2000) of the variously directed "flows" of these "energies" usually fell back upon overtly hydraulic metaphors, such as "damming", "channeling", and "flooding", revealing what was probably the fundamental source (dare we say "wellspring"?) of mental imagery, as it was with the explicitly humoral theories of the late antiquity. Strategic models, on the other hand, have not been known historically by any other common name. Modern "optimality" models all represent strategic models, but not all strategic models presume any strict optimality. Paradoxically, the underlying military metaphor is also rarely used overtly, even in the study of aggression.

Among the better-known hydraulic models are the psychodynamic theories of Freud (1915), the ethological theories of Lorenz (1957) and Tinbergen (1951), to some extent, the drive-reduction theories of Hull (1943) and Spence (1956), and the highly influential Frustration-Aggression Hypothesis, rooted in Psychoanalytic thinking, adapted by the learning theorists (e.g., Dollard *et al.*, 1939), and developed by the Social Psychologists. A common feature of these models is that the motivational energy or excitation is presumed to be essentially endogenous, coming from *within* the organism. External stimuli or conditions serve only to facilitate ("trigger", "discharge", "release", "dissipate"), inhibit ("repress", "suppress", "block"), or redirect ("sublimate", "displace", "channel") the object of this motivational energy. The outpouring of some discrete quantity of this phlogiston-like fluid is regulated by various intrapsychic plumbing fixtures and waterworks ("cathexes", "anticathexes", "releasing mechanisms", "inhibitory potentials"), whether innate or acquired through experience. The following excerpt perhaps best captures the spirit of this general idea (Lorenz, 1957, pp. 289-290):

> All these behavior patterns respond more readily if they have not been released for some time. The threshold value of releasing stimuli decreases during quiescence. Moreover, an instinctive movement that is not "used" over a long period literally becomes a "motive." It causes motor unrest in the organism as a whole, and induces it to search actively for the releasing stimulus situation... "Something" is accumulated (generated) rhythmically and continually, and used up by the consummation of an instinctive act...

The more traditional metaphor of the external *stimulus*, which figuratively "goads" an otherwise inert organism into reaction, is therefore superseded by that of the "releaser", which unlocks an accumulated store of pent-up energy within. Thus, not only is the behavioral organization of a fixed action pattern biologically prepared, but its motivational impetus is also fundamentally endogenous. The external environment merely occasions its performance.

One is reminded of the scenario in the movie, *Sudden Impact*, in which Homicide Detective "Dirty" Harry Callahan, armed with a .44 Magnum revolver, warns the last survivor of a gang of fleeing suspects, "Go ahead: make my day!" The implication is that minimal provocation might be required to release a fully prepared pattern of violent behavior which would only incidentally be "caused" by the suspect's resistance. It afterwards comes as no surprise that this fictional detective invariably finds ample opportunities to discharge his favorite firearm in the course of going about his normal business. It is clearly only a matter of adequate opportunity. Furthermore, if Lorenz were correct about "vacuum activity", he might eventually fire his weapon for no external reason whatsoever if sufficiently deprived of reasonable provocation.

Similarly, the Frustration-Aggression hypothesis, originally anchored in Freudian theory and advanced through learning theory by Dollard *et al.* (1939), originally relied on the notion of a "released" internal energy. Freud, apparently borrowing ideas from Newton's Third Law, argued that a portion of the chemical energy ingested by an individual transduces into "psychic energy," which builds up over time – and must be released in some form. Any impediment to an important goal triggers a release of this energy as an internal state – arousal – which the individual experiences as frustration.[1] Arousal, in its raw form, incites the individual to aggress directly against the impediment(s). If direct aggression is not possible, then the individual *displaces* aggression overtly or covertly onto other persons, organisms, or objects. The release of overt or covert aggression decreases the arousal state driving it – hence reinforcing the associated activity.[2]

The Frustration-Aggression hypothesis treats all forms aggression as equivalent. In so doing, the hypothesis strongly predicts that aggression in *any form* will decrease all other forms of aggression (Dollard, Doob, Miller, Mowrer, & Sears, 1939). Moreover, the hypothesis suggests that, once discharged, it will take time for the "psychic energy" to rebuild.[3] During that time, this view predicts a "latency period" during which impediments to a goal will not trigger frustration or aggression, a time in which the same impediments will partially trigger frustration and aggression, and a time still later in which the impediment will fully trigger frustration and aggression. Although most modern versions of the hypothesis do not predict "vacuum activity", this hydraulic "psychic energy" model provides predictions quite similar to those provided by Konrad Lorenz and by the *Dirty Harry* movies. Unfortunately, the data have been unkind to these predictions.

In contrast, strategic models represent aggression as purely *instrumental*, not as an inevitable conflict looking for a place to happen. As in international diplomacy, the use of force is seen as a potential means to a specified end. Indeed, it is one tool among many, and typically *not* the instrument of choice. The reason for this strategic restraint in the use of force is generally not presumed to be altruism towards the victim, but the inevitable fact that aggressive action usually entails a certain nontrivial cost and/or risk to the perpetrator. Thus, most strategic models of aggression implicitly predict the minimization of either cost or risk in the instrumental use of violence. Thus, the initiation, graded escalation, and eventual

---

[1] More formally, frustration occurs when "an interference with the occurrence of an instigated goal-response at its proper time in the behavior sequence [occurs]" p. 7.

[2] Currently, most who accept the Frustration-Aggression hypothesis do not accept the idea that frustration leads inevitably to aggression; in contrast, many accept the idea that aggression requires some form of frustration to drive it.

[3] Hence the fully discredited notion of "catharsis"

termination of aggressive action is expected to be closely monitored and controlled by the perpetrator with respect to the attainment of pre-specified objectives. Whereas the organism is expected in hydraulic models to avail itself of any opportunity to discharge as much of its repressed hostility as possible (unless otherwise inhibited), excessive force is construed in strategic models as not only unnecessarily destructive to the victims (who might themselves be of some future instrumental utility), but inefficient, wasteful, and downright imprudent for the perpetrator.

The motivational and cognitive learning theories of Tolman (1925), and the functional and stochastic perceptual theories of Brunswik (1952, 1955), although not designed specifically as models for aggression, are historical examples of strategic models. Virtually all optimality theories in modern sociobiology and behavioral ecology are overtly strategic in both inspiration and in character (*cf.*, Alcock, 1989). Indeed, it could be suggested that whereas the properties of hydraulic models reflects an industrial-era emphasis on the rational management and engineering of unruly natural impulses by distant organizational hierarchies, those of strategic models reflect the postindustrial or information-era emphasis on precise command, control, and communications by integrated cybernetic networks (*cf.*, Haraway, 1991). Thus, the postmodern focus is more on the *method* than the *madness*. The angry and volatile image of "Dirty Harry" as an emotional powder keg is superseded by the cold and calculating figure of *The Terminator* and his precise mission parameters.

Exploring the extensions of these rival metaphors reveals some of the basic operating characteristics that have been most widely thought to be the underlying mechanisms of aggression. A case in point is the varying interpretation of the nature of aggressive inhibition, disinhibition, and escalation. For example, hydraulic models tell us that a normal individual spontaneously generates and accumulates a store of aggressive "action-specific energy", and that only the presence of either innate or acquired inhibitions prevent the expression of dangerously violent behavior. Hydraulic models also require the presence of metaphorical safety valves for "letting off some steam" by releasing controlled amounts of aggressive energy in harmless but vigorous alternative pursuits. The relaxing of normal inhibitions to achieve this controlled prophylactic release is thus an inherently dangerous affair ("do not try this at home!") that may require the supervision of a trained mental health professional. Many social interventions, for example, seek to redirect aggressive energy into friendly neighborhood games of basketball that might have otherwise gone into brutal gang violence. Unfortunately, increasing the general basketball proficiency of inner city youths has so far seemed to have no appreciable impact upon the rate of violent crime. Furthermore, hydraulic models also require some mechanism for converting physical energy into "psychic" or "psycho-hydraulic" energy, which has never been adequately specified and which has never been found.

For example, what was formerly among the most popular theories of the effects of alcohol on aggressive behavior, and now called the *alcohol disinhibition fallacy*, was implicitly based on the assumptions of the hydraulic model. In this theory, alcohol produced spontaneous expressions of violent behavior by disabling the natural inhibitions which normally keep aggression suppressed. No other explanation for the outburst of violence was presumably needed other than that the normal restraints had been artificially lifted. The proverbial floodgates had been opened; the inebriated little Dutch boy had pulled his finger from the dyke. Although a plausible hypothesis, under the assumptions of the hydraulic model, the evidence has not been kind to this theory.

There are other, more sophisticated, versions of the alcohol disinhibition hypothesis that can be made within the framework of a strategic model of aggression. Within the context of strategic models, inhibition need not function to completely suppress or abolish aggressive behavior, but rather to modulate it adaptively with respect to the attainment of the presumed ultimate behavioral objectives (Brunswik's *distal achievements*). This strategic inhibition of aggression can work through any or all of various complementary mechanisms: (1) the processing of internal cues related to the control of physiological arousal for the optimal expenditure of biophysical energy (*real* energy, measurable in calories), (2) the processing of external cues relating to the achievement of behavioral objectives, and (3) the processing of external cues relating to the monitoring of either the costs or risks of the aggressive action. The strategic expectation is that perceptual cues to such factors as excessive physiological arousal, the early achievement of behavioral objectives, or the incursion of excessive cost or risk will be inhibitory to either continued or escalated aggression (*cf.*, Steele & Southwick, 1985; Bushman & Cooper, 1990). Alcohol use can clearly interfere with any or all of these cognitive inhibitory functions. For example, alcohol's interference with normal inhibitory functions has been shown to generalize well from antisocial to prosocial behaviors (Steele, Critchlow, & Liu, 1985), but not to nonsocial behaviors (Hull & Bond, 1986).

Indeed, the second mechanism also leaves a place for traditional ethological interpretations of the aggressive inhibition produced by the species-typical ritualized gestures of submission produced by the victim that often signals the achievement of social objectives to the perpetrator. This mechanism may be of particular importance in alcohol's facilitation of domestic violence against women or children, where the perpetrators and the victims are so often physically mismatched. Thus, failure to process cues for early social submission may commonly lead to the counterstrategic use of excessive physical force. In addition, the failure to process cues to the malicious or neutral intent of ones' potential adversary may also interfere with strategic modulation of instrumental aggression (Zeichner & Pihl, 1980). There is also evidence that alcohol use impairs the perpetrator's judgment of the consequences of his actions (Zeichner & Pihl, 1979). This would clearly interfere with the operation of the third mechanism in the monitoring and management of costs and risks. Thus, this third mechanism may also function in alcohol's facilitation of sexual violence, a behavior which is known to be extremely sensitive to risk and social costs in normal men. It would also interfere with the perpetrator's perception of strategically relevant information, such as the possible criminal and legal implications of his domestic violence as well as the direct and indirect damage, both physical and psychological, done to what may be his own biological offspring (*cf.*, Figueredo & McCloskey, 1993).

Thus, the alcohol disinhibition hypothesis becomes both plausible and empirically defensible if applied to the expected mechanisms of *strategic* inhibition rather than to their traditional hydraulic counterparts. The predictions of alcohol disinhibition theory under the strategic model of aggression, however, are very different. Alcohol use would not be expected to produce spontaneous aggression where no preexisting conflict was in evidence. Alcohol use would instead be expected to produce maladaptive and strategically counterproductive escalations of aggressive action where the behavioral objectives had already been achieved or where excessive risks or costs had been incurred. Thus, it matters very much what metaphors we use in our conceptions of aggression when we uncritically accept their implications in our extensions of the alternative theories for the hypothetic-deductive generation of the divergent model predictions required for strong inference (Platt, 1964).

We adopt the strategic model as the more tractable model for cross-disciplinary knowledge integration based on evolutionary psychological principles. This is because it is manifestly more plausible to predict the probable influence of the emergent forces at ascending levels of biological and social organization upon the strategic options and contingencies available to the behaving individual than upon some metaphorical hydraulic mechanism that is presumably completely internal to the organism. The integration of our knowledge must therefore focus on how any hypothesized causal influence at any level of organization ultimately impinges on the potential use of violence by the individual as a viable strategic option.

The heuristic use of the strategic model does not require a quixotic view of the individual as that of a rational decision-maker. Instead, it leads us to explore personological (individual difference) characteristics that might significantly impair or warp rational choice, such as cognitive distortions or deficits. Indeed, it leads us to explore individual characteristics that might impair not just the planful formulation, but the very execution of optimal strategies. Furthermore, the strategic model leads us to realize that "rational" (adaptive) choices may not be the same for everyone, but might instead be significantly moderated by personological characteristics that differentially suit individuals to exploiting the potentials of particular strategies. Thus, different options might present different Gibsonian *affordances* to different individuals, depending on the varying characteristics of those individuals. This means that identical circumstances might present different affordances to different individuals. On the other hand, the strategic model does not necessarily reduce aggression to an individual trait or pathology. The environment in which an individual is operating produces the material contingencies that codetermine the relative efficacies of the different adaptive strategies available, including aggressive ones. For example, it is possible that certain familial, social, economic, or political structures create environments that generally favor the strategic use of violence, regardless of individual variation. On the other hand, it is also possible that certain environments differentially impact the viability of the strategic options available to different individuals within them according to each individual's disproportionate prior possession of strategically relevant characteristics. Thus, the strategic model formulates the problem of aggression as the product of a complex person-situation interaction.

THE BEHAVIORAL ECOLOGY OF RISK

Behavioral ecology and Economics define risk mathematically as increased variance in outcomes. Outcomes may be distributed symmetrically about a mean. Hence it may be adaptive, under certain circumstances, to take so-defined risks. With a mean expected outcome or *payoff* of zero, there is no a priori theoretical reason to avoid taking such risks consistently because there is no consistently expected *loss* associated with outcomes.

Not all risks are symmetrically distributed about the mean, however, with an equal likelihood of better and worse outcomes. Many risks are skewed systematically toward negative outcomes, with few positive possibilities to recommend them. Social science normally labels these "risky" behaviors, more properly "risk-taking" behaviors, deeming these behaviors ill advised. Risk taking behaviors, defined this way, have the statistical expectation of producing on the average, a net loss rather than a net gain.

The standard social sciences generally do not distinguish between risk-taking behaviors that increase the outcome variance and those that reduce the outcome mean. This places undue emphasis upon *costs* and ignores expected *benefits* of risk-taking, whether real or perceived. By conflating variable payoffs and expected losses, social science becomes insensitive to potential motivations behind risk-taking. Standard social sciences thereby typically treat risk-taking as pathological and in need of preventive interventions.

Prospect Theory (Kahneman & Tversky, 1979), a descriptive theory based on the choices that most people actually make under conditions of uncertainty, is a proximate-level theory of the behavioral mechanisms that people actually exhibit, rather than an ultimate-level theory of the real-world functionality or "rationality" of these responses. Most individuals from normative samples exhibit a pattern called loss aversion, which is a psychological overvaluing of the cost of losses as compared to the benefit of gains. Traditional social science reflects this general attitude regarding the relative merits of risk-taking. Non-normative samples of socially deviant individuals may or may not deviate from this general pattern. The obvious prediction from evolutionary thinking, contrary to the seemingly normative consensus, is that, for some individuals under certain specific circumstances, it is contingently adaptive to take these risks.

Although a distinction between proximate and ultimate causation is by now well-known, there are related terminological ambiguities that produce added conceptual difficulties. In the *proximate* terminology of behavioral psychology, for example, the "stimulus" usually consists of peripheral sensory input to the organism, just as the "response" usually consists of peripheral motor output from the organism. In the *ultimate* terminology of behavioral ecology, however, the environment to which the organism adapts usually consists of objective features external to the organism and presumably independent of its subjective experience. For example, there may be substantial differences between the hedonic (pain/pleasure) and the fitness (cost/benefit) outcomes of any given behavior. Thus, the psychological use of "stimulus" and "response" terminology interchangeably for proximal and distal as well as subjective and objective referents creates difficulties in the description of behavioral evolution.

Probabilistic Functionalism (Brunswik, 1952, 1955), a meta-theoretical framework from ecological psychology, clearly distinguishes between: (a) the proximal stimulation received by an organism and the distal state of the environment that ultimately produces it; and (b) the proximal reaction or response produced by an organism and the distal achievement that the proximal reaction, in turn, ultimately produces in the environment. For that reason, proximal "stimuli" are often referred to as *cues* (to external states) and proximal "responses" as *means* (to external ends). This distinction acknowledges that an array of multiple proximal *cues* emanate from any given distal event, as well as an array of multiple proximal *means* that can converge upon any given distal outcome. Although the cues or means within each such array may be functionally intersubstitutable, they may differ appreciably in either their *veridicality* as indicators or their *instrumentality* as effectors. In short, the veridicality and instrumentality of cues and means may be organized hierarchically.

We can quantify these hierarchical relations using differential *ecological validities* and *functional utilizations*. The *ecological validity* of any given *cue* is the degree of association between a sensed proximal stimulus (a cue) and actual physical characteristics of the distal environmental event independent of the utilization of that cue by the organism. The *functional utilization* of any given *cue* is the relation between a proximal stimulus received and degree of utilization by the organism of that cue as an indicator of the specified distal event independent of the objective state of the environment. The *ecological validity* of any given *means* is the relation between a proximal response and the distal achievement presumably produced in the environment, independent of utilization of that means by the organism. The *functional utilization* of any given *means* is the relation between a proximal response effected and its use by the organism as an effector of the specified distal achievement, independent of the causal efficacy of that means on the environment.

Thus, Brunswikian ecological psychology distinguishes the economic concept of "risk" as an objective contingency of the external environment from the psychological concept of "risk-taking" propensity as a measure of an organism's tendency to interact with environmental contingencies. The ecological validity of a specific "risk" *contingency* can tell us, in terms of fitness costs, benefits, and the trade-offs among them, if and to what degree a specific risk-taking behavior might be adaptive; the functional utilization of a specific "risk-taking" *behavior* can tell us the organism's propensity to engage in that behavior under specified environmental conditions.

From this perspective, the measure of behavioral adaptation is the match between functional utilization and ecological validity. Presumably, behavioral evolution, by means of genetic preparedness, and behavioral development, by means of epigenetic plasticity and flexibility determine the degree of match between functional utilization and ecological validity (Figueredo, Hammond, & McKiernan, 2006). Furthermore, Probabilistic Functionalism describes these relations as *stochastic*, making that framework useful for the study of risk and risk-taking. This view also acknowledges that any discrepancies that might exist among the extant environment and the environment in which the behavior evolved and developed would produce varying degrees of mismatch between ecological validity and functional utilization.

THE RELATIVE TIMING OF EXPECTED COSTS AND BENEFITS

The fact that the costs and the benefits of a certain risk-taking behaviors may be displaced in time is another factor that influences a scientific perspective on risk-taking. Specifically, some behaviors produce *short-term gains* but *long-term losses,* a condition sometimes labeled a *contingency trap*. Social sciences generally tend to regard long-term thinking and planning as desirable and short-term thinking and planning as undesirable. In contrast, behavioral ecologists and economists tend to regard discounting future losses in favor of more immediate gains, under certain circumstances, as adaptive. Similar to an invariable preference for risk-averse behavior, discounting the benefits of immediate gains in contrast to a dread of future losses is normative position taken by the social sciences.

A contingency trap is a special case of mismatch between the timing of expected gains and losses. The four possible synchronies and asynchronies between costs and benefits can be cross-tabulated, as shown in Table 1. This cross-tabulation shows how the relative timing of costs and benefits can be *synchronous*, as when either short-term costs are exchanged for short-term benefits or long-term costs are exchanged for long-term benefits, or *asynchronous*, as when either short-term costs are exchanged for long-term benefits or long-term costs are exchanged for short-term benefits.

Table 1. Synchronies and Asynchronies in Costs and Benefits of Risk-Taking

		Cost	
		Short-Term	Long-Term
Benefit	Short-Term	Synchronous	Asynchronous
	Long-Term	Asynchronous	Synchronous

The contingency table indicates that the relative adaptive values of short- and long-term costs and benefits determine the objective adaptiveness of risk-taking in any given context, or the *ecological validity* of the risk-taking behavior relative to maximizing net fitness payoffs. It is clear, however, that relative hedonic values subjectively assigned by any given individual to short- and long-term costs and benefits may determine that individual's actual risk-taking behavior within any given context, or the *functional utilization* of that risk-taking behavior by that individual in the context. Furthermore, the table suggests that, although mismatch between validity and utilization may occur, one cannot always assume the risk-taking behavior to be maladaptive, even in the case of asynchronous timeframes of costs and benefits. Under some circumstances, discounting future losses in favor of more immediate gains is the more adaptive strategy; conversely, under other circumstances, discounting immediate gains in favor of future losses is more adaptive strategy. Hence, presuming that one or the other set of relative valuations is inherently or universally superior to the other is unwise.

This view is neutral toward risk taking behavior, neither advocating nor condemning it. The stance permits us to view the etiology and maintenance of risk-taking behavior dispassionately, permitting an examination of both the negative consequences and positive incentives that might underlie risk-taking behavior. Such a view permits a comprehensive look at the entire *natural history* of risk-taking behavior within a socio-ecological context.

A NATURAL HISTORY OF RISK-TAKING

A risk-taking propensity does not appear to be domain-specific, but instead generalizes across many different areas of life (Donovan & Jessor, 1985). Moreover, risk-taking behaviors, and the physical and social consequences often associated with them, rarely occur in isolation but instead tend to cluster – that is, occur non-randomly among socioecological contexts and correlate strongly with situations that a Western culture characterizes as *stressful*. For example, father-absence during early childhood and stressful home circumstances such as dysfunctional parental relationships and low socioeconomic status correlate strongly. Father-absence and the associated stressful home circumstances and subsequent offspring risk-taking behaviors such as sexual precociousness, poor parenting behavior, poor academic performance, suicide attempts, and violent offending also strongly correlate. An entire cluster of high-risk sexual behaviors in teens includes sexual intercourse before the age of 15, sexual intercourse six or more times in the past six months, rarely or never using birth control, multiple sexual partners, friends in gangs, criminal behavior, and alcohol and/or illicit substance abuse. In turn, both experiencing teen pregnancy and causing it (by impregnating others) and stressful offspring life outcomes such as contracting sexually transmitted diseases, developing mood and anxiety disorders, experiencing young motherhood or fatherhood, dropping out of high school, chronic unemployment or underemployment, low socioeconomic status, welfare dependence, and the intergenerational transmission of poverty strongly correlate. In short, it is difficult to make a clear distinction between the risk-taking behaviors themselves and the environmental circumstances in which they are imbedded. This is perhaps because the risk-taking behaviors in question tend to reproduce these same circumstances (such as father-absence) in the next generation.

Our data indicate that these social and ecological contexts, the clusters of behaviors and outcomes associated with them, serve as proxies for a single latent multivariate construct (Figueredo *et al.*, 2006). If these contexts, behaviors, and outcomes reflect a single latent multivariate construct, then changing a specific, or even a set of behavioral strategies within the cluster, without changing the contexts in which they occur, will be ineffective.

Traditional social science theories have not provided adequate causal explanations for the existence of these clusters, and they have not provided either pure or applied guidance for those who wish to address these problems systematically. For that guidance, we turn to evolutionary biology.

INTRODUCTION TO LIFE HISTORY THEORY

Life History Theory (LHT) is a mid-level theory that describes the strategic allocation of bioenergetic and material resources between two major components of fitness, Somatic Effort, which anchors one end of the first dimension of this trade-off, and Reproductive Effort which anchors the second dimension of this trade-off. *Somatic Effort* refers to resources devoted to survival of the individual organism; *Reproductive Effort* refers to resources devoted to production of new organisms as vehicles devoted to perpetuation of the individual's genes. The major Reproductive Effort dimension is further partitioned into two major components, Mating Effort and Parental/Nepotistic Effort. *Mating Effort* anchors one end of a dimension measuring resources devoted to acquiring and retaining sexual partners; whereas *Parental/Nepotistic Effort* refers to resources devoted to enhancing the survival of existing offspring and other genetic relatives. Thus, a life-history strategy allocates an individual's bioenergetic and material resources among the competing demands of survival and reproduction.

LHT provides a unique perspective on both the environmental and behavioral contexts in which high-risk behaviors may occur. The fast-slow (r-K) continuum represents a covarying range of reproductive behavioral strategies inversely relating life-history traits such as fecundity and parenting. LHT predicts that, all else being equal, species living in harsh (high-risk of mortality), unpredictable, and uncontrollable environments evolve clusters of "fast" life history traits – traits associated with fast reproductive rates – nominal parental investment, and relatively brief inter-generation times. In contrast, species living in predictable, stable, and relatively safe and controllable environmental conditions evolve clusters of "slow" life history traits associated with slow reproductive rates, extensive parental investment, and extended inter-generational times. Hence, the fast-strategist is a short-term planner, taking benefits opportunistically with little regard for long-term consequences. In contrast, the slow-strategist is a long-term planner, delaying immediate gratification in the service of future eventualities.

This theoretical framework also provides a unique perspective on *why* clusters of risk-taking behavior tend to occur under stressful environmental circumstances. *Unpredictable* events are especially stressful by virtue of interfering with the organism's ability to solve adaptive problem such as avoiding or escaping future aversive events. The relation between behavior and outcome defines an *uncontrollable*: Whether an organism responds or not in any particular way is irrelevant to the likelihood of the outcome. Although an event can be predictable without being controllable, controllable events are predictable by definition. Controllability can thus be seen as a special case of predictability, and an unpredictable environment is therefore also uncontrollable. It is an axiom of LHT that unpredictable and uncontrollable environments favor the evolution of "fast" life-history strategies. Therefore, under those circumstances, what traditional social sciences consider "risk" or "risk-taking" behaviors might actually be adaptive, in terms of both accepting a higher variance in outcomes and discounting potential future losses. It is important to recognize that, in purely Darwinian terms, a "slow" strategy is neither superior nor inferior to a "fast" one: superiority depends on the ecology in which the organism is situated.

LIFE HISTORY, SOCIAL DEVIANCE, AND RISK-TAKING

Figueredo *et al.* (2006) described an integrated theory of individual differences that traces the behavioral development of life history from genes to brain to reproductive strategy, providing evidence that a single common factor, the K-Factor, underpins a variety of life-history parameters, including an assortment of sexual, reproductive, parental, familial, and social behaviors. A wide array of cognitive and behavioral psychometric indicators is associated with this factor, including traits at the individual, familial, and societal levels. In addition, Figueredo and collaborators developed multivariate measurement models of the common factor underlying social deviance (d), which includes delinquency, substance abuse, sexual promiscuity, self-destructive risk-taking behaviors, impulsive behaviors, Machiavellianism, and Psychopathy.

Using well-established neuropsychological tests sensitive to self-control, which governs the domain of impulsiveness versus delay of gratification, we are examining the prediction that certain mental abilities (e.g., executive functions) underpinning self control are essential to a slow life history strategy, but may inhibit social deviance. Specifically, we predict an incompatibility between a slow life-history strategy and social deviance and, if the requisite mental abilities are present, a slow life history strategy will suppress social deviance. Thus, a slow life history may serve as a protective factor against the development of social deviance and associated risk-taking behaviors. Conversely, we predict compatibility between a fast life history strategy and social deviance. In this case, a fast life history strategy serves as a permissive factor, especially if the executive functions underpinning self-control are not fully developed. In this view, a combination of a *behavioral preferences* (fast or slow life history strategy) and a set of *mental abilities* (associated with self-control or lack thereof) adaptively modulate the development of an entire cluster of high-risk behavioral strategies within the broader construct of social deviance.

LHT proposes that the root cause of individual variation in behavior lies in the harshness and unpredictability of the physical and social environments, which favor the development of fast life-history strategies (Ellis *et al.*, in press). This perspective implies that the developmental causes of social deviance, although biologically prepared, are not immutable. It also implies that addressing any single high-risk behavior in isolation, independent of the clusters within which they occur or to the exclusion of other aspects of these clusters is, by definition, inadequate; instead, one needs to address the social and behavioral contexts in which risk behaviors occur. Furthermore, one needs to identify the causal mechanisms of *proximate* mediation that translate these *ultimate* or functional evolutionary causes (e.g., life history strategy) into high-risk behavior.

THE K-FACTOR AND MENTAL ABILITIES

Does a slow life history entail a *behavioral preference* or a *mental ability*? For example, personality is generally deemed to be a set of behavioral preferences, whereas intelligence is generally deemed to be a set of mental abilities. Could a "slow" life history entail both? Why would systematic preferences evolve without the supporting abilities to implement them?

Sefcek, Miller, and Figueredo (2005; Sefcek, 2007) found that a "slow" life history, as indicated by the Arizona Life History Battery, measuring the K-Factor and General Intelligence, as measured by APM-18 (a short form of the Ravens Advanced Progressive Matrices), the Shipley Vocabulary and Abstractions Tests, the Mill-Hill Multiple Choice Sets A and B, and Scholastic Aptitude Tests do not correlate taken individually or in a multivariate composite. MacDonald, Figueredo, Wenner, and Howrigan (2007; Figueredo, MacDonald, Wenner, & Howrigan, 2007) replicated this negative result in an independent sample and found that K and higher Executive Functions, as measured by Dysexecutive Questionnaire, (Malloy & Grace, 2005), the Brief Rating Inventory of Executive Function A (Gioia, Isquith, Retzkaff & Espy, 2002),, and the Executive Function Questionnaire correlate significantly (Wenner, Jacobs, & Nagaran, 2007). Wenner, Figueredo, Rushton, & Jacobs (2007) more recently replicated both the correlation of K with higher Executive Functions and the lack of significant correlation of K with General Intelligence. In addition, Wenner and collaborators found that higher Executive Functions and Social Deviance (d), as measured by a set of behavioral self-report scales, including the D-20 Delinquency Short Form, the LEQ-R (adapted from Zuckerman), and the DAST measure of substance abuse correlate negatively.

Consistent with this finding, Gladden, Sisco, and Figueredo (2008; Gladden, Sisco, & Figueredo, 2007) found that several of these same convergent indicators of a "slow" life history strategy correlated negatively and significantly with an extensive inventory of self-reported sexually coercive behaviors, as well as with the Primary and Secondary Psychopathy Scales (Levenson, Kiehl, & Fitzpatrick, 1995), the Short-Form Machiavellianism Scale (Christie & Geis, 1970), and the Buss-Perry Aggression Questionnaire (Buss & Perry, 1992). Furthermore, Andrzejczak, Jones, Smith, Montero, & Figueredo (2007) found that various convergent indicators of a "slow" life history and a short-form measure of Emotional Intelligence correlate significantly (adapted from Andrade, Navarro, & Yock, 1999).

Primary and Secondary Psychopathy have been associated with deficits in emotional and cognitive empathy (Heym & Lawrence, 2007), respectively, which tie these findings to Emotional and Social Intelligence. Furthermore, a general Social Deviance factor, including measures of lack of positive peer influence, antisocial behavior, deficits in self-control, impulsivity, lack of future orientation, and risk-taking, correlate with systematic deficits in performance-based measures of Executive Functions, including elements of the Wisconsin Card Sort and a Modified Stroop Test (Frías-Armenta et al., 2005; Figueredo et al., 2005). Current research is underway to determine if a "slow" life history strategy and performance on the University of Magdeburg Social Intelligence Test (SIM) (Süß, Weis, & Seidel, 2005; Weis & Süß, 2007), a performance-based measure of Social Intelligence correlate positively.

Thus far, these preliminary data suggest that Executive Functions are positively associated with a "slow" Life History (K) and negatively associated with Social Deviance. It is therefore reasonable to predict that Executive Function mediates the proximate-level neuropsychological link between life history strategies, social deviance, and "risk-taking". If either life-history strategy or social deviance entails a set of mental abilities and not just a set of correlated behavioral preferences, then the problem of Risk (both scientific and social) becomes considerably more difficult to address through proximate interventions.

RISK-TAKING AND EXECUTIVE FUNCTIONS

The constellations or clusters of deviant or antisocial behaviors we have described strongly resemble *pseudopsychopathy*, the unreliability, impulsive antisocial acts, sexual excesses, crude humor, disregard for social propriety, control of behavior by immediate environmental contingencies (immediate gratification), stereotypy, and impulsivity associated with orbital frontal brain damage (e.g., Harlow, 1848, 1868; Stuss & Benson, 1986). This cluster reflects the behavioral clusters that occur in individuals with a varying propensity toward risk taking. Under ordinary circumstances, a strong relation between measures of Executive Function and level of risk tolerance (or risk taking) exists.

Plain common sense, the independence of measures of *general intelligence (g)* and Executive Function, and clinical observations tell us that both g and Executive Function "protects" individuals at high risk of antisocial behavior. High intelligence diminishes the risk of criminal behavior (but not necessarily risky behavior) in men, independent of social status or education (Kandel et al., 1988; Lynam, Moffitt, & Stouthamer, 1993; White, Moffitt, & Silva 1989). Moreover, deficits in Executive Function predict teacher and parents reports of a child's level of self control (Beaver, Wright, & Delisi, 2007), pathological gambling (Kalechstein, Fong, Rosenthal, Davis, Vanyo & Newton, 2007), and systematic changes in risk taking as a function of aging (Deakin, Aitken, Robbins, & Sahakian, 2004). Conversely, offender groups demonstrate lower executive capacity than controls (Bergeron & Valliant, 2001); a single dose of methylphenidate normalizes the risk-taking behavior of both frontotemporal dementia patients and children diagnosed with ADHD (e.g., Fitzgerald & Demakis, 2007).

Hence, data anchored in a number of unique methods, designs, statistical approaches, and laboratories detect consistent relations among measures of life history strategy, specific Executive Functions, intact or damaged Frontal Cortices, and constellations of high-risk behavior, social deviance, and delinquency. Importantly, these life-history-related traits are statistically independent of measures of generalized intelligence and working memory.

Central to this framework is the evidently enhanced executive functioning of slow life history strategists, and more specifically, a superior capacity for rule governance. Executive functions include abilities to plan, inhibit or delay responding, initiate behavior, and shift between activities flexibly. These abilities all involve rule governance. Rule governance, the control of behavior through verbal statements rather than through the direct experience of specific environmental contingencies, permits individuals to respond adaptively in a variety of different contexts without requiring previous experience with every possible set of circumstances. The fundamental role of rule governance in social deviance, as mediated by executive functions, is discussed.

EXECUTIVE FUNCTION, RULE GOVERNANCE AND BEHAVIORAL REGULATION

As do the traditional social sciences, Western cultures value self-control. Our most cherished values, the control of aggression, risk taking, alternative life styles – social deviance in general – center on the ability of an individual to either suppress or purportedly channel such activities into personally and socially productive venues – that is, to lead autonomous and focused lives. The way in which individuals do this has been the focal point of a good deal of research activity since the 'decade of the brain' began. The emerging consensus is that a set of mental abilities, centered in the frontal lobes of the human brain, play a principal role in controlling the self and behavior. These abilities have, by consensus, taken the name *Executive Functions*.

Executive functions are "…the high-level cognitive processes that facilitate new ways of behaving, and optimize one's approach to unfamiliar circumstances" (Gilbert & Burgess, 2008, p. R110). According to theory, we engage these processes, which consist of processes known as inhibition, shifting, and updating (Miyake, Friedman, Emerson, Witzki, Howerter, & Wager, 2000)., when we make a plan for the future, switch from one behavioral tactic to another, or even when we resist temptation. Theories concerning executive function distinguish between *higher level* controlled processing and *lower level* automatic processing.

Controlled processing refers to mental operations that one brings to bear during encounters with unique environmental contingencies (i.e., adaptive problems) in which one cannot access clear or well-established behavioral activities to solve the problem - or during conflict situations – for example when one "realizes" that current behavioral tactics are not producing optimal outcomes. In short, controlled processing seems to occur during ambiguous, inconsistent, or non-routine situations. Automatic processing, in contrast, refers to habitual activities – activities that appear to center on procedural kinds of behaviors, riding a bicycle, using a knife to cut meat, sitting quietly while someone lectures. These well-rehearsed over-learned activities occur in familiar, unambiguous, non-conflicting, routine situations.

By most accounts, control of automatic processes interact primarily *top-down*. That is to say, we use our Executive Functions to modulate the lower-level automatic processes controlling behavior. These higher-level processes might lead us to attend only to particular parts of an environment and thereby behave consistently in the face of an apparently stereotyped ecological niche or to respond flexibly to relatively new environments – equipping us with the ability to adapt to the dynamics of that niche. Of course, the lower level automatic processes "talk to" the higher-level Executive Functions (bottom-up interactions) – but theoretically the major influence flows from the higher-level to the lower-level processes.

Norman and Shallice (1986; see also Duncan, 2001a, 2001b, and Miller & Cohen, 2001) suggested that experientially established schemas serve as the control mechanism for automatic behaviors. According to these authors, environmental stimuli *or* output from the Executive Systems – composed of the various Executive Functions may trigger these schemas. When environmental contingencies clearly specify the required activity, salient environmental events trigger the appropriate schema – which serves to guide the appropriate (automatic) behavior. When environmental contingencies do not clearly specify the required activity, Executive Functions such as planning (updating), inhibition, and shifting work in concert to active other possibly more relevant schema (some might say to shift the base-rate of various behavioral tactics), and then monitor the impact of the altered base-rate, eliminating what does not work and preserving what does.

All of this is good and well; humans appear to have acquired a way to use the Executive Functions to short-circuit the trial-and-error learning studied so extensively by the early behaviorists – the processes that other species seem to require to acquire habits. To examine that short circuit, we must turn to another literature – that of rule-governance.

We fell into this particular field of study when we read a remarkable study by Galizio (1979). He demonstrated that instructions (*rules*) could come to control behavior even in the face of contradictory environmental contingencies. He set up an operant situation, placed people on a schedule of reinforcement that produces a highly distinctive pattern of responding, told them they were on a different schedule – and observed that the behavior responded to the rule not to the actual environmental contingencies. These people behaved as if they were under the control of the contingency described by the rule rather than the actual extant environmental contingency. In so doing, the participants' behavior was both maladaptive and irrational.

Interpreted in our own unique way, we began to think that rules, as given by other human beings, are typically expressed – either explicitly or implicitly – as *if-then* statements. The *if* part of the statement typically specifies a behavioral strategy or behavioral tactic; the *then* part of the statement typically specifies an outcome of the strategy or tactic. We then noticed that the consequence (the *then* part of the statement) serves to alter the probability of the antecedent tactic (the *if* part of the statement) – that is, to change the base-rate of a particular class of behavior. This change in base-rate appeared to us to be one of the fundamental functions of the Executive System.

As we thought about this, we began to realize (all too slowly) that direct environmental contingencies do not control the majority of human activities; instead, rules control them – rules typically provided by other human beings. Compliance with those rules bypasses the need for direct trial-and-error learning (Doll, Brehm, Zucker, Deaver-Langevin, Griffin, & Hickman, 2000). As importantly, compliance with those rules lead to the control of aspects of behavior known as aggression, risk taking, alternative life styles – social deviance in general. With that, we began to ask, "Do Executive Functions govern rule governance?" In addition, we asked, "Will individual differences in the quality of Executive Functions relate directly, and by inference, influence what the field has come to know as *self control*?"

In short, to us it appears there is a reliable relationship between general self-control, as a function of rule governance, and an individual's level of Executive Function. The lower the level of Executive Function, the more directly the individual responds to immediate extant adaptive problems, environmental conditions, and behavioral outcomes – a general characteristic of the impulsive, short-time-horizoned fast LH strategies. The higher the level of Executive Function, the more the individual responds to long-term adaptive problems, environmental conditions, and behavioral outcomes – a general characteristic of the planful, long-time-horizoned slow LH strategist (Wenner, Figueredo, Rushton, & Jacobs, 2009).

This theoretical framework differs in subtle but important ways from Gottfredson's and Hirschi's (1990) General Theory of Crime (*GTC*), in which impulse control (or lack thereof) figures prominently in the etiology of social deviance. The *GTC* is essentially a hydraulic model, as described above, in which individuals are presumed to universally possess antisocial impulses which require inhibition, and it is differential inhibition between different individuals that causes individual differences in socially deviant behavior. In contrast, our conceptual framework is a strategic model, in which individuals might differ in both the nature and the degree of their impulsiveness as well as their ability to regulate their own behavior according to their life history strategy. The concept of rule governance provides a positive heuristic for behavioral self-regulation in addition to the negative one implied in traditional conceptions of impulse control.

CONVERGENT AND DIVERGENT INTEREST SOCIAL STRATEGIES

Traditional social science models of social deviance do not adequately distinguish between behavioral dispositions that tend to produce harm to the self and those that tend to produce harm to others. This is perhaps because those behaviors generally tend to be highly correlated with each other, for reasons that have not been made completely clear. "Risk-Taking" behaviors are generally deemed to produce harm to the self, although our theoretical analysis indicates that this may not either necessarily or universally be the case. "Antisocial" behaviors are generally deemed to produce harm to others, but whether they do or do not produce harm to the self is also open to question.

For example, Malamuth's (1996) *Confluence Model* describes a generalized disposition towards rape as being influenced by multiple specific pathways (hence the term, "Confluence"), but these pathways (roughly representing promiscuity and hostility) are ultimately driven by an even more generalized disposition towards relationships with members of the opposite sex. Malamuth suggests two general sexual strategies at opposite ends of a continuum: (1) a *convergent interest* sexual strategy; and (2) a *divergent interest* sexual strategy. Specifically, males following the convergent interest strategy see their reproductive interests and those of the female as mutually consistent, or *mutualistic*, and base their intersexual relationships on this perceived "common ground" of shared interests. In contrast, males following the divergent interest strategy see their reproductive interests and those of the female as mutually inconsistent, or *antagonistic*, and base their intersexual relationships on this perceived conflict of interests.

Malamuth (1998) suggests that the selection of these strategies during development might be biased by different life history (LH) strategies. He uses different terminology, but suggests that slow LH strategists are more prone to adopt convergent interest (mutualistic) sexual strategies and that fast LH strategists are more prone to adopt divergent (antagonistic) sexual interest strategies. This is evidently because convergent interest (mutualistic) strategies are more consistent with long-term sexual relationships and cooperative biparental care whereas divergent interest (antagonistic) strategies are clearly inconsistent with these long-term reproductive tactics.

In the proposed extension of this model beyond the sexual and into the general social domain, we further suggest that slow LH strategists are more prone to adopt otherwise equivalent convergent interest *social* strategies and that fast LH strategists are more prone to adopt otherwise equivalent divergent interest *social* strategies. Malamuth also suggests, although cautiously, that a generalized competitive or cooperative disposition may exist, but does not develop this idea much further.

Our own research on the K-Factor indicates that slow LH strategists are more likely to engage in reciprocally altruistic relationships with both kin and non-kin, as well as with both romantic (not just sexual) partners and with their offspring. Slow LH strategists clearly prefer long-term and cooperative *social* as well as *sexual* relationships, which are evidently easier and more profitable to maintain in their characteristically more stable, predictable, and controllable environments. Convergent evidence from game-theoretic analyses indicates that unstable or shorter-term (especially one-shot) social interactions are likely to lead to more "defection" (aka "cheating") than cooperation.

Our own research on the K-Factor has also characterizes LH strategies as associated with different attachment styles, with slow LH strategists having secure attachment styles and fast LH strategies having any of several insecure attachment styles (e.g., anxious or avoidant). Recall that Bowlby (1969) related these attachment styles with *internal working models* of self-other relationships, which have been extended to generalized sexual and social relationships, and not just parent-child bonds (e.g, Pietromonaco & Feldman-Barret, 2000). Recently, researchers (e.g., Tremblay & Dozois, 2009) described entire *early maladaptive schemas* that seem to reflect these different internal working models and are evidently influenced by the many of the same proposed developmental factors. Belsky, Steinberg, and Draper (1991) associated *insecure* attachment with a *mistrustful* internal working model and an *opportunistic* interpersonal orientation and associated *secure* attachment with a *trusting* internal working model and a *reciprocally-rewarding* interpersonal orientation. Ross and Hill (2002) have also associated insecure childhood attachment and a mistrustful internal working model to an *unpredictability schema* which they define as "a pervasive belief that people are unpredictable and the world is chaotic" (p. 458). They further associate the unpredictability schema to an external locus of control, helplessness, causal uncertainty, decreased interpersonal trust, decreased sense of coherence, decreased future orientation, and decreased delay of gratification, as well as increased impulsivity, increased sensation-seeking, and increased risk-taking behaviors, such early sexual activity, risky sexual behavior, adolescent pregnancy and childbearing.

LH theory does not regard these *social schemata*, if they may be called that, as particularly "maladaptive", but instead as contingently adaptive in different environments. Specifically, such schemata might be adaptive in the various environments where LH strategies evolve and develop. Furthermore, in evolutionary terms, these schemata might ultimately boil down to Malamuth's convergent and divergent interest strategies.

Moreover, it is unclear to what extent these "early" schemas are the environmentally-determined product of the specified developmental conditions and to what extent they are evolved and heritable strategies spuriously associated with those developmental conditions by gene-environment (G-E) correlations (presumably generated by the strategic dispositions of the parents, which may be genetically transmitted to the offspring). Hence, the social schema hypothesis is beset by the same nature/nurture confounds that afflict the much-disputed father-absence effect.

Either way, this general theory of convergent and divergent interest social strategies provides a highly parsimonious explanation for what our group consistently finds inverse relationships between slow LH strategy and socially conflictive attitudes and behaviors such as: (1) intrasexual competitiveness; (2) negative androcentrism; (3) negative ethnocentrism; (4) sexually coercive behaviors; and (5) intimate partner violence.

Furthermore, this general theory serves as an alternative hypothesis that is complementary to the idea that Executive Functions (EF), and specifically Behavioral Self-Regulation (aka "Impulse Control"), mediate the effects of slow LH strategies. The latter idea posits that fast LH strategists lack the requisite *mental abilities* to suppress socially deviant/nonconforming behaviors, which they might otherwise inhibit. The convergent and divergent interest social strategies theory instead posits that slow and fast LH strategists possess different *behavioral preferences* or general dispositions in social and sexual interactions, based on different social cognitive schemata. These two mechanisms are not mutually exclusive, because evolutionary thinking predicts that both traits should coevolve and reinforce each other, in spite of the fact they represent two theoretically distinct causal pathways.

A structural equations model developed by Wenner, Figueredo, Rushton, and Jacobs (2009) illustrates this combination of factors nicely, as displayed in Figure 1. In this model, the Slow LH (K) factor is measured by the Arizona Life History Battery; the General Mental Ability (g) factor is measured by the mean subscales of the Shipley IQ test; the Executive Functions (EF) factor is measured by the Dysexecutive Questionnaire, the Brief Rating Inventory of Executive Function A, and the Executive Function Questionnaire; the Psychopathic Attitudes factor is measured by the Lilienfeld Psychopathy Scales, the Risk-Taking Questionnaire, and Impulsive Behaviors; and the Socially Deviant Behaviors factor is measured by the Life Experiences Questionnaire - Revised, the D-20 Delinquency Short Form, and the Drug Abuse Screening Test. Within this model, both Slow LH and General Mental Ability contribute significantly and independently to Executive Functions; Executive Functions inhibit Psychopathic Attitudes; and Psychopathic Attitudes contribute positively to Deviant Behaviors, but Executive Functions and General Mental Ability both serve to partially inhibit these tendencies from being expressed in overt socially deviant behavior. The model fits quite well ($X^2(3) = 6.074^{ns}$, $CFI = .967$, $RMSEA = .077$) and all of the pathways are statistically significant ($p<.05$). Consistently with our other recent findings (e.g., Wenner, Figueredo, Rushton, & Jacobs, 2007), there was no significant correlation between slow LH and general mental ability, so no free correlation among the exogenous variables was either specified or required by the model.

This model illustrates how both slow LH and general mental ability ultimately drive some of the more specific mental abilities (Executive Functions) and behavioral preferences (Psychopathic Attitudes) that contribute to Social Deviance across a variety of intrasexual, intersexual, and general social situations entailing both potential harm to self and harm to others.

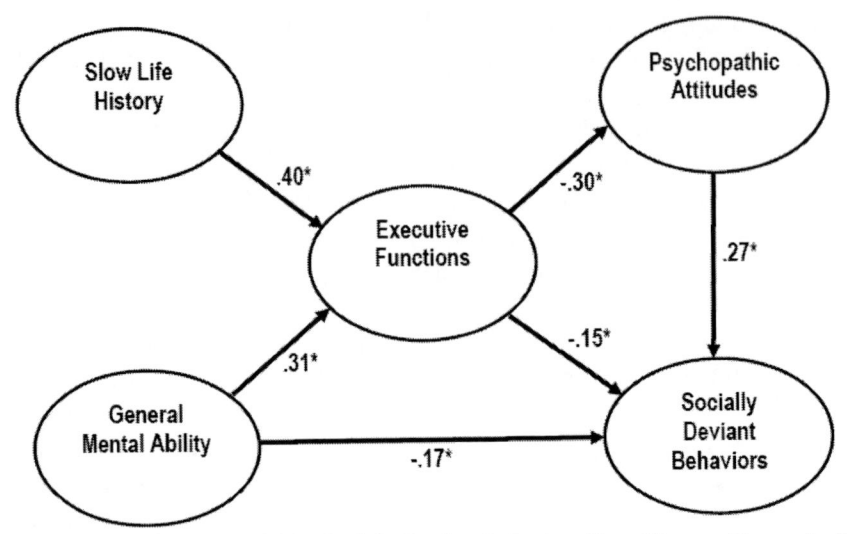

Figure 1. A Structural Equations Model for Socially Deviant Behaviors (from Wenner, Figueredo, Rushton, & Jacobs, 2009).

THE PROXIMATE AND ULTIMATE RELATIONS BETWEEN HARM TO SELF AND HARM TO OTHERS

These considerations help elucidate why behavioral dispositions that tend to produce harm to self and harm to others are normally conflated in the traditional social science conceptions of social deviance. Bluntly put, behavioral preferences (or dispositions) and the mental abilities (or deficiencies) that tend to produce harm to self are quite consistent with dispositions and abilities that tend to lead to harm to others.

Fast LH strategy is expected to be associated with a divergent interests (antagonistic) social strategy which tends to bring individuals into conflict with others. Fast LH strategy is also associated with apparent "deficits" in behavioral self-regulation (Executive Functions or Impulse Control) that facilitate the inhibition of aggressive impulses in situations of social conflict, where mutual strategic interference is occurring among individuals. Better self-regulation might facilitate non-aggressive and cooperative solutions to such social conflicts of interest, but these skills are evidently less well-developed in fast LH individuals, perhaps due to strategic disuse or neglect throughout development. Therefore, the combination of the characteristic behavioral preferences and suite of mental abilities of different LH strategies create both ultimate-level and proximate-level phenotypic (and perhaps even genetic) correlations between behaviors promoting harm to others and those seemingly promoting harm to self.

Objectively, divergent interests (antagonistic) social strategies are inherently riskier than convergent interests (mutualistic) social strategies due to the increased risk of intraspecific aggression (retaliation) they apparently occasion. Socially conflictive behaviors in response to real or perceived conflicts of interests with others reflect back upon the perpetrator in producing risk of harm to the self. Regardless of LH strategy, a target of aggression more than likely strikes back in response to the aggression. Furthermore, the same conditions of environmental harshness and unpredictability that foster the evolution and development of fast LH strategies (Ellis *et al.*, in press) also foster that of divergent interests (antagonistic) social strategies according to both early maladaptive schema theory (Tremblay & Dozois, 2009) and evolutionary socialization theory (Belsky, Steinberg, & Draper, 1991) and simultaneously foster that of greater risk-taking propensities according to unpredictability schema theory (Ross & Hill, 2002). Harm to others and potential harm to self are therefore intimately intertwined in multiple ways and at multiple levels that are difficult to disentangle in the real world.

CONCLUSIONS

The coordination of a coherent life history strategy involves a set of behavioral preferences *and* specific mental abilities. The logic of life history theory, anchored in principles of natural and sexual selection, specifies conditions under which these preferences and abilities will or will not interact. For example, impulse control is not relevant to social deviance unless one actually experiences deviant impulses that need control. Delay of gratification is not a problem if one has no long-term aspirations requiring short-term sacrifices. Risk-taking is not maladaptive if a short life-span obviates the possibility of long-term adverse consequences. What is maladaptive is a lack of coordination between preferences and abilities. Selection for life history strategies will produce *coadapted* behavioral preferences and mental abilities, internally consistent strategies that function together adequately. Our task, and that of the field, is to identify the critical preferences and abilities and to determine how they interact to coordinate a coherent life history strategy.

The main contribution of the present chapter has therefore not been to identify either high time preferences, reduced executive functions, or antagonistic and divergent interests social schemata as predictors of social deviance, because these various contributing factors had already been separately identified. Instead, the main contribution of the present chapter has been to bring them all together under the common rubric of reproductive life history strategy as the ultimate cause and adaptive explanation for their convergent and interdependent effects. This fundamental insight represents a necessary first step in constructing a behavioral ecology of social deviance.

REFERENCES

Alcock, J. (1989). *Animal behavior: An evolutionary approach (4th ed.).* Sunderland, MA, US: Sinauer Associates.

Andrade, X., Navarro, O., & Yock, I. (1999). *Construcción y validación de una prueba para medir inteligencia emocional.* Unpublished "Licenciatura" Thesis, School of Statistics, University of Costa Rica.

Andrzejczak, D.J., Jones, D.N., Smith, V., Montero, E., & Figueredo, A.J. (2007). Ethnocentrism and life history strategy. Paper. In Figueredo, A. J., (Chair), Correlates of life history strategy. Annual Meeting of the Human Behavior and Evolution Society, Williamsburg, Virginia.

Beaver, K. M., Wright, J. P., & Delisi, M. (2007). Self-Control as an executive function. *Criminal Justice and Behavior, 34*, 1345-1361

Belsky, J., Steinberg, L., & Draper, P. (1991). Childhood experience, interpersonal development, and reproductive strategy: An evolutionary theory of socialization. *Child Development, 62*, 647-670.

Benedict, R. (1934). Anthropology and the abnormal. *The Journal of General Psychology, X*, 59-80.

Bergeron, T. K., & Valliant, P. M. (2001). Executive function and personality in adolescent and adult offenders vs. non-offenders. *Journal of Offender Rehabilitation, 33(3)*, 27-45.

Bowlby, J. (1969). *Attachment and loss: Vol. 1. Attachment.* New York: Basic.

Brunswik, E. (1952). The conceptual framework of psychology. In *International encyclopedia of unified science (Vol. 1)*. Chicago: University of Chicago.

Brunswik, E. (1955). Representative design and probabilistic theory in a functional psychology. *Psychological Review, 2*, 193-217.

Bushman, B. J., & Cooper, H. M. (1990). Effects of alcohol on human aggression: An intergrative research review. *Psychological Bulletin, 107(3)*, 341-354.

Buss, A., & Perry, M. (1992). The aggression questionnaire. *Journal of Personality and Social Psychology, 63*, 452-459.

Christie, R. & Geis, F. (1970). *Studies in Machiavellianism.* New York: Academic Press.

Deakin, J., Aitken, M., Robbins, T., Sahakian, B. J. (2004). Risk taking during decision-making in normal volunteers changes with age. *Journal of the International Neuropsychological Society, 10(4)*, 590-598.

Doll, B., Brehm, K., Zucker, S., Deaver-Langevin, J., Griffin, J., Hickman, A. (2000). Contrasting procedures for empirical support of traditional and population-based mental health services. *Psychology in the Schools, 37(5)*, 431-442.

Dollard, J., Doob, L., Miller, N., Mowrer, O. H., & Sears, R. (1939). Frustration and aggression. New Haven: Yale University Press.

Donovan, J. E. & Jessor, R. (1985). Structure of problem behavior in adolescence and young adulthood. *Journal of Consulting and Clinical Psychology, 53*, 890-904.

Duncan, J. (2001a). An adaptive coding model of neural function in prefrontal cortex. *Nature Reviews Neuroscience, 2(11)*, 820-829.

Duncan, J. (2001b). Frontal lobe function and the control of visual attention. In J. Braun, C. Koch, & J. L. Davis, (Eds.),Visual attention and cortical circuits (pp. 69-88). Cambridge, MA: The MIT Press.

Ellis, B.J., Figueredo, A.J., Brumbach, B.H., & Schlomer, G.L. (2009). Mechanisms of environmental risk: The impact of harsh versus unpredictable environments on the evolution and development of life history strategies. Human Nature, 20, 204-268. [view pdf]

Figueredo, A. J., & McCloskey, L. A. (1993). Sex, money, and paternity: The evolutionary psychology of domestic violence. *Ethology and Sociobiology, 14*, 353-379.

Figueredo, A. J., Frías-Armenta, M., Valdez, P., Nava, M. G., Borrani, J., Contreras, M., Vega, B., & Ríos, D. (2005). Executive function and juvenile delinquency: Preliminary data. Paper. In Figueredo, A.J., (Chair), Life history strategy and mental abilities. Annual Meeting of the International Society for Intelligence Research, Albuquerque, New Mexico.

Figueredo, A. J., Hammond, K. R., & McKiernan, E. C. (2006). A Brunswikian evolutionary developmental theory of preparedness and plasticity. *Intelligence, 34(2)*, 211-227.

Figueredo, A. J., MacDonald, K. M., Wenner, C., & Howrigan, D. (2007). Executive functions, general intelligence, life history, and temperament. Paper. Annual Meeting of the International Society for Intelligence Research, Amsterdam, The Netherlands.

Figueredo, A. J., Vásquez, G., Brumbach, B. H., Schneider, S. M. R., Sefcek, J. A., Tal, I. R., Hill, D., Wenner, C. J., & Jacobs, W. J. (2006). Consilience and life history theory: From genes to brain to reproductive strategy. *Developmental Review, 26,* 243-275.

Fitzgerald, K., & Demakis, G. (2007). The neuropsychology of antisocial personality disorder. *Disease-a-Month, 53,* 177-183

Freud, S. (1915). Instincts and their Vicissitudes. In J. Strachey (Trans. & Gen. Ed.) in collaboration with A. Freud, assisted by A. Strachey & A. Tyson, *Standard Edition of the Complete Psychological Works of Sigmund Freud,* Vol. 14, 1957, pp. 111-140. London: Hogarth Press.

Freud, S. (2000). *The Standard Edition of the Complete Psychological Works of Sigmund Freud* (James Strachey, Ed.). Boston: W. W. Norton & Company.

Frías-Armenta, M., Valdez, P., Nava, M. G., Borrani, J., Figueredo, A. J., Contreras, M., Vega, B., & Ríos, D. (2005). *Funciones ejecutivas y delincuencia juvenil: datos preliminares.* In Frías-Armenta, M., & Corral-Verdugo, V., (Eds.), *Niñez, Adolescencia, y Problemas Sociales.* Mexico: CONACYT-UniSon. Pp. 267-278.

Galizio, M. (1979). Contingency-shaped and rule-governed behavior: Instructional control of human loss avoidance. *Journal of the Experimental Analysis of Behavior, 31(1),* 53-70.

Gilbert, S. J., & Burgess, P. W. (2008). Executive function. *Current Biology, 18(3),* R110-R114.

Gioia, G., Isquith, P., Retzkaff, P. D., & Espy, K. A. (2002). Confirmatory factor analysis of the Behavioral Rating Inventory of Executive Function [BRIEF] in a clinical sample. *Child Neuropsychology, 8,* 294-257.

Gladden, P.R., Sisco, M., & Figueredo, A.J., (2008). Sexual Coercion and Life History Strategy. *Evolution and Human Behavior,* 29, 319-326

Gladden, P. R., Sisco, M., & Figueredo, A. J. (2007). Life history strategy, competitive disadvantage, or by-product: A test of multiple evolutionary hypotheses of sexual coercion. Paper. In Figueredo, A. J., (Chair), Correlates of life history strategy. Annual Meeting of the Human Behavior and Evolution Society, Williamsburg, Virginia.

Gottfredson, M. R., & Hirschi, T. (1990). *A general theory of crime.* Stanford, CA: Stanford University Press.

Haraway, D. J. (1991). *Simians, Cyborgs, and Women: The Reinvention of Nature.* New York: Routledge.

Harlow, J. M. (1848). Passage of an iron rod through the head. *Boston Medical and Surgical Journal, 39,* 389-393. (Republished in *Journal of Neuropsychiatry and Clinical Neuroscience, 11,* 281-283)

Harlow, J. M. (1868). Recovery from a passage of an iron bar through the head. *Publications of the Massachusetts Medical Society, 2,* 327-347.

Heym, N., & Lawrence, C. (2007). The relationship between psychoticism, empathy and aggression. Paper. 13th Biennial Meeting of the International Society for the Study of Individual Differences, Giessen, Germany.

Hinde, R. A. (1960). Energy models of motivation. *Symp. Soc. exp. Biol., 14,* 199-213.

Hull, C. L. (1943). *Principles of Behavior: An Introduction to Behavior Theory.* Oxford, England: Appleton-Century.

Hull, J. G., & Bond, C. F. (1986). Social and behavioral consequences of alcohol consumption and expectancy: A meta-analysis. *Psychological Bulletin, 99(3),* 347-360.

Kahneman, D., & Tversky, A. (1979). Prospect theory: An analysis of decision under risk. *Econometrica,* XLVII (1979), 263-291.

Kalechstein, A. D., Fong, T., Rosenthal, R. J., Davis, A., Vanyo, H., & Newton, T. F. (2007). Pathological gamblers demonstrate frontal lobe impairment consistent with that of methamphetamine-dependent individuals. *Journal of Neuropsychiatry and Clinical Neuroscience, 19,* 298-303.

Kandel, E., Mednick, S. A., Kirkegaard-Sorensen, L., Hutchings, B., Knop, J., Rosenberg, R., Schulsinger, F. (1988). IQ as a protective factor for subjects at high risk for antisocial behavior. *Journal of Consulting and Clinical Psychology, 56(2),* 224-226.

Levenson, M. R., Kiehl, K. A., & Fitzpatrick, C. M. (1995). Assessing psychopathic attributes in a noninstitutionalized population. *Journal of Personality and Social Psychology*, 68, 151-158.

Lorenz, K. (1957). The nature of instinct. In Schiller C.H., (ed.), *Instinctive Behavior: The development of a Modern Concept.* New York, NY: International Universities Press.

Lorenz, K. (1966). *On Aggression.* London, UK: Methuen & Co.

Lynam, D., Moffitt, T. E., Stouthamer-Loeber, M. (1993). Explaining the relation between IQ and delinquency: Class, race, test motivation, school failure, or self-control? *Journal of Abnormal Psychology, 102(2),* 187-196.

MacDonald, K. M., Figueredo, A. J., & Wenner, C., & Howrigan, D. (2007). Life history strategy, executive functions, and personality. Paper. In Figueredo, A. J., (Chair), Correlates of life history strategy. Annual Meeting of the Human Behavior and Evolution Society, Williamsburg, Virginia.

Malamuth, N. M. (1996). The confluence model of sexual aggression: Feminist and evolutionary perspectives. In Buss, D. M., & Malamuth, N. M., (Eds.), *Sex, power, conflict: Evolutionary and feminist perspectives*, pp. 269-295. New York, NY: Oxford University Press.

Malamuth, N. M. (1998). The confluence model as an organizing framework for research on sexually aggressive men: Risk moderators, imagined aggression, and pornography consumption. In Geen, R. G., & Donnerstein, E., (Eds.) *Human aggression: Theories, research, and implications for social policy*, pp. 229-245. San Diego, CA: Academic Press.

Malloy, P., & Grace, J. (2005). A Review of rating scales for measuring behavior change due to frontal systems damage. *Cognitive and Behavioral Neurology, 18,* 18-27.

Miller, E. K., Cohen, J. D. (2001). An integrative theory of prefrontal cortex function. *Annual Review of Neuroscience, 24,* 167-202.

Miyake, A., Friedman, N. P., Emerson, M. J., Witzki, A. H., Howerter, A., & Wager, T. D. (2000). The unity and diversity of executive functions and their contributions to complex "frontal lobe" tasks: A latent variable analysis. *Cognitive Psychology, 41,* 49–100.

Norman, D. A., & Shallice, T. (1986). Attention to action: Willed and automatic control of behaviour. In R. Davidson, G. Schwartz, & D. Shapiro, (Eds.), *Consciousness and self regulation: Advances in research and theory, Vol. 4* (pp. 1–18). New York: Plenum.

Pietromonaco, P. R., & Barrett, L. F. (2000). The internal working models concept: What do we really know about the self in relation to others? *Review of General Psychology, 4(2)*, 155-175.

Platt, J. R. (1964). Strong Inference. *Science, 146(3642),* 347-353.

Ross, L. T., & Hill, E. M. (2002). Childhood unpredictability, schemas for unpredictability, and risk taking. *Social Behavior and Personality, 30,* 453–474.

Sefcek, J. A. (2007). *A life-history model of human fitness indicators.* Unpublished Doctoral Dissertation, University of Arizona.

Sefcek, J.A., Miller, G., & Figueredo, A. J. (2005). General intelligence, life-history, and covitality: A test of evolutionary hypotheses. Paper. In Figueredo, A. J., (Chair), Life history strategy and mental abilities. Annual Meeting of the International Society for Intelligence Research, Albuquerque, New Mexico.

Spence, K. W. (1956). *Behavior theory and conditioning.* New Haven, CT: Yale University Press.

Steele, C. M., & Southwick, L. (1985). Alcohol and social behavior: I. The psychology of drunken excess. *Journal of Personality and Social Psychology, 48(1),* 18-34.

Steele, C. M., Critchlow, B., & Liu, T. J. (1985). Alcohol and social behavior: II. The helpful drunkard. *Journal of Personality and Social Psychology, 48(1),* 35-46.

Stuss, D. T. & Benson, D. F. (1986). The frontal lobes. New York: Raven Press.

Süß, H.-M., Weis, S., & Seidel, K. (2005). Soziale Kompetenzen. In H. Weber & T. Rammsayer (Hrsg.), Handbuch der Persönlichkeitspsychologie und Differentiellen Psychologie (Handbuch der Psychologie). Göttingen: Hogrefe.

Tinbergen, N. (1951). *The Study of Instinct.* Oxford, UK: Oxford University Press.

Tolman, E. C. (1925). Behaviorism and purpose. *Journal of Philosophy, 22, 36-41.*

Tremblay, P. F., & Dozois, D. J. A. (2009). Another perspective on trait aggressiveness: maladaptive schemas. *Personality and Individual Differences,* 46(5-6), 569-574.

Weis, S., & Süß, H.-M. (2007). Reviving the search for social intelligence – A multitrait-multimethod study of its structure and construct validity. *Personality and Individual Differences, 42(1)*, 3-14.

Wenner, C., Figueredo, A. J., Rushton, J. P, & Jacobs, W. J. (2007). Executive functions, general intelligence, life history, psychopathic attitudes, and deviant behavior. Paper. Annual Meeting of the International Society for Intelligence Research, Amsterdam, The Netherlands.

Wenner, C., Figueredo, A. J., Rushton, J. P, & Jacobs, W. J. (2009). Profiling approaches to life and experience. Manuscript in preparation.

Wenner, C., Jacobs, W. J., & Nagaran, K. (2007). The executive functions questionnaire. Manuscript in preparation.

White, J. L., Moffitt, T. E., & Silva, P. A. (1989). A prospective replication of the protective effects of IQ in subjects at high risk for juvenile delinquency. *Journal of Consulting and Clinical Psychology, 57(6),* 719-724.

Zeichner, A., & Pihl, R. O. (1979). Effects of alcohol and behavior contingencies on human aggression. *Journal of Abnormal Psychology, 88(2),* 153-160.

Zeichner, A., & Pihl, R. O. (1980). Effects of alcohol and instigator intent on human aggression. *Journal of Studies on Alcohol, 41(3)*, 265-276.

Chapter 2

EXECUTIVE FUNCTIONS, ATTENTION AND JUVENILE DELINQUENCY

Martha Frías-Armenta[1], Pablo Valdez-Ramírez[2], Guadalupe Nava-Cruz[2], Aurelio J. Figueredo[3] and Victor Corral-Verdugo[4]

[1] University of Sonora, Hermosillo, Mexico.
[2] Nuevo León Autonomous University, Monterrey, Mexico.
[3] University of Arizona, Tucson AZ, USA.
[4] University of Sonora, Hermosillo, Mexico.

ABSTRACT

This chapter is aimed at elucidating whether juvenile delinquents have poorer executive functioning in inhibition, flexibility, and attention, than control adolescents. Seventy-five Mexican teenagers participated in a study. The total sample was divided into three groups, one consisting of minors institutionalized by a juvenile court for serious offenses (N=24), another reported for antisocial behavior (n=24) and a control group from the general population (N=27) that was matched by sex, age and schooling to the juvenile court group. Demographic variables were considered and executive functions were assessed by means of the Wisconsin Card Sorting Test, and the Shifting Criteria Stroop Test- a modified version of the Stroop test- and the Continuous Performance test. T-tests were conducted to compare group means between the delinquent and control groups, and between juveniles having committed serious offences and those with statutory offenses. An ANOVA (GLM procedure) was also conducted to compare the three groups: the control group, the juveniles with serious offenses, and the juveniles with statutory offenses. Results showed means differences in some tasks of the Wisconsin test between the institutionalized adolescents and the control group. There were no significant differences in the STROOP test between the control group and the delinquent group. However, significant differences in inhibitory tasks were found between juveniles with serious and statutory offenses. Differences were also found in some indicators of selective and sustained attention, and tonic and phasic alertness, between the control group and the delinquent minors. Results are discussed in regard to minors' inability to respond adequately to the social environment, which results from neuropsychological impairment.

INTRODUCTION

Juvenile delinquency is one of the most serious problems that human societies currently face worldwide. The Annual Report on Violence and Health (Krug, Dahlberg, Mercy, Zwi, & Lozano, 2002) indicates that the world rate of homicide perpetrated by men aged between 15 and 29 years is 19.4 per 100,000 persons, and in the year 2000 juvenile violence caused 199,000 (9.2 per 100,000) deaths. Death rates were higher in Latin America (34.4 per 100,000) and in Africa (17.6 per 100,000). In Mexico the average ratio is 15.3 (per 100,000) for combined males and females, 27.8 (per 100 000) for males and 2.8 (per 100 000) for females. Around the world for each youth homicide there are 20-40 victims of non-fatal violence (Krug, Dahlberg, Mercy, Zwi, & Lozano, 2002), and 15.5% of arrests for violent crime are for juveniles under the age of 18 years in the United States (Crime in the United States, 2003). In 2004, 12.1 % of clearances for violent crime and 18.9 for property crime involved juveniles (Crime in the United States, 2004). In the same year, 195,468 juveniles were arrested for drug abuse violations in the United States. In 1997, 58,720 minors were arrested in Mexico, and in 1998 the number was of 56,448 for different types of offenses (Instituto Nacional de Estadística, Geografía e Informática, INEGI, 2004). These data only represent the young people that were accused and arrested. Yet, there are few studies in Latin America and in Mexico concerning the causes of juvenile delinquency.

Juvenile delinquency is influenced by multiple factors, such as biological, psychological, and social (Geis, 2000; Gottfredson & Hirschi, 1990). Recently, some researchers (Moffit, 1993a; Raine, Buchsbaum, & LaCasse, 1997; Glaser 2000; Teichner & Golden, 2000) have argued that a delay in brain maturation may produce impairment in attention and executive functioning. This impairment could be a cause of learning difficulties, low grade achievement, or behavioral disorders which make youths abandon school, get involved in antisocial groups, and engage in delinquency. According to this argument, chronic delinquents present some neuropsychological delay, especially in executive functions and attention, during the early stages of adolescence, making them more vulnerable to engage in antisocial behavior when exposed to it (Beaver, Wright, & Delisi, 2007). Adolescents showing poor inhibitory control and impulsivity are more in risk to become early-onset offenders (Carroll, Hemingway, Bower, Ashman, Houghton, & Durkin, 2005). Control over emotions and behavior is exercised by cognitive executive-functions. Indeed, cognitive development reduces youth's likelihood of future delinquency (Ngai & Cheung, 2005).

It is well-known that antisocial behavior and risk-seeking increase during adolescence. Evolutionary theories explain risk-taking in adolescence as likely necessary because it increases reproductive opportunities (Steinberg, 2007; see also Figueredo & Jacobs, this volume). Risk-seeking in puberty is associated to remodeling dopaminergic pathways and accompanied by an increase in oxytocin receptors. However, a number of factors transform sensation-seeking in antisocial behavior (Steinberg, 2008). Recent studies suggest that decision making is a combination of cognitive control and socio-emotional factors (Bechara, 2005).

Juvenile delinquency is also associated to attentional problems. Phamn, Vanderstukken, Philippot, and Vanderlinden (2003) examined criminal psychopaths, using D-II Cancellation, Porteus Maze, Modified Wisconsin Card Sorting, Stroop Color Word Interference, Trail Making, and Tower of London tests, finding selective attention and specific executive function deficits among psychopaths. Attention problems are also associated with antisocial behavior and substance use (Fleming, Harachi, Cortes, Abbott, & Catalano, 2004).

Attention plays an important role in learning, academic and social functioning (Herba, Tranah, Rubia, & Yule, 2006). It makes adaptive behavior possible in everyday constant demands on the cognitive and emotional systems by selecting, prioritizing and integrating competing challenges and opportunities (Berger, Kofman, Livneh, & Henik, 2007). The ability to pay attention and respond to internal and external stimuli is fundamental in planning behavior. Attention also allows movements to be voluntary selected and started (Bonilla & Fernández-Guinea, 2006).

The above-mentioned studies show some correlates of neuropsychological functioning and antisocial behavior. As far as we know, there is no research investigating the relationship between the delay in the development of executive functions (EF) and antisocial behavior in adolescents in Mexico. Since there are some environmental influences in the development of self-regulation such as quality of attachment and parenting strategies and styles, it is important to confirm if this relationship exist in countries other than the industrialized ones, where this research has been conducted (Berger, Kofman, Livneh, & Henik, 2007; Paschalla, & Fishbein, 2002). Some studies have shown differences in brain development between sexes (Andersen, 2002; Davies & Rose, 1999; Blakemore & Choudhury, 2006). They compared the volume of gray matter in the frontal lobes and found that it increases in pre-adolescents with a peak of 12 for boys and 11 for girls (Blakemore & Choudhury, 2006). In addition, gender covaries with delinquency. Moffit (1990), in a revision of the literature, mentions that few studies investigating neuropsychological factors related to delinquency control the sex factor. Thus, the study reported in this chapter includes both-sex participants to control for possible sex variations. Since school experience modifies the organization and development of human brain, school grades should also be controlled. In addition, age was controlled because during infancy and adolescence an accelerated development of the brain occurs and the prefrontal neural architecture continues changing until late adolescence (Blakemore & Choudhury, 2006; Gómez-Pérez & Ostrosky-Solís, 2006) and it exerts significant influence on neuropsychological functioning. Since some inconsistencies are found in the literature on EF and antisocial behavior, this investigation tries to clarify the specific subcomponents of executive functions analyzed. The present study was aimed at analyzing the executive functions of inhibition and flexibility by using two tests: the Wisconsin Card Sorting Test (WCST) and the Shifting Criteria Stroop Test (SCST), a modified version of the Stroop Test. Attention, in turn, was assessed by using the continuous performance test. Most of the antecedent studies have assessed brain damage as a condition indicating impairment in executive functions, whereas the study we present in this chapter takes into account the perspective of development of some EF rather than the approach focusing on damage of the prefrontal cortex as correlate of antisocial behavior in adolescents. Also this study analyzes the differences between juveniles committing felonies and misdemeanors.

EXECUTIVE FUNCTIONS

Executive functions refer to a person's capacity to identify an objective, to establish a goal, to build a plan to reach that goal, to organize the way to reach it, to perform actions according to the plan, to evaluate the consequences of actions, and to change behavior according to results (Godefroy, 2003). Ishikawa and Raine (2003, p. 281) define executive functions as "higher-order cognitive processes involving initiation, planning, cognitive flexibility, abstraction and decision making that together allow the execution of contextually appropriate behavior." The abilities of goal formation, planning, carrying out goal-directed plans, and effective performance are the four components that conceptualize executive functions (Jurado & Rosselli, 2007). Executive functions are crucial for the regulation of behavior, self-control, decision making and problem solving (Luria, 1974; Strayhorn, 2002). In addition, executive functions allow adaptation before changes in the environment, shifting conduct to diverse situation, and the inhibition of inappropriate behaviors. Creating a plan, initiating and preserving its performance until its completion are part of executive functions (Jurado & Rosselli, 2007).

These capacities are regulated by the frontal lobes, especially by the prefrontal (anterior) areas. The development of the prefrontal cortex is thought to play an important role in the maturation of higher cognitive abilities (Casey, Tottenham, Liston, & Durston, 2005; Wallis, 2007). Patients with prefrontal damage may perform well on diverse cognitive tasks and intelligence tests (Ardila, Pineda, & Rosselli, 2000; Lezak, Howieson, & Loring, 2004), but fail to adjust their behavior to many situations requiring self-control, problem solving, or making decisions according to social demands (Luria, 1986; Valdez, Nava, Tirado, Frías, & Corral, 2005). Beaver, Wright, & Delisi (2007) indicate that prefrontal cortex lesions may result in executive dysfunctions including low self-control. Prefrontal areas develop slowly, being one of the last areas of the brain completing maturation (Toga & Thompson, 2005); there is some evidence that these brain areas mature around the ages of 21 to 24 years (Hudspeth & Pribram, 1992; Spreen, Risser, & Edgell, 1995).

Children perform worse than adults on higher cognitive tasks. Brain regions associated with more basic functions such as motor and sensory processes mature first, followed by areas controlling thoughts and action (Valdez et al., 2005). Tasks with lesser cognitive demands do not seem to show age-related differences (Booth, et al. 2003). Olesen, Nagy, Westerberg, and Klingberg, (2003) demonstrated the importance of maturation of the prefrontal-parietal connectivity in the performance of a working memory task. Adolescence underlies risk-taking and novelty-seeking behavior (Bjork *et al.*, 2004), and this could be related to a retarded maturation of the prefrontal cortex which means a lag in the development of executive functions.

ATTENTION

Although attention lacks a precise definition, it could be conceived as the cognitive process that implies the capacity for responding to the environment, to select a sensorial signal, and a specific response, as well as the capability to sustain a response to stimuli over time (Valdez, 2005). Attention is also defined as the ability to responding to environmental changes and internal psychobiological states (Cohen, 1993). Attention selects the information that allows access to the working memory (Knudsen, 2007). However, the literature in psychology relates attention to a diverse set of cognitive process or abilities, and while some researchers conclude that attention is theoretically incoherent (Tucha, Tucha, Laufkotter, Walitza, Klein, & Lange, 2008), others conceive it as a non-unitary process comprising a series of smaller elements (Cohen, 1993). In addition, different kind of studies (neuroanatomical, clinical, neuroimaging, and neuropsychological) disclose that attention is not a single function (Tucha, Tucha, Laufkotter, Walitza, Klein, & Lange, 2008). Zimmermann and Leclercq (2002) consider attention as a multidimensional cognitive capacity.

Posner and Rafal (1987) propose a model of attention suggesting four fundamental components: tonic and phasic alertness, selective attention and vigilance. Valdez *et al.* (2005) define alertness as the general capacity of the organism to respond to environmental stimuli. It could be divided into two different types: tonic and phasic. Tonic is related to general awakening during the day, while phasic is the increased attentiveness after a warning signal or when the environment requires a response. Selective attention is the ability to attend to a stimulus, ignoring others. It implies, also, the capacity to emit a response while inhibiting others (Driver, 2001). Vigilance refers to the capacity to sustain attention for long periods of time (Posner & Rafal, 1987). Selective attention contributes to the analysis of the most important events in the environment; therefore it helps to decision making processes (Valdez *et al.*, 2005).

EXECUTIVE FUNCTIONS AND ANTISOCIAL BEHAVIOR

Eslinger, Flaherty-Craig and Benton (2004) found that the prefrontal cortex is indispensable in early and later psychological development. Individuals with prefrontal-cortex damage exhibit some degree of cognitive alteration; most of them show emotional, social and self-control deficits. The authors concluded that these findings support the idea of a fundamental importance of prefrontal cortex maturation in prolonged cognitive, social-emotional, and self-control development. Murderers present abnormal cortical and subcortical brain processes, suggesting that these may predispose them to violence (Raine, Buchsbaum & LaCasse, 1997). Critchley *et al.* (2000), in a study conducted with violent inpatients and a control group, found that violent patients had reduced neuronal density and abnormal phosphate metabolism in the prefrontal lobe, compared to nonviolent control subjects. In the same study these authors showed that lesions to the prefrontal cortex generally increase aggressive behavior.

A study examining executive functions of criminal violent offenders demonstrated a dual impairment in inhibitory cognitive control. The participants were deficient in both their shifting attention and in their ability to alter behavior in response to fluctuations in the emotional significance of stimuli (Bergvall, Wessely, Forsman, & Hansen, 2001). Inhibition is related to antisocial behavior since individuals cannot stop their actions when circumstances indicate that they are inappropriate (Hawkins & Trobst, 2000). Glaser (2000) found that early neuromotor deficits (indicating anomalous brain development) interacting with unstable family environmental factors increase the risk of violent behavior. Barratt,

Stanford, Kent, and Felthous (1997) reported that incarcerated inmates for violent crimes have poorer performance on most neuropsychological tests. Prefrontal cortex dysfunction underlies the risk for suicidal behavior and substance abuse in young adults (Tarter, Kirisci, Reynolds, & Mezzich, 2004). Phamn, Vanderstukken, Philippot, and Vanderlinden (2003) examined criminal psychopaths, using D-II cancellation, Porteus Maze, Modified Wisconsin Card Sorting, Stroop Color Word Interference, Trail Making, and Tower of London tests, finding selective attention and specific executive function deficits among psychopaths.

Low inhibitory regulation magnifies the risk of substance abuse; this low inhibition is manifested as irritability, reactive aggression, impulsivity, and sensation seeking (Young et al., 2000). Adolescents showing poor inhibitory control and impulsivity are more in risk to become early-onset offenders (Carroll et al., 2005). Control over emotions and behavior is exercised by cognitive executive-functions. Cognitive development reduces youth's likelihood of future delinquency (Ngai & Cheung, 2005). Brower and Price (2001), in a revision of the literature, found that deficits in executive functions may increase the likelihood of future aggression. It seems that the mechanism by which executive functions may increase violence is through control of impulsivity (Brower & Price, 2001).

Lueger and Gill (1990) administered neuropsychological tests to 21 juvenile delinquents and a control group. Their results showed that conduct-disordered adolescents presented more errors in the WCST (Wisconsin Card Sorting Test) and, in general, performed more poorly on measures related to prefrontal lobe functioning. The delinquent group exhibited higher number of perseverations, more sustained attention errors, and poorer sequential motor memory.

Juveniles with frontal disorders are in higher likelihood of displaying violent behavior (Golden, Jackson, Peterson-Rohne, & Gontkovsky, 1996). Also, neuropsychological deficits have been observed in aggressive adolescents (Teichner & Golden, 2000). Broomhall (2005) studied executive function deficits in 25 violent offenders, separating instrumental and reactive offenders, finding that the reactive group was significantly impaired on higher-order executive functions, whereas the instrumental group was no significantly different from the control group. However, the latter group showed a tendency to be selectively impulsive on several executive functions depending on the task. Cauffman, Steinberg, and Piquero (2005) combined variables based on Gottfredson's and Hirschi's self-control theory with neuropsychological and physiological factors, finding that serious juvenile offenders evidence lower resting heart rate, poorer performance on tasks that activate cognitive functions, mediated by prefrontal cortex; in addition, juveniles score lower in self-control measures. Girls with conduct disorders perform more poorly on executive functions, in visospatial and in academic achievement domains; they exhibit a lower general intelligence than control groups after adjusting for demographics (Pajer, Chung, Leininger, Wang, Gardner, & Yeates, 2008). Poor neuropsychological functioning is linked to aggressive behavior (Séguin, Nagin, Assaad, & Tremblay, 2004). Children with conduct disorder (CD) were found to be significantly impaired in executive functioning after attention deficit- hyperactivity disorder (ADHD) symptoms and socioeconomics status were controlled (Toupin, Déry, Pauzé, Mercier, & Fortin, 2000; Baving, Rellum, Laucht, & Schmidt, 2006).

However, Laakso, Gunning-Dixon, Vaurio, Repo-Tiihonen, Soininen and Tiihonen (2002) found no significant correlations between overall prefrontal cortical volumes and the degree of psychopathology, concluding that volume deficits previously observed could be more related to alcoholism or differences in education than to antisocial personality disorder.

Another study conducted with subjects exhibiting antisocial personality disorder did not find performance deficits on classical tests of frontal executive functions (Dinn & Harris, 2000). Nevertheless, those subjects presented higher neurological deficits on measures sensitive to orbitofrontal dysfunction compared to control subjects. Loeber, Pardini, Stouthamer-Loeber, and Raine (2007) examined cognitive, physiological and psychological factors and delinquency risk factors in a community sample and found that none of the cognitive (verbal IQ, Spatial IQ, verbal memory, visual memory, executive functions), physiological (skin conductance responding, and resting heart rate [HR]), parenting (positive parenting, supervision, physical punishment and parental stress) or community (housing quality and community crime) factors predicted resistance to delinquency. The significant predictors of delinquency were child risk factors (prevalence of tobacco, alcohol or marijuana use, drug selling, interpersonal callousness, runaway, race, attitude towards delinquency, likelihood of getting caught, truancy) or peer models (peer delinquency). The Cognitive Assessment System (CAS) was used to measure executive functions in 111 male adolescent offenders. Results showed that antisocial adolescents were significantly below the standards for planning and successive processing (Enns, Reddon, Das, & Boukos, 2007). Morgan and Lilienfeld (2000) conducted a meta-analysis of studies related to antisocial behavior and executive functions finding a robust relationship between them especially in inhibition and motor control. However, they found inconsistencies in other results and recommend more research on specific neuropsychological deficits.

ATTENTION AND ANTISOCIAL BEHAVIOR

The attention deficit hyperactivity disorder (ADHD) has been associated to conduct disorders (CD), oppositional deviant disorder (ODD), and mood disorders (Wilens *et al.* 2002). Posner (2007), in a study of preschool children, found comorbidity of ADHD with ODD, communication and anxiety disorders. ADHD is also related to substance abuse (Kirisci, Tarter, Vanyukov, Reynolds, & Habeych, 2004), aggression, and violent behavior (Paschalla, & Fishbein, 2002). Other study showed that subjects with ADHD were significantly more anxious and poorly socialized than a control group (Young & Gudjonsson, 2006). ADHD has also been related to persistent criminal offending (Moffit, 1990). Problem behavior is linked significantly to attention problems, assessed through teacher observation (they registered whether children paid attention, were easily distracted, and stood on tasks) in the classroom (Fleming, Harachi, Cortes, Abbott, Catalano, 2004). Several studies reported that ADHD prevail between 30% and 45% of juvenile delinquents (Teichner & Golden, 2000; Rosler *et al.*, 2004). ADHD was found in 13% of juvenile female delinquents as compared to 1% of the control group (Dixon, Howie, & Starling, 2004). A study conducted in Sweden with juvenile delinquents found that ADHD is seemingly related to crime volume rather than to severity (Dalteg & Levander, 1998). Rey, Sawyer, Prior (2004) compared aggressive and delinquent adolescents and children with a non-aggressive control group, finding that the aggressive group exhibited higher levels of ADHD, which decreased when children became older, with the exception of the inattentive subtype. This suggests differences in the pattern of comorbidity for aggression, delinquency and subtypes of ADHD. Such results seem to indicate a relationship between attention and delinquency. Other studies suggest deficits in selective attention in children with ADHD, especially in the early filtering aspect, measured by direct reflections of brain activity (Kenemans, Bekker, Lijffijt, Overtoom, Jonkman, & Verbaten, 2005). Also, children with ADHD present an inability to sustain attention, measured by a continuous-performance task (Barkley, 1997; Jensen & Cooper, 2002), and impairment in selective attention. However, Van Der Meere (2002) claims that hyperactive children differ from controls in terms of declined task performance and this difference depends on the conditions of the stimuli, and this condition appear when a slower presentation rate is used. Inability to maintain attention is also related to impulsivity; impulsive subjects exhibit an alteration in alertness in simple reaction time tasks; in addition they display a shorter reaction time (Bayle *et al.*, 2006). Adults with conduct disorder syndrome exhibit impairment in sustained attention in a continuous performance task, which results in an increase in errors (Epstein, Johnson, Varia, & Conners, 2001).

The abovementioned literature suggests significant relations between attention, executive functions and delinquency. Therefore the aim of this chapter is to study the display of executive functions -flexibility, inhibition and attention- in juvenile delinquents controlling by age, school grade, and gender.

METHOD

Participants

The total sample was constituted by 75 adolescents divided into three groups: one consisting of juveniles receiving treatment in a juvenile-court confinement center ($N=24$) at the city of Hermosillo, in northwestern Mexico (population=600,000), another reported for antisocial behavior ($N=24$) and a control group from the general population ($N=27$) at that same city, which was matched by sex, age and schooling to the group receiving treatment. The control group was selected to match the age of the juvenile delinquents; therefore, the former were recruited from afternoon schools, where students are older than those attending regular (morning) schools.

We interviewed all the juveniles that were in the courts at the time the project was conducted. The mean age for the total sample was 14 years old (SD=1.35). Twenty percent of the participants in the juvenile delinquent group were females and 80% males. Those that reported brain damage, brain surgery, epilepsy, and the ones under treatment of drugs affecting the nervous system were excluded.

Instruments

A questionnaire was used to obtain demographic variables such as income, educational level, occupation and unemployment rate of participants and of their family, and number of family members. The Wisconsin Card Sorting Test (Heaton, Chelune, Talley, Kay, & Curtis, 1983), and the Shifting Criteria Stroop Test (Valdez, 2005), Continuous Performance Test were the neuropsychological tools that we used.

The Wisconsin Card Sorting Test (WCST)

Consists of 64 stimulus cards (Wright, Waterman, Prescott, & Murdoch-Eaton, 2003), each having a combination of 4 characteristics: shape (circle, triangle, star, or cross), color (red, blue, yellow, or green) and number (one, two, three, or four). Sets of 4 cards are presented sequentially to the participant, who is required to select one card from a set of 4, with no information about the classification category. The tester provides feedback for each response (i.e., correct or incorrect), depending on the subjects matching the cards according to the established category. After 10 consecutive correct responses, the experimenter changes the criterion without telling the participant. Patients with frontal lobe damage commit more perseverative errors in this test compared to controls, although this test does not differentiate among patients with frontal or non-frontal damage (Lezak, Howieson, & Loring, 2004).

Shifting Criteria StroopTest (SCST)

Consists of a card (letter size) with 48 words (4 columns of 12 words each) (font=arial, size=28). Words were 4 names of colors (blue, brown, red, green) written in incongruent colors (for example, "red" is written with green color ink). Half of the words were marked with a dot at its left and were distributed through the card. Each participant must tell aloud and as fast as possible each word, by columns, according to the following tasks:

1. Reading. Read the words without considering the color in which they are written.
2. Color naming. Tell the color of the words.
3. Shifting criteria 1. Read the words marked with a dot on its left, and tell the color of the words that are not marked by a dot.
4. Shifting criteria 2. Tell the color of the words marked with a dot on its left, and read the words that are not marked by a dot.

The first two tasks are similar to the Stroop test (MacLeod, 1991), the latter two tasks have been designed to evaluate one component of executive functions: set shifting (adjusting behavior to changes in the requirements) (Miyake et al., 2000). College students, 18-25 yrs old, required less than two minutes to complete each shifting criteria task, with a maximum of 10 errors in each task; whereas patients with prefrontal lesions required more than 2 minutes; they produced more than 10 errors, and some were unable to complete these tasks (Valdez, 2005).

Continuous Performance Test

A modified version of the Continuous Performance Test (Riccio, Reynolds, Lowe, & Moore, 2002) was utilized to measure attention. Participants were required to use three fingers (index, middle, and annular) to press 1, 2, and 3 respectively on the computer keypad. They had to press 1 on any number (except "9") appearing at the center of the computer screen; to press 2 when a "9" appeared, and 3 when a "4" appeared after "9". There were 27 blocks of 20 stimuli each (14 numbers different from "9", 4 numbers "9", and 2 numbers "4" after "9". The stimulus duration was 100 milliseconds, and the inter-stimulus interval varied around 1200 milliseconds (1000, 1100, 1200, 1300 and 1400). The stimuli within the block and between the blocks were randomized. Font and size of the numbers were Arial 60; a 14" monitor was situated 60 cm in front of the participant. There were, in total, 540 stimuli and the total task duration was 11 minutes and 42 seconds. According to definitions explicited in Posner and Rafal's (1987) model, responses to numbers different from "9" were taken as indicators of tonic alertness, responses to "9" were taken as indicators of selective attention, responses to "4" after "9" were taken as indicators of phasic alertness, and three continuous responses of the task were taken as indicators of vigilance (concentration) or sustained attention.

Procedure

First, the authorization of the president of the Minor Tutelary Counsel (Juvenile Court) was granted in order to obtain access to the court's building to administer the instruments to the institutionalized minors. The control group participants were interviewed at the school they attended to and those arrested were interviewed in the buildings were they were confined. Clinical psychologists, trained in neuropsychological assessment and psychological interview, administered the tests. This took approximately 80 to 100 minutes. The voluntary consent was obtained from both groups and from minors and their parents and they were advised that they could stop the interview at any moment they wished. First, we interviewed arrested juveniles; an appointment for the administration of the instruments was set for each participant. The administration of the tests was individual and we controlled for any disturbances during the settled time.

Data Analysis

Univariate analyses were conducted to estimate means and standard deviation of the observed variables. Then, we ran an independent sample t–test to estimate group differences (delinquents vs. non-delinquents) in neuropsychological tasks. Afterwards, a delinquency categorical variable was constructed that categorized offenders into two groups: those with felonies or serious crimes and those with misdemeanors or minor crimes. Because of unequal Ns in our groups we decided to use a General Linear Model (GLM) procedure to perform the analysis of variance (ANOVA) needed to assess the differences between the 3 groups: the control group, delinquents with serious crimes, and delinquents with minor crimes. Subsequently, we ran an independent sample t-test to compare juveniles with serious crimes against juveniles with minor crimes.

RESULTS

Table 1 shows mean differences in some demographic characteristics of the participants. Statistically significant mean differences between groups resulted only in "suspended in school for discipline problems" (X^2=15.27, p =.0009).

Table 1. Group differences in demographics characteristics

	Frequency Control	Frequency Experimental	X2	p
Ocupation, besides				
Student	0	5	8.04	NS
Left hand	5	3	0.02	NS
Drink cofee	18	12	0.00	NS
Smoke	2	16	23.59	NS
Alcohol	2	3	0.89	NS
Drugs	0	18	35.53	NS
School counseling	4	5	1.03	NS
Dificulties to read or write	3	3	0.27	NS
Dificulties between right-left	10	1	5.13	NS
Quit school	4	22	33.01	NS
Suspended in school for discipline	11	21	15.27	0.0009
Arrested for any crime	0	30	75.00	NS

T-tests in neuropsychological tasks indicated statistically significant group differences in WSCT total errors ($t=-2.01$, $p=.04$), WCST non- perseverative errors ($t=-2.47$, $p<.01$), WCST, percentage of non-perseverative errors ($t=-2.28$, $p<.02$), WCST, percentage of conceptual responses, ($t=2.36$, $p<.02$), and number of categories completed ($t=2.17$, $p<.03$). No differences were found between the control and the experimental groups in the STROOP test (see Table 2).

The ANOVAs showed statistically significant differences in the STROOP test performances for time-color ($F=3.71$, $p<.02$), time color less time word ($F=4.32$, $p<.01$), and word errors ($F=3.38$, $p<.03$), among juvenile delinquents with serious offenses, juvenile delinquents with minor offenses, and the control group. *T*-tests comparing juvenile delinquents with serious offences and minor offences showed significant differences in time-color ($t=2.33$, $p<.02$), time color less time word ($t=2.77$, $p<.01$), and word errors ($t=2.14$, $p<.04$).

The Continuous Performance Test presented group differences on percentages of correct responses in tonic alertness ($F=8.11$, $p<0.001$), % of correct responses in selective attention ($F=6.79$, $p<0.002$), % of correct responses in phasic alertness ($F=3.99$, $p<0.023$), % of correct responses in general ($F=7.80$, $p<0.001$), total omissions ($F=4.00$, $p<0.02$), percent of total omissions ($F=4.00$, $p<0.02$), amount of series of 3 or more errors ($F=3.24$, $p<0.04$), SD of corrects responses ($F=3.63$, $p<0.03$), and SD of reaction time ($F=4.55$, $p<0.01$) indicating group differences in attention components. A post-hoc test showed that percent of correct tonic, phasic and selective attention were significantly lower in the institutionalized group and the amount of series of 3 or more errors were higher for the institutionalized group (see Table 4).

Table 2. Differences between groups (control and delinquents) in neurops. Tests

Variables	Control Means	SD	Experimental Means	SD	T	DF	p
WSCT							
WCST, Total of errors	35.42	20.02	44.86	19.87	-2.01	73	.04
WCST, % errors	30.24	13.85	36.47	13.60	-1.92	73	.05
WCST, perseverative responses	18.44	10.56	22.30	9.50	-1.61	73	.11
WCST, % perseverative responses	15.94	7.59	18.20	6.60	-1.33	73	.18
WCST, perseverative errors	16.57	9.96	20.66	8.16	-1.86	73	.06
WCST, % perseverative errors	14.23	7.27	16.89	5.54	-1.70	73	.09
WCST, non perseverative errors	17.20	10.97	24.46	14.47	-2.47	73	.01
WCST, % no perseverative errors	14.73	826	19.74	10.62	-2.28	73	.02
WCST conceptual responses	66.04	17.14	58.56	17.98	1.81	73	.07
WCST, % conceptual responses	60.52	17.35	50.59	18.44	2.36	73	.02
Number of categories completed	4.95	1.66	4.10	1.66	2.17	73	.03
Iintents to compl category	20.80	26.47	23.16	21.90	-0.40	73	.68
STROOP							
Time word	25.91	7.08	27.07	6.80	-0.70	73	0.4
Time color	59.86	10.28	63.13	11.39	-1.29	73	0.2
Time color less time word	33.95	10.38	36.07	11.82	-0.82	73	0.4
Time point word	67.28	13.95	72.17	15.58	-1.42	73	0.1
Time point color	77.13	15.65	83.97	17.95	-1.75	73	0.1
T. point word less time point color	144.42	27.73	156.13	31.13	-1.71	73	0.1
Total time	230.20	38.99	246.33	40.65	-1.73	73	0.1
Word errors	0.31	0.73	0.57	0.77	-1.45	73	0.1
Color errors	5.78	4.59	7.30	5.23	-1.33	73	0.2
Word point errors	6.24	4.67	7.53	4.55	-1.18	73	0.2
Point color errors	12.87	9.21	13.60	9.01	-0.34	73	0.7
P. Word er. less point color errors	19.11	11.94	21.13	11.08	-0.74	73	0.4
Total errors	25.20	14.41	29.00	13.55	-1.15	73	0.2

Table 3. Differences in neuropsychological test means between delinquents with serious offenses and delinquents with minor offenses

Variables	Minor Means	SD	Serious Means	SD	t	DF	p
STROOP							
Time word	27.78	7.36	26.00	6.00	.69	28	.49
Time color	59.44	9.64	68.67	11.94	-2.33	28	.02
Time color less time word	31.67	10.66	42.67	10.64	-2.77	28	.01
Time point word	69.33	15.33	76.42	15.60	-1.23	28	.22
Time point color	86.11	18.48	80.75	17.37	.79	28	.43
T. point word less time point color	155.44	31.74	157.17	31.55	-.14	28	.88
Total time	242.67	41.816	251.83	39.99	-.59	28	.55
Word errors	.33	.48	92	.99	-2.14	28	.04
Color errors	6.50	4.52	8.50	6.14	-1.02	28	.31
Word point errors	6.94	4.95	8.42	3.91	-.86	28	.39
Point color errors	15.78	10.02	10.33	6.27	1.67	28	.10
P. Word errors less p. color errors	22.72	12.06	18.75	9.39	.96	28	.34
Total errors	29.56	13.18	28.17	14.63	.27	28	.78

Table 4. Group differences in attention components

Variable	Mean (SD) Control	Minor offenses	Institutionalized	Mean squared DF=2	F	Sig
% of correct tonic	88.55	88.69	77.23	863.86	8.11	.001
	(7.6)	(9.7)	(11.26)			
% of selective	66.63	59.49	50.19	1525.72	6.79	.002
	(1.32)	(1.65)	(1.52)			
% of correct phasic	70.91	74.14	58.87	1568.24	3.99	.02
	(22.71)	(12.28)	(22.21)			
% of correct gen	79.90	77.02	67.93	971.32	7.80	.001
	(9.59)	(10.13)	(13.51)			
Lineal tendency correct	.01	03	.06	.072	.64	.52
	(.34)	(.35)	(.29)			
Reaction time tonic	475.08	468.68	466.28	533.64	.12	.88
	(56.63)	(66.56)	(73.90)			
Reaction time selec	557.84	567.58	546.03	2795.65	.58	.56
	(58.49)	(52.40)	(91.62)			
Reaction time phasic	453.61	452.13	444.48	594.22	.068	.93
	(92.58)	(67.81)	(113.50)			
Reaction time gen	495.28	492.93	481.58	1329.65	.32	.72
	(55.72)	(63.16)	(72.44)			
Tend gen reaction time	-.13	-.19	-.11	.040	.39	.67
	(.32)	(.30)	(.33)			
Total omissions	31.59	33.79	52.79	3348.54	4.00	.02
	(23.33)	(27.53)	(35.26)			
% total omissions	5.85	6.25	9.77	114.83	4.00	.02
	(4.32)	(5.09)	(6.53)			
3 or more errors	1.37	2.13	3.96	44.30	3.24	.04

Table 4. (Continued)

Variable	Mean (SD)			Mean squared DF=2	F	Sig
	Control	Minor offenses	Institutionalized			
	(1.59)	4.27	(4.64)			
SD of corrects	2.17	2.46	2.76	2.20	3.63	.03
	(.57)	(.92)	(.81)			
SD of reaction time	200.95	218.22	243.73	11694.95	4.55	.01
	(47.14)	(42.13)	(61.22)			

CONCLUSION

Results of our study showed significant differences in some of the indicators of executive functions between institutionalized and non-institutionalized minors. Group differences in non-perserverative errors and percent of non-perserverative errors in the Wisconsin test were found between juvenile delinquents and the control group. These differences provided complex information. We expected differences in perserverative errors because this task represents behavioral flexibility. Individuals with pre-frontal damage evidence impairments in this function, showing limited flexibility in their behavior. Our hypothesis was that juvenile delinquents would show less flexibility because they had developmental delays in executive functions. However, with these data we cannot confirm such hypothesis. In addition, the data show group differences in percentages of conceptual-level responses. This result presumably reflects troubles in the sorting strategy, indicating potential problems in concept formation, conceptual flexibility and ability to use clues. It could indicate that juvenile delinquents are unable to cope with a simple problem and that they use inappropriate rules to solve it (Enns, Reddon, Das, & Boukos, 2007). These results are also consistent with previous reports documenting these deficits in executive functions in juvenile delinquents (Moffit, 1993b).

No group differences were found between the control group and juvenile delinquents in STROOP test indicators. However, significant differences appeared when juveniles with serious offenses and juveniles with minor offences were compared. These differences show that serious offenders have difficulties in displaying inhibitory functions. Therefore, two distinct groups of juvenile offenders result, and the impairment of executive functions is present only in those minors that engage in serious offences, indicating that neuropsychological delay is related only to that kind of offending (Moffit, 1993b; Cauffman, Steinberg, & Piquero 2005). On the other hand, juveniles with minor offenses seem to be more similar to the control group. One explanation could be that juveniles institutionalized by minor offenses are sometimes arrested for statutory offenses such as truancy, antisocial behavior or related conducts that are common in non-delinquent juveniles.

Results of our study also seem to show the presence of significant differences in attention components between institutionalized, non-institutionalized antisocial, and control group of minors. The institutionalized group performed worse on selective attention, which indicates that juvenile delinquents cannot select environmental information to respond adequately to social stimuli. Attention problems could difficult the decision-making process in everyday demands because these minors might be unable to effectively select, integrate and prioritize the stimuli to responding before environmental demands. Selective attention is important to goal-directed behavior because the selection of environmental stimuli will focus on choosing the available alternatives, and finding the satisfactory response to social demands (Cohen, 1993). Differences in selective attention between juvenile delinquents and control group have been previously reported in the literature (Cauffman, Steinberg, & Piquero, 2005; Fleming, Harachi, Cortes, Abbott, & Catalano, 2004).

We also found that adolescents from the institutional setting exhibited less alertness represented by less percentage of correct tonic and phasic responses. It seems that alertness functions as a modulating influence on other attentional components, thus selective components of attention may be not independent from the intensity component indicated by alertness (Sturm & Willmes, 2001). The neural system regulates alertness (increasing or decreasing it) depending on the evaluated needs. In this sense, adolescents with a reduction of alertness will have selective attention problems.

In addition, the institutionalized adolescents presented more series of 3 or more errors, which is a sign of problems to sustain attention. Sustained attention requires the capacity to select a response over time (Cohen, 1993). Subjects with problems in sustained attention are able to select some stimuli or responses but neglect others, which causes behavioral problems. Other studies associate conduct disorder to sustained attention (Epstein, Johnson, Varia, Conners, 2001). The inability to maintain attention is also related to impulsivity (Bayle *et al.*, 2006).

These findings indicate that adolescents with attention impairment do not respond adequately to environmental stimuli (specially the social ones), which might result in behavior problems, making them vulnerable to criminal behavior. This situation does not imply that deficiencies in attention cause crime, but that they can interfere in processing information from the environment, producing inappropriate responses of juveniles to social demands or a impulsive decision making. According to researchers, the function of attention is to select/decide the most adequate action, based on the characteristics of stimuli (Munar, Rosselló, & Sánchez-Cabaco, 1999). Thus, impairment in attention would produce inadequate responses to specific social stimuli. Since attention provides adaptation to everyday demands, a lack in this function will result in adolescents' maladjustment (Berger, Kofman, Livneh, & Henik, 2007).

Moreover, our results indicate a differential effect of attention problems on the kind of offense committed. Juveniles arrested for felonies differ in the displayed components of attention from juveniles reporting antisocial behavior, and both groups differ from the control group. Moffit (1990) had also found subgroups among juvenile delinquents. It seems that attention deficits are more pronounced in more violent offenders, causing their deficient adjustment to social requirements.

To some extent, these results suggest that juvenile offenders may find difficulty in controlling their behavior as well as in effectively detecting and using clues to inhibit their impulses. They also indicate impairment in their ability to constantly change responses to environmental demands, as Broomhall (2005) suggest, following his results, which showed that juvenile offenders are unable to responding with flexible behavioral changes.

A number of studies indicate that early neuropsychological development contributes to the prediction of later behavioral outcomes (Nigg, Quamma, Greenberg, & Kusche, 1999). Behavioral problems are thought to be related to failure of the regulatory control (executive) process (Barkley, 1997). Similarly, Toupin, Déry, Pauzé, Mercier, & Fortin (2000), when comparing children with CD (conduct disorders) with controls, found that CD children were impaired in 4 to 5 executive function measures after controlling for ADHD.

Our findings, which are, to some extent, similar to those reported in the literature, are not definitive; yet, they provide evidence that serious-offender juveniles manifest impairment in inhibition and flexibility functions as well as in attention. The neuropsychological perspective provides a framework for the explanation of juvenile delinquency, additional to the more classical perspectives. It emphasizes the role of internal factors (neural processing) along with external explanations (environmental clues and demands), stressing that the internal approach does not constitute a sufficient explanation. More research is necessary in order to evaluate serious juvenile offenders, following these results and their implications. In doing this, it is necessary to consider larger samples in order to produce clearer results. However, the main contribution of our study is that it shows differences in attention and executive functions between diverse groups of juvenile delinquents. Most of the studies compare delinquents with a control group of non-antisocial juveniles; yet, it seems that there are different categories within the more general classification of delinquents. This could be one of the reasons why the results of the literature related to executive functions are inconsistent. It is necessary to continue exploring this possibility in the future.

These results might also suggest that the detection of impairments in executive functions and treatment at early stages of childhood are a viable alternative approach to juvenile-delinquency prevention.

REFERENCES

Andersen P. (2002). Assessment and development of executive function (EF) during childhood. *Child Neuropsychology,* 8(2), 71 –82.

Ardila, A., Pineda, D., & Rosselli, M. (2000). Correlation between intelligence test scores and executive function measures. *Archives of Clinical Neuropsychology,* 15(1), 31-36.

Barkley, R. A. (1997). Behavioral inhibition, sustained attention, and executive function: Constructing a unified theory of ADHD. *Psychological Bulletin, 121,* 65-94.

Barratt, E. S., Stanford, M. S., Kent, T.A., & Felthous, A.R. (1997). Neuropsychological and cognitive psychophysiological substrates of impulsive aggression. *Biological Psychiatry, 41,* 1045–1061.

Baving, L., Rellum, T., Laucht, M., & Schmidt, M.H. (2006). Children with oppositional-defiant disorder display deviant attentional processing independent of ADHD symptoms. *Journal of Neural Transmission,* 113, 685-693.

Bayle, F. J., Daban, C., Willard, D., Bourdel, M.C., Olie, J. P., Krebs, M. O., & Amado-Boccara, I. (2006). Specific pattern of attentional changes in impulsive individuals. *Cognitive neuropsychiatry,* 11(5), 452-464.

Beaver, K. M., Wright, J. P., & Delisi, M. (2007). Self-Control as an Executive Function: Reformulating Gottfredson And Hirschi's Parental Socialization Thesis. *Criminal Justice and Behavior,* 34, 1345-1361.

Bechara, A. (2005). Decision making, impulse control and loss of willpower to resist drugs: A neurocognitive perspective. *Nature Neuroscience, 8,* 1458-1463.

Berger, A., Kofman, O., Livneh, U., & Henik, A. (2007). Multiciplary perspectives on attention and the development of self-regulation. *Progress in Neurobiology*, 28, 256-286.

Bergvall, A. H., Wessely, H., Forsman, A., & Hansen, S. (2001). A deficit in attentional set-shifting of violent offenders. *Psychological Medicine*, *31*, 1095-1105.

Bjork, J. M., Knutson, B., Fong, G. W., Caggiano, D. M., Bennett, S. M., and Hommer, D. W. (2004). Incentive-elicited brain activation in adolescents: Similarities and differences from young adults. *Journal of Neurosciences*, *24*, 1793-1802.

Blakemore, S. J., & Choudhury, S. (2006). Development of the adolescent brain: implications for executive function and social cognition. *Journal of Child Psychology and Psychiatry*, 47(3/4), 296–312.

Bonilla, J., & Fernández-Guinea, S. (2006). Neurobiología y Neuropsicología de la conducta antisocial. *Psicopatología Clínica, Legal y Forense*, 6, 67-81.

Booth, J. R. et al. (2003). Neural development of selective attention and response inhibition. *Neuroimage 20*, 737-751.

Broomhall, L. (2005). Acquired Sociopathy: A neuropsychological study of executive dysfunctions i violent offenders. *Psychiatry, Psychology and Law*, 12, 367-387.

Brower, M. C., & Price, B. H. (2001). Neuropsychiatry of frontal lobe dysfunction in violent and criminal behavior: a critical review. *Journal of Neurology, Neurosurgery and Psychiatry*, 71, 720-726.

Carroll, A., Hemingway, F., Bower, J., Ashman, A., Houghton, S. & Durkin, K. (2005). Impulsivity in Juvenile Delinquency: Differences Among Early-Onset, Late-Onset, and Non-Offenders. *Journal of Youth and Adolescence*, *35*(4), 517-527.

Casey, B. J., Tottenham, N., Liston, C., & Durston, S. (2005). Imaging the developing brain: What have we learned about cognitive development? *Trends in Cognitive Science*, *9*, 104-110.

Cauffman, E., Steinberg, L., & Piquero, A. (2005). Psychological, neuropsychological, and physiological correlates of serious antisocial behavior in adolescence: The role of self-control. *Criminology*, 43, 133-176.

Cohen, R. A. (1993). The neuropsychology of attention. New York: Plenum Press.

Crime in the United States: Uniform Crime Reports. (2003). US Department of Justice. Federal Bureau of Investigation. Washington, D.C.20535. http://www.fbi.gov/cius_2003/pdf/03scc1.pdf.

Crime in the United States: Uniform Crime Reports. (2004). US Department of Justice. Federal Bureau of Investigation. Washington, D.C.20535. http://www.fbi.gov/cius_2003/pdf/03scc1.pdf.

Critchley, H.G., Simmons, A., Daly, E. M. Russell, A., Amelsvoort, T. Robertson, D. M., Glover, A., Murphy, D. G.M. (2000). Prefrontal and medial temporal correlates of repetitive violence to self and others. *Journal of Society of Biological Psychiatry, 47*, 928-934.

Dalteg, A. & Levander, S. (1998). Twelve Thousands crimes by 75 boys: A 20 year follows up study of childhood hyperactivity. *The Journal of Forensic Psychiatry*, 9, 39-57.

Davies, P. & Rose, J. (1999). Assessment of Cognitive Development in Adolescents by Means of Neuropsychological Tasks. *Developmental Neuropsychology*, 15, 227-249.

Dinn, W. M., & Harris, C. L. (2000). Neurocognitive function in antisocial personality disorder. *Psychiatry Research, 97*, 173-190.

Dixon, A., Howie, P. & Starling, J. (2004). Psychopathology in female juvenile offenders. *Journal of child psychology and psychiatry,* 45 (6), 1150-1158.

Driver, J.,(2001). A selective review of selective attention research from the past century. *Journal of the British Psychological Society,* 92, 53-98.

Enns, R. A., Reddon, J. R., Das, J. P. & Boukos, H. (2007). Measuring executive function deficits in male delinquents using cognitive assessment system. *Journal of Offender Rehabilitation,* 44, 43-63.

Epstein, J, N., Johnson, D. E., Varia, I. M., & Conners, K. C. (2001). Neuropsyehological assessment of response inhibition in adults with ADHD. *Journal of Clinical and Experimental Neuropsychotogy,* 23,362-371.

Eslinger, P. J., Flaherty-Craig, C. V., and Benton, A. L. (2004). Developmental outcomes after early prefrontal cortex damage. *Brain and Cognition,* 55, 84-103.

Fleming, C. B., Harachi, T. W., Cortes, R. C., Abbott, R. D., & Catalano, R.F. (2004). Level and change in reading scores and attention problems during elementary school as predictor of problem behavior in middle school. *Journal of Emotional and Behavioral Disorders,* 12 (3), 130-144.

Geis, G. (2000). On the absence of self-control as the basis of general theory of crime: A critique. *Theoretical Criminology,* 4, 35-53.

Glaser, D. (2000). Child abuse and neglect and the brain-a review. *Journal of Child Psychology and Psychiatry,* 41, 97-116.

Godefroy, O. (2003). Frontal syndrome and disorders of executive functions. *J Neurol,* 250, 1-6.

Golden, C. J., Jackson, M. L., Peterson-Rohne, A., and Gontkovsky, S. T. (1996). Neuropsychological Correlates of violence and aggression: A review of clinical literature. *Aggression and Violent Behavior,* 1, 3-25.

Gómez-Pérez, E. & Ostrosky-Solís, F. (2006). Attention and memory evaluation across the life span: heterogeneous effects of age and education. *Journal of Clinical and Experimental Neuropsychology,* 28(4), 477-494.

Gottfredson, M. R., and Hirschi, T. (1990). *A general theory of crime.* Stanford, CA: Stanford University Press.

Hawkins, K. A., & Trobst, K. K. (2000). Frontal lobe dysfunction and aggression: Conceptual issues and research findings. *Aggression and Violent Behavior,* 5, 147-157.

Heaton, R., Chelune, G., Talley, J., Kay., & Curtiss, G. (1997). *Wisconsin card sorting test.* Manual de aplicación. Madrid: TEA Ediciones.

Herba, C. M., Tranah, T., Rubia, K., & Yule, W. (2006). Conduct problems in adolescence: Three domains of inhibition and effect of gender. *Developmental Neuropsychology,* 30(2), 659-695.

Hudspeth, W. J., & Pribram, K. H. (1992). Psychophysiological indices of cerebral maturation. *Int J Psychophysiol,* 12(1), 19-29.

Instituto Nacional de Estadística, Geografía e Informática, INEGI. (2004). Sistema de Consulta para la información Censal. México, D.F.: Instituto Nacional de Estadística, Geografía e Informática.

Ishikawa, S. S., & Raine, A. (2003), Prefrontal deficits and antisocial behavior: A causal model. In B. B. Lahey, T. E. Moffitt, & A. Caspi (Eds.), *Causes of conduct disorder and juvenile delinquency* (pp. 277-304). New York: Guilford

Jensen, P. S., & Cooper, J. R. (2002). Attention Deficit and Hyperactivity Disorder: State of the Science, Best Practices. Kingstown, New Jersey: Civic Research Institute.

Jurado, M. B., & Rosselli, M. (2007). The Elusive Nature of Executive Functions: A Review of our Current Understanding. *Neuropsychological Review, 17*, 213-233.

Kenemans, J. L., Bekker, E. M., Lijffijt, M., Overtoom, C. C. E., Jonkman, L.M., & Verbaten, M. N. (2005). Attention deficit and impulsivity: Selecting, shifting and stopping. *International Journal of Psychophysiology, 58*, 59-70.

Kirisci, L., Tarter, R. E., Vanyukov, M. Reynolds, M., & Habeych, M. (2004). Relation between cognitive distortions and neurobehavior disinhibition on the development of substance use during adolescence and substance use disorder by young. adulthood: a prospective study. *Drug and Alcohol Dependence, 76*, 125–133.

Knudsen, E. I. (2007). Fundamental components of attention. *Annual Review of Neuroscience, 30*, 57-78.

Krug, E. G., Dahlberg, L. L., Mercy, J. A., Zwi, A. B., & Lozano, R. (2002). World Report on Violence and Health (WHO). Retrieved June 20, 2006, from: http://www.who.int/violence_injury_prevention/ violence/world_report/en/full_en.pdf.

Laakso, M. P., Gunning-Dixon, F.,Vaurio, O., Repo-Tiihonen, E., Soininen, H. & Tiihonen, J. (2002). Prefrontal volumes in habitually violent subjects with antisocial personality disorder and type 2 alcoholism. *Psychiatry Research Neuroimaging, 114*, 95-102.

Lezak, M. D., Howieson, D. B., & Loring, D. W. (2004). *Neuropsychological assessment* (4th Ed.). New York: Oxford University Press.

Loeber, R., Pardini, D. A., Stouthamer-Loeber, M. and Raine A. (2007). Do cognitive, physiological, and psychosocial risk and promotive factors predict desistance from delinquency in males? *Development and Psychopathology*, 19, 867-887.

Lueger, R., & Gill, K. (1990). Frontal-Lobe cognitive dysfunction in conduct disorder adolescents. *Journal of Clinical Psychology, 46*, 698-705.

Luria, A. R. (1974). *El cerebro en acción*. Barcelona: Martínez Roca.

Luria, A. R. (1986). *Las funciones corticales superiores del hombre*. México: Fontamara.

MacLeod, C. M. (1991). Half a century of research on the Stroop effect: an integrative review. *Psychol Bull, 109*(2), 163-203.

Miyake, A., Friedman, N. P., Emerson, M. J., Witzki, A. H., Howerter, A., & Wager, T. D. (2000). The unity and diversity of executive functions and their contributions to complex "Frontal Lobe" tasks: a latent variable analysis. *Cognit Psychol, 41*(1), 49-100.

Moffit, T. E., (1990). Juvenile delinquency and attention deficit disorder: Boys' developmental trajectories from age 3 to age 15. Child Development, 61, 893-910.

Moffit, T. E. (1993a). Adolescent-limited and life course-persistent antisocial behavior: A developmental taxonomy. *Psychological Review, 100*, 674-701.

Moffit, T. E. (1993b).The neuropsychology of conduct disorder. *Development and Psychopathology, 5*, 135-151.

Morgan, A. B., & Lilienfeld, S. O. (2000). A meta-analytic review of the relation between antisocial behavior and neuropsychological measures of executive function. *Clinical Psychology Review, 20*, (1), 113–136.

Munar, E., Roselló, J., & Sánchez-Cabaco (1999). *Atención y percepción*, Alianza: Madrid.

Ngai, N., & Cheung, C. (2005). Predictors of the likelihood of delinquency: A study of Marginal Youth in Hong Kong, China. *Youth & Society, 36*, 445-470.

Nigg, J. T., Quamma, J. P., Greenberg, M. T., & Kusche, C. A. (1999). A two-year longitudinal study of neuropsychological and cognitive performance in relation to behavioral problems and competencies in elementary school children. *Journal of Child Abnormal Psychology,* 27 (1), 51-63.

Olesen, P. J., Nagy, Z., Westerberg, H., & Klingberg, T. (2003). Combined analysis of DTI and FMRI data reveals a joint maturation of white and grey matter in a fronto-pariental network. *Cognitive Brain Research, 18,* 48-57.

Pajer, K., Chung, J., Leininger, L., Wang, W., Gardner, W., and Yeates, K. (2008). Neuropsychological Function In Adolescent Girls With Conduct Disorder. *American Academy of Child and Adolescent Psychiatry, 47,* 416-425.

Paschalla, M. J., & Fishbein, D. H. (2002). Executive cognitive functioning and aggression: a public health perspective. *Aggression and Violent Behavior, 7,* 215–235,

Phamn, T. H., Vanderstukken, O., Philippot, P., & Vanderlinden, M. (2003). Selective Attention and Executive Functions Deficits Among Criminal Psychopaths. *Aggressive Behavior, 29,* 393-405.

Posner, M. I., & Rafal, R. D. (1987). Cognitive theories of attention and rehabilitation of attentional deficits. In M.J. Meier, A. L. Benton, and L. Diller, *Neuropsychological rehabilitation.* New York: The Guilford Press.

Posner et al. (2007). Clinical Presentation of Attention-Deficit/Hyperactivity Disorder in Preschool Children: The Preschoolers with Attention-Deficit/Hyperactivity Treatment Study (PATS). *Journal of child and adolescent psychopharmacology,* 17 (5), 547-562.

Raine, A., Buchsbaum, M., & LaCasse, L. (1997). Brain abnormalities in murderers indicated by positron emission tomography. *Society of Biological Psychiatry, 42,* 495-508.

Rey, J. M., Sawyer, M. G., & Prior, M. R. (2005). Similarities and differences between aggressive and delinquent children and adolescents in a national sample. *Australian and New Zealand Journal of Psychiatry,* 39, 366-372.

Riccio, C. A., Reynolds, C. R., Lowe, P. & Moore, J. J. (2002). The continuous performance test: a window on the neural substrates for attention? *Archives of Clinical Neuropsychology,* 17(3), 235-272.

Rosler, M., Retz, W., Retz-Junginger, P., Hengesch, G., Schneider, M., Supprian, T., et al. (2004). Prevalence of attention deficit-/hyperactivity disorder (ADHD) and comorbid disorders in young male prison inmates. European archives of psychiatry and clinical neuroscience, 254(6), 365-371.

Spreen, O., Risser, A. H., & Edgell, D. (1995). *Developmental neuropsychology.* New York: Oxford University Press.

Steinberg, L. (2007). Risk taking in adolescence: New perspectives from brain and behavioral science. *Current Directions in Psychological Science,* 16, 55-59.

Steinberg, L. (2008). A social neuroscience perspective on adolescent risk-taking. *Developmental Review*, 28, 78-106.

Strayhorn, J. M., Jr. (2002). Self-control: theory and research. *Journal of the American Academy of Child Adolescet & Psychiatry, 41*(1), 7-16.

Tarter, R.E., Kirisci, L., Reynolds, M., & Mezzich, A. (2004). Neurobehavior disinhibition in childhood predicts suicidal potential and substance use disorder by young adulthood. *Drug and alcohol dependence,* 76, 45-52.

Teichner, G. & Golden, C. (2000). The relationship of neuropsychological impairment to conduct disorder in adolescence: A conceptual review. *Aggression and Violent Behavior*, 5, 509-528.

Toga, A. W., & Thompson, P. M. (2005). Genetics of brain structure and intelligence. *Annual Review of Neuroscience*, 28, 1-23.

Toupin, J., Déry, M., Pauzé, R., Mercier, H., & Fortin, L. (2000). Cognitive and familial contributions to conduct disorder in children. *Journal of Child Psychology and Psychiatry, 41,* 333-344.

Tucha, L., Tucha, O., Laufkotter, R., Walitza, S., Klein, H. E., & Lange, K. W. (2008). Neuropsychological assessment of attention in adults with different subtypes of attention-deficit/hyperactivity disorder. *Journal of Neural Transmission,* 115, 269-278.

Valdez, P. (2005). *Manual de la Prueba Stroop con Criterio Cambiante*. Monterrey: Facultad de Psicología, Universidad Autónoma de Nuevo León.

Valdez, P., Nava, G., Tirado, H., Frías, M., & Corral, V. (2005). Importancia de las funciones ejecutivas en el comportamiento humano: implicaciones en la investigación con niños. In M. Frías & V. Corral (Eds.), *Niñez, adolescencia y problemas sociales* (pp. 65-81). México: CONACYT-UniSon.

Van Der Meere, J. J. (2002). The role of Attention. In S. Sandberg (Eds.). Hyperactivity and Attention Disorders in Childhood. London: Cambridge University Press.

Wallis, J. D. (2007). Orbitofrontal Cortex and Its Contribution to Decision-Making. *Annual Review of Neuroscience*, 30, 31-56

Wilens, T., Biederman, J., Brown, S., Tanguay, S., Monuteaux, M. C., Blake, C., & Spencer, T. J. (2002). Psychiatric Comorbidity and functioning in clinically referred preschool children and school-age youths with ADHD. American Academy Child & Adolescent Psychiatry, 4, 262–268.

Wright, I., Waterman, M., Prescott, H., & Murdoch-Eaton, D. (2003). A new Stroop-like measure of inhibitory function development: typical developmental trends. *Journal of Child Psychology and Psychiatry,* 44(4), 561-575.

Young, S., Stallings, M., Corley, R., Krauter, K., and Hewin, J. (2000). Genetic and environmental influences on behavior desinhibiton. *American Journal of Medicine and Genetics, 96,* 684-695.

Young, S., & Gudjonsson, G. H. (2006). ADHD symptomatology and its relation with emotional, social and delinquents problems. *Psychology Crime and Law*, 12(5), 463-471.

In: Bio-Psycho-Social Perspectives on Interpersonal Violence   ISBN: 978-1-61668-159-3
Editors: M. Frías-Armenta et al., pp. 51-77   © 2010 Nova Science Publishers, Inc.

Chapter 3

A STUDY OF PERSONALITY TRAITS IN UNDERGRADUATES: ALEXITHYMIA AND ITS RELATIONSHIP TO THE PSYCHOPATHIC DEVIATE

José Moral de la Rubia[*]
Universidad Autónoma de Nuevo León, Mexico.

ABSTRACT

The aim of the study presented in this chapter is to analyze the relationship between alexithymia and psychopathy deviation, also clarifying the role that depression plays in this relationship and to observe possible gender differences in alexithymia and psychopathy deviation. Alexithymia was assessed by using 20-items from the Toronto Alexithymia Scale (TAS-20), psychopathic deviation was measured with the MMPI clinical scale 4 (PD), and depression with the MMPI clinical scale 2 (D). The sample included 84 male and 275 female undergraduate students attending a psychology school in the northeast of Mexico, and the scales were administered by trained psychologists. Pearson's product-moment correlation, partial correlation, multiple linear regression, Student's t-test for independent samples and path analysis were conducted for data analysis. The psychopathic deviate variable correlated with the TAS-20 *difficulty in identifying feelings* factor in the total sample, which approached statistical significance in the sample of males. Depression correlated significantly with psychopathic deviate (PD), with the TAS-20 total score and with its first two factors *difficulty in describing feelings* (DDF) and *difficulty in identifying feeling* in the total sample. In the females' sample, depression showed the same pattern of correlations. In the males' sample, depression correlated with psychopathic deviate and with DIF; the correlation with TAS-20 total score approached statistical significance. The TAS-20 *externally oriented thinking* (EOT) factor resulted independent from depression in the three samples. After controlling the depression effect on the correlation between psychopathic deviate and DIF, this turned out non significant. In the regression model depression resulted the only significant predictor. Using path analysis, estimated by Maximum Likelihood, two models presented good fit: In one model, depression predicted psychopathic deviation, while depression

---

[*] Monterrey, Nuevo León, México, jose_moral@hotmail.com

determined the difficulty in identifying feelings and psychopathic deviation, in the other model. Additional models where the TAS-20 and the difficulty in identifying feelings factor were determinants of psychopathic deviation did not exhibit goodness of fit. Significant differences by gender in psychopathic deviate and the TAS-20 externally oriented thinking (EOT) factor were obtained, in which male's means were higher. It is concluded that alexithymia and psychopathic deviation are two different concepts, weakly related, and mediated by depression, at least, in an undergraduate's sample. This study deepens and clarifies the concepts of alexithymia and psychopathy. It also shows some difficulties in estimating differences by gender with the MMPI clinical scale 4 (psychopathic deviate).

INTRODUCTION

Legal experts identify psychopathy and addictions as two risk factors in the problem of violence. The prevalence of antisocial personality disorders in the population is approximately 3% in males and 1% in females (DSM-IV, 1994); but about 30 to 50% in incarcerated males (Raine & Sanmartín, 2000) and around 30% in female offenders (Louth, Hare, & Linden, 1998). In cases of child abuse, 35% of these situations involve alcohol or substance abuse (Raine & Sanmartín, 2000). Psychopathy and addictions are interacting variables. Antisocial personality disorder is a risk factor for addictions. 30 to 40% of people with an antisocial personality disorder meet substance abuse or dependence criteria (DSM-IV, 1994). On the other hand, alcohol and stimulants reduce impulsive control in psychopaths, with 50% of women abusers showing this character disorder (Raine & Sanmartin, 2000). Therefore, the study of possible psychopathic determinants is fully justified in the research field of interpersonal violence, which is the central topic of this book.

Alexithymia is one possible psychopathic determinant since there is literature on the subject that differentiates and relates both concepts. This chapter focuses on the relationship between alexithymia and psychopathic deviation, taking into consideration two intermediate variables from a psychometric standpoint and from studies of personality: depression and gender. Our approach considers alexithymia as a psychopathic determinant that would rely on a character structure of the inability to understand and control emotions, and to make contact with the human environment, and also as a cause of antisocial behavior (Keltikangas-Järvinen, 1982; Poser, 2000; Sifneos, 2000; Wastell & Booth, 2003). Empirical data support this hypothesis. A significant rate of alexithymia among incarcerated populations and the population with an antisocial personality disorder has been found, as compared to the general population (Keltikangas-Järvinen, 1982; Sayar, Ebrinc, & Ak, 2001). This correlation is significant only in relation to the *difficulty in identifying feelings* factor in incarcerated people (Louth, Hare, & Linden, 1998). Although no study focuses exclusively in the general population, Wastell and Booth (2003) report a moderate-to-low correlation between alexithymia and Machiavellianism; therefore, a weak moderate association is expected between alexithymia and psychopathic deviation in the general population.

Although there is a clear association between alexithymia and depression (Honkalampi *et al.*, 1999, 2000) as well as between depression and antisocial behavior (APA, 2000), it is necessary to elucidate whether or not depression intervenes in the relationship between alexithymia and psychopathy in the general population. In other words, it is necessary to demonstrate that individuals with psychopathic traits and depression are those that show a clear tendency to score higher in alexithymia, resulting alexithymia and psychopathy independent from each other without mediation from depression. The differential role of gender in alexithymia, depression and psychopathic deviation should be also contrasted.

ALEXITHYMIA: CONCEPT, MEASUREMENT AND EXPLANATORY MODELS

Sifneos coined the term "alexithymia," a neologism that literally means "lack of words to express feelings." In 1967, Sifneos used the term for the first time during his lecture "*Clinical observations on some patients suffering from a variety of psychosomatic diseases*", at the 7th European Conference on Psychosomatic Research held in Rome. He used it again in 1972 during a symposium on the role of emotions in the etiology of psychosomatic disorders organized by the *Ciba Research Foundation,* in London. This paper was later published in the monograph "*Short term psychotherapy and emotional crisis*" (Sifneos, 1972). However, in the article "*The prevalence of alexithymic characteristics in psychosomatic patients*" published in 1973 by the *Psychotherapy and Psychosomatics* magazine, Sifneos incorporates the concept and presents and implements a scale for it, the *Beth-Israel Psychosomatics Questionnaire* (BIQ). The importance of alexithymia in the research of affective processing deficits was established in 1976 during the International Conference of Psychosomatic Diseases in Heidelberg. Within the psychosomatic literature, Nemiah and Sifneos (1970) define the concept as a lack of the fantasy function that is evidenced by a poor emotional conscience, difficulty in expressing feelings, lack of daydreams, night dreams with scarce symbolic material and an externally-oriented thinking style with no contact with the internal personal world.

In regard to construct measurement, the BIQ clinical interview of Sifneos (1973) prevailed up until the mid eighties as well as projective techniques such as the Rorschach test (Vogt, Burckstrummer, Ernot, Meyer, & Rad, 1977) and the *Archetypal Test-9* (AT-9) (Demers-Desrosiers, 1982), the *Scored Archetypal Test-9* (SAT-9) (Cohen, Demers-Desrosiers & Catchlove, 1983) and the TAT (Taylor & Doody, 1982). The first psychometrical scales showed poor results, such as the *Schalling-Sifneos Personality Scale* (SSPS) by Apfel and Sifneos (1979), the *MMPI-Alexithymia Scale* by Kleiger and Kinsman (1980) and Shipko and Noviello (1984) and the *Analog Alexithymia Scale* (AAS) by Faryna, Rodenhauser, and Torem (1986).

In 1985, Taylor, Ryan, and Bagby reported a Likert-type scale with good psychometrical properties: the *26-item Toronto Alexithymia Scale* (TAS-26). This scale has four orthogonal factors that account for 32% of the total variance, which agrees with the construct's content: difficulty in identifying feelings, oral difficulty in expressing feelings, poor fantasy and externally-oriented thinking. The scale shows internal consistency, as indicated by a Cronbach's alpha coefficient of .62, a temporal stability of $r=.82$ after one week, and $r=.75$ after five weeks. In the years that followed, the TAS-26 took over empirical research due to several replications in different countries and cultures, with highly converging results (Rodrigo, Lusiardo & Normey, 1989, Rodrigo & Lusiardo, 1992, in Uruguay; Paez & Velasco, 1993, in Spain; Pasini, Delle-Chiaie, Seripa, & Ciani,1992, in Italy; and Troop, Schmidt & Treasure, 1995, in England; among others).

Bagby, Parker, and Taylor (1994) revised the scale improving its psychometric properties and published the TAS-20. Again, they obtained strong valid results (Bagby, Taylor & Parker, 1994) and good reliability indexes. The internal consistency increased up to .81 and a temporal stability of .77 was achieved over a period of three weeks. The third factor was eliminated due its significant correlation with the Social Desirability factor measured by the *Social Desirability Scale* by Crowne and Marlowe (1960), reducing the scale down to 20 items with a three orthogonal factor structure (difficulty in identifying feelings, difficulty in expressing feelings and externally-oriented thinking). Through a confirmatory factor analysis, the authors illustrate an excellent adjustment of the three-factor structure in two different samples at the same time: a control population and a clinical sample. These results have been reproduced in several countries (Parker, Bagby, Taylor, Endler, & Schmit, 1993, in Germany, Canada, and USA; Pandey, Mandal, Taylor, & Parker, 1996, in India; Loas, Parker, Otmani, Verrier, & Fremaux, 1997, in France; Martínez-Sánchez, 1996 and Moral & Retamales, 2000, in Spain; Paéz., Martínez-Sánchez., Velasco, Mayordomo, Fernández, & Blanco, 1999, in Spain and other Spanish-speaking countries; Moral, 2008, in Mexico; among others).

Taylor, Bagby, and Parker (1997), in their book *"Disorders of affect regulation: Alexithymia in medical and psychiatric illness"*, established that alexithymia is a health risk factor associated with emotional dysregulation found in several diseases such as depression, addictions, eating disorders, panic disorder, post-traumatic stress disorder, somatization, and other medical illnesses associated with psychological factors.

With regard to its etiology, data concerning the genetic and environmental determining factors of alexithymia have been produced. So far, there is only one early study about genetic determinants in twins conducted by Heiberg and Heigberg (1977, 1978), which has been criticized for its lack of control samples. There is also evidence of environmental determinants. Even though the first contributions were of a psychodynamic and theoretical nature (McDougall, 1974; Krystal, 1979) research shortly assumed an empirical character. For instance, a special emphasis was made on the early rejection bond or the lack of connection between baby and mother as a consequence of alexithymia or the mother's emotional clinical symptoms (McDougall, 1974, 82), or an alexithymic family environment where the individual internalizes a type of emotional function (Onnis & Di Genaro, 1987, 1994), or a traumatic childhood or adult experience (Krystal, 1979, 88; Berenbaum, 1996; Honkalampi, Koivumaa-Honkanen, Antikainen, Haatainen, Hintikka, & Viinamäki, 2004). At the same time, the neural bases of alexithymia have been studied, emphasizing a dysfunction in the connection between the two cerebral hemispheres (Hoppe & Bogen, 1977; Parker, Taylor, & Bagby, 1992), or a problem of emotional signals filtering at the geniculum, as well as a processing deficit at the basal-medial prefrontal lobe level (Schore, 1996; Lane, Ahern, Schwartz, & Kaszniak, 1997). Current studies support the existence of an automatic cognitive bias that ignores internal and interpersonal emotional information (Lundhl & Simonsson-Sarnecki, 2002).

DEFINITION OF PSYCHOPATHY

Pinel (1809), a French psychiatrist, disserted about "mania without delirium." The author referred, with this concept, to people with a normal intellectual function, but behaving in constant conflict with legal and moral standards. In a similar way, the British psychiatrist Prichard (1835) mentioned "moral madness," a concept that dominated psychopathology during the 19th century. The American psychiatrist Partridge (1930) criticized the concept of "moral imbecility" and referred to "sociopathy" or "antisocial deviation in social relations," introducing the current meaning of the term as a personality disorder. This new concept was used in 1952, in the first edition of the Diagnostic and Statistical Manual (DSM) of the American Psychiatric Association (APA, 1952), wherein it appeared under the label of "sociopathic personality disorder, antisocial reaction". After the second edition (APA, 1968), it was known as "antisocial personality disorder" (APD). This term is still used, as we can see in the third edition (APA, 1980), the third edition revised (APA, 1987), the fourth edition (APA, 1994), and the fourth edition revised (APA, 2000) texts.

The diagnostic criteria that currently appears in the DSM-IV-TR for the antisocial personality disorder are: [A] A general pattern of contempt and violation of others' rights that appears at 15 years old, as indicated by three (or more) of the following seven items: (1) a failure to adapt to social standards in relation to legal conduct, as it is indicated by the repetition of acts that usually end up in an arrest; (2) dishonesty, indicated by continuous lying, the use of aliases, conning others to obtain a personal benefit or for pleasure; (3) impulsiveness or an inability to plan for the future; (4) irritability and aggressiveness, indicated by continuous physical fights or aggressions; (5) imprudent carelessness for his own safety and others'; (6) a persisting irresponsibility, indicated by the inability to keep a job or handle economic obligations; (7) remorselessness, indicated by indifference toward or justification for harming, mistreating or stealing others. [B] The subject is younger than 18 years old. [C] There is evidence of a dissocial disorder beginning before the age of 15. [D] Antisocial behavior is not exclusive of a schizophrenic or maniac episode. This definition is very similar to the dissocial personality disorder applied during the tenth edition of the International Classification of Diseases (ICD-10), published in 1992 by the World Health Organization (WHO).

STUDIES ON THE RELATIONSHIP BETWEEN ALEXITHYMIA AND PSYCHOPATHY

Psychopathy is characterized by a noticeable lack of empathy, emotional disconnection, impulsiveness, and a marked hostility. In turn, alexithymia is not only characterized by the difficulty in identifying and expressing feelings, but also by a lack of empathy and a high impulsiveness and psychosomatic tendency. Also, the etiology of both diagnoses shows an early maternal rejection and a lack of maturity in the brain routes and regions that regulate conscience and emotional control (especially the tract that connects the basal-medial prefrontal lobes to the amygdales). This creates a convergence between both concepts resulting in an interesting subject: the relationship between psychopathy and alexithymia. Also, one question arises: Could psychopathy be considered a type of alexithymia?

Sifneos (2000) suggests that alexithymia is the personality trait found in leaders implicated in political crimes or even genocide such as Hitler, Eichmann, and Hess. Cruelty arises from an affective disconnection and specific, literal thinking. Based on the transcriptions of daily conversations or interrogations with these individuals, the author describes them as individuals completely devoid of emotions; avoiding all contact with their internal self; shallow, and prone to get involved in long, boring, and confusing monologues on technical, construction or weapon matters.

In a similar line of thinking, Wastell and Booth (2003) criticize the Machiavellian volitional approach and propose an alternate alexithymic model, a disconnection of feelings and an inability to connect emotionally with others. As a consequence, they treat others as objects and manipulate them to satisfy egocentric goals. To support this hypothesis, in a sample of 27 men and 73 women, first-year psychology students at the Macquarie University of Sydney (Australia), they found that Machiavellianism (*Machiavellianism Scale* by Christie & Geis, 1970) significantly ($p<.01$) correlated with alexithymia (TAS-20) ($r=.48$) and its three factors (DIF, $r=.43$; DDF, $r=.40$; and EOT, $r=.30$). At the same time, TAS-20 and its three factors negatively correlated with empathy (*Empathy Scale for Adult* by Feshbach & Lipian, 1987). The authors concluded that Machiavellianism is a strategy to dwell in an interpersonal world of feelings. A world where the Machiavellian individual is a misfit due to a deficit in the processing of emotional signals, since persistent intimate relationships need some appropriate affective modulations and expressions. Because (s)he is unable to implement these relational processes, (s)he treats people as objects.

Keltikangas-Järvinen (1982) carried out a study on psychopathic personality in Helsinki, Finland, using the Rorschach test and the TAT. The study compared a sample of 68 men imprisoned for violent crimes to 64 men without any criminal or psychiatric record. Both samples were made up by young men (the average age for prisoners was 28.5 years, and 24.1 for the control sample), with elementary education (6.7 years of education for prisoners, and 8.4 years for the control sample). Aggression, inability to daydream, and inability to expressing feelings stand out as differences. The author concluded that the inability to daydream and the inability to express feelings support the hypothesis of alexithymia among criminals. She attributed this pathology to a fixation at the pre-genital level and to the mother-child relationship disorder.

Louth, Hare, and Linden (1998) found a prevalence of 30% of psychopathic traits (*Psychopathy CheckList-Revised* (PCL-R) by Hare, 1991) and 32% of alexithymic traits (TAS-26) in a sample of 37 female delinquents from Vancouver, Canada. They also found that PCL-R as well as TAS-26 were significantly correlated ($p<.01$) to a history of violence (.60 and .49, respectively). However, only 3 women shared psychopathic and alexithymic traits. Once the correlation between both scales was estimated only the difficulty in identifying feelings factor of the TAS-26 was significantly correlated to the total score ($r=.33$) and to the second factor of impulsive, antisocial, and unstable lifestyle ($r=.38$) of the HPCL-R. The authors concluded that in spite of an apparent conceptual similarity, psychopathy and alexithymia are different clinical constructs.

Sayar, Ebrinc, and Ak (2001) conducted a study with recruits from the military service at a Turkish military hospital in Istanbul. In the group of soldiers with antisocial personality disorder (DSM-IV) (excluded from the military service due to an antisocial behavior), they found a mean significantly higher in the TAS-26 ($\overline{X}=41 \pm S_{\overline{X}}=8.5$) than in the control group of soldiers ($\overline{X}=14.8 \pm S_{\overline{X}}=9$) ($t_{(88)}=14.01$, p=.000). In the joint sample of 90 subjects, they did not obtain a significant correlation between the TAS-26 and the remaining psychological measures administered: depression (BDI by Beck, Ward, Mendelson, Mock., & Erbaugh,,1961), hopelessness (BHS by Beck, Weissman, Lester, & Trexler, 1974), anxiety (STAI by

Spielberger, Gorsuch, & Lusahene, 1970) and possible psychopathology (BSI by Derogatis, 1992); but they noticed a higher mean in the TAS-26 among individuals of a lower social class ($t_{(88)}$=2.294, p<.05) and lower schooling ($t_{(88)}$=2.287, p<.05). They argue that alexithymia may develop through social ways, which means that it may originate from a failure in the socialization process.

Moriarty, Stough, Tidmarsh, Edger, and Dennison (2001) compared 15 teenage sexual offenders from Sydney, Australia, and 49 young men without criminal or psychiatric records, in the same age group. They assessed three emotional-intelligence skills (attention to feelings, emotional clarity, and restoration of mood states) using the *Trait Meta-Mood Scale* (TMMS) (Salovey, Mayer, Goldman, Turvey, & Palfai, 1995), alexithymia using the TAS-20 (Bagby, Parker & Taylor, 1994), empathy using the *Interpersonal Reactivity Index* (IRI) (Davis, 1980), interpersonal problems using the *Inventory of Interpersonal Problems-32* (IIP-32) (Barkham, Hardy, & Startup, 1996) and openness to emotions and experience using the *Openness* factor of the *NEO-PI-R* (Costa & McCrae, 1992). By using a discriminant analysis, 89.9% of the subjects were correctly classified. Sexual offenders were characterized by a higher number of aggressive and violent conflicts (IIP-32), for paying more attention to their feelings (TMMS), for more confusion in their feelings (TMMS), as well as for a less ability to restore negative emotions and maintain positive emotions (TMMS). The authors propose to focus on the treatment of these traits.

A review of the literature on the subject revealed that alexithymia and psychopathy are two perfectly distinguishable concepts, moderately related in the criminal population and less likely to appear in the control population. The correlation is more obvious in the difficulty in identifying feelings factor of alexithymia and in poor empathy. However, it is possible that this relation might be considerably mediated by depression. Since alexithymia is strongly related to depression (Honkalampi *et al.*, 1999, 2000) there are critics opposed to the concept of alexithymia as a personality trait, who propose to consider alexithymia as a kind of depressive disorder (Wise *et al.*, 1988). At the same time, there is an indication that during adolescence, dissocial behavior is frequently related to masked depression and dysthymia (Wicks-Nelson & Israel, 1997) and the MMPI scale 4 (psychopathic deviation) show a significant correlation to the MMPI scale 2 (depression), even moderately high (r=.60) with the MMPI additional scale D1 (subjective depression) by Harris and Lingoes (1955).

Gender is another significant factor in the association between alexithymia and psychopathy, even within the possible mediation of depression. The concept of alexithymia has been criticized for being a communication style related to the masculine gender (O'Neil, Good, & Holmes, 1995). On the contrary, American community studies have shown that the prevalence of depression doubled in women and the antisocial personality disorder is three times higher in men than in women (DSM-IV, 1994). This would indicate that the association between psychopathy and alexithymia is mediated by the male gender and that depression and the absence of alexithymia is mediated by the female gender. However, the measurement of alexithymia by the TAS-26 and the TAS-20 shows a very low bias effect in regard to gender. There is usually an equivalence of means between men and women in the total score and its factors, except in the externally-oriented thinking factor where men score slightly higher (Parker, Taylor, & Bagby, 1989; Dion, 1996, Paez *et al.*, 1999). It must be also pointed out that there is no mean difference between men and women (Schuler, Snibbe, & Buckwalter, 1994) in psychopathic traits within the control population (with no criminal or psychiatric records), defined as a continuum (measured by the scale 4 of the MMPI, for instance) and not as a clinical dichotomy (presence or absence of an antisocial personality disorder, for example, according to DSM-IV criteria).

OBJECTIVES AND HYPOTHESIS

The aims of this study were: (1) to study the association between alexithymia and psychopathy, (2) to establish the effect of depression in the association between alexithymia and psychopathy, and (3) to observe gender differences among alexithymia, psychopathy and depression.

According to these three objectives and upon the examination of the literature on the subject of alexithymia and psychopathy, we expected: (1) a slight association between alexithymia and psychopathy; (2) a fairly higher association between psychopathy and depression, with a lower intensity in the association between alexithymia and psychopathy by eliminating the effect of depression; (3) a statistic difference between men and women in the externally-oriented thinking factor of alexithymia and in psychopathic deviation, where men average higher, but a statistic equivalence in the total score of alexithymia and difficulty in identifying and expressing emotional factors, where men's means are higher, except in the difficulty in identifying feelings factor.

Social and cultural factors are not considered in this study, even though they are essential to this issue. Social criticism has not only suggested the possibility that alexithymia is a communication style related to the male gender, but also a style of communication related to lower classes. This criticism is partly based on the distribution of psychosomatic diseases within the lower social-class group and the presence of more serious psychosomatic diagnoses found in men (Borens, Grosse-Schulte, Jaensch & Kortemme, 1977; Lesser, Ford, & Friedman, 1979; Smith, 1983). However, based on epidemiological data obtained from the TAS as a measurement for alexithymia, the hypothesis stating that the concept should be limited to a communication style particular to a demographic group, either men or lower social class, can be rejected (Parker, Taylor, & Bagby, 1989; Pasini *et al.*, 1992). It has also been proposed that alexithymia is an invention introduced by the Western society and the middle class, in contrast with some forms of corporal emotional expression more present in eastern societies and western lower social class. This statement is discredited by cross-cultural congruence and interclass of the alexithymia assessment by the TAS-20 (Sivak & Wiater, 1997). Nevertheless, alexithymia estimates, using alternative methods such as neuroimaging and neurocognitive techniques, can reveal new and unknown aspects.

METHOD

This is a correlational study with a non-experimental transversal design that uses a non-probabilistic sampling with a large incidental sample (Hernandez-Sampieri, Fernández-Collado & Baptista, 2006).

Participants

Only 359, out of 362, subjects assessed with TAS-20 and MMPI yielded complete data. Thus, three cases were eliminated from the statistical calculation. The sample consisted of first-year psychology students selected for admission to college in June 2003. The average age was 17.65 years with a standard deviation of 2.32 years. The age range was 16 to 36. Seventy six percent were women and 24% men. Ninety eight percent were single and 2% were married or cohabitating. Ninety eight percent were financially dependent from their parents and 2% were emancipated. Only 80% had no paid job and 20% worked part-time.

Instruments

Alexithymia

We used the Likert type *20-item Toronto Alexithymia Scale* by Bagby, Parker, and Taylor (1994), which has been validated in the Mexican population by Moral (2008). Five out of the 20 items are reverse-scored (4, 5, 10, 18 and 19). According to an exploratory factor analysis, the Mexican version of the TAS-20 had a three orthogonal factor structure that accounted for 38% of the total variance: (1) difficulty in expressing feelings (DDF) (2, 4, 11, 12, and 17); (2) difficulty in identifying feelings (DIF) (1, 3, 6, 7, 9, 13 and 14), and (3) externally-oriented thinking (EOT) (5, 8, 10, 15, 16, 18, 19 and 20). These factors (defined as a single sum of items) were interrelated. The highest correlation were between the first and second factors ($r=.57$) and the lowest correlations were between these and the third factor. The scale showed internal consistency ($\alpha=.82$) and was reliable for 6 months ($r=.70$), as well as its first two factors: difficulty in expressing and identifying feelings ($\alpha=.80$ and $r=.55$ and $\alpha=.78$ and $r=.61$, respectively). The third factor had a low reliability ($\alpha=.53$ and $r=.36$). The 20 items were discriminant and reliable. Each item had a range of 6 possible points (0 to 5), each end with three points but no intermediate point. The scale distribution adjusted to a normal mean curve of 25 and a standard deviation of 12. The asymmetrical distributions of its three factors were slightly positive.

Psychopathic Deviation

It was assessed using the MMPI Scale 4 developed by Hathaway and McKinley in 1944. Its 50 items estimate the rejection to social norms and standards, indifference to the rights of others, dishonesty, amorality, lack of acceptance of authority, poor impulse control with violent outbreaks, family and relationship conflicts, guilt externalization, extroversion and narcissism. The scale exhibits an acceptable internal consistency of .60 and a high temporal stability of .80 over one week. It correlates, with values from .65 to .40, to the scales 8 (Schizophrenia), 6 (Paranoia), and 9 (Hypomania) of the MMPI; and with values from .40 to .20 to the MMPI scale 2 (Depression). The scale is a good criterion for the prediction of crimes and misdemeanours, as well as drug abuse among students and workers (Hathaway & McKinley, 1967).

Depression

This factor was assessed using the MMPI scale 2 developed in 1942 by Hathaway and McKinley. Its 60 items estimate feelings of sadness, sorrow and guilt, anhedonia, pessimism, psychomotor inhibition, poor concentration and low self-esteem. The scale shows an internal reasonable consistency of 0.64 and a high temporal stability of 0.76 over one week. It accurately classifies 92% of depressive patients (Hathaway & McKinley, 1967).

Scales 2 and 4 of the MMPI are used in direct scores due to the lack of standards for Mexican samples. The *gender* variable was handled as a dichotomy: man and woman.

Data Analysis

Linear associations between psychopathic deviation (the MMPI scale 4) and alexithymia (the TAS-20 and its three factors) were estimated using Pearson's linear correlation. The techniques of partial correlation, multiple linear regression and path analysis using linear structural equations were used in order to determine the effect of depression on the relationship between alexithymia and psychopathic deviation. The mean difference by gender in alexithymia and psychopathic deviation was established using Student's t tests for independent samples. Variance equality between both samples was previously contrasted using Levene's test to assume homoscedasticity. Groups with high or low psychopathic deviation traits (defined by percentiles 80 and 20) in the TAS-20 and its three factors were compared using Student's t tests. The significance level was set at values of p lower than or equal to .05 to reject the null hypothesis. When the values of p are lower than or equal to .075, we assume an approximation to statistical significance, even though other authors increase the margin up to .099. This qualification of approximation to statistical significance is more relevant with small samples or when there is an imbalance in the number of subjects in comparative groups. In these cases, the statistical-contrast tests incur more in the type II error, that is, they support the null hypothesis when it is false. Our case is that of samples matched with a disparate number of subjects (García-Cruz, 2002; Osterwalder, 2002). Structural equations are estimated using the Maximum Likelihood method from the correlation matrix, leaving residuals independent; every analyzed variable is manifest with the exception of the residuals. Statistic estimates were obtained using the SPSS 16 program, except for the path analysis that was conducted using the STATISTICA 7 SEPATH module (Steiger, 1995). AMOS 7 (Arbuckle, 1997) was also used to obtain the estimates of the models. Tables of parameters and fit indices came from STATISTICA 7 and figures from AMOS 7. We must point out that fit and parameter results coincide with both programs.

RESULTS

Correlations between Alexithymia and Psychopathic Deviation

The MMPI scale 4 (psychopathic deviation) only correlates significantly with the second factor of the TAS-20 (difficulty identifying feelings) in the total sample (n=359) (r=.124, p=.018). In the male sample, the correlation approximates statistical significance (p=.065).

Although its value was as high as $r=.202$, the test loses power due to the smaller size of the sample (n=84) (see Table 1).

Table 1. Correlations between the TAS-20 and its three factors
and the MMPI clinical scale 4 (Psychopathic deviate)

Alexithymia	MMPI Scale 4 (Psychopathic deviate)					
	Total sample (n=359)		Men (n=84)		Women (n=275)	
	r	P	R	P	R	P
TAS-20	.074	.163	.092	.406	.065	.283
DDF	.053	.310	.109	.322	.037	.537
DIF	.124	.018	.202	.065	.096	.113
EOT	-.025	.638	-.126	.255	.008	.897

TAS-20: Total score of the 20-items Toronto Alexithymia Scale. DDF: Difficulty in describing feelings. DIF: Difficulty in identifying feelings. EOT: Externally oriented thinking style.

Mean Differences in Alexithymia between High and Low PD Score Groups

Another method used to estimate the relation between psychopathic deviation and alexithymia involved a means comparison between both extreme groups of psychopathic deviation in alexithymia. First, 26 was taken as the cutting point of the MMPI scale 4. This value corresponds to a T score of 80 in the American sample of Hathaway and McKinley (1967). A means equivalence was obtained in the total score of the TAS-20 in the total sample ($p=.527$), in males ($p=.484$), and females ($p=.806$). With no significant difference, the group with a higher psychopathic deviation (PD≥26) had a higher mean score in alexithymia. Only the second factor of the TAS-20 (difficulty in identifying feelings) approximates statistic significance in the total sample ($p=.067$) and in the male sample ($p=.975$). The group with the higher psychopathic deviation is the one that tends to be in the lead (see Table 2).

As we have just mentioned, the 26 score corresponds to percentiles 60-65 of the Mexican sample and a T score of 80 in the Hathaway and McKinley's (1967) American sample. The 28 score was used as the cutting point that corresponds to the percentile 80 of the Mexican sample and a T score of 85 in the American sample. Although there were values of mean differences as high as 3, the big difference in group size makes it difficult to reach a significant result. In the total score of the TAS-20 there are means equivalence in the total sample (p=.107), in the male sample (p=.209), and in the female sample (p=.213). Subjects in the group with the most psychopathic features stand out. The biggest difference appeared in the difficulty in identifying feelings factor, in the total and in the male sample (see Table 3).

The Effect of Depression in the Relationship
between Alexithymia and Psychopathy

In the combined sample ($n=359$), the correlation between psychopathic deviation and depression is significant and stronger ($r=.205$) than between psychopathic deviation and difficulty in identifying feelings ($r=.124$). At the same time, there is a significant and direct correlation between depression and alexithymia ($r=.231$) and their first two factors of difficulty in expressing and identifying feelings (DES $r=.265$ and DIS $r=.199$). These correlations were quite similar to those obtained in the female sample ($n=275$), where depression correlated directly and significantly ($p<.01$) with the TAS-20 total score ($r=.252$) and its two first factors (DES, $r=.286$ and DIS $r=.196$) and with psychopathic deviation ($r=.166$). In the male sample ($n=84$), due to its smaller size, depression only correlated significantly with psychopathic deviation ($r=.350$, $p=.001$) and with difficulty in expressing feelings ($r=.264$, $p=.015$). Also, its correlation was closer to statistical significance with the TAS-20 total score ($r=.211$, $p=.054$). In males, depression is independent from difficulty in expressing feelings ($r=.159$, $p=.148$). The third TAS-20 factor (externally-oriented thinking) is independent from depression in the three samples (see Table 4).

Table 2. Differences on the TAS20 y its three factors means by groups of low and high scores (centiles 20 and 80) at the MMPI scale 4 (Psychopathic deviate)

Samples	Alexi-thymia	Mean ± Standard deviation		Levene's test		Student's test		
		PD<26 (n=213)	PD≥26 (n=149)	F	P	t	df	p
Total (n=359)	TAS20	24.39 ± 11.89	25.21 ± 12.83	.770	.381	-.632	360	.527
	DDF	7.95 ± 5.29	8.01 ± 6.16	4.324	.038	-.096	360	.923
	DIF	7.89 ± 5.40	9.01 ± 6.15	1.056	.305	-1.835	360	.067
	EOT	8.54 ± 4.45	8.19 ± 4.55	.386	.535	.729	360	.467
		PD<26 (n=56)	PD≥26 (n=28)	F	P	t	df	p
Men (n=84)	TAS20	25.14 ± 11.46	27.04 ± 11.99	.012	.913	-.703	82	.484
	DDF	8.14 ± 4.84	8.89 ± 6.15	2.277	.135	-.611	82	.543
	DIF	7.29 ± 5.20	9.54 ± 5.75	.000	.997	-1.803	82	.075
	EOT	9.71 ± 4.96	8.61 ± 4.76	.184	.669	.976	82	.332
		PD<26 (n=156)	PD≥26 (n=119)	F	P	t	df	p
Women (n=275)	TAS20	24.11 ± 12.10	24.48 ± 12.88	.428	.513	-.246	273	.806
	DDF	7.90 ± 5.47	7.73 ± 6.19	2.203	.139	.245	273	.807
	DIF	8.13 ± 5.47	8.78 ± 6.23	.942	.333	-.915	273	.361
	EOT	8.08 ± 4.16	7.97 ± 4.44	1.264	.262	.196	273	.845

TAS-20: Total score of the 20-items Toronto Alexithymia Scale. DDF: Difficulty in describing feelings. DIF: Difficulty inidentifying feelings. EOT: Externally oriented thinking style PD: Psychopathic deviate.

Table 3. Differences on the TAS20 and its three factors' means by groups of low and high scores (centiles 15 and 85) at the MMPI scale 4 (Psychopathic deviate)

Samples		Mean ± Standard deviation		Levene's test		Student's test		
		PD<28 (n=273)	PD≥28 (n=89)	F	P	T	df	P
Total (n=359)	TAS20	24.13± 12.01	26.55± 12.95	.988	.321	-1.618	360	.107
	DDF	7.66 ± 5.24	8.94 ± 6.71	14.396	.000	-1.654	124.96	.101
	DIF	8.06 ± 5.61	9.25 ± 6.07	.436	.510	-1.696	360	.091
	EOT	8.41 ± 4.38	8.36 ± 4.85	1.065	.303	.099	360	.921
Men (n=84)		PD<26 (n=56)	PD≥26 (n=28)	F	P	T	df	P
	TAS20	24.97 ± 10.92	28.94 ± 13.89	2.082	.153	-1.265	82	.209
	DDF	7.94 ± 4.70	10.18 ± 7.04	7.239	.009	-1.242	19.77	.229
	DIF	7.54 ± 5.08	10.00 ± 6.56	.458	.501	-1.678	82	.097
	EOT	9.49 ± 4.74	8.77 ± 5.60	.221	.640	.545	82	.587
Women (n=275)		PD<26 (n=156)	PD≥26 (n=119)	F	P	T	df	P
	TAS20	23.73 ± 12.27	25.86 ± 12.80	.275	.600	-1.248	273	.213
	DDF	7.55 ± 5.42	8.62 ± 6.69	8.114	.005	-1.212	103.86	.228
	DIF	8.20 ± 5.73	9.04 ± 6.02	.223	.637	-1.057	273	.291
	EOT	7.98 ± 4.13	8.20 ± 4.69	1.582	.210	-.376	273	.708

TAS-20: Total score of the 20-items Toronto Alexithymia Scale. DDF: Difficulty Describing Feelings. DIF: Difficulty identifying feelings. EOT: Externally oriented thinking style PD: Psychopathic deviate.

Table 4. Correlations between the TAS-20 and its three factors and the MMPI scale 4 (Psychopathic deviate) with the MMPI scale 2 (depression)

Alexithymia	MMPI Scale 2 (Depression)					
	Total sample (*n*=359)		Men (*n*=84)		Women (*n*=275)	
	R	P	R	P	r	P
TAS-20	.231	.000	.211	.054	.252	.000
DDF	.265	.000	.264	.015	.286	.000
DIF	.199	.000	.159	.148	.196	.001
EOT	.043	.420	.037	.738	.079	.190
PD	.205	.000	.350	.001	.166	.006

TAS-20: Total score of the 20-items Toronto Alexithymia Scale. DDF: Difficulty Describing Feelings. DIF: Difficulty identifying feelings. EOT: Externally oriented thinking style PD: Psychopathic deviate.

The correlation between psychopathic deviation and depression reaches a higher magnitude in the male sample ($r=.350$) and, as in the total sample, it surpasses the correlation between difficulty in identifying feelings and depression ($r=.264$). In the female sample, the value is the lowest ($r=.166$), and it is surpassed by the correlation between depression and difficulty in identifying feelings ($r=.196$). Thus, the relationship between depression and psychopathy is more obvious in men (see Table 4).

When controlling the effect of depression on the relationship between difficulty in identifying feelings and psychopathic deviation ($r_{DIF, PD(D)} = .087$), using the partial correlation technique, this correlation resulted non-significant ($p=.100$) (See Table 5).

Table 5. Partial correlations between TAS-20 and its three factors and the MMPI scale 4 (psychopathic deviate) controlling the MMPI scale 2 (depression)

Alexithymia	MMPI Scale 4 (Psychopathic deviate)					
	Total sample (n=359)		Man (n=84)		Women (n=275)	
	r_p	P	r_p	p	r_p	P
TAS-20	.0277	.600	.0197	.859	.0243	.689
DDF	-.0008	.988	.0189	.866	-.0106	.861
DIF	.0869	.100	.1581	.153	.0656	.276
EOT	-.0343	.516	-.1482	.181	-.0054	.929

TAS-20: Total score of the 20-items Toronto Alexithymia Scale. DDF: Difficulty in describing feelings. DIF: Difficulty in identifying feelings. EOT: Externally oriented thinking style.

In the male sample, where the correlation between psychopathic deviation and difficulty in identifying feelings ($r=.202$) approximates a statistic significance ($p=.065$), when it comes to control the effect of depression through partial correlation this decreases and it is not significant ($r_{DIF, PD(D)} = .158, p=.153$) (see Table 5).

Likewise, in a linear regression model calculated by the Enter method, which predicts the MMPI Scale 4 (psychopathic deviation) using the MMPI Scale 2 (depression) and the second factor of the TAS-20 that corresponds to the difficulty in identifying feelings as predictors, only depression resulted significant (Beta=.187, t=3.570, p=.000) in the combined sample (see Table 6). These two variables were used as predictors because they were the only ones with a significant correlation with the criteria, while the TAS-20 total score as well as the scores of DDF and EOT factors were excluded.

Table 6. Linear regression Model by the Enter method

R^2=.049 (N=359)	Non-standardized coefficients		Standardized coefficients	t	P
	B	Standardized Error	Beta		
(Constant)	20.727	1.075	-	19.275	.000
D	.171	.048	.187	3.570	.000
DIF	0.061	.037	.089	1.652	.099

Dependent Variable: Psychopathic deviation. Predictor variables: D = MMPI Depression scale. DIF = TAS-20 Difficulty in identifying feelings factor.

Using a path analysis, we tested a model where depression determines the difficulty in identifying feelings as well as psychopathic deviation, while difficulty in identifying feelings determines a psychopathic deviation (Model 1), this latter path was not significant and the fit indices cannot be calculated due to the lack of degree of freedom (see Figure 1 and Tables 7 and 8).

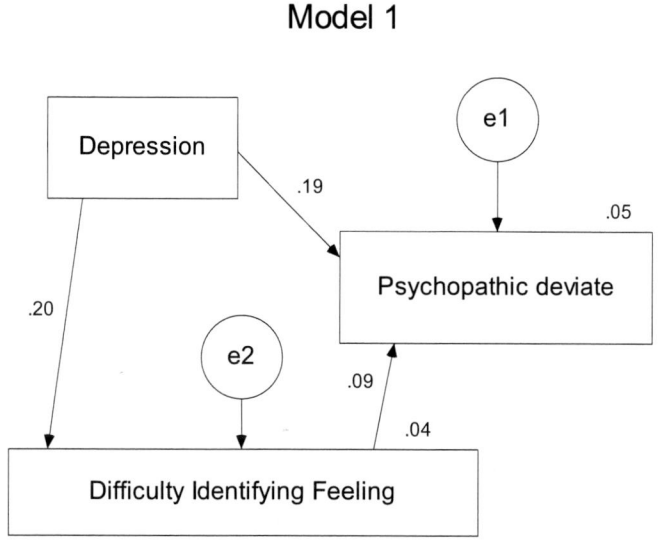

Model 1

Figure 1. Model 1: Determination of psychopathic deviation.

There was a good fit in the model where psychopathic deviation and difficulty in identifying feelings are two manifest endogenous variables determined by depression, specified as an exogenous variable (Model 2). All its determination paths are significant and the fit indices resulted acceptable (see Figure 2 and Table 7 and 8).

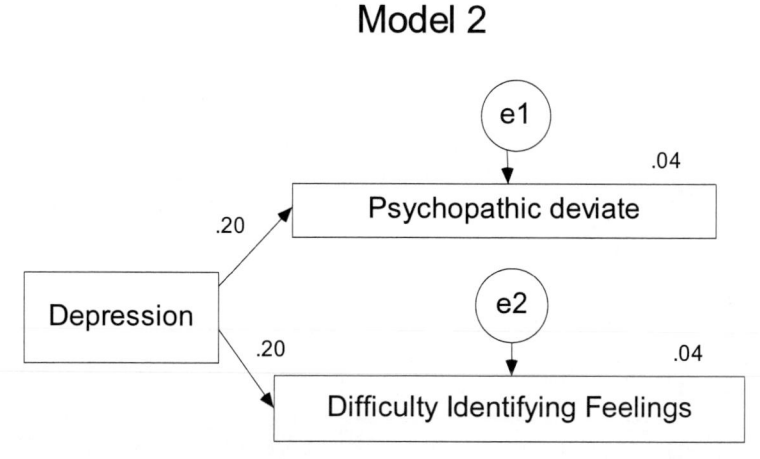

Model 2

Figure 2. Model 2: Determination of psychopathic deviate.

In the regression model where depression and difficulty in identifying feelings determine a psychopathic deviation (Model 3), the latter path is not significant and the fit indices are not as good as those obtained for model 2. Also, this model contemplates the correlation between depression and a difficulty in identifying feelings that is, indeed, significant (see Figure 3 and Tables 7 and 8).

Model 3

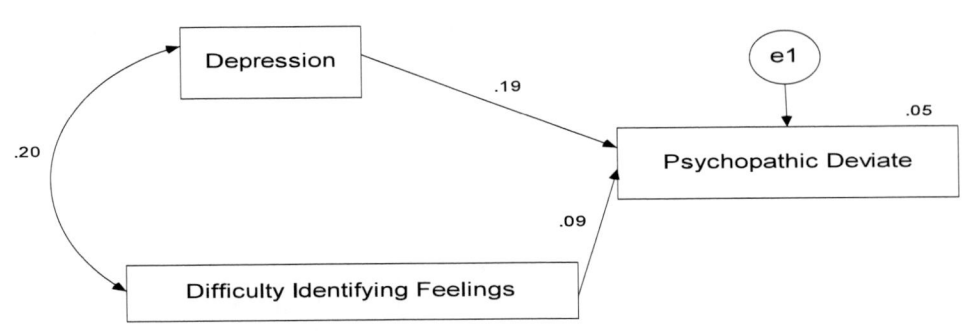

Figure 3. Model 3: Determination of the psychopathic deviate.

The fit improved when the model was calculated, again, without determining psychopathic deviation through the difficulty in identifying feelings (Model 4). This model resulted better than the second one (Model 2). The explained variance of psychopathic deviation in both models (2 and 4) is 5%, thus very low (see Figure 4 and Tables 7 and 8).

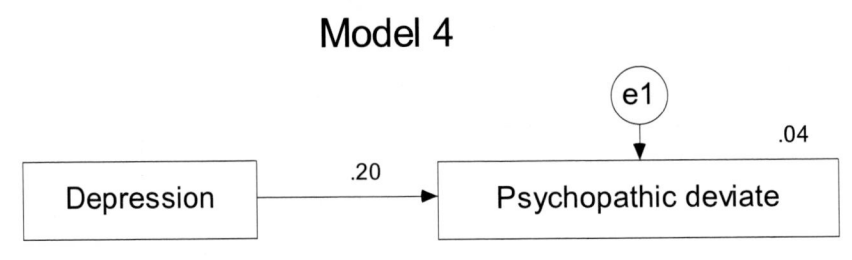

Model 4

Figure 4. Model 4: Determination of psychopathic deviate.

Table 7. The determination path parameter estimates of the 4 models

Models	Determination path	Parameter estimate	Standard error	t statistic	p-level	% var.
M1	[MMPID]-1->[MMPIPD]	0.187	0.051	3.642	0.000	PD 4.9%
	[MMPID]-2->[DIF]	0.199	0.051	3.932	0.000	
	[DIF]-3->[MMPIPD]	0.087	0.052	1.663	0.096	PD 3.9%
M2	[MMPID]-1->[MMPIPD]	0.205	0.050	4.059	0.000	PD 4.9%
	[MMPID]-2->[DIF]	0.199	0.050	3.932	0.000	
M3*	[MMPID]-1->[MMPIPD]	0.188	0.050	3.719	0.000	PD 4.9%
	[DIF]-2->[MMPIPD]	0.087	0.050	1.697	0.090	
M4	[MMPID]-1->[MMPIPD]	0.200	0.000	8.825	0.000	PD 4.2%

[ ]: manifest variable, MMPID: MMPI scale 2 (depression), MMPIPD: MMPI scale 4 (Psychopathic deviate), DIF: TAS20 difficulty identifying feelings factor.

*M3: STATISTICA does not allow the involvement of endogenous manifest variables in undirected relations. AMOS does not have this restriction.

Table 8. Fit indices of the 4 models calculated by Maximum Likelihood (ML)

Fit indices	Interpretation Good	Interpretation Bad	Models M1	M2	M3	M4
Basics summary statistics						
FD	≤2	>3	0	0.008	0.040	0.001
MLχ2 (df)			0 (0)	2.735 (1)	14.55 (1)	0.336 (1)
P	≥.05	<.01		0.098	0.000	0.562
MLχ2/df	≤2	>3	1	2.735	14.550	0.336
RMS SR	≤.05	>.075	0	0.034	0.083	0.023
Non-centrality based indices (point estimate)						
PNCP	≤1	>2		0.005	0.037	0.000
RMS EA	≤.05	>.075		0.069	0.192	0.000
GPI	≥.95	<.85		0.997	0.976	1.000
AGPI	≥.90	<.80		0.981	0.857	1.000
Other simple sample indices						
GFI	≥.95	<.85		0.995	0.974	0.999
AGFI	≥.90	<.80		0.970	0.846	0.997
NFI	≥.95	<.85		0.916	0.556	0.978
NNFI	≥.95	<.85		0.825	-0.367	1.000
CFI	≥.95	<.85		0.942	0.544	1.000
Δ	≥.95	<.85		0.945	0.573	1.000

Models: D=depression, DIF=Difficulty identifying feelings y PD=Psychopathic deviate. M1 (D→PD y DIF, DIF→PD), M2 (D→PD y DIF), M3 (D y DIF→PD) y M4 (D y DIF→PD).

Fit indices: DF: Discrepancy function, MLχ2: ML chi-square, df: degrees of freedom, p-level: probability of MLχ2, RMS SR: Standardized Root Mean Square Residual, PNCP: Population non-centrality parameter, RMS EA: Steiger-Lind's root mean squared of approximation error de, GPI: Population gamma Index, AGPI: Adjusted Population gamma Index, GFI: Joreskog's Goodness Fit Index, AGFI: Joreskog's adjusted Goodness Fit Index, NFI: Bentler-Bonett's normed Fit index, NNFI: Bentler-Bonett's Non-normed Fit index, CFI: Bentler's comparative fit index & Δ: Bollen's delta.

Comparing TAS-20 Means by Gender, Its Three Factors and Psychopathic Deviation

In regards to TAS-20 and its three factors, the only significant difference ($p<.05$) was observed in the third factor between men and women. Men showed a more externally-oriented thinking trait than women (p=.024). Although not a statistically significant value ($p<.10$), women produced a higher mean in the difficulty in identifying feelings, while the total score for alexithymia and for difficulty in expressing feelings were higher among men.

Since women had a score of 8% superior to men in the psychopathic deviation scale (24.56 ± 3.78), due to the inclusion of more items, their mean is higher (25.19 ± 4.06) than men's (24.56 ± 3.78), without obtaining any statistically significant value (p<.10). However, as expected, men scored significantly higher than women (23.17 ± 3.74) ($t_{(357)}$=2.974, p=.000) when females' scores were reduced 8% (see Table 9).

Table 9. Differences of the TAS-20, its three factors and the MMPI scale 4 (Psychopathic deviation) between men and women

Alexithymia	Men Mean ± SD	Women Mean ± SD	Levene's test F	p	Student's t-test t	df	P
TAS-20	25.98 ± 11.68	24.27 ± 12.42	.499	.481	1.123	360	.262
DDF	8.54 ± 5.43	7.83 ± 5.78	.341	.560	1.011	360	.313
DIF	8.15 ± 5.54	8.41 ± 5.79	.310	.578	-.359	360	.720
OET	9.28 ± 4.90	8.04 ± 4.27	.740	.390	2.270	360	.024
PD	24.56 ± 3.78	25.19 ± 4.06	.522	.470	-1.256	357	.210
PD*	24.56±3.78	23.17±3.74	.008	.928	2.974	357	.003

TAS-20: Total score of the 20-items Toronto Alexithymia Scale. DDF: Difficulty in describing feelings. DIF: Difficulty in identifying feelings. EOT: Externally oriented thinking style PD: Psychopathic deviate. PD* The women's MMPI scale 4 was reduced in 8% (PD) scores before conducting the means contrast.

Table 10. Correlations between corrected PD scores and TAS-20 and its three factors

Alexithymia	PD* Total sample (n=359) R	p	Man (n=84) R	p	Women (n=275) r	P
TAS-20	.088	.095	.092	.406	.075	.213
DDF	.064	.224	.109	.322	.081	.181
DIF	.120	.022	.202	.065	.094	.121
EOT	.006	.903	-.126	.255	.023	.708

TAS-20: Total score of the 20-items Toronto Alexithymia Scale. DDF: Difficulty in describing feelings. DIF: Difficulty in identifying feeling. EOT: Externally oriented thinking style. PD* The women's MMPI scale 4 was reduced in 8% (PD) scores before conducting the means contrast.

The results of the correlations between alexithymia and psychopathic deviation do not differ when the correlations are calculated while female scores in the MMPI Scale 4 were reduced 8%. In the combined male and female samples (n=359), a weak and significant correlation with the difficulty in identifying feelings (r=.120, p=.022) was observed. The other two factors and their relation to the total score are independent. No changes were observed in the male sample (n=84). Only the correlation with the difficulty in identifying feelings is closer to statistic significance (r=.202, p=.065). No correlation is significant in the female sample (n=275) (see Table 10).

CONCLUSION

Psychopathy (assessed with the MMPI-Scale 4), in its relation with alexithymia (measured with the TAS-20) only correlates weakly with the difficulty in identifying feelings factor in this sample of Mexican students. The higher the score in psychopathic deviation the most difficulty in identifying feelings was found. This correlation appears significant only in the combined sample while is close to significance in the males' sample. In the females' sample, no correlation was found between alexithymia and psychopathy. These results coincide with the proposed hypothesis. As in the sample of Canadian women of Louth et al.

(1998), there was no relation between the TAS-20 as total score and its three factors, and psychopathic deviation, but a correlation was indeed present with depression in this sample of Mexican women. Likewise, as reported in the studies with males conducted by Keltikangas-Järvinen (1982) in Finland, and Moriarty *et al.* (2001) in Australia, the Mexican sample analyzed in this study emphasized the difficulty in identifying feelings -or emotional confusion factor- in relation to psychopathy. Using two samples of Turkish soldiers, one made up by subjects diagnosed with antisocial personality disorder (DSM-IV) and the other as a control sample, Sayar, Ebrinc, and Ak (2001) found a means difference in the total score of the TAS-26, but no correlation was found between the TAS-26 as total score and depression (BDI). In the Mexican sample of our study, only the difficulty in identifying feelings come closer to the statistic significance taking 26 as the cutting point in psychopathic deviation, which corresponds to percentile 60-65, in the Mexican sample, and a T score of 80, in the American sample of Hathaway and McKinley (1967). These results are similar to those obtained with the Turkish sample. The only difference between both studies is the absence of correlation between alexithymia and depression in the Turkish data, and the significant correlation in the Mexican data, which is the most common result.

In our study, depression resulted related to the total score of the TAS-20 and to its first two factors (difficulty in describing and identifying feelings) in the joint and female samples. In the male sample, the relation between depression and the difficulty in describing feelings approximates statistic significance. Thus, the externally-oriented thinking factor is clearly independent from depression. It must be pointed out that the relation between depression and alexithymia is more apparent in women than in men. On the other hand, the relation between psychopathic deviation and alexithymia is more obvious in men than in women. This agrees with culturally expected gender differences.

By controlling the depression level through partialization in the correlation between psychopathic deviation and the difficulty in identifying feelings (the only significant correlation in the joint sample), the correlation is not longer significant; whereas in the male sample, there was only an approximation to statistical significance, where this correlation decreases even more and it clearly becomes non significant. Whereas when trying to predict the psychopathic deviation score, using depression and the difficulty in identifying feelings as predictors, only depression resulted significant in the regression model. Finally, when comparing path models that regard the difficulty in identifying feelings factor as the determinant of psychopathic deviation, these showed maladjustment. This supports the hypothesis that psychopathy and alexithymia are two different, yet weakly related constructs, and that this relation is mediated by depression. These results not only confirm the proposed hypothesis but contribute to a solid corpus of findings that relate the total score of the TAS-20, and its first two factors, to depression (Taylor *et al.*, 1997). We must point out that strong data have been gathered on behalf of the conceptual distinction between depression and alexithymia through follow-up studies of cases and the temporal consistency of results (Parker, Bagby, & Taylor, 1991; Muller, Bühner, & Ellgring, 2003). It has also been proposed to make a distinction between primary alexithymia and secondary alexithymia in the affective diagnosis (Honkalampi *et al.*, 2004), overcoming the criticism of reducing alexithymia to a form of depression.

The data in this Mexican study show that alexithymia and psychopathy are clearly distinguishable from each other, and also that psychopathy cannot be reduced to an alexithymic type. Empathic, affective-expressive and modulation deficits belong to a completely different nature. An alexithymic subject may be considered as an adaptable, physiologically stressed person when facing emotional situations or intense emotional conflicts, with a dull social expression as well as someone dismissing his/her personal style of attachment. On the contrary, a psychopath is a rebellious transgressor, who seduces and deceives through affective modulation; he/she tries to control the will of others, and provoke emotions in his/her victims; exploits and manipulates his/her interpersonal relationships. This reflects a knowledge and conscious control of emotions, very different from a true alexithymic individual who tends to be an isolated individual from his social group, singled or with a dead married life. Thus, in prison or within a criminal group, the alexithymic subject would be the victim or the weakest link in a group of inmates, whereas the psychopath would probably be the leader. According to Louth et al. (1998), alexithymia can be related to crime. Based on the conceptual analysis of both constructs we can hypothesize that alexithymia may be sporadically related to crime or as a survival mode and, in the case of psychopathy, with a more regular character or an antisocial mode.

These results and conclusions are also close to the study of Bach et al. (1994) who tried to determine the role of alexithymia in clinical and personality disorders. They used a sample of 182 out-patients from Viennese hospitals and clinics and determined DSM-III-R diagnoses through a Structured Clinical Interview for DSM-III-R (SCID) and the Revised Personality Diagnostic Questionnaire (PDQ-R). Alexithymia was measured using the TAS-26. These authors did not find any relationship between alexithymia and any axis I diagnosis, but found an association with the dependent, avoidative and schizoid personality disorder categories. This makes alexithymia a personality disorder closer to unstable introvert subjects or indifferent introvert subjects unconnected to an antisocial personality disorder. According to Poser's analysis (2000), the perfect prototype of an alexithymic subject would be the main character in Albert Camus' "The Stranger". It might not be right to simply consider Hitler or Eichmann as alexithymic subjects according to Sifneos (2000), or Machiavellian persons as alexithymic individuals according to Wastell and Booth (2003). These cases can show alexithymic traits, but may be overlapped or subordinated to other more dominant traits such as Machiavellian, narcissistic and/or antisocial traits which constitute what Paulhus and Williams (2002) designate as "the dark triad of personality". In a sample of 37 female inmates, Louth et al. (1998) found that both alexithymia and psychopathy coincide as diagnostic traits only in an 8% of the sample; when this two personality disorders were present they appeared separately in a third of the sample. We can imagine that the female alexithymic criminal clearly differs in bonds, social skills and dangerousness from a psychopathic woman. Consequently, rehabilitation programs would require a differential approach for these two types of inmates.

Using the raw scores from the MMPI scale 4, men and women showed no difference at the middle level of psychopathic deviation traits. Also, the point-biserial correlation between gender and MMPI scale 4 (PD) is not significant; and by estimating the means difference of psychopathic deviation between men and women, using depression as a covariant, in a covariance analysis model, this resulted non significant. The data in this non-clinic sample of psychology students reflect congruently independence between gender and psychopathic deviation, which coincide with previous results reported by Schuler, Snibbe, & Buckwalter (1994) in T scores. In the tables to convert raw scores into T scores without adding the K scale correction (Hathaway & McKinley, 1967), raw and T scores are higher in women. The raw scores of women are three points higher than those of men at the range from 1 to 5 of T

scores; there is a two point difference at the range from 6 to 14 of *T* scores; there is a match at the range from 15 to 25; and there is a two-point difference at the range from 26 to 40. In cases of inequality, the *T* score is higher for women, having in turn a higher raw score. The highest raw score in women is 50 and 46 in men. Also, the minimum score in women is 2 and 1 in men. These differences are due to marked female's traits in responses to the scale. The median corresponds to a raw score of 14 in both samples, which is a false equivalence due to differential ranks of points. The scale overrates the trait in women, and underestimates it in men. Due to the 8% difference in the scales (44 points for men as opposed to 50 points in women), we decided to reduce the females' total score an 8% to obtain an equivalent rank to those of men. After this reduction, there was a significant difference in contrasting means, as expected according to epidemiologic studies (APA, 2000); also, the correlation of gender with the psychopathic deviation scale (PD) resulted significant with 2.4% of shared variance. The correlation is more defined if the effect of depression is controlled through covariance analysis.

Regarding alexithymia, there was only a difference between men and women in the third factor, which is independent from both depression and psychopathy. Men tend to have less contact with their internal personal world and focus more on external references in their arguments and decision-making processes. This is the most solid difference found in cross-cultural studies (Dion, 1996; Paez & Casullo, 2000). These data support TAS-20 as an alexithymic measure quite independent from gender.

When administering the Prototypic Alexithymic Profile (Haviland & Reise, 1996) and the Psychopathic Profile (Reise & Oliver, 1994) to a sample of 42 historic political leaders, Haviland, Sonnie, and Kowert (2004) in their California Q-set study, they clearly distinguished both concepts. These authors point out that prototypic alexithymic as well as psychopathic individuals share a lack of empathy as well as of self-understanding and reflective introspection. However, prototypic alexithymic subjects are anxious, over-controlled, submissive, boring, ethically consistent and socially agreeable individuals. On the contrary, prototypic psychopaths seem to be anxiety-free, impulsive, dominant, charming, fun, amoral, quarrelsome and disagreeable individuals.

There are important limitations to this study that we must point out: (1) The reliability and validity indexes of the two MMPI scales used are acceptable, although these could be improved using additional scales such as the BDI-2 (Beck, Steer, & Brown, 1996) for depression and the Hare's PCL-R (1991) for psychopathy; (2) The MMPI scales 2 and 4 were analyzed using raw scores since there are no standards developed for Mexico. The range would expand with the *T* scores and we would even achieve a closer approximation to a normal distribution; (3) Out of the 6 measures used, only the total score of the TAS-20 fits a normal curve (Z_{K-S}=1.280, p=.076). With the 5 remaining variables we can reject the normality null hypothesis. By violating the assumed normality the validity of the parametric tests used decreases. Mathematic transformations of the scores were conducted (with logarithmic functions and square root); variables were closer to normality but this was not reached and the results were invariant; so we decided to present the estimates with the direct scores; (4) the third factor of TAS-20 showed a slightly lower reliability and the distribution of the three TAS-20 factors were asymmetric. Perhaps, if we use another measuring instrument such as the *Bermond-Vorst Alexithymia Questionnaire* (BVAQ) (Vorst & Bermond, 2001), originated in Amsterdam (Holland), the psychometric properties could be improved in evaluating alexithymia, as shown by studies conducted in English and French samples (Zeck, Luminet, Rime & Wagner, 1999); (5) the male sample was rather small and proportionally unbalanced in relation to the female sample, which decreases the power of the statistical tests; (6) Subjects filled out questionnaires during a selection process, which may affect the sincerity of their responses. However, the levels of scales' validity of the MMPI, as considered by American standards (PT) (Hathaway & McKinley, 1967), are adequate: [L=(PB=5, PT=53), F=(PB=8, PT=61), K=(PB=13, PT=53)]; and the study of temporal stability for the TAS-20, applied to our sample six months later, yielded a high correlation (r=.70).

In conclusion, alexithymia and psychopathy are two perfectly distinguishable concepts, with a weak relation mediated by depression, at least in a sample of university students. Psychopathy is more related to depression than to alexithymia. The TAS-20 appears as a fairly independent measure of gender, except for its third externally-oriented thinking factor that shows a male bias. This factor is clearly independent from depression and psychopathy in men as well as in women, thus it does not influence the subject of study under consideration. As expected, according to epidemiological studies, there is a gender difference at the psychopathic deviation level, averaging more in men by reducing women scores by 8% to adjust the differential range of the scale for both genders. We can ascertain that psychopathy cannot be reduced to alexithymia and that it is not a type of alexithymia.

REFERENCES

American Psychiatric Association (APA) (1952). *Diagnostic and statistical manual of mental disorden (DSM)*. Washington, DC: APA.

American Psychiatric Association (APA) (1968). *Diagnostic and statistical manual of mental disorden (2^a. ed.) (DSM-II)*. Washington, DC: APA.

American Psychiatric Association (APA) (1980). *Diagnostic and statistical manual of mental disorden (3^a. ed.) (DSM-III)*. Washington, DC: APA.

American Psychiatric Association (APA) (1987). *Diagnostic and statistical manual of mental disorden (3^a. ed. Rev.) (DSM-III-R)*. Washington, DC: APA. Versión española. Ed. Masson, Barcelona (1995).

APA (American Psychiatric Association) (2000). *Diagnostic and statistical manual of mental disorden (4^a. ed.) (DSM-IV)*. Washington, DC: APA. Versión española. Ed. Masson, Barcelona (1995).

American Psychiatric Association (APA) (1994). *Diagnostic and statistical manual of mental disorden (4^a. ed. Revised Text). (DSM-IV-TR)*. Washington, DC: APA. Versión española. Ed. Masson, Barcelona (2002).

Apfel, R. J. & Sifneos, P. E. (1979). Alexithymia: Concept and measurement. *Psychotherapy and Psychosomatics*, *32*(1-4), 180-190.

Arbuckle, J. L. (1997). AMOS. *Behaviormetrika*, *24*, 85-87.

Bach, M., de Zwaan, M., Ackard, D, Nutzinger, D. O., & Mitchell, J.E. (1994) Alexithymia: relationship to personality disorders. *Comprehensive Psychiatry*, *35*(3), 239-243.

Bagby, R. M., Parker, J. D. A. & Taylor G. J. (1994). The twenty-item Toronto alexithymia scale-I. Item selection and cross-validation of the factor structure. *Journal of Psychosomatic Research*, *38*(1), 23-32.

Bagby, R. M., Taylor, G. J., & Parker, J. D. A. (1994). The twenty-item Toronto alexithymia scale-II. Convergent, discriminant and concurrent validity. *Journal of Psychosomatic Research*, *38*(1), 33-40.

Barkham, M., Hardy, G. E., & Startup, M. (1996) The structure, validity and clinical relevance of the inventory of interpersonal problems. *British Journal of Medical Psychology, 67*, 171–85.

Beck, A. T., Steer, R. A., & Brown, G. K. (1996). *Beck Depression Inventory- 2nd Edition Manual*. San Antonio, Texas: Psychological Corporation.

Beck, A. T., Ward, C. H., Mendelson, M., Mock, J., & Erbaugh, J. (1961). An inventory for measuring depression. *Archives of General Psychiatry*, *4*, 561-571.

Beck, A. T., Weissman, A., Lester, D., & Trexler, L. (1974). The measurement of pessimism: The Hopelessness Scale. *Journal of Consulting and Clinical Psychology*, *42*, 861-865.

Berenbaum, H (1996). Childhood abuse, alexithymia and personality disorder. *Journal of Psychosomatic Research*, *41*, 585-595.

Borens, R., Grosse-Schulte, E., Jaensch, W., & Kortemme, K. H. (1977). Is Alexithymia but a social phenomenon? An empirical investigation in psychosomatic patients. *Psychotherapy and Psychosomatics*, *28*(1-4), 193-198.

Christie, R., & Geis, F.L. (1970). *Studies in Machiavellianism*, New York: Academic Press.

Cohen, K. R., Demers-Desrosiers, L. A., & Catchlove, R. F. H. (1983). The SAT9: A Quantitative Scoring System for the AT-9 Test as a measure of symbolic function central to alexithymic presentation. *Psychotherapy and Psychosomatics*, *39*(1), 77-88.

Costa, P. T, Jr., & McCrae, R. R. (1992). *Revised NEO Personality Inventory and Five-Factor Inventory Proffesional Manual*. Odessa, Florida: Psychological Assessment Resources.

Crowne, D. P., & Marlowe, D. (1960). A new scale of social desirability independent of psychopathology. *Journal of Consult Clinical Psychology*, *24*, 349-354.

Davis, M. H. (1980) Measuring Individual Differences in Empathy: Evidence for a Multidimensional Approach. *Journal of Personality and Social Psychology*, *44* (1), 113-126.

Demers-Desrosiers, L. A. (1982). Influence of alexithymia on symbolic function. *Psychotherapy and Psychosomatics*, *38*, 103-12.

Derogatis, L. R. (1992). *The Brief Symptom Inventory (BSI). Administration, scoring and procedures manual*. Los Angeles, California: Clinical Psychometric Research Inc.

Dion, K. L. (1996). Ethnolinguistic correlates of alexithymia: toward a cultural perspective. *Journal of Psychosomatic Research*, *41*(6), 531-539.

Faryna, A., Rodenhauser, P., & Torem, M. (1986). Development of an Analog Alexithymia Scale: Testing in a nonpatient population. *Psychotherapy and Psychosomatics*, *45*(4), 201-206.

Feshbach, N. D., & Lipian, M. (1987). *The Empathy Scale for Adult (ESA)*. Los Angeles: University of California.

García-Cruz, J. A. (2002). Inferencia y significación estadística. En E. Palacián y J. Sancho (eds.), *Actas de la Décima Jornada para el Aprendizaje y la Enseñanza de las Matemáticas* (vol. 2, pp. 457-466). Tenerife: Universidad La Laguna.

Hare, R. D. (1991). *The Hare Psychopathy Clecklist – Revised*. Toronto: Multi-Health Systems.

Harris, R. E., & Lingoes, J. C. (1955). *Subscales for the MMPI: an aid to profile interpretation* (Mimeographed materials). San Francisco, C.A.: University of California, Department of Psychiatry.

Hathaway, S. R., y McKinley, J. (1967). *Minnesota Multiphasic Personality Inventory: Manual for administration and scoring*. New York: Psychological Corporation.

Haviland, M. G., Sonnie, J. L., & Kowet, P. A. (2004). Alexithymia and psychopathy: Comparison and application of California Q-set prototypes. *Journal of Personality Assessment, 82*(3), 306-316.

Heiberg, A. N., & Heiberg, A. (1977). Alexithymia an inherit traits? A study of twins. *Psychotherapy and Psychosomatics, 28* (1-4), 221-225.

Heiberg, A. N., & Heiberg, A. (1978). A possibility genetic contribution to the alexithymia trait. *Psychotherapy and Psychosomatics, 30*(3-4), 205-210.

Hernández-Sampieri, R., Fernández-Collado, C., y Baptista, L. (2006). Introducción a la metodología de la investigación (4ta edición). México: McGraw-Hill Interamericana.

Honkalampi, K., Hintikka, J., Tanskanen, A., Lethonen, J., & Viinamäki, H. (2000). Depression is strongly associated with alexithymia in the general population. *Journal of Psychosomatic Research, 48*, 99-104.

Honkalampi, K., Koivumaa-Honkanen, H., Antikainen, R., Haatainen, K. Hintikka, J., & Viinamäki, H. (2004). Relationships among alexithymia, adverse childhood experiences, sociodemographic variables and actual mood disorder: A 2-year clinical follow-up study of patients with major depressive disorder. *Psychosomatics, 45*(3), 197-204.

Honkalampi, K., Saarinen, P., Hintikka, J., Virtanen, V., & Viinamäki, H. (1999). Factors associated with alexithymia in patients suffering from depression. *Psychotherapy and Psychosomatics, 68*, 270-275.

Hoppe, K. D., & Bogen, J. E. (1977). Alexithymia in twelve commissurotomised patients. *Psychotherapy and Psychosomatics, 28*, 148-155.

Keltikangas-Jarvinen, L. (1982). Alexithymia in violent offenders. *Journal of Personality Assessment, 46*, 462-467.

Kleiger, J. H., & Kinsman, R. A. (1980). The development of an MMPI alexithymia scale. *Psychotherapy and Psychosomatics, 34*, 17-24.

Krystal, H. (1979). Alexithymia and psychotherapy. *American Journal of Psychotherapy, 33*, 17-31.

Krystal, J. H (1988). *Integration and self-healing: Affect, trauma and alexithymia*. Hillsdale: Analytic Press.

Lane, R. D., Ahern, G. L., Schwartz, G. E., & Kasznjak, A. W. (1997). Is alexithymia the emotional equivalent of blindsight? *Biology Psychiatry, 42*, 834-844.

Lesser, I. M., Ford, C. V., & Friedman, C. T. (1979). Alexithymia in somatizing patients. *General Hospital of Psychiatry, 1*(3), 256-261.

Loas, G., Parker, J. D. A., Otmani, O., Verrier, A., & Fremaux, D. (1997). Confirmatory factor analysis of the French translation of the 20-item Toronto Alexithymia Scale. *Perceptual and Motor Skills, 83*, 1018.

Louth, S. M., Hare, R. D., & Linden, W. (1998). Psychopathy and alexithymia in female offenders. *Canadian Journal of Behavioural Science, 30*(2), 91-99.

Lundhl, L.-G., & Simonsson-Sarnecki, M. (2002). Alexitimia and cognitive bias for emotional information. *Personality and individual differences, 32*, 1063-1075.

Martínez-Sánchez, F. (1996). Adaptación española de la Escala de Alexitimia de Toronto (TAS-20). *Clínica y Salud, 7*(1), 19-32.

McDougall, J. (1974). The psychosoma and psychoanalytic process. *International Review of Psychoanalysis, 1,* 437-442.

McDougall, J. (1982). Alexithymia: a Psychoanalytic viewpoint. *Psychotherapy and Psychosomatics, 38,* 81-90.

Moral, J. (2008). Propiedades psicométricas de la Escala de Alexitimia de Toronto de 20 reactivos en México. *Revista Electrónica de Psicología Clínica de Iztacala, 11*(2), 97-114. Retrived on November, 2, 2008, from: http://www.iztacala.unam.mx/carreras/psicologia/psiclin/principal.html

Moral, J., & Retamales, R. (2000). Estudio de validación de la escala de Alexitimia de Toronto (TAS-20) en muestra española. *Revista Electrónica de Psicología, 4*(2). Retrived on November, 2, 2008, from: www.psiquiatria.com/psicologia/vol4num2/art_3.htm.

Moriarty, N., Stough, C., Tidmarsh, P., Edger, D., & Dennison, S. (2001). Deficits in emotional intelligence underlying adolescent sex offending. *Journal of Adolescence, 24*(6), 743-751.

Muller, J., Bühner, M., & Ellgring, H. (2003) Relationship and differential validity of alexithymia and depression: A comparison of the Toronto Alexithymia Scale and self-rating depression scales. *Psychopathology, 36,* 71-77.

Nemiah, J. C., & Sifneos, P. E. (1970). Affect and fantasy in patients with psychosomatic disorders. En O.W. Hill (editor), *Modern Trends in Psychosomatic Medicine.* (Vol. 2) (pp. 26-35). London, Butterworths.

O'Neil, J. M., Good, G. E., & Holmes, S. (1995). Fifteen years of theory and research on men's gender role conflict: New paradigms for empirical research. En R. E. Levant & W. S. Pollack (Eds.) *A new psychology of men.* New York: Basic Books.

Onnis, L., & DiGenaro, A. (1987). Alexitimia: una revisione critica. *Medicina Psicomática, 32,* 45-64.

Onnis, L., DiGenaro, A., et al. (1994). Sculping present and future: a systemic model applied to the psychosomatic families. *Family Process, 33,* 341-355.

Organización Mundial de la Salud/World Health Organization (1992). *CIE 10. Décima Revisión de la Clasificación Internacional de las Enfermedades. Trastornos mentales y del comportamiento. Descripciones clínicas y pautas para el diagnóstico.* Madrid: Meditor.

Osterwalder, J. J. (2002). The p value as the guardian of medical truth, illusion or reality? *European Journal of Emergence Medicine, 9,* 283-6.

Páez, D., & Casullo, M. M. (2000). Presentación de las propiedades psicométricas de la Escala de Alexitimia de Toronto (TAS-20) en comunidades de habla hispana y otros países. En D. Páez y M. M. Casullo (Eds.), *Cultura y alexitimia* (p.199-203). Buenos Aires, Argentina: Paidós.

Paéz, D., Martínez-Sánchez, F., Velasco, C., Mayordomo, S., Fernández, I., & Blanco, A. (1999). Validez psicométrica de la Escala de Alexitimia de Toronto (TAS-20): un estudio transcultural. *Boletín de Psicología, 63,* 55-76.

Páez, D., & Velasco, C. (1993). Alexitimia: una revisión de los conceptos, de los instrumentos y una comparación con la represión. En D. Páez (Ed.), *Salud, expresión y represión social de las emociones* (pp. 195-235). Valencia: Promolibro.

Pandey, R., Mandal, M. K., Taylor, G. J., & Parker, J. D. (1996). Cross-cultural alexithymia: development and validation of a Hindi translation of the 20-Item Toronto Alexithymia Scale. *Journal of Clinical Psychology, 52*(2), 173-176.

Partridge, G. E. (1930). Current conceptions of psychopathic personality. *American Journal of Psychiatry, 10*, 53-99.

Parker, J. D. A., Bagby, R. M., & Taylor, G. J. (1991). Alexithymia and depression: Distinct or overlapping constructs? *Comprehensive Psychiatry, 32*, 387-394.

Parker, J. D. A., Bagby, R. M., Taylor, G. J., Endler, N. S., & Schmitz, P. (1993). Factorial validity of the 20-ítems Toronto Alexithymia Scale. *European Journal of Personality, 7*, 221-232.

Parker, J. D. A., Taylor, G. J., & Bagby, R. M. (1989). The alexithymia construct: relationship with sociodemographic variables and intelligence. *Comprehensive Psychiatry, 30*(5), 434-441.

Parker, J. D. A.; Taylor, G. J., & Bagby, R. M. (1992). Relationship between conjugate lateral eye movements and alexithymia. *Psychotherapy and Psychosomatics, 57*(3), 94-101.

Pasini, A., Delle-Chiaie, R., Seripa, S., & Ciani, N. (1992). Alexithymia as related to sex, age, and educational level: results of the Toronto Alexithymia Scale in 147 normal subjects. *Comprehensive Psychiatry, 33*(1), 42-46.

Paulhus, D. L., & Williams, K. (2002). The dark triad of personality: Narcissism, machiavellianism, and psychopathy. *Journal of Research in Personality, 36*, 556-568.

Pinel, Ph. (1809). *Traité medico-philosophique sur l'aliénation mentale*. Paris: Chez J. Ant. Brosson.

Poser, S. (2000). The unconscious motivation to become a murderer in Camus' The Stranger. *Modern Psychoanalysis, 25*(2), 259-267.

Prichard, J.C. (1835). *Treatise on insanity*. London: Sherwood, Gilbert and Piper.

Raine, A., & Sanmartín, J. (2000). *Violencia y psicopatía*. Madrid: Editorial Ariel, S.A.

Rodrigo, G., & Lusiardo, M. (1992). Factor structure of a Spanish version of the Toronto Alexithymia Scale. *Psychotherapy and Psychosomatics, 58*(3-4), 197-201.

Rodrigo, G.; Lusiardo, M., & Normey, L. (1989). Alexithymia: reliability and validity of the Spanish version of the Toronto Alexithymia Scale. *Psychotherapy and Psychosomatics, 51*(3), 162-168.

Salovey, P., Mayer, J. D., Goldman, S., Turvey, C., & Palfai, T. (1995). Emotional attention, clarity, and repair: Exploring emotional intelligence using the Trait Meta-Mood Scale. En J. W. Pennebaker (Ed.), *Emotion, disclosure, and health* (pp. 125-154). Washington, DC: American Psychological Association.

Sayar, K., Ebrinc, S., & Ak, I. (2001). Alexithymia in patients with antisocial disorder in a military hospital setting. *The Israel Journal of Psychiatry and Related Sciences, 38*, 2, 81-86.

Schore, A. N. (1996). The experience-dependent maturation of a regulatory system in the orbital prefrontal cortex and the origin of developmental psychopathology. *Developmental Psychopathology, 8*, 59-87.

Schuler, C. E., Snibbe, J. R., & Buckwalter, J.G. (1994). Validity of the MMPI Personality Disorder scales (MMPI-PD). *Journal of Clinical Psychology, 50*(2), 220-227.

Shipko, S., & Noviello, N. (1984). Psychometric properties of self-report scales of alexithymia. *Psychotherapy and Psychosomatics, 41*(2), 85-90

Sifneos, P. E. (1967). Clinical observations on some patients suffering from a variety of psychosomatic diseases. Proceedings of the 7th European Conference in Psychosomatic Research. *Acta Medica Psychosomatica, 1*, 3-11.

Sifneos, P. E. (1972). *Short term psychotherapy and emotional crisis.* Cambridge, Massachusetts: Harvard University Press.

Sifneos, P. E. (1973). The prevalence of alexithymic characteristics in psychosomatic patients. *Psychotherapy and Psychosomatics, 22*, 255-262.

Sivak, R., & Wiater, A. (1997). *Alexitimia, la dificultad para verbalizar afectos. Teoría y clínica.* Buenos Aires, Argentina: Paidós.

Sifneos, P E (2000). Alexithymia, clinical issues, politics and crime. *Psychotherapy and Psychosomatics, 69,* 3, 113-115.

Smith, G. R., Jr. (1983). Alexithymia in medical patients referred to a consultation/liaison service. *American Journal of Psychiatry, 140*(1), 99-101.

Spielberger, C. D., Gorsuch, R. L., & Lusahene, R. E. (1970). *Manual for State-Trait Anxiety Inventory.* California: Consulting Psychologists.

Steiger, J. H. (1995). Structural Equation Modeling (SEPATH.) En *Statistica 5. Computer software and manual* (Volume III, pp. 3539-3688). Tulsa, OK: StatSoft, Inc.

Taylor, G. J., Bagby, R. M., & Parker, J. D. A. (1997). *Disorders of affect regulation: Alexithymia in medical and psychiatric illness.* U.K.: Cambridge University Press.

Taylor, G. J. & Doody, K. F. (1982). Psychopatology and verbal expression in psychosomatic and psychoneurotic patients. *Psychotherapy and Psychosomatics, 38,* 121-127.

Taylor, G. J., Ryan, D. P., & Bagby, R. M. (1985). Toward the development of a new self-report alexithymia scale. *Psychotherapy and Psychosomatics, 44*(4), 181-199.

Troop, N. A., Schmdit, U. H., & Treasure, J. L. (1995). Feelings and fantasy in eating disorders: a factor analysis of the Toronto Alexithymia Scale. *International Journal of Eating Disorders, 18*(2), 151-157.

Vogt R., Burckstrummer, G., Ernot, T., Meyer, K., & Rad, M. von (1977). Differences in phantasy life of psychosomatic and psychoneurotic patients. Psychotherapy *and Psychosomatics, 28,* 98-105

Vorst, H. C., & Bermond, B. (2001) Validity and reliability of the Bermond-Vorst Alexithymia Questionnaire, *Personality and Individual Differences, 30*(3), 413-434.

Wastell, C., & Booth, A. (2003). Machiavellianism: An alexithymic perspective. *Journal of Social and Clinical Psychology, 22*(6), 730-744.

Wicks-Nelson, R., & Israel, A.C. (1997). *Psicopatología del niño y del adolescente* [3ra edición]. Madrid: Prentice Hall.

Wise, T. N., Jani, N. N., Kass, E., Sonnenschein, K., & Mann, L. S. (1988). Alexithymia: Relationship to severity of medical illness and depression. *Psychotherapy and Psychosomatics, 50,* 68-71.

Zeck, E., Luminet, O., Rimé, B., & Wagner, H. (1999). Alexithymia and its measurement: confirmatory factor analyses of the 20-item Toronto Alexithymia Scale and the Bermond-Vorst Alexithymia Questionnaire. *European Journal of Personality, 13,* 511-532.

In: Bio-Psycho-Social Perspectives on Interpersonal Violence   ISBN: 978-1-61668-159-3
Editors: M. Frías-Armenta et al., pp. 79-99   © 2010 Nova Science Publishers, Inc.

Chapter 4

SELF-CONTROL, SELF-REGULATION, AND JUVENILE DELINQUENCY

Martha Frías-Armenta[1], Jorge Borrani[2], Pablo Valdez[2], Hugo Tirado[2] and Xochitl Ortiz Jiménez[2]*

[1] Universidad de Sonora (Mexico).
[2] Universidad Autónoma de Nuevo León (México).

ABSTRACT

Several theories have been proposed to explain delinquency; some include environmental factors and others consider personal variables. Personal, cognitive, and emotional deficits have been associated to delinquent or antisocial behavior. It has been argued that low self control is an internal system that manages antisocial behavior; self control is also understood as a tendency to pursue instant gratification. Besides, self-regulation has been related to violent behavior. Self regulation is conceptualized as the capacity to modulate emotions, attention and behavior; this concept has also been linked to emotional control. Effortful control is another term used for emotional regulation, which is associated to modulation of emotional reactivity and behaviors. Control or regulation of emotions and cognitions are the factors related to delinquent behavior. The aim of this chapter is to test a model including self-control and self-regulation as predictors of antisocial behavior. The sample was integrated by 164 participants, 58 were juvenile delinquents internalized in an institution and 106 were selected from the general community in a northern Mexican city. All of them reported some kind of antisocial behavior. Scales investigating impulsivity, risk, self-regulation and antisocial behavior were administered to the participants. The data were analyzed using structural equation modeling. Two factors were constructed: *self –control*, with impulsivity, sensation seeking, and risk indicators, and *self –regulation*, with indicators of emotional volatility, emotional intensity and activity regulation. Both factors exhibited a negative effect on antisocial behavior. We conclude that self-control is an important factor in the prediction

---

* Correspondence regarding this chapter should be sent to: Martha Frías Armenta, Departamento de Derecho, Universidad de Sonora, Blvd. Luis y Encinas y Rosales S/N, Hermosillo, Sonora, 8300, Mexico. E-mail: marthafrias@sociales.uson.mx

of antisocial behavior; however there are additional variables that should be included in explanatory models of juvenile delinquency in prospective studies.

INTRODUCTION

Around the world, 199,000 homicides of young people were produced in 2000 (The Annual Report on Violence and Health 2002; Krug, Dahlberg, Mercy, Zwi, & Lozano, 2002). From January to May, 2008, 4048 adolescents were incarcerated in treatment centers of Mexico (Secretaría de Seguridad Pública, Consejo de Menores, 2008). Katzmann (2002) details that in the United States 309 juveniles out of 100,000 are arrested due to violent crime, including homicide, aggravated assault, and robbery. The Unified Reporting Program (UCR) of that country report 1,560,289 arrests of juvenile offenders (Burfeind & Bartusch, 2006). The FBI indicates that the arrest of juveniles for murder increased 2.8 percent in 2007 compared to 2006 and the total arrest frequency for juveniles resulted in 9,347,086 cases (Crime in the United States, 2007). In Rome, according to the police, 2 percent of juveniles committed a crime (Roucek, 1970). Israel sources indicate that the rate of violent injuries in young people is 196 per 100,000 (Krug, Dahlberg, Mercy, Zwi, & Lozano, 2002). England estimated an annual increase of delinquency of 5 and 6% (Maguire, Morgan & Reiner, 2002).

Cognitive and emotional deficits have been associated to children and adolescent violent or antisocial behavior. One of most cited theories is Gottfredson & Hirschi's (1990) low self control theory. A number of studies have tried to demonstrate the relationship between low self-control and delinquency, with some of them failing and other succeeding. Gottfredson & Hirschi (1990) argue that low self control is the crucial factor predicting delinquency. However, the existence of additional explanatory variables has been demonstrated. Emotional self-regulation is, for instance, associated to antisocial behavior. Emotions can change the way the individual interact with the environment and emotions can also change motivations. Moreover, emotional regulation correlates with adaptive functioning; that is, emotional control helps in responding adequately to social requirements, and helps to interact with society. Alternatively, emotional disregulation could incite violence (Valiente, Lemery-Chalfant, & Reiser, 2007). Low self control and self regulation are causes of violence in young people (Gottfredson & Hirschi, 1990).

A number of studies relate self control to delinquency; however, the relationship between emotional self-regulation has not been studied, and there is no study combining both self control theory and self-regulation in a due explanatory model. Therefore, the objective of this chapter is to test a model that includes both predictors of antisocial behavior.

SELF- CONTROL THEORY

Gottfredson, & Hirschi (1990) proposed the Low Self Control Theory. This argues that self control is an internal system that manages antisocial behavior. Low self control is also understood as a tendency to pursue instant gratification (MacDonald, Piquero, Valois, & Zullig, 2005). Thus, it is assumed that this trait tends to be stable across time (Marcus, 2004). Individuals lacking self-control are impulsive, risk taking, of volatile temper, and tend to get involved in criminal acts because they cannot anticipate/think the long term consequences of their behavior (Gottfredson, & Hirschi.2009). The Classical Theory of Crime (CTC) establishes that humans have a natural tendency to seek pleasure and search for their immediate satisfaction, crime being an uncontrolled propensity for gratification while self control restrains this tendency, (Muraven, Pogarsky, & Shmueli, 2006). Consequently, CTC assumes that human beings have a natural tendency to be aggressive and that criminals follow this natural propensity (Idem). According to this theory, two key factors explain criminal conduct: low self-control and opportunity (Cauffman, Steinberg, & Piquero, 2005). Hirschi and Gottfredson (1994) define self-control as "the tendency to avoid acts whose long term costs exceed the momentary advantages." Individual differences in self-control determine participation in criminal activities, low self-controlled individuals are impulsive, insensitive and risk-taking and more prompt to be involved in criminal acts (Gottfredson & Hirschi, 1990). Therefore, individuals do not seek the opportunity for crime; they act when the possibility arises, and low self-control persons are more likely to offend. Thus, individuals with low self control tend to respond immediately to the environment; they are active, physical, adventuresome, and insensitive to suffering and to the needs of others, pursue immediate pleasure, and are tolerant to physical pain. In addition, classical control theories argue that criminals are not restrained by social norms and posit that they are asocial (Gottfredson, & Hirschi, 2009). The weakness of criminals social bonds are related to criminal behavior and similarly legal norms do not exert influence on criminals. Thus, these theories establish that criminals are insensitive to social and legal norms. In this sense, empirical research has also demonstrated that self-control is a relevant factor in predicting criminal and deviant behavior (Pratt, & Cullen, 2000). However, in these studies self-control has been defined in several forms, which could cause inconsistent results. In some of them self control is highly related to criminal behavior and in others this relation is nonexistent.

Gottfredson & Hirschi (2009) suggest that the main predictor of self-control is an ineffective child-rearing practices. Parents have to inculcate self-control to their children, and they have to follow some procedures to reach that goal, such as supervision, recognition, and regulation of deviant behavior. Inappropriate parenting fails in creating self control in children (Burfeind, & Bartusch, 2005). Empirical studies have shown that parents' conduct and supervision, as well as their rearing practices are important factors in preventing delinquency from occurring and in eliminating its sources (Ngai & Cheung, 2005; Frías-Armenta, Ramirez, Soto, Castell, & Corral-Verdugo, 2000). Parental warmth and concern are indispensable conditions for effective child rearing (Gottfredson & Hirschi, 2009). Mother's competences and father's interactions with family are also related to juvenile delinquency inhibition (McCord, 2009). The straight of the parent-child relationship also prevent juvenile delinquency from being developed (Burfeind, & Bartusch, 2005). Valiente, Lemery-Chalfant, and Reiser (2007) assessed the effect of parental effortful control (the ability to control dispositional reactivity) on externalized behavior and found a negative relationship between these two constructs.

Family environment and childrearing practices play an important role in child behavior problems. Consequently, harsh parenting has been associated to antisocial behavior and delinquency. Family separation and family violence facilitate juvenile delinquency (Ngai & Cheung, 2005). A longitudinal study conducted by Rebellon and Van-Gundy (2005) found that child abuse was a predictor of violent and property crimes. Besides, antisocial behavior is one of the short term consequences of child abuse (Frías, Ramírez, Soto, Castell, & Corral,

2000). Other studies indicate that a history of child abuse increases the risk for antisocial behavior in adolescence and adulthood (Cicchetti & Manly, 2001; Lansford, Dodge, Pettit, Bates, Crozier, & Kaplow, 2002). Another longitudinal study by Gushurst (2003) reported that 74% of adolescents who had been abused presented at least one of the following problems: high levels of aggression, anxiety, depression, problems with the police, runaway, gang involvement, unwanted pregnancy, compared with 43% of the adolescents who had not been abused. In addition, the likelihood of being arrested on charges of violent acts was 1.9 times higher for child abuse victims than for the controls. Experimenting abuse during childhood has been related to carrying arms during adolescence (Leeb, Barker, & Strine, 2007). Victims of child abuse present a higher risk of developing psychopathology, depression (Putnam, 2003) and aggressive behaviors (Baldry, 2007). Aversive and inept parenting and inconsistent discipline are also related to juvenile delinquency (Meeus, Branje, & Overbeek, 2004).

Social control is indirectly related to individual self-control through parental supervision (Gottfredson & Hirschi, 2009). During childhood, such supervision prevents further involvement in antisocial behavior or criminal acts from occurring (Hoffman, 2002). The recognition of deviant behavior is an essential component of supervision; parents should be able to distinguish the lack of self control of their children in order to monitor their behavior (Gottfredson & Hirschi, 2009). Burfeind & Bartusch (2005) argue that criminal parents possess a deviant lifestyle; they drink excessively, steal things, etc.; thus they will not be able to recognize the antisocial acts of their children. Parental imprisonment is related to juvenile delinquency; parent-child separation is a risk factor for antisocial behavior, apparently it affects the quality of care, also producing stigma, and the reduction of family income (Murray & Farrington, 2005). Supervision and discipline is almost inexistent in families with separated or imprisoned parents. Moreover, parents that stay at home might use harsh corrective methods or inconsistent punishment (Burfeind & Bartusch, 2006). Control theories stress the need of sanctions to misbehavior for the prevention of criminal behavior (Idem). Formal or direct control is established by the imposition of formal rules, supervision, and sanction. However, punishment it not always desirable; disapproval from valuable people could be a more potent sanction. Control theories are concerned with the informal social control exerted by the family, friends and other members of the community (Idem). Parental supervision is also considered as an informal social control for children.

Hirschi (2009) proposes the Control Theory of Delinquency trying to elucidate the factors that reduce delinquency. According to such theory, individuals that develop social bonds to people (parents) or conventional institutions (schools) are less likely to engage in delinquency. The establishment of these bonds prevents delinquency from occurring because crime put people in danger to lose both their social position and bonds gained. Four bounds are expected to prevent delinquency: attachment, commitment, involvement and belief. Attachment consists of the affection of the individual towards other(s) as a member of society; it is the internalization of social norms. Social norms are shared by the group the individual belongs to, and they establish an external influence: the perception of what others are doing or what they should do (Schultz, 2002). Grasmick and Bursik (1990) operationalize the concept of social norm as the loss of respect from socially valuable people (friends or acquaintances) since violating a social norm is to act contrary to the desires, standards, and customs of other members of society. The internalization of the social norm has been operationalized as personal norm. A personal norm has been identified as a sentiment of moral obligation (Schwartz, 2002). In these terms, social norms indicate the external pressure (the perception of what others are doing or what they have to do), and personal norms are the internalized self-expectations (what I should do). Therefore, attachment is the dimension related to the individuals' bond to conventional social norms and its internalization as a personal norm to prevent criminal behavior from occurring.

Commitment is defined by Hirschi (2009) as the fear of consequences. People invest money, education, and social bonds to acquire a reputation; the fear to destroy their reputation prevents them from being involved in criminal acts. Individuals assess the costs and benefits of criminal behavior, based on their status. When the cost exceeds the benefits, crime is not committed. Rational choice theory also establishes a similar hypothesis, indicating that crime likelihood will expand when an individual encounters a suitable situation whose expected benefits surpass costs and risks (Wortley & Mazarolle, 2008). The process of living in a society pursuing a conventional status is identified as commitment to conformity and it will prevent crime. Involvement in conventional activities is a deterrent of delinquency because people do not have time to engage in criminal activity (Hirschi, 2009). For juveniles, the time they spent in conventional activities for satisfying their recreational interest makes the difference in terms of juvenile delinquency. Informal or unconventional activities in leisure time for adolescent may create a set of values that inhibit delinquency (idem). Sharing a universal value system in society constitutes the beliefs dimension of the control theory of crime. It is assumed that every person is socialized in a group wherein they define what is good or wrong (Idem). Self-categorization theory (Sigala, Burgoyne, & Webley, 1999), in turn, proposes that social identity is the way people are socialized. This theory establishes that there are three levels of abstraction that can be used to categorize identity: personal identity (the being as individual), social identity (the being as member of a group), and intra-species identity (oneself as part of the human race). Each level is as valid as the subsequent (or precedent); the being is also defined as "individual" and "social member of the group." In essence, people are more prone to be influenced by whom they consider members of their relevant self-categorization (Hornsey, 2008). These influences mean that the points of view and behavioral tendencies of the members of the group are going to be internalized as their social convictions (Abrams & Hogg, 1990). Control theory indicates that variations in the internalization of norms exist: the less a person believes in obeying society's rules, the more likely that s/he will violate them (Hirschi, 2009). Self-categorization theory argues that internalization is affected by the group's identification. According to this theory, criminal behavior will depend on the identification of the group, the attachment with the group, the level of internalization of social norms and the fear of losing the social status inside the group. Social Control theories (SCT) indicate that behavior is motivated by external consequences, which are perceived as punishments and rewards (Tyler, 2006). Classical theories established that criminality is a natural tendency of humans. This propensity is indicated by two variables: low self control and opportunity; however, for social control theories, behavior can be controlled by external consequences. Theorists such as Hirschi (2009) recognize the role of environmental factors in the emergence and maintenance of self-control. Therefore, parental practices and supervision could help to develop this individual's capacity.

IMPULSIVITY

Gottfredson and Hirschi (2009) proposed some elements to identify self-control and impulsivity is one of the key components of their theory. Dickman (1990) defines impulsivity as the tendency to deliberate less than most people before engaging in action; it is also a characteristic of people that act without thinking of the risk of their behavior (Miller, Joseph, Tudway, 2004). Impulsivity has been also defined as the incapacity to forecast consequences, to wait, and to inhibit inappropriate behaviors (Reynolds, Ortengren, Richards, & de Wit, 2006). In addition, it is conceived as lack of self-control and a tendency to immediate gratification (Carrasco, Barker, Tremblay, & Vitaro, 2006). Impulsivity is associated with responding before a question is concluded, with difficulty in waiting turn, and with interrupting others (Enticott & Ogloff, 2006).

The structure of impulsivity has been discussed in regard to the unidimensionality or multi-dimensionality of the construct. Some researchers characterize three different components: the first is structured by the tendency to manifest spontaneous thoughts and behaviors, the second as the propensity to be disorganized and unprepared in everyday activities, and the third as carefree attitudes and behaviors (Miller, Joseph, & Tudway, 2004). Whiteside and Lynam (2001) studied impulsivity and found four facets: urgency, premeditation, perseverance, and sensation seeking and they defined urgency as the tendency to feel strong impulses, premeditation as the tendency to think about the consequences of acts before engaging in them, perseverance is the ability to remain focused in a task, and sensation seeking is the tendency to look for exciting activities. Reynolds, Penfold, and Patak (2008) evaluated the dimensions of impulsivity in a group of adolescents and identified three behavioral elements: Impulsive decision-making, impulsive inattention and impulsive disinhibition. Therefore, impulsivity has been rather conceptualized as a multifaceted construct including verbal, cognitive and behavioral dimensions (Avila, Cuenca, Felix, Parcet, & Miranda, 2004).

Cognitive and behavioral impulsivity has been related to delinquency (Avila, Cuenca, Felix, Parcet, & Miranda, 2004) and has been seen as a key aspect of violence, aggression, and substance abuse (Vigil-Colet & Codorniu-Raga, 2004). Impulsivity is positively related to substance abuse and drug consumption (Slater, 2003). Smokers, cocaine users, alcoholics, and opiate addicts score higher on impulsive measures and behavioral inhibitions tasks (Reynolds, Richards, Horn, & Karraker, 2004). Billieux, Van der Linden, and Ceschi, (2007) used the Impulsive Behavior Scale and Questionnaire Smoke Urges in 40 undergraduate students and found that the urgency dimension of impulsivity was significantly related to smoking craving. Impulsivity and sensation seeking also predict unsafe driving (Dahlen, Martin, Ragan, & Kuhlman, 2005). Children and adolescents consuming drugs show higher rates of impulsivity (Moeller & Dougherty, 2002).

Impulsive aggression has been described as an affective emotional response. Stanford, Houston, Villemarette-Pittman, and Greve, (2003), in a study conducted with 80 psychiatric aggressive patients, found that they exhibited higher scores in personality pathology, impulsivity, anger, psychoticism, neuroticism and hostility. Carrasco, Barker, Tremblay, and Vitaro (2006) examined personality traits in 868 adolescent boys finding impulsivity and extraversion traits being related to antisocial behavior. A longitudinal study conducted with 400 boys, measuring impulsivity and antisocial behavior, showed an association between antisocial behavior and behavioral impulsivity (White, Moffitt, Caspi, Bartusch, Needles, & Stouthamer-Loeber, 1994). Fossati, Barratt, Carretta, Leonardi, Grazioli, and Maffei (2004) conducted a study with 747 undergraduate students and found that the impulsivity facets were linked to different aggressive dimensions. Offenders showed significant differences in diverse measures of impulsivity in a research investigating 129 adolescents, 86 institutionalized and 43 regular school students (Carroll, Hemingway, Bower, Ashman, Houghton, & Durkin, 2006). Impulsivity also increases health risk behaviors such as alcohol use and smoking (Grano, Virtanen, Vahtera, Elovainio, & Kivimaki, 2004). Another study showed that both behavioral and cognitive impulsivity were associated to delinquency (Herba, Tranah, Rubia, & Yule, 2006). Impulsive children also exhibit sensation seeking behaviors (Gatzke-Kopp, Raine, Loeber, Stouthamer-Loeber, & Steinhauer, 2002).

SELF-REGULATION

Self-regulation is conceptualized diversely in the literature. Rafaelli and Crockett (2003) define it as the capacity to regulate emotions, attention and behavior, while Dawes, Tarter and Kirisci (1997) use the term *behavioral self-regulation* defining it as the level of control of individuals' reactivity or activity before environmental stimuli, which can be manifested as inattention, impulsivity, and hyperactivity. This concept has also been related to emotional control (Zeanah, 2005). Effortful control is another term used for emotional regulation, which is associated to the modulation of emotional reactivity and behaviors (Valiente, Lemery-Chalfant, & Reiser, 2007). Individuals with high EC tend to voluntarily control their attention and behavior.

Eisenberg and Fabes (1998) argue that self-regulated individuals are social competent and pro-social, even if they experience negative emotions. Rafaelli & Crockett (2003) studied sexual risky behaviors in adolescents and found that self-regulation was associated with sexual risk taking. The lack of children effortful control correlated with children problem-behaviors (Valiente, Lemery-Chalfant, & Reiser, 2007). Attentional control is considered another aspect of EC, which is also associated to delay in gratification (Sethi, Mischel, Aber, Shoda, & Rodriguez, 2000). Behavioral self regulation is also related to substance abuse (Dawes, Tarter, & Kirisci, 1997).

Emotion regulation is one recent paradigm for studying emotions, and it is defined as the way a person uses emotional experiences for adaptive functioning (Thompson, 1994). This contruct has been linked to emotional control and coping strategies for modifying emotion reaction (Galambus & Costigan, 2003). Emotional regulation is understood as the way individuals deal with their feelings and how they reach positive emotions and modulate distress (idem). This theory also establishes that flexibility and responsiveness are necessary skills for the control of emotions, and another skill included is the awareness of emotional states, the capacity to understand others' emotions, and empathy (Thompson, 1994). Adolescents are more able than children to regulate their emotions, and they can assume the point of view of others (Galambus & Costigan, 2003). Emotional regulation includes strategies to modify, intensify, dismiss, or transform emotional reactions to adapt to social requirements. Therefore, it is contextual dependent, since different environments represents diverse emotional challenges. Emotional regulation will depend on the goals of the individual and the environmental requirements (Thompson, 1994). Campos, Mumme, Kermoian, and Campos (1994) consider emotional regulation as an interpersonal phenomenon rather than an intrapsychic one. It is argued that beliefs about the availability of support and the likelihood of others' response will facilitate emotional regulation throughout constructing strong relations with others (Thompson, 1994). The ability to experience emotions and the control of intensity and duration is also conceived as emotional regulation (Zeanah, 2005). Alternatively, emotional disregulation is defined as the impairment of the control of emotional practices and expression (Zeanah, 2005).

Emotions could function as a contextual factor for parenting (Forgatch & Stoolmiller, 1994). The parent-child relationship is essential for emotional development (Oatley & Jenkins, 2006). Warm parenting creates an affective atmosphere that helps children to develop skills to manage emotions, and emotion regulation is essential for the adaptation to social environments.

EMOTIONS

The definition of emotion has proven difficult to establish. A number of researchers conceive it as a psychological state that prepares the organism to react adaptively to different relevant physical conditions for survival (Ortiz, Ramirez, & Valdez, 2009). Kelley (2005) indicates that emotion involves "motivational states, shaped by natural selection that allows modulation of physiological and behavioral responses ensuring survival, reproduction and fitness" which corresponds to valence affective states (Ortony & Turner, 1990). Frijda (1986) defines emotions as the "change in readiness for action". However, it is also considered as a communication process from one member of the species to another (Barlow, 2004). Communication patterns have the same signal value within species. Campos *et al.* (1994) consider emotion as the process that establishes, maintains, changes, and terminates the individual relation with the environment or other matters. Emotions are also conceived as states that are elicited by rewards and punishments (Rolls, 2005).

Emotions are viewed as the essential motivation for human behavior (Izard, 1998). Emotions may change the way people act (Posner, 2001); abilities, preferences, and beliefs are sometimes modified during emotional states. Moreover, there are emotional dispositions that moderate these emotional states (Posner, 2001). In addition, it is possible both to "cultivate" emotional dispositions and to control emotions (Cacioppo & Gardner, 1999). Emotions are also seen as intense and adaptive changes in response to an environmental stimulus (Adolphs, 2005). Adolphs (idem) argues that emotions are "representational states" because they characterize the connotation for the organism's homeostasis of a set of sensory inputs and behavioral outputs.

Charles Darwin hypothesized that a small number of emotional states were innate and present from birth in humans (Zeanah, 2005), showing consistencies across and within species (Barlow, 2004). There are six to nine universal human expressions. However, these universal expressions could be subject to modification through socialization (Izard & Read, 1982). Some behavioral mechanisms establish a quick and appropriate (i.e., adaptive) response accompanying an emotion. For instance, escape from an imminent physical danger is the best possible reaction. However, controlling emotional reactions serves better the individuals' adaptation in facing social stimuli, regardless of their perceived dangerous nature. Darwin also pointed out that humans express emotions in the same way from childhood to adulthood (Idem). Evidence has been found of three emotional states in two year-old babies (Izard & Read, 1982). Emotion facial expression seems to be consistent across cultures (Idem). Thus, innate emotional states have been called *primary emotions*, while the emotions that individuals acquire through their lifespan are identified as *secondary emotions* (Damasio, 1995). Ultimately, any stimulus possesses an affective meaning (Simon, 1997). Since emotions regulate social behavior in groups they are also considered as a social adaptation (Adolphs, 2005). Humans have to survive within a social group and self-regulation of emotions is a tool for adaptation of this social group. Emotions as adaptive processes are diverse in different cultures; one stimulus may elicit distinct emotions in people from different cultures because its differential meaning. Emotions are seen as signals ruling social communication (Adolphs, 2005). Emotions are also related to long term plans since individuals evaluate and select the available rewards and their costs, avoiding punishments (Rolls, 2005).

Additionally, the discussion continues about the independence of cognition from emotion, in which some researchers consider emotions as a separate mechanism (Zajonc, 1984) and others believe that emotions and cognition are functions of the same system (Lazarus, 1984). Lazarus (1991) argues that cognition precedes emotions because individuals evaluate emotions before a behavioral response. Since differential neuroanatomical structures have been identified for emotion and cognition, appraisal and affect are often uncorrelated: affective reactions can be manifested without appraisal. Therefore, some emotional states can be invoked without the mediation of a cognitive process (Zajonc, 1984).

Considering these results offered by the literature, the aim of this study is to analyze the relationship between self-control, self-regulation and antisocial behavior. Having this in mind, we specified and tested a model including self-control and self-regulation as predictors of antisocial behavior in juvenile delinquents.

METHOD

Participants

The sample included 164 participants; 58 were juvenile delinquents internalized in a juvenile court) and 106 were selected from the general community of a middle-sized Mexican city (population = 700,000 inhabitants). All of them reported some kind of antisocial behavior. The mean age for the total sample was 14 years old, 13.82 (SD=1.35) for the control group and 14.33 (SD=1.34) for minors at the juvenile court. Twenty four percent of the participants in the juvenile delinquent group were females and 76% were males.

Instruments

Self Regulation

Self-regulation was assessed using Raffaelli and Crockett's (2003) scale, which consists of 14 items based on the theory that self regulation is a multi-dimensional construct. The items measured emotional volatility and intensity, and activity regulation, using a 5 point scale, ranking from 0 to 4, where 0=Totally disagree and 4=Totally agree. Raffaelli and Crockett (2003) conducted a confirmatory factor analysis, which indicated construct validity of the instrument. These items are intended to assess emotional volatility, attention and activity regulation. In the pilot study an alpha of .86 was obtained.

Risk Taking

The Grasmick et al.'s (1993) instrument was used. The instrument includes 4 items in a 7-point scale (0="never", 1="once", 2="two times"… to 6="more than 20 times") detailing risky actions. Vazsonyi, Pickering, Junger, and Hessing, (2001) reported an alpha of .62 for the instrument.

Impulsivity

This construct can be defined as the tendency to respond quickly to a specific stimulus without thinking or evaluating the possible consequences of such responding. Grasmick et al's (1993) scale was used to assess it. This instrument includes 19 items with 7 point-scale response options from 0 to 6, 0 meaning "never", 1 "once", 2 "two times"… to 6 "more than 20 times" the individual reported actions such as acting impulsively, acting without thinking, planning trips, etc. Varsonyi, Pickering, Junger, and Hessing (2001) reported an alpha of .62 for this scale. We piloted it with high school students obtaining an alpha of .86.

Antisocial Behavior

Twenty six items of the antisocial behavior scale by Grasmick *et al.* (1993) were utilized. They were first piloted with high school students, obtaining a Cronbach's alpha of .70. By responding to this scale, participants have to select an option out of 7 points, ranking from 0 to 6, where 0 indicates "never" and 6 "more than 20 times" they engaged in a particular antisocial action during the last six months. "Steal something," "damage public property," "smoke," and "avoid paying for something consumed" are examples of this scale's items.

Procedure

The authorization from the president of the Minor Tutelary Counsel (Juvenile Court) was obtained in order to have access to the Court's building for the administration of the instruments to the institutionalized minors. This authorization was granted by school principals for the control group. Clinical psychologists, trained in psychological interview, administered the instruments in approximately 15 to 20 minutes. The voluntary consent to participate was obtained from both groups, minors and their parents, and they were advised that they could stop the interview at any moment. The arrested juveniles were interviewed first; once we obtained the demographic data of this group we located the participants for the control group and they were interviewed at the school they were attending.

Data Analysis

First, we conducted univariate analysis (means, standard deviations, minimum and maximum values) from the demographic data and the scales used as well as Cronbach's alphas to indicate internal consistency for those scales. Indexes of each sub-scale were computed (an index is the average response of the sub-scale items). Three indexes of the self-regulation scale (emotional volatility, emotional intensity, and activity regulation) were computed as well as five indexes of antisocial behavior (general deviance, thief, assault, school problems, and property crimes) and four indexes for impulsivity and risk seeking (motor impulsivity, no plan impulsivity, sensation seeking and risk taking). In addition, a structural equation model (SEM) was specified to estimate the relationships between self-control, self-regulation and antisocial behavior. The specified hypothetical model considered the direct and indirect effects of self-regulation and self-control on antisocial behavior. In order to test the pertinence of this hypothesized model, goodness of fit indicators were considered. These indicators show whether the specified relations in the model are supported by the data, and included the statistical indicator χ^2, expecting a non-significant p value ($p > .05$) associated to this indicator. Practical indicators were also considered, including the Non-Normed Fit Index (*NNFI*) and the Comparative Fit Index (*CFI*)) which are expected to produce a value higher than .90 (Bentler, 2006). To assess the reasonable error of approximation in terms of goodness of fit, the index root mean squared error (RMSEA) was obtained, requiring a <.08 value (Browne & Cudeck, 1993).

RESULTS

The univariate statistics of the scale of risk's items (means and standard deviations) are shown in Table1.

Table 1. Univariate statistics from responses to the risk scale

Items	N	Mean	sd	Min	Max
Experimenting risk-taking	162	2.06	1.535	0	4
Taking risks for fun	162	1.78	1.527	0	4
Do things that cause problems	162	1.44	1.532	0	4
Having fun is more important	162	1.14	1.367	0	4

Table 2 exhibits the univariate statistics of the impulsivity scale. The highest mean was for "having an active life (mean 3.07).

Table 2. Univariate statistics from responses to the impulsivity scale

Items	N	Mean	sd	Min	Max
Start a work without planning	158	1.73	1.35	0	4
Think what to do before starting it	158	2.95	1.24	0	4
Acting impulsively	158	2.01	1.35	0	4
Spending no time for planning	158	2.11	1.30	0	4
Having new and excitement experiences	158	2.30	1.44	0	4
Planning before starting a new job	158	2.89	1.17	0	4
Traveling without planning routs and times	158	2.62	1.45	0	4
Getting into new situations	158	1.85	1.46	0	4
Doing things just for emotion	158	1.80	1.49	0	4
Changing interest frequently	158	1.99	1.24	0	4
Doing scaring things	158	2.07	1.48	0	4
Trying anything even if it is dangerous	158	1.90	1.53	0	4
Having a very active life	158	3.07	1.25	0	4
Doing craziness just for fun	158	2.02	1.54	0	4
Exploring a strange place	158	1.50	1.55	0	4
Prefer unpredictable friends	158	1.97	1.44	0	4
Excitation without thinking consequences	158	1.63	1.36	0	4
A crazy person	158	1.66	1.51	0	4
Likes parties without inhibitions	158	1.56	1.59	0	4

In turn, Table 3 displays univariate statistics for the self-regulation scale. "Very active" (mean=2.15, range 0 to 4), "swift change of humor" (mean =2.14, range 0 to 4), and "worries too much" were the items with the highest means.

Table 3. Univariate statistics from responses to the self-regulation scale

Items	N	Mean	sd	Min	Max
Suddenly changes humor	162	2.14	1.369	0	4
Fearful and anxious	162	1.79	1.480	0	4
Feels happy	162	1.40	1.497	0	4
Cries frequently	162	.99	1.35	0	4
Nervous or stressed	162	1.67	1.44	0	4
Irritable	162	1.61	1.45	0	4
Strong Temperament	162	1.45	1.53	0	4
Problems to concentrate	162	1.46	1.37	0	4
Confounding feelings	162	1.86	1.39	0	4
Acts without thinking	162	1.49	1.48	0	4
Difficulty to stop thinking	162	1.88	1.48	0	4
Very active	162	2.15	1.50	0	4
Worries too much	162	2.05	1.51	0	4

Table 4 presents the univariate statistics of the antisocial scale. The highest levels of antisocial behavior were for fights (mean=2.26, range 0 to 4) and goes out without permission (mean=1-87, range 0 to 4). Finally, Table 5 exhibits the means, standard deviation, and alphas of all the scales. All alphas were higher than .70, which is considered an appropriate internal consistence.

Table 4. Univariate statistics from responses to the risk-taking scale

Items	N	Mean	sd	Min	Max
Gets inside forbidden place	136	1.10	1.740	0	4
Goes out without permission	136	1.87	2.139	0	4
Does not return money	136	.88	1.417	0	4
Dirties the streets	136	1.57	2.053	0	4
Cheats a cashier	136	.43	1.203	0	4
Bothers unfamiliar persons	136	1.12	1.795	0	4
Cheats	136	1.01	1.671	0	4
Takes tires' air off	136	.66	1.545	0	4
Lies about age	136	.68	1.464	0	4
Makes inappropriate calls	136	.60	1.307	0	4
Avoids to pay	136	.70	1.405	0	4
Starts alarms	136	.75	1.429	0	4
Damages public places	136	.60	1.390	0	4
Abuses animals	136	.95	1.502	0	4
Graffiti	136	1.15	2.092	0	4
Destroys things of another person	136	1.07	1.696	0	4
Makes heavy jokes	136	1.49	1.901	0	4
Answers wrong to an authority	136	1.32	1.805	0	4
Smokes in a prohibited place	136	.77	1.789	0	4
Refuses to do homework	136	1.32	1.763	0	4
Fights	136	2.26	2.329	0	4
Threats people to get Money	136	.62	1.674	0	4
Gets into a close store	136	.47	1.377	0	4
Uses fake money	136	.55	1.343	0	4
Steals things to a family member	136	.56	1.349	0	4
Steals something of little value	136	.78	1.538	0	4

Table 5. Means and reliabilities of all used scales

Scale	N	Mean	SD	Alpha
Risk	136	6.42	4.46	.74
Impulsivity	136	39.63	14.29	.86
Self-regulation	136	21.95	11.50	.86
Antisocial behavior	136	25.28	29.24	.95

Figure 1 shows the results of the structural model; all the proposed factors seem to evidence convergent construct validity of the used measures, manifested by the salient and significant values of the factor loadings. Self- control affected positively antisocial behavior (structural coefficient = .25) self-regulation had a direct effect on antisocial behavior (structural coefficient = .29) as well as on self-control (structural coefficient = .55). The practical goodness of fit indicators met the required criterion values, evidencing the adequacy of the tested model. Although the X^2 was significant ($\chi^2(43) = 80.68$; $p < .000$), the practical indexes demonstrated that the model fit the data (Bentler, 2006).

CONCLUSION

The General Theory of Crime considers self-control as a unique determinant of criminal behavior (Gottfredson & Hirschi, 1990). However, research results indicate a limited explanatory power of the former variable on the variance of the latter; this would indicate the existence of additional variables predicting antisocial behavior. Marcus (2004) argues that behavior is the product of intricate determinants from different sources. Criminal behavior is initiated and maintained by multiple determinants and self-control is just one of these factors. Marcus also indicates that investigations trying to demonstrate that self-control is a unique variable predicting criminal behavior have failed, although other studies have supported and documented the uni-determined nature of criminal actions (Gottfredson & Hirschi, 1990; Pratt & Cullen, 2000).

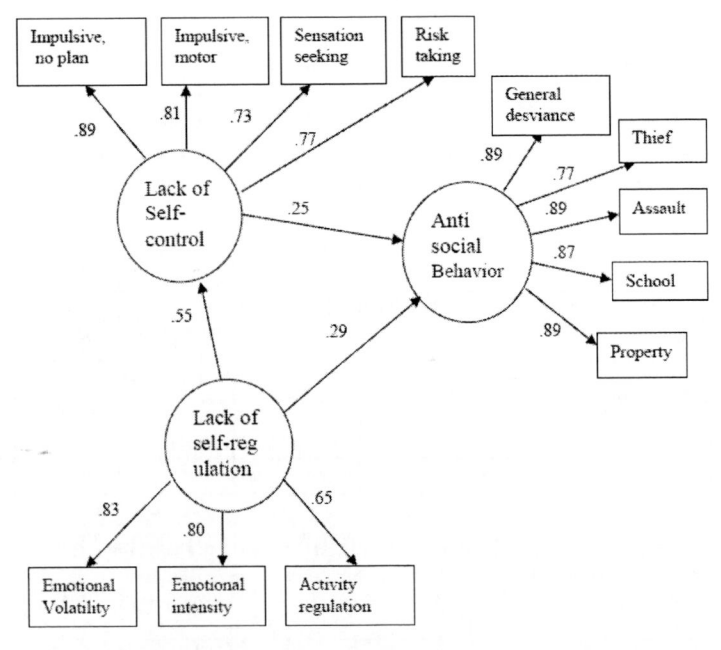

Figure 1. Model of self control and antisocial behavior. All structural coefficients and factor loadings are significant at at $p < .05$. Goodness of fit: $X^2 = 102.28$ (51 df), $p = 0.00$; NFI =. 93 NNFI =.95, CFI = .96, RMSEA= .07; R^2 =. 23.

Low self-control is clearly an important predictor of delinquent behavior (Pratt & Cullen, 2000; Vitacco & Rogers, 2001). Nevertheless, these studies explain less than 20% of the variance in such behavior (Vazsonyi, Pickering, Junger, & Hessing, 2001). In view of the abovementioned results, we were committed to study the explanatory role of variables other than self control, yet also including this important determinant in our model of antisocial behavior.

Since theory establishes that individuals lacking self control are impulsive and risk taking (Gottfredson & Hirschi, 1990), in the study reported in this chapter these variables constituted a "lack of self control" factor. Low self-controlled individuals seek for immediate pleasure and cannot control their impulses. This tendency to instant gratification leads them to commit acts of deviance.

Although in the original model (Gottfredson & Hirschi, 1990) emotional regulation or temper is proposed as being part of the construct of self control, in our study emotional control seems to constitute a separate factor, yet highly correlated to impulsivity and risk taking. Results showed that emotions affect self-control, which replicates previous findings indicating that emotion regulates cognition and changes the way people act (Posner, 2001). However, self-regulation also directly predicted antisocial behavior.

Our model contains a component of emotional stability which had not been previously included in the theory. Emotions could be developed through life span to respond more adequately to social stimuli; in this sense, emotion is also seen as part of an adaptive process aimed at adjusting people's responses to social requirements. The more the individual develops emotional regulation the more (s)he gets adapted to social life and avoids antisocial behavior. Antisocial individuals are incapable to control their behavior or emotions.

However, the phenomenon of delinquency is complex and should instigate the searching for multiple factors explaining delinquency. This chapter analyzed some individual factors related to antisocial behavior: self-control and self-regulation, which explained almost a quarter of antisocial behavior variance.

Self control theory also assumes that ineffective childrearing practices often result in low self–control in children. Parental supervision and support help to develop cognitive and emotional regulation. In addition, negative emotions within family predict antisocial behavior in minors (Forgatch & Stoolmiller, 1994). Therefore, it is important to include in future testing of models these variables as correlates of children self-control and antisocial behavior.

Social and governmental responses to adolescents' antisocial behavior have included the creation of formal institutions for their attention and treatment; juvenile tribunals are one of them. These tribunals were firstly instituted more than a century ago; however, nowadays the question is whether or not they have been effective in preventing youth violence. It is true that children need specialized institutions. Yet, it is also true that those institutions have failed in stopping an increased juvenile criminal behavior. A change in perspective is necessary, and this can be guided by pertinent research and the participation of the diverse social and professional instances involved in this serious community problem. Sharing perspectives among psychologist, sociologists, courts, correctional institutions, defense attorneys, media, schools teachers, social workers, private institutions, and communities is crucial to find a solution (Katzmann, 2002). As a number of studies have demonstrated, using a unique theoretical perspective is not the appropriate way: the problem persists and its severity increases. Thus, the solution involves the implementation and evaluation of multiple programs containing results from scientific scrutiny. Diverse theories and approaches have to be tested, developing interventional programs based on these theories. In this chapter, the importance of emotional and cognitive self-control was demonstrated, which can provide clues for the development of treatments/interventions, in which adolescents learn to control their emotions and to be able to foresee the long-term consequence of their acts. The natural tendency to getting instant gratification could be reversed teaching them self-control through appropriate training, parental supervision and support.

REFERENCES

Abrams, D., & Hogg, M. A. (1990). Social identification, self-categorization and social influence. *European Review of Social Psychology, 1*, 195-228.

Adolphs, R. (2005). Could a robot have emotions?: Theoretical perspectives from social Cognitve Neuroscience. In J-M. Fellous & M. A. Arbib (eds), Who Needs Emotions?: The Brain Meets the Robot. (pp.9-25). New York,: Oxford University Press.

Avila, C., Cuenca, I., Felix, V., Parcet, M. A., & Miranda, A. (2004). Measuring impulsivity in school-aged boys and examining its relationship with ADHD and ODD ratings. *Journal of Abnormal Child Psychology*, 32, 295–304.

Baldry, A. C. (2007). "It does affect me": Disruptive behaviors en preadolescents directly and indirectly abused at home. *European Psychologist, 12,* 29-35.

Barlow, D. H. (2004). Anxiety and its disorders: The nature and treatment of anxiety and panic. New York: Guilford Press.

Billieux, J., Van der Linden, M., & Ceschi, G. (2007). Which dimensions of impulsivity are related to cigarette craving? Addictive Behaviors, 32(6), 1189-1199.

Browne, M. W., & Cudeck, R. (1993). Alternative ways of assessing model fit. In K. A. Bollen & J. S. Long (Eds.), *Testing structural equation models* (pp. 136-162). Thousand Oaks, CA: Sage.

Burfeind, J. W., & Bartusch, D. J. (2006). Juvenile Delinquency: An integrated approach. Ontario, Canada: Jones and Bartlett Publishers.

Cacioppo, J. T., & Gardner, W. L. (1999). Emotion. *Annual Review of Psychology, 50,* 191-214.

Campos, J.J., Mumme, D. L., Kermoian, R., & Campos, R. G. (1994). A functionalist perspective on the nature of emotion. Monographs of the Society for Research in Child Development, 59, 284–303.

Carrasco, M., Barker, E.D., Tremblay, R. E., & Vitaro, F. (2006). Eysenck's personality dimensions as predictors of male adolescent trajectories of physical aggression, theft and vandalism. Personality and Individual Differences 41, 1309–1320.

Carroll, A., Hemingway, F., Bower, J., Ashman, A., Houghton, S., & Durkin, K. (2006). Impulsivity in Juvenile Delinquency: Differences Among Early-Onset, Late-Onset, and Non-Offenders, *Journal of Youth and Adolescence,35 (4), 519–529.*

Cauffman, E., Steinberg, L., & Piquero, A. R. (2005). Psychological, neuropsychological and physiological correlates of serious antisocial behavior in adolescence: the role of self-control. Criminology, 43, 133-175.

Cicchetti, D., & Manly, J. T., Eds. (2001). Operationalizing child maltreatment: Developmental process and outcomes (Special issue). *Development and Psychopathology, 13.*

Crime in the United States (2007). Retrieved on July 2009 from: http://www.fbi.gov/ucr/cius2007/arrests/index.html.

Dahlen, E. R., Martin, R. C., Ragan, K., & Kuhlman, M.M. (2005). Driving anger, sensation seeking, impulsiveness, and boredom proneness in the prediction of unsafe driving. Accident Analysis and Prevention, 37, 341–348

Damasio, A. R. (1995). Toward a neurobiology of emotion and feeling: Operational concepts and hypothesis. The Neuroscientist, 1, 19-25.

Dawes, M. A., Tarter, & R. E. Kirisci, L. (1997). Behavioral self-regulation: Correlates and 2 year follow-ups for boys at risk for substance abuse. Drug and Alcohol Dependence, 45, I65 – 176.

Dickman, S. J. (1990). Functional and dysfunctional impulsivity: Personality and cognitive correlates. Journal of Personality and Social Psychology, 58(1), 95-102.

Eisenberg N, Fabes RA. 1998. Prosocial development. In *Handbook of Child Psychology. Social, Emotional, and Personality Development,* ed. W Damon, N Eisenberg (ser. ed). 3:701–78. New York: Wiley & Sons.

Enticott, P. G., & Ogloff, J. R. P. (2006). Elucidation of impulsivity. Australian Psychologist, 41(1): 3-14.

Forgatch, M. S., & Stoolmiller, M. (1994). Emotions as contexts for adolescents delinquency. Journal of Research on Adolescence, 4(4), 601-614.

Fossati, A., Barratt, E. S., Carretta, I., Leonardi, B., Grazioli, F., & Maffei, C. (2004). Predicting borderline and antisocial personality disorder features in nonclinical subjects using measures of impulsivity and aggressiveness. Psychiatry Research, 125, 161–170.

Frías, M., Ramírez, J., Soto, R., Castell, I., & Corral, V. (2000). Repercusiones conductuales del maltrato infantil: Un estudio con grupos de alto riesgo. En AMEPSO (Ed.), *La Psicología Social en México*, Vol. 8. México: AMEPSO.

Frijda, N. H. (1986). The emotions. New York: Cambridge University Press.

Galambus, N. L., & Costigan, C. L. (2003). Emotional and personality development in adolescence. In R.M. Lerner, M. A. Easterbooks, and Mistry, J. (Eds), I. B. Weiner, (Ed. In chief), Handbook of Psychology, Developmental Psychology, vol. 6. Pp.251- 372. New Jersey, John Wiley & Sons, Inc.

Gatzke-Kopp, L. M., Raine, A., Loeber, R., Stouthamer-Loeber, M., & Steinhauer, S. (2002). Serious delinquent behavior, sensation seeking, and electrodermal arousal. Journal of Abnormal Child Psychology, 30, 477–486.

Golden, C. J., Jackson, M. L., Peterson-Rohne, A., & Gontkovsky, S. T. (1996). Neuropsychological correlates of violence and aggression: a review of the clinical literature. Aggression and Violent Behavior, 1(1), 3-25.

Gottfredson, M. R., & Hirschi. T. (1990). *A General Theory of Crime.* Stanford, CA: Stanford University Press.

Gottfredson, M. R., & Hirschi.T. (2009). The nature of criminality: Low self-control. In F. R. Scarpitti, A. L. Nielsen, & J. M. Miller (Eds.), Crime and Criminals: Contemporary and Classic Readings in Criminology (pp. 272-288). New York: Oxford University Press.

Grano, N., Virtanen, M., Vahtera, J., Elovainio, M., & Kivimaki, M. (2004). Impulsivity as a predictor of smoking and alcohol consumption. *Personality and Individual Differences, 37,* 1693–1700.

Grasmick, H., Title, C., Bursick., & Arneklev, B. (1993). Testing the core empirical implication of Gottfredson and Hirschi's General Theory of Crime. *Journal of Research in Crime and Delinquency, 30,* 5-29.

Grasmick, H. G., & Bursik, R. J., Jr. (1990). Conscience, significant others, and rational choice: Extending to deterrence model. *Law and Society Review, 24,* 837-861.

Herba, C. M., Tranah, T., Rubia, K., & Yule, W. (2006). Conduct Problems in Adolescence: Three Domains of Inhibition and Effect of Gender. *Developmental Neuropsychology, 30*(2), 659–695.

Hirschi, T. (2002). Causes of delinquency. New Jersey: Transaction publishers.

Hirschi, T. (2009). A control Theory of delinquency. In F. R. Scarpitti, A. L. Nielsen, & J. M. Miller (Eds.), Crime and Criminals: Contemporary and Classic Readings in Criminology (pp. 272-288). New York: Oxford University Press.

Hirschi, T., & Gottfredson, M. R. (1994). The Generality of Deviance. In T. Hirschi and M. R. Gottfredson (eds) *The Generality of Deviance,* pp. 1–22. New Brunswick, NJ: Transaction Publishers.

Hoffmann, J. P. (2002). A Contextual Analysis of Differential Association, Social Control, and Strain Theories of Delinquency. *Social Forces,* 81(3):753-785.

Hornsey, J. M. (2008). Social Identity Theory and Self-categorization Theory: A Historical Review. *Social and Personality Psychology Compass, 2*(1), 204–222.

Izard, C. E., & Read, P. B. (1982). Measuring emotions in infants and children. New York: Cambridge University Press.

Izard, C. E, (1998). Emotions and facial expressions: A perspective from differential emotions theory. In J. A. Russell & J. M. Fernández-Dols, G. Mandler. The psychology of facial expression. Cambridge, UK: Cambridge University Press.

Katzmann, G. S. (2002). Securing Our Children's Future: New Approaches to Juvenile Justice and Youth Violence. Washington, D.C. Brookings Institution Press.

Kelley, A. E. (2005). Neurochemical networks encoding emotion and motivation: evolutionary perspective. In J-M. Fellous & M. A. Arbib (eds), Who Needs Emotions?: The Brain Meets the Robot. (pp.29-77). New York,: Oxford University Press.

Krug, E. G., Dahlberg, L. L., Mercy, J. A., Zwi, A. B., & Lozano, R. (2002). World Report on Violence and Health (WHO). Retrieved on June 20, 2006, from: http://www.who.int/violence_injury_prevention/violence/world_report/en/full_en.pdf.

Lansford, J. E., Dodge, K. A., Pettit, G. S., Bates, J. E., Crozier, J., & Kaplow, J. (2002). Long-term effects of early child physical maltreatment on psychological, behavioral, and academic problems in adolescence: A 12-year prospective study. *Archives of Pediatrics and Adolescent Medicine, 156,* 824–830.

Lazarus, R. S. (1984). On the primacy of cognition. American psychologist, 39(2), 124-129.

Lazarus, R. S. (1991). Cognition and motivation in emotion. American Psychologist, 46(4), 352-367.

Leeb, R. T., Barker, L. E., & Strine, & T. W. (2007). The effect of childhood physical and sexual abuse on adolescent weapon carrying. *Journal of Adolescent Health, 40(6),* 551-558.

MacDonald, J. M., Piquero, A. R., Valois, R. F., & Zullig, K. J. (2005). The Relationship Between Life Satisfaction, Risk-Taking Behaviors, and Youth Violence. *Journal of Interpersonal Violence,* 20; 1495-1514.

Maguire, M.,Morgan, R., & Reiner, R. (2002). Manual de Criminología. México: Oxford University Press.

Marcus, B. (2004). Self-control in the General Theory of Crime: *Theoretical implications of a measurement problem. Theoretical Criminology,* 8(1), 33–55.

McCord, J. (2009). Family relation, Juvenile delinquency, and adult criminality. In F. R. Scarpitti, A. L. Nielsen, & J. M. Miller (Eds.), Crime and Criminals: Contemporary and Classic Readings in Criminology (pp. 272-288). New York: Oxford University Press.

Meeus, W., Branje, S., & Overbeek, G.J. (2004). Parents and partners in crime: a six-year longitudinal study on changes in supportive relationships and delinquency in adolescence and young adulthood. Journal of Child Psychology and Psychiatry 45(7),1288-1298.

Miller, E., Joseph, S., & Tudway, J. (2004). Assessing the component structure of four self-report measures of impulsivity. Personality and Individual Differences, 37, 349–358

Moeller, F. G., & Dougherty, D. M. (2002). Impulsivity and Substance Abuse: What Is the Connection? Addictive Disorders Their Treatment, 1, 3-10.

Moffitt, T. E. (2003). Life-course-persistent and adolescence-limited antisocial behavior: A 10-year research review and a research agenda. In Benjamin B. Lahey, Terrie E. Moffitt and Avshalom Caspi (eds.). Causes of Conduct Disorder and Juvenile Delinquency. New York: Guilford Press.

Muraven, M., Pogarsky, & G. Shmueli, D. (2006). Self-control depletion and the General Theory of Crime. *Journal of Quantitative Criminology*, 22, 263–277.

Murray, J., & Farrington, D. P. (2005). Parental imprisonment: effects on boys' Antisocial behavior and delinquency through the life-course. Journal of Child Psychology and Psychiatry 46(12), 1269–1278.

Ngai, N., & Cheung, C. (2005). Predictors of the likelihood of delinquency: A study of marginal Youth in Hong Kong, China. Youth & Society, 36, 445-470.

Oatley, K., & Jenkins, J. M. (2006). Understanding Emotions. Oxford, UK: Wiley-Blackwell.

Ortiz, X., Ramírez, C., &Valdez, P. (2009). Ritmos circadianos en la motivación y la emoción. En P. Valdez Ramírez (Ed.), Cronobiología Respuestas Psicofisiológicas al tiempo. (pp. 213-225). Nuevo León México: Universidad Autónoma de Nuevo León.

Ortony, A., & Turner, T. J. (1990). What´s basic about basic emotions? Psychological review, 97(3), 315-331.

Posner, E. A. (2001). Law and Emotions. *Georgetown Law Journal*, 89, 1977-1993.

Pratt, T. C., & Cullen, F. T. (2000). The empirical status of Gottfredson and Hirschi's general theory of crime: A meta-analysis. *Criminology*, 38, 931-964.

Putnam, F. W. (2003). Ten-year research update review: Children sexual abuse. *Journal of the American Academy of Child and Adolescent Psychiatry, 42,* 269-278.

Rafaelli, M., & Crockett, L. (2003). Sexual risk taking in adolescence: The role of self regulation and attraction to risk. *Developmental Psychology, 39,* 1036-1046.

Rebellon, C. J., & Van-Gundy, K. (2005). Can control theory explain the link between parental physical abuse and delinquency? A longitudinal analysis. Journal of research in crime and delinquency, 42, 247-274.

Reynolds, B., Ortengren, A., Richards, J. B., & de Wit, H. (2006). Dimensions of impulsive behavior: Personality and behavioral measures. Personality and Individual Differences, 40, 305–315

Reynolds, B., Richards, J. B., Horn, K., & Karraker, K. (2004). Delay discounting and probability discounting as related to cigarette smoking status in adults. Behavioral Processes, 65, 35-42.

Reynolds, B., Penfold, R. B., & Patak, M. (2008). Dimensions of Impulsive Behavior in Adolescents: Laboratory Behavioral Assessments. Experimental and Clinical Psychopharmacology, 16(2), 124–131.

Rolls, E. T. (2005). What are emotions, why do we have emotions, and what is their computational basis in the brain. In J-M. Fellous & M. A. Arbib (eds), Who Needs Emotions? The Brain Meets the Robot. (pp.117-146). New York,: Oxford University Press.

Roucek, J. S. (1970). Juvenile delinquency. New York: Philosophical reading.

Schultz, P.W. (2002). Knowledge, information, and household recycling: Examining the knowledge-deficit model of behavior change. In T Dietz & P. Stern (Eds.), *New Tools for Environmental Protection: Education, Information, and Voluntary Measures* (pp. 67-82). Washington, DC: National Academic Press.

Schwartz, S. (2002). ¿Existen aspectos universales en la estructura y contenido de los valores humanos? In M. Ros & V. Gouveia (Eds.), *Psicología Social de los Valores Humanos*. Madrid: Biblioteca Nueva.

Secretaría de Seguridad Pública de México, Consejo de Menores, (2008). *Transparencia focalizada de prevención y readaptación social: Estadísticas penitenciarias*. Retrived on June, 10, 2009, from: http://www.ssp.gob.mx/portalWebApp/ShowBinary? nodeId=/ BEARepository/365162//archivo

Sethi, A., Mischel, W., Aber, J., Shoda, Y., & Rodriguez, M. L. (2000). The role of strategic attention deployment in development of self-regulation: Predicting preschoolers' delay of gratification from mother-toddler interactions. Developmental Psychology, 36, 767–777.

Sigala, M., Burgoyne, C., & Webley, P. (1999). Tax communication and social influence: Evidence from a British simple. *Journal of Community and Applied Social Psychology, 9,* 237-241.

Simon, V. M. (1997). La participación emocional en la toma de decisiones. Psicothema, 9(2), 365-376.

Slater, M. D. (2003). Sensation-seeking as a moderator of the effects of peer influences, consistency with personal aspirations, and perceived harm of marijuana and cigarette use among younger adolescents. Substance Use and Misuse, 38, 865-880.

Stanford, M. S., Houston, R. J., Villemarette-Pittman, N. R., & Greve, K. W. (2003). Premeditated aggression: clinical assessment and cognitive psychophysiology. Personality and Individual Differences, 34, 773–781.

Taylor, C.S. (1996). *The unintended consequences of incarceration: Youth development, the juvenile corrections system, and crime*. Presented at Conf. Vere Inst. Harriman, NY.

The Political Constitution of the United Mexican States. (2009). Retrieved on March 25, 2009 from: http://www.cddhcu.gob.mx/LeyesBiblio/

Thompson, R. (1994). Emotion regulation: A theme in search of definition. In N. Fox (Ed.), The development of emotion regulation: Biological and behavioral considerations. *59*(2–3, Serial 240). *Monographs of the Society for Research in Child Development.*

Tyler, T. R. (2006). *Why People Obey The Law*. New Jersey: Princeton University Press.

Valiente, C., Lemery-Chalfant K., & Reiser, M. (2007). Pathways to Problem Behaviors: Chaotic Homes, Parent and Child Effortful Control, and Parenting. Social Development, 16(2), 249-267.

Vazsonyi, A., Pickering, L., Junger, M., & Hessing, D. (2001). An empirical test of a general theory of crime: a four-nation comparative study of self-control and the prediction of deviance. *Journal of Research in Crime and Delinquency, 38*, 2, 91-131.

Vigil-Colet, A., & Codorniu-Raga, M. J. (2004). Aggression and inhibition deficits, the role of functional and dysfunctional impulsivity. Personality and Individual Differences, 37(7), 1431-1440.

Vitacco, M. J., & Rogers ,R. (2001). Predictors of adolescent psychopathy: The role of impulsivity, hyperactivity, and sensation seeking. Journal of American Academy of Psychology and Law 29(4): 374–382.

White, J. R., Moffitt, T. E., Caspi, A., Bartusch, D. J., Needles, D. J., & Stouthamer-Loeber, M. (1994). Measuring Impulsivity and Examining Its Relationship to Delinquency. Journal of Abnormal Psychology, 103(2), 192-205.

Whiteside, S. P., & Lynam, D. R. (2001). The five factor model and impulsivity: Using a structural model of personality to understand impulsivity. Personality and Individual Differences, 30, 669–689.

Wortley, R., & Mazarolle, L. (2008). Environmental Criminology and Crime Analysis. Portland, Oregon: William Publishing.

Zajonc, R. B. (1984). On the primacy of affect. American psychologist, 39(2), 117-123.

Zeanah, C.H. (2005). Handbook of Infant Mental Health. New York: Guilford Press.

In: Bio-Psycho-Social Perspectives on Interpersonal Violence ISBN: 978-1-61668-159-3
Editors: M. Frías-Armenta et al., pp. 101-121 © 2010 Nova Science Publishers, Inc.

Chapter 5

CHILD MALTREATMENT, SELF REGULATION, AND PARENTING[1]

José Concepción Gaxiola Romero and Martha Frías Armenta
University of Sonora, Mexico.

ABSTRACT

Family is a group constituted by individuals linked with ties of kinship and affection, wherein children grow and develop. Caring and educating children are parents' duties. However, quite often, family is not the optimum environment for the development of children, especially when it creates and maintains attitudes and conflicts that act against the emotional and physical stability of minors. Child abuse occurs frequently within families and it causes short and long term consequences. However, in several victims of child abuse the negative effects never appear; thus, it is assumed that a number of factors protect them against these negative consequences. A protective factor is something that, in relation or in interaction with risk, reduces the likelihood of psychosocial problems. Social support is one of these variables. The aim of this study was to identify the protective function of social support and the effects of dispositional resilience and self-regulatory skills on the intergenerational transmission of child abuse. An inventory with various scales was constructed, assessing demographic variables such as mothers' age and marital status, monthly family income, separate income for each partner, partner's current occupations, mothers' and fathers' education, history of abuse, resilience, parenting styles, self-regulation and social support. The data were analysed using structural equation modelling. The resulting model confirms a negative relation between lack of self-regulation and resilience, so that the higher the lack of behavioural self-regulation the lower the resilience. In this research child abuse history was positively related to negative parenting. Findings are discussed in relation to the developmental system theory.

---

[1] This research was made possible thanks to CONACYT retention funds 2008-2009.

INTRODUCTION

Family has been conceived as a positive setting for development and growth of their members (United Nations Organization, 1989); unfortunately that is not always the case. Child maltreatment occurs in families and represents one of the most frequent health problems in the world with short and long term physical and psychological consequences (World Health Organization, 2002). The World Health Organization (1999, pp. 15-16) defined child maltreatment as "all forms of physical and/or emotional ill-treatment, sexual abuse, neglect or negligent treatment or commercial or other exploitation, resulting in actual or potential harm to the child's health, survival, development or dignity in the context of a relationship of responsibility, trust or power."

Child maltreatment regularly occurs in family, in the context of disciplinarian practices administered by parents or relatives living and interacting with children (UNESCO, 2005). According to UNICEF (2007), every year, 80,000 children die in Latin America as a consequence of family violence, and 70% of violence perpetrated against children and adolescents happen in families.

Mexico does not possess precise and specific data on child maltreatment; yet in 2004 the government accepted and registered 22,842 cases throughout the country (Instituto Nacional de Estadísticas Geografía e Informática , 2004). In Sonora, a northwestern state, according to local government there were 1197 child maltreatment occurrences in 2005 (Gabriel Baldenebro Patrón, Procurador de la Defensa del Menor y la Familia, personal communication, 2005).

Child maltreatment produces a number of physical and psychological sequelae. The physical consequences include diverse injuries, short and long term physical harm, susceptibility to health problems, and death (WHO, 2002). The psychological consequences of child maltreatment are characterized by interpersonal, cognitive, emotional and behavioural problems, substance abuse, and an increasing rate of health services demand (Hodson, Newcomb, Locke, & Goodyear, 2006; Kaplow & Widom, 2007).

There is empirical evidence that child maltreatment may result in long term consequences, one of them called *the intergenerational transmission of child abuse*. This implies that mothers with a child-maltreatment history are in the risk of reproducing abusive behaviors with their own children (Frías 2002; Gaxiola & Frías, 2005; Simons, Withbeck, Conger, & Chyi-In, 1991). It has been reported that a third of mothers with child abuse history maltreats their children and develops harsh parenting practices towards them (Kaufmann & Zigler, 1993; Oliver, 1993). However, these results also indicate that seventy percent of mothers do not do that, so that it could be presumed that those mothers are rather utilizing more positive parenting styles. Fortunately, there is evidence that positive parenting can be transmitted intergenerationally to break the (also) intergenerational cycle of child abuse, (Belsky, Jaffe, Sligo & Woodwart, 2005).

Developmental Psychology analyses the psychological problems that are present during human development (Cicchetti & Toth, 1998). This field studies the risk and protective factors for the developmental process of the child where every syndrome is seen in a successive developmental period (Sameroff, Lewis, & Miller 2000). According to theory, the interplay between the biological, psychological, and social contextual aspects affects the life span in different ways (Cicchetti, 1993; Cicchetti & Toth, 1998). These may produce individual responding differences that culminate in adaptive or maladaptive behavioral patterns (Cicchetti & Dawson, 2002; Cicchetti & Sroufe, 2000). Then, it may be stated that child maltreatment affects differentially the physical and psychological development of victims.

Developmental psychopathology is an integral framework of research within the field of development psychology, yet it is not based upon a unified theory; rather, it seeks to integrate the achieved knowledge from scientific findings at multiple levels of analysis (Cicchetti & Blender, 2004). Developmental psychopathologists "move" across the analysis of pathology and adaptation over life span, and the analysis of risk and protective factors associated to both conditions (Cichetti & Hinshaw, 2003; Cicchetti & Walker, 2001). The investigation of risk and pathology can enhance the comprehension of normal development (Sroufe, 1990).

Developmental systems theory (DST), as described by Masten (2006), is a conceptual framework in the field of developmental psychopathology. DST posits that individuals are living systems in continuous interaction with the contexts wherein they are embedded, which include family, peers, schools, jobs and larger systems such as culture. This theory constitutes a dynamic, non-reductionist, integrative, and multidisciplinary approach to describe, explain, and optimize ontogenetic change (Lerner, 2002; Overton, 2006).

Lerner (2005) argues that developmental systems theory has nine main characteristics:

1. Relational theory. The developmental systems conception transcends the Cartesian dichotomous discussions of mechanical determinism like nature-nurture, gene-environment or biology-culture. Development is influenced by the interplay of biological, psychological, social and cultural variables. Systemic integrations replace dichotomizations or reductionist points of view of the developmental system.
2. Integration of levels of organization. Development is an integration of systems, and not the result of a reductionist vision. The levels of organization are fused from the biological and psychological through the cultural and historical.
3. There is a mutually influential individual-context relation in ontogeny. The regulations of development occur as a consequence of mutually influential connections between all levels of the developmental system.
4. Individual-context emphasis. Individual-context relations are the basic unit of analysis of development. The integration of the individual to the context and the influences of the context on the individual are the fundamental unit of analysis of development.
5. Plasticity in development. In development, there is potential for systematic change and variation in individual trajectories.
6. Relative plasticity. The probability of change in developmental trajectory depends on variations in contextual conditions. Sometimes those variations facilitate change; sometimes they can constrain the change.
7. There is diversity in development. The particular combination of variables among the integrated levels of organization accounts for the differences across individuals and groups.
8. Promotion of positive development. Based on the relative plasticity of development, the promotion of positive human development could be achieved by working in the strengths of individuals and contexts.

9. Multidisciplinarity. The complexity of development across its levels of organizations requires the study and collaboration of different disciplines.

Masten and Coatsworth (1995), in considering this framework, establish that individuals have self-organizing, self-regulatory and self-righting properties, and they also have the task of maintaining their functioning while adapting to the contexts where they live. Individuals, while regulating their behavior, influence the behavior of others and are influenced by them in a reciprocal manner. Self-regulation of behavior, in this theory, is one of the most important individual variables, which transforms the individual in an important agent of his/her own development.

Two more assumptions derived from general systems theory (Bertalanffy, 1962) are basic in the developmental systems theory: Equifinality and multifinality principles (Cichetti & Rogosh, 1996). Equifinality emerged from the observation that in any open system a diversity of pathways may lead to the same result, and multifinality implies that any component may function differently, depending on the particular organization of a due system. These principles take into account the flexibility and variability of behavior in development which are basic for understanding the principle of resilience, establishing that even in a history of risk it is possible to find adaptive behaviors in individuals living in harsh conditions.

According to developmental systems theory, parenting is displayed by living systems influenced by internal and external interactions across development. In that sense, the influences of parenting can be short-termed or long-termed and they can be determined in a dynamic nature, reflecting multicausality and multiple pathways according to developmental principles. Children and parents are fused structurally and functionally in a multilevel system going from biological to socio-cultural tiers of organization; parents influence other levels of the developmental system and are reciprocally influenced by those variables (Lerner, 2002). There is continuity in human development from infancy to adulthood, but history of development is modulated by present contextual relations (Masten, 2006). The research in this framework needs to analyze the dynamics of those multiple relations in development and the association of past experiences with present contextual conditions.

Spencer, Samuelson, Blumberg, McMurray, Robinson, and Tomblin (2009) posit that developmental processes unfold over time, and therefore cannot be viewed in isolation; the processes we caught in research have a history that extend back in time; finally, the activity of individuals reflect the integration of experiences occurring over short periods of time or years (Adolph, Robinson, Young, & Gill-Alvarez, 2008).

In the context of developmental systems theory, risk and protective factors are dynamic in nature, and they can be found in multiple and diverse systems influencing the behavior at different levels. According to the multifinality principle, individuals living the same circumstances can take different directions in behavior results; some can be adapted, others not (Cicchetti & Rogosh, 1996). That is the core principle of resilience: that some individuals facing risk factors in their development do not experience its adverse consequences, and they behave adaptively in some developmental areas. There is some sort of individual choice in this pathway and it is hypothesized that it could be due to self-regulation behavior.

There are two perspectives in the integrative framework of developmental psychopathology; one is the study of abnormal behavior, the other is the investigation of adaptive behavior and variables associated to both conditions (Masten, 2006). The focus in abnormal behavior studies is on the negative consequences of conditions that affect human development (e.g. child maltreatment); the emphasis in adaptative behavior, instead, is on variables that promote behavioral health, sometimes under risk conditions.

Because of the multilevel dynamics of the variables associated to behavioral results in development it is necessary the use of multivariate research procedures, such as structural equation modeling (Bentler, 2006) to study those situations or contextual circumstances. Also, it is needed research to ascertain how the interaction among the complexity of variables in a developmental process could influence individual characteristics, and the adaptive or maladaptive behavioral processes (Cicchetti & Dawson, 2002).

If we study the variables associated to child maltreatment, resilience and parenting in its complexity, it will be possible to generate preventive and rehabilitative programs to promote positive development in individuals living in risk conditions. This strategy, in synthesis, can improve community's health and prevent the incidence of new problems from occurring (Masten, 2001). The selection of the variables associated to resilience can have the potential to be strengthened to modify the course of individual development into more positive pathways. These strategies can inspire the fields of education, social policy, and social work and go beyond the traditional vision that is characterized by vulnerability emphasis, recognizing the importance and benefits that can be obtained when a positive promotion of resilience is reinforced (Munist, Santos, Kotliarenco, Suárez, Infante, & Grotberg, 1998).

PARENTING STYLES

Parenting styles can be defined as the framework wherein child rearing practices are articulated. They imply a constellation of communication attitudes toward children that builds an emotional climate in which parents' behaviors are expressed (Darling & Steinberg, 1993).

Baumrind (1967; 1991) develops a classification of parenting styles, widely accepted in research, according to responsivity and demands expressed in every day interactions with children. Such classification results in three different parenting styles: the authoritarian, the authoritative and the permissive.

The authoritarian style is characterized by high demands and low responsivity, and a tendency to use harsh parenting strategies like verbal and physical punishment in the context of disciplinary interactions with children. Authoritarian parents expect their orders to be obeyed without explanation and are prone to monitor their children's activities carefully for meeting high expectations, often difficult to achieve. The authoritarian style has been associated, in children and adolescents, with an academic performance lower than controls, and problems in familiar and socially adaptative behavior (Bean, Bush, McKenry, & Wilson, 2003; Mupinga, Garrison & Pierce, 2006).

In regard to the permissive style, Maccoby and Martin (1983) describe passive parents as showing low demands and high responsivity (indulgent parents), or low demands and low responsivity. Passive parents avoid confrontations, do not monitor children's conduct, and actively evade childrearing responsibilities. The lack of supervision and commitment in passive parents can produce deficient adaptation to social and school norms (Englund, Luckner, Whaley, & Egeland, 2004; Rey & Plapp, 1990).

The authoritative style, the most positive one, is characterized by high demands in the context of high responsivity. Authoritative parents often monitor and establish clear standards for their children's behavior; they administer supportive rather than punitive disciplinarian methods and expect their children to be assertive, socially responsible and cooperative in daily interactions. The authoritative style in children and adolescents is associated with psychosocial adaptation, social and cognitive competence and positive behaviors (Jeynes, 2003; Kaufmann, Gesten, Santa, Salcedo, Rendina-Gobioff, & Gadd, 2000).

A mother with child abuse history that utilizes authoritative strategies presumably has developed herself under the influence of protective factors. A protective factor is something that, in relation or interaction with risks, reduces the probability of psychosocial problems (Little & Mount, 1999). Protective factors are those variables that buffer, attenuate or decrease the negative effects of adversity linked to risk factors (Muller & Lemieux, 2000; Zielinsky & Bradshaw, 2006). Social support from peers, relatives and neighbours are among the most salient protective factors to child maltreatment as mentioned by relevant literature.

Social Support

Humans are social, so that they are integrated into collective systems with complex interdependent relationships that serve many regulatory and protective roles (Masten & Obradovic, 2007). According to Bolger and Patterson (2003), in the context of childhood maltreatment the ability to benefit from interpersonal relationships is an important factor in predicting positive adaptation. The development of supportive relationships with adults and friends outside the immediate family system can afford instrumental (e.g. money, place to live) and emotional resources before problems originated inside family (Crouch, Milner, & Thompsen, 2001). Social support has been found to be a powerful protective factor against child-maltreatment experiences (Muller & Lemieux, 2000; Gaxiola & Frías, 2008). Social support can also provide information of more positive practices, alternative to child maltreatment (Garbarino & Kostelny, 1995) and could serve as a positive influence to parents in risk (Garbarino, 1995).

Social support manifests its buffering effects when it affects the stress perception and provides protective resources (Vranceanu, Hobfol, & Johnson, 2007). According to Armstrong, Birnie and Ungar (2005), social support could produce protective effects because it is associated with wellbeing and quality of parenting.

Neighborhood Characteristics

Neighborhood is an important unit of analysis because it may affect the social and psychological conditions of individuals living within its boundaries. The definition of neighborhood includes the geographical and social aspects of a particular community (Garbarino, 1985) and it implies informal social support and social ties (Garbarino, Kostelny & Barry, 2002). It has been found that neighborhood conditions act as a stressor or support for families at risk of child maltreatment practices (Coulton, Crampton, Irwin, Spilsbury, & Korbin, 2007); for example, children whose parents lived in neighborhoods that were low in social cohesion and informal social control were less likely to be resilient (Jaffe, Caspi, Moffitt, Polo- Tomás, & Taylor, 2007).

Secure and positive neighborhoods can promote personal development, psychological wellness and stimulate health interactions within the family, and among families and the broad social context (Gracia & Musitu, 2003; Korbin, 2003). Neighborhood advantage does not exert a direct effect on child maltreatment protection, but moderates the relationship between household stability and adaptation (DuMont, Widom, & Czaja, 2007).

Child maltreatment research has found that social isolation is a prominent characteristic of children's abusers (Gracia & Musitu, 2003), so it is important to study the indirect effects of neighborhood in child maltreatment research.

As a result of the influence of protective factors some individuals can be resilient to negative consequences of risk factors, presumably because there are some individual developmental pathways to competent adaptation, in spite of the exposure to conditions of adversity (Masten, Burt, Roisman, Obradovic, Long, & Tellegen 2004).

RESILIENCE

In general, resilience is a concept related to positive adaptation[2] in the context of challenge (Masten & Gerwitz, 2006). It implies that some individuals have relatively good outcomes despite suffering risk experiences, and relative resistance to circumstances of adversity (Rutter, 2006). Resilience is not a trait; it is a product, inferred from the interplay of buffering protective variables with risk factors experienced across psychological development. The final product of resilience is adaptability to adverse situations; it means flexibility of adaptation.

Resilience could be inferred from individuals who master normative competence in developmental tasks despite their experiences of adversity (Luthar, Cichetti & Becker, 2000). There is not a unique way to measure resilience competence; it depends on individuals' age and positive living activities that are functional in their time, culture and life circumstances. Tusaie & Dyer (2004) conceive resilience as a dynamic process that involves a personal negotiation through life and that fluctuates across time, developmental stage, and context.

One of the challenging questions in resilience is: Who decides or defines the criteria for judging good adaptation? (Masten & Obradović, 2006). To avoid the subjective use of normative social judgments and social values of dominant individualistic cultures in the definition of desirable and undesirable outcomes, criticised by some authors (Frydenberg 2002; Ungar 2003), it is proposed to use competences that research has proved to be functional in developmental psychology[3]. It won't totally eliminate normative decisions, because science is ultimately a social product but, at least, it could reduce the complication of decision making when choosing the subjective appropriateness of a cultural competence.

Three criteria are needed to establish the conclusion of resiliency; one is the presence of risk; second, is the evaluation of individual dispositional variables; and, third, is some measure of competence in a developmental task. In the context of child maltreatment

---

[2] Sameroff and Rosemblum (2006) say that: "Mental illness is the opposite of resilience in that behaviour does not change with the situation. There is poor regulation of affect, behavior, and cognition. Healthy individuals may become saddened by the death of a relative but then move on, whereas depressives are saddened in all situations" (p. 117).

[3] A similar suggestion was established by Olsson et al. (2003), when reviewing the literature of resilience as an outcome characterized by particular patterns of functional behavior.

resilience competence can be measured as an authoritative parenting style (Gaxiola & Frías, 2008), because according to empirical data, this style has the most positive results on child and adolescent social adjustment (Baumrind, 1991).

DISPOSITIONAL VARIABLES

Dispositional variables in resilience contexts are the individual ways to cope with adverse situations; they constitute a history result of the interaction with risk[4] and protective factors. Dispositional factors are tendencies or propensities to act (Ryle, 1949) and include collections of actions and events, not behaviors themselves (Ribes, 1990); these variables probabilize behavioral phenomena, for example resiliency. In that sense, resilience is an inference, a result of the interaction of individual dispositional factors and it can be measured using the procedures derived from the statistical tradition of latent-variables assessment (Bentler, 2006). This conceptualization avoids the misconceptions around the status of resilience conceived as a trait with all the causal internalization which is implicit in it (e.g. Reivich & Shatte, 2002).

Some dispositional variables related to resilience can be mentioned, collected from the literature of individually protective factors (Olsson, Bond, Burns, Vella, & Sawyer, 2003); for example: coping, positive attitude, humor sense, empathy, flexibility to accepting negative experiences, perseverance, religiosity, self-efficacy, optimism, and goal orientation.

The resilience phenomenon is multi-determined (Luthar, Cichetti, & Becker, 2000), so that it is necessary to establish multivariate models to know the paths and processes in which the influencing variables affect to each other. Structural equation modelling is a powerful tool in this enterprise (Bentler, 2006), because in a single model the protective and risky factors, as well as the targets or processes of the resilience variable can be specified and tested (Gaxiola & Frías, 2008; Serbin & Karp, 2004).

SELF-REGULATION

Self-regulation is a central concept in social cognitive theory and can be defined as the capacity to interact with the environment, to learn and regulate thoughts and behaviors, to adjust the performance and to alter the environment in order to meet certain standards (Bandura, 1986). In general, self-regulation is conceptualized as the capacity to regulate own emotions, attention and behavior (Block & Block, 1980). When individuals face contextual and personal demands, they need to control attention, behavior and affective states to attain desired goals (Zimmerman, 2000). The development of the self-regulation capacity represents a major achievement of childhood, which is related to social, behavioral and academic competence (Gillmore & Cuskelly, 2005); for that reason, individuals who lack effective and flexible skills of self-regulation are at risk of experiencing a variety of personal and socials

---

[4] Even risk coped in controlled situations could be positive in psychological development, because it is expected to act as an inoculation process. For additional commentaries about this, see Rutter, M. (2007). Resilience, competence, and coping. *Child Abuse & Neglect, 3*, 205-209.

difficulties (Caspi, Henry, McGee, Moffitt, & Silva 1995; Cleary & Zimmerman, 2004; Pelletier, Dion, & Reid, 2004).

An association between resilience and self-regulation, mediated by positive emotion, has been reported (Tugade & Fredrickson, 2004). In fact, resilience research in its origins (Block & Block, 1980) had been related to personality and regulation. In the concept of ego resiliency it is defined as "the dynamic capacity of an individual to modify his/her modal level of ego-control, in either direction, as a function of the demand characteristics of the environmental context" (p. 48). Ego resilience involves adaptation resources to changing circumstances and flexible use of problem-solving strategies where regulation plays a central role. It is expected that resilient individuals can be flexibly adapted to environmental changing circumstances and stress (Eisenberg, Fabes & Spinrad, 2006).

Self regulation is a complex mechanism of adaptation with a neuro-biological basis but influenced by the environment, especially by the characteristics of the relationship with parents during infancy (Demetriou, 2000). Parenting interactions in the context of warmer disciplinarian practices expose children to new regulatory skills and provide opportunities to engage in effective regulatory experiences; contrarily, physically punitive parenting practices may interfere with the development of effective self-regulatory strategies by reducing the opportunity and motivation to engage in effective regulatory experiences (Colman, Hardy, Albert, Raffaelli, & Crocket, 2006). Eisenberg et al. (2001) report that persistence during challenges, frustration tolerance, and compliance with caregiver demands are the bases of successful emotional self-regulation in early childhood. It has been reported that high levels of maternal warmth and low levels of physically punitive discipline at age 4-5 are associated with a greater capacity for self-regulation at age 8-9 (Colman et al., 2006). These associations indicate that the development of self-regulation is open to caregiver influence during childhood. In fact it has been found that problems in learning and self-control often begin in the preschool years and are related to the quality of available parenting (Masten & Gewirtz, 2006).

Eisenberg, Champion, and Ma (2004) proposed a theory to link self-control, regulation, emotionality, and resiliency. The theory posits that there are two types of control: 1) reactive control, which is characterized by less voluntarily, automatic, reflexive, and unintentional processes, and 2) effortful control, characterized by voluntary and goal-oriented control processes. Only effortful control represents the behaviour regulation and resilience characteristics.

In the context of parenting, self-regulatory skills may have a relationship with resilience because of its implications in the adaptability and control of behavior (Eisenberg, Champion & Ma, 2004). For that reason, probably people with high self-regulatory skills tend to be more resilient than their counterparts with lower self-regulatory measures.

For the reasons exposed, the aim of this study is to identify the protective function of social support and the effects of dispositional resilience and self-regulatory skills in the intergenerational transmission of child abuse.

Hypothesis

On the basis of existant theory and empirical research, we stated the next hypothesis: self regulated behavior may affect the dispositional individual characteristics of resilience and parenting of mothers with child abuse history.

METHOD

Participants

Participants in this investigation included 132 mothers with children attending elementary school. The selection criterions were: a) To have a child in elementary school, b) Voluntarily agree to participate in the investigation, and c) To have a child- abuse history. Previous to the application of the instruments the informed consent to be filled, including the objectives, procedures and ethical considerations of this research was presented to all participants and signed by them.

Instruments

An inventory with various scales assessing, in the first part, demographic variables like mothers' age and marital status, monthly family income, separate income for each partner, partner's current occupations, and mothers' and fathers' education was built. The second part assessed the following variables:

History of Abuse
In order to determine mother's abuse history, six items from the Conflict Tactics Scale (Straus, 1979, 1990) were administered. The items measured the frequency of abuse tactics perpetrated by parents, when the mothers of this study were children (less than twelve years old). The scale was responded by considering seven options: 1(once), 2 (two times), 3 (three to five times), 4 (six to seven times), 5 (eleven to twelve times), 6 (more than twenty times), and 7 (zero). In previous studies with samples of similar characteristics, Cronbach's alphas of .80 (Frias, 2002) and .83 (Gaxiola & Frías, 2005) resulted from using this scale (Frías, 2002).

Social Support
It was measured with a scale specially constructed for this study. It includes eight items concerning the social support inside family and social support provided by the neighborhood around family. The scale provides response options ranging from completely agree (1) to completely disagree (5).

Parenting Styles
A translation and adaptation to Spanish of the Parenting Styles Inventory (Robinson, Mandelco, Olsen, & Hartr, 1993) was administered to all participants. This instrument was validated with a Mexican sample (Gaxiola, Frías, Cuamba, Franco, & Olivas, 2006) and

includes 62 items assessing authoritative, authoritarian and permissive parenting styles (Baumrind, 1967, 1991). The options in this scale are: never (0), sometimes (1), about half of the time (2), very frequently (3), and always (4). Robinson *et al.* (1993) reported an alpha of .91 from the authoritative dimension, .86 from the authoritarian and .75 from the passive style.

Resilience

In order to assess resilience, a 24-item scale (IRES, Gaxiola, Frías, Hurtado, Salcido, & Figueroa, *in press*) was constructed and administered including questions about personal dispositional variables associated with resilience: coping, positive attitude, sense of humor, empathy, flexibility, perseverance, religiosity, self-efficacy, optimism, and goal orientation. The response options are: nothing (1), a little (2), regularly (3), much (4) and totally (5), which identify the stated personal characteristics.

Self-Regulation

Self-regulation was measured with 30 items from the Behavioral Regulation Scale extracted from the Behavior Rating Inventory of Executive Function-Adult Version (Gioia, Isquith, Retzkaff, & Espy, 2002). These items evaluate the inhibition, shift, emotional control and self-monitoring functions of respondents, using seven options: never (0), occasionally (1), sometimes (2), often (3), very often (4), frequently (5), almost always (6).

Procedure

The sample was selected from mothers with children attending elementary schools in different sectors of the city. The contact was established through the school's principals. The aim of the research was explained to these principals; if they agree to participate, they established contact with teachers, who, in turn, sent a letter to mothers inviting them to participate in the study, following a scheduled program.

Previous to informant consent signing, the interview was conducted by trained research assistants in the classrooms of the elementary schools. Voluntary participation, the content of questionnaire and the research objectives were communicated by interviewers to every mother of the sample. The interview took about 30 minutes.

Although all the mothers were interviewed, the sample was selected only by considering to those meeting the history of abuse criterion.

Data Analysis

Data were analyzed using univariate statistics, means and standards deviations for continuous variables and frequencies for discrete variables. Frequency analyses were conducted with categorical demographic variables such as educational level, marital status, and professional level of respondents. In addition, a structural equation model (SEM) was specified and tested including direct and indirect relations between the variables (Bentler, 1990). A SEM is characterized by two components: the measurement model and the structural model. The former consists of the validation of the administered measures trough confirmatory factor analysis, and the latter is contained in the path trajectories between latent variables. A SEM includes observed and latent variables wherein coherent factors related to the studied behavioral aspects should emerge from inter-relations between items, deemed to indicate each latent variable. Observed variables are indicators or manifest variables, while latent variables are the constructs or factors which are inferred from their corresponding indicators (Corral, Frías, & González, 2001).

In our tested model, protective factors, indicated by institutional support, neighbors support, family and friends support, affect resilience, indicated by positive attitude, sense of humor, perseverance, religiosity, optimism, and goal-oriented behavior. Protective factors affect, at the same time, the lack of self-regulation formed by inhibition, shift, self-monitoring, and emotional control. Lack of self-regulation affects both resilience and negative parenting indicated by authoritarian and passive styles. Finally, child abuse history is related to negative parenting.

The goodness of fit of the theoretical model is also tested (Bentler, 2006). Goodness of fit indicators are intended to determine whether the model being tested should be accepted or rejected. Three types of goodness of fit indicators are, at least, recommended (Garver & Mentzer, 1999): 1) the statistical indicator chi-squared (χ^2); 2) practical indicators, such as the nonnormed fit index (NNFI) and the comparative fit index (CFI); and 3) the root mean squared approximation of error (RMSEA). An acceptable χ^2 indicating goodness of fit exhibits a nonsignificant associated p (>.05) value. In turn, NNFI and CFI with values >0.90 indicate good fit, while a RMSEA of a <0.08 value, and a ratio χ^2/d.f. of 3 or less indicates an acceptable fit. Bentler (1990) developed the CFI index as a noncentrality parameter to overcome the limitation of sample size effects.

RESULTS

Table 1 describes the demographic data of the sample. There is much variability in family income (*S.D.* $ 1007.1 U.S. Dollars) because the sample was selected from different socio-economic strata of the city.

In regard to the marital status of respondents the majority of the sample was married (84.8%) and only 3.8% were divorced; 50.8 % are housewives, 12.1% are employees and 12.1% are professionals.

Table 2 resumes the Cronbach's alphas of the dimensions used in the structural model. All the alphas are .60 or above; so, they were considered acceptable (Nieva & Sorra, 2003).

Structural Model

In the structural model (see figure 1) the protective factor was indicated by the variables institutional support (factor *loading* =.27), support from neighbors (.87), and family and friends support (.53). The resilience factor emerged from positive attitude (.80), sense of humor (.54), perseverance (.84), religiosity (.52), optimism (.72), and goal-oriented behavior (.77). The lack of self-regulation factor was indicated by inhibition (.80), shift (.73), self-monitoring (.78) and emotional control (.90). Finally, negative parenting was indicated by authoritative (.82) and passive parenting (.66).

In the pathways of the structural model, lack of self-regulation resulted negatively related to resilience (-.33), while lack of self-regulations was positively related to negative parenting (.61), and child abuse history was positively associated to negative parenting (.17). We did not find a significant statistical relation between protective factors and lack of self-regulation.

The model explains 14% of the variance in resilience and 49 % of variance in negative parenting. Goodness of fit indicators produced a χ^2 value of 142.03 (97 df), p=0.001, and values of NNFI=.92 and CFI=.94. The practical indicators evidenced that the data supported the specified model of relations between variables.

Table 1. Demographic data

Variable	M	SD
(N= 132)		
Age	37.3	5.03
Own income*	321.3	486.1
Partner's income*	994.0	914.7
Family income*	1281.2	1007.1
Number of children	2.6	0.9
Schooling in years	12.6	3.1
Partner's schooling in years	12.8	3.5
Time living with partner	13.2	5.5
Age of son or daughter selected	9.2	1.7

* US dollars (monthly) based in a parity of $13.35 Mexican pesos per dollar.

Tabla 2. Cronbach´s alphas of the scales used in the study

Dimensions	Cronbach´s alpha
Abuse history	.81
Parenting styles	.72
Protective factors	.71
Resilience	.92
Self-regulation	.90

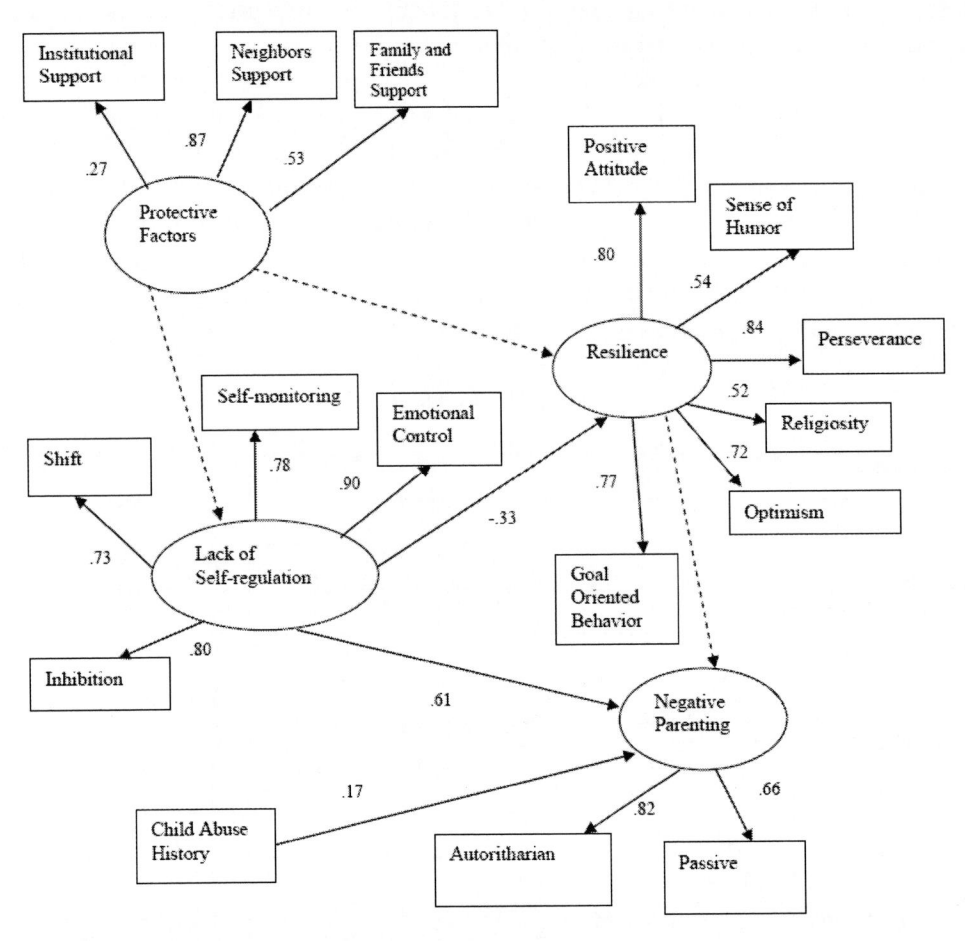

χ^2 = 142.03 97 G. de L. p = 0. 001 BBNFI =. 84 BBNNFI =.92 CFI = .94 RMSEA= .06 R^2 =. 14.
Figure 1. Structural model of protective factors, self-regulation and resilience to child abuse history.

CONCLUSION

Our tested structural model support the idea that a negative relation between the lack of self-regulation and resilience exists, so that the higher the lack of self-regulation of behavior the lower the resilience. This finding is in line with previous studies' outcomes wherein self-regulation strategies are linked to resilience because resilience implies behavioral control (Tugade & Frederickson, 2007).

Our data also support the theory stating the central position of self-regulation in the modulation of behavior (Masten & Coatsworth, 1995), specifically in the association between self-regulation and the dispositional characteristics of resilience. Since self-regulation is shaped in the development and integration of ontogeny (Colman *et al.*, 2006; Ruff & Rothbart, 1996) longitudinal research intended at finding the process implicated in the multilevel dynamics of the self-regulation of behavior and resilience in development is needed. Its results would potentiality allow to know how to improve individual resilience.

Lack of self-regulated behavior in our structural model was associated to negative parenting. As expected, in this research respondents' inhibition, shift, emotional control and self-monitoring -as indicators of self-regulation- played a significant role in parenting. The strategies of control and adaptation before changes are crucial to overcome the everyday task of parenting (Darling & Stainberg, 1993). Parents that show difficulties in self-monitoring are at risk of displaying negative parenting styles.

In this study, child abuse history was positive related to negative parenting. This relation evidences the influences of child abuse history on current parenting styles. This finding has been reported in previous studies by our research group (Frías, 2002; Gaxiola & Frías, 2005). Studies on the long-term consequences of child abuse evidence the negative effects of child abuse history on own children, when the circumstances of parenting overpass the capacity of adaptation of victims. The development of parenting styles reflects the integration of experiences occurring over years as indicated by developmental systems theory (Adolph, Robinson, Young, & Gill-Alvarez, 2008; Spencer *et al.*., 2009); and the continuity of human development from infancy to adulthood (Masten, 2006).

Although developmental systems theory establishes that all the assessed variables may influence resilience and the self-regulated behavior in a multilevel action, some of these variables failed in producing a significant structural effect on their target variables. In this study we did not find a significant relationship between protective factors (assessed as social support) and self-regulation, which could be explained by some recent findings that link self-regulation to the left frontal hemisphere EEG activity (Curtis & Cicchetti, 2003). In this sense, it is likely that self-regulation systems are more associated to frontal cerebral activity than to environmental support. That reason could sustain, also, the lack of statistical significant relation between protective factors and resilience. In fact, resilience explained variance by the model was only of 14%. Previous research indicates that resilience implies the action of ordinary neurobiological systems; when these systems associate to self-regulatory capacity of the human brain they are working properly. Resilience results as the individual learns and develops (Masten & Obradović, 2006). Further research is necessary in this promising area.

One of the limitations of this study was the self-reported nature of our data. In future studies, it will be interesting to assess parenting styles as a competence, using structured interactions between parents and children, also linking the dispositional resilience with the observed measures. Yet, and in spite of the mentioned limitation, our results seem to indicate that self-regulated behavior has important links with resilience and parenting.

REFERENCES

Adolph, K. E., Robinson, S. R., Young, J. W., & Gill-Alvarez, F. (2008). What is the shape of developmental change? *Psychological Review, 115,* 527–543.

Armstrong. M. I., Birnie-Leftcovitch, & Ungar, M. T. (2005). Pathways between social support, family well being, quality of parenting, and child resilience: what we know. *Journal of Child and Family Studies, 14,* 269-281.

Bandura, A. (1986). *Social foundations of thought and action: A social cognitive theory.* Englewood Cliffs, NJ: Prentice- Hall, Inc.

Baumrind, D. (1967). Child care practices anteceding three patterns of preschool behavior. *Genetic Psychology Monographs, 75,* 43–88.

Baumrind, D. (1991). Parenting styles and adolescent development. In J. Brooks-Gunn, R. Lerner y A. C. Petersen (Eds.): *The encyclopedia of adolescence* (pp. 746-758). New York: Garland.

Bean, R. A., Bush, K. R., McKenry, P. C., & Wilson, S. M. (2003). The impact of parental support, behavioral control, and psychological control on the academic achievement and self-esteem of African American and European Adolescents. *Journal of Adolescent Research, 5,* 523-541.

Belsky, J., Jaffe, S. R., Sligo, J., & Woodwart, L. (2005). Intergenerational transmission of warm-sensitive-stimulating parenting: a prospective study or mothers and fathers of 3-years-olds. *Child Development, 2,* 384-396.

Bentler, P. M. (1990). Comparative fit indexes in structural models. *Psychological Bulletin, 107,* (2), 238-246.

Bentler, P. M. (2006). *EQS 6 Structural Equations Program Manual.* Encino, CA: Mulivariate Software Inc.

Bertalanffy, L. V. (1962). *Modern theories of development: An introduction to theoretical biology* New York: Harper & Row. (Original work published in German in 1933).

Block, J. H. & Block, J. (1980). The role of ego-control and ego-resiliency in the organization of behavior. In W. A. Collins (Ed.), *The Minnesota Symposia on Child Psychology,* Vol. 13, pp. 39—101. Hillsdale, NJ: Erlbaum.

Bolger K. E. & Patterson C.J. (2003). Sequelae of child maltreatment: Vulnerability and resilience. In: S.S. Luthar, Editor, *Resilience and vulnerability: Adaptation in the context of childhood adversities*, Cambridge University Press, Cambridge, UK, pp. 156–181.

Caspi, A., Henry, B., McGee, R. O., Moffitt, T. E., & Silva, P. A. (1995). Temperamental origins of child and adolescent behavior problems: From age three to age fifteen. *Child Development, 66,* 55-68.

Cicchetti, D. (1993). Developmental psychopathology: Reactions, reflections, projections. *Developmental Review, 13,* 471–502.

Cicchetti, D., & Blender, J. A. (2004). A multiple-levels-of-analysis approach to the study of developmental processes in maltreated children. *Proceedings of the National Academy of Sciences, 101*(50), 17325–17326.

Cicchetti, D., & Dawson, G. (2002). Multiple levels of analysis [Special issue]. *Development and Psychopathology, 14*(3), 417–666.

Cicchetti, D., & Hinshaw, S. P. (Eds.). (2003). Conceptual, methodological, and statistical issues in developmental psychopathology: A special issue in honor of Paul E. Meehl [Special issue]. *Development and Psychopathology, 15*(3), 497–832.

Cicchetti, D., & Rogosch, F.A. (1996). Equifinality and multifinality in developmental psychopathology. *Development and Psychopathology, 8,* 597–600.

Cicchetti, D., & Sroufe, L. A. (Eds.). (2000). Reflecting on the past and planning for the future of developmental psychopathology [Special issue]. *Development and Psychopathology, 12*(3), 255–550.

Cicchetti, D., & Toth, S. L. (1998). Perspectives on research and practice in developmental psychopathology. In W. Damon (Ed.), *Handbook of child psychology* (5th ed., Vol. 4, pp. 479–583). New York:Wiley.

Cicchetti, D., & Walker, E. F. (Eds.). (2001). Stress and development: Biological and psychological consequences [Special issue]. *Development and Psychopathology, 13*(3), 413–753.

Cleary, T. J., & Zimmerman, B. J. (2004). Self-regulation empowerment program: A school-based program to enhance self-regulated and self-motivated cycles of student learning. *Psychology in the Schools, 41*(5), 537-550.

Colman, R. A., Hardy, S. A., Albert, M., Raffaelli, M., & Crocket. L. (2006). Early predictors of self-regulation in middle childhood. *Infant and Child Development 15* (4), 421–437.

Corral, V., Frías, M., & González, D. (2001). *Análisis Cuantitativo de Variables Latentes.* Colección textos académicos, No. 13, Mexico: Editorial UniSon.

Coulton, C. J., Crampton, D. S., Irwin, M., Spilsbury, J. C., & Korbin, J. E. (2007). How neighborhoods influence child maltreatment: A review of the literature and alternative pathways. *Child Abuse and Neglect, 31*, 11-12.

Curtis, W. J., & Cicchetti, D. (2003). Moving research on resilience into the 21st century: Theoretical and methodological considerations in examining the biological contributors to resilience. *Development and Psychopathology, 15,* 773–810.

Crouch, J. L., Milner, J. S., & Thomsen, C. (2001). Childhood physical abuse, early social support, and risk for maltreatment: current social support as a mediator of risk for child physical abuse. *Child Abuse and Neglect, 1,* 93-107.

Darling, N., & Steinberg, L. (1993). Parenting style as a context: an integrative model. *Psychological Bulettin, 113,* 487-496.

Demetriou, A. (2000). Organization and development of self-understanding and self-regulation: Toward a general theory. In M. Boekaerts, P. R. Pintrich, & M. Zeidner (Eds.), *Handbook of selfregulation* (pp. 209– 251). San Diego, CA: Academic.

DuMont, K. A., Widom, C. S., & Czaja S. J. (2007). Predictors of resilience in abused and neglected children grown-up: The role of individual and neighborhood characteristics. *Child Abuse and Neglect, 31*, pp. 255–274.

Eisenberg N, Champion C, & Ma Y. (2004). Emotion-related regulation: An emerging construct. *Merrill-Palmer Quarterly, 50* (3), 236–259.

Eisenberg, N., Fabes, R. A., & Spinrad, T.L. (2006). Prosocial behavior. In: N. Eisenberg, W. Damon, R. M. Lerner (Eds.). *Handbook of child psychology: Vol. 3, Social, emotional, and personality development* (6th ed., p.p. 646-718), New York: Wiley.

Eisenberg, N., Gershoff, E. T., Fabes, R. A., Shepard, S. A., Cumberland, A. J., Losoya, S. H., et al. (2001). Mothers' emotional expressivity and children's behavior problems and social competence: Mediation through children's self-regulation. *Developmental Psychology, 37,* 475–490.

Englund, M. M., Luckner, A. E., Whaley, G. J., & Egeland, B. (2004). Children's Achievement in Early Elementary School: Longitudinal Effects of Parental Involvement, Expectations, and Quality of Assistance. *Journal of Educational Psychology, 4,* 723–730.

Frías, M. (2002). Long- term effects of child punishment on Mexican women: a structural model. *Child Abuse and Neglect, 26,* 371-386.

Frydenberg, E. (2002). *Beyond coping: Meeting goals, visions, and challenges.* NY, US: Oxford University Press.

Garbarino, J. (1985). An ecological approach to child maltreatment. In L. E. Pelton (Ed.), *The social context of child abuse and neglect* (pp. 228-267). New York: Human Sciences Press.

Garbarino, J. (1995). *Raising children in a socially toxic environment.* San Francisco: Jossey-Bass.

Garbarino, J., & Kostelny, K. (1995). Parenting and public policy. In M. H. Bornstein (Ed.), Handbook of parenting: Vol. 3. *Status and social conditions of parenting* (pp. 419-436). Mahwah, NJ: Erlbaum.

Garbarino, J., Kostelny, K., & Barry, F. (2002). Neighorhood-based programs. In Trickett, P. K., y Schellenbach, C. J. (Eds.), *Violence Against Children in the Family and the Community* (pp. 287-314). Washington DC: American Psychological Association.

Garver, M. S. & Mentzer, J.T. (1999). Logistics research methods: Employing structural equation modeling to test for construct validity, *Journal of Business Logistics, 20*, (1), 1999, 33-57.

Gaxiola, R. J., & Frías, A. M. (2005). Las consecuencias del maltrato infantil: un estudio con madres mexicanas. *Revista Mexicana de Psicología, 22*, 363-374.

Gaxiola, R. J., & Frías, A. M. (2008). Un modelo ecológico de factores protectores del abuso infantil: un estudio con madres mexicanas. *Medio Ambiente y Comportamiento Humano, 9*, 13-31.

Gaxiola, R. J., Frías, A. M., Cuamba, O. N., Franco, B. J. D., & Olivas, S. L. C. (2006). Validación del cuestionario de prácticas parentales en una población mexicana. *Enseñanza e Investigación en Psicología, 11* (1), 115-128.

Gaxiola, R.J. C., Frías, A. M., Hurtado A. M. F., Salcido, N. L. C., & Figueroa, F. M. (in press). Validación del inventario de resiliencia (IRES) en una población del nororeste de México. *Enseñanza e Investigación en Psicología*.

Gilmore, L. A. and Cuskelly, M. (2005) The Measurement of Self-Regulation from Ages 2 to 8. In L. A. Gilmore, and M. Cuskelly (Eds.) *Proceedings 40th APS Annual Conference*, Melbourne, Australia. Retrived on August 10, 2009 from: http://eprints.qut.edu.au

Gioia, G., Isquith, P., Retzkaff, P.D., & Espy, K.A. (2002). Confirmatory factor analysis of the Behavioral Rating Inventory of Executive Function [BRIEF] in a clinical sample. *Child Neuropsychology, 8*, 294-257.

Gracia, E., & Musitu, G. (2003). Social isolation from communities and child maltreatment: A cross-cultural comparison. *Child Abuse and Neglect, 27*, 153-168.

Hodson, C., Newcomb, M. D., Locke, T. F., & Goodyear, R. K. (2006). Childhood adversity, poly-substance use, and disordered eating in adolescent Latinas: Mediated and indirect paths in a community sample. *Child Abuse and Neglect, 30*, 1017–1036.

INEGI, Instituto Nacional de Estadísticas Geografía e Informática (2004). Encuesta Nacional Sobre la Dinámica de las Relaciones en los Hogares, 2003. Aguascalientes, México: INEGI.

Jaffe, S. R., Caspi, A., Moffitt, T. E., Polo- Tomás, & Taylor, A. (2007). Individual, family, and neighborhood factors distinguish resilient from non-resilient maltreated children: A cumulative stressors model. *Child Abuse and Neglect, 31*, 231-253.

Jeynes, W. (2003). A meta-analysis the effects of parental involvement on minority children's academic achievement. *Education and Urban Society, 2*, 202-218.

Kaplow, J. L., & Widom, C. S. (2007). Age of Onset of Child Maltreatment Predicts Long-Term Mental Health Outcomes. *Journal of Abnormal Psychology, 116*, 176–187.

Kaufmann, D., Gesten, E., Santa, R. C., Salcedo, O., Rendina-Gobioff, G., & Gadd, R. (2000). The relationship between parenting style and children's adjustment: The parents' perspective. *Journal of Child and Family Studies, 2*, 231–245.

Kaufman, J., & Zigler, E. (1993). The intergenerational transmission of abuse is overstated. In R.J. Gelles y D.R. Loseke (Eds.) *Current controversies on family violence* (pp. 209-221). Newbury Park, CA: Sage.

Korbin, J. E. (2003). Neighborhood and community connectedness in child maltreatment research. *Child Abuse and Neglect, 27*, 137-140.

Lerner, R. M. (2002). *Concepts and theories of human development* (3rd ed.). Mahwah, NJ: Lawrence Erlbaum Associates.

Lerner, R. M. (2005). Promoting positive youth development: Theoretical and empirical bases. White paper prepared for: Workshop on the Science of Adolescent Health and Development, National Research Council, Washington, DC. September 9, 2005. National Research Council/Institute of Medicine. Washington, D.C.: National Academy of Sciences. Retrived on August 12, 2009, from: http://ase.tufts.edu/iaryd/documents/pubPromotingPositive.pdf

Little, M., & Mount, K. (1999). Prevention and Early Intervention with Children in Need. Ashgate, Aldershot.

Luthar, S. S., Cicchetti, D., & Becker, B. (2000). The construct of resilience: A critical evaluation and guidelines for future work. *Child Development, 71*, 543–562.

Maccoby, E. E., & Martin, J. A. (1983). Socialization in the context of the family: parent–child interaction. In P. H. Mussen (Series Ed.) & E. M. Hetherington (Vol. Ed.), *Handbook of child psychology*: Vol. 4. Socialization, personality, and social development (4th ed., pp. 1–101) New York: Wiley.

Masten, A. S. (2006). Developmental psychopathology: Pathways to the future *International Journal of Behavioral Development, 30* (1), 47–54.

Masten, A. S. (2001). Ordinary magic: Resilience process in development. *American Psychologist, 56*, 227-238.

Masten, A. S., Burt, K. B., Roisman, G. I., Obradovic, J., Long, J. D., & Tellegen, A. (2004). Resources and resilience in the transition to adulthood: Continuity and change. *Development and Psychopathology, 16*(4), 1071–1096.

Masten, A. S., & Coatsworth, J. D. (1995). Competence, resilience, and psychopathology. In D. Cicchetti y D. Cohen (Eds.), *Developmental psychopathology: Vol. 2. Risk, disorder, and adaptation* (pp. 715-752). New York: Wiley.

Masten, A. S., & Gerwitz, A. H. (2006). Resilience in development: The importance of early childhood. Retrieved on May 8, 2009, from: www.child-encyclopedia.com/documents/Masten-GewirtzANGxp.pdf

Masten, A. S. & Obradović, J. (2006). Competence and Resilience in Development. *Annals of the New York Academy of Sciences, 1094*, 13-27.

Masten, A. S., & Obradović, J. (2007). Disaster preparation and recovery: lessons from research on resilience in human development. *Ecology and Society* 13*(1)*: 9. [online] URL: http://www.ecologyandsociety.org/vol13/iss1/art9/

Muller, R. T., & Lemieux, K. E. (2000). Social support, attachement, and psychopathology in high risk formerly maltreated adults. *Child Abuse and Neglect, 24*, 883-900.

Munist, M., Santos, H., Kotliarenco, M. A. Suárez, O. E., Infante, F., & Grotberg, E. (1998). *Manual de identificación y promoción de la resiliencia en niños y adolescentes*. PAHO and WHO Eds., Washington, D.C.

Mupinga, E. E., Garrison, M. E. B., & Pierce, S. H. (2006). An exploratory study of the relationships between family functioning and parenting styles: The perceptions of mothers of young grade school children. *Child Abuse & Neglect, 30*, 599–617.

Nieva, V.F., & Sorra, J. (2003). Safety culture assessment: a tool for improving patient safety in healthcare organizations. *Quality Safe Health Care*, 12 (supl), ii17-ii23.

Oliver, J. E. (1993). Intergenerational transmission of child abuse: Rates, research, and clinical implications. *American Journal of Psychiatry*, 150, 1315-1324

Olsson, C. A., Bond, L., Burns, J. M., Vella, B. D. A. & Sawyer, S. M. (2003). Adolescent resilience: a concept analysis. *Journal of Adolescence, 26*, (1), 1-11.

Overton,W. F.(2006). Developmental Psychology: Philosophy, Concepts, Methodology. In R. M. Lerner (Ed.). Theoretical models of human development. Volume 1 of Handbook of Child Psychology (6th ed.). Editors-in-chief: W. Damon & R. M. Lerner. Hoboken, NJ: Wiley.

Pelletier, L. G., Dion, S. C., & Reid, R. (2004). Why do you regulate what you eat? Relationships between forms of regulation, eating behaviors, sustained dietary behavior change, and psychological adjustment. *Motivation and Emotion, 28*(3), 245-277.

Reivich, K., & Shatte, A. (2002). *The resilience factor*. New York: Broadway Books.

Rey, J. M., & Plapp, J. M. (1990). Quality of perceived parenting in oppositional and conduct disordered adolescents. *Journal of the American Academy of Child and Adolescent Psychiatry, 29,* 382–385.

Ribes, E. (1990). *Problemas conceptuales en el análisis del comportamiento*. Trillas, México.

Robinson, C. C., Mandelco, S., Olsen, F., & Hartr, C. H. (1995). Authoritative, authoritarian, and permissive parenting practices: Development of a new measure. *Psychological Reports, 77,* 819-830

Rutter, M. (2006). The promotion of resilience in the face of adversity. In A. Clarke-Stewart & J. Dunn (Eds.), *Families count: Effects on child and adolescent development* (pp. 26–52). New York & Cambridge: Cambridge University Press.

Ryle, G. (1949). *The concept of mind*. New York: Barnes and Noble.

Rutter, M. (2007). Resilience, competence, and coping. *Child Abuse & Neglect, 3*, 205-209.

Sameroff, A. J, Lewis, M., & Miller, S.M. (2000). Handbook of developmental psychopathology. New York: Academic plenum press.

Sameroff, A. J., & Rosenblum, K. L. (2006). Psychosocial constraints on the development of resilience. *Annuary fo New York Academy of Sciences, 1094,* 116-124.

Serbin, L. A., & Karp, J. (2004). The intergenerational transfer of psychosocial risk: mediators of vulnerability and resilience. *Annual Review of Psychology, 55,* 333-363.

Simons, R. L., Withbeck, L. B., Conger, R. D., & Chyi-In, W. (1991). Intergenerational transmission of harsh parenting. *Developmental Psychology*, 27, 159-171.

Spencer, J. P., Samuelson, L. K., Blumberg, M. S., McMurray, B., Robinson, S. R., & Tomblin, J. B. (2009). Seeing the World Through a Third Eye: Developmental Systems Theory Looks Beyond the Nativist–Empiricist Debate. *Child Development Perspectives, 3,* (2), Pages 103–105.

Sroufe, L. A. (1990). Considering normal and abnormal together: The essence of developmental psychopathology. *Development and Psychopathology, 2,* 335–347.

Straus, M. A. (1979). Measuring intrafamily conflict and violence: The Conflict Tactics (CT) Scale. *Journal of Marriage and the Family, 41,* 75-88.

Straus, M.A. (1990). The Conflict Tactics Scale and its critics: An evaluation and new data on validity and reliability. In M.A. Straus, and R.J: Gelles. (Eds.) *Physical Violence in American Families: Risk factors and adaptations to violence in 8,145 families.* New Brunswick, N J: Transactions Publishers.

Tussaie, K., & Dyer, J. (2004). Resilience: a historical review of the construct. *Holistica Nurse Practice, 18,* 3-10.

UNESCO (2005). Web site of the General Secretary of Violence Studies Against Children (*http://www.violencestudy.org/r27*) & J. E. Durrant. Corporal punishment: prevalence, predictors and implications for child behaviour and development. In S. N. Hart (ed.), *Eliminating Corporal Punishment* (París, UNESCO), 52 -53.

UNICEF (2007). Informe sobre el Estado Mundial de la Infancia. Retrived August, 26, 2007, from: http://argijokin.blogcindario.com/2007/02/06086-unicef-en-el-mundo-seis-millones-de-menores-son-sometidos-a-actos-de-violencia familiar.html

Ungar, M. 2003. Qualitative contributions to resilience research. *Qualitative Social Work* 2(1), pp. 85-102.

UNO/United Nations Organization (1989). *Convention. on the rights of the child.* Office of the high commissioner for human rights. Geneva, Switzerland. Retrived on May, 5, 2007, from: http://www.unhchr.ch/spanish/html/menu3/b/k2crc_sp.htm

Vrancenau, A. M., Hobfol, S. E., & Johnson, R. (2007). Child multi-type maltreatment and associated depression and PTSD symptoms: The role of social support and stress. *Child Abuse and Neglect, 1,* 71-84.

WHO/World Health Organization (1999). *Report of the Consultation on Child Abuse Prevention.* World Health Organization, Social Change and Mental Health, Violence and Injury Prevention, Geneva, pp. 15-16. Retrieved on March, 8, 2003, from: http://www.anppcan.org/anppcan/deftext.htm

WHO/World Health Organization (2002). *World report on violence and health.* Geneva, Switzerland. Retrived on January 10, 2005, from: http://www.who.int/violence_injury_prevention/violence/world_report/en/

Zielinsky, D. S., & Bradshaw, C. P. (2006). Ecological influences on the sequelae of child maltreatment: A review of the literature. *Child Maltreatment, 11,* 48-62.

Zimmerman, B. J. (2000). Attaining self-regulation: A social cognitive perspective. In M. Boekaerts, P. R. Pintrich, & M. Zeidner (Eds.), *Handbook of self-regulation* (pp. 13–39). San Diego, CA: Academic Press.

PART ONE B): CONTEXTUAL VARIABLES

In: Bio-Psycho-Social Perspectives on Interpersonal Violence   ISBN: 978-1-61668-159-3
Editors: M. Frías-Armenta et al., pp. 125-142   © 2010 Nova Science Publishers, Inc.

Chapter 6

ENVIRONMENTAL FACTORS IN HOUSING HABITABILITY AS DETERMINANTS OF FAMILY VIOLENCE

Victor Corral-Verdugo[*], *Martha Frías-Armenta and Daniel González-Lomelí*
Universidad de Sonora, Mexico

ABSTRACT

In approaching the issue of family violence, most specialists acknowledge the crucial influence of environmental factors on the emergence and sustenance of such a type of interpersonal violence. The Ecological Model of human development assumes that people's violence at home is influenced by a number of overlapping contextual levels, from the most proximal *microsystem*, containing the house and the family, to the most global *macrosystem* including social norms and cultural conventions. In turn, Crimen Prevention Through Environmental Design (CPTED), one more theoretical perspective, establishes that a proper household design is a deterrent against aggressions from sources *outside* residential settings. However, neither the Ecological Model nor CPTED have so far addressed the topic of the effect of habitability conditions on family violence. A number of authors have suggested that housing habitability is an important factor for quality of life, family functioning and a potential inducer of domestic violence. Household habitability is also assumed to determine family's quality of life and interrelations; subsequently, it could influence parents-children interactions as well as marital/couple functioning. Housing habitability is conceived as the set of psycho-environmental dimensions of a household. Those dimensions include overcrowding, privacy, noise, illumination, depth and temperature, among other conditions. According to a number of psycho-environmental authors, negative conditions in housing habitability could be inductive of family violence through the generation of stress and related situations that predispose aggressive interactions. In spite of this suggestion, no empirical

---

[*] Correspondence regarding this chapter should be sent to: Victor Corral-Verdugo, Departamento de Psicología y Ciencias de la Comunicación, Universidad de Sonora, Blvd. Luis y Encinas y Rosales S/N, Hermosillo, Sonora, 8300, Mexico. E-mail: victorcorralv@gmail.com

studies have been so far conducted for addressing the relation between psycho-environmental factors of housing habitability and family violence. The aim of this chapter is to present antecedents and results of a study on housing habitability and its impact on family child maltreatment and interpartner abusive behaviors. After reviewing theories and previous research on housing habitability and family relations, methods, results and conclusions of an empirical study are presented. Scales investigating negative habitability conditions (poor illumination, lack of privacy, lack of depth, noise, and extreme temperature) were administered to participants (200 Mexican housewives) at their households. In addition, they responded to an instrument investigating child maltreatment and interpartner aggressive episodes, which constituted a single factor of family violence. Housewives also provided demographic information. Results were processed within a structural-equation model, which showed that negative habitability conditions of the household significantly and positively predicted family violence. A higher socioeconomic status correlated with a perceived better housing habitability while younger participants perceived those conditions as being worse than older individuals. Implications of these results are discussed in terms of paying attention to the physical housing design as a promoter of family positive functioning.

INTRODUCTION

Family violence (FV), also known as domestic violence, comprises diverse ways with which a person within a family relation causes harm to another. Wallace (2005) defines FV as "any act or omission by persons who are cohabiting that result in serious injury to other members of the family." (p.2). Family violence includes child maltreatment and aggressive behaviors between members of a sexual partnership (interpartner violence). Abuse amongst siblings and maltreatment to elder family members are also included in this category. Child victimization at home consists of both direct maltreatment and witnessing violence between parents (Kalil & Harris, 2003; Merrill, Thomsen, Crouch, May, Gold, & Milner, 2005). These two situations result in negative consequences for children. From a child's perspective, the abuse received from her/his parents/caretakers constitutes a direct type of violence, while witnessing inter-parental violence is an indirect type of violence (Davies, DiLillo, & Martínez, 2004; Margolin & Gordis, 2000; Straus, Hamby, Boney-McCoy, & Sugarman, 1996).

The World Health Organization (WHO, 1999, p. 15) defines child maltreatment as behavior that "constitutes all forms of physical, and/or emotional ill-treatment, sexual abuse, neglect or negligent treatment or commercial or other exploitation, resulting in actual or potential harm to the child's health, survival, development or dignity in the context of a relationship of responsibility, trust, or power."

In Mexico, the Child Maltreatment Prevention Program received in the year 2002 23,585 reports of child abuse and neglect, of which 13,332 cases were confirmed (DIF, 2004). The National Institute of Statistics, Geography and Informatics (INEGI, 2007) informed that during 2002 24,563 reports were received; 32,218 in 2003 and 38554 during 2004. Clearly, this is a growing phenomenon.

In regard to interpartner violence the data are no more encouraging. Jayaraman (2004) establishes that at least one-third of all women have experienced domestic violence (by their husbands/family members) in their lifetime. In the Mexican Sonora State 49.8% of women had experienced at least one violent incident from her sexual partner during the last 12 months, as revealed by INEGI (2007), the Mexican Census Boureau. A survey, also conducted by INEGI in the Federal District, indicated that 30% of families suffered from some type of family violence, such as emotional maltreatment, intimidation, or physical or sexual abuse committed by a family member (Violencia y Maltrato, México, 2006). Nonetheless, one more study indicates that, in Mexico, 70% of women report some type of domestic violence (Violencia Doméstica, 2006).

Victimization from one parent to another (indirect violence) seems to be a key variable for understanding behavioral problems in children. Some studies demonstrate that, when parents are victimized, children are at serious risk of developing conduct problems (Litrownik, Newton, Hunter, English, & Everson, 2003; Morrel, Dubowitz, Kerr, & Black, 2003; Thompson, 2007). Moreover, research findings point out at a co-occurrence of the direct and indirect victimization, which worsen the effects of violence on children (English, Marshall, & Stewart, 2003). Children experiencing multiple types of maltreatment are at higher risk of developing conduct problems (Sternberg, Baradaran, Abbott, Lamb, & Guterman, 2006).

Unfortunately, the direct violence significantly covaries with the indirect manifestation. Slep and O'Leary (2005) found that in 45% of the investigated cases, child maltreatment co-occurred with interpartner violence. Other authors calculate that these two phenomena co-occurrence varies between 30% and 60% (Knickerbocker, Heyman, Slep, Jouriles, & McDonald, 2007). In this sense, looking for the subjacent causes of one manifestation of FV could lead to explaining the remaining types of domestic violence.

Among the predictors of family violence, the pertinent literature has focused on *personal determinants* such as a history of abuse experienced by the perpetrator (Ehrensaft, Cohen, Brown, Smailes, Chen & Johnson, 2003), beliefs on the efficacy of punishment as a disciplinary method (Corral-Verdugo, Frías-Armenta, Romero, & Muñoz, 1995), a low self-steem, impulsiveness, negative affectivity and deficiencies in coping with stress (Pianta, Egeland & Erickson, 1989), and alcohol consumption (Jewkes, Levin, & Penn-Kekana, 2002), among others.

ENVIRONMENTAL DETERMINANTS OF FAMILY VIOLENCE

The literature also mentions environmental factors as determinants of domestic violence. Yet, Fincham (2000) alerts that contextual factors are not focal in the empirical papers that deal with family violence determinants. Herrenkohl and Herrenkohl (2007) also criticize the fact that it is practically unknown the influence of environmental stressors on abuse/neglect and exposure to domestic violence.

This sounds odds, because most theoretical approaches to the family violence problem highlight the importance of the proximal environment (house, neighborhood) in the genesis of interpersonal aggressive behavior among family members. Garbarino and Gaboury (1992), for instance, acknowledge that the design, amount and level of maintenance of housing result in differential (good/bad) contexts for child development. Garbarino's work was influenced by Urie Bronfenbrenner's (1979) Ecological Model which concedes a paramount relevance to contextual factors in the explanation of child development. Since some of these factors are negative, the resulting developmental outcomes in children are negative as well.

Bronfenbrenner (1979, 1997) proposed a nested model whereby the developing person is surrounded by four environmental levels including: (a) *the microsystem*: the most proximal environment, which typically is the family; (b) *the mesosystem*: that includes the relationship between the family and other principal settings (extended family context, neighborhood) in which human development occurs; (c) *the exosystem*: contexts which are external to the developing person but still affect him/her, because these are environments in which other family members participate in. For example, in the case of children, their parents' workplace is an exosystem. Finally, the *macrosytem* includes broad policies, ideological values, cultural norms and institutional patterns of a particular society.

According to the ecological theory, children and families experience a variety of negative effects from a number of overlapping risk factors that interact within and across various levels of the environment, including the family and surrounding community (Bronfenbrenner and Morris, 1998; Cicchetti and Lynch 1993). Cicchetti and Lynch stress the role played by potentiating risk and compensatory factors within the microsystem, macrosytem, and exosystem levels of the environment, while Sameroff, Bartko, Baldwin, Baldwin, & Seifer (1998) show that adverse outcomes in children result from diverse additive or accumulative environmental factors. However, as Herrenkohl and Herrenkohl (2007) point out, tests of the ecological perspective have yet to account adequately for the range of experiences within abusive families and the combined, enduring impact of multiple forms of family violence. One of these (untested) experiences has to do with the housing habitability conditions that are present in abusive families.

Crimen Prevention Through Environmental Design (CPTED) provides one more theoretical and practical standpoint for understanding the relationship between family violence and contextual features. Crowe (2000, p. 46) asserts that "the proper design and effective use of the built environment can lead to a reduction in the fear and incidence of crime, and an improvement in the quality of life." Cozens (2008) reinforces this idea, establishing that CPTED is aimed at proactively prevent crime, as compared to the reactive and often ineffective strategies of most justice systems.

Among the CPTED most used strategies that have proved to be effective in reducing crime rates, Cozen mentions *territorial reinforcement*, which includes symbolic barriers (i.e., signage) and real barriers (e.g., fences, divisions between public and private spaces), access control and surveillance. He also includes *natural surveillance* as CPTED measure, which is provided by windows and design that promotes capable guardianship in an area. *Natural access control* to an area, including security personnel and mechanical access control is also used as a CPTED strategy. Finally, routinely *maintaining the built environment* (i.e., maintenance of the physical condition and image of the built environment), and *activity support* (i.e., the use of design and signage to encourage intended patterns of usage of public space). Although CPTED has been successfully used as a basis to promote crime prevention in neighborhoods and cities –that is, *outside* homes- it is strange that this strategy has not been tested *inside* households, in preventing aggressive and violent behaviors.

Emery (1989) and Emery & Laumann-Billings (1998) provide some instances of contextual factors affecting family violence. Among those factors, they point out at some community characteristics such as high levels of unemployment, community violence, and inadequate housing conditions. In this regard, Kakar (1998) mentions that within the general culture of most societies a subculture exists that tolerates the use of violence from childhood through adulthood. Also cultural frameworks such as disciplinary punitive beliefs, as well as the legal institutions tolerating disciplinary punishment, influence domestic violence (Frías-Armenta & McCloskey, 1998). Most of the mentioned factors are socio-cultural and a minimum effort has been devoted to studying the effect of physical housing factors on family violence. A special subject of interest should be the perception of those physical characteristics constituting housing habitability, and how those perceptions affect family dysfunction. Although a marked interest is manifested in residential satisfaction (i.e., satisfaction with the home-environment characteristics) among psycho-environmental researchers (see Bell, Greene, Fisher, & Baum, 2005), such interest is not complemented with investigative efforts aimed at elucidating how such satisfaction correlates with positive family interactions.

HOUSING HABITABILITY AND FAMILY VIOLENCE

As abovementioned, the search for factors associated to domestic violence has paid little attention to the socio-physical environment in which family interactions are displayed. Housing characteristics are logical candidates since they constitute the immediate environment for those interactions. Some authors suggest that housing habitability is an important factor for families' quality of life, in which healthy and prosocial interrelations among family members play a relevant role. Thus, according to these authors, housing habitability might be inductive of family violence (Holman & Stokols, 1994; Landázuri & Mercado, 2004). In a similar vein, Paglioni (2006) establishes that the prevention and eradication of domestic violence should consequently start with the protection of women's right to adequate housing. Although it is assumed that housing habitability does not affect quality of life in a global way (i.e., in all of its components such as health, job quality of life, free time, etc.) it does determine family quality of life and relations (Monsalvo & Vital 1998) so that this habitability could influence good interactions between parents and children and between sexual partners.

Housing habitability is defined as the set of psycho-environmental dimensions of a household. Those dimensions include *overcrowding*, which is conceived as a subjective state or psychological experience generated by individual's demand of space, which exceeds the available space (Hombrados, 2000). One more dimension of habitability is *privacy* or the capacity of a person or group to selectively regulate the amount and intensity of social interactions in a due socio-environmental context, in addition to regulating the flow of information produced in such interactions (Altman, 1975). Besides, habitability dimensions shaped by physical aspects are mentioned, including *noise*, or undesirable sound, house's *illumination*, and house's *temperature*. One more dimension is the household's *depth*, defined as the distance between sectors within the house (Landázuri & Mercado, 2004). According to Holman and Stokols (1994) negative housing habitability conditions could induce domestic violence by generating stress and other situations predisposing aggressive interactions at home. Herrenkohl and Herrenkohl (2007) also suggest that stress is the mediating mechanism between physical housing conditions and family violence.

The relation between temperature and domestic violence has been one of the few investigated in the framework of the association between housing habitability factors and aggressive family interactions. Mitchell (1991) found a significant relationship between temperature and domestic violence but, interestingly, this was stronger in poor than in economically affluent neighborhoods. A previous study by Harries and Stadler (1988) had demonstrated that assaults in Dallas, Texas, correlated significantly with temperature only in the medium and low-socioeconomic status neighborhoods (see also Rotton & Cohn, 2002). Since poorer neighborhoods contain the less desirably housing-habitability conditions it is likely than this association might be mediated by the physical conditions of households.

Also, overcrowding and lack of privacy have been studied in relation to domestic violence. Herrenkohl and Herrenkohl (2007) recently measured a series of family stressors, including overcrowding in the household, housing problems, lack of privacy, among others, which they grouped into a factor they called "external constraints." This factor slightly but significantly correlated with three forms of child maltreatment: physical, sexual and neglect. A stronger association between these external constraints and a factor that included marital problems and conflict was also found.

There are also studies considering additional housing aspects, relating them with domestic violence. For instance, Baker, Cook, and Norris (2003) found that more than a third of women that had experienced domestic violence reported housing problems like late paying rent, skipping meals and threatened with eviction. Also, the Children, Youth, and Family Consortium (2001, p. 1) established that "families are at risk... when they live in temporary housing, spend more than 1/3 of their income for shelter, live in deteriorating housing conditions or feel unsafe in their homes and neighborhoods." The consortium includes extreme stress as a negative outcome of these housing conditions, which increases the likelihood of child abuse and neglect, as well as marriage problems.

Additional studies on the topic of family violence and contextual factors show that some demographic variables such as mothers' age could affect their interactions with their children, manifested as more frequent child maltreatment among younger women (Connelly & Straus, 1992). Age could also influence interpartner violence: it has been found that younger couples are at more risk than older ones (Canadian Centre for Justice Statistics, 2000). Poverty has also been documented as a determinant of family violence (Berger, 2005). It is possible that, at least partially, these effects might be mediated by housing habitability conditions since younger and poorer couples live in houses of lower habitability quality.

We decided to assess housing habitability conditions from the perspective of participants in an empirical study, since, according to a number of authors, "objective" (i.e., physical) measures of habitability sometimes do not correspond with people's assessments (i.e., perceptions) of their household quality and conditions. Heywood and Naz (1990) also found that the majority of participants in a survey saw the quality of their house in a more favorable light than professional surveyors, and many people who live in households classified – according to experts- as unfit are satisfied with their house (Clapham, 2005). Since contextual factors affect people's behavior through the mediation of perceptual processes (Gaspar de Carvalho, Palma, & Corral-Verdugo, in press) participants' perceptions of their house habitability conditions should be more adequate for our research purposes than either the objective measures of physical household's dimensions or the professionals' assessments of habitability.

Although diverse authors point to a potential link between housing habitability and family violence, we have not detected empirical studies investigating this relationship so far. As illustrated before, some empirical research has been conducted regarding the influence of isolated aspects such as temperature, overcrowding, and lack of privacy on domestic violence, but no study addressing housing habitability as a whole has been produced.

Thus, based on relevant theories and these antecedents, we decided to study the link between domestic violence and housing habitability characteristics. These included privacy, illumination, overcrowding, depth, extreme temperatures (cold house in winter, hot house in summer). In addition, we studied the self-reported parental violence towards children and towards their sexual partners, as well as demographic variables.

METHOD

Participants

Two hundred housewives were interviewed; they were selected as participants from three socio-economic (high, middle, low) strata, which were representative of Hermosillo, a northwestern Mexican city. The housewives should have had at least a year living with a sexual partner, and being mothers of a child with ages between 4 and 15 year-old. As Table 1 indicates, the age mean for these participants was 32 years, while their schooling level mean was 11.12 years and their monthly family income was in average 1,600 U.S. dollars.

Table 1. Descriptive statistics of demographic variables

Variables	N	Minim	Maximum	Mean	SD
Age	200	18	62	32.00	9.43
Schooling (years)	200	3	25	11.20	3.32
Family income (Dlls)	198	140	9000	1168.01	407.62

Instrument

We administered an instrument based on items generated by Landázuri and Mercado (2004), which address factors of habitability, to be responded by the studied housewives. The measure included nine items assessing *overcrowding* with a 0-to-4 response options, where 0 = easy, sufficient, everything, impossible; and 4 = difficult, insufficient, nothing, possible, which were the options for items assessing perceived human concentration in the house and ease of navigation throughout its spaces. Examples of these items include: "Moving through my house is…easy/difficult," "The space in my house is…enough/insufficient"

The instrument also contained items assessing *privacy*, considering the same 0-to-4 scale of response, which evaluated situations such as conducting activities without being disturbed, finding places to get isolation, etc. "At home, I can develop my activities without being disturbed" and "Privacy at home is adequate" are examples of privacy items.

In addition, four items assessing the perception of *interior noise* at the household were included, plus two items measuring *exterior noise*, which were responded with a 0 (does not listen, nothing) to 4 (does listen, always). "I can hear the T.V. and radio noises from my neighbors' houses" is an example of the former, and "Normally, the noise within my house is high" is an example of the latter.

One item evaluating the household's illumination level (0 = bad... 4 = good) was administered; besides, one more item indicating how much hot in summer and how much cold in winter the house is (0 = not... 4 = too much) were used. Two open items assessing *depth* were also utilized; one measuring the number of doors to be crossed through to get the most private place in the household, and another assessing the distance from the entrance door to that most private place.

Finally, two scales assessing family violence were administered; one measuring parental violence towards children (or child maltreatment), which included 7 item from Straus' (1979) Conflict Tactics Scales (CTS), describing episodes of physical and psychological violence against children to which women responded using a 0 (never) to 6 (more than twenty times in the past year). The second set of measures was also based on Straus' (1979) CTS and assessed interpartner violence with 60 items (30 "from your partner towards you" and 30 "from you towards our partner"). Tables 2 and 3 show the items used to asses family violence.

The socio-demographic assessed variables were age, schooling level and monthly family income.

Procedure

The selected households were visited and the instrument was administered to the participants, after obtaining their informed consent to engage in our study. In cases where the participant was the mother of more than one child, the researcher randomly selected one, who was, subsequently, the reference for responding to the child maltreatment scale.

Data Analysis

We obtained univariate statistics for every used item and the sociodemographic variables. In order to estimate the reliability of the administered scales, we conducted internal consistency analyses, indicated by Cronbach's alphas. After verifying an adequate reliability, the means of these scales were used to calculate indexes (i.e., the average response to the set of items constituting a scale). The "depth" index was calculated from averaging responses to its two measures, without obtaining its internal consistency. The correlation between these two measure was $r = .32$ ($p < .01$).

All the indexes were entered in a structural equation model, using the EQS statistical package (Bentler, 2006). The specified model hypothesized high and significant interrelations between the items "bad illumination", "house hot in summer", "house cold in winter", and the indexes "overcrowding", "noise at home", "house depth", and "privacy" which were assumed to be influenced by a "negative habitability conditions" factor. In turn, child maltreatment, violence against women, and violence against men, at home, constituted the indicators of the "family violence" factor. Before building these two factors, additional internal consistency analyses were conducted for each, and two correlation matrixes were obtained. Then, the structural model was estimated. We predicted that the "negative habitability conditions" factor would significantly affect the "family violence factor." Also, we specified correlations between the socio-demographic variables age and SES (an index constructed from averaging family monthly income and schooling level). As it is common practice in these cases, we obtained goodness of fit indicators for the specified/estimated structural model. These indicators included the statistic X^2 indicator, and the practical goodness of fit indexes *NNFI*, *CFI* as well as the *RMSEA* indicator.

RESULTS

Table 2 shows some univariate statistics of the items assessing child maltreatment. The highest levels of this abusive conduct corresponded to "shouted, yelled, or screamed at him/her" (mean = 1.95, range 0 to 6) and "slapped or spanked him/her" (mean = 1.65). The least admitted maltreating behaviors were "threatened him/her with a knife or gun" (mean = .39) and "Burned or scalded him/her" (mean = .42).

Table 2. Univariate statistics from responses to the child maltreatment scale

Items	N	Mean	sd	Min	Max
Slapped or spanked him/her	197	1.56	1.57	0	6
Shouted, yelled, or screamed at him/her.	197	1.95	1.90	0	6
Pushed him/her out of house or room	199	0.68	1.24	0	6
Pushed, grabbed, or shoved him/her	198	1.00	1.34	0	6
Burned or scalded him/her	197	0.42	1.05	0	6
Kicked, bit, or hit him/her	197	0.49	1.14	0	6
Threatened him/her with a knife or gun	197	0.39	1.02	0	6

In turn, Table 3 exhibits the univariate statistics extracted from responses to the instruments assessing inter-partner violence. Women reported their being victimized by their partners, especially in receiving psychological maltreatment; yet, extreme forms of physical abuse (burned, attempted to strangle her, hit with an object, etc.) were also reported, though not as frequently as the less severe forms of abuse. Interestingly, women also reported their practicing violent behaviors against their romantic/sexual partners. Although these aggressive manifestations were less frequent than the ones practiced by their partners, the difference seems to be non salient.

In Table 4, the univariate statistics of all items assessing the housing habitability dimensions are presented. Responses to items revealed low levels of overcrowding reported by respondents as indicated by scores around 1 (in a 0 to 4 scale, where 0 represents no overcrowding and 4 high overcrowding). The respondents' perception of privacy seems to be in intermediate (around 2.5) levels, between the extremes 0, indicating perfect privacy, and 4, referring to a null privacy. Participants also reported their living in low-noisy houses, as indicated by levels of responses around 1.5, where 0 means no noise and 4 indicates high or frequent noise. The levels of perceived illumination and temperature were also intermediate between the extremes 0 (bad illuminated, very hot in summer, very cold in winter house) and

4 (good illuminated, fresh in summer, warm in winter house). The household's depth was indicated by about two doors to get the most private place at home from the entrance, and an average of 6.5 meters to cover such a distance.

Table 3. Univariate statistics from responses to the violence against women scale

During the last 12 months...	Her partner to her		Her to her partner	
Items	*Mean*	*SD*	*Mean*	*SD*
Shouted or yelled at partner	2.40	2.01	2.23	1.95
Has thought about leaving him/her	1.11	1.81	1.25	1.78
Has felt criticized	1.85	2.08	1.69	1.90
Has felt ignored	1.66	2.02	1.57	1.94
Insulted or swore at him/her	2.03	2.19	1.77	2.06
Refuses to talk about problems	1.46	1.94	0.92	1.51
Has left violently the room	1.31	1.81	1.05	1.65
Told him/her something to cause trouble	1.01	1.66	0.71	1.45
Threatened her/him telling will hit her/him	0.70	1.40	0.58	1.33
Threw to her/him an object	0.66	1.31	0.65	1.31
Pushed, grabbed her/him violently	0.85	1.45	0.60	1.28
Slapped her/him	0.58	1.12	0.66	1.26
Kicked, hit or bit her/him	0.53	1.22	0.41	1.08
Hit or tried to hit her/him with an object	0.52	1.25	0.45	1.15
Has threatened her/him with committing suicide	0.39	1.11	0.25	0.87
Has tried to strangle her/him	0.36	1.03	0.24	0.84
Has threatened her/him with a gun	0.33	0.99	0.23	0.83
Has stabbed or shot her/him with a pistol	0.25	0.94	0.21	0.74
Has hit her/him during some minutes	0.39	1.06	0.38	1.13
Has forced her/him to have sexual relations	0.53	1.22	0.29	0.94
Has forced her/him to have oral or anal sex	0.34	0.91	0.34	1.10
Has threatened her/him saying will hurt children	0.39	0.98	0.39	1.14
Has threatened her/him taking children	0.45	1.14	0.53	1.29
Has hurt killed a pet	0.36	0.98	0.28	0.98
Has told her/him (s)he will kill her/him	0.32	0.95	0.28	0.84
Has torn her/his cloth or broken some object	0.45	1.16	0.31	0.85
Has burned her/her with a cigarette	0.23	0.81	0.25	0.86
Has invaded her/him intimacy	1.24	1.98	0.84	1.50
Had to look for a doctor	0.27	1.01	0.18	0.72
He/she did some of these while being pregnant	0.53	1.15	0.44	1.10

Table 4. Univariate statistics of housing habitability items

SCALE/variables	mean (sd)	min	max
OVERCROWDING			
Navigating through my house is (easy/difficult)	1.13 (1.32)	0	4
The available space at home is (enough/insufficient)	1.47 (1.43)	0	4
Hinders when moving through house (everything/nothing)	1.59 (1.34)	0	4
There is space on the corridors (impossible/possible)	1.57 (1.45)	0	4
Enough space opening main door (insufficient/sufficient)	1.53 (1.42)	0	4
Accessing from living room to WC is (easy/difficult)	1.15 (1.33)	0	4
Accessing dining room from kitchen is (easy/difficult)	0.78 (1.17)	0	4
Moving from the fridge to the zinc is (easy/difficult)	0.99 (1.33)	0	4
Accessing the rest room from bedrooms is (easy/difficult)	1.04 (1.29)	0	
PRIVACY			
Can find silence when I need it (always/never)	2.43 (1.34)	0	4

Can engage in activities, not disturbed (always/never)	2.49 (1.34)	0	4
Can do anything, neighbors unaware (always/never)	2.62 (1.36)	0	4
Can control access around house (possible/impossible)	2.30 (1.54)	0	4
Privacy at home is (adequate/inadequate)	2.59 (1.43)	0	4
Rest without noise (possible/impossible)	2.18 (1.56)	0	4
Listen bedrooms conservations (possible/impossible)	2.11 (1.49)	0	4
Accessing WC without being seen (impossible/possible)	2.02 (1.57)	0	4
Noises from bathrooms (much/little)	2.51 (1.49)	0	4
Close windows to not be heard (never/always)	2.53 (1.48)	0	4
Close curtains to not be seen (never/always)	2.20 (1.56)	0	4
EXTERIOR/INTERIOR NOISE			
Neighbors' TV and radio (not listened/listened)	1.29 (1.41)	0	4
Close Windows to avoid outside noise (never/always)	1.65 (1.49)	0	4
Speak not loudly (never/always)	1.08 (1.30)	0	4
Neighbors' voices (not heard/heard)	1.41 (1.41)	0	4
House's interior noise is (much/little)	1.91 (1.47)	0	4
Interior noise disturbs me (never/always)	1.60 (1.31)	0	4
INTERIOR NOISE, ILLUMINATION, TEMPERATURE			
House's illumination is (bad/good)	2.69 (1.42)	0	4
House in summer is (very hot/fresh)	2.04 (1.48)	0	4
House in Winter is (very cold/warm)	2.07 (1.45)	0	4
DEPTH			
Doors to cross to get most private place	1.96 (0.95)	0	5
Distance (mts.) from entrance to most private place	6.69 (5.14)	0	28

Table 5 presents the means, standard deviations, minimum and maximum values and the reliabilities of all used scales. It can be seen that the lowest alpha value was .76 for the "noise at home" scale, while the highest internal consistency was found in the inter-partner violence instruments.

Table 5. Means and reliabilities of all used scales

Scale	N	Mean	SD	Min	Max	Alpha
Overcrowding	200	1.25	.91	0	4	.86
Privacy	200	1.64	.82	0	4	.78
Noise at home	200	1.49	.94	0	4	.76
Child maltreatment	200	0.92	.91	0	6	.80
Violence against women	200	0.77	.86	0	6	.94
Violence against men	200	0.67	.78	0	6	.94

Since we specified and tested two factors within the structural equation model, we also obtained their internal consistency by using indexes and items as indicators. The negative habitability conditions factor produced an alpha = .81, while the family violence factor resulted in an alpha = .83 (see Table 6).

Table 6. Means and reliabilities of factors used in the structural model

Variable	N	Mean	SD	Min	Max	Alp
Habitability conditions						.81
In summer, house is hot	200	2.04	1.48	0	4	
In winter, house is cold	200	2.07	1.45	0	4	
Overcrowding at home	200	1.25	0.91	1	4	
Noise at home	200	1.49	0.91	1	4	
Illumination	200	1.32	1.41	1	4	

Table 6. (continued)

Privacy at home	200	1.64	0.82	1	4	
Family violence						.83
Child maltreatment	200	0.92	.91	0	6	
Violence against women	200	0.77	.86	0	6	
Violence against men	200	0.67	.78	0	6	

Table 7 shows the interrelations among the habitability conditions. All the indicators of this factor were saliently and significantly interrelated (excepting "depth" and "cold house"), indicating that there were bases for presuming the existence of a factor subjacent to those interrelations. The negative correlations indicate links between a "positive" habitability condition (e.g., "privacy") and a "negative" one (e.g., "noise"), while positive correlations indicate associations between two "positive" or between two "negative" conditions.

We also obtained the correlation matrix for the indicators of family violence. High and significant interrelations between child maltreatment and the two forms of inter-partner violence were found, as well as a salient and significant correlation between these two types of inter-spouse abuse (see Table 8).

Table 7. Correlation matrix of habitability indicators*

	Crowd.	Priva.	Noise	Depth	Illum.	Hot	Cold
Overcrowding	-----						
Privacy	-.61	----					
Noise	.52	-.73	----				
Depth	-.26	.27	-.29	----			
Illumination	-.49	.41	-.40	.20	----		
Hot house	.46	-.42	.36	-.22	-.42	----	
Cold house	.33	-.35	.24	.01	-.32	.69	----

*All correlations are significant at $p < .05$, excepting the one between depth and cold house.

Table 8. Correlation matrix of family violence indicators*

	Ch. Maltr.	Viol. Women	Viol. Men
Chid maltreatment	-----		
Violence against women	.62	----	
Violence against men	.58	.66	----

*All correlations are significant at p <.05.

The structural model results are shown in figure 1. Both (habitability and family violence) factors highly and significantly ($p < .05$) loaded on their corresponding indicators. In the case of the habitability factor, these loadings were negative for the "positive" indicators (i.e., illumination, privacy, and depth), and positive for the "negative" indicators; therefore this factor was labeled "negative habitability conditions." Also, the family violence factor coherently emerged from the significant interrelations among child maltreatment, violence against women and violence against men, as expected.

A high and significant structural coefficient resulted between the negative habitability factor and family violence. This suggests that aggressive episodes among family members are incited, at least partially, by inadequate housing conditions. In turn, the negative housing conditions negatively correlated with the participant's age and SES.

The goodness of fit indicators evidence that the data support this theoretical model of relations between variables (X^2 = 104.7 [61 df], p <.0004; $NNFI$ = .90, $RMSEA$ = .06). The R^2 for family violence was .32.

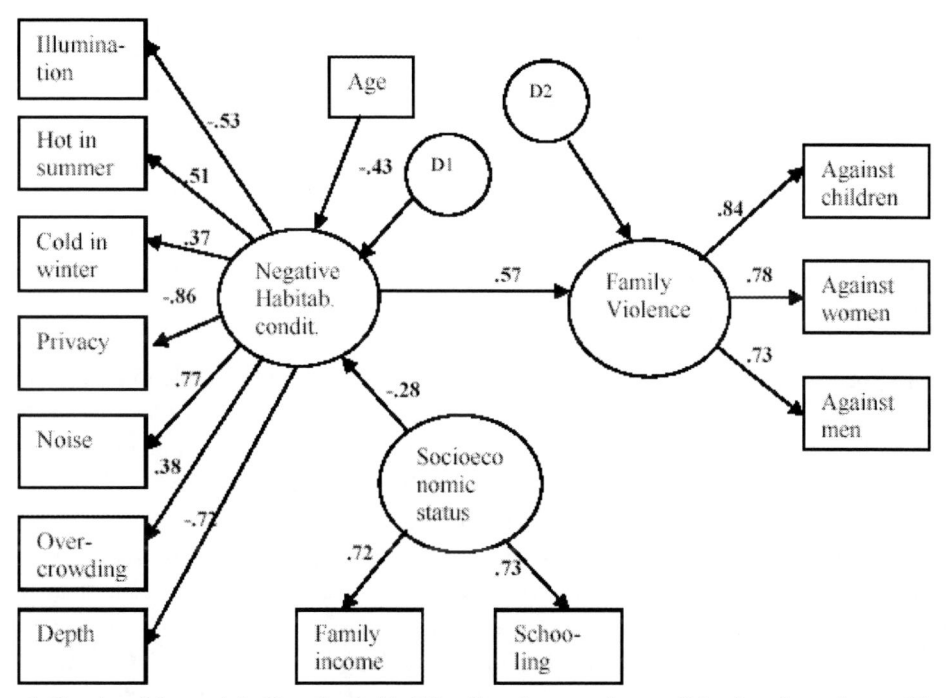

Figure 1. Results of the model of housing habitability (housing negative conditions) as determinant of family violence. All structural coefficients and factor loadings are significant at p < .05. Goodness of fit: *Chi-square* = 104.762 (61 *df*), *p*=.0004; *NNFI* = .90; *CFI* = .91; *RMSEA*=.06. Family violence's *R-Square* = .32.

CONCLUSION

The study described in this chapter was aimed at modeling and investigating the potential association between housing habitability and family violence. Explanations of those kinds of interpersonal violence assume that environmental factors significantly influence aggressive behaviors among family members, in addition to the effects that personal or dispositional variables exert on child maltreatment and interpartner violence.

The environmental explanations of domestic violence consider that contexts of daily living affect the way family members interact with each other. According to Bonfenbrenner's (1979) Ecological Theory, children's development is negatively influenced by adverse family, neighborhood, and general socio-cultural conditions. These adverse conditions also affect interpartner relations. However, although the physical conditions of a home are fundamental components of the microsystem/family environment, a review of the pertinent literature reveal that the influence of those conditions on domestic violence has not been sufficiently studied within the framework of the Ecological Theory.

Family violence is considered to be a form of crime in cultures that have legislated to prevent it. Theories such as Crimen Prevention Through Environmental Design (CPTED) establish that a proper design and effective use of the built environment can lead to a reduction in the incidence of crime. This theory explicitly acknowledges that factors of housing habitability may be inductive of aggressive (and criminal) behaviors. Unfortunately, most studies and interventions using CPTED as a conceptual standpoint are solely intended at studying how a "proper" house design prevents external (i.e., out of family) aggressive and criminal behaviors from occurring and harming the integrity of family members. A lack of studies investigating how household design inhibits child abuse and interpartner violence is noticed.

Based on literature proposals suggesting the association between housing habitability and domestic violence, we assessed the reports that a sample of Mexican housewives provided regarding their committing abusive behavior against their children as well as their experiencing violent interactions with their romantic/sexual partners. We also measured a series of variables presumably indicating habitability conditions, which were reported by housewives in a Mexican city. Some of those variables were negative conditions such as overcrowding, noise, and extreme temperatures, while others were positive conditions as in the case of privacy, household's depth, and illumination.

Not surprisingly, we found that women reported that family interactions include child abuse and interpartner aggressive interactions. After a factor analysis we also found that the resulting latent variable -subjacent to the interrelations among the habitability conditions- loaded negatively on the "positive" housing conditions. Therefore, we concluded that the resulting latent variable was a "negative habitability conditions" factor. Since the different manifestations of family violence also showed high and salient interrelations, we also constructed a "family violence" factor with the mother's self-reported maltreatment to their children and the also self-reported inter-partner violence as indicators. So, our results confirmed the already known fact that child abuse and interpartner aggressive interactions are highly and significantly interrelated (Ehrensaft *et al.*, 2003; Slep & O'Leary, 2005). These findings also confirmed our main hypothesis regarding a significant influence of habitability on domestic violence.

The fact that, in this study, the negative habitability conditions significantly correlated with family violence seems to imply that housing habitability indeed affect family relations. These environmental variables accounted by for a third of the variance of child maltreatment and inter-partner violence episodes. The lack of privacy and depth in the household, a poor illumination, an excessive noise, overcrowding, cold in summer and hot in winter, become undesirable factors for family members, probabilizing family violence.

We do not have reasons to suppose that the effect of these negative conditions is direct on the family members' interactions with each other. On the contrary, it is very likely that intervening factors mediate this relation. For instance, Herrenkohl and Herrenkohl (2007) conceive the negative housing design and physical factors that incite family violence as "family stressors," suggesting that these habitability factors promote stress in the first place, which would be followed by violent, aggressive behaviors between family members. We failed in assessing this intervening process so that a further study measuring stress levels among children and –specially- adults at home is required in order to confirm the supposition of a causal path of effects linking these three factors in the sequence: habitability conditions → stress → family violence.

In addition to the abovementioned findings, the negative habitability conditions were related to a low schooling level, low income and youth of the interviewed housewives. This indicates that families with less economic affluence and the younger cannot afford households with optimum habitability levels and, consequently, they are more exposed to both a negative environment at home and to violent situations that such an environment incites. Thus, poorer families are special targets of interventional programs aimed at improving both habitability conditions and family interactions.

CPTED and the Ecological Model offer appropriate theoretical frameworks to explain how habitability conditions influence family violence. These conceptual frameworks could also serve as standpoints in the implementation of interventional programs aimed at improving habitability conditions that promote a positive family functioning. CPTED has been successful in deterring violence against families from *external* sources; it should also be effective in preventing aggressive behavior *within* families. If our findings were to be replicated, a "proper" household design should include conditions allowing privacy, illumination, isolation from extreme temperatures and external noise, depth, and enough space to avoid overcrowding to family members, so that the internal sources of violence are minimized as much as the external threats can be. The ecological model, in turn, is suited to investigate habitability factors, within the microsystem, which influence both negative parenting practices as well as violent interactions between sexual/romantic partners at home.

The data here presented suggest the formulation of new hypotheses regarding the mechanisms of family violence, by considering socio-physical environmental factors that explain such a manifestation of interpersonal aggressive behavior, in addition to those variables that have traditionally been studied within models of family dysfunction.

REFERENCES

Altman, I. (1975). *The environment and social behavior*. Monterey, CA: Brooks/Cole Publishers Company.

Baker, C., Cook, S., & Norris, F. (2003). Domestic violence and housing problems. *Violence Against Women, 9*, 754-783.

Bell, P.A., Greene, T.C., Fisher, J.D., & Baum, A. (2005). *Environmental Psychology*, 5th Edition. Mahwah, NJ: Lawrence Erlbaum.

Bentler, P. (2006). *EQS, Structural Equations Program Manual*. Encino, CA: Multivariate Software Co.

Berger, L. (2005). Income, family characteristics, and physical violence toward children. *Child Abuse & Neglect*, 29, 107-133.

Bronfenbrenner, U. (1979). *The ecology of human development: Experiments by nature and design*. Cambridge, MA: Harvard University.

Bronfenbrenner, U. (1997). Ecological models of human development. In M. Gauvain & M. Cole (Eds), *Readings on the Development of Children*. New York, NY: Freeman.

Bronfenbrenner, U., & Morris, P. A. (1998). The ecology of developmental processes. In W. Damon (Ed.) *Handbook of child psychology (5th ed.)*. New York: Wiley.

Canadian Centre for Justice Statistics (2000). *Family violence in Canada: A statistical profile*. Otawa: Statistics Canada.

Children, Youth, and Family Consortium (2001). *Affordable housing and family wellbeing.* Children, Youth and Family Consortium: Retrieved on June, 2009 from: http://www.cyfc.umn.edu/policy/issues/briefings/housing.pdf.

Cicchetti, D., & Lynch, M. (1993). Toward an ecological/transactional model of community violence and child maltreatment: Consequences for children's development. *Psychiatry, 56,* 96–118.

Clapham, D. (2005). *The meaning of housing. A pathways approach.* Bristol: The Policy Press.

Connelly, C.D., & Straus, M.A. (1992). Mother's age and risk for physical abuse. *Child Abuse & Neglect, 26,* 709- 718.

Corral, V., Frías, M., Romero, M., y Muñoz, A. (1995). Validity of a scale of beliefs regarding the 'positive' effects of punishing children: A study of Mexican children. *Child Abuse and Neglect, 19,* 669-679.

Cozens, P. (2008). *Crime prevention through environmental design.* In R. Wortley and L. Mazerolle (Eds.), Environmental Criminology and Crime Analysis. Portland, OR: Willan Publishing.

Crowe, T. (2000). *Crime Prevention Through Environmental Design: Applications of Architectural Design and Space Management Concepts.* 2nd ed., Butterworth-Heinemann, Oxford.

Davies, C. A., DiLillo, D., & Martínez, I. G. (2004). Isolating adult psychological correlates of witnessing parental violence: Findings from a predominant Latina sample. *Journal of Family Violence, 19*(6), 377-385.

DIF (2004). Datos Estadísticos del Programa de Prevención al *Maltrato Infantil* del Sistema Nacional de Desarrollo Integral de la Familia (DIF- PRENAM). Retrieved January 6, 2005 from: http://www.dif.gob.mx/inegi/nino2004.pdf.

Ehrensaft, M., Cohen, P., Brown, C., Smailes, E., Chen, H., & Johnson, J. (2003). Intergenerational transmission of partner violence: A 20-year prospective study. *Journal of Consulting and Clinical Psychology, 71,* 741-753.

Emery, R.E. (1989). Family violence. *American psychologist, 44,* 321-328.

Emery, R.E. & Laumann-Billings, L. (1998). An overview of the nature, causes, and consequences of abusive family relationships. Toward differentiating maltreatment and violence. *American psychologist, 53,* 121-35.

English, D. J., Marshall, D. B., & Stewart, A. J. (2003). Effect of family violence on child behavior and health during early childhood. *Journal of Family Violence, 18,* 43-57.

Fincham, F.D. (2000). Family violence: a challenge for behavior therapists. *Behavior Therapy, 31,* 685-693.

Frías-Armenta, M., & McCloskey, L.A. (1998). Determinants of harsh parenting in Mexico. *Journal of Abnormal Child Psychology, 26,* 129-139.

Garbarino, J. & Gaboury, M. (1992) *Introduction.* In J. Garbarino (Ed.). Children and families in the social environment. Chicago: Aldine Transaction.

Gaspar de Carvalho, R., Palma, J. & Corral-Verdugo, V. (In press). Why do people fail to act? Situational barriers and constraints on pro-ecological behavior. In V. Corral-Verdugo, C. García-Cadena, & M. Frías-Armenta, M. (Eds.), *Psychological Approaches to Sustainability. Current trends in theory, research, and applications.* New York: Nova Sciences Publ.

Harries, K.D., & Stadler, S.J. (1988). Heat and Violence: New Findings From Dallas Field Data, 1980-1981. *Journal of Applied Social Psychology, 18*, 129-138.

Herrenkohl, T. & Herrenkohl, R. (2007). Examining the Overlap and Prediction of Multiple Forms of Child Maltreatment, Stressors, and Socioeconomic Status: A Longitudinal Analysis of Youth Outcomes. *Journal of Family Violence, 22*, 553-562.

Heywood F, & Naz M. (1990). Clearance: The View from the Street. Birmingham: Housing Community Forum.

Holman, E. & Stokols (1994). The environmental psychology of child sexual abuse. *The Journal of Environmental Psychology*, 14, 237-252.

Hombrados, M.I. (2000). Hacinamiento. En J.I. Aragonés y M. Amérigo, *Psicología Ambiental*. Madrid: Pirámide.

INEGI. (2007). Retrieved July, 2007 from: http://www.inegi.gob.mx/est/ contenidos/ espanol/rutinas/ept.asp? t=mvio03&c=3371.

Jayaraman, R. (2004). *Modeling Domestic Violence*. Center for Economic Studies. University of Munich. Mimeo.

Jewkes, R., J. Levin, & L. Penn-Kekana (2002). Risk Factors for Domestic Violence: Findings from a South African Cross-sectional Study. *Social Science and Medicine* 55, 1603–70.

Kakar, S. (1998). *Domestic abuse: public policy/criminal justice/ approaches towards child, spousal and elderly abuse*. Bethesda, MD: Austin & Winfield, Publishers.

Kalil, A., & Harris, L. (2003). Domestic violence and children's behavior in low income families. *Journal of Emotional abuse, 3*, 75-101.

Knickerbocker, L., Heyman, R. E., Slep, A. M., Jouriles, E. N., & McDonald, R. (2007). Co-occurrence of child and partner maltreatment: Definitions, prevalence theory and implications for assessment. *European Psychologist, 12*(1), 36-44.

Landázuri, A.M. & Mercado, S. (2004). Algunos factores físicos y psicológicos relacionados con la habitabilidad interna de la vivienda. *Medio Ambiente y Comportamiento Humano*, 5, 89-113.

Litrownik, A. J., Newton, R., Hunter, W. M., English, D., & Everson, M. D. (2003). Exposure to family violence in young at risk children: A longitudinal look at effects of victimization and witnessed physical and psychological aggression. *Journal of Family Violence, 18*, 59-73.

Margolin, G. & Gordis, E. B. (2000). The effects of family and community violence on children. *Annual Review of Psychology, 51*, 445-479.

Merrill, L. L., Thomsen, C. J., Crouch, J. L., May, P., Gold, S. R., & Milner, J. S. (2005). Predicting adult risk of child physical abuse from childhood exposure to violence: Can interpersonal schemata explain the association? *Journal of Social and Clinical Psychology, 24*, 981-1002.

Mitchell, M.F. (1991). *The effects of weather and routine activity on domestic disputes across ecological areas in Charlotte, North Carolina: 1986*. Unpublished masther's thesis, Southern Illinois University, Carbondale.

Monsalvo, J., & Vital, A. (1998). *Habitabilidad de la vivienda y calidad de vida*. Tesis de Licenciatura Inédita, Facultad de Psicología, U.N.A.M.

Morrel, T. M., Dubowtiz, H., Kerr, M. A., & Black, M. M. (2003). The effect of maternal victimization on children: A cross-informant study. *Journal of Family Violence, 18,* 29-41.

Organización Mundial de la Salud /OMS (2002). *World report on violence and Health*. Ginebra: World Health Organization.
Paglione, G. (2006). Domestic violence and housing rights: A reinterpretation of the right to housing. *Human Rights Quarterly, 28*, 120-147.
Pianta, R. B., Egeland, B., & Erickson, M. F. (1989). The antecedents of maltreatment: Results of the Mother-Child Interaction Research Project. In D. Cicchetti & Carlson (Eds.), *Child maltreatment: Theory and research on the causes and consequences of child abuse and neglect* (pp 203- 253). New York: Cambridge University Press.
Rotton, J. & Cohn, E. (2002). Climate, weather, and crime. In R.B. Bechtel & A. Chruchman (Eds.), *Handbook of Environmental Psychology*. New York: Wiley.
Sameroff, A. J., Bartko, W. T., Baldwin, A., Baldwin, C., & Seifer, R. (1998). Family and social influences on the development of child competence. In M. Lewis & C. Feiring (Eds.), *Families, risk, and competence*. Mahwah, NJ: Lawrence Erlbaum.
Slep, A. M., & O'Leary, S. G. (2005). Parent and partner violence in families with young children: Rates, patterns and connections. *Journal of Consulting and Clinical Psychology, 73*, 435-444.
Sternberg, K. J., Baradaran, L. P, Abbott, C. B, Lamb, M. E., & Guterman, E. (2006). Type of violence, age, and gender differences, in the effects of family violence on children's behavior problems: A mega-analysis. *Developmental Review, 26,* 89-112.
Straus, M. (1979). Measuring Intrafamily Conflict and Violence: The Conflict Tactics (CT) Scales. *Journal of Marriage and the Family, 41*, 75-88.
Straus, M., Hamby, S., Boney-McCoy, S., & Sugarman, D. (1996). The revised Conflict Tactics Scales (CTS2): Development and preliminary psychometric data. Journal of Family Issues, 17, 283-316.
Thompson, R. (2007). Mother's violence victimization and child behavior problems: Examining the link. American Journal of Orthopsychiatry, 77(2), 306-315.
Violencia doméstica. (2006). Retrived on May, 15, 2006, from: http://www.arte-sana.com/espanol_statistics2.htm.
Violencia y maltrato en México. (2006). Retrieved on May, 2006, from: http://www.unicef.org/mexico/programas/violencia.htm
Wallace, H. (2005). *Family violence: Legal, medical & social perspectives, 4e*. Boston: Allyn & Bacon.
World Health Organization/ WHO (1999). *Report of the Consultation on Child Abuse Prevention*. World Health Organization, Social Change and Mental Health, Violence and Injury Prevention, Geneva, pp. 15-16. Retrieved on March 8, 2003 from: http://www.anppcan.org/anppcan/deftext.htm.

In: Bio-Psycho-Social Perspectives on Interpersonal Violence   ISBN: 978-1-61668-159-3
Editors: M. Frías-Armenta et al., pp. 143-165   © 2010 Nova Science Publishers, Inc.

Chapter 7

THE ROLE OF FAMILY COMMUNICATION AND SCHOOL ADJUSTMENT IN ADOLESCENTS' VIOLENT BEHAVIOR

María Elena Villarreal-González[1],
Juan Carlos Sánchez-Sosa[1] and Gonzalo Musitu-Ochoa[2]

[1] Universidad Autonoma de Nuevo Leon, Mexico[1].
[2] Universidad Pablo de Olavide de Sevilla, Spain.[2]

ABSTRACT

This chapter elaborate on the roles that family communication and school adjustment play in the prevention of adolescents' violent behavior. Our study analyzed the relation between familial (functioning, communication), school (academic expectations and performance) and social (integration and participation) factors and adolescents' violent behavior mediated by social self-esteem and psychological disorders (depressive symptomatology and perceived stress). The results show an indirect effect of familial, school and community variables on adolescents' violent behavior mediated through social self-esteem and psychological disorder.

INTRODUCTION

During the last years, violence in schools became a problem firmly confirmed in Mexico, although it was previously detected in countries like the United States, Sweden, Norway, United Kingdom and Spain. Such a problem concerns administrative and educational

---

[1] Correspondence: María Elena Villarreal González, Universidad Autónoma de Nuevo León, Facultad de Psicología, Mutualismo 110, Colonia Mitras Centro Monterrey, Nuevo León, CP 64460, México; tel.: +52 (81) 8333 8233, fax: +52 (81) 8333 8222, email: psiquemalena@yahoo.com.mx

[2] This research has been prepared within the PSI2008-01535/PSIC Research project framework "School violence: Victimization and social reputation in adolescence", supported by the Ministry of Science and Innovation of Spain".

authorities, parents and society in general due to its implications and consequences. This is a problem that has acquired a considerable dimension since the 70s. Even though it is true that in our country its incidence is still low, we observe how adolescents, day after day, are more frequently involved in violent behaviors at school.

Adolescence has been defined by several authors as a transitional period wherein an individual life changes from childhood to youth (Frydenberg, 1997). Usually, the scientific literature identifies this stage as one of primordial importance through the biopsychosocial development, since adolescence exhibits a series of characteristics that are hard to find in other phases of the vital cycle. Among those characteristics, there are two standing out: briefness and fastness changes are produced. This is a period in which the individual finds a moment of searching an image he does not yet know, in a barely understandable world, and in a body (s) he starts to discover. If physiological changes are evident, psychological ones are too obvious as well.

The scientific psychological study of adolescence started at the end of the XIX Century (Mussen, Conger, & Kagan, 1982). A significant figure in the study of adolescence is, without doubt, Stanley Hall (1904), who, at the beginning of the 20th Century was considered as the father of the scientific study of adolescence, which he labelled a "storms and conflicts phase", as well as one implying physical, mental and emotional strong potentials.

Coleman and Hendry (2003) consider adolescence as a transitory period, and they summarize a series of implications such transition brings: an enthusiastic expectation for the future; a feeling of sorrow due to the loss of (childhood) state; an anxiety feeling with regards to the future; an important psychological readjustment; an ambiguous situation about social position during the transition.

This transition is going to provoke changes in adolescents' relationships with others, as well as changes in their school environment, since teenagers are passing from elementary to secondary school, and in many occasions this is the moment they need to make decisions about their academic and professional future, playing in this way a crucial role so as to define themselves (Musitu, Buelga, Lila, & Cava, 2001).

It seems that the adolescence stage is progressively delayed, so that subjects between 12 to 20 years old are included already in this stage. This period is generally divided in three stages, each one defined by their own features. The first one is called first adolescence (it includes 12 to 14 years old subjects); the second is middle adolescence (including 15 to 17 years old subjects), and the last stage is called delayed adolescence (that goes from 18 to 20 years old).

Among the peculiarities of the stages mentioned before, it can be indicated that most of the biological and physical type changes occur in first adolescence. Sudden and frequent mood fluctuations occur in middle adolescence. Moreover, the self-consciousness level of teenagers is very high; consequently, they feel a great worry about how they are perceived by others. Finally, during delayed adolescence there is a risk of being involved in deviate behaviors, such as drug consumption, aggressive or violent behavior (Musitu, Buelga, Lila, & Cava, 2001).

As we have observed, it is in adolescence when individuals are more involved in violent behavior, as stated by Estévez, Jiménez and Musitu (2007). They mention that violent behavior at school is manifested in multiple ways: brazenness with teachers; interruptions during classroom hours; vandalism and material damage toward other classmates' objects, like scratching notebooks, or toward school material like writing desks or breaking glasses;

physical aggressions to teachers and to other students; isolation from classmates; and even in some cases, though less frequently, sexual harassment. Most of these behaviors occur in all elementary and secondary teaching schools, both public and private, although not all happen with the same assiduity. The most frequent are those related to threats and insults, followed by rejection and social exclusion (i.e., to set apart a classmate from the rest in order to isolate him/her), and finally, we found the acts implicating direct physical aggressions like beating peers.

Since the first studies conducted in the 80s, the importance of familial and school environment has been established so as to explain violent behavior (Olweus 1998; Gazquez, Cangas, Perez-Fuentes, Padilla & Cano, 2007). Eccles, Midgley, Wigfield, Buchanan, and Reuman (1993) affirmed that violent behavior must be considered as a more specific matter of development which includes factors such as school and the immediate familial environments. Popper and Steingard (1996) have suggested, under this framework, that a weak person-environment adjustment for the adolescent (at home or at school), may explain the increase of this type of behavior in adolescence. These authors show that as children grow up and obtain a higher educational level, they want more participation at school and in family decision making. However, if they have few opportunities in this regard, they get involved in risky behaviors in order to express their autonomy needs. Adolescent deviant behavior is, consequently, explained by a school and family failure in assuming the increasing autonomy and control needs of the adolescent.

One of the aspects related to violent behavior is that adolescents are generally associated, at their school environment, to equally deviant subjects, who accept them and who exhibit similar behavior, values and attitudes (Hymel, Wagner, & Butler, 1990). This association contributes to the preparation of own codes and standards that reinforce their behaviors and increase the likelihood that deviation get worse (Fergusson, Woodward, & Horwood, 1999; Simons, Wu, Conger, & Lorenz 1994; Vitaro, Brendgen, & Tremblay, 2000). In this way, these adolescents satisfy their need to feel integrated and accepted, and at the same time they give in to the group pressure, assuming a violent behavior. Once this group is integrated, the positive interactions with other peers are limited, leading both to isolation and violence (Espelage, Holt, & Henkel 2003; Fergusson, Woodward, & Horwood, 1999). The association to equally deviant peers in the rejected group may be due to two causes: on one side, it may be the result of problems related to pairs of previous ages, aspect that, on the other side, restricts the child contact to equally non-deviant individuals, and reinforces the adolescent feeling of social competence in the deviant peers group.

As abovementioned, adolescence is a great transformations period in different spheres of life, such as physical, social, cognitive and psychological. Moffitt (1993) emphasizes on the fact that in adolescence a maturity "period" or "jumping" happens. It is a moment defined as hard and complex, both for the young individuals themselves and for their parents, since the adolescent is presumptuously living a transition towards his/her personal maturity, in which (s)he experiences a series of new situations and social readjustments, as well as his/her own independence search. Consequently, adolescents thrive in a time characterized by personal indefiniteness that at the same time comes with the hope of conquering the adult status and of being far from childish roles.

Moffitt (1993) proposed the existence of two antisocial adolescents' ways: (1) transitory and (2) persistent. According to relevant research, the last one, which involves the minority of the population, is characterized by an early and persistent appearance (even from pre-school age) of a set of behavioral problems that would be stepped up frequently and severely; and although they change their expressions according to age, clearly correspond to the kind of problem studied. For example, pre-school aggression could be manifested as tantrum in school age; as destruction and aggression to others, in adolescence. Moffit (op. cit.) states that transitory ways in adolescence pertain to most of the young that ever had been involved in violent activities, and are characterized by a lack of obvious behavioral problems during their childhood. The confluence of these two groups would explain why there are especially high participation rates in violent behavior during adolescence. The disappearance of the transitory group would explain the fall observed in these rates after adolescence. There are a series of explanatory models of school violent behavior, which we will explain in the following sections.

THEORETICAL APPROACHES TO VIOLENT BEHAVIOR

The main approaches analyzing violent-behavior causes can be grouped into two big theoretical aspects: active or biological theories, and reactive or environmental theories. Active or biological approaches consider aggressiveness as an organic or innate component of the person, basic for adaptation processes; from this perspective, aggression is considered as having a positive function, and the task of education mainly consists of focusing their expression on socially acceptable behaviors. On the contrary, reactive or environmental theories stand out the environment role and the importance of learning process in the violent behavior of human beings (Mackal, 1983).

The main active or biological theories: genetic, ethological, psychoanalytical, personality, frustration and sign-activation theory are presented in the following paragraphs.

Genetic theory emphasizes the importance of genetic predisposition and hereditary aspects during violent behavior development, and it states that aggressive behavior is triggered as a consequence of a series of biochemical processes occurring internally in the organism, in which hormones play a decisive role. It has been demonstrated, for instance, that noradrenaline is a causal agent of aggression (Haller, Makara, & Kruk, 1997).

The ethological theory stated by Lorenz (1978) considers aggression to be an innate reaction based on unconscious impulses, biologically adapted, that have been developed as the species evolved. The purpose of aggression is the surviving of both the person and the species.

Psychoanalytical theory sustains that aggressiveness is a basic instinctive component coming from a reaction facing libido-blocking, which results in a series of negative internal affections that the person is incapable to exteriorize. If the individual is not able to release this energy, aggression comes up (Freud, 1973). Personality Theory, in turn, considers that personality factors as impulsiveness and self-control determine peoples' involvement in aggressive behaviors (Gottfredson & Hirschi, 2009).

According to Dollard, Miller, Doob, Mowrer, and Sears' (1939) Frustration Theory, all aggressive behavior is the consequence of a previous frustration. Sign-activation Theory is based on the assumptions of Frustration Theory; Berkowitz (1996) considers that frustration emerges when a person feels (s)he is going to loose what (s)he wants; frustration provokes anger, activates the body and prepares it for aggression.

Hereinunder we will explain the main reactive or environmental theories: social learning, social interaction, sociological and ecological theories.

Social Learning Theory, proposed by Bandura (1977), considers violent behavior as the result of learning from observation and imitation. From this perspective, important models for the person, like parents and friends are especially relevant. It has been demonstrated that parents occasionally promote and tolerate aggressive behaviors; and, in some cases, both parents and friends approve of this kind of behaviors, so that teenagers and children obtain the social benefit of respect and popularity when they behave aggressively, which increases the likelihood of still behaving violently.

Vigotsky's (1979) Social Interaction Theory emphasizes the interactive character of human behavior, and considers that these behaviors are the result of interaction between individual characteristics of the person and social context circumstances that surround him/her. The core is the familial and school roles. In this way, a deficiency in familial socialization, poor quality relations between parents and children, social rejection problems of peers and the affiliation to deviant peers are extremely important factors that will increase the probability that an adolescent gets involved in violent behaviors.

Sociological Theory underlines violence as a product of cultural, political and economical characteristics of society. Factors like poverty, marginalization, intellectual development difficulty, exploitation or subjugation are paramount factors. This behavior emerges from the deviant behavior of persons integrating society (Durkheim, 1938).

The Ecological Theory proposed by Bronfenbrenner (1979) considers that persons are immersed in an interconnected community, organized into four main levels: the macrosystem, the exosystem, the mesosystem and the microsystem. The *Macrosystem* refers to culture and the historic moment the person lives in, including ideological aspects and predominant values of her/his society. The *Exosystem* refers to those social environments in which the adolescent does not actively participate, but what is happening in such environments may affect their closer environments. The *Mesosystem* is related to all the existent interactions between the different contexts. Finally, the *Microsystem* refers to immediate contexts of the adolescent, meaning family and school, including all the activities, roles and interpersonal relations experienced by the individual in his/her more immediate environment. This approach stands out behavioral problems that cannot be due only to the person, but they need to be considered as a result of an interaction between behavior and his environment (in the case of adolescence, the familial, school and social environment). This presumes the need of examining the problematic behavior in the context it emerges from (in our case, in the classroom or school).

ECOLOGICAL THEORY AND ADOLESCENTS' VIOLENT BEHAVIOR

From all the proposed theories, the perspective we consider as the most appropriate to understand violent behavior is the Bronfenbrenner's ecological approach, since the study of school violence problems must take into account that it is caused by multiple, complex and iter-related factors, and that they need to be analyzed in terms of interaction between person adjustments and different contexts in which the adolescent is developing (Díaz-Aguado, 2002).

Sánchez-Sosa and Villarreal-González (2009) agree with the approach when affirming that it is necessary to specify and test explanatory models that, from a field perspective, integrate contextual (family, school and community) and personal variables, so as to obtain a higher heuristic capacity in explaining unfit behaviors.

One of the variables of the microsystem that is more frequently related to adolescent psychosocial adjustment is family communication (Musitu, Buelga, Lila & Cava, 2001; Rodrigo et al., 2004). The interest in analyzing familial variables would derive, in consequence, not only from its direct possible influence on school violence, but also from the fact that family can display certain individual variables directly related to these behaviors.

Estévez, Musitu, and Herrero (2005) found that adolescents who inform their having communication problems with their parents experience higher depression and stress symptoms (psychological disorders); on the other hand, an open communication with parents is positively associated to children's school self-esteem, which at the same time, is negatively related to depression and stress.

Both familial communication problems and conflicts between parents and children have been associated to different adjustment indexes in adolescence. In this way, positive and fluid familial communication has been related to psychological well-being, a higher self-esteem and a positive self-concept of adolescents in different aspects like emotional, social and academic ones (Musitu & Molpeceres, 1992).

The studies indicate that mothers are generally described as more open to listening problems and feelings of their children (Forehand & Nousiainen, 1993; Noller & Callan, 1991; Shek, 2000). Nonetheless, adolescents declare having more conflicts with their mother than with their father, although at the same time, they declare to have more positive interactions with her (Jackson, Bijstra, Oostra, & Bosma, 1998; Noller & Callan, 1991). Therefore, the existing data suggest that the interaction between mothers and children is more frequent and close, but at the same time more conflictive (Oliva & Parra, 2004).

Multi-causality of violent behavior during adolescence seems to be caused not only by multiple risk factors combination in different levels of human development, but also by historical, social and cultural processes affecting differently to some young generations from their early childhood. Violence affecting adolescents and the young, making them delinquents, increases enormously health services and social assistance costs; reduces productivity and property value; disorganizes a series of essential services and deteriorates society structure (Pattishall, 1994).

In addition to familial environment, school exosystemic environments represent a significant scenario in adolescents' life, and consequently their experience in these settings seems to be an important factor related to adjustment and violence. A crucial characteristic of formal education is the students' participation in a system they are part of (Musitu, 2002).

What it is usually found is that students barely intervene in decisions concerning organizational aspect of their school, which influence both school's culture and the teaching/learning process, even though they do experience the consequences derived from those decisions. This contradiction is especially important when students reach adolescence, since in this stage their desire to taking part in decision-making processes increases, and at the same time they experience a higher questioning about established rules. Moreover, the distinctive characteristics of the teaching centers organization, together with their culture, influence the students' perception of their school, as well as the expression of disruptive behaviors (Fernández, 1993; Henry, Guerra, Huesmann, Tolan, Van Acker, & Eron, 2000). A poor organization of standards and rules, an authoritarian orientation versus democracy of the school, and students overcrowding in classrooms stand out as the main factors provoking this kind of undesirable behaviors in the school context (Khoury-Kassabri, Benbenishty, Astor, & Zeira, 2004).

These behaviors inhibit the normal teaching process and affect seriously the interpersonal relations of teachers and students (Olweus, 1998, 2005; Smith & Brain, 2000; Trianes, 2000). Their high incidence (Cerezo, 1999; Ortega & Mora-Merchan, 2000; Solberg & Olweus, 2003), as well as the negative consequences experienced by both victims and aggressors (Estévez, Musitu, & Herrero, 2005; Guterman, Hahn, & Cameron, 2002), have incited the increase in studies aimed at analyzing factors influencing their development, mainly during the adolescence stage in which these behaviors result more serious and problematic.

School violence seriously affects teaching-learning process in classrooms, as well as the existing social relations thereof, both between classmates and between students and teachers. More specifically, some researchers stand out that school violence exerts a triple impact on school functioning (Trianes, Sánchez, & Muñoz, 2001): it provokes to giving up its primary-concern objective (knowledge transmission), since the attention now focuses on disciplinary measures, and it causes to leave behind human formation objectives (socialization to everyone), since the attention is translated into those students who show more discipline problems.

Violent behavior at school is a kind of behavior in which the main actors are children and adolescents, and which is carried out in schools and institutes, that is, in scenarios where they spend several hours per day, during a number of years. Therefore, a violent/aggressive student at school is the one whose behavior supposes the breaking of school and social standards that regulate classroom and educational centers' interactions, by expressing to others some punishable behaviors (Marin, 1997).

Regarding school adjustment, Moral, Sánchez-Sosa and Villarreal González (2009) found significant correlations between academic performance and lack of intention to continue studying at the university level. They also found that high school students exhibit better grades than those from middle school. These authors state that the reason could be that they are motivated by a higher maturity level and, to a lesser extent, by the influence exerted by the intention to attending university, situation expected to be more defined in high school students. Likewise, in regards to familial communication, findings suggest that child-mother relations are more influential than the child-father ones when dealing with school adjustment/adaptation.

In addition to contextual factors, personal or psychological variables are extremely important in explaining school violence. Musitu, Buelga, Lila and Cava (2001) argue that self-esteem is the way every person evaluates his/her self-image, and it represents the consequences of his/her internal dialogue kept when he/she values his/her surrounding world and his/her position in society. This is a resource people count upon to face hard situations and vital events through their lifespan. Generally, a high self-esteem during adolescence is indicated as an important protective factor in facing emotional problems and behavioral difficulties (Cava, Musitu, & Vera, 2000; Harter, 1990). However, its relation is not completely clear when dealing with adolescents' violent behavior (O'Moore & Kirkham, 2001), since some authors establish that aggressive adolescents exhibit a lower self-esteem, while others state that aggressors usually show a positive self-esteem (Olweus, 1998).

Therefore, the objective of our study is to analyze the relation between familial, school and social factors and adolescents' violent behavior mediated by social self-esteem and psychological disorders (depressive symptomatology and perceived stress). The familial variables taken into account in this study included familial functioning (emotional bond and adaptability between members) and father-child and mother-child familial communication (communication opening). The school variables included academic expectations and performance. Social variables refer to members' integration and participation. With regards to psychosocial variables, in this study we considered the social self-esteem dimension (one of the AF5 multidimensional scale factors) which deals with how the adolescent perceives himself before his friends, as well as psychological disorders, indicated by depressive symptomatology and perceived stress, and, finally, violent behavior at the classroom. We suppose that these familial, school, social and personal variables can contribute jointly, indirectly and/or directly to explaining violent behavior in adolescents.

METHOD

Participants

We considered public schools of two cities in the Northeast of Mexico, two middle schools and two high schools, located in the municipalities of San Nicolás de los Garza and Escobedo, both limiting with Monterrey, Capital of the State of Nuevo León. One middle school and one high School from each Municipality were selected; the total population of these 4 educational institutions is 6,412 students, distributed in 24 middle-school groups and 21 from high school. The sample size chosen was of 1,285 students distributed into 20 groups, 10 for middle school and 10 groups for high school, using a stratified random sampling, considering the students proportion per semester, groups and shift. The sample size was calculated by nQuery Advisor 6.0, establishing that the maximum variables to be included in a predictive model would be 20, with a determining coefficient of .05[3] and a power[4] of .90.

Instruments

In selecting the instruments, we considered their theoretical fitness to the study, as well as the existing scales' validity and reliability, responding in this way to the objectives established in this research. The scales went through an examination process, being reviewed by four experts in violent behavior matters in order to avoid biases, and once observations to the questionnaire were corrected by the specialists, a pilot test was conducted with 30 students aged from 13 to 16 years old so as to determine how clearly and accurately the instruments were understood.

---

[3] The determination coefficient refers to the explained variance percentage. In order to assure the correct sampling size it is a little value (Elashoff, 2005).
[4] Power: probability that results are statistically significant at a specified reliability level (Elashoff, 2005). Elashoff, J. (2005). nQuery Advisor Version 6.0. User's guide. Los Angeles, CA: Statistical Solutions Ltd.

Family Apgar Scale

Smilkstein, Ashworth, Montano (1982) Family Apgar Scale was used to measure familial functionalism, composed of 5 Likert-type items, it is known as APGAR since it makes reference to five components of familial function, assessing the following characteristics: 1) *Adaptability*, which refers to the use of intra and extra-familial resources so as to solve problems when family stability is threatened by stress during a crisis time; 2) *partnership*, involving the participation in making decisions and responsibilities, defines the power level of family members; 3) *growth*, which refers to the possibility of reaching emotional and physical maturity, and self-realization of family members by mutual support; 4) *affection*, including the relation between love and care existing among family members; and at last, 5) *resolve*, which refers to commitment or determination to dedicate time (space, money) to family members. This is a scale that may be administered either by the interviewer or to be filled out directly by the interviewed person. It is composed of 5 items, with three options each, scored from 0 to 2 points distributed as 0 (almost never), 1 (sometimes) and 2 (almost always); its total range goes from 0 to 10. It has been used in studies for family assessment in cases of alcoholism and a scoring of > 6 as functional and of < 6 as dysfunctional has been proposed. Severe dysfunction would be indicated by scores of 0 to 3; while 4 to 6 is considered as moderate dysfunction and 7 to 10 as familial functionality. Results seem not to be influenced by the cultural level of the interviewee, and the instrument has been used with children as young as 10-11 years old.

Parents-Children Scale

Barnes and Olson (1982) Parents-Children Scale is an adaptation conducted by the Lisis Group (Psychology College at the Universidad de Valencia). This scale is composed of 20 items and two sub-scales evaluating child-mother and child-father communication. Items responses vary from 1 (never) to 5 (always). The two sub-scales present a two-factor structure: the first indicates an opening level in communication (positive, free, comprehensive and satisfactory communication) and, the second one, the presence of problems in communication (critical and/or negative and not very effective communication). Concerning the reliability of the questionnaire, appropriate levels of internal consistency are indicated (from .87 and .86 to mother and father, respectively). Opening in communication with the mother refers to the existence of a fluid communication between mother and child. It has to do with the presence of a positive communication in the mother-child dyad, based on freedom, free interchange of information, comprehension and satisfaction experienced during the interaction. Its reliability is of .89. Problems in mother's communication refer to the existence of communication disturbances between mother and her child. Such problems have to do with an excessively critical or negative (or not very effective) communication in the dyad. In this way, it is centered on aspects like resistance to share information and affection, or a negative interactive style. Its reliability is of alpha=.64. The opening in communication with the father refers to the existence of a fluid communication between father and child. Its reliability is of alpha=.91. Problems in communication with the father refer to the existence of communication troubles between father and child. Its reliability is of alpha=.66.

School Adjustment Scale

It was created by Moral, Sánchez-Sosa and Villarreal-González (2009) and is composed of 10 items, in a Likert-type format (from 1=completely disagree to 6=completely agree). The scale range goes from 10 to 60; the higher the scoring, the higher the school adjustment. It is composed of 3 factors, which explain 59.59% of the variance. The first factor, defined by five items (6, 7, 8, 9 and 10), is denominated "school integration problems" (reflecting school-environment adjustment problems). The second factor is defined by three items (1, 2 and 5) and is denominated "academic performance." The third factor, "academic expectations," is indicated by two items (3 and 4, lack of intention to continue studying at the university). The psychometric properties are the following: the reliability for school integration is .85; for academic performance, .78; and for academic expectations .85. The reliability of the global scale is alpha=.76 (Moral, Sánchez-Sosa & Villarreal-González 2009).

Social Community Support Scale

It was produced by Gracia, Herrero and Musitu (2002), and is composed of 20 items; thirteen are written in a positive way (2,3,5,6,7,8,10,12,14,15,17,18,19) and seven are negative (1,4,9,11,13,16,20). The original factorial structure assesses the community integration dimensions, community participation and social support in informal systems and it is directed to 11-12 years old adolescents. The instrument addresses the dimensions of community-integration, community participation and social support in informal nets. The psychometric properties of the instrument reveal a Cronbach Alpha coefficient for the general scale of .76; for the dimension of community integration is of .88; for participation is of .86 and for social supports in informal nets resulted of .85.

Self Esteem

The Questionnaire of Self-esteem Evaluation in Adolescents (Gracia & Musitu, 1999) is composed of 30 items responded with a Likert-type scale from 1 (never) to 5 (always). It evaluates 5 dimensions: academic, social, emotional, familial and physical. The higher the score in each of the mentioned factors, the higher the self-concept. The dimensions refer to the following aspects: a) academic self-esteem: opinion the individual has about his own academic performance; b) social self-esteem: it refers to the opinion the individual has about his own social relations; c) emotional self-esteem: it refers to the opinion the individual has about his own emotions; d) familial self-esteem: it deals with the evaluation the individual produced concerning his familial relations; e) physical self-esteem: items dealing with the opinion the individual has about his own physical characteristics. The alpha of the global whole scale was = .81. For the subscales the alphas were: academic/labor = .88; social = .69; emotional = .73; familial = .76 and physical = .74.

Depressive Symptomatology

The scale of depressive symptomatology is a Spanish adaptation of the Center for Epidemiologic Studies Depression Scale (CESD; Radloff, 1977) conducted by the Lisis group (Universidad de Valencia). Radloff original instrument is composed of 20 items, in a range from 0 to 3, and a route from 20 to 60. The adapted instrument, a Likert type scale, was extended from 4 to 5 response options (never, almost never, sometimes, frequently and very frequently). So, unlike the original scale, the route of adaptation goes from 20 to 100. Out of the 20 items, 16 are written in a direct way (1,2,3,5,6,7,9,10,11,13,14,15,17,18,19,20) and 4 have an opposite meaning (4,8,12,16). The scale evaluates the symptomatology normally associated to depression, but it does not evaluate depression itself. The higher the score in this scale the most frequent the depressive symptoms. It shows an internal consistency of .89.

Perceived Stress Scale

The PSS was elaborated by Cohen, Kamarak, and Mermelstein (1983). This scale assesses the level in which situations of life are evaluated as stressing. The instrument is composed of 14 items, scored from 0 (never) to 4 (very frequently) and a 0 to 56 route. A study carried out in Spain by Remor (2006) showed a reliability of .81.

Violent Behavior

To measure violent behavior, we used Rubini and Pombeni's (1992) Criminal Behavior Scale, adapted to Spanish by Musitu *et al.* (2001). This scale evaluates 19 violent and victimized behaviors in the last three years, considering transgression to social standards or school regulations. The scale of responses varies from 1 (never) to 5 (many times). Both the original questionnaire and the Spanish adaptation have been successfully administered to samples of the general population of adolescents in England (Emler & Reicher, 1995), Italy (Palmonari, Pombeni, & Kirchler, 1992) and Spain (Musitu *et al.*, 2001). The reliability of dimensions shows an alpha of .84 for violent behavior in classroom/disruptive and .82 for victimization.

Procedure

To obtain the data, the authorization of the educational institutions' authorities was requested, explaining them the research objective. Later, the authorization from teachers and principals was granted, explaining also to them the research objectives. Once this was done, every selected group was visited and the students' authorization to participate was requested, letting them know that they had been randomly selected to be part of the study. We also explained to them that our goal with this work was to know what young people think about different subjects, like family, school, and friends. They were free to refuse if they were not willing to participate. Once the questionnaire was filled out, the students deposited it in a box placed on a classroom's desk.

Data Analysis

A structural equation model was specified and tested using the EQS 6.0 (Bentler, 2006) program, to analyze the relation between latent factors and observed variables. Based on theory and empirical data, the designed model was composed of 6 factors, as follows:

- Factor 1, the familial context latent variable was indicated by three observed variables: familial functioning, opening in mother communication and in father communication. Familial functioning is composed of 5 items from Smilkstein,

Ashworth, and Montano (1982) APGAR Scale: Are you satisfied with the help you receive from your family when you have a problem?, Do your family discuss the home problems you have?; Are important decisions made conjointly at home?; Are you satisfied with the time your family and you spend together?; Do you feel your family loves you? Opening in mother and father communication by Barnes and Olson (1982), was composed of the items: Can I talk to them about what I feel without feeling uncomfortable?; Do I believe what they are telling me?; Do they pay me attention when I talk to them?; Can they know how I feel without asking me?; Do we get along?; If I had problems, could I tell them to my parents?; Do I easily show my affection?; Am I careful with what I say, when I ask questions?; Do they respond me honestly?; Do they try to understand my point of view (the way I see things)?; Do I think it is easy to talk to them about my problems?; Can I express my real feelings?

- Factor 2, the school integration latent variable was indicated by two observed variables that refer academic expectations in the items: Do I plan to finish high school?; Am I interested in applying for university? Concerning academic performance, the indicator items were: Do I think I am a good student?; Do I enjoy doing my school homework?; I have good grades. All of these items are from the school adjustment scale (Moral Sánchez-Sosa & Villarreal-González 2009).
- Factor 3, the community context: It makes reference to two observable variables (community integration, and community participation). The community integration items were: I do not like my neighborhood; I feel very happy in my neighborhood; I am appreciated by people from my neighborhood; I feel my neighborhood as if it was mine; there are persons in my neighborhood that help me to solve my problems; In my neighborhood I can find people who help me to feel happy; In my neighborhood, I would ask for counseling to solve my problems; In my neighborhood, I can find someone that listen to me when I feel bad; in my neighborhood, I find many satisfactory things; In my neighborhood, I can be encouraged and can improve my mood when I feel bad. With regards to community participation items: I collaborate (alone, with my family, with friends...) in associations or in activities organized in my community or neighborhood; I participate in sport, cultural, religious groups of my neighborhood; I generally participate if volunteers are required in my neighborhood for carrying out any activity (for example, at church...). All of these items were extracted from the community social support scale by Gracia, Herrero and Musitu (2002).
- Factor 4, the social self-esteem latent variable. The items pertaining to this dimension include: Do I easily make friends?; Am I a friendly person?; Am I happy? Do I have a lot of friends? All of these items come from the AF5 self-esteem scale by Gracia and Musitu (1999).
- Factor 5, psychological disorder, composed of perceived stress (Cohen *et al.*, 1983) and depression symptomatology (Radloff, 1977) whole scales.
- Factor 6, violent behavior. This latent variable was composed of two violent dimensions with 13 items: I have painted or damaged school walls; I stole objects from my classmates or from school; I have insulted or deceived on purpose to teachers; I have damaged professors' cars; I have made a classmate gets wrong in homework, on purpose; I have been aggressive and hit my peers; I have bothered or annoyed the teacher in class; I have broken windows glasses of my school; I have

insulted aggressively to my teachers; I have tore notes and works from my peers; I have provoked conflicts and problems in class; I have responded aggressively to my teachers; I have provoked conflicts and problems between my colleagues. With respect to victimization, the items were: Someone in school saw me sulkily; somebody insulted me or beat me; somebody stole something from me; Someone makes fun of me at classroom, or they hurt me; somebody from school offended my family; somebody at school blamed on something I had not done. All of these items belong to the violent behavior and victimization scale by (Rubini & Pombeni, 1992).

RESULTS

The demographic data of the sample are presented in Table 1, we can observe that 1285 students – 650 men, representing a 50.5%, and 635 women, representing a 49.5% of the total sample participated.

Table 1. Distribution of frequencies by variable category: Gender

		Frecuency	Percentage
Valid	Men	650	50.5
	Women	635	49.5
Total		1285	100.0

In table 2, the students distribution by educational levels is observed: 634 students were in middle school (49.5%), and 651 attended high school (50.5%), being statistically equivalent percentages.

Table 2. Participants percentage according to educational levels

		Frequency	Percentage
Valid	Secondary school	634	49.3
	High school	651	50.7
Total		1285	100.0

In table 3, we present more specifically the distribution of participants in this study, classifying them in early adolescence, from 12 to 14 years old, with 455 students, represented by a (35.4%); middle adolescence, from 15 to 17 years old, with 790 students, by a (61.5%), and advanced adolescence, from 18 to 21 years old, with 40 students, represented only by a (3.1%). As we can see, population is concentrated between early and middle adolescence.

Table 3. Participants' percentage according to age

		Frequency	Percentage
Valid	12-14 years old	455	35,4
	15-17 years old	790	61.5
	18-21 years old	40	3,1
	Total	1285	100.0

In Table 4 the frequencies and percentages of reported violent behavior are observed. A 15.85% of students show violent behavior.

Table 4. Violent behavior

	Violent Behavior	Frequency	Percentage
Valid	Violent	191	15.85
	Non violent	1094	84.15
Total		1285	100.0

With regard to victimization behavior, we show in table 5 the frequencies and percentages. As we can observe, a 20.54% of the subjects report victimization.

Table 5. Victimization behavior

	Victimization Behavior	Frequency	Percentage
Valid	Victimized	255	20.54
	Non victimized	1,030	79.46
Total		1285	100.0

In table 6, the descriptive statistics of observed variables and normality tests are shown.

Table 6. Descriptive statistics and normality test

Scales and subscales	Possible score	Mean	Median	DT	α	K-S	Sig.
Familial variables							
Opening in communication with mother	12 - 60	44.68	46	11.02	.92	2.66	.000
Opening in communication with father	12 - 60	39.97	41	13.39	.94	2.28	.000
Familial functioning	5 - 15	12.30	13	2.43	.80	6.09	.000
School variables							
Academic performance	3 - 18	12.06	12	3.50	.78	3.32	.000
Academic expectations	2 -12	10.19	12	2.74	.85	11.2	.000
Community variables							
Community integration	10 - 40	26.29	27	6.56	.80	2.08	.000
Community participation	4 - 16	8.86	9	3.26	.79	2.96	.000

Personal variables							
Social self-esteem	5 - 25	19.34	20	4.07	.78	3.29	.000
Depressive symptomatology	20 - 100	47.65	46	12.64	.87	2.38	.000
Perceived stress	0 - 56	24.25	25	6.36	.83	3.37	.000
Dependent Variables							
Violent behavior	13 - 65	19.03	15	8.63	.93	8.40	.000
Victimization	6 - 30	10.26	9	4.67	.85	6.36	.000

** The correlation is significant at a 0.01 level (bilateral).
* The correlation is significant at 0.05 level (bilateral).

In table 7, we show the Pearson's correlations of all the variables object of this study.

In figure 1, the goodness of fit of the estimated model and the statistical significance of the coefficients are presented. Robust estimators were used because of deviation from normality of the data (Mardia normalized coefficient: 47.39). The proposed model fit well the data, as indicated by the following indexes: CFI= .95, IFI= .95, GFI= .95, NNFI= .94, and RMSEA= .042. For CFI, IFI and GFI indexes, values higher than .90 are considered acceptable, and for the RMSEA index, values lower than .05 are adequate (Batista & Coenders, 2000). This model explains 66% of the variance in violent behavior.

The results of the structural model show that familial context is related to school environment (β= 0.179, p<0.001), and to community context (β= .078, p<0.001), and school environment, at the same time is related to community context (β= 0.377, p<0.001). Familial context is negatively related to violent behavior, through the mediation of psychological disorder, depressive symptomatology and perceived stress (β= -0.413, p<0.001), and this one is positively linked to violent behavior (β= 0.186, p<0.001), and the present of this psychological disorder is positively associated to violent behavior in classroom. With respect to school context, performance and academic expectations, they are positively related to social self-esteem (β= 0.123, p<0.001), and this one at the same time to violent behavior in the classroom (β= 0.158, p<0.001), that is, the performance and academic expectations foster social self-esteem, but this self-esteem is a risk variable in violent behavior in the classroom. The community context is directly and positively related to social self-esteem (β= 0.314, p<0.001), and negatively to psychological disorder (β= - 0.155, p<0.001), and the last one to violent behavior in the classroom.

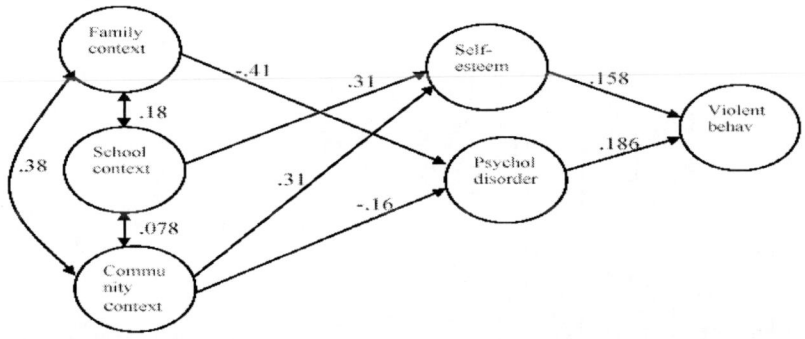

Figure 1. Violent behavior explanatory model. Goodness of fit: CFI=.95; IFI=.95; GFI=.95; NNFI=.94; RMSEA=.04.

Table 7. Person variables correlations

		1	2	3	4	5	6	7	8	9	10	11	12
1.Open comm. with the mother	Corr	1											
2.Open comm. with the father	Corr	.507**	1										
3.Familial functioning	Corr	.560**	.506**	1									
4.Academic performance	Corr	.286**	.204**	.256**	1								
5.Academic expectations	Corr	.233**	.118**	.159**	.505**	1							
6.Communn integration	Corr	.225**	.230**	.260**	.197**	.090**	1						
7.Community participation	Corr.	.194**	.187**	.192**	.165**	.013	.490**	1					
8.Social self-esteem	Corr	.151**	.144**	.126**	.114**	.084**	.172**	.139**	1				
9.Perceived stress	Corr	-.305**	-.267**	-.333**	-.253**	-.176**	-.273**	-.143**	-.238**	1			
10.Depressive S.	Corr	-.333**	-.334**	-.398**	-.268**	-.157**	-.260**	-.141**	-.202**	.556**	1		
11.Violent behavior	Corr	-.112**	-.053**	-.113**	-.121**	-.193**	-.008	.037	-.143**	.123**	.058*	1	
12.Victimization	Corr	-.076*	-.071*	-.102**	-.064*	-.146**	-.038	.046	-.161**	.168**	.170**	.666*	1

** The correlation is significant at 0.01 level (bilateral).

* The correlation is significant at 0.05 level (bilateral)..

CONCLUSIONS

This study analyzed contextual and personal variables influencing adolescents' violent behavior at classroom. The obtained results showed an indirect relation of familial, school and community variables with violent behavior mediated through social self-esteem and psychological disorder, which exhibited a direct and significant effect on the dependent variable.

In regard to familial context, we have found the references of a number of authors (McGee, Williams, Poulton, & Moffitt, 2000; Formoso, González, & Aiken, 2000; Johnson, LaVoie, & Mahoney, 2001) indicating that a high cohesion and adaptability between family members, as well as the opening in familial communication with both parents is negatively related to the presence of depressive symptomatology and perceived stress, and then to violent behavior. Likewise, the studies conducted by Jackson et al. (1998); Luengo, Otero-López, Mirón, and Romero (1995); Loeber et al. (2000); Musitu, Buelga, Lila and Cava (2001); Megías et al. (2002, 2003); Secades, & Fernández-Hermida (2003), which indicate that adolescents involved in violent behaviors at the classroom also reflect communication problems with their parents. Similarly, in the results of our research, we have confirmed that subjects who commit less antisocial actions are characterized by a more open and fluid communication with their parents. In this sense, familiar communication seems to be a protective factor against individual's adjustment problems. This effect has been also reported, among others, by Musitu, Buelga, Lila, and Cava (2001); Muñoz-Rivas & Graña (2001); Secades & Fernández -Hermida (2003).

We have seen how the familial context produces an indirect relation to violent behavior at the classroom through a direct, negative and significant relation to psychological disorder. So, familiar relations have an indirect effect on violent behavior, through mediation of psychological disorder, in such a way that familiar relations perform as a distal explanatory factor of violent behavior in the classroom, while perceived stress and depressive symptomatology act as explanatory proximal factors. Concerning school environment and community context, the data indicate indirect effects on violent behavior, both mediated by social self-esteem. Martínez, Murgui, Musitu, & Monreal (2008) have stressed the importance of students' perception of school as an unfair environment and their indifference towards academic activities, which seem to function favoring their engagement in violent acts. School violence could be one of adolescents' responses to an environment they consider unfair and useless for their lives, and on which, they feel powerless to produce minimum changes. In this study we found that school integration problems, as well as poor academic expectations and a low academic performance are associated to violent behavior. These studies converge with different authors' findings indicating that school failed experiences frequently constitute a risk factor; meanwhile school achievement represents a protective factor.

The adolescent's attitude toward school is also important. If (s)he finds it as a pleasurable and useful space for his personal development he will commit with learning objectives (Seydlitz & Jenkins, 1998). School violence may be an adolescents' response to an environment they consider unfair and not very useful, and on which, additionally, they feel powerless to exert a minimum influence.

In reference to the community context, adolescents feel more integrated to their community or neighborhood if they have a feeling of being an active member of the social group. This provides a sense of identity to them so that young people might overestimate their social area: by generating a perception of their ability to make friends, and overestimating the number of friends they have. Regarding psychosocial variables, the model confirmed the references reported in different studies (Musitu, Jiménez, & Murgui, 2007; Martínez-Anton, Buelga, & Cava, 2007; Cava, Musitu, & Murgui, 2006; Cava & Musitu, 2001; Cava, Musitu, & Vera, 2000) in regard to the mediating role played by self-esteem in explaining a number of behavioral problems.

As Fierro (1998) establishes, the adolescent develops a strong commitment with her/his group, by accepting preferences, fashions and styles. That explains why, if among the activities that provide cohesion to the group violent behaviors are found, the adolescent will feel strongly pressed to engage in such actions, keeping in this way the desired social self-esteem before his peers (Musitu, Buelga, Lila & Cava, 2001).

Another plausible explanation for this direct relation between social self-esteem and violent behavior is the one suggested by authors based on the perspective of adolescents' temporary trajectory. According to these researchers, violent or criminal behaviors must be interpreted in terms of an identity search. Such an identity is constructed within the peer's group, and by an image the subject acquires from his/her social environment. Consequently, keeping or handling such image in its more significant context will constitute the main social objective of the adolescents' deviate activities (Palmonari, Pombeni, & Kirchler, 1992; Moffitt, 1993; Coleman & Hendry, 2003).

Nonetheless, these results must be interpreted cautiously due mainly to the transversal character of the data, which, as it is well known, does not allow establishing causal relations. In future research, it would be interesting to incorporate the temporal dimension as well as to analyze the stability of the relations observed in this study. Moreover, the use of self-reports might implicate certain bias derived from the fact of being the informer the subject himself. In this sense, it would be convenient to include measures from alternative sources, like parents or teachers. Nonetheless, we believe that the results obtained in this study might contribute to a better understanding of family and school factors in the prediction of violent behavior, and might contribute also with ideas both for professional practice and for interventional programs at the school level.

Finally, we consider that in these programs, the connection between familial communication and school-adjustment must be emphasized in order to provide for adolescents the necessary resources helping them to reduce the likelihood of being involved in school violent acts, and, at the same time, to promote the development of a more satisfactory school experience.

REFERENCES

Bandura, A. (1977). *Social learning theory*. Englewood Cliffs, NJ: Prentice-Hall.

Barnes, H., & Olson, D. H. (1982). Parent adolescent communication scale. En D. H. Olson, H. McCubbin, H. Barnes, A. Larsen, M. Muxen, y W. Wilson (Eds.), *Family Inventories: Inventories Used in a National Survey of Families across the Family Life Cycle* (pp. 33-48). St. Paul: University of Minnesota Press.

Batista, J.M., & Coenders, G. (2000). *Modelos de ecuaciones estructurales.*Madrid: La Muralla.

Bentler, P. M. (2006). *EQS structural equations program manual.* Encino, CA: Multivariate Software.Barnes.

Berkowitz, L. (1996). *Agresión: Causas, Consecuencias y Control.* Bilbao: Desclée de Brouwer.

Bronfenbrenner, U. (1979). *The ecology of human development: Experiments by nature and design.* Cambridge: Harvard University Press (ed. cast.: *Ecología del desarrollo humano.* Barcelona: Paidós, 1987).

Cava, M. J., & Musitu, G. (2001). Autoestima y percepción del clima escolar en niños con problemas de integración social en el aula. *Revista de Psicología General y Aplicada,* 54 (2), 297-311.

Cava, M.J., Musitu, G., & Murgui, S. (2006). Familia y violencia escolar: el rol mediador de la autoestima y la actitud hacia la autoridad institucional. *Psicothema,* 16 (4), 674-679

Cava, M.J., Musitu, G., & Vera, A. (2000). Efectos directos e indirectos de la autoestima en el ánimo depresivo. *Revista Mexicana de Psicología,* 17, 151-161.

Cerezo, F. (1999). *Conductas agresivas en la edad escolar.* Madrid: Pirámide.

Cohen, S., Kamarak, T., & Mermelstein, R. (1983). A Global Measure of Perceived Stress. *Journal of health and social behaviour,* 24, 385-396.

Coleman, J. C., & Hendry, L. B. (2003). *Psicología de la adolescencia.* Madrid: Morata.

Díaz-Aguado, M. J. (2002). *Convivencia escolar y prevención de la violencia.* Madrid: Publicaciones del Ministerio de Educación y Ciencia, CNICE.

Dollard, J., Doob, L., Miller, N., Mowrer, O., & Sears, R. (1939). *Frustration and Aggression.* New Haven: Yale University Press.

Durkheim, E. (1938). *The rules of sociological method.* Glencoe: The Free Press.

Eccles, J. S., Midgley, C., Wigfield, A., Buchanan, C. M., & Reuman, D. (1993). Development during adolescence: the Impact of stage-environment fit on adolescents' experiencees In schools and families. *American Psychology,* 48, 90-101.

Emler, N., & Reicher, S. D. (1995). *The social psychology of adolescent delinquency.* Oxford, UK: Basil Blackwell.

Espelage, D. L., Holt, M. K., & Henkel, R. R. (2003). Examination of peer group contextual effects on aggression during early adolescence. *Child Development,* 74, 205-220.

Estévez, E., Musitu, G., & Herrero, J. (2005). The influence of violent behavior and victimization school on psychological distress: the role of parents and teachers. *Adolescence,* 40(157), 183-196.

Estévez, E., Jiménez, T., & Musitu, G. (2007). *Relaciones entre padres e hijos adolescentes.* Valencia, España: NauLibres.

Fergusson, D. M., Woodward, L. J., & Horwood, L. J. (1999). Childhood peer relationship problems and young people's involvement with deviant peers in adolescence. *Journal of Abnormal Child Psychology,* 27, 357-370.

Fernández, M. (1993). La profesión docente y la comunidad escolar: Crónica de un desencuentro. Madrid: Morata.

Fierro, A. (1998). Desarrollo social y de la personalidad en la adolescencia. En M. Carretero; J. Palacios y A. Marchesi (Eds.), Psicología Evolutiva. *Adolescencia, madurez y senectud.* Madrid: Alianza.

Forehand, R., & Nousiainen, S. (1993). Maternal and paternal parenting: critical dimensions in adolescent functioning. *Journal of Family Psychology,* 7, 213-221.

Formoso, D., González, N. A., & Aiken, L. S. (2000). Family conflict and children's internalizing and externalizing behavior: Protective factors. *American Journal of Community Psychology*, 28, 175-199.

Frydenberg, E. (1997). *Adolescent Coping*. London: Routledge.

Freud, S. (1973). *Más allá del principio del placer*. En Freud, S; *Obras completas*. Tomo III. Madrid: Biblioteca Nueva.

Frydenberg, E. (1997). *Adolescent Coping*. London: Routledge.

Gázquez, J.J., Cangas A.J., Pérez-Fuentes, M.C., Padilla, D., & Cano, A. (2007). Percepción de la violencia escolar por parte de los familiares: un estudio comparativo en cuatro países europeos. *Internacional Journal of Clinical and Health Psychology*, 7, 93-105.

Gottfredson, M. R., & Hirschi.T. (2009). The nature of criminality: Low self-control. In F. R. Scarpitti, A. L. Nielsen, & J. M. Miller (Eds.), Crime and Criminals: Contemporary and Classic Readings in Criminology (pp. 272-288). New York: Oxford University Press.

Gracia, E., Herrero, J., & Musitu, G. (2002). *Evaluación de recursos y estresares psicosociales en la comunidad*. Madrid: Síntesis.

Gracia, F., & Musitu, G. (1999). *Autoconcepto Forma 5*. Madrid: TEA.

Guterman, N.B., Hahm, H.C., & Cameron, M. (2002). Adolescent victimization and subsequent use of mental health counselling services. *Journal of adolescent Health*, 30, 336-345.

Hall, S. (1904). *Adolescence, its Psychology and its relations to Psychology, Anthropology, Sociology, Sex, Crime, Religion and Education*. Nueva York: Appleton.

Haller, J., Makara, G., & Kruk, M. (1997). Catecholaminergic involvement in the control of aggression: hormones, the peripheral sympathetic, and central noradrenergic systems. *Neuroscience and Behavioral Reviews*, 22, 85-97.

Harter, S. (1990). Causes, correlates and the functional role of global selfworth: a life-span perspective. En J. Kolligian y R. Sternberg (eds.): *Perceptions of competence and incompetence across the life-span* (pp. 67-98). New Haven, CT: Yale University Press.

Henry, D., Guerra, N., Huesmann, R., Tolan, P., Van Acker, R., & Eron, L. (2000). Normative influences on aggression in urban elementary school classrooms. *American Journal of Community Psychology*, 28 (1), 59-81.

Hymel, S., Wagner, E., & Butler, L .J. (1990). Reputational bias: View from the peer group. En S.R. Asher y J.D. Coie (Eds.), *Peer rejection in childhood* (pps. 156-186). New York: Cambridge University Press.

Jackson, S., Bijstra, J., Oostra, L., & Bosma, H. (1998). Adolescents' perceptions of communication with parents relative to specifics aspects of relationships with parents and personal development. *Journal of Adolescence*, 21, 305-322.

Johnson, H. D., LaVoie, J. C., & Mahoney, M. (2001). Interparental conflict and family cohesion: Predictors of loneliness, social anxiety, and social avoidance in late adolescence. *Journal of Adolescent Research*, 16, 304-318.

Khoury-Kassabri, M., Benbenishty, R., Astor, R. A., & Zeira, A. (2004). The contributions of community, family, and school variables to student victimization. *American Journal of Community Psychology*, 34, 187–204.

Loeber, R., Drinkwater, M., Yin, Y., Anderson, S. J., Schmidt, L. C., & Crawford, A. (2000).Stability of family interaction from ages 6 to 18. *Journal of Abnormal Child Psychology, 28 (4),* 353-369.

Luengo, A., Otero-López J., Mirón, L., & Romero, A. (1995). *Análisis psicosocial del consumo de drogas en los adolescentes gallegos.* Santiago de Compostela: Xunta de Galicia.

Lorenz, K. (1978). Sobre la agresion : el prendido mal.madrid : Siglo XXI

Mackal, P. K. (1983). *Teorías psicológicas de la agresión.* Madrid: Ediciones Pirámide. (Edición original 1979).

Marín, M. (1997). *Psicología social de los procesos educativos.* Sevilla: Algaida.

Martínez-Ferrer, B., Murgui-Pérez, S., Musitu-Ochoa, G., & Monreal-Gimeno, M. (2008). El rol del apoyo parental, las actitudes hacia la escuela y la autoestima en la violencia escolar en adolescentes. *International Journal of Clinical and Health Psychology,* 3, 679-692.

McGee, R., Williams, S., Poulton, R., & Moffitt, T. (2000). A longitudinal study of cannabis use and mental health from adolescence to early adulthood. *Addiction,* 95, 491-503.

Megías, E., Elzo, J., Rodríguez San Julián, E., Navarro, J., Megías Quirós, I., & Méndez, S. (2002). *Hijos y padres: Comunicación y conflictos.* Madrid: FAD.

Megías, E., Elzo, J., Rodríguez San Julián, E., Navarro, J.; Megías Quirós, I. & Méndez, S. (2003). *Comunicación y conflictos entre hijos y padres.* Madrid: FAD.

Moffitt, T. E. (1993). Adolescence-limited and life-course-persistent antisocial behavior: A developmental taxonomy. *Psychological Review,* 100 (4), 674-701.

Moral, J., Sánchez-Sosa, & Villarreal González M. (2009). Propiedades psicométricas de la escala breve de ajuste escolar (EBAE) desarrollada en México *Revista Enseñanza e Investigación en Psicología,* Número especial, 657-662.

Muñoz-Rivas, M. J., & Graña, J. L. (2001). Factores familiares de riesgo y de protección para el consumo de drogas en adolescentes. Psicothema, 13 (1), 87-94

Musitu, G. (2002). Las conductas violenta en las aulas de los adolescentes: El rol de la familia. *Aula Abierta,* 79, 109-138.

Musitu, G., Buelga, S., Lila, M., & Cava, M. J. (2001). *Familia y adolescencia.* Madrid: Síntesis.

Musitu, G., & Molpeceres, M.A. (1992). Estilos de socialización, familismo y valores. *Infancia y Sociedad, 16,* 67-101.

Musitu, G. Jiménez, T., & Murgui, S. (2007). Funcionamiento familiar, autoestima y consumo de sustancias en adolescentes: un modelo de mediación. *Revista de salud pública de México,* 49 (1), 3-10.

Mussen, P. H.; Conger, J. J., & Kagan, J. (1982). *Desarrollo de la personalidad en el niño.* México: Trillas.

Noller, P., & Callan V. (1991). *The adolescents in the family.* London: Routledge.

Oliva, A., & Parra A. (2004). Contexto familiar y desarrollo psicológico durante la adolescencia. En E. Arranz: *Familia y desarrollo psicológico.* Madrid: Prentice Hall.

Olweus, D. (1998). *Conductas de acoso y amenaza entre escolares.* Madrid: Morata.

Olweus, D. (2005). Bullying en la escuela: datos e intervención. En J. Sanmartín (ed.): *Violencia escuela.* Valencia: Centro Reina Sofía para el estudio de la violencia.

O'Moore, M., & Kirkham, C. (2001). Self-esteem and its relationship to bullying behavior. *Aggressive Behavior, 27,* 269-283.

Ortega, R., & Mora-Merchán, J.A. (2000). *Violencia escolar. Mito o realidad.* Sevilla: Mergablum.

Palmonari, A., Pombeni, M. L., & Kirchler, E. (1992): Evolution of the self-concept in adolescence and social categorization processes. *European Review of Social Psychology,* 3, 285-308.

Pattishall, E. (1994). A research agenda for adolescent problems and risk-taking behaviors. In R. Ketterlinus, y M. Lamb (Eds.), Adolescent problem behaviors: Issues and research (pp.209-217). New Jersey: Lawrence Erlbaum.

Popper, C., & Steingard, M. (1996). Trastornos de inicio en la infancia, la niñez o la adolescencia. En R. Hales (Dir.), *Tratado de Psiquiatría.* Barcelona: Ancora.

Radloff, S. (1977). The CES-D scale: A self-report depression scale for research in the general population. *Applied Psychological Measurement,* 1, 385-401.

Remor, E. (2006). Psychometric Properties of a European Spanish Version of the Perceived Stress Scale (PSS). *The Spanish Journal of Psychology,* 9, 86-93.

Rodrigo, M.J., Máiquez, M.L., García, M., Mendoza, R., Rubio, A., Martínez, A., & Martín, J.C. (2004). Relaciones padres-hijos y estilos de vida en la adolescencia. *Psicothema, 16*(2), 203-210.

Rubini, M., & Pombeni, M.L. (1992). *Cuestionario de conductas violenta en el aulas.* Mimeo. Universidad de Bolonia, Facultad de Ciencias de la Educación. Area de Psicología Social.

Sánchez-Sosa, J., & Villarreal-González, M. (2009). El factor psicológico de los desordenes alimenticios: Una perspectiva de campo. *Revista Enseñanza e Investigación en Psicología,* Número especial, 37-42

Secades, R., & Fernández Hermida, J. R. (2003). Factores de riesgo familiares para el uso de las drogas: Un estudio empírico español. En J. R. Fernández Hermida y R. Secades (Coods.), *Intervención familiar en la prevención de las drogodependencias* (pp. 57-111). Madrid: Ministerio del Interior.

Seydlitz, R., & Jenkins, P. (1998). The influence of family, friends, schools, and community on delinquent behavior. In T. Gullota, G. Adams, y R. Montemayor (Eds.), *Delinquent violent youth. Trends and interventions* (pp. 129-134). Thousand Oaks: Sage.

Shek, D. T. L. (2000). Differences between fathers and mothers in the treatment of, and relationships with, their teenage children: perceptions of Chinese adolescents. *Adolescence, 35,* 135-145.

Simons, R. L., Wu, C., Conger, R. D., & Lorenz, F. O. (1994). Two routes to delinquency: Differences between early and late starters in the impact of parenting and deviant peers. *Criminology, 32,* 247-275.

Smilkstein, G., Ashworth, C., & Montano, D.(1982).Validity and reliability of the Family APGAR as a test of family function. *Journal of Familiar Practice.* 15: 303-11.

Smith, P. K., & Brain, P. (2000). Bullying in schools: lessons from two decades of research. *Aggressive Behavior, 26*(1), 1-9.

Solberg, M., & Olweus, D. (2003). Prevalence estimation of school bullying with the Bully/Victim Questionnaire. *Aggresive Behavior, 29,* 239-268.

Hall, G. S. (1904). *Adolescence: Its psychology and its relations to physiology, anthropology, sociology, sex, crime, religion, and education (Vols. I & II).* New York: D.Appleton & Co.

Trianes, M.V. (2000). *La violencia en contextos escolares.* Málaga: Aljibe.

Trianes, M.V., Sánchez, A., & Muñoz, A. (2001). Educar la convivencia como prevención de violencia interpersonal: perspectivas de los profesores. *Revista Interuniversitaria de Formación del Profesorado, 41,* 73-93.

Vigotsky L. S. (1979). *El Desarrollo de los Procesos Psicológicos Superiores.* Barcelona: Crítica

Vitaro, F., Brendgen, M., & Tremblay, R. E. (2000). Influence of deviant friends on delinquency: searching for moderator variables. *Journal of Abnormal Child Psychology, 28,* 313-325.

Chapter 8

VIOLENT OFFENDERS: A QUALITATIVE STUDY OF MURDEROUS VIOLENCE IN VENEZUELA

Alejandro Moreno
Popular Investigations Center, Venezuela.

ABSTRACT

The author, who has lived up to 30 years in Caracas' poor neighborhoods and written many articles and books with the Popular Investigations Center's team (that him founded and directs), offers a brief, yet complete report about assassin violence in Venezuela. After a quick review of the main quantitative aspects, he analyzes in depth the qualitative dimension of this phenomenon, approaching the violent subjects' closer motivations. Once he rules out easy causal interpretations, and detects the well founded personal/social origins of that violence, the author suggests some possible corrective interventions. He also explains what has been done by the Church and several private institutions regarding such a problem; as well by organizations whose attitude contrasts with the State's one, which seems not to be taking care of their citizens at all.

INTRODUCTION

When the Peruvian Association for Peace Studies (APEP) invited the Andres Bello Catholic University (UCAB) of Caracas in 1989 to join the Latin American institutions researching about violence in our countries (Ugalde, 1993) many doubted that such matter belonged to our social reality. Yet, the UCAB adhered to the project. Two years after its progress two things changed: "One, the reality of violence and its interest, perception and suffering of the population." (Idem).

During the last thirty years, criminal violence, especially lethal violence has being growing and expanding on an accelerated rhythm so that no inhabitant of this country feels that (s)he and his/her relatives are out of danger.

The new generations, the Venezuelans under forty years, have borne in mind this violence throughout all the journey of their personal history, being an almost normal part of their social everyday landscape, occupying ample spaces in all the information fields, and getting into a good part of the familiar conversations of every sector in our society. They have not known another world and, as a consequence, violence may seem a normal companion of existence.

According to the spokesman of the Institute of Investigations of Coexistence and Citizen's Security –Incosec- Luis Ferrer (2008), violence "...is experiencing a process of adoption in the public opinion" in a manner that people are starting to consider it as part of their daily lives; something which they must learn to deal with. For we, those who live in *barrios* (slums), the noise of shots and pistols -if not more powerful weaponry- whether they are triggered far or close, at the street or behind the forthcoming alley, produce a dry and sharp echo that reaches the hills or the walls of our house; a sound that is no longer a surprise and that does not frightens anyone. It forms part of the enviromental music, just like the bark of a dog or the roar of a motorcycle.

Nevertheless, as popularly said, there were better times. Those who agree can validate what Briceño León states. Briceño-León (2005), director of the Venezuelan Observatory of Violence, the more prestigious Venezuelan institution in violence studies says: "In two decades the population did not doubled, but homicides were multiplied by ten. The number of homicides in the early 80's oscillated around 1,300; twenty years later they reach 13,000." Briceño estimated 13,157 homicides committed in Venezuela during 2007, which gives a rate of 49 murders per 100,000 habitants; while the rate in the world is 8.8 per 100,000.

As the author posited during a conference at the Central University of Venezuela, in December 9th, 2008, the Venezuelan government stopped providing public accounts on violence since 2004; so, the official numbers can vary, although a little, from one report to another. As a a matter of fact, researchers access "official" numbers through non-official routes and have to apply some corrections to them since the calculating procedures used by the governmental institutions of security leave in the shade very important data.

For example, results calculated by the Observatory indicate 14,600 murders, which raise the rate of homicides up to 52 (Reyes, 2009). An idea of what is happening in 2009 can be traced in the numbers picked up by the press during the six weekends that preceded the moment at which this chapter was written. These are numbers exclusive to Caracas, a city that, according to official numbers, has 3,205,463 inhabitants.

It is remarkable that between the dawn of Friday the 13th and Monday 16th on February, 2009, 63 homicides took place (Rodríguez, 2009a); 18 of them occurred on Friday night (Rodríguez, 2009b). We have to consider that on Sunday 15th it was celebrated the referendum on the constitutional amendment which gave the president the right to appear indefinitely as candidate to new elections, a circumstance in which everyone expect that these numbers could be heavily kept secret. During the following weekend the number of deaths resulted 57 (Murolo, 2009). March began with 65 murders (Rodriguez, 2009c). During the next weekend from March 6th to 8th, 20 Caracas natives were murdered (La Voz, 2009) while, on the subsequent weekend, March 13th to 15th another 37 were slained (El Nacional, 17-3-2009). Within the first three months of the current year, homicides increased 31% in contrast with the same trimester of the previous year (Rodriguez, 2009d).

PAST AND PRESENT OF VIOLENCE IN VENEZUELA

It cannot be stated that Venezuela was previously an ocean of interpersonal peace. In every society, lethal violence has always been present since humankind exists. We knew the typical rural violence, the violence that occurs by rage explosions, by quarrels of honor between male victims, due to past hostilities between clans and families, and due to the distribution of inheritances, land seizure, borderlines, etc. There was also a hot and passional violence, oriented towards a well-known and identified victim; however, urban violence was hardly known. From time to time it arose exceptionally and on unexpected situations.

Since the second half of the twentieth century Venezuela got transformed swiftly into an almost completely urban country, going from an eighty percent of rural to an urban population, a process that was carried out without great social or interpersonal conflict.

In this new urban scene, the first kind of violence was political, where the murder of opponents during the dictatorship of Perez Jiménez was followed by the killing of government officials, including police officers. During the days of the guerrilla, as Ugalde has called it, a directed and instrumental violence (Ugalde, 1993) had been used as a specific mean to secure defined aims. It was violence explained by itself, it was not posed as a way for understanding problems, but served only as a justification.

During the last three decades we are witnessing a savage violence that does not seem to have any direction or a precise instrumentality so that, in the words of España (1993, p. 14) "it is not born from groups of interests or political, economic or cultural factions who use violence to defend themselves or to dominate a community. On the contrary, it is about disproportionate actions and reactions towards the context where it happens, lacking a specific objective or transcending beyond the necessity of the direct aggressor", a violence that, as the same author states, "has become crazy" (Idem. p.13) because "it does not know norms or reasons that may allow engaging in a dialogue with it" (ibidem. p. 14).

Basic Questions

Then, is it a violence that does not raise an explanation because is unjustified, although it causes misunderstanding problems. It is not enough to say that it is crazy. What does this madness mean? Is it truly totally irrational or has an intrinsic rationality? An internal logic? One that would allow us to include its birth, course and opening; to think about limits and rectifications? Is it born from hidden and polluting underground sources or does it suddenly falls like a storm that grows and shapes itself from its own movement?

These questions arise from the anguish that affects us before the perception that none of us is free from danger; it hangs over us like a sword, as a threat and imminence. Moreover, we see the disagreement, impotence or perhaps the incapacity and, what is worse, the carelessness and lack of interest, apathy of the institutions who are incumbent to stop and control it, and so to protect defenseless citizens.

Routes of Answer

Three paths have been pointed out by specialists: identification, amount and sources. In the field of identification, knowledge had to travel through an intricate forest of varieties, diversifications, qualities, degrees, generalization, particularitities and shades. Violence reveals itself as diverse and multiple, omnipresent, infiltrated in all interstices of everyday life, and impregnating all our relations. We perceive it as physical, psychological, verbal, nonverbal; by gender, adult, against children, structural, social, personal, grave, light, intermediate, bearable, unbearable, justified, unjustified, defensive, offensive, of injuries, mortal; as homicide, assassination and many etceteras. But, which one really distresses us? The one that threatens our lives and tranquility? The one we are obligated to defend ourselves against? The radically intolerable because its tolerance is mortal?

Certainly, there is no single type of violence that could be considered as ethical and humanly tolerable; although with many of these, humanity has always coexisted and, in certain societies, it has managed to eliminate at least temporarily or to maintain within certain limits.

When societies live moments like this, as we are currently living in Venezuela, it is inevitable to establish priorities. Although every kind of violence requires attention, it is clear that criminal, deadly violence, the one that every day threatens and takes away the life of many Venezuelans, demands our interest and study.

Consequently, the Center of Popular Research addresses lethal violence as part of its study's subjects, wherein a wide range of publications and diffusion are available (Moreno, 2007). That violence will be the core subject of this work.

Among the different types of violence included in the WHO classification (2002) our researchers have focused on the "non-fortuitous, deliberate, physical, deadly and unfair (that is, not in self-defense, for example), and therefore criminal violence."

Criminal violence in Venezuela has been object of numerous investigations and exchange of ideas between social scientists, politicians, clergy and the population; people who are worried about its increase, spread and danger. The study and reflection revolve around quantitative and statistical aspects of this phenomenon (Briceño-Leon *et al.*, 1997; Briceño-Leon & Pérez-Perdomo, 2000) and the explanations of psychological (Vethencourt, 1962; Pedrazzini & Sanchez, 1990; 1992), sociological (Briceño-Leon, 1997; 2000, Cisneros & Zubillaga, 1997), anthropological (Ferrándiz, 2005), criminalistic (Del Olmo, 1997; Santos, 1997; Ponce, 1993) and multidisciplinary (Briceño-Leon, 2001) types; all according to theories considered as valid in other latitudes, although not taking into account the way of being and living of Venezuelans.

There are many quantitative studies in this matter. Because official data are not very reliable, as I already indicated, this deficiency is fulfilled with effectiveness not only by the press but, mainly, by university institutions and other organisms working along with official institutions, like the Laboratory of Social Sciences at the Central University of Venezuela and the Observatory. In numerous publications (2007, 2009) I found abundant information on the numerical evolution of lethal crime in Venezuela during the second half of the XX century and its incidence, its forms, the age of victims and victimizers, its social impact and everything that has to do with statistics of diverse type.

When exploring the causes of violence, the attention of scholars easily focuses on general causes and topics. We have been told that, through out all our history, since the Spanish conquest, violence is preminent; one that evidentiates the structural violence of human society according to the historical accomplishments and situations of exclusion, oppression, poverty and injustice that are present in Latin America and our country. This is especially evident in the unequal distribution of wealth, in the life at the districts lacking the most needed services and in the supposedly dominant dysfunctional families in popular sectors, in the mass media as promoters of images and stories where blood and death, alcohol and drugs reign without control. The list of causes and conditions that could be related to criminal violence nowadays can be almost interminable.

It is certain that violence could be considered as multicaused, so that none of the adduced determinants explain it as a whole, but, do they all together explain violence totally? If the answer to the latter question is positive, can something effective be performed against it? First of all, and this has always be stressed because it seems to be forgotten frequently, it is not possible to speak of "causes", *sensu stricto*, in explaining a phenomenon. It is rather necessary to speak about circumstances, conditions, tendencies, possibilities or multiple, diverse, coincident, interrelated probabilities; all of them at the most govern, but do not determine, a motivation, an integration of shared experiences, a social factor or a set of factors that exceptionally activate, and are capable to explain the phenomenon in question.

Although people are conditioned by the so called structural violence of a determined society, being capitalistic, exploitative or of any other specification, only a few of its members are involved in killing people. It is the conduct of this small group which needs to be explained. The violence of the social structures, for the case that occupies our attention, explains too much to us and therefore does not explain anything at all.

The same can be said of the conditions of poverty and exclusion wherein popular sectors live. These affect Venezuelans from those sectors, but only a group of them is devoted to extremely violent crime. Poverty and exclusion, just like other conditions, do not determine it. They do not explain what happens when Héctor Blanco, one of the subjects of our investigation, says: "When I was fifteen years old, I already had committed six homicides" (Moreno et al., 2007, p. 314), or: "when I was fourteen-year old I began to get into trouble, I began to shot people" (Idem, p. 309) and, yet, Ismael, the opposite case, (Ibidem, pp. 798-825) was abandoned and without family since he was three years old, and he never killed anybody and today he is a dedicated educator of *niños de la calle* (children in street situation).

The society in which both have lived has been the same oppressive, corrupt, exploitative and structurally violent, and even the circumstances of exclusion and marginality has been far worse for Ismael than for Héctor. It is here where social psychology, together with urban cultural anthropology, sociology and the philosophical reflection located in this reality and the hermeneutic understanding of their reality, can help us explain and understand such discrepancy.

METHODOLOGICAL APPROACHES

Most of the efforts aimed at understanding the kind of violence we are referring to are mainly descriptive, because they concentrate on its manifestations, processes and incidences, as well as on the social structures wherein it appears. But different questions emerge from those who have been in contact with the characters of that violence, not only witnesses but also researchers that intend to understand the popular Venezuelan way-of-life.

Violence is understood from their actors, but how is it within violent subjects? If the majority of people live in the same circumstances and they do not engage in violent offending, what kind of people does? How are they like? How are they related? What are their deepest desires? What is their vital project? Moreover, where do we need to look at to find their internal world? If not as a whole, at least in the possibly maximum of complexity.

And secondly, once we find that searched place: How to approach it so that we can arrive not only to a description but to an understanding of the internal dynamics, the logic, if it exists, that governs the delinquents' development and understanding of the world? The subject of our preoccupation has been the life of the violent offenders. However, that life is "in them", not only in the individual schemata but also in the type of "violent assassins", including the popular way-of-life that they belong to, because violent people of popular origin are the ones that interest us.

If, as Ferrarotti (1981) states, every person is the synthesis of the social processes (living) into the individual, from the general to the specific; besides, if in every person the society which he belongs exists, if all the groups where life happens and in which this runs, and if in a person a society can be known, then that "where" is the life of everyone of these actors. That life history is complete and fulfilled. In the history-of-life of any one of the violent assassins violence can be found from its inside and vital concreteness.

We selected the life stories of fifteen assassins' of popular origin from different places of Venezuela and several ages, mainly young people, all men, because 98% of the delinquent assassins are male and 70% are between 16 and 30 years (Briceño-Leon, et al., 2009). The number of life stories obeys to the desire of finding variety and contrasting diversities.

The history of life is the place where we have looked at for murderous violence, since its making to present date. When the story is told by the actor, who we call "historian" (not "interviewed" or informer) we will find behind a "co-historian" (instead of "interviewer" or "investigator").

For the procedure of analysis -or study method- we have considered that its understanding is hermeneutic, not of a text but of life practices. When doing hermeneutics of a text, we ask for the aspects not clearly appearing on it; the aspects without which the text would not be the one that it is. So we access its implicit, not yet conscious, meaning of the culture, the symbolic world where the text has its positivity (Moreno, 1998). In the same way, we ask for the group meanings -constituent of the "violent delinquents" group- providing consistency to life practices that take the place in texts and oral writings; an exercise that otherwise would not have taken place nor had another form of existence. In this way we applied hermeneutics to this social investigation.

PROFILE OF THE VENEZUELAN VIOLENT DELINQUENT OF POPULAR ORIGIN

We performed an elaborate profile of violent delinquents of popular origin in Venezuela, from their structure and inner process of structuring. This would allow us to think about ways and procedures for action, and elaboration of feasible projects for prevention and correction.

I will select the aspects of this profile that seem more significant to us, the investigators, as aspects marked as the "centers of meaning and sense" that yield unity to life and guide actors to this violence. We began with the last element in our investigation: the concept. This is the result of a long study that, once elaborated, appears to us like the integrating nucleus in everyone that exerts the kind of violence we try to deal with.

If we look at the life of delinquents from the perspective of the social life lived by the majority of people, from the shared norms of coexistence that guarantee a safe and minimally comfortable human existence, they would seem absolutely irrational. Instead, if we observe them from the inside; if we see them as living beings and consider the rules by which they produce their quotidian living, as well as the underlying system of meanings, we will find a principle of organization, a unity of sense in their multiple actions, experiences and conducts which provides an inner rationality, an intrinsic logic conforming a specific way of living.

In order to provide name and conceptual content to this integration we elaborated the construct "form-of-life". The expression "form of life" exists and is used in diverse senses. That is why we re-elaborated it, because we arrived to it not from linguistic expression, neither from a theory nor from an idea but from the life history of our subjects, their practices and directions. The criminal violence form-of-life is, then, the structure that constitutes a violent subject, which is praxical, existential, conceptual, even semantic; it is a way to give meaning to the world that he lives in, a way of living, a life style, a form of existence, a system of conditions of life in his present time and to his future possibility, a form of interacting with society, a way to do, a reasoning of his process in time; that is to say, a history.

Because the purpose of our work is to study violent Venezuelan delinquent of popular origin from their own interpretation, we have selected them.

The Venezuelan popular world-of-life is constituted (Moreno, 1997, 1998a, 1998b, 2002, 2008) as a system of meaning sustained by common practices wherein people who coexist (*convivientes*), grounded on a primary practice from which all the others receive the sense and act like the dynamic center of organization that shapes the life of the Venezuelan popular communities. This primary practice of way-of-life is the "convivial relation of matricentered affective tone."

The meanings that transform criminal violence into a form-of-life or into worlds-of-life are deviant, transgressor, distorting, out of the norms, and extreme. In the same way a crazy individual can only become mad according to his culture; these subjects live in a world ruled by their codes, but they cannot be mad according to their practices.

Their abnormality is mainly found in the distortion and extra limitation of the world-of-life' cultural features. Convivial relation, the central meaning of the popular world-of-life, is distorted in the criminal violence form-of-life, as this practice is merely a utilitarian instrument, manipulated only to achieve egocentric goals and not for a positive coexistence. Furthermore, the typical easiness whereupon the Venezuelan of popular origin changes his compromises (usually taken by "irresponsibility") becomes an absolute denial of every commitment or absolute irresponsibility.

This means that delinquents of popular origin practice a very different criminal violent form-of-life than the form-of-life of a violent criminal who belongs to another world-of-life.

We have seen this in the history of all of them. Thus, for example, the way gangs of delinquents gather does not follow the conformation of groups governed by a functional work's division and a strict hierarchy in the distribution of power, as happens with classic gangs (according to conventional literature on the subject). In our case, the reproduction of relational weaves ruled by affective entailment belongs to popular daily life, where affection works as solidarity and complicity for crime. In this way, Venezuelan gangs will be much less stable that classic bands, since they are more exposed to conflicts and internal violence, and governed by temporary circumstantial agreements instead of planned, rationally maintained projects in time, and coherently executed.

Therefore, it will be very different the way in which society and the State will have to deal with a "Venezuelan" type gang from the way that other societies and states have, according to their own types.

The concept "violently criminal form-of-life" allows us to synthesize the organic multiplicity of the phenomenon and to distinguish the violent cases that fit perfectly in it as the persons characterized by this form-of-life from those that have a circumstantial temporary link. We have called the first ones "violent structural delinquents", and the latter "circumstantial" or "accidentally violent delinquents".

The differences between them are very important. While structural delinquents never leave that form-of-life, persisting on it until they perish, generally violent and early (Mendoza, 2008), circumstantial delinquents get rehabilitated, integrating themselves sooner or later to social normality, many times without specialized intervention.

AFFIRMATION OF THE SELF IN SEARCHING FOR RESPECT

"I didn't want them to bring me down" (Moreno, 2007, p. 311). With this phrase Hector explains and justifies his conduct of extremely violent delinquent and his decision to begin "shooting people. Paj, paj! [bang, bang!]", according to his own words.

The interpretative analysis of his history-of-life shows us that this decision of not accepting anything that he can understand like submission, prevails like a masterful line, rulling all his conduct from the first years to the present.

Héctor accomplishes the central meaning in the histories of our subjects: to affirm his self over and against all the limits that can be displayed to him. Everyone, with their own ways, and according to their personalities and personal histories, confirm this rule. The limit is, mainly, the others.

Frank, on the other hand, makes it clear also with these words: "I wanted to kill him because in my mind that thought was present; because I do not allow nobody's bringing me down" (Id. 547). What do they understand by submission? Anything that means some type of control, whether familiar, communitarian, social, legal, rational or affective. Before any attempt of control, it raises, like a defense, the brutal and extreme attack, directed to the destruction of what is perceived as an obstacle to the expansion of the self. The last and unquestionable justification of all violent conduct is referred in the dominium of the personal self, to the will of eliminating any obstacle, difficulty or adversity. There is no reference to family, needs, poverty or interests or to any group of mates or friends. In any case, family and group will be instruments for the affirmation of the personal self.

The whole thing is about exalting the self in front of the community and society, without limitations, gaining "respect" through fear and the unavoidable submission of the others, as well as the recognition of their superiority obtained no matter how.

Respect

It is exposed very well by Héctor: "All began because they also brought me down and...it arrived a moment where I said 'It's enough'... I saw that the *malandros* (popular criminals, thugs) were respected, all of them were respected, and those "chamitos" (kids) wanted to put me under and I got tired... I bought a pistol... from there, they gave me one slap and I shot down four times the chamo (guy), as a result of that, I began to commit a lot of homicides... when I was fifteen years old, I already had six homicides" (Ib. pp. 311-312).

Respect is not an attitude or condition that the violent offender expresses towards the other; on the contrary, is the others' attitude towards him that he is able to gain by means of fear and inescapable submission. So, they recognize his superiority and undisputed importance. Respect is obtained by imposition and exhibition of power. Thus, at a second moment, respect and power are integrated into a unit.

"I had the power", says Alfredo (Ib. 47). To have power is to be above, over everyone. They dominate; that is the point about "having power" for them, but at the same time they are dominated by it because they cannot do anything but to seek and keep exercising it.

Power has consequences: the person stands out, he is recognized and is important, but mainly, he does not have anybody over him. There is no speech about power in their lives, maybe a few expressions; but its practice is permanent. They do to exercise power as a recurrent practice but as life risking, especially in jail.

Power is not sustained with a purpose, although its goal is the achievement of goals; power is maintained by itself, by the affirmation and expansion of the self. In this sense, power and will are identified. When power is achieved "it is well". The group of Alfredo has power in jail and, therefore, they are well. Power is not necessarily linked to violence, although it consists of the practical ability to exert it; it has to do with the conditions of possibility of "being well", with living better at the moment (they are never worried about future) and having access to goods that, otherwise, would be out of reach. Not only material, but also intangible goods like safe movility, others' do not messing with him, respect for who he is, be admired and recognized. It is about power, an instrumental relation distorting the experience and practice of the Venezuelan relational conviviality, for it implies the others as exploited, where the central goal of violent criminal life is "respect".

On different paths, Zubillaga (2001) coincides with us in identifying the demand and search for respect in violent young people, who are the population in her study; respect is essential for the construction of identity in that type of adolescents.

"In the field, respect constitutes an ideal value orienting the action of these young people. In the field of its translation into interactions, respect constitutes a personal outcry of recognition and ascendancy that is considered as adhered to the person, concretely to the masculine identity" (Idem, pp. 582-583).

But this demand for recognition and ascendancy is imposed: young people demand respect but they do not grant it. Respect ceases to represent an intersubjective capacity of recognition to constitute pure demand of a subject that prevails" (Ibidem). All this is related as a constant feature, common among them since childhood: rebellion to the authority. This rebel attitude is practiced in many ways; some openly against familiar/school authority, some more concealed, but always taking advantage of every chance of eluding it.

If, during childhood, dealing with authority is conflictive, during adolescence this rejection is clear as well as an attitude of locating themselves in the verge, which also becomes absolutely clear. This process ends in adulthood with total immersion in criminal violence.

Nevertheless, authority will be always present in their lives as an exclusively repressive instance, out or within jail. Since their very first experience, authority itself (a firm and affectionate guide) has been replaced by a working power as real arbitrariness (maternal, paternal or both; a demand imposed by emotional reaction and not by rational calculation), which produces a concrete ability to live on the basis of domination and destruction. José does not complain about how his uncle treated him but instead he states that he "lived enslaved" (Moreno et al., 2007, p. 176).

They soon pass to a world of the street and delinquent gangs, wherein there is no authority, but pure power. Power, as an exercise for imposition, starts as a desire and then becomes practical, that is, abusive; a violent exercise that allows surpassing every control and limit.

In their later life, authority disappears. They will never respect anybody else and only put themselves under authority when having no more option. Nobody (family, policemen, judges, guards of any kind, stronger delinquents) will be recognized by them as authority, but only as instances of power to which they have to submit. Among the youngest ones this situation exacerbates until paroxysm. Héctor not only rebels in a manifest, violent manner but rebellion comes to be a structural part of its way-to-be in the world.

The Way (*La Vía*)

Structurally violent delinquents perceive their way-of-life as a destiny which they cannot escape from. They express this perception with a meaningful word: "The Way" (la vía). Paradoxically, these violent delinquents, who live in absolute egocentric arbitrariness, feel themselves like a toy of destiny, dominated by external forces. At the same time, this serves as an excuse, an alibi for them to commit their crimes. So fate liberates them from all responsibility because crime does not produce any feeling of guilt but pride.

What appears like total freedom, as a chance to accomplish every desire without imposed control or limits, paradoxically draws a very rigid line in life, impossible to leave, to which they feel indissolubly bounded. Extreme freedom like inevitable slavery: that is the essence of *the way*.

Thus, the way and destiny are identified. The way, indeed, is fatal or, rather, there is fatality in it. It is not what you do, but what happens to you. Once in the way, life no longer depends on its actor, it depends on the way itself. If you give yourself to it, you cannot leave the way. All delinquents in our study at some time of their life, as much in childhood as then, had the opportunity to correct their course and leave the "way", but they have not taken that chance.

How does this form-of-life originate? It does not emerge from poverty, hunger or social marginality. Many of the contents and meaning of the history-of-life of Venezuelans of popular origin, as well as the experience of coexistence in *barrio*'s ambiences, reveal us a hunger history in Venezuela.

Nevertheless, we do not have histories, like in medieval Europe, of massive starvation across the country and devastation of what they find in their way. We don't have news of hunger and poverty as a source for generalized robberies, nor popular insurgencies. We had these, but by other reasons and not by strictly popular origin. We have histories of sackings, but they cannot be attributed to hunger or pure poverty. Other factors have been decisive in those events.

There is no consensus among researchers; many of them do not consider poverty to be the decisive factor. España (2005) indicated in a conference at the University of Carabobo: "I will point out some things about the relation between poverty and criminal problems, social deviation and criminality; and I will foretell in order to demystify this relationship, sometimes that common knowledge associates mechanically". However, it is clear that a poor environment since birth offers a fertile ground to those who are more inclined to undertake a criminal violent life. Poor origins close the possibility of acquiring, legally, sumptuary, pleasant, not absolutely necessary goods demonstrated as symbols of status and success in the affirmation of the self. "The thing was about stealing n' dressing fine; having women. And being the big daddy as it was desire ... having them all" said Alfredo (Moreno et al., 2007, p.40). Those who are impelled to obtain these things are not left other way but through crime. This is deduced clearly from our study and it confirms what was said by Briceño-Leon and others (2001).

In our study, only in one case (Juan Antonio's) poverty (extreme, almost absolute) appears, together with others, like the decisive factor in his induction from childhood to delinquency. In the rest of our subjects, neither hunger nor the search to satisfy basic needs is on the basis of their histories of crime and violence, as indicated in our analysis of every history-of-life.

The Determining Factor

Others are the main factors. One, barely emphasized and suspected, is the torment, the sufferings during the first stages of life, that is to say, the received violence which is transformed into administered violence toward others.

The suffered violence is not necessarily in the form of cruelty and physical mistreatment or strong and abundant blows. Only Juan Antonio is an exception. The violence that our subjects suffer since childhood takes the form of abandonment with multiple variations: absence of father or mother or both, negligence, disregard, rejection. Alfredo says: "they were like 'niggering' me" (Moreno et al., 2007, p. 40).

Excepting Juan Antonio's case, in which intra-family violence was absolutely brutal and cruel during his childhood, we did not find in our study any family being more violent than others. We found, however, delinquent families, abandoning families, neglected families, weak internal links families, families with scarce affective solidity. It is *abandonment* -in which, who abandon is not replaced by anybody else, especially when the mother fails to accomplish her culturally established function (providing affection, attention, and her vital significance for the child's experience) -the most influential factor, one among other keys to understand the making of the violent delinquent's personality.

Their histories can be defined as histories of absences, of certain absences that are basic: absence of a solid family, a significant mother, positive affection, binding relations, attention, significant presences. All this shapes a background of a deep pain into the person, a pain that hurts; only from time to time is conscious, a background of suffered violence that sustains his disposition to activate violence. One that originates the exacerbated necessity of extreme recognition revealed in their thirst for respect (as described above), power and dominant presence.

So they feel irresistibly driven to get what "big daddies", the "bourgeoisie", the "rich" own, especially what these enjoy; for having and enjoying it means gaining relevance, recognition, importance, prominence, affirmation and expansion of the self. José explains this way how he left his family in order to get involved into the criminal world: "...but, because I was disquiet, I have always liked, I have liked the good thing, I came, I got annoyed of that (the work), and..." (Moreno *et al.*, 2007, p. 179).

All of them, with the exception of Juan Antonio, state that what they wanted was "to dress fine." Not that they did not have anything to dress, but that they wished to show up and enjoy luxury.

Getting well dressed is a current yearning in all young men and not only the so young ones in our popular sectors. Among the delinquents, this goes too far. To get well dressed is not only to walk clean and decent, but, in addition, walking showy and even luxurious. To get well dressed is not to walk elegantly, in the aesthetic sense of the term, but to wear expensive dresses of recognized quality by its brand. Perhaps in another aesthetic sense, more centered on appearance that on harmony of the forms. Get dressed motley rather than elegantly.

What is the goal pursued by the obsession of getting showy and brand clothes? Social psychologists say they are looking for affiliation, that is, for being accepted and welcomed. In the normal Venezuelan, the objective is to sympathize, like others, to be appreciated, to stand out of the average people, to produce sexual attraction, to be received everywhere, that is to say, affiliation is understood as the joyful interpersonal relation.

In the delinquent all that is exasperated and transformed into exhibiting himself as someone of an importance superior to all competitors, by showing off a higher success in life than anybody.

What can ordinarily be an instrument of social acceptance, for him becomes a mean of domination, imposition, forced submission, of more subjugating power; this in relation to other delinquents that he tries to keep out of competition. Before society this means an imposition of his successful presence. Society does not accept him, but it must recognize that he is able to achievement within their parameters of success, although by deviate means.

CRIMINAL VIOLENCE THROUGH TIME

The history-of-life of our subjects delineates a succession of the different ways in which the criminal violence way-of-life has been appearing through the last fifty or sixty years. In the *barrios* it is usually spoken of the *"malandro Viejo"* (old thug) different from the *"malandro nuevo"* (new thug). This corresponds, according to our history-of-life, to the experience of popular communities in their struggle with *"malandros"* (thugs).

We found in our study three cases that represent the three moments in the evolution of criminal violence:

- Old form; personified in Jose
- Medium form; personified in Alfredo
- New or actual form; personified in Héctor.

Between the "old form" and "new form" the differences are very clear and possible to be identified. In the "medium form" the limits are more diffuse: remains of the old mix with signs of the new one.

In the "old form" murder is not displayed like a feat, but a valuable action that is brave or cold or ruthless, which confirms the delinquent's worth. This appears indeed through the narration as the true meaning, but is not explicitly manifested along the speech; it does not appear as an actor's glory. It is narrated like a "necessity" produced by circumstances, like something inevitable if the executor wanted to be saved from "the worse thing," like the necessary elimination of a serious danger. The fearless emphasis is not on murder itself, but on the "manner" to perform it; in other words, in the ability to do it, the intelligence to plan it, the cleverness to discover the other's weak points, the firmness of the decision at the precise moment, etc.

In the "medium form" murder is not certainly a glorious act, but it is not concealed as product of the inevitable "thing." The will to do it is confessed without modesty and told with indifference, without guilty or regret. An attitude of lightness and indifference is rather discovered before the murder.

In the "new form", the murder is a glorious feat by itself. The emphasis is on the capacity to assassinate several times. The number of murders in relation to age is very important. The more the deaths he has, the younger the subject is, the worthier he is for admiration. Murdering more people equates the youngest ones with "los más cartelúos" (the most badass) and, even, that can put them above them. For the "new ones" murder is an achievement and they are proud of it; for them, murderous violence is shameless, totally cold, unmotivated (or with banal motives), almost mechanical; the result of a device working automatically.

For Héctor, one more death is a simple decision. It does not need explanation, justification, reason; it is performed and that's it. It is a pure exercise of power on life and death. He kills "people", as he says, just because he wants.

In the "old form", these fields were limited in such a way that any of these actions were imposed to another or confused. In the "new form," robbery, assault and murder superimpose, go together: I rob you and I kill you or, if you are lucky, I hurt you, for example, in the feet. This represents a radical, frightful change for everybody. Violence has become bloodier, more aggressive, and implacable. The "new ones" already have no control, no limit, and no emotion.

The "old delinquent" kept up the looks in front of his community, although everybody knows about his condition. The "medium" only takes care of his pals, colleagues, or the members of his group, where a murder does not mean a big deal. The "new one" does not care because the community does not concern him and each murder is a blazon in the group.

All this depends much on social control. We are not speaking of the police or governmental control, but of society and community's control. This control has not only diminished throughout time, since the 50's to nowadays, but at present time it has disappeared or become ineffective and weak.

The "old ones" were under a very hard and effective social control. By social control we mean the opinion of people, the way to deal with them, the non-expressed conditions but present in the relational practices in order to not make notice, deny assistance, etc.

The community knew that someone was a delinquent, they knew his misdeeds, but they also accepted him if displayed some conditions of respect (for example, not glorifying himself because his crimes, not committing crimes within the community and protecting it against external criminals, not scandalizing children, etc.), that is to say, he observed certain rules and kept up appearances. If he did not fulfill these rules, if he was not good with the community, they elaborated mechanisms to punish him effectively, either by police or by the neighbors.

Social control has disappeared as a real, operative force, due to several reasons, such as the proliferation of delinquents, increased access to new and more powerful guns, the criminals' shorter age (more instinctive, less reflexive), the absolute loss of human respect, the inefficacity of police to control crime and the danger of resorting to them, etc.

The "old criminal" had some needs of being accepted, a feeling inculcated to him by both family and neighborhood. To the "new one" it does not matter absolutely if he is accepted or not. The acceptance is replaced by his brutal and direct capacity to impose himself, to have the total power on anyone, pure "desire"; power like death instinct in a pure state. If for the "old" the other had some importance the other is completely annulled for the "new." They only worry about themselves. They are integral assassins.

Before this new reality and without effective police protection, the community has no other mean than lynching. In the old days, lynchings were very rare and took place only at critical moments; nowadays, they happen more often than what is said, believed and known. One could think that these terrible novelties are product of the diffusion of drugs between youngest. Drugs possibly have an influence, that is for sure, but both the "old" and "medium" delinquents used drugs and murdered, and they did not arrived to this point. The "old one" moves from community to community. He leaves the familiar community and enters the contemporary young people's gang or something major. When he falls totally in the life of crime, he enters into a group of delinquents which even form a community and live in the same house of vicinity and regularly break the law as a group; at least while the police does not disarticulate them.

The "medium" becomes part of a group of the street and lives in a migratory way. He joins others transitorily to form a task group that dissolves once the "job" is finished. He is free, less tied to commitments but he breaks the law in group. The "new one" does not coexist. He may circumstantially join in groups of two, three or little more; although he has "panas" (buddies), especially when they kill people, he essentially acts by himself. The "new one" is mainly, a solitaire. The "old" one is on alert with the police both when he acts alone or in group. According to the "old", the police is not an organization that tolerates delinquents or that is capable of dealing with them. The "mediums" come into terms with the police. At this point, police commit the same crimes than delinquents do; they are distinct only because of their different procedures, and if police prosecute criminals, they do not serve and protect citizens. The "new one" flees from the police because he is not even able to come to terms with them in crimes. Sometimes, he even faces them. They are competition.

In such a way, criminal violence becomes autonomous from society. In "old times" delinquency was not apart from society, the "barrial" community (the slums), police, and citizens' opinion. That situation did not prevent crime, but hindered it by setting some rules. Although it was ill and dangerous to community, the delinquents belonged to it in the same way as lepers, mad or mentally retarded people did. Society had elaborated control mechanism for delinquents (isolation, reclusion and even reintegration where possible), leaving them some spaces where they could learn to live; anyway, they could not get rid of or become independent from society.

Nowadays, the "new ones" have become totally autonomous. None of the old rules and social mechanisms exerts any pressure on them any longer. In addition, there are no ties with cultural values, the popular world-of-life's meaning, all what has been conceptualized as "human" in tradition, those aspects still present to some extent in the "old ones". This autonomy is a total uprooting, as it is not supported on anything, including family, the mother, a friend, Earth, nature, dignity, humanity, but on his own mechanisms of action.

How a Structurally Violent Delinquents Is Formed

"Old", "medium" and "new" delinquents follow the same path. Since childhood they have a week relation with the central figures of their families, especially with their mother, the family's affective center. This can be defined as a belonging deficit; indeed, they don't perceive themselves as completely belonging to their families.

They also demonstrate, throughout all their childhood, a disoriented, conflictive behavior before their family, school and neighborhood. Their bad conduct at school causes their exclusion from educational centers, where they spend short periods; thus, they leave studies very early. When he was 11, Alfredo had not finished second degree: "They also put me in the school; they expelled me in a week, for I shot a *guapo* (cocky guy) there, I gave him two blows. They expelled me", says José (Moreno *et al.*, 2007, p. 170).

At the neighborhood they are perceived like problematic: they are authors of small robberies progressively more important, they "martillean" (bum off) close neighbors, cause destructions, etc. Very early they begin to separate from family. This has different manifestations: they pass from the family of origin to the family of some relative, like their grandmother, some uncle, of whom they also separate soon to return transitorily to the original one, either to pass to streets; others, however, pass directly from family to the street.

The separation from family is progressive and in order to be in the street they need to follow some steps. They spend some days with family, go to the community's streets; then they return to family to sleep and go back into the street, where they spend the night in an abandoned car, and so on for a time in which the street predominates over the house.

During the next step, the young stays away for a long time far from their family, joining to some gang of young ones in a house they cohabit with for a period of time or circumstantially. Finally, it comes the total loosening from the family remaining in the community, or leaving it to enter a gang, were they find an already established group or an entirely new one, made with some fellows in his same situation. From this moment, they are already completely incorporated into the criminal way-of-life and the development of their histories is already signed. The first homicide marks a decisive time. The first killing experience seems to break barriers, opening the possibilities to future homicides. We would say with Bandura (1987) that it awakes the perception of "self-efficacy", facilitating the performance of criminal behaviors. All the controls and moral limits are then surpassed.

The Nonstructural or Circumstantial Violent Delinquents

We selected those that recover from delinquency, leaving and reincorporating themselves to normal life within the popular society. What are their distinguishing characteristics?

First of all, they live a protected childhood within the house, where there is a mother who somehow fulfills their basic needs. They have a mother and a house; thus a sense of belonging.

They have the experience of belonging to a family and a home. Not only having a family but also belonging to it. They lived a strong bond, not only with the mother but also with siblings. They speak about them in plan of brothers and sisters, not as co-victims like Juan Antonio.

We find a religious sense, popular, with a God. Not as an accomplice or obliging being, but like an aid who does not replace the responsibility of who commits an action. A belief in God that we could describe as "adequate" from the Catholic point of view. This is not a compliant God, who accept and deals with crime, as we have found in others, nor a magical God, to whom attribute all material salvation, but a God that helps and still demands freedom, responsibility, decision and effort to who trusts Him.

Our circumstantial delinquents left home and mother during the adolescence (not before, as it happens with the others), considering it as a negative experience and feeling guilt about it. They express it with the popular terms of who accuses himself: "no le hacía caso" (I didn't obey her"), "me desaté" ("I untied").

The others express this separation with indifference, even as an achievement, never in terms of guilt or regret (even if they can, sometimes, show these feelings to impact on the listener). Although they detach themselves from their family and mother, this remains as a background. Even if the mother is absent, her presence exists, as a lived experience and security of encounter when he wants coming back to her.

In these histories, there is also a non-denying father, who is a non-negative influence, although representing always a secondary meaning compared with the mother; this is a typical matricentric family's father (Moreno, 1997b). Nevertheless, the father tries to play the roles of guidance, responsibility, protection and discipline in the life of his son; despite that he might be separated from the family, constituting a different (new) and even distant one.

They stay at school during the first years until adolescence. They finish elementary school and even complete some courses in High School. In adolescence they leave school and start developing criminal conducts.

Education had much importance. They remember and value it and they try to resume study, years later, or at least consider it although they may decide that no longer it is the time. Early education stays as a background of moral guidance that resurges during times of reflection and maturity.

Regarding the others, there is the impression that all educational attempts arrive late and results are inefficient. At some moment of their life there are attempts to help them with advices, even punishments, with the idea of teaching them a skilled occupation, with attempts to learn the value of work, a discipline. Nevertheless, these remedies arrive when the oriented criminal way-of-life is already defined and does not prove to have an effect. All of them had some contact with school, an educative institution, a friend of the family or some influence in familiar means of regenerative type, but the important thing is that nothing of these has been significant to them. It does not mean anything.

Delinquency does not define them; it seems rather an accident, although it continues throughout their lives. Neither Alberto (Moreno et al., 2007) nor Nelson (Idem) live like delinquents or violent people; something that is evident in all the others although they do not express it in these terms. They do not belong to the delinquency nor delinquency belongs to their lives; they go through it as those who go through bad events in life, but they do not remain. For that reason they are recoverable. Where there is family, where there is mother, and soon wife, the insertion in the criminal life is temporary although it lasts for some time. They do not become part of the criminal act; they always describe it from the outside, because they are at the margin of crime, not inside.

The way they narrate it denotes were they stand. It is a narration conducted from outside; they are always located in an external position in regards to the criminal act. They do not belong to that form-of-life. They pass through that way-of-life, they meddle, introduce themselves momentarily, were they can last more or less a long time, but, if we study their history-of-life, they enter and leave, they are not the "pertaining ones" like the others.

They have never committed crimes driven only by the desire of having the things of the rich people (like in the majority of our other cases), but by obey other things: the group, the fun, the necessity to defend itself, etc. Something important that distinguishes them from the other cases is that they assume responsibilities: they lie down the guilt on their deviations to themselves, while the other always finds a guilty person.

They also use a relational language, instead of the others', who use a self-centered language. Here the expression is centered in the interpersonal relation as their way to live. Their history comes as a present, a narrated relation. Here we have subjects impregnated of the Venezuelan popular world-of-life sense. Their prior responsibility is with their families, as well as with the others and relatives' suffering, instead of keeping fixed on their self. This attitude is very significant because we did not find it in the other delinquents.

They also look at their victims in a different way. These are not any "güevones" (any fools), "bugs", "chigüires" (*capibaras*: stupids), "venaos" (*deers*: dummies, naives, unawares), as it was seen with the other criminals; for them they are human beings that have rights and do not have the right to be though. They are capable of putting in somebody else's shoes.

For them the relationship they have with their family has a special importance: they feel identified among its members, something to which they belong to. This link with the good world that allows them to live in the bad world of crime and jail is what opens the possibility for regeneration and frees them from entering completely in the world of crime. This link preserves an island of health in their interior.

They not only begin to work, but also learn to work seriously; thus feeling pleased about that. Satisfaction in work is a good sign indicating that this may be their project for a future life. The change seriously starts from this satisfactory experience. The meaning of popular world-of-life comes back to life after beingn clouded for some time, dominated by the criminal form-of-life.

They never present themselves like protagonist's feats, groups or amazing stories. They are totally distinguished from other subjects of this study. Neither as protagonists nor as self-centered, but as people included in the flow of life.

To those who regenerate themselves, an important factor comes to their lives when entering into the adulthood: a woman with whom they establish a more or less stable couple relation. In the life of the others, women do not play any important role, for them they do not mean anything beyond the satisfaction of a desire or need, or for being the mothers of some children with whom they really do not have any relation. Women do not influence their lives in any case.

The life of our two "regenerated" subjects coincides in this matter, according to the experience of those who live in *barrios*. The trajectory of our *malandros* neighbors, for those who had a woman in a stable relationship, who was affectively significant in their lives, let them to leave crime and came back to normal life. The type of woman had much to do with it as well as the capacity of affective entailment of the subject.

It must be a woman they met outside the world of delinquency, a woman not tied to that world, reluctant to get involved in it, not giving in to the pressure that violent delinquents exerts on her in order to get some company in their misdeeds and drug consumption.

In this couple relationship, but not outside of it, children have great importance. Woman and children represent an anchorage to common life; a completely effective factor when becoming their fundamental centers of meaning. Through them these subjects usually recover a positive relation with their mothers and their original family. Here, women's task is to keep them in the house, distant from criminal life.

THE VIOLENT ONE HAS HIS COMMUNITY AND COMMUNITY HAS ITS VIOLENT ONES

The "new" delinquents' autistic behavior, their conduct aside the community, takes to the extreme their tendency to break the law. They have the certitude of not living beyond the 20-25 years, show no fear to death and act like suicidal terrorists that cannot be stopped by any threat, danger or punishment. Therefore, in desperate cases (much more frequent than it is usually recognized), communities feel driven to resort to the terrible lynching.

Nevertheless, this exceptional situation does not overcome the relationship between local communities and violent delinquents that live with them. In every set of concrete circumstances, the *malandro* has his community, and each community has its *malandro*.

Studies do not pay attention to this. It is commonly assumed that violent delinquents can only be rejected by nonviolent people living in the same community. On the contrary, violent delinquents and "normal" people are used not only to coexist in a common physical space (usually little and crowded, a narrow alley between overlapped houses), but to share many social linkages; for them they are relatives, *compadres* (close friendship), *paisanos* (coming from the same place in the country), neighbors; they see each other almost every day, in a party, at the bus stop, just joking or arguing. Complex networks of human relationships where the violent delinquent coexists with healthy people as well as with others like him.

From our study we can determine some clues to understand this complex relationship between the violent delinquent and the community. José's history-of-life provides the first element for this understanding. How Jose and his group of delinquents proceed in their community?

- they used to go outside the *barrio* to make their misdeeds,
- the group had a boss, Jose, who controlled all his pals, "very psychopaths", according to his expression,
- they crossed the district "to share", to take beer, as "healthy people",
- they helped "all the ones that needed, that had a necessity".

- the boss, the greater delinquent, became responsible "of any bad thing that happened in the *barrio*",
- the boss calls "to account" to the one disobeying his orders, usually accepted by everyone,
- as a consequence, robberies were not committed in the *barrio*, and drugs were not consumed before children,
- in any case, robbed things were given back and the boss was in charge to beat the robber with the butt of his pistol, or to compensate the robbery with some drug he managed as the main *jíbaro* ("dealer"),
- delinquents keep this control for they need to be safe in their communities; if they were committing crimes they would be putting themselves in danger.
- So the great delinquent gained the respect and esteem from "everybody".

This way the great delinquent - greater by being boss and by age- was respected and ruled fundamental norms of coexistence, not dictated by anybody, but implicit in the daily life of the *barrio* and necessary so that the community had peace and the delinquent had security. It was established, then, a non declared but effective covenant between the "*malandro*" and his close neighbors: the community does not denounce, allows his presence like he was any other inhabitant, shares diversion and communication, conceals his crimes that everybody knows well, and even takes advantage of the merchandise robbed by him. In retribution, it is protected from any act of robbery and violence coming from external agents and young delinquents.

The relationship between the "*malandros*" and the community is not only pacific, but warm. The demands imply an effective control, exerted by the community onto its delinquents. This control neither is absolutely social nor governmental; it consists of people's opinions, treatment, relational practices, the boundaries of tolerance, etc. Two set of needs come to negotiation: delinquent's (security, consideration, respect and refuge) and community's (peace, security non provided by the police in popular sectors).

Thus, the *malandro* has a community where to live in, and the community has its "*malandros*", as also has its *recogelatas* (begger), its *borrachín* (habitual drunk), its madman on the streets, its *Portuguese* or priest. In such a way, the community has to deal with *malandros* when the State is not able to guarantee social coexistence; by this we are not referring only to the official institutions dedicated to the problem of delinquency (police, for instance), but to those who are expected to be provided with the most essential services (for example, nobody knows when, where or how water will come to the *barrio*).

Let's see the case of a guy who lives in my barrio, who is also a part of a research project still in process. Yovani (Moreno, 2009) is twenty-eight years old. He has surpassed, then, the critical age of the twenty-five and he is coming to be a "*malandro viejo*", an exceptional survivor. He speaks little and with a few persons organizes with intelligence and sobriety; he is ruthless and cold when the circumstances demand it. He became the strong man of his *barrio*. He gained that position by eliminating "*a punta de plomo*" (by gun means), that is to say, by shooting down seven or eight competitors.

He dominates all the drug market and manages his pals' violence and criminal activities. He could be a band boss respecting his neighbors who stays like a parasitic body of the community without taking part in anything neither negative nor positive. It's not like that. He incarnates a figure similar to Jose's that we already knew.

First of all, in the community everything works out well and peacefully because Yovani never messes with anybody at the place. Once cleared the panorama, people are better, cool, because he and his guys removed all the strangers and those who hide in the *barrio* because they were being chased from other places. In addition he does not admit anybody to get in from outside. The implicit pact returns to work.

With the *malandros,* pacts can be done in the relational plots of the Venezuelan popular world-of-life. And those pacts are safe, while those made with the police are not. For the inhabitants of the *barrio* Yovani and his fellows are more reliable than policemen. This reality may be terrible but is the one that exists; the one lived by the popular areas' neighbors. In 2007 the police committed 381 murders; these figures arrived to 509 during the past year, increasing by 33.59% (Molina, 2009).

What can people do to coexist with their *"malandros"*? They are theirs. How can they treat them? Why not to deal with them? When the community accepts its *"malandros"* and considers them as their own, they understand their flows and security. Although this does not stop delinquents from keeping assassinating and committing crimes, the community is not directly affected by those activities. On the other hand, *malandros* integrate themselves into the activities of the *barrio*, they participate and collaborate. Therefore, the phenomenon must be studied deeper. Understanding it like a simple delinquent's tyranny, like a brutal exercise of violence in order to submit by fear a population, may explain a few cases, but neglects the need for order, rationality, peace and security demanded by every human in order to stay alive; a necessity satisfied by irregular means when institutional legality is not working.

EFFORTS TO PROVIDE AN ANSWER TO THE VIOLENCE SITUATION

During the last ten years, the Venezuelan government has not considered the fight against murderous violence among its priorities. Edwin Rojas, Director of the Ministry of Justice for Crime Prevention, shamelessly said that "other public policies are priority" (Rojas, 2009). Now he announces an "armored plan" of security, but only a few in Venezuela may think of it as something more than a mere statement for the mass media. The government's absence is reflected in 14,600 assassinations in Venezuela during 2008. It is difficult to believe a so huge irresponsibility.

The absence of the State is aggravated by the uncontrolled proliferation of fire arms released by security officers themselves, both policemen and military, who sell or rent the guns in exchange for sharing the profits from criminal acts, (González, 2009); also the absolute impunity (92% of the murders in Venezuela are not investigated), the widespread drug's selling and consumption, the venality of the judges, the abuse in jails (described by the prisoners themselves as "alive men's cemeteries"), and other multiple deficiencies that would be long to enumerate. Besides, the population cannot do anything, because even the simplest denunciation means the denouncer's death sentence. In spite of that, many institutions are dedicated to crime prevention, especially with the youngsters and children.

Violence is especially dangerous and seductive for young men (14-18 years) who left school, but are not working because laws do not allow them or the absence of jobs. The Church, mainly (but not exclusively) has created a wide network of centers aiming to yield them opportunities for a professional education. Special attention must be paid to street children, a situation materialized in many ways, whose numbers are not well known. Also there is a great variety of institutions, most of them nongovernmental that have started very creative programs, with little or no official aid.

A very important group (of which only their communities and its inner institutions can take care of) is made by the great majority of children and adolescents without personal, direct experience with violence, although surrounded by it. Because they only attend school half a day, then spend a lot of time at the streets, while their parents are absent, mainly because they work. These kids can be modeled by delinquents they meet every day, displaying power, success, prestige, material goods, drug consumption and money. These youngsters do not receive official attention; however, private institutions (especially the Church when this have presence in the community) offers them a variety of extra-curricular activities, thus promoting sports, excursions, meeting places, courses, night activities and vacations on weekends and holidays.

Some private initiatives have been undertaken to rehabilitate young murderous delinquents. Despite its publicity, there are only a few and they have been ineffective. The "Alcatraz" project, conducted by a sugar and rum industrialist, is the best known and has been even praised by the President of the Republic; nevertheless, its area of influence is limited and external evaluations show that the results are far from the proclaimed goals.

Future does not appear very encouraging in Venezuela. An even higher increase of criminal violence may be foressen throughout the passing of time if we consider the rising progression since the late 90's.

REFERENCES

Bandura, A., (1987), Pensamiento y Acción, Buenos Aires, Martínez Roca. (1986, *Social Foundations of Thought and Accion*, New Jersey, Prentice-Hall).

Briceño-León, R. et al (1997). La emergente cultura de la violencia en Caracas. *Revista de Economía y Ciencias Sociales*, UCV. Caracas.

Briceño-León, R., Pérez Perdomo, R. et al. (2000). La Violencia en Venezuela. Un fenómeno capital. In: Banco Interamericano del Desarrollo (Ed.). *Asalto al Desarrollo*, Washington: BID.

Briceño-León, R., (comp.) (2001). Violencia, sociedad y justicia en América Latina, Buenos Aires: FLACSO.

Briceño-León, R. (2005), Dos décadas de violencia en Venezuela, en: Varios, "Violencia, criminalidad, terrorismo", Caracas: Fundación Venezuela Positiva.

Briceño-León, R., & Avila, O. (Eds.) (2007). Violencia en Venezuela. Caracas: Lacso.

Briceño-León, R. et al. (2009). Inseguridad y violencia en Venezuela – informe 2008- , Caracas: Lacso-Alfa.

Cisneros, A., & Zubillaga, V. (1997). La violencia desde la perspectiva de la víctima: la construcción social del miedo. *Espacio Abierto*, 6, 1.

Del Olmo, R. (1997), La pobreza, ingobernabilidad y violencia en Venezuela, *Revista Relación Criminológica*, 12.

El Nacional, (2009). En Caracas hubo 37 muertes el fin de semana. El Nacional, 17-3-2009

España, P. (1993). Introducción. In: Ugalde, L. et al. *La Violencia en Venezuela*. Caracas: Monte Avila

España. L. P. (2005), La pobreza, ingobernabilidad y violencia en Venezuela, *Revista Relación Criminológica*, 12.

Ferrándiz, F. (2005). Venas abiertas: africanos y vikingos entre los jóvenes espiritistas venezolanos. In: Ferrándiz, F. *Jóvenes sin Tregua*. Barcelona, Anthropos.

Ferrarotti, F. (1981). *Storia e storie di vita*. Bari: La Terza.

Ferrer, L. (2008). Violencia Ciudadana Naturalizada. El Nacional. September 18.

González, D. (2009). Mercal de balas. El Nacional, August 7.

La Voz. (2009). 20 muertes violentas en Caracas. Diario La Voz, 9-3.

Mendoza, R. (2008). Morir antes de los 18. Tal Cual, 25-7-2008.

Molina, T. (2009). En 33,59% aumentaron asesinatos cometidos por policías en 2008, El Nacional 3-4.

Moreno, A. (1997a), Desencuentro de mundos, *Heterotopía*, 2, 11-37.

Moreno, A. (1997b), La familia popular venezolana. Caracas: Centro Gumilla-CIP.

Moreno, A. (1998a). El pueblo venezolano, Acontecimiento y sentido, *Heterotopía*, 1/2, 7-25.

Moreno, A. (1998 b). Historia-de-vida de Felicia Valera. Caracas: CONICIT.

Moreno, A. (2002). Buscando Padre. Caracas-Valencia: UC-CIP.

Moreno, A. (2007). Y salimos a matar gente. Maracaibo: LUZ, CIP

Moreno, A. (2008a) ¿Padre y Madre? Caracas: CIP.

Moreno, A. (2008b). El Aro y la Trama (5th edit). Miami: Convivium Press.

Moreno, A. (2009). El malandro y su comunidad: violencia en el barrio. In: Briceño-León, R., Avila, O., & Camardiel, A. (Eds), *Inseguridad y Violencia en Venezuela*, 274-292.

Murolo, D., (2009). Se reportan 57 asesinatos hasta el martes en Caracas, El Nacional, 25-2.

Pedrazzini, Y., & Sánchez, M. (1990). Nuevas legitimidades y violencia urbana en Caracas, *Nueva Sociedad*, sept-oct.

Pedrazzini. Y. & Sáchez, M. (1992). Malandros, bandas y niños de la calle, cultura de urgencia en las metrópolis latinoamericanas, Caracas: Vadell Hermanos.

Pérez Perdomo, R. et al. (1997). Magnitud de la violencia delictiva en Venezuela, *Espacio Abierto*, 8, 1.

Ponce, M. G. (1993). Drogas y Violencia en Venezuela. In: Ugalde L., et al (Eds,). *La Violencia en Venezuela*. Caracas: Monte Avila.

Reyes, T. (2009). Caracas, la capital más violenta de América Latina. El Universal.

Rodríguez, G., (2009a). Fin de semana de referendo. El universal, 17-2.

Rodríguez, G. (2009b). Reportan 18 asesinatos en Caracas. El Universal, 15-2.

Rodríguez, G. (2009c). Asesinada una persona por hora. El Universal, 3-3.

Rodríguez, G. (2009d). Aumentaron 31% los homicidios en el primer trimestre de 2009. El Universal 2-4.

Rojas, E. (2009). Otras políticas públicas eran prioridad en los primeros años, El Universal, 29-3.

Romero, A. (2002). Informatización y Privatización del control social: respuestas al miedo y a la violencia delictiva, *Sociologías*, 8, 2.

Santos Alvis, T. (1997). Repensando la violencia desde la criminología, *Espacio Abierto*, 6, 1.

Ugalde, L. (1993). Presentación. In: Ugalde et al, *La Violencia en Venezuela*. Caracas: Monte Avila.

Vethencourt, J. L. (1962). Psicología de la Violencia, *Gaceta APUCV*, Sept-Dec.
Zubillaga, V. (2001). Exclusión, masculinidad y respeto: algunas claves para entender la violencia en adolescentes en barrios, *Nueva Sociedad,* 173, 34-48.

Part Two:
Institutional Violence

In: Bio-Psycho-Social Perspectives on Interpersonal Violence ISBN: 978-1-61668-159-3
Editors: M. Frías-Armenta et al., pp. 193-215 © 2010 Nova Science Publishers, Inc.

Chapter 9

ENVIRONMENTAL AND PERSONAL VARIABLES PREDICTING SCHOOL BULLYING: A STUDY WITH MEXICAN ADOLESCENTS

Victor Corral Verdugo, Blanca Fraijo-Sing[*], Martha Frías-Armenta and César Tapia–Fonllem
Universidad de Sonora, Mexico.

ABSTRACT

Bullying in schools has been recognized as a serious problem affecting both the normal development and the wellbeing of children. Around the world, 20% of school children are involved in bullying behavior. In Mexico there is no exact statistics about the problem but many teachers and students report this problem in diverse forms. The aim of this chapter is to elucidate some of the factors that predict bullying at schools. The sample of this study was constituted by 126 teachers from 24 cities, towns and communities of the Sonora State, in northern Mexico. Five components of the "Sample Survey for Teachers and Other Staff about Bullying" (Ministry Of Education, Ontario) were used. They included the sub-scales of type of abuse, context, actions, moment and abusive conduct at school. In addition, demographic variables were considered. The instrument was administered at the schools where teachers were taking academic training courses. Univariate analyses from the demographic data and the scales used were performed; also we conducted reliability analysis for each scale. An index for the time of abuse was created, and parcels of action taken (to deal with bullying), perception of bullying, and bullying were calculated. Finally a structural equation model was specified to estimate the relationship between context -as exogenous variable- and action taken, perception, and time of bullying -as intermediate variables- which presumably affect the bullying dependent variable. Results indicated that the context of abuse had a direct effect on the perception of bullying, action taken and time of abuse, and these variables produced a direct effect on the dependent variable bullying. Results are discussed in terms of the effect of context on bullying and the reactions of teachers. Theory on

---

[*] Correspondence to Blanca Fraijo-Sing, Departamento de Psicología, Universidad de Sonora, Rosales y Luis Encina, S/N, Hermosillo, Sonora, 83000, Mexico. E-mail: bfraijo@sociales.uson.mx.

antisocial behavior suggests that offenders seek the opportunities to engage in criminal, antisocial behaviors. As our data reveal, some places, school time and actions taken by teachers could create or facilitate these opportunities for bullying.

INTRODUCTION

Around the world, a substantial number of children report being bullied at school and this kind of misbehavior has been recognized as a serious threat affecting children development and wellbeing. Schools have become risky places. In these surroundings students adopt certain attitudes and conduct that would not subsist if these risks were not present. In present times, the notion that places like family or school are safe and that they form good citizens has radically changed. Schools are one of the most important environments for the development of human beings. It is presumed that it is here where students will acquire the abilities and competences necessary to enable them to incorporate into a productive community. Schools are also expected to reinforce positive models of conduct (altruism, honesty, work habits) that theoretically are passed down from students' families to younger individuals. Notwithstanding, research data appear to indicate that school environments do not necessarily transmit those models of civil conduct (and on many occasions, not even the expected intellectual capacities).

A study of 28 European and North America countries, using a random sample of schools, showed that the prevalence of bullying victimization among students ranged from 5% to 40%, the average of occurrence among all these countries being 17%. The highest incidence was in Lithuania (average 39.8%), with the percentage of bullying for boys being of 41.4% and of 38.2% for girls (Due et al., 2005). Another study reported that physical and verbal victimization in primary or elementary schools ranges from 8% to 46% across the world, whereas the incidence of bullying others ranges from 3% to 23% (Woods, & Wolke, 2003). In Finland, one out of ten children is exposed to bullying at school (Kaltiala-Heino, Rimpelä, Marttunen, Rimpelä, & Rantanen, 1999). In addition, 25.9% of boys in Israel report being bullied at their schools (Due et al., 2005). Nansel, Overpeck, Pilla, Ruan, Simons-Morton, & Scheidt (2001) measured the prevalence of behaviors of abusive children in the United States in a sample of 15, 686 students from 6th to 10th years at private and public schools, using the definition of the World Health Organization. They administered the surveys during the spring of 1998. Results showed that 29.9% of children were implicated in some act of bullying; 13.0% abused others, 10.6% were victims, and 6.3% were both abusers and victims. One more study showed that one out of five students in the United States recognize themselves as bully and one out of four self-reported being bullied (Whitted, & Dupper, 2005). In Australia 23.7% of students bullied others, 12.7 were bullied and 21.5% were both bullied and bullied others; only 42% had no reported their being involved in bullying (Forero, McLellan, Rissel, Bauman, 1999). There is also a high rate of bullying in Ireland: 76% of students reported their being victimized by peers (Mc Guckin, & Lewis, 2006). Forty percent of high school students in Turkey experienced or participated in bullying (Alikasifoglu, Erginoz, Ercan, Uysal, & Albayrak-Kaymak, 2007). Thirty nine percent of students in Greece admitted being bullied in schools (Greek Institute of Mental Health, 2000). Olweus (1995) estimated that 15% of the students between first and ninth grades were involved in bullying in the Scandinavian countries. In China, a comprehensive study of 7025 primary school children found that 24% of the respondents reported that they bullied another child (Wong, Lok, Lo, & Ma, 2008).

In Latin-America, few studies exist showing the incidence of this phenomenon; in one research conducted in Brazil, 60% of the students of high schools reported having bullied other students (Desouza, & Ribeiro, 2005). Forty seven percent of middle-school students in Chile reported being bullied (Fleming, & Jacobsen, 2009).

Bullying causes physical harms (such as stomach ache, headache, backache, and dizziness) and psychological problems (bad temper, sleep deficit, feeling nervous, morning tiredness, loneliness, helplessness, depression, lower self-esteem, suicidal ideas, and bed wetting) and, in most severe cases, suicide (Due *et al.*, 2005; Kaltiala-Heino, Rimpelä, Marttunen, Rimpelä, & Rantanen, 1999; Rigby, 2000). It is also associated to psychosomatic symptoms and poor mental health (Forero, McLellan, Rissel, Bauman, 1999). Bullying also has a negative effect on the learning environment at schools; and it is an antecedent of more violent behaviors (Whitted, & Dupper, 2005). Bullies and victims participate in risky behaviors, they report higher rates of alcohol, drug use and weapon carrying (Kaltiala-Heino, Rimpela, Rantanen, Rimpela, 2000). Bullying also has long term effects; Giora, Gega, Landau, and Marks (2005) found that victims of bullying develop anxiety disorders and have problems with substance use in adulthood. Bullying presents continuity from elementary school through high school and college. Chapell, Hasselman, Kitchin, Lomon, Maclver, and Sarullo (2006) conducted a longitudinal study of students from elementary school to college and found that 53.8% of bullies in college were bullies in high school and in elementary school. Bullying is associated with internalizing problems; for example, girl victims develop eating disorders (Bond, Carlin, Thomas, Rubin, & Patton, 2001). The most preoccupant effect of bullying is that children feel fear to attend school; some studies reported that children stay at home to avoid bullying or are frightened during their school day (Glew, Rivara, & Feudmer 2000). In addition, victims of bullying cannot concentrate in school work and drop out of school (Ferguson, San Miguel, Kilburn, Jr., & Sanchez, 2007).

There are few studies conducted in Mexico about this phenomenon, therefore, the knowledge about the causes and consequences of this problem is scarce. This study is aimed at elucidating some of the factors predicting bullying at schools. Its results could help to develop effective intervention programs.

DEFINITIONS

Bullying is recognized as any frequent aggressive behavior intended to cause physical or psychological harm and it makes use of imbalance of power (Limber, 2002). Due *et al.* (2005, p. 129) define bullying as "a deliberate, repeated or long term exposure to negative acts performed by a person o group of persons regarded of higher status or greater strength than the victim." According to Olweus (1993), bulling refers to the exposition of a person to negative actions of one or more persons with the intentions to injure or to hurt him/her. Bullying behavior should have the conscious desire of hurt and put in stress another person (Oyaziwo, 2006). Bullying is also defined as any form of child aggression intended to harm another child perceived as unable to defend himself or herself (Glew, Rivara, & Feudmer, 2000). Bullying is also deemed as a kind of aggression, and it is defined as the harassment or attacks received by a child from one or several children (Salmivalli, Kaukiainen, Kaistaniemi, & Lagerspetz, 1999).

The abusers are known as bullies; they repeat the negative behaviors more frequently and usually create unbalance between conflicting behaviors, while never perceiving the reality or the consequences of their conducts (Craig, 1998; Whitney & Smith, 1993). A narrow definition is proposed by Elliott, Hamburg, and Williams (1998), which is related to the intention of threat or cause physical harm, injury or intimidation to another person. Bullying is the coercion of others by fear or threat; it includes verbal (threats, nicknames, insults), physical (assault, theft, kick, push, to take the money of others, slap, puncture, etc), social (exclusion of peer group) or other forms of violence or manipulation acts (Due *et al.*, 2005). The imbalance of power and frequency distinguishes bullying from other forms of aggression (Desouza, & Ribeiro, 2005). Technologies provide other kind of bullying: the digital bullying, which consists of sending threatening messages via cell phones or computer; also, bullies create hate-filled web pages of the victims, including personal information (Aluedse, 2006).

Some researchers include relational violence as this kind of manipulation acts, involving interpersonal manipulative actions (Yoon, Barton, & Taiariol, 2004). Researchers also divide direct from indirect bullying; direct bullying includes the physical, psychological and verbal aggression, while the purposed actions leading to social exclusion or damage to child status or reputation are considered as indirect bullying (Whitted, & Dupper, 2005; Crick & Grotpeter, 1995). There are two other kinds of bullying: racial and sexual. Sexual bullying consists of passing unwanted notes, jokes, pictures, starting rumors of sexual nature, graving private parts, or forcing to engage in sexual behavior. Racial bullying includes making racial slurs, mocking victims' culture, or making offensive gestures (Whitted, & Dupper, 2005).

Olweus (1994) distinguishes three elements of the definition: a) negative actions, b) power differential, and c) repetition. Negative actions are considered as the intention to cause harm on other individual. The power differential implies that children cannot defend themselves and, to complete the definition, harassment should occur repeatedly over time. According to this definition a single incident does not constitute bullying. However, some researchers argue that it is difficult to determine this latter element (Beran, 2008). Bullying can occur in any social environment, school, work, neighborhoods, etc.

In bullying, the participants are the bully, the victim and the observer. Each of them plays a role in the relation. The bully is the abuser, the victim is the person who is abused and the observers can play different roles in the abuse; sometimes they are an active part of the abuse assisting the bullies; others acts as neutral and others try to help the victim.

THEORIES

Several theories have been developed for the explanation of bullying. Some are centered on individual factors and others include family and situational factor. The most inclusive theory is Bronfenbrenner's (1987) Ecological Model (EM), which considers all the variables representing the contexts wherein the individual develops. Bullying occurs in one of those contexts and EM determines its main components.

Evolutionary Psychology also offers a perspective, according to which all organisms are programmed to seek and acquire the necessary resources to survive, because they are limited creatures and are forced to compete for them. In this perspective, bullying is a means to obtain resources and dominance (Rigby, 2002).

In addition, Egotism Hypothesis argues that violence or aggression is a result of threaded egotism; it suggests that disproportionate beliefs about personal superiority might be more prone to find threats and, for that reason, cause aggression (Salmivalli, Kaukiainen, Kaistaniemi, & Lagerspetz, 1999). Bullying as a kind of aggression is interpreted under Egotism Hypothesis.

Social Relation Theory indicates that bullying derives from the power relations and roles of the group. Bullying is not an isolated behavior; it reflects social relations and attitudes to the bully's peers. Each participant in bullying plays a role; some are active-aggressive (bullies) or passive (victim); others act as aggressive (assisting or reinforcing the bully), or pro-social (defending the victim) (Salmivalli, Kaukiainen, Kaistaniemi, & Lagerspetz, 1999).

Social Coping Model states that behavior is a result of a problem-solving event (Dussich & Maekoya, 2007). It is based on the child evaluation of the problem, the availability of resources, and the memory of success with similar coping strategies. Child behavior will depend on the coping skills available and his/her social support. Thus, bullying or victimization will depend on the coping skills of the subjects; if they lack them, they will be a victim of a bully.

Attachment Theory, in turn, establishes that children internalize working models based on repetitive interactions with their caregivers; so, these models are developed during the first years of life. Bowlby (1988) defines working models as a set of rules for processing social information based on early attachment experiences. The internal working model continues influencing the child throughout lifespan, providing the foundation of self-efficacy, beliefs, affect-regulation strategies, self-concept and behavioral strategies (Bowlby, 1969). A negative attachment may represent a precursor of a maladaptive cognitive style. Contrarily, healthy parent-child relationships develop a positive working model, which provides children with a safe support to explore their environment (Bowlby, 1988). In this sense, the way the child relates with peers is determined by the early attachment relationship with their caregivers (Rigby, 2002). Insecurely attached adolescent tend to be more aggressive, hostile and antisocial (Ducharme, Doyle, & Markiewicz, 2002). Attachment Theory has been re conceptualized as relationship schemas that are developed in the early life years and guide the interpersonal relations in the lifespan (Baldwin, 1992). A study conducted in Virginia assessing attachment, school climate, aggressive attitudes and bullying behavior in 110 students noticed an indirect effect of attachment through aggressive attitudes to bullying (Eliot &. Cornell, 2009).

Social Disorganization Theory assures that individual involvement in deviant behavior depends on environmental factors such as concentration of poverty, residential mobility, etc. (Elliott, Wilson, Huizinga, Sampson, Elliott, & Rankin, 1996). A similar process occurs at the school environment: some factors challenge its functioning and dismiss school climate; some of the mentioned variables are student-teacher ratio, location of school, etc. (Bradshaw, Sawyer, & O'Brennan, 2009). Larger school size is linked with higher rates of aggressive behavior (Stewart, 2003); however the teachers/students proportion is more related to violence in schools (Khoury-Kassabri, Benbenishty, Astor, & Zeira, 2004) than school size; a larger rate will decrease the possibility of teachers' supervision and increase the opportunity of bullying. A high concentration of students with conduct problems is another factor that disrupt school climate; the group of aggressive students alters school rules and environment (Koth, Bradshaw, & Leaf, 2008). Mobility is another indicator of social disorganization; theory argues that mobile individuals are not attached to the norms of the community and they are more prompt to participate in deviant acts. Similarly, a high mobility of students in schools interrupts the rhythm and predictability of their environment (Wilson, 2004). The change into a new school requires that the student learn new rules, adjust to educational content and culture; the exclusion or low involvement to a new school could support aggressive attitudes and behavior (Bradshaw, Sawyer, & O'Brennan, 2009). Special education placements may also contribute to school bullying because they represent inequality: special education children are labeled differently from their peers (White, & Loeber, 2008). White and Loeber (2008) found that youths placed in special education programs presented several risk factors for bullying and delinquency.

Ecological Theory claims that bullying derives from the individual characteristics of the child and socio-environmental characteristics of the school (Andreou, Didaskalou, and Vlachou, 2007). This theory argues that the contributions of cognition to aggression depend on the child interactions with the environment (Bandura, 1986). Bullying is perceived as a group phenomenon and peers are seen as powerful moderators of behavior. For instance, some children assist the bullying when someone has started it (assistants); others provide positive feedback (reinforcers); others remain silent and could approve the bullying (outsiders), while others confront the bully and help the victim (defenders). These patterns of conduct have been seen stable in different situations (Andreou, Didaskalou, & Vlachou, 2007). This explanation is very close to social relation theory in the way it describes participants.

Ecological Theory provides an ampler framework for the explanation of bullying because this behavior would be the result of the influence of various contextual systems. Bronfenbrenner (1987) proposes an ecological perspective regarding the development of human behavior. This perspective conceives the ecological environment as a set of systems structured in different levels and each level contains the subsequent ones. Bronfenbrenner denominates those levels the *microsystem*, the *exosystem* and the *macrosystem*. The microsystem constitutes the immediate level wherein the individual develops (usually, family); the exosystem comprises an ampler context like school, community or neighborhood; finally, the macrosystem constitutes the culture and subculture in which the person lives. Belsky (1993) proposes one more system, implying the personal characteristics of the individual; the *ontosystem*. According to Bronfenbrenner (1987) the capacity to shape a system depends on the existence of social interconnections between these systems. Interdependence between the characteristics of the individual, family, social reality and culture predicts violent or aggressive behavior.

Some of the individual variables associated with bullying behavior include aggressive attitudes, lack of empathy, and depression (Espelage & Swearer, 2003). Aggressive attitudes in middle school children predict successive violent behavior and bullying (McConville, & Cornell, 2003). Substance use has been associated with school bullying as well (Carlyle & Steinman, 2007). Bullying can be also viewed as a component of general antisocial behavior; between 35% and 40% of the students characterized as bullies have been arrested at age 24 (Olweus, 1995). It has also been reported that bullies are overly aggressive, impulsive, oppositional, destructive and having problems in processing social information (Smokowski,

& Kopasz, 2005). Bullies are considered deficient in their ability to interpret and handle social information. Their social interaction with peers could respond to this problem of processing social information (Gini, 2006). In addition, it has been found that bullies lack social skills and show poorer school achievement (Andreou, 2001).

Family can work as an effective and positive context of human development or, alternatively, it can play a destructive or disruptive role (Bronfenbrenner, 1987). In criminology, family instability, disintegration and disruption constitute a central part in the explanation of delinquency development (Wells & Rankin, 1991). Family conflicts, the loss of parents, and the lack of child-rearing abilities are factors that could take part in the development of antisocial behavior and delinquency (Widom, & Ames, 1994). McCord (2001) argues that parents or caretakers forge criminals through their rearing practices in three forms: 1) by the transmission of values through their own actions and the actions that they approve, 2) by the lack of leagues with and between the members of the family, and 3) by establishing the legitimacy of antisocial actions, through the methods that they use to satisfy their desires. Children learn that what it is valued within the family environment is good or bad for the rest of society.

Parenting styles are also related to children's behavior; child victimization in home is associated to bullying behavior (Dussich & Maekoya, 2007). Permissive parental style has been linked to bullying; the lack of supervision and attention allows disruptive behaviors of children (Smokowski, & Kopasz, 2005). Aggressive children are exposed to inconsistent discipline and physical punishment from their parents (Carney, & Merrell, 2001). Vygotsky (1978), who developed the Social Development Theory, suggested that child development depends on social interactions and bullying is a product of the interactions of the child with his/her family. Physically abused children reproduce the abusive relationship with their peers, as victims or abusers (Swinforde, DeMaris, Cernkovich, & Giordano, 2000). Dussich and Maekoya (2007) argue that physical punishment causes two kinds of effects on human relationships: first, children learn the power relationship, which means that some persons try to dominate others through aggression, and; second, they find that one part of the relationship is vulnerable, lonely, and powerless. Olweus (1993), in his early research, noted that some family factors influence bullying; parents of bullies were more tolerant to aggressive behavior. The aggressive authoritarian style may lead to children to imitate aggressive behavior in the case of bullies: on the one hand, the response to coercive parenting may result in beliefs and strategies about power and relationships; on the other hand, parents who promote collaborative decision-making with their children model more pro social behavior (Nation, Vieno, Perkins, and Santinello, 2007). Parental models about how to shape and maintain a relationship may result in patterns of human relations (Curtner-Smith, 2000). Theories about parenting and bullying are inconsistent; however, research indicates that parents who are inconsistent, permissive or fail to control children aggressive behavior may promote bullying behavior. Studies have indicated that bullies came from families with parents who are authoritarian, hostile, rejecting, and have poor problem-solving skills (Ma, 2001). Dussich and Maekoya (2007) conducted a comparative study among Japan, South Africa, and The United States, and found that physically-abused children had more likelihood of being involved in bullying behavior.

The exosystem is the second level in Bronfenbrenner's (1987) model and is formed by the community. It includes the institutions mediating between the cultural and the familiar systems and is structured by school, church, mass media, recreational institutions and organisms of security. School constitutes a preponderant part in the environment of young people; they remain a substantial part of their time in this place, which contributes to children intellectual, emotional, and social development. School is the place wherein young people acquire knowledge, but also it is the setting where they are trained for social relations and where they are exposed to varied social norms, rules and customs of their community. The form in which school exerts its influence on students is through its policies, which are reflected in the establishment of rules and their endorsement. A relation between school environment, delinquency and violent behavior exists; a positive school climate allows prosocial relations between students and professors, and among students (Angenent & Man, 1996). It is likely that children in schools learn patterns of antisocial and criminal actions and that some stimuli of the school context promote more than others the appearance and the maintenance of those negative actions. The school climate is one of the most important contexts of coexistence for adolescents with their peers and it is also the place in which they receive more influence from those peers. A negative school environment can lead students to antisocial behavior, as has been show by Lotz and Lee (1999).

School norms also predict bullying; some schools have clear rules, discipline policies and their strict application. However, when schools lack regulations or the application of them is arbitrary, students may perceive that authorities excuse inappropriate behavior. This also occurs when teachers do not intervene in cases of bullying, which can be seen as a part of the school's normal climate (Desouza & Ribeiro, 2005). School physical environment also may influence social interactions in this context (Boulton, 1999).

Positive school environments may prevent bullying from occurring; these environments promote social interactions with teachers and peers. A study found that tougher discipline and intensive supervision decrease bullying (Ma, 2001). On the contrary, Bradshaw, Sawyer, O'Brennan, (2009), in a study conducted in Maryland with 22,178 students, found that school-related indicators of disorder (student-teacher ratio, suspension rate, student mobility, concentration of student poverty) predicted bullying in schools. Khoury-Kassabri, Benbenishty, Astor, and Zeira, (2004) carried out a national study in The United States and found that the perception of students about fairness in their school, clarity of rules, and discipline consistency from school authorities are the most important predictors of school violence. Thus, negative school climate increases the risk for violence (Wilson, 2004), while emotional support from teachers causes a more positive behavior in students (Bru, Stephens, & Torsheim, 2002). Student participation in decision-making processes at school is also linked to a positive environment and to less aggressive acts; student- teacher relationship is important in reducing school violence as well (Nation, Vieno, Perkins, and Santinello, 2007). Bullying is higher in boys and girls that score high in misconduct and believe that teachers will not punish them (Desouza, & Ribeiro, 2005).

The community contextual settings also influence school violence; neighborhoods with less social cohesion and greater economic disadvantage increase the risk for aggressive behavior in schools (Tolan, Gorman-Smith, & Henry, 2003).

The macrosystem includes much further of the immediate situation that affects the person. It is the amplest context, embracing the social organization, the systems of beliefs and the lifestyles that prevail in a culture or subculture (Bronfenbrenner, 1987). Integration in society is part of the acculturation of individuals into conventional institutions, norms and customs (Angenent & Man, 1996). Positive attitudes to use aggression for solving conflicts have been related to bullying (Eliot & Cornell, 2009). Children may bully because they have a negative view of the victims and they accept this kind of behavior. Students with positive attitudes towards bullying engage more frequently in bullying (Boulton, Trueman, & Flemington, 2002).

BEHAVIOR AND BEHAVIORAL SETTINGS

The manner in which school environments shape behavior has been studied by environmental psychologist; among the earliest works in this area are those by Barker (1968) and Barker and Wright (1951). These researchers began by observing children individually in the diverse environments where they developed and found that children behaved differently depending on *where they were*. This research led to the establishment of a new area of investigation aimed at studying "behavioral settings," which are conceived as a group of behavioral patterns linked to a specific context. The establishment of this new research unit was due to the findings of Barker and Wright who demonstrated that behavior was linked/associated to the setting where it took place.

Researchers, in a consistent manner, registered that behaviors always occurred in a specific time and place and that people behaved according to those specific spatial-temporal contexts. So important is the context in which a behavior occurs, that people in an environment can change (i.e., they may be removed from it) and still the new people in that environment will behave *the same* way (Bechtel, 1997). Accordingly, it has been demonstrated that students respond with better grades and conduct in environments that are more 'humanly" designed; in other words, in places where students are treated fairly and with dignity. Bechtel (1997) suggests that an adverse school environment is a factor that significantly influences on spawning delinquency, due to the fact that it does not fulfill its function in guiding youngsters who attend schools.

Environmental criminology indicates that behavior results from a person-situation interaction and that the environment plays an essential role propitiating crime and determining its course, so that a particular kind of environment influences the possibility of offending (Wortley & Mazarolle, 2008). Therefore, crime not only results from individual variables but also from contextual factors. On the one hand, the environment shapes the lifestyle of the offender, creating her/his needs and motives (Wortley & Mazarolle, 2008) and, on the other hand, it offers opportunities to commit a crime (Cornish & Clarke, 2006). According to the Rational Choice Theory, the immediate environment is the source of information the individual uses to decide his/her committing a crime; the motivated criminal evaluates the opportunities based on the likelihood of rewards, the required effort and the risks involved. Thus, crime results from motivations, desires and preferences of the offender, combined with environmental opportunities and constraints (Clarke & Cornish, 2001). This theory also establishes that crime is more likely to occur if the offender converges with a suitable victim in absence of guardians; in other words, the offender needs to find a target in an appropriate setting (Felson, 2000). The process varies depending on the right targets, the time and the space in the scenery of crime (Felson & Poulsen 2003). In this sense, victims and offenders must converge in space and time for a crime to occur. Therefore, crime extends when an individual with some criminal inclination encounters a suitable target in a situation enough to activate the readiness potential, meaning that the expected benefits surpass the cost and risks.

Environmental criminology also indicates that crime occurs in a setting created by the urban appearance. The urban scenery (roads, land use, entertainment areas, and shopping areas) develops routines and creates suitable areas for crime. This scenery is called "crime generators," and involves areas in which a large number of unrelated person converge for different activities (Brantingham & Brantingham, 2008). Brantingham and Brantingham (2008) argue that crime is clustered and is influenced by crime generators. Some researchers (Jeffery, 1977; & Newman, 1972) establish that crime can be controlled by properly designed spaces. Elements that prompt the "normal" use of space discourage the abnormal or illegitimate use (Cozens, 2008).

Some places and situations propitiate bullying more than others; children are more frequently bullied during recess at school. In this time there are more opportunities, since more vulnerable children are present as well as less supervision and less structured activities are noticed (Rigby, 2002).

VICTIMS' CHARACTERISTICS

Sometimes it is difficult to differentiate victims from bullies, because frequently bullies become victims and victims become bullies (Ma, 2001). Ma (2001) conducted a study in a Canadian province and proved this victim-bully circle to be real. Some students are solely victims or bullies, but some are classified as bully-victim. Studies around the world indicate about 10% of incidence of this cycle (Ma, 2001; Alikasifoglu, Erginoz, Ercan, Uysal, & Albayrak-Kaymak, 2007). Carlyle and Steinman (2007) in a study conducted in The United States found that 7% of the students were victims and bullies, and depressive affect was associated with victimization.

Olweus (1993) argues that victims are students with few friends and overprotected by their parents. Victims are usually more anxious and insecure than students in general; they are also cautions, sensitive, and quiet (Olweus, 1995). They lack social skills, rarely defend themselves, exhibit low self-esteem, high social anxiety, and fear to negative peer evaluation (Slee, 1994). Nation, Vieno, Perkins, and Santinello (2007) conducted a national survey with 4386 students from 243 middle and secondary schools in Italy and found that chronically-bullied students had lower social competence. The findings also suggested that disempowered students by teachers may balance by oppressing (bullying) or become a victim. The lack of personal power has been also associated with bullying victimization. The majority of the victims are considered submissive, but some of they are also aggressive, and lack communication and assertive skills (Smokowski, & Kopasz, 2005). Another study showed that victims had poorer emotional and social adjustment, which causes that they have great difficulty to make friends, fewer relationships with peers, and loneliness (Nansel, Overpeck, Pilla, Ruan, Simons-Morton, & Scheidt 2001). Victims see themselves as insignificant, unattractive and unintelligent (Carney & Merrell, 2001). Victims are unable to report the victimization, which could cause to be the target of recurrent abuse (Olweus, 1995).

INTERVENTION PROGRAMS

In response to school violence, policies, programs or strategies to reduce or prevent this problem have been elaborated. The prevention programs have been classified as targeted or universal (Orpinas, Horne, & Staniszewski, 2003). The targeted are directed to students at risk of perpetuating aggressive behavior or to individuals who already committed violent acts. The universal programs are designed to prevent the problem; they are designed for every person at school settings.

One strategy aimed to eliminate the problem is zero tolerance policies; however, its fairness has resulted controversial and it has not proved to be effective in reducing violence or in improving schools' environment (Skiba, 2000). Moreover, it has been criticized because it does not solve the problem and does not seek strategies to reach it, also sending a message to the students that they will not be heard (Orpinas, Horne, & Staniszewski, 2003).

A conflict resolution skill program for students, teachers and parents is one of the universal strategies designed to prevent bullying. This approach has been providing mixed results. Some interventions directed to teachers have reduced violence in schools and created a positive climate between teachers and students. However, it has not been effective in family intervention (Ialongo, Poduska, Whertamer, & Kellam, 2001). Parental involvement in schools programs directed to teach the use of conflict resolution skills in daily life has been very effective in preventing bullying (Kenny, McEachem, & Aluede, 2005).

Other universal programs are designed to change school climate. They establish clear rules and consequences for breaking them, and the positive behavior is rewarded, identifying and working with school values (Orpinas, Horne, & Staniszewski, 2003). Positive multicultural environments involving respect and tolerance for everyone have been encouraged to reduce violence (Aluedse, 2006). A better supervision is necessary, especially during recess and lunch (Garrett, 2003). Empathy training has also been used to help victims and bullies; it teaches students to understand others' feelings and to treat peers with gentleness (Aluedse, 2006). This training has been effective in reducing aggressiveness in schools.

Olweus (1994) argues that a combination of strategies reduces approximately 50% of bullying; it consists of parental and teacher involvement, supervision and vigilance, the elaboration of clear and firm rules against bullying. Teaching assertiveness and problem-solving skills to victims, bullies, and parents increase students' and teachers' social competence, and changes school climate. A warmth climate with strict application of the rules and non-aggressive consequences for bullying behavior has been effective in reducing bullying. Although more intervention programs are directed to prevention of bullying, it is argued that they should pay attention to victims. Some programs are directed to help victims to be more assertive, to express their feelings and to seek help in appropriate times (Varjas, Meyers, Henrich, Graybill *et al.*, 2006).

General recommendations to prevent bullying and intervene in bullying cases have been established. A number of them are attributable to Olweus (1993) and others to Allensworth, Lawson, Nicholson *et al.* (1997) and Edmonson and Hoover (2008). Some of the recommendations are:

1. Involvement of parents, teachers and other adults. These include training school staff and volunteers, and networking community organizations. The promotion of community activities and the media is encouraged.
2. Training to understand bullying , which also provides anti-bullying education
3. Modeling positive behaviors. Desirable behavior is demonstrated in role playing, art work, songs and awards.
4. Establishment of school rules against bullying.
5. Teaching problem-solving skills and decision-making methods. They consist on anger management, empathy building, friendship making, and problem-solving skills.
6. Talking to bullies, victims and parents.

Ecological theory suggests that individual intervention will not be effective, since bullying behavior comprise at set of systems. Therefore, the efforts should be directed to reach all the intervening contexts. The community and family involvement are required as well as the participation of students and school personnel in the prevention or intervention program for bullying. Even in a school context the students' group participation is necessary to change and maintain behavior. The students' group could encourage the change (Andreou, Didaskalou, and Vlachou, 2007). Therefore, the objective of our study was to investigate the contextual and personal variables related to school bullying.

METHOD

Participants

The sample of this study was constituted by 126 teachers at 24 cities, towns and communities of the state of Sonora, Mexico. Eighty participants were female and 46 male. The average age of the sample was 31 years old (S. D.= 6,9, ranking from 22 to 52 years old). The participants have been working as teachers for an average of 8 years (S. D.= 6,1, ranking from 1 to 28). Teachers reported the socioeconomic level of the neighborhood at the school where they work, 2 schools were placed in conditions of extreme poverty (1,6%), 45 were situated in communities considered low class (35,7%), 44 of schools were located in lower middle class neighborhoods (34,93%), 25 in middle-class (19,84%) and 10 in upper middle class locations (7,93%). All of the teachers worked in public schools of the Sonora State Educational System, with 66% of them working in the elementary level of education.

Instruments

Five components of the instrument "Sample Survey for Teachers and Other Staff About Bullying" (Ministry Of Education, Ontario) were used. The Type of abuse, Context, Actions, Moment and abusive Conduct in school sub-scales were included; in addition, demographic variables were assessed: they included the city or locality of work, age, gender, educational level of the school and the socioeconomic context of the work place. The translation of the instrument into Spanish was conducted by a professional translator.

Table 1. Educational levels of the participating teachers

Educational level	Frequency	%	% accumul
Preschool	15	11.93	11.9
Elementary	83	65.97	77.90
Middle school	18	14.48	92.38
High school	01	00.89	93.27
Elementary and middle	03	02.38	95.65
Preschool and elementary	01	00.89	96.54
College	05	03.46	100.00
Total	126	100.00	100.00

Procedure

The instrument was administered at the schools where teachers were taking diverse educational advanced training courses during the vacation period of winter 2008. Teachers were approached at their classrooms; the interview took 30 minutes.

Data Analysis

Univariate analyses (means, standard deviations, minimum and maximum values) from the demographic data and the scales used were performed; also we conducted reliability analysis for every scales (see Table 3). An index for the time of abuse was created, and parcels for action taken, perception of bullying, and bullying were constructed. An index is the mean of responses to items of a scale. Finally a structural equation model (SEM) was specified to measure the relationships between context, as exogenous variable, and action taken, perception, and time of bullying as intermediate variables on the dependent variable bullying.

A SEM contains two models: the measurement model and the structural model. The first is fundamentally a confirmatory factor analysis wherein the relations between the observed variables and its corresponding factors are specified and tested (Bryant & Yarnold, 1998). The structural model estimates the covariances between the constructed factors, as well as between manifest variables and latent factors. In this study, the measurement model was created from the relationship between indexes and their corresponding latent variables. Four latent variables were specified: perception of the abuse, context, teachers' actions taken and bullying. Two indicators of goodness of fit were considered, the statistical and the practical ones. The statistical indicator was chi-square (X^2), which assesses the difference between the theorethical and the saturated model of variables' interrelations. X^2 is expected to produce a low and non-significant value ($p > .05$) if the theoretical model were to be not different from the saturated. However, this indicator is susceptible to sample size and it often results significant in function of the number of participants. To control this vulnerability the practical indicators are considered. These indicators control the effect of sample size on the significance level in the comparison of the two models. The practical indexes we used here were the non-normed fit index (NNFI) the comparative fit index (CFI) and the Bentler-Bonnet non-normed fit index (BBNNFI); a value higher than .90 is expected for these indicators (Bentler, 2006). The index root mean squared error of approximation (RMSEA) was utilized to measure the reasonable error of approximation in terms of goodness of fit, requiring a value less than .08 (Browne & Cudeck, 1993).

Results

Table 2 shows frequencies of bullying at the schools. Physical and verbal abuse were the most reported form of aggression (99%), while the least frequent was bullying for religion preferences (55%). Also a large percentage of the respondents reported bullying from social discrimination (95%).

Table 2. Frequencies and percentages of abuse

Kind of abuse	Frequencies and percentage				
	Never	Almost Never	Sometimes	Almost always	Always
Variables					
Physical	1(0.8%)	6(4.8%)	45(36%)	39(31%)	33(26%)
Verbal	1(0.8%)	9(7.1%)	44(35%)	31(25%)	40(32%)
Social Discrimination	6(4.8%)	29(23%)	51(40.5%)	23(18.3)	14(11.1%)
Electronic	54(43%)	38(30.2%)	23(18.3%)	6(4.8%)	2(1.6%)
Raze culture Discri.	35(28%)	43(34.1%)	29(23.7%)	11(8.7%)	6(4.8%)
Sex (sexual preference)	37(29%)	35(27.8%)	36(28.6%)	9(7.1%)	8(6.3%)
Religion	56(44%)	42(33.3%)	20(15.9%)	4(3.2%)	2(1.6%)
Gender	40(32.%)	40(31.7%)	31(24.6%)	11(8.7%)	3(2.4%)

All scales' alphas were higher than .60 as it is shown in Table 3. Teachers perceived that racial discrimination (mean=3.5) is more frequent than any other kind of bullying. The more reported places for the occurrence of bullying were the yard of the school (mean= 2.9) and the classroom (mean=2.8). The time of abuse is weekends (weekend programs) (mean=3.3); during the break (mean=2.9) and after school (mean=2.9) were also frequently reported. The most reported action taken is development and establishment of class rules (mean=2.8), increasing the supervision in the school (mean=2.5) and class discussion about abuse (mean=2.5).

Table 3. Descriptive statistics and scales' alphas

Variable	n	x	sd	min.	max.	Alpha
Perceptions of the problem at school						0.85
The child who physically abuse	125	3.1	.86	1	4	
The child who verbally abuse	124	3.1	.82	1	4	
The child who discriminates socially	124	2.7	.90	1	4	
The child who threatens by electronic means	118	2.1	1.0	1	4	
The child who discriminates racially	123	3.5	.94	1	4	

The child who sexually molest	123	2.3	1.0	1	4	
The child who bothers by type of religion	122	2.0	.90	1	4	
The child who bothers by appearance	122	2.8	.84	1	4	
There is a high level of bullying	121	2.3	.89	1	4	
Dedicates time and resources taking care problems	123	2.8	.82	1	4	
In relation to other priorities, we dedicated efforts	123	2.8	.74	1	4	
Invested most of time & possible resources	124	2.5	.80	1	4	
Kind of abuse						0.87
Physical abuse	124	2.7	.92	0	4	
Verbal abuse	125	2.8	1.0	0	4	
Social discrimination	123	2.0	1.0	0	4	
By electronic means	123	.89	.98	0	4	
Discrimination due to race or culture	124	1.2	1.1	0	4	
Due to sex preferences	125	1.3	1.1	0	4	
Due to religion preferences	124	.82	.92	0	4	
Due to gender	125	1.1	1.0	0	4	
Context or place of bullying						0.91
Classroom	124	2.8	1.3	0	5	
Hall	117	1.6	1.9	0	5	
Entrances and exits at school	122	2.5	1.4	0	5	
Library	121	1.0	1.5	0	5	
Computer center	121	1.5	1.5	0	5	
Gymnasium or field of game	120	2.6	1.4	0	5	
Restrooms	121	2.5	1.5	0	5	
School bus	120	.99	1.8	0	5	
Yard of the school	121	2.9	1.1	0	5	
Way to school, roundtrip	123	2.7	1.9	0	5	
Store of the school or recess	122	2.6	1.5	0	5	
School parking	122	1.6	2.0	0	5	
Surrounding places of the school	120	2.5	2.0	0	5	
Time of abuse						0.72
Before school	122	2.6	1.3	1	5	
During class	123	2.4	1.0	1	5	
During break time	123	2.9	.95	1	5	
After school	122	2.9	1.3	1	5	
Weekends	121	3.3	1.7	1	5	
Actions against bullying						0.92
Prevention committee	124	1.4	.88	1	4	
School assembly and newspaper	124	1.7	.86	1	4	
Higher student supervision outside classroom	124	2.5	.66	1	4	
Rules and school policies about abuse	124	2.2	.88	1	4	
Personnel formation about abuse	124	1.9	.93	1	4	
Reorganization of physical places	124	1.8	.89	1	4	
Class discussion about abuse	124	2.5	.79	1	4	
Material in curriculum about prevention	123	1.8	.92	1	4	
Class exercises and written works	123	2.2	.85	1	4	
Development & establishment of class rules	123	2.8	.45	1	4	
Intervention and support of classmates	123	2.3	.85	1	4	
Participation of students in the committee	123	1.5	.90	1	4	
Student activities	122	1.6	.94	1	4	
Individual advise to students (bullies)	122	2.1	.93	1	4	
Individual advise to victims	121	2.0	.99	1	4	
Group advise to students (bullies)	122	1.9	.94	1	4	
Group advise to victims	122	1.8	.98	1	4	

Table 3. (Continued).

Variable	n	x	sd	min.	max.	Alpha
Special workshops to victim groups	122	1.4	.94	1	4	
Information to parents	122	2.0	.91	1	4	
Seminars and school presentations	122	1.5	.90	1	4	
Invitation parents participate in prevention	122	1.9	.98	1	4	
Meetings with community leaders	121	1.4	.83	1	4	
Diffusion mass media school Achievements	123	1.5	.86	1	4	
Invitation to community organizations and leaders to participate in school activities	123	1.5	.89	1	4	

Results of the structural model are shown in figure 1; circles represent the latent variables and rectangles the observed variables. The relations between variables are represented by the arrows of the figure. Continuous lines represent statistically significant relations ($p < .05$). The path coefficients are expressed as standardized regression (*beta*) weights. The four proposed latent variables were significantly (t>1.96, $p < .05$) related to their observed variables. The context of abuse had a direct effect on perception of abuse (structural coefficient .56), action taken (structural coefficient .20) and time (.55), and these variables directly and significantly influenced the dependent variable bullying (perception of abuse, structural coefficient .64, action taken .25 and time .23). Context had an indirect effect on bullying through these variables.

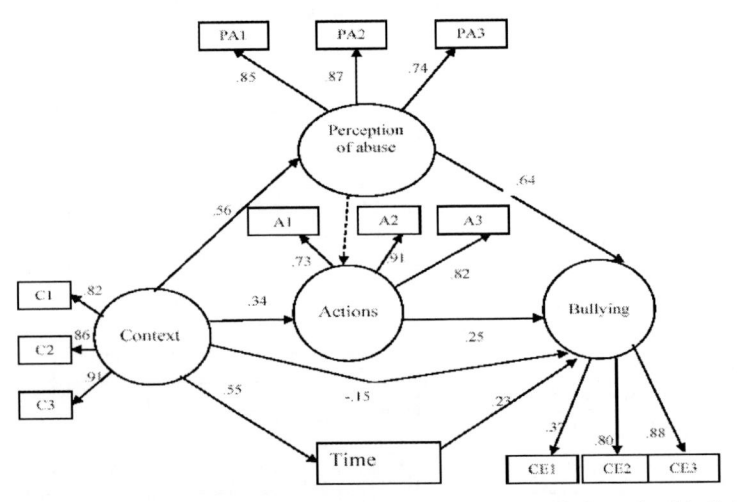

Figure 1. Results of the model of environmental and personal variables prediction school bullying. The structural coefficients and factor loadings with continued lines are significant at $p < .05$. Goodness of fit: Chi-square = 74.12 (57 df), p=.06; NNFI = .91; CFI = .97; RMSEA=.05. R-Square = .47.

CONCLUSION

Results of the study presented in this chapter seem to reinforce the main tenets of theories explaining bullying behavior. These results showed a direct effect of context of bullying on the perception of abuse, actions taken and time of abuse, which, in turn, affected bullying. These findings indicate that the physical environment exert an influence on the behavior of students and teachers. Newman's theory (1972) argues that environmental spaces indirectly affect criminal behavior and Jeffery (1977) claims that the design of the environment influences behavior (Wortley & Mazarolle, 2008). The effect of the context on the time of bullying is explained by Rational Choice Theory: abusers perceive environmental clues that facilitate bullying; they choose the appropriate places and time for abuse. According to this theory, offenders seek the places and time that offers less risk to commit the abusive behavior (Cornish & Clarke, 2006). Another interpretation could be that in these times and places is when and where most students keep together at school, socializing and probably exerting pressure to engage in abusive behaviors. Situations may exert social pressure on individuals to perform inappropriate behaviors. Environmental criminologists argue that criminal behavior occurs when the opportunities are present in a given space and time. Bullying occurs more frequently at school yards during recess. These results are similar to others found by analogous studies (Rigby, 2002); bullying takes place in unsupervised areas and because bullies find opportunities. The context also predicts teachers' perception of bullying, indicating that teachers perceive differently aggressive actions of the students in more informal environments as the school yard: the same action could be evaluated as less violent than in the classroom. Action taken for the teacher was also predicted by context, meaning that aggressive behavior during recess could be interpreted as "playing", but a similar behavior at the classroom could be not tolerated. Teachers seem to be stricter at the classroom than outside.

The action taken by teachers also had a direct effect on bullying. Bullying increase could depend on teachers' actions. If these actions are not administered with regularity or equity they may create an unlawful environment (Desouza & Ribeiro, 2005). It has been found that the inexistence of regulations or their unjust application could cause that students perceive their inappropriate behavior as justified by teachers. Bullying was also affected by the perception of abuse: if teachers perceive that bullying is minor they could not pay so much attention to it. Bradshaw and colleagues (2007) found that teachers tend to underestimate the abuse; yet this could be permeated by the context where abuse occurs.

Time had a direct effect on bullying, as environmental criminology considers. Criminal or antisocial behavior, in this case bullying, occurs when opportunities are present, in this case during break time at school. In addition, the effect of context on bullying was indirect, which could imply that the setting affords the occasion for bullying, although the context does not directly causes it. These results evidence the complexity of the problem and can guide future research.

Our study did not consider either individual or family variables of bullies; therefore it should be replicated including these variables. Ecological theories indicate that behavior is a result of the combination of individual, family, social and cultural factors (Bronfenbrenner, 1987). In addition, it is important to consider multi-informant reports of behavior; in this study we considered teachers' reports but it is important to analyze the opinion of students and parents.

Several research strategies have been implemented in diverse countries approaching bullying and most of them recognize that the problem is multifactorial; thus interventions should follow its complex nature. Some successful interventions have considered the Ecological Model, including family and community aspects, in the intervention. One mechanism used to encompass the participation of all the contextual systems implicated in bullying has been called "Participatory Action Research," which includes researchers, educators, families, students, and communities (Leff, Angelucci, Goldstein, Cardaciotto, Paskewich, & Grossman, 2007). This kind of programs promotes ecological participation and validity. The intervention programs in our cultural (Mexican) reality would also be well served by considering the findings we presented here: The context where bullying occurs more frequently is the school yard; therefore actions should be implemented aimed at eliminating the opportunities for bullies at these settings, for example more supervision during recess. Teachers should also pay more attention to certain behaviors that are apparently (or are perceived) as games, but that could be (sometimes subtle) forms of bullying. Promoting cooperative behavior, empathy among students could also decrease bullying. Families, schools and communities should work together to provide a safer environment to young people.

Education is considered a fundamental right for children (Convention of the right of the Child, 1989; Mexican Constitution, 2009). Safety in schools should be part of this fundamental right. No child should feel fear from attending school, or from being harassed or degraded.

REFERENCES

Alikasifoglu, M., Erginoz, E., Ercan, O., Uysal, O., & Albayrak-Kaymak, D. (2007). Bullying behaviours and psychosocial health: results from a cross-sectional survey among high school students in Istanbul, Turkey. *European Journal of Pediatrics,* 166, 1253–1260.

Allensworth, D., Lawson, E., Nicholson, L., *et al.* (Eds). (1997). *Schools and health: Our nation's investment.* Washington, DC: National Academy Press.

Aluedse, O. (2006). Bullying in Schools: A form of child abuse in schools. *Educational Research Quarterly,* 30(1), 37-41.

Andreou. E. (2001). Bully/victim problems and their association with coping behavior in conflictual peer interactions among school-age children. *Educational Psychology,* 21 , 5 9 - 66.

Andreou, E., Didaskalou, E., and Vlachou, A. (2007). Evaluating the Effectiveness of a Curriculum-based Anti-bullying Intervention Program in Greek Primary Schools. *Educational Psychology, 27, 693–711.*

Angenent, H., & Man, A. (1996). Background Factors of Juvenile Delinquency. New York.:Peter Lang Publishing.

Baldwin, M. W. (1992). Relational schemas and the processing of social information. *Psychological Bulletin, 112,* 461-484.

Barker, R. (1968). *Ecological Psychology.* Standford, CA: Standford University Press.

Barker, R., & Wright, H. (1951). One boy's day. New York: Row Peterson.

Bandura, A. (1986). *Social foundations of thought and action: A social cognitive theory.* Englewood Cliffs, NJ: Prentice Hall.

Bechtel, B. (1997). Environment & Behavior. Thousand Oaks, Ca.: Sage Publications.

Belsky, J. (1993). Etiology of child maltreatment, a developmental-ecological analysis. *Psychological Bulletin*, *114* (3), 413-434.

Beran, T. (2008). Stability of Harassment in Children: Analysis of the Canadian National Longitudinal Survey of Children and Youth Data *The Journal of Psychology, 142*(2), 131–146.

Bond, L., Carlin,J. B., Thomas, L., Rubin, K., & Patton, G. (2001). Does bullying cause emotional problems: A prospective study of young teenagers. *British Medical Journal. 323.* 480-483.

Boulton, M. J. (1999). Concurrent and longitudinal relations between children's play ground behavior and social preference, victimization and bullying. *Child Development,* 70(4), 944-954.

Boulton, M. J., Trueman, M., & Flemington, I. (2002). Associations between Secondary School Pupils' Definitions of Bullying, Attitudes towards Bullying, and Tendencies to Engage in Bullying: age and sex differences. *Educational Studies, 28* (4),*353-370.*

Bowlby, J. (1969). *Attachment and loss: Vol. 1. Attachment.* New York: Basic Books.

Bowlby, J. (1988) *A Secure Base: Parent-Child Attachment and Healthy Human Development.* London: Basic Books

Bradshaw, C, P., Sawyer, A. L., & O'Brennan, L. M. (2007). Bullying and peer victimization at school: Perceptual differences between students and school staff. *School Psychology Review, 36,* 359-380.

Bradshaw, C. P., Sawyer, A. L., & O'Brennan, L. M. (2009). A Social Disorganization Perspective on Bullying-Related Attitudes and Behaviors: The Influence of School Context. *American Journal Community Psychology,* 43, 204–220.

Brantingham, P. & Brantingham, P. (2008). Crime pattern Theory. In R. Wortley, & L. Mazarolle, (eds). Environmental Criminology and Crime Analysis. Portland, Oregon: William Publishing

Bronfenbrenner, U. (1987). La ecología del desarrollo Humano. Barcelona, España: Ed. Paidós

Browne, M. W. & Cudeck, R. (1993). Alternative ways of assessing model fit. In: Bollen, K. A. & Long, J. S. (Eds.) *Testing Structural Equation Models.* pp. 136–162. Beverly Hills, CA: Sage

Bru, E., Stephens, P., & Torsheim, T. (2002). Students' perceptions of class management and reports of their own misbehavior. *Journal of School Psychology,* 40, 287-307.

Bryant, F., & Yarnold, P. (1998). Principal–components analysis and exploratory and confirmatory factor analysis. In L. Grimm & P. Yarnold (Eds.), *Reading and understanding multivariate statistics* (pp. 99–136). Washington, DC, USA: American Psychological Association.

Carlyle, K. E. & Steinman, K. J. (2007). Demographic differences in the prevalence, co-occurrence, and correlates of adolescent bullying at school. *Journal of School Health,* 77, 623-629.

Carney, A, G.. & Merrell.K.W. (2001). Bullying in schools: Perspectives on understanding and preventing an international problem. *School Psychology international, 22,* 364-382.

Chapell, M. S., Hasselman, S. L., Kitchin, T., Lomon, S. N., MacIver, K. W., and Sarullo, P. L. (2006). Bullying in elementary school, high school, and college. *Adolescence, 41(164),* 633-648.

Clarke, R. V. & Cornish, D. B. (2001). Rational Choice. In R. Paternoster and R. Bachman (eds). Explaining Criminals and Crime: Essays in contemporary Criminological Theory. Los Angeles, CA: Roxburry.

Convention of the right of the Child(1989). UNICEF. Retrieved on September 29 2009 from: http://www.unicef.org/crc/fulltext.htm

Cornish, D. B. & Clarke, R. V. (2006). Rational Choice perspective. In S. Henry and M.M. Lanier (eds). The Essential Criminology Reader. Boulder, CO: Westview Press.

Cozens, P. (2008). Crime prevention Through environmental design. . In R. Wortley, & L. Mazarolle, (eds). Environmental Criminology and Crime Analysis. Portland, Oregon: William Publishing

Craig, W. M. (1998). The relationship among bullying, victimization, depression, anxiety and aggression in elementary school children. *Personality and Individual Differences,* 24, 123– 130.

Crick, N. R., Casas, J. F., & Hyon-Chin, K. (1999). Relational and physical forms of peer victimization in preschool. *Developmental Psychology,* 35, 376–385.

Crick, N. R. & Grotpeter J. K. (1995) Relational aggression, gender, and social-pyschological adjustment. *Child Development,* 66, 710-722

Curtner-Smith, M. E. (2000). Mechanisms by which family processes contribute to school-age boy's bullying. *Child Study Journal,* 30, 169–186.

Desouza, E. R. & Ribeiro, J. (2005). Bullying and Sexual Harassment Among Brazilian High School Students *Journal of Interpersonal Violence,*20(9), 1018-1038.

Ducharme, J., Doyle, A. B. & Markiewicz, D. (2002) 'Attachment Security with Mother and Father: Associations with Adolescents' Reports of Interpersonal Behavior with Parents and Peers', *Journal of Personal and Social Relationships* 19: 203–31.

Due, P., Holstein, B. E., Lynch, J., Diderichsen, F., Gabhain, S. N., Scheidt, P., & Currie, C., and the health behavior in school-aged children bulling working group. (2005). Bullying and symptoms in school-aged children: International comparative cross sectional study in 28 countries. *European Journal of Public health,* 15 (2), 128-132.

Dussich, J. P. J. & Maekoya, C. (2007). Physical Child Harm and Bullying-Related Behaviors: A Comparative Study in Japan, South Africa, and the United States *International Journal of Offender Therapy and Comparative Criminology,* 51(5), 495-509.

Edmondson, L. and Hoover, J. (2008). Process Evaluation of a Bullying Prevention Program:A Public School-County Health Partnership. *Reclaiming Children and Youth,* 16(4), 25-33.

Eliot, M. &. Cornell, D. G.(2009). Bullying in Middle School as a Function of Insecure Attachment and Aggressive Attitudes. *School Psychology International;* 30; 201-214.

Elliott, D. S., Hamburg, B. A., & Williams, K. R. (1998). *Violence in American schools.* New York: Cambridge University Press.

Elliott, D. S., Wilson, W. J., Huizinga, D., Sampson, R. J., Elliott, A.,& Rankin, B. (1996). The effects of neighborhood disadvantage on adolescent development. *Journal of Research of Crime and Delinquency,* 33, 493–517.

Espelage, D. L. & Swearer, S. M. (2003). Bullying in American Schools: A social Ecologial Perspective on Intervention and Prevention. New Jersey: Lawrence Erlbaum Associates Publishers.

Felson, M. (2000). The Routine Activity Approach: A very Versatile Theory of Crime. In R. Paternoster and R. Bachman (eds) Explaining Criminals and Crime: Essays in *Contemporary Criminological theory.* Los Angeles, CA: Roxbury.

Felson, M. & Poulsen, E.(2003). Simple indicators of crime by time of day. *International Journal of Forescasting*, 19, 595- 601.

Ferguson, C. J., San Miguel, C., Kilburn, J. C. Jr., & Sanchez, P. (2007). The Effectiveness of School-Based Anti-Bullying Programs A Meta-Analytic Review. *Criminal Justice Review*, 32 (4), 401-414.

Fleming, L. C. & Jacobsen, K. H. (2009). Bullying and Symptoms of Depression in Chilean Middle School Students. *Journal of School Health*, 79(3), 130-137.

Forero, R., McLellan, L., Rissel, C., & Bauman, A. (1999). Bullying behavior and psychosocial health among school students in New South Wales, Australia: cross sectional survey, *British Medical Journal*, 319; 344-348.

Garrett, A.G. (2003). Bullying in American schools: Causes, preventions and interventions. Jefferson, NC: McFarland &Co.

Gini, G. (2006). Social cognition and moral cognition in bullying: What's wrong? *Aggressive Behavior*, 32, 528-539.

Giora, A., Gega, L., Landau, S., & Marks, I. (2005). Adult recall of having being bullied in attenders of an anxiety disorder unit and attenders of a dental clinic: A pilot controlled study. Behavior Change, 22(1), 44-49.

Glew, G., Rivara, E, & Feudmer, C. (2000). Bullying: Children hurting children. *Pediatrics in Review*, 21,183-190.

Greek Institute of Mental Health. (2000). *International research of school population health: Greek students* (A. Kokkevi, Ed.). Athens: Institute of Mental Health.

Ialongo, N. S., Poduska, J., Werthamer, L., & Kellam, S. (2001). The distal impact of two first-grade preventive interventions on conduct problems and disorder in early adolescence. *Journal of Emotional and Behavioral Disorders*, 9, 146-160.

Jeffery, C. R. (1977). Crime Prevention Through Environmental Design. Bervely Hills, CA: Sage.

Kaltiala-Heino, R., Rimpelä, M., Marttunen, M., Rimpelä, A., & Rantanen, P. (1999). Bullying, depression, and suicidal ideation in Finnish adolescents: school survey. *British Medical Journal*, 319, 348-351.

Kaltiala-Heino, R., Rimpela, M., Rantanen, P., & Rimpela, A. (2000). Bullying at school: an indicator of adolescents at risk for mental disorders. *Journal of Adolescence*, 23(6), 661-674.

Kenny, M.C., McEachem, A.G., & Aluede, O. (2005). Female bullying: Prevention and counseling interventions. In O. Aluede, A.G. McEachem & M.C. Kenny (Eds.). Peer victimization in schools: An international perspective (pp. 13-19). New- Delhi, India: Kamla- Raj Enterprises.

Khoury-Kassabri, M., Benbenishty, R., Astor, R. A., & Zeira, A. (2004). The contributions of community, family, and school variables to student victimization. *American Journal of Community Psychology*, 34(3/4), 187–204.

Koth, C. W., Bradshaw, C. P., & Leaf, P. J. (2008). A multilevel study of predictors of student perceptions of school climate: The effect of classroom-level factors. *Journal of Educational Psychology*, 100, 96–104.

Leff, S. S., Angelucci, J., Goldstein, A. B., Cardaciotto, L., Paskewich, B., & Grossman, M. (2007). Using a participatory action research model to create a schoolbased intervention program for relationally aggressive girls: The Friend to Friend Program. In J. Zins, M. Elias, & C. Maher (Eds.), *Bullying, victimization, and peer harassment: Handbook of*

prevention and intervention in peer harassment, victimization, and bullying (pp. 199-218). New York: Haworth Press.
Limber, S. P. (2002). *Addressing youth bullying behaviors*. Published in the Proceedings of the Educational Forum on Adolescent Health on Youth Bullying. Chicago: American Medical Association.
Lotz, R., & Lee, L. (1999). Sociability, school experience, and delinquency. *Youth & Society*, 31, 199-223.
Ma, S. (2001). Bullying and Being Bullied: To What Extent Are Bullies Also Victims? *American Educational Research Journal, 38(2), 351–370.*
McConville, D. & Cornell, D. G. (2003). 'Aggressive Attitudes Predict Aggressive Behavior in Middle School Students. *Journal of Emotional and Behavioral Disorders*, 11, 179–187.
McCord, J. (2001). Forging Criminals in the Family. En W. Kluber (Ed.) Handbook of Youth and justice. New York: Academic/Plenum Publishers.
Mc Guckin, C., & Lewis, C. A. (2006). Experiences of school bullying in northern ireland: data from the life and times survey. *Adolescence, 41(162), 313-320.*
Nansel, T. Overpeck, M. Pilla, R. Ruan, W., Simons-Morton, B., & Scheidt, P. (2001). Bullying Behaviors among US Youth: Prevalence and Association with Psychosocial Adjustment. *Journal of the American Medical Association,* 285, 2094-2100.
Nation, M., Vieno, A., Perkins, D. D., and Santinello, M. (2007). Bullying in School and Adolescent Sense of Empowerment: An Analysis of Relationships with Parents, Friends, and Teachers. *Journal of Community & Applied Social Psychology,* 18, 211–232.
Newman, O. (1972). Defensible space: Crime Prevention Through Urban Design. New York: Msmillan.
Olweus, D. (1993). Bullying at school: What we know and what we can do (pp. 353– 365). USA: Blackwell.
Olweus, D. (1994). Annotation: Bullying at school: Basic facts and effects of a school based intervention program. *Journal of Child Psychology and Psychiatry, 35,* 1171–1190
Olweus, D. (1995). Bullying or peer abuse at school: Facts and intervention. Current directions in *Psychological Science,* 4, 196-200.
Orpinas, P., Horne, A. M., & Staniszewski, D. (2003). School Bullying: Changing the problems by changing the school. *School psychology Review,* 32(3), 431-444.
Oyaziwo,A.(2006) Bullying in school:A Form of Child Abuse in Schools. *Educational Research Quarterly, v30* n1 p37-49
Rigby, K. (2000). Effects of peer victimization in schools and perceived social support on adolescent well-being. *Journal of adolescence*, 23, 57-68.
Rigby, K. (2002). New perspectives on bullying. Philadelphia, PA: Jessica Kingsley Publishers.
Salmivalli, C., Kaukiainen, A., Kaistaniemi, L., & Lagerspetz, K. M. J. (1999). Self-Evaluated Self-Esteem, Peer-Evaluated Self-Esteem, and Defensive Egotism as Predictors of Adolescents' Participation in Bullying Situations. *Personality and Social Psychology Bolletin,* 25, 1268-1278.
Skiba, R. J. (2000) Zero tolerance: zero evidence: An análisis of school disciplinary pratice. Indiana Education Policy Center. Retrieved on august 8 2008, from: http://www.indiana.edu/~safeschl/ztze.pdf

Slee, P. T. (1994). Situational and interpersonal correlates of anxiety associated with peer victimization. *Child Psychology and Human Development, 25,* 97–107.

Smokowski, P. R., & Kopasz, K. H. (2005). Bullying in School: An Overview of Types, Effects, Family Characteristics, and Intervention Strategies. *Children & Schools, 27*(2), 101-110.

Stewart, E. A. (2003). School social bonds, school climate, and school misbehavior: A multilevel analysis. *Justice Quarterly, 20*(3), 575–604.

Swinforde, S. P., DeMaris, A., Cernkovich, S. A., & Giordano, P. C. (2000). Harsh physical discipline in childhood and violence in later romantic involvements: The mediating role of problem behaviors. *Journal of Marriage and Family 62,* 508-519.

Tolan, P. H., Gorman-Smith, D., & Henry, D. B. (2003). The developmental ecology of urban males' youth violence. *Developmental Psychology, 39*(2), 274–291.

Varjas, K., Meyers, J., Henrich, C. C, Graybill, E. C, Dew, B. J., Marshall, M. L., et al. (2006). Using a participatory culture-specific intervention model to develop a peer victimization intervention. *Journal of Applied School Psychology, 22,* 35-57.

Vygotsky, L. S. (1978). *Mind and society: The development of higher mental processes.* Cambridge, MA: Harvard University Press.

Wells, L.E., & Rankin, J. H. (1991). Families and Delinquency: A meta-analysis of the impact of Broken Homes. *Social Problems, 38,* 71-93.

White, N. A., & Loeber, R. (2008). Bullying and Special Education as Predictors of Serious Delinquency, *Journal of Research in Crime and Delinquency,* 45(4), 380-397

Whitney, I., & Smith, P. K. (1993). A survey of the nature and extent of bullying in junior/middle and secondary schools. Educational Research, 35, 3–25.

Whitted, K. S., & Dupper, D. R. (2005). Best Practices for Preventing or Reducing Bullying in Schools. *Children & Schools,* 17(3), 167-175

Widom, C. S., & Ames, A. (1994). Criminal consequences of childhood sexual victimization. *Child Abuse & Neglect, 18,* 303-318.

Wilson, D. (2004). The interface of school climate and school connectedness and relationships with aggression and victimization. *Journal of School Health, 74,* 293–299.

Wong, D.S.W., Lok, D. P. P., Lo, T.W., & Ma, S. K. (2008). School Bullying Among Hong Kong Chinese Primary Schoolchildren. *Youth & Society, 40*(1), 35-54.

Woods, S., & Wolke, D. (2003). Direct and relational bullying among primary school children and academic achievement. *Journal of School Psychology, 42,* 135-155.

Wortley, R., & Mazarolle, L. (2008). Environmental Criminology and Crime Analysis. Portland, Oregon: William Publishing.

Yoon, J. S., Barton, E., & Taiariol, J. (2004). Relational Aggression in Middle School: Educational Implications of Developmental Research. *The Journal of Early Adolescence,* 24; 303-318.

In: Bio-Psycho-Social Perspectives on Interpersonal Violence ISBN: 978-1-61668-159-3
Editors: M. Frías-Armenta et al., pp. 217-232 © 2010 Nova Science Publishers, Inc.

Chapter 10

VIOLENCE IN PRISON: INSTITUTIONAL CONSTRAINTS AND INMATE'S AGRESSIVENESS

Rui Abrunhosa Gonçalves[*]
University of Minho, Braga, Portugal.

ABSTRACT

This chapter tries to illustrate two different kinds of violence within prisons. The one that is performed by the institution and can be directly linked with the "pains of imprisonment" (e.g., Sykes, 1958), and the other related to the interactions that prisoners establish with the institution, staff and among themselves. First, we describe the most common prison stressors and emphasize their effects on the prisoners' well being and their ability to cope with them. Afterwards, relevance is given to the types of violent interactions that occur between inmates: physical, sexual, psychological, economical and social. A third issue addressed concerns prison-staff problems and how they affect the staff's relationship with prisoners and the institutional climate. A theoretical framework either linked to the environmental stress approach in the first case, or to a risk-factor analysis in the second case is discussed, thus providing some possibility of designing interventions for reducing both dimensions of prison violence. Finally, issues concerning the discussion about more recent forms of punishment such as "supermax prisons" are addressed.

INTRODUCTION

Prison is, by definition, a violent place. It was outlined to contain dangerous persons and its architecture was designed to establish clear boundaries between "good people and evil people" (Foucault, 1975). The first prison buildings were places where prisoners were caged and tortured and left to die in awful conditions. Nowadays, we can see some prisons that are confounded in the urban net while others stand up for their grandiosity. Small or huge places

---

[*] Associate professor at the School of Psychology, University of Minho, Braga, Portugal. E-mail: rabrunhosa@psi.uminho.pt

to confine people for few days or endless time, in various conditions, some of them outrageous, degraded and inhuman while others presenting several features that are common in our houses (heating, private TV, computers, etc.).

The asymmetries between prisons are related mostly to the social conditions of their countries and their management, and the use of imprisonment can be divided, according to Coyle (2004), in five groups. A first group, stemming from developing countries that were former African colonies, disregard the importance of prison, which in many cases was not a cultural inheritance of their own, and the idea of confining healthy men in places where they cannot be productive seem strange to these societies. In fact, most of these countries struggle with basic economic needs and spending money on building a prison is not a priority. In this sense, innovative ideas in sentences mainly stressing the use of work on the behalf of the community or strategies of restorative justice with the victims, become ways of healing wounds between different ethnic groups involved in massive killing such as occurred in Rwanda some years ago. On the opposite side we can find prisons ruled by prisoners where violence and abuse prevail and where staff seems only preoccupied with the external security of the building. Many Latin American countries are representative of this group, whose prisons tend to present massive physical degradation. The third group is composed, mainly, by the former countries of the Soviet Union either on Eastern Europe or Central Asia. Overcrowding represents the main problem there, with all the associate issues of illnesses, especially tuberculosis; which in 2002 affected 10% of the Russian prisoners (e.g., Kalinin, 2002, cited in Coyle, 2004). The recent political changes towards democracy in these countries are forcing them to promote penal reforms in order to reduce the use of imprisonment, Russia being the head of this political will. The majority of Western Europe countries compose a fourth group that sees prison as the ultimate penal resource. In these countries government and societies acknowledge that prison cannot serve as a tool to solve problems such as drug abuse or mental illness. Rates of incarceration tend to diminish in these countries and the use of alternative measures to prison such as electronic monitoring is raising progressively thus permitting new forms of dealing with criminality (see Walmsley, 2005). Finally, some countries like USA seem to see prison as the principal resource for most social problems, thus putting behind bars lots of individuals touched by economical disadvantages, poverty, homelessness and minority group belonging. And this is the main reason why the USA is the country with the highest rate of imprisonment that also leads to serious problems of overcrowding. Among western European countries, England, Wales and Spain also seem to endorse this penal policy of putting behind bars everyone who becomes a social problem (e.g., Coyle, 2004; King, 2007). This appalling evidence should raise ethical problems in the minds of those who rule prisons either directly (wardens and prison guards) or indirectly (secretary of justice/government).

PRISON AS A SOURCE OF VIOLENCE

A. The Place

In his seminal work about life in prison, Sykes (1958) points to the fact that serving time is only one of "the pains of imprisonment." Several others are documented through his work and half a century later some of them persist, while others were minimized and others are product of the evolution of penology and penitentiary laws (e.g., Johnson & Toch, 1982; Liebling & Maruna, 2005). In this part of the chapter we will try to emphasize how prison can be a source of violence by itself, focusing initially on his institutional weight and secondly on the role played by prison staff.

Prison might be defined as a place of stress (e.g., Johnson & Toch, 1982). Susan Saegert (1976) conceived it as a model of environmental stress involving six aspects that can be applied to prison environments. The first aspect refers to the *physical threats* of the environment. In this sense environments might be threatening due to their harsh conditions of living (e.g., very high or very low temperature, humidity, air pollution…) and prisons, specially old facilities are a good example of "acclimatized environments" being cold in the winter and hot in summer. Several studies acknowledge the existence of a relationship between individual mood changes and differences in temperature, namely when it increases, and also the growth of crime rates, violent crimes in particular (e.g., Anderson & Anderson, 1984; Bell & Green, 1984; Cohn, 1990; Rotton & Frey, 1985). Prison architecture is another extension of this stressor. In fact, prisons are designed according to the notion of functionality, utility and discipline, and little attention is paid to issues of comfort or well-being; although, more recent constructions, built at the end of 20th century, are trying to dismiss this assumption (e.g., Fairweather, 1980; Jewkes & Johnston, 2007; Spens, 1994). Furthermore, the housing conditions provided in prisons are, in some cases, very troublesome with prisoners having to share the cell space with other fellow inmates or being assigned to dormitories that are even more stressful. For those who are assigned to single cells, the experience of total isolation might also turn out to be very problematic.

The second aspect referred by Saegert is *stimulus information overload*, which is particularly linked to the problem of prison overcrowding. In fact, inmates are confronted with an environment where privacy is not possible and in most cases they have to share the cell with other prisoners. They are forced to live and interact with persons that are in most cases complete strangers to them and cope with frustration of not being allowed to do what they want, even simple things. Numerous studies have proved the deleterious effects of prison overcrowding on the physical and mental health of the prisoners, their aggressiveness and suicide attempts (e.g., Cox, Paulus, & McCain, 1984; McCain, Cox, & Paulus, 1976, 1980; Ostfeld, Kasl, D'Attri, & Fitzgerald, 1987). At the same time, prisoners are also forced to make choices or decisions in limited time, mostly related to their need of compromise, either to official rules of the prison or inmates subculture, thus putting them under great pressure. Additionally, things might get worse if negative stimuli comes in an unpredictable or uncontrolled way, frequently and intensively, as in the case of violent attacks from other prisoners that are, also, frequently in crowded facilities (e.g., Farrington & Nuttall, 1980) promoting permanent fear and insecurity feelings. However, a recent review paper suggests that the relationship between crowding and prisoner's misconduct should be taken more cautiously in light of several observed methodological flaws (e.g., Steiner & Wooldredge, 2009). In any case, these authors do not deny the influence of the former on the latter but suggest that this issue could be enlighten if a more rigorous evaluation of the type of involved offenders could take place.

Saegert (1976) also points to the fact that certain environments can have qualities that might enhance frustration and aggression following Berkowitz's theory (e.g., Berkowitz, 1962). One of such qualities is *inflexibility or rigidity*, which is a feature that all prisons portray through their straight rules and incapacity of promoting change, because many propose modifications that pose threats to the "status quo." In fact, prison rules emphasize procedural rigidity all the way, transforming simple demands in a rosary of bureaucratic steps whose goal surpasses the mere "need to control", excuse to become an attempt to force the petitioner to desist of his/her intent.

Consequently, one can also argue about the extent of *meaningful messages or experiences* that prison may provide for inmates. As stated above, prison environments are more prone to provide antisocial learning than pro-social attitudes, since in most cases prisoner's rewarding is only associated to "cooperative" behaviours such as snitching. Being constantly criticized or being only praised by displaying attitudes and behaviours that are contrary to inner beliefs, might enhance frustration and low self-esteem. Besides, due to their low social class background, prisoners are less prepared to cope with adversity. So it is acceptable that some violent outbursts displayed by them might be a consequence of the poor rate of meaningful gratifications that prison provides and the frustration associated to it. Additionally, one might also argue that the success of prison smuggling could be explained by the appeal that such products, albeit innocuous in some cases, can provide in the "meaningless world" of prison.

Saegert (1976) further emphasizes that the *quality of the relationships* that the individual establishes with the environment might also represent a source of stress. In fact, some environments are more demanding to the individual, while others provide mostly stereotyped clues. Prison fits in the last group, either you see it from the formal (administrative) side or from the informal (inmate's code) side. Newcomers are forced to choose between these two ways and the decision can be based on previous prison experiences or being yet associated to an active criminal career. Adaptation to prison is, again, the issue and prisoners might adopt extreme positions – mirroring the criminal subculture or adopting the formal code – or try to survive in a compromise between these two opposite worlds. Whatever the decision might be, risks are always present but it is clear that possibilities of obtaining absence leaves or early release from prison depend on the ability of the prisoner to avoid violent incidents and to remain far from the criminal subculture's influence.

Finally, and in opposition to the first aspect, Saegert (1976) argues that stress may also be induced by *lack of adequate stimulation*. In fact, prisons are characterized, in most cases, for providing less relevant information and simultaneously forcing the individuals to cope with unwanted or even pernicious information as stated above. Places where people are deprived from adequate stimulation, tend to promote social alienation, emotional withdrawn and mental illness, which is what occurs under "solitary confinement" doctrine.

The above stated dimensions might be overcome through a more adequate prison planning, involving their architecture but also their functioning. Prisons that are not conceived as huge concrete blocks but allocate fewer inmates, provide a more proximal approach between guards and prisoners and contribute to a more positive way of reinsertion, thus reducing the overall deleterious effects of imprisonment (e.g., Farbstein, & Wener, 1982; Johnson & Toch, 1982; Liebling & Maruna, 2005; Wener, Frazier, & Farbstein, 1987).

B. The Staff

At least once a year, when the report from International Amnesty is available, complaints about the existence of acts of violence perpetrated by staff, mainly by prison guards, upon prisoners is referred in several countries. The events occurred in Abu Ghraib Prison revalidated the results of the Stanford Experiment held more than three decades ago by Zimbardo and colleagues (e.g., Haney, Banks & Zimbardo, 1973; Zimbardo, Haney, Banks, & Jaffe, 1973), whose parallel the author efficiently noted in his recent book (e.g., Zimbardo, 2007). More recently, Lurigio (2009) goes beyond Zimbardo's reflections and points out "seven lessons" that should inform future prison administrations. All these lessons focus on the need of providing effective tools in order to prevent events such as the ones that took place in Abu Ghraib, which should no longer occur. The first one has to do with an adequate selection of prison officers, where traditional screening through psychological testing does not seem reliable in order to identify the most suitable for the job. The second one is the importance of assuming a role based on the relevance of status identity and all the features that reinforce such identity (uniform, weapons, mirrored sunglasses, etc.). In fact, as Goffmann (1961/1986) noted, the loss of identity, for those who entered the so-called "total institutions", consisted of, among other things, the current clothes which were substituted by uniforms, and the names by numbers. Prisons are environments that reinforce the separation between guards and inmates assigning specific roles for both groups and making sure that the boundaries between them should not be crossed. And one of the ways of establishing such separation is stressing the differences by incorporating all the features of that identity in an obsessive way, violence among them. On the contrary, developing a sense of tolerance towards deviance, seeing one's job as a way of promoting adequate models of social reinsertion can lead inmates towards change, instead of reinforcing their criminal identity.

Another feature pointed by Lurigio (2009) acknowledges the situational effect on behavioural change. In fact, adaptation to prison relies on the need of compromise between formal and informal rules and some prisoners cannot succeed in doing this either because of their prior mental health problems or their personality antisocial traits. Attention should be paid to what extent does confinement represents, a way of amplifying these negative features and what prison administration can do about this.

Lurigio (2009) also stresses the issue of leadership. If an institution is ruled by a person who approves, even tacitly, the use of violence as a way of dealing with people, it is almost certain that violent acts will become frequent. This was what the Milgram's experiences have told us about obedience to authority (e.g, Milgram, 1974) and that one is not responsible for one's acts when they are acknowledged and sponsored by superiors. Similarly, absence of leadership is also conducive to a general chaos leaving power at one's own hands. Consequently, prisons are places where the need for adequate leadership and monitoring of personnel must be strongly encouraged in order to prevent power abuses and impunity.

A leadership that reinforces or overlooks violent behaviours from the personnel, leads to a generalizing effect of bystander apathy displayed by other officers. In fact, in these kinds of environments the most sadistic elements tend to assume leadership and impose their own code of conduct, leaving the other personnel between two choices: following them or not to interfere. Assuming that the last choice is more reassuring and guilty absent implies confirming in some way the findings of Asch's (1956) experiment on conformity, but in the opposite sense. Here, officers defend themselves under the assumption that if no one acts, why should I? So, the lesson to draw is that being an observer or choose not to interfere is, also, a crime that should be punished.

When people are deprived from their rights and try to protest or fight back there can be two ways of dealing with the matter. Either we acknowledge them, reason and try to provide a fair solution by engaging in a dialogue with the prisoner, or we reinforce our rules uprising the control and harshening the procedures. In prisons, the vicious cycles tend to mount in the absence of adequate leadership and measures to end violence, and protests from prisoners tend to be seen as threats to authority thus deserving harsher punishment. In this case, the message to prison administrators should be the emphasis on the need to reassure that prisoners and guards have their own legal rights and when an inmate makes use of them, he is exerting a legal right and not necessarily "attacking" the guards. These, in turn, must not redirect their frustrations towards other inmates as expiatory goats. Also, the ability to empty circumstances that can evolve to sources of potential conflict should be a priority in running a prison.

Finally Lurigio (2009) stresses the importance of using negative outcomes to promote altruistic behaviour and change in a positive sense. That is what Zimbardo did more then thirty years ago, when after debriefing he promoted future health programs in prison facilities. That is probably what is under the political measures implemented by the present USA Administration in relation to Guantanamo. Consequently, bearing in mind the influence of situational factors over dispositional features as an enduring idea should be a duty to everyone working in prisons.

PRISONERS AS A SOURCE OF VIOLENCE

The second part of this chapter deals with the other source of violence that occurs in prison settings: the one that is perpetrated by inmates between themselves and against the staff. We don't intend to say that this type of violence is inherent to the offender's personality and has nothing to do with the place where he/she is confined. It is clear, from precedent pages, that we support the importance of situational factors in explaining general behaviour and especially prison violence. However, we also think that certain types of prisoners are more prone to display violent attitudes and behaviours either to their fellow inmates or to the staff. These attitudes and behaviours might be catalogued in different groups and consequently we can also envisage different features in perpetrators and victims.

A. Violence among Prisoners

Following Bowker's (1982) presentation, we can identify five types of victimization practised between prisoners. The first one and the most recognizable is *physical aggression*. Several reasons can be traced for this type of violence: 1) to achieve or reinforce status in the informal hierarchy of the prison; 2) retaliation, to prove one's masculinity against insinuations or previous attacks; 3) to promote a cathartic effect related to the constant tension that prison life promotes; 4) to obtain goods from the victim (e.g., drugs, cigarettes, money, etc.); 5) as a warning of intimidation to those who fail to pay their debts (namely drugs the aggressor had already obtained for them); and 6) to force the administration to act according to the prisoner's desires (e.g., be transferred to another prison, obtain a favourable job inside the facility, etc.).

Another kind of violence in prison, not as evident as physical aggression but far more traumatic is *sexual victimization*. Here the goal of the aggressor might be, similarly to the case before expressed, "to teach a lesson to those who don't pay their debts", but may also represent a simple expression of power. Certain inmates are more prone to be sexually attacked in the prison: child abusers, white young males, middle class individuals, newcomers to prison, those who cooperate with the administration ("rats" and "snitches"), those presenting less physical attributes or some mental or physical handicap, those who exhibit effeminate attitudes, those who lack street surviving skills and those who have been already victims of sexual assaults are at higher risk (e.g., Alarid, 2000; Beck, 1994; Bowker, 1982; Dumond, 2000).

Psychological victimization might be identified as the most common among all violent interactions between prisoners. It has several advantages because it is much harder to prove and it can provide the offender with the same profit. The most common manifestations of this type of victimization are subtle distortions or verbal manipulations of the facts to create a state of anxiety and worry in the victim. Spreading rumours about the masculinity of the individual or his/her loyalty to the inmate's code are good examples of theses strategies. Also very common is to provide inaccurate information about relatives or create suspicions regarding the fidelity of the prisoner's wife or girlfriend. Indeed, prisoners attained by psychological aggression tend to be more careless, and often fail to protect adequately their goods and provisions thus being more prone to be robbed or sexually attacked. Finally, prisoners attained by psychological victimization may get involved in provocations and aggressive acts against the staff, instigated by informal leaders that through this strategy may create a mutiny without being, at the end, clearly identified.

The *economic victimization* is the most ancient forms of prison victimization and relies on the importance that prohibition of certain objects or goods represents for the prisoners. All sorts of smuggling objects from the outside have been revealed throughout the years but others emerge. At present, drug trafficking is by far the most serious problem in this area, due to the fact that a large percentage of inmates are drug consumers/abusers. Cell phones also represent one of the goods that are most valuable in prisons but they are more difficult to conceal from inspection than drugs.

Finally we can assume that there is a *social victimization* (e.g., Bowker, 1982), mainly based on what is determined by the environment that provides the inmate population. In fact, prisons reflect to certain degree the free society, and the differences that occur outside. Delinquency and crime are mostly a product of suburban or degraded quarters, where gangs emerge assuming their racial and ethnic identity or their local neighbourhood and the rivalry towards other groups from other parts of the city. They are frequently involved in street fights and when they are in prison conflicts and violence also persists. So, social victimization in prison means that one is victimized not for what he does (or does not) but for what he socially stands for (e.g., Wolff, Shi, & Blitz, 2008).

Violence between prisoners might be conceived as a product of their antisocial personalities but also as an enduring problem of lack of authority and unwillingness to promote adequate forms of separation and segregation of high-risk offenders. Quay's (1984) Adult Internal Management System is a good example of providing clear guidelines to deal with this subject. In fact, one can divide, on the basis of psychological and psychometric evaluation, prisoners who are more prone to victimize – namely the psychopaths – from others who are more at risk to become victims (drug dependants, mentally ill, conventional inmates, etc.) and allocate them in independent facilities or cell blocks. According to the same classification, it is possible to provide different types of programmes regarding their criminogenic needs and potential for change (e.g., Hollin & Bilby, 2007).

B. Inmate Violence Towards Staff

Evidence concerning assaults to prison staff perpetrated by inmates is quite scarce. A study by Kratcoski (1988) described seven factors (location, shift of occurrence, officer work experience, officer's sex, inmate's age, presence of staff during the assault and assaults on officers after being threatened) related to the occurrence of aggressions on prison staff. Only two of these variables present significant results: assault on guards was associated with younger inmates and newer officers where the most likely targets.

A study by Light (1991) tried to identify the motivations behind inmate-on-staff aggressions. After analysing a total of 694 incidents, the author identified at the top of the list 26% of random acts of violence. Second, 13% of the inmates responded aggressively to direct commands from the staff such as an order to leave an area. Third, inmates considered that 11% of their misconducts were simply protests for being treated unfairly.

Gaes and McGuire (1985) identified prison overcrowding as the most important variable in explaining the assaults but also that non-White prisoners had a higher rate of staff assaulting, while McCorkle, Miethe, and Drass (1995) concluded that poor prison management was the best predictor of prison violence. Briggs, Sundt and Castellano (2003) provided mixed results when analysing staff assault among several "supermax" prisons in different American States, because the effect found either was positive, negative or null. Following this, Lahm (2009) conducted a large-scale study with 1054 inmates from 30 prisons in three states. Prisoners responded to self-report questionnaires voluntarily, and institutional information was collected from the State's Department of Corrections. Inmates were subject to report if they engaged in a non-serious/non deadly assault on a prison staff member during the last 12 months. This dependent variable was related to several factors concerning the individual (e.g., age, race, etc.), his criminal issues (e.g., type of offence, time served, prior convictions) and institutional data (e.g., overcrowding, proportion of non-white prisoners, etc.), among others. Four percent of the sample revealed having committed an assault on a staff member.

The results showed that younger prisoners convicted by a violent offence were more prone to attack the guards, and that they tend to do so more near the end of their sentences and most frequently in prisons where the proportion of non-white prisoners was higher and the ratio guards-prisoners larger. Thus, results suggest that some dispositional variables may play an important role on staff assault along with situational cues associated with the prison conditions. In fact, one interesting issue revealed by this study was that inmates tend to be more assaulting by the end of their sentences, thus contradicting the idea that with the passage of time they "settle down" according to process of conformity to the prison rules described by early prison sociologists (e.g., Clemmer, 1940; Garabedian, 1963; Wheeler, 1961).

METHOD

Participants

As a part of our own research, we analysed the relationship between drug abuse and misconduct in prison leading to the administration of punishments. A sample of 79 male prisoners (age: $M = 31.5$; $SD = 9,99$) from a local Portuguese prison was divided in two groups: 39 were drug abusers and the other 40 had no present or past history of drug abuse. Drug trafficking was the most salient crime ($n = 33$; 41,8%) followed by crimes against property (theft and robbery: $n = 25$; 31,6%) and crimes against persons (homicide, physical assaults and sexual crimes: $n = 21$; 26,6%).

Procedure

The study was conducted through institutional records search, analysing a period of four years. During this time 69 infractions were recorded. One third of them (23) were committed against the staff, while the other two thirds were aggressions between inmates, destruction of property and rule-breaking attitudes. The 69 infractions were committed by 36 (45,6%) out of the 79 inmates. Of these 36 prisoners, 29 (80,6%) were drug abusers and they were responsible for 55 infractions, which gives a rate of 1.9 infractions per inmate.

The research hypothesis was that drug abuse offenders had a more violent behavioural pattern in prison; therefore they present a heavier disciplinary record. Additionally, other variables were considered (age, civil status, academic level, criminal record, crime committed, penal situation, having a job in prison).

Results show that offenders with drug problems were indeed those who commit more infractions and get punished more often. Additionally, those who were recidivists and already convicted were most likely to misbehave in the prison. Finally those who committed crimes against persons were the less likely to engage in disciplinary problems. Of the socio-demographic variables, only civil status yielded significant differences since single or divorced inmates presented a high similar prevalence of infractions in contrast to those who were married. While discussing these results, we acknowledge the relationship between drug abuse and prison violence, and a past criminal record as important elements that shape criminal careers which are associated to antisocial personality traits (e.g., Farrington, 2003; Smith, 2007). On the other hand, being effectively sentenced to prison after serving some time in the remand condition ends the period of incertitude, where most prisoners adopt a false and dissimulated image. The convicted prisoner might now stop faking and assume his true nature because his situation is already defined (e.g., Gibbs, 1982; Toch, 1992). Finally, marriage may represent a sign of engaging on compromise and responsibility, thus signifying a protective factor against antisocial behaviour (e.g., Sampson & Laub, 1993).

RESULTS

Table 1 accounts only the variables that presented significant associations related to the 69 infractions.

Table 1. Significant associations between the prevalence of infractions recorded and variables considered

VARIABLES	N	M	SD	F	P
Drug Condition:				23.539	.000
Drug Abusers	39	2.28	1.05		
Non Drug Abusers	40	1.30	.72		
Criminal Record:				7.298	.008
Recidivists	36	2.11	1.70		
Remands	43	1.51	.80		
Penal Situation:				8.370	.005
Convicted	44	2.07	1.07		
Preventive	35	1.43	.85		
Crime Committed:				5.708	.005
- Drug Trafficking	33	1.82	1.04		
- Crimes Against Property	25	2.20	1.12		
- Crimes Against Persons	21	1.24	.54		
Civil Status:				3.017	.055
Married	34	1.47	.75		
Single	36	2.0	1.07		
Divorced	9	2.11	1.45		

Additionally, results show that inmates who were drug abusers were most likely to be young (F = 2,052; p = .05), single (F = 5,422; p = .05), mostly recidivists (F = 16,328; p = .000) and already serving effective prison sentences (F = 12,228; p = .001) for drug related crimes or crimes against property (F = 12,327; p = .000). Thus, analysing all these variables as a whole, we noticed a great overlap between being a drug abuser inmate and a violent inmate. However, when we track the distribution of 55 infractions committed by the drug abuse offenders along four years of prison already served (see Figure 1) the distribution of the data clearly shows that the vast majority of the infractions occurred in the first year of prison (63,6%), dropped less than half in the second year (25,5%) and was residual in the last two years.

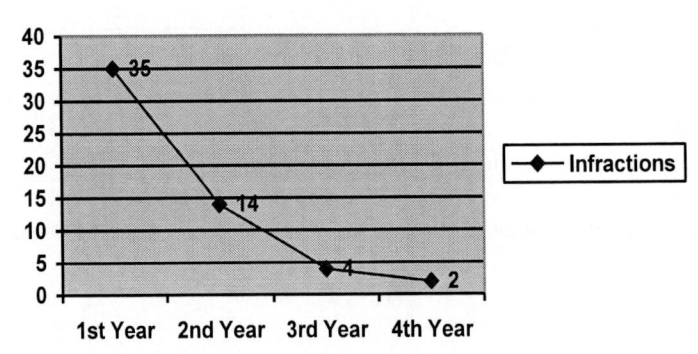

Figure 1. Infractions (n = 55) committed by drug abuse offenders distributed along the four years of prison.

These facts reinforce the idea that adaptation to prison is probably a more relevant phenomenon to explain the prevalence of violent acts perpetrated by inmates towards staff ratter than their specific inner condition and that the first months/year of "doing time" represent a particularly vulnerable period (e.g., Gibbs, 1982; Toch, 1992). This vulnerability can also be related to other "prison problems" such as suicides, violent outbursts or mental illness symptoms (e.g., Harvey, 2005; Liebling, 2007; Toch & Adams, 2002). In fact, findings already reported by Lahm (2009) concerning an increase of violence towards the end of the sentence might be more associated with inner characteristics of some prisoners (e.g., psychopaths) that are negatively correlated with prison adjustment (e.g., Gonçalves, 2004), independently of the time location of the sentences they are serving.

CONCLUSION

Several years ago, Andrew Rutherford (1991) pointed that the problems of prisons can be conceived according to a "penal trinity": the capacity of the prison, the conditions of the prison and the population of the prison.

As reported by numerous studies (e.g., Ostfeld, Kasl, D'Attri, & Fitzgerald 1987; Steiner & Wooldredge, 2009; Walmsley, 2005), overcrowding still persists as one of the most important "pains of the imprisonment" (e.g., Sykes, 1958; Toch & Adams, 1982) thus influencing the social climate of the prisons and the ability to provide more adequate services to the prisoners, either in terms of providing more security (by preventing assaults from other inmates) or assuring them a more individualized and purposeful treatment avoiding the prison deleterious effects.

Overcrowded prisons might also be understaffed prisons thus conducting to inappropriate conditions of serving sentences and inadequate ways of prisoners' surveillance, with guards often exhibiting unnecessary force and creating a climate of tension and violence, reminding Zimbardo's experience (e.g., Haney, Banks, & Zimbardo, 1973; Zimbardo, Haney, Banks, & Jaffe, 1973). When prison conditions are deficient there is also a possibility that prisoners become more intolerant, provocative and violent, enhancing the number of prison occurrences that end in disciplinary charges.

Moreover, there is also considerable evidence that the great majority of prisoners present antisocial personality traits associated with drug abuse problems. Additionally some of them show active symptoms of mental illness. All these features require adequate treatment but mainly early screening to prevent further negative outcomes such as suicide attempts or violent attacks towards staff or other prisoners. Instruments such as the Jail Screening Assessment Tool (JSAT: Nicholls, Roesch, Olley, Ogloff, & Hemphill, 2005) seem to be of great assistance. Furthermore it is clear from studies on adaptation to prison (e.g., Toch & Adams, 2002; Zamble & Porporino, 1988) that individuals tend to reproduce in prison their habitual functioning in the free world and so those who were more violent and disruptive outside will probably present more problems while serving sentences. Thus, it is important to combine screening strategies with procedures of classification and separation of inmates to assure a meaningful drop of incidents either between prisoners or between them and the staff.

In any case, criminal policy is heading in two separate ways. Some countries, with the USA at the top, feel that imprisonment is a valid answer to a majority of social problems ranging from poverty to mental illness and that is why their rate of imprisonment continues to mount (see, Walmsley, 2005). These are also the countries where most investment has been carried out in the construction of "supermax" prisons where problems didn't cease to appear (see The Prison Journal, 2008, Special Issue on Supermax Prisons; King, 2005). In Europe, countries like Sweden, Norway, Finland or Denmark show a habitual low rate of imprisonment contrary to other countries where imprisonment rates are traditionally very high (e.g., Russia, Czech Republic, Latvia) while other countries (e.g., England, Wales, Spain) seem to encompass the USA tendency and present a substantial growth in their rates of imprisonment (see King, 2007; Walmsley, 2005). Additionally, other European countries (e.g., Portugal and Lithuania) are consistently diminishing their imprisonment rates over the past years, but it is not clear if this decrease is due to a change in criminal policy, to promote community based interventions rather than institutionalising the criminals or to simply find a way of diminishing cost in prisons' budget. In fact, several analysis point to the high cost of maintaining people in prison (e.g., Prison Reform Trust, 2007) – values varying between 70 USD to 200 USD of inmate per day costs – which was an argument to launch prison privatisation several years ago (e.g., Beyens & Snacken, 1996; Mehigan & Rowe, 2007).

If eighteen century prison reformers like John Howard or Jeremy Bentham could return from their graves, they will probably be quite surprised to see that XXI century prisons are not very different from those they knew. In fact, as we have been arguing, nowadays prisons continue to reflect some pernicious effects on inmates, thus failing to provide meaningful rehabilitation. On the other hand, prisoners continue to present several risk factors either internal (e.g., drug abuse, antisocial personality traits and beliefs) or/and external (poverty, social/ethnic minorities backgrounds, low school level). It seems that over these years, prisons and prisoners remain resistant to change and accumulate problems over problems. But several guidelines can be outlined to minimize or even overcome theses conditions and to provide effective crime reduction and diminish "the pains of imprisonment": we can start by remembering that prisons are not asylums so they are not adequate to treat mental illness or shelter homeless people; secondly, addictions represent mostly a problem for mandatory health care and not judicial procedure; thirdly, more attention should be paid to the effects that imprisoned women, who are mothers, may provoke on their offspring; fourthly, using or enhancing the use of more adequate systems of evaluating risk and dangerousness for prisoner's assignments may contribute to diminish violent interactions in the prison; also it is crucial that staff, namely guards, should be involved in the correctional treatment procedures rather than being solely "instrumental repressors" (e.g., Bennett, Crew, & Wahidin, 2008); and, finally, it is crucial to develop more regular and efficient cost-benefit analysis. As Toch (2005) vividly points out, we can be in control of the prison without the need of constantly reminding who controls the prisoners.

REFERENCES

Alarid, L. F. (2000). Sexual assault and coercion among incarcerated women prisoners: Excerpts from prison letters. *The Prison Journal, 4*, 391-406.

Anderson, C. A. & Anderson, D. C. (1984). Ambient temperature and violent crime: tests on the linear and curvilinear hypothesis. *Journal of Personality and Social Psychology, 46*, 91-97.

Asch, S. E. (1956) Studies of independence and conformity: A minority of one against a unanimous majority. *Psychological Monographs, 70* (Whole no. 416).

Beck, G. (1994). Self reported bullying among imprisoned young offenders. *Inside Psychology, 2,* 16-21.

Bell, P. A. & Green, T. C. (1984). Thermal stress: physiological, comfort, performance and social effects of hot and cold environments. In Gary W. Evans (Ed.), *Environmental Stress* (pp. 75-104) Cambridge: Cambridge University Press.

Bennett, J., Crew, B., & Wahidin, A. (2008).*Understanding prison staff*. Devon: Willan.

Berkowitz. L. (1962). *Agression: A social psychological analysis*. N. Y.: McGraw Hill.

Beyens, K., & Snacken, S. (1996). Prison privatization: An international perspective. In R. Matthews and P. Francis (Eds.), *Prisons 2000 – an International perspective on the current state and future of imprisonment* (pp.240-265). London: Macmillan Press.

Bowker, L. H. (1982). Victimizers and victims in American correctional institutions. In R. Johnson & H. Toch (Eds.), *The pains of imprisonment*. (pp. 63-76). London: Sage.

Briggs, C. S., Sundt, J. L., & Castellano, T. C. (2003). The effect of supermaximum security prisons on aggregate levels of institutional violence. *Criminology, 41*, 1341-1376.

Clemmer, D. (1940). *The prison community*. New York: Holt.

Cohn, E. G. (1990). Weather and crime. *British Jounal of Criminology, 30*, 51-64.

Coyle, A. (2004). Prison reform efforts around the world: the role of prison administrators. *Pace Law Review, 24,* 825-832.

Cox, V. C., Paulus, P. B. & McCain, G. (1984). Prison crowding research. The relevance for prison housing standards and a general approach regarding crowding phenomena. *American Psychologist, 39*, 1148-1160.

Dumond, R. W. (2000). Inmate sexual assault: The plague that persists. *The Prison Journal, 4*, 407-414.

Edgar, K. & O'Donnell, I. (1998). Assault in prison. *British Journal of Criminology, 38*, 635-650.

Fairweather, L. (1980). The evolution of the prison. In *Prison architecture* (13-40). London: Architectural Press.

Farbstein, J. & Wener, R. E. (1982). Evaluation of correctional environments. *Environment and Behavior, 14*, 6, 671-694.

Farrington, D. P. (2003). Developmental and life-course criminology: Key theoretical and empirical issues. *Criminology, 41*, 221-255.

Farrington, D. P. & Nuttal, C. P. (1980). Prison size, overcrowding, prison violence and recidivism. *Journal of Criminal Justice, 8*, 221-231.

Foucault, M. (1975). *Surveiller et punir. Naissance de la prison.* Paris: Gallimard.

Gaes, G. & McGuire, W. (1985). Prison violence: The contribution of crowding versus other determinants of prison assault rates. *Journal of research in Crime and Delinquency, 22*, 41-65.

Garabedian, P. G. (1963). Social roles and process of socialization in the prison community. *Social Problems, 11* (2), 140-152.

Gibbs, J. J. (1982). The first cut is the deepest: Psychological breakdown and survival in the detention setting. In R. Johnson & H. Toch (Eds.), *The pains of imprisonment* (97-114). Beverly Hills: Sage.

Goffman, E. (1986). *Asylums* (13th ed.). London: Penguin Books. Originally published in 1961 by Anchor Books, Doubleday, N. Y..

Gonçalves, R. A. (2004). Adaptation to prison and psychopathy. In R. A. Gonçalves (Ed.), *Victims and offenders* (pp.71-81). Brussels: Politeia.

Haney, C. Banks, W. C. & Zimbardo, P. G. (1973). Interpersonal dynamics in a simulated prison. *International Journal of Criminology and Penology, 1*, 69-97.

Harvey, J. (2005). Crossing the boundary: The transition of young adults to prison. In A. Liebling and S. Maruna (Eds), *The effects of imprisonment* (pp. 232-254). Devon: Willan.

Hollin, C. & Bilby, C. (2007). Addressing offending behaviour: "What works" and beyond. In Y. Jewkes (Ed.), *Handbook on prisons* (pp. 608-628). Devon: Willan.

Jewkes, Y. & Johnston, H. (2007). The evolution of prison architecture. In Y. Jewkes (Ed.), *Handbook on prisons* (pp. 174-196). Devon: Willan.

Johnson, R. & Toch, H. (Eds.) (1982). *The pains of imprisonment*. London: Sage.

King, R. D. (2005). The effects of supermax custody. . In A. Liebling and S. Maruna (Eds), *The effects of imprisonment* (pp. 118-145). Devon: Willan.

King, R. D. (2007). Imprisonment: Some international comparisons and the need to revisit panopticism. In Y. Jewkes (Ed.), *Handbook on prisons* (pp. 95-122). Devon: Willan.

Kratcoski, P. (1988). The implications of research explaining prison violence and disruption. *Federal Probation, 52*, 27-32.

Lahm, K. F. (2009). Inmates assault on prison staff. A multilevel examination of an overlooked form of prison violence. *The Prison Journal, 89*, 131-150.

Liebling, A. & Maruna, S. (Eds) (2005). *The effects of imprisonment*. Devon: Willan.

Liebling, A. (2007). Prison suicide and its prevention. In Y. Jewkes (Ed.), *Handbook on prisons* (pp. 423-446). Devon: Willan.

Light, S.C. (1991). Assaults on prison officers: International themes. In M. Braswell, R. Montgomery Jr., & L. Lombardo (Eds.), *Prison violence in America* (pp. 207-224). Cincinnati, OH: Anderson.

Lurigio, A. J. (2009). The rotten barrel spoils the apples: How situational factors contribute to detention officer abuse towards inmates. *The Prison Journal, 89 (Supplement)*, 70S-80S.

McCain, G., Cox, V. C. & Paulus, P. B. (1976). The relationship between illness complaints and degree of crowding in a prison environment. *Environment and Behavior, 8*, (2), 283-290.

McCain, G., Cox, V. C. & Paulus, P. B. (1980). *The effect of prison crowding on inmate behavior*. Washington D. C.: National Institute of Justice.

McGurk, B. J. & McDougall, C. (1991). The prevention of bullying among incarcerated delinquents. In P. K. Smith and D. Thompson (Eds), *Practical approaches to bullying*. London: Fulton.

McCorkle, R. C., Miethe, T., & Drass, K. A. (1995). The roots of prison violence: A test of the deprivation, management and not-so-total institutions model. *Crime and Delinquency, 2*, 197-221.

Mehigan, J., & Rowe, A. (2007). Problematizing prison privatization: An overview of the debate. In Y. Jewkes (Ed.), *Handbook on prisons* (pp. 356-376). Devon: Willan.

Milgram, S. (1974). *Obediance to authorithy: An experimental view*. NY: Harper Collins.

Nicholls, T. L., Roesch, R., Olley, M. C., Ogloff, J. R. P., & Hemphill, J. F. (2005). Jail Screening Assessment Tool: Guidelines for mental health screening in jails. Vancouver: Simon Fraser University, Mental Health Law and Policy Institute.

Ostfeld, A. M., Kasl, S. V., D'Attri, D. A. & Fitzgerald, E. F. (1987). *Stress, crowding and blood pressure in prison*. N. J.: Lawrence Erlbaum.

Prison Reform Trust, (2007). *Bromley briefings prison factfile*. December. Available on www.prisonreformtrust.org.uk

Quay, H. C. (1984). *Managing adult inmates: Classification for housing and housing assignments*. College Park, Md.: American Correctional Association.

Rotton, J. & Frey, J. (1985). Air pollution, weather and violent crimes: concomitant time-series analysis of archival data. *Journal of Personality and Social Psychology, 49*, 1207-1220.

Rutherford, A. (1991). Introduction. In D. Whitfield (ed.), *The state of prisons — 200 years on* (1-12). London: Routledge.

Saegert, S. (1976). Stress-inducing and reducing qualities of environments. in A. M. Proshansky, W. A., Ittelson and L. G. Rivlin (Eds.), *Environmental psychology: people and their physical settings* (2nd ed.) N. Y.: Holt, Rinehart and Winston.

Sampson, R. J. & Laub, J. H. (1993). *Crime in the making: Pathways and turning points through life*. Cambridge, MA: Harvard University Press.

Smith, D. J. (2007). Crime and the life course. In M. Maguire, R. Morgan and R. Reiner (Eds), *The Oxford handbook of criminology* (4th edn.) (pp.641-683). Oxford: Oxford University Press.

Spens, I. (1994). *Architecture of incarceration*. London: Academy Editions.

Steiner, B. & Wooldredge, J. (2009). Rethinking the link between institutional crowding and inmate misconduct. *The Prison Journal, 89*, 205-233.

Struckman-Johnson, C. & Struckman-Johnson, D. (2000). Sexual coercion rates in seven midwestern prison facilities for men. *The Prison Journal, 80*, 379-390.

Sykes, G. (1958). *The society of captives*. Princeton: Princeton University Press.

The Prison Journal (2008). *Special Issue on Supermax Prisons, 88*, 3-176.

Toch, H. (1992). *Mosaic of despair: Human breakdowns in prison*. NJ: Princeton University Press.

Toch, H. (2005). Reinventing prisons. In A. Liebling and S. Maruna (Eds), *The effects of imprisonment* (pp. 465-473). Devon: Willan.

Toch, H. & Adams, K. (2002). *Acting out: Maladaptive behaviour in confinement*. Washington, DC: American Psychological Association.

Walmsley, R. (2005).*World prison population list (6th ed.)*. London: International Centre for Prison Studies.

Wener, R., Frazier, W. & Farbstein, J. (1987). Building better jails. *Psychology Today, 21*, (6), 40-49.

Wheeler, S. (1961). Socialization in correctional communities. *American Sociological Review, 26*, 679-706.

Wolff, N., Shi, J., & Blitz, C. L. (2008). Racial and ethnic disparities in types and sources of victimization inside prison. *The Prison Journal, 88*, 451-472.

Zamble, E. & Porporino, F. (1988). *Coping behaviour and adaptation in prison inmates*. N.Y.: Springer-Verlag.

Zimbardo, P. G., (2007). *The Lucifer effect: How good people turn evil*. NY: Random House.

Zimbardo, P. G., Haney, C., Banks, W. C. & Jaffe, D. (1973). *The psychology of imprisonment: Privation, power and pathology*. Stanford: Stanford University Press.

Chapter 11

MEDIA EFFECTS ON ANTISOCIAL BEHAVIOR IN CHILDREN AND ADOLESCENTS

Pablo Espinosa and Miguel Clemente
Universidad de La Coruña, Spain.

ABSTRACT

There is mounting evidence on the effects of media on antisocial and aggressive behaviour. This chapter reviews current research on the topic, which has focused on how media violence effects on arousal, affect, cognition and behaviour. Most evidence comes from television and video games research and the differential effects of these two types of media on the individual are examined. Additional evidence from studies on the Internet effects and music and lyrics is also provided. The main short and long-term effects of media violence are also discussed, suggesting different explanatory models. Another important distinction examined relates to the types of violence displayed on the media. Most of the effects of media violence relate to the development, over-learning and reinforcement of aggression-related knowledge structures, including hostile attribution bias, aggressive actions against others, expectations of violence, positive attitudes towards violence, the belief that violence is acceptable and appropriate to solve problems, and desensitization. Although aggressive and antisocial behavior is affected by media violence, there is also evidence that a raw amount of media use, regardless of its violent content, has an impact on behavior. The social perspective of the individual mediates the relation between raw media use and behavior. This is explained in terms of the lack of role-taking opportunities that media provide, compared to other sources of socialization. The inability to adopt another's perspective and the lack of opportunities for cognitive de-centering and the reduction of egocentric bias limit the adolescent's capacity to calculate the consequences of own behavior. It also limits his/her understanding of the needs, feelings, desires, purposes, and worries of other people. Individuals in this situation would be unable to grasp the most direct consequences of their behavior and, consequently, would be more likely to engage in antisocial conducts.

INTRODUCTION

Media is currently one of the major sources of socialization for children and adolescents (and probably adults too), together with family, peers, school and other social institutions. Media contents and the amount of time children and adolescents are exposed to it deserve attention because of the potential effects it can have on cognition, emotions and behavior. It is estimated that American children from ages 8 to 18 use different types of media on an average of 5 hours per day, specifically, they watch TV 2 ½ hours, listen around 1 ½ hours of music and play video games about 20 minutes (Roberts, Foehr, Rideout, & Brodie, 1999). This length of time is similar to the time they spend at school, but they are exposed to media all year, including weekends and holidays.

It is also relevant to consider the contents of media they are exposed to, since they spend more than 50% of their leisure time watching TV and 61% of the programs contain violence (Browne & Hamilton-Giachritsis, 2005), and even 50% of the news in TV news programs depicted varied forms of violence (Johnson, 1996). In television the level of violence is five violent acts per hour during prime time, whereas the exposition to cartoons gets from 20 to 25 acts of violence per hour (Sweet & Singh, 1994). Similarly, Wilson, Smith, Potter, Kunkel, Linz, and Colvin, (2002) state that children's TV programs contain more violence than adult films with up to 30 violent acts per hour. Furthermore, Yomota and Thompson (2000) found that 64 movies from a sample of General Public–rated animation films included a violent act on average; violence in these movies lasted 11.8% of its length. Still, children TV programs are not the only source of TV violence they are exposed to; research shows that almost 75% of children aged 3 through 8 years old watch TV programs that are not specifically child-oriented (Von Feilitzen, 1990).

Regarding video, computer, electronic and arcade games (hereafter video games), 88% of children aged 8-18 years in the US play video games at least occasionally. The average amount of videogame playing is 13.2 hours per week, higher in males (16.4 hr/week) than in females (9.2 hr/week) (Gentile, 2009). Not long ago, a study that used a sample of children aged 2-17 years (Gentile and Walsh, 2002) found that the average amount of game playing was 7 hr/week (males play 13hr/week and females 5 hr/week). The age range in these two studies is very different, but the increase in video game habits is nevertheless informative.

Videogames contain more violence than TV programs. Haninger and Thompson (2004), in a review of teen-rated videogames content, found that 94% depicted some kind of violence and violent content last 36% of game time on average. Furthermore, Thompson and Haninger (2001) found that 64% of General Public-rated videogames contain some sort of violence. In general, a consistent finding in experimental and correlational research, supported by meta-analytical studies, shows that children and teens who are exposed to violent media tend to act more aggressively (Anderson & Bushman, 2001, 2002b; Anderson & Dill, 2000; Bushman & Anderson, 2001; Huesmann, Moise-Titus, & Podolski, 2003). Derksen and Strasburger (1996) summarize media effects of violence, antisocial behavior, and aggression in the media in the following categories: *1)* displacement of healthy activities, *2)* modeling of inappropriate behavior, *3)* disinhibition, *4)* desensitization, *5)* aggressive arousal, and *6)* association with risk taking behavior. Similarly, Urra, Clemente and Vidal (2000), and Clemente & Vidal (1996) review the following effects of violence displayed in media: *1)* learning aggressive attitudes and behaviors, *2)* desensitization towards violence, *3)* fear of being a victim of violence, *4)* fostering cognitive justification processes for violent behaviors, *5)* cognitive association via a priming effect, and *6)* transference of excitability. Media violence is also related to poorer executive functioning and self-control, especially in adolescents who have a history of aggressive-disruptive behavior (Kronenberger *et al.*, 2005).

Also, frequent exposure to media violence may lead to cognitive distortions (Richmond & Wilson, 2008). Cognitive distortions interfere with moral standards, which act as an internal control that inhibit inappropriate behavior. These moral standards are acquired over the course of socialization and act as guiding principles in order to judge own behavior and self-regulate actions. People self-regulate and refrain from violence because these moral standards act as aggression inhibitors. In some circumstances these standards are overridden, and people "disengage" from their regular moral standards and engage in blameworthy behaviors. Moral disengagement is a cognitive distortion technique that focuses on redefining negative behavior into positive behavior (or at least not so negative behavior) as a way of escaping self-conscious blaming of their behavior (Bandura, Barbaranelli, Caprara, & Pastorelli, 1996).

Bandura describes eight mechanisms of moral disengagement: moral justification, sanitizing language, advantageous comparison, displacement of responsibility, diffusion of responsibility, distortion of possible consequences, attribution of blame, and dehumanization (Bandura, Barbaranelli, Caprara, Pastorelli, & Regalia, 2001). People use one or more of these mechanisms to justify unjustifiable behavior. For instance, vandalism can be justified by displacement of responsibility ("I was drunk"); diffusion of responsibility ("everyone else was also doing it during the protest"); or attribution of blame ("I got carried away, I wouldn't have even thought of it if it wasn't for the others").

Richmond and Wilson (2008) found that the relation between media violence and aggression is partially explained by moral disengagement, which provokes distorted attitudes towards violence. These distorted attitudes can involve a positive perception of violence, hostile attribution bias or an underestimation of its consequences. This finding is congruent with Anderson's General Aggression Model (GAM, Anderson & Dill, 2000), which states that repeated exposure to media violence on the long term reinforces aggression-related knowledge structures (attitudes, beliefs, perceptual and behavioral schemata).

There is controversy on whether media violence has a greater impact on children with emotional difficulties. It has been argued that violent media exposure affects more vulnerable children. In their review, Mitrofan, Paul, and Spencer (2009) found mixed results that precluded any conclusion on whether violent media enhances aggression more on children with emotional and behavioral difficulties. So, the hypothesis is that in order to be affected by violent contents in the media, a child would necessarily have other predisposing dispositional factors, yet it has not a straightforward support.

OVERVIEW OF VIOLENCE EFFECTS ACROSS TYPES OF MEDIA

TV Watching

The specific effects of violence on TV have been widely studied. Pennell and Browne (1999) indicate that violence on television can affect behavior in several ways: *1)* through imitation of violent roles and acts of aggression, *2)* triggering aggressive impulses in predisposed individuals, *3)* desensitizing feelings of sympathy towards victims, *4)* creating an indifference to the use of violence, and *5)* perceiving violent acts as a socially acceptable response to stress and frustration. Other evidence suggests that television violence increases hostile behavior (Browne & Hamilton-Giachritsis, 2005; Zillmann & Weaver, 1997), arousal towards aggression (Bushman, 1998), and acceptance of violence as a mean of conflict resolution (Zillmann & Weaver, 1997). Similarly, Vidal, Clemente, and Espinosa (2003) confirm that under 18's those who spend more hours watching TV, value violence more positive, bothemotionally and cognitively. Osofky and Osofky (1998) suggest that continued exposure to violence may cause youngsters to identify less with victims of violence and more with perpetrators.

The influence of TV on violence is not limited to childhood, Johnson, Cohen, Smailes, Kasen, and Brook (2002), report that males (but not females) who watch more TV during early adolescence, at age 14, are more prone to being violent towards others, although no effect was found for other types of antisocial or criminal behaviors. Furthermore, during young adulthood (age 22) watching TV is related to more aggressive behaviors both in men and women. Nevertheless, agreement on these findings is not unanimous. Savage (2004), in a methodological review, strongly criticized the methodological shortcomings of many studies that claim a link between television and violent criminal behavior. Other authors, like Grooves (1997) also doubt the relationship between television and actual behavioral consequences, and Felson (1996) warned about the possible "sponsor effect" in this type of research. He argues that an experimenter who shows violent films creates a permissive atmosphere likely to affect antisocial behavior as a whole (both aggressive and non-aggressive antisocial behavior).

On the other hand, research on TV exposure effects is not limited to aggression related behaviors, Collins *et al.,* (2004) showed that heavy exposure to sexual content on television relate, strongly, to teens' initiation of sexual intercourse. Chandra *et al.*, (2008) also found that watching sex on TV was related to teen pregnancy. In their study, with 12-17 years-old the proportion of teens who became pregnant or were responsible for a pregnancy was two times greater among those exposed to high levels of televised sexual content (90th percentile) than those exposed to low levels (10th percentile).

Video Game Playing

A large body of research examined the specific effects of violent video games on children and young people. Some positive aspects have been identified such as classroom learning, language teaching, fostering friendship, and being an aid in therapy with children. Unfortunately, a range of negative aspects have also been described: addiction, physical symptoms (soreness in joints), social isolation, low self esteem and aggression (see Colwell & Payne, 2000), and obesity, especially in young girls, although this effect is probably linked to sedentary activities (Vandewater, Shim, & Caplovitz, 2004).

It has been argued that exposure to violent video games increases aggressive thoughts, hostile attribution bias, aggressive affect, aggressive behavior, cardiovascular arousal and other aggression related phenomena (Anderson, 2004; Anderson & Dill, 2000; Dill &Dill, 1998; Gentile, Lynch, Linder, & Walsh, 2004; Kish, 1998). This is also true for young children (Funk, Hagan, Schimming, Bullock, Buchman, & Myers, 2002; Griffiths, 1999), who become more aggressive after playing or watching a video game. Anderson and Dill (2000) also found that violent video games are positively related to aggressive behavior, and violent and non-violent delinquency (although the effect was stronger for violent delinquency, 0.46 vs. 0.31 for non-violent delinquency), and this effect was stronger in males and individuals with aggressive tendencies. Anderson and Dill found that academic achievement is negatively related to the overall amount of time spent using computer games. In general, the summary of evidences suggests that violent videogames are positively related to aggressive behavior (Anderson & Dill, 2000, Collwell & Payne, 2000).

Other authors, like Wiegman and van Schie (1998) argue that, while they find no relation between video game playing and aggressiveness, there is a significant negative correlation with prosocial behavior. Anderson and Bushman (2001) and Anderson (2004) also report this negative link with prosocial behavior. In any case, according to Anderson (2004) the effects of violent media on cognition, affect and behavior are underestimated. He compared methodologically sound research with other research with potential weaknesses, finding that, although results were significant in both cases, methodologically sound research produced larger effect sizes.

DIFFERENCES BETWEEN TV VIEWING AND VIDEO GAME PLAYING EFFECTS

Many studies found differences between TV and videogames, generally resulting stronger effects in videogames. For instance, it was found that videogame effects on arousal (Brooks, 2000) and violence are stronger than those of movies or television (Dill & Dill, 1998). The reason of this impact is that violent videogames have unique features compared to other media violence (Dill & Dill, 1998):

Videogames provide direct rewards for aggressive action in the game (points, levels, special equipment). This characteristic enhances their addictive nature. The reinforcing characteristics of videogames can promote learning and enacting aggressive behavior patterns (Anderson & Dill, 2000; Collwell & Payne, 2000). In order to succeed and get rewards, players must identify and choose violent strategies. Repeated violence choices resulting in a continuous cycle of reward (Funk, Baldacci, Pasold, & Baumgardner, 2004).

Identification with the aggressor and the subsequent increase in the chances of behaving violently is potentially higher, especially in the "first person perspective" and in games were the player could choose from a variety of customizable characters.

Videogames are increasingly realistic in graphic and sound, combined with extreme violent action. Some video games have a higher budget than Hollywood films and they are developed with minute detail.

The user of a video game is on an active role, and there is more control by the player (Collwell & Payne, 2000), whereas in other media, like TV, the user is passive. The players create video gameactions, rather than simply be their recipients. This can lead to a higher chance of developing aggressive behavior patterns, and facilitate the rehearsal of specific behavioral skills and patterns, like hitting the opponent (Anderson & Dill, 2000).

In the case of people with an aggressive personality, their aggressive behavioral patterns are more developed, then can be easily activated and their social perception patterns are equally biased towards interpreting social events aggressively or in an aggression-enhancing way. These individuals perceive more violence than there really is and expect problems to be resolved violently. Violent videogames presumably make aggressive patterns and thoughts more accessible than TV (Anderson & Dill, 2000; Kiewitz & Weaver, 2001).

In line with Dill and Dill (1998) and Brooks (2000), Clemente, Espinosa, and Vidal (2008) found that video games are a significant predictor of antisocial aggressive behavior, while television is not. A plausible explanation is that video games, due to their rewarding nature, are more reinforcing and addictive than television. Since video games allow the rehearsal of behavioral patterns, and because most video games do not promote prosocial behavior (most games are competitive in nature or cooperative on a very limited trade-off basis) the chances are that the behavioral patterns acquired through interactive media are very self-centered. Limited, self-centered, cognitive and behavioral patterns strongly reinforced will likely lead to antisocial behavior.

Internet Use

There is less research being conducted on the specific effects of the Internet on children and youth's socialization. Among the effects of exposure to the Internet on users, it was found that the characteristics of regular Internet users and non-regular Internet users differ in a variety of ways. The more time they spend online the more they loose social contact; expend less time with other media, more time at home and less time buying in regular stores (Nie & Erbring, 2000). Similarly, Gracia-Blanco, Vigo-Anglada, Fernández-Pérez, and Marcó-Rabonés (2002) underline that the usual problems derived from being online are negative effects on social and family relationships, reduction of other daily activities, losing working or studying time, an increase in the desire for being online, lose track of time while online and feeling guilty for those negative effects.

A key variable in the study of the Internet effects is the degree of involvement of the individual in online activities. In this sense, Loges and Jung (2001) propose the concept of "Internet connectedness" as a measure of importance of the Internet in an individual's everyday life. Loges and Jung (2001) together with Jung, Qiu, and Kim (2001) argue that the relationship between a person and the Internet is not properly reflected in traditional measures such as hours spent online. Connectedness is not defined as the different uses a person gives to the Internet but rather as socially structured relation between the individual and the communication environment.

This construct would be composed of three dimensions:

1. History and context (when and where gets online);
2. Scope and intensity (amount of access, variety of goals and interests in the Internet); and
3. Centrality in one's life (impact on one's life and extent to which one would miss the Internet if it were no longer available).

Wether Internet connectedness or other construct are able to capture the use of the Internet as a means of socialization it would be very useful to measure the impact of this media on behavior and cognition.

MUSIC

Media violence doesn't necessarily need to be displayed on a screen. Rubin, West, and Mitchel (2001) found correlational evidence that consumers of rap and heavy metal music report a more hostile attitude than consumers of other genres. Due to the correlational nature of this study, conclusions cannot be drawn about the directionality of this relationship (musical genres can make people more hostile vs. hostile people tend to choose certain musical genres). There can even be other confounding variables at stake, being a fan of a music movement depends on more variables than the nature of the lyrics, such as outlooks, attitudes and values. In an experimental setting, listening to aggressive relative to neutral song lyrics increased short-term aggressive thoughts and hostile feelings (Anderson, Carnagey, & Eubanks, 2003). Still, music is not the most violent media. Only 15% of music videos contain physical violence (Smith & Boyson, 2002), although there are no accounts of the proportion of violent song lyrics or other types of violence in either lyrics or music videos.

EFFECTS OF SHORT-TERM AND LONG-TERM EXPOSURE TO MEDIA VIOLENCE

A major distinction on media violence research has been the effects provoked by short-term vs. long-term exposure. Most of the effects, already shown, relate to the effects of a long exposure to media violence on affect, cognition and behavior. Generally, more attention has been paid in the effects of long-term exposure; as a consequence short-term exposure is assumed to dissipate more or less quickly. While this assumption may be accurate, to some extent, it is still interesting to differentiate both kinds of effects, since effects of short-term exposure have actual consequences to the individual and the repeated accumulation of effects caused by a short-term exposure may have a longer-lasting impact.

SHORT-TERM EXPOSURE EFFECTS

Anderson and Dill (2000) affirm that violent video games may increase aggression in the short term whenever they prime aggressive thoughts, increase hostile feelings or arousal. Barlett and Rodeheffer (2009) state that media violence produces a variety of short-term effects, including an increase in heart rate, especially when it is realistic. Media violence also provokes an increase in aggressive thoughts, aggressive feelings and heart rate (arousal), although repeated exposure shows that these effects stabilize; they do not change after the initial increase. In other words, once individuals have been aggressively primed, there is no additional effect of a continuedly violent video game play.

Recent research (Uhlmann & Swanson, 2004) also shows that associations with the self can predict a number of violent behaviors and these associations can be facilitated by a short-term exposure to violent media. Playing a violent video game over a short period of time (10 min.) resulted in an automatic association of the self with aggressive traits and actions. Exposure to violent media thus influences automatic associations with the self. An explanation for this result is that exposure to violent games temporarily primes alternative aggressive self-representations of the multiple possible selves, some of them are more accessible than others.

Desensitization is a variable strongly related to exposure to media violence. Usually, desensitization is studied as a mechanism that provokes changes on media user's attitudes towards violence and victims, after a long-term or chronic media violence exposure. Nevertheless, desensitization to media violence also has a short-term impact. Even a brief exposure to media violence may alter physiological and affective reactions to violence and cause increased aggression, reduce sympathy to victims of violence, and a decreased probability of helping victims, even though it is not yet clear how this short-term mechanism works. Bushman and Anderson (2009) state that after viewing a violent movie or playing a violent video game, people take longer to help a stranger apparently in distress. This delay is explained as a desensitization to violence, since it provokes various short-term effects including decrease attention to violent events, failure to recognize an event as an emergency, reduction of the perceived seriousness of an injury or that the emergency exists. Furthermore, feelings of personal responsibility are diminished when desensitization leads to decrease sympathy for the victim, increase a belief that violence is normative, and decreases negative attitudes toward violence. Repeated exposure to media violence over a short period of time reduces the psychological impact of media violence temporarily and desensitizes viewers to violence, reducing its psychological impact. Viewers tend to feel less sympathy towards the victims of violence and actually enjoy more violence portrayed in the media (Fanti, Vanman, Henrich, & Avraamides, 2009).

As for the duration of short term effects, there is evidence from Barlett, Branch, Rodeheffer, and Harris (2009) that the immediate effects of violent game plays on aggressive feelings and thoughts last less than 4 minutes, and between 4 and 9 minutes for arousal. These three internal state components mediate the relation between violent media and aggressive behavior so it can be argued that the short-term effects of violent game play on behavior can dissipate quickly. It takes from 10 to 20 minutes of game play to stimulate this increase in aggressive thoughts, feelings and arousal.

LONG-TERM EXPOSURE EFFECTS

In addition to those already described, there are a number of effects related to the length of exposure to violence in any setting, and a long-term exposure to violence is assumed in order to play a role in the onset of dysfunctional behavior. Adolescents exposed to greater amounts of videogame violence are more hostile, have more arguments with teachers, are oftently involved in physical fights and get worse grades at school. Furthermore, adolescents low in hostility but high in violent videogame exposure get involved in more fights than high hostile adolescents who are low in exposure to violent video games (Gentile, Lynch, Linder, & Walsh, 2004).

Anderson and Dill (2000) affirm that long-term exposure to violent content may result in the development, over-learning and reinforcement of aggression related knowledge structures. These structures include hostile attribution bias, aggressive actions against others, expectations of violence, positive attitudes towards violence, the belief that violence is acceptable and appropriate to solve problems, and desensitization. As stated, desensitization is a variable widely used in research on media violence. Media violence can have an impact on desensitization in the long run. A distinction can be made between two types of desensitization, emotional and cognitive. Emotional desensitization occurs when there is a reduction in emotional reaction to events which would typically elicit a strong response (empathy if the situation involves a person). Cognitive desensitization happens when people change the belief that violence is uncommon, and unlikely from the belief that violence is common and inevitable. Both types of desensitization decrease the likelihood that violent behavior will either be censured, including owns'. When desensitization occurs, the process of moral evaluation is disrupted because the individual fails to perceive or respond to the cues present in the situation to elicit the moral evaluative process (the individual fails to see he is after a social problem or moral situation). In this situation, actions may be taken without considering their moral implications. Lack of empathy and pro-violence attitudes may imply a previous desensitization to distress. With these two important components, the moral evaluation process can be affected by exposure to violence in real life or media (Funk *et al.*, 2004).

Exposure to video game violence is associated to lower empathy in 10-years-old, and video game and movie violence exposure are associated to stronger pro-violence attitudes in children of this age. Violent video games contribute to the development of positive attitudes towards violence because games make violence seem common and acceptable and desensitize the player to real-life consequences of violence. Also, violent video games can impair empathy, since empathy is not adaptive in violent games, and moral evaluation is often non-existent, whereas violence is continuously rewarded (Funk *et al.*, 2004).

Another variable related to long-term exposure to media violence is hostile attribution. Krahé and Möller (2004) found that exposure and attraction to violent games were related to hostile attribution. Processed information based on aggressive scripts can lead to the development of a hostile attributional style, that is, to interpret ambiguous stimuli as hostile or aggressive. When hostile intent is attributed to other person's ambiguous actions and results in reactive aggressive behavior, the link between perception of hostility and aggression is reinforced, following a flawed logic or a sort of self-fulfilling prophecy ("He was looking funny at me, I hit him and there was a fight, so I was right in hitting him first because there was going to be a fight"). This hostile attribution bias may start a cycle, resulting in the long-term stability of aggressive behavior. This relation was mediated by aggressive normative beliefs. Thus, the use of violent video games has a long-term effect on aggressive behavior via the acceptance of aggressive norms.

Finally, results of longitudinal studies on media violence are of greater interest. Across longitudinal studies long-term television violence influences aggressiveness (Pennell & Browne, 1999; Eron, Huesmann, Lefkowitz, & Walder, 1996; Anderson *et al.*, 2008) and crime (Huessman et al., 2003). In their longitudinal study, Huessman et al. (2003) found that the correlation between aggressiveness and TV violence exposure was about .20 ($p<.01$) for men and women. For instance, males who were exposed to more TV violence during childhood were three times more likely to beat their partner or having been arrested for a crime. These effects were established after controlling variables like dispositional aggressiveness, intellectual capacity, social status and parental variables such as aggressiveness, TV use and discipline style in parents. Wallenius and Punamäki (2008) also found a link between digital game violence and direct aggression longitudinally and synchronously, moderated by parent-child communication in interaction with sex and age. Among young male children or female children with poor parent-child communication, video game violence predicted aggression. Additionally, in a 30-month longitudinal study with adolescents, Möller and Krahé (2009) found that the combination of exposure to video game violence, normative beliefs sanctioning violence and hostile attribution bias predicted physical and relational aggression synchronously. Longitudinally, violence exposure predicted physical aggression, aggressive norms and hostile attribution bias. It is worth noting that game violence predicted aggression 30 months later, but aggressive behavior did not predict game use in the posttest, hinting at the directionality of the relationship.

EXPLANATORY MODELS

Several recent models account findings previously presented. According to Bandura's social cognitive theory of mass communication (Bandura, 1994), observational learning does not automatically lead to actual imitation of target behavior. It rather leads to the inference of rules of conduct that can be applied under different circumstances. This extrapolation of rules is called abstract modelling. Through this kind of modelling it is how viewers may adopt certain values that for example, might influence attitudes towards aggression. Berkowitz (1990), within his cognitive-neoassociationistic model affirms that violent media, automatically prime aggressive thoughts and feelings, which in turn prime aggressive action tendencies. Repeated exposure to violent media may make aggressive thoughts and actions permanently accessible, increasing the probability that an individual would choose to behave violent, especially when provoked or frustrated. Individuals higher in aggressive traits would have a cognitive-associative network more linked to aggression and when exposed to violence they would more readily accept violence alternatives to conflict resolution (Zillman and Weaver, 1997).

Huesmann (Huessman, Moise-Titus, & Podolski, 2003) proposes that the socio-cognitive observational learning theory or script-based model assumes that as children get older, social behavior and cognitive patterns which they acquire vicariously from their family, peers, community and media become more complex and abstract. Watching violence habitually in their environment makes children more likely to attribute hostility to other's behaviors, which makes them more likely to behave aggressively. In time, normative beliefs on which social behaviors are appropriate become internalized and work as filters to limit inappropriate behaviors. These normative beliefs are influenced by children behavior and other behaviors in their environment, including those in the media. In the long run, exposure to violence fosters aggressive problem-solving patterns, hostile attribution biases, and normative beliefs approving of violence.

The GAAM (General Affective Aggression Model) and more recently the GAM (General Aggression Model) (Anderson & Dill, 2000; Anderson & Bushman, 2001), state that through the use of violent media, especially videogames, individuals rehearse aggressive patterns that teach and reinforce vigilance against enemies, aggressive behaviors towards others, expectances that others will act aggressively, positive attitudes towards the use of violence, and belief that violent solutions are appropriate. As the individual becomes more aggressive, his/her environment reacts to this, and the kind of people willing to interact with this individual, the type of interactions maintained, and the kind of social situations accessible to him/her, change. While interactions with other aggressive individuals may increase, the rest of interactions would worsen. The GAM also accounts media violence with cognitive and arousal effects, teaching the individual how to fight, making aggressive cognitions more accessible (both aggressive behavioral patterns and aggressive perceptive schemata, see also Buselle, 2003 and Anderson, Camagey, & Eubanks, 2003), increasing excitability and an aggressive affective state. The long-term effects of violent media come from the development, rehearsing and finally automatization of aggressive knowledge structures and perceptual schemata. Anderson and Bushman (2002a) includes in this knowledge, structures, stable cognitive factors related to human aggression, which have been widely researched, like hostile perception, hostile expectancies and hostile attribution. He also includes narcissistic self-esteem as a factor positively related to aggression and values that entail the acceptance of violence as a means of conflict resolution (i.e. honor).

Finally, the downward spiral model (Slater, Henry, Swaim, & Anderson, 2003) proposes some interesting perspectives that explain the concurrent effects of media violence and aggressiveness in individuals. According to this model, aggressiveness and media violence are mutually reinforcing, both leading to the other and producing aggregate effects over time. The media effects on antisocial behaviors would be most acute in individuals more vulnerable to this type of behaviors (males, less socially and culturally inhibited, or individuals with high sensation seeking tendencies). So a young person with aggressive tendencies would be prone to seek violent content in the media, this would increase and reinforce his/her aggressive tendencies and start again the cycle of seeking further violent content repeatedly.

TYPES OF VIOLENCE DISPLAYED IN THE MEDIA

It has been suggested that there would be different effects on behavior, affect and cognition according to the types of aggression displayed on the screen. One primary distinction can be made between realistic and unrealistic violence. In this case, Barlett and Rodeheffer (2009) affirm that realistic, compared to unrealistic, violence causes an increase in heart rate, but it provokes no changes in aggressive thoughts. This is consistent with the hypothesis of aggressive priming, which states that it is enough to prime violence, regardless of its realism, to increase aggressive thoughts. Differences between types of aggression have also been hypothesized for justified versus unjustified aggression and direct versus indirect aggression.

In the first case, socially justified violence can be defined as violence used to protect a victim, to defend a moral value or to prevent some kind of wrongdoing, whereas socially unjustified violence is committed with selfish, unlawful or evil intent or gratuitous violence.

Vidal, Clemente, and Espinosa (2003) in a study were children of age 13 watched video fragments of socially justified and unjustified violence and completed pre and post-tests of attitudes towards violence. They found that media violence is better valued and it is more attractive after watching it on film, especially when it is justified. In a recent study, Clemente, Espinosa, and Vidal (2009) found a correspondence between early adolescents' who self-perceived traits and those perceived the main character of a film, exerted socially justified violence and with whom participants felt identified. Self-perceived traits were opposed to those perceived in the main character's opponents. These results suggest that being identified with an attractive violent character that performs socially justified violence, may result as a character they identify with violence. In video games, violence is also presented as justified, without negative consequences and even funny (Funk, Baldacci, Pasold, & Baumgardner, 2004). In this respect, Richmond and Wilson (2008) suggest that justified violence in media may have a greater impact than "senseless" violence, since it possibly promotes the assimilation of distorted attitudes towards violence more efficiently (portraying violence as an acceptable means of resolving conflicts, for instance).

As for the distinction between direct and indirect aggression, direct aggression is a type of aggression were the perpetrator does not tries to minimize the possibility of discovery by the victim in order to avoid consequences. It can be physical or verbal, but the perpetrator does not take any measure to prevent a response from the victim. In contrast, indirect aggression is a manipulative form of aggression often initiated under anonymity. The perpetrator minimizes the cost of harming others. Thus, the perpetrator does not confront the target of the aggression and often uses the established peer network. Even if discovered, the perpetrator leaves room for deceptive strategies such as denial or creating alternative explanations of an event in order to be exonerated from any blame. Examples include gossiping, ignoring, dirty looks, spreading secrets, ostracizing others from the group, disparaging comments, non-verbal aggression (i.e., rolling eyes, negative body posture) or otherwise hurting or manipulating other people's feelings (Coyne & Whitehead, 2008; Ostrov, Gentile, & Crick, 2006).

Indirect aggression has been rarely examined in media research. Nevertheless, Coyne and Archer (2004) state that indirect aggression is extremely common in adolescents' popular TV programs. It rates higher than physical violence. In fact, more than 90% of the UK programs show indirect aggressions. Even Disney films portray an average of 9.23 acts of indirect aggression per hour, and this is a low rate among children's films (Coyne & Whitehead, 2008). On TV, females are more often portrayed as indirectly aggressive and males as directly aggressive. Acts of indirect aggression are often carried out by attractive characters, rewarded and justified. The high amount and portrayal of female indirect aggression on media might have an influence on subsequent female aggression, confirming the gender linked-hypothesis that states that females would use more indirect aggression often than males so that they can fulfill gender-specific social goals, whereas males they rely more on direct aggression (Crick & Grockpeter, 1995).

Indirect aggression on media can influence both direct and indirect aggressive behaviors. Coyne, Archer, and Eslea (2004) found that after watching videos showing either direct or indirect aggression, participants were more, directly and indirectly, aggressive towards an irritating confederate compared to a control group who watched a non-aggression video. In another study, Coyne et al. (2008) found that participants who previously watched a direct or indirect aggression video, gave louder noise blasts to adversaries in a competitive computer game, compared to those who viewed a non-aggressive video. There was no difference in the loudness of the blast between participants who viewed either aggression videos. Hence, indirect aggression in the media effects may be as influential as direct aggression.

Further evidence comes from a two-year longitudinal study with preschoolers. Ostrov, Gentile, and Crick (2006) found that media exposure predicted various types of aggression and prosocial behavior. Watching television was associated longitudinally and synchronously with indirect aggression, but only for females. In contrast, watching television was associated longitudinally and synchronously with direct aggression, but only for males. Perhaps children are being exposed to gender-specific aggression models from a very early age, and identification with same-gender role model leads to learning different aggressive schemas and tactics.

GENDER DIFFERENCES IN MEDIA VIOLENCE EFFECTS

Several gender differences moderate the link between TV and aggression. Huessman *et al.*, (2003), found that TV violence is related to direct aggression in males and indirect aggression as females. Kiewitz and Weaver (2001) also found that gender moderates the impact of violent media on violence perceptions and interpersonal conflicts. In general, males prefer more violent content in media than females (Valkenburg & Soeters, 2001). However, it has been found interesting results that indicate otherwise. In a study by Clemente, Espinosa, and Vidal (2008) with adolescents, males reported a higher frequency of aggressive behaviors, and also their pattern of media use differed from females. Males spent more time using computers, although the TV and Internet use, and preference for violent video/PC games was not statistically different from girls. Very interestingly, females' aggression was predicted by the amount of media use, whereas males' aggression was not. In males, aggression was predicted by preference for violent media. It may be that males' socialization patterns are more associated with media use, especially as regards to computer use, as it has been traditionally more male oriented, with male oriented games, male characters in games and video games being considered more "male toys". Thus, for males, a higher or lower amount of used media would not make a difference in terms of behavioral effects and a difference in their exposure to violent media. As for females, computer appeared to be more off-trend. So the amount of usage did make a difference. This result suggests a difference in media socialization between males and females. This may due because males have a higher baseline of aggressive behavior, they need more stimuli to experience an increase in their aggressive behaviors, while simple exposure to media is enough for females. Due to the correlational nature of the study, it cannot be ruled out that aggressive males have a preference for violent media, and not only for consuming more media, while aggressive females have a tendency for using more media, not just media with violent content (or a tendency for engaging in activities more akin to male socialization, in terms of media use).

PROSOCIAL CONTENT IN THE MEDIA

Violence in media is highly prevalent, but some studies have also examined the effects of prosocial contents displayed in media and their potentially positive effects. A few examples of these effects and explanations are discussed in the following lines. For instance, it has long been established that media can be highly effective in changing consumers' habits, generally through commercials. In this line, media has often been used to promote changes in public health risk behaviors. An unfavorable portrayal of habits or behaviors can influence people's social perception and reduce the acceptability of certain behaviors, such as driving under the influence of alcohol (Yanovitzky & Stryker, 2001).

Another evidence of the effects of media on prosocial behavior comes from Morgan, Movius, and Cody (2009), who found that after watching TV dramas that encourage organ donation, viewers who were not previously organ donors were more likely to donate organs, especially if they were emotionally involved in the narrative. Also, Greitemeyer (2009) found that listening to songs with prosocial lyrics (relative to neutral lyrics) increased the accessibility of prosocial thoughts, leding to more interpersonal empathy and fostered helping behavior towards people in need. Thus, prosocial lyrics were found to affect cognition, emotion and behavior. Anderson's General Aggression Model (GAM; Anderson & Dill, 2000; Anderson & Bushman, 2001) proposes that media exposure affects cognition, emotion (affect and arousal) and ultimately behavior. The General Learning Model (GLM) proposed by Buckley and Anderson (2006) has been developed to provide a wider range of explanation on different media effects based on the structure of the GAM. Expanding on GAM, the GLM proposes that media effects can also be positive, rather than only negative. Whereas media violence is related to aggression, prosocial media would promote prosocial behavior.

EFFECTS OF THE AMOUNT OF MEDIA USE IRRESPECTIVE OF CONTENT

Most research and models proposed in the literature look at the relation between violent media content and aggressive or antisocial behavior, while research on the raw effects of media on violent behavior has been scarce in comparison. There can certainly be a huge difference between violent and non-violent media contents, nevertheless there is a great amount of evidence suggesting a link between media violence and aggression performed by young viewers; however, evidence not as straightforward as it is would be desired. For instance, some studies found an effect on males or females and other studies yield contradictory results (Anderson & Dill, 2000).

There are positive effects of using video games in children and adolescents, like classroom learning, language teaching, fostering friendship and as an aid in children therapy. Unfortunately, negative aspects have also been described: addiction, physical symptoms (soreness in joints), social isolation, low self-esteem and antisocial behaviors such as aggression (Colwell & Payne, 2000). Another general negative effect it is addiction to media, and in particular, video games. It is estimated that 8.5% of video game players are addicted (Gentile, 2009) and a similar rate (9.9%) was found in Spain (Tejeiro-Salguero & Bersabé-Morán, 2002). These gamers spend twice as much time playing compared to non-pathological gamers and show attention problems. Video game addiction significantly predicts poorer school performance.

Gentile *et al., (*2004) argue that regardless of content, the amount of video game play can negatively affect children and youths by displacing other activities. Video games and other media can take the place of other habits such as study, reading, family interaction, and social play with peers. Therefore, it is important to examine videogame play in the context of other media habits. Despite findings on the negative effects of amount of game play in school performance, Gentile found no relation between the amount of media use and physical aggression; although we reviewed abundant evidence that points in the opposite direction.

Primary evidence relating raw amount of media use and antisocial and aggressive behavior comes from neuroscience research. It has been reported that video game use can affect the brain, particularly the prefrontal cortex. The prefrontal cortex is linked to morality, creativity, flexibility and making decisions in ambiguous situations. Damasio (1999) reported that damage to this area of the brain, early in life, results in antisocial behavior and an inability to recognize antisocial behaviors as immoral. Mathews, Kronenberger, Wang, Lurito, Lowe, and Dunn (2005), state that video game playing suppresses the activation of the prefrontal cortex during problem solving, turning the brain activation into one that looks like of an aggressive delinquent.

Other evidences come from Johnson, Cohen, Smailes, Kasen, & Brook (2002), who found that high amounts of TV viewing in adolescence (they did not measure content and used the raw amount of TV viewing) predicted an increase in aggressive behavior in adulthood. Santisteban, Alvarado, and Recio (2007) also offer evidence that aggressive behavior relates to global amount of TV viewing and video game playing, together with other habits like homework dedication and leisure activities like reading. Ostrov, Gentile, and Crick (2006) research did discriminate between media contents. They argue that while violent media is indeed associated with aggression, violence-free media is not without risks. They found that exposure to educational media is not always only associated to positive behaviors. In particular, children exposed to educational media showed and increase in indirect aggression in a two-year follow-up. This finding suggests that too much media consumption, regardless of content, may have negative consequences to peer relationships.

Gentile and Gentile (2008) propose characteristics in video games that make them ideally suited to be highly effective educational tools. They summarize these characteristics in seven dimensions:

- Video games have clear objectives, often distributed along different game levels. This setup is very appropriate to adjust the learning acquisition to the prior knowledge skills of the learner and his/her learning pace.
- Video games require learning to be active with practice and feedback until the required behaviors are mastered. Practice to achieve a high standard of performance is predictive of how much is remembered later.
- Once mastered, knowledge and skills in the game are practiced to provide over-learning. Through over-learning, knowledge and skills become automatized and consolidated in memory, so the gamer can advance to focus on comprehending new information.
- Objectives in the game are reinforced both extrinsically (in-game bonuses, points, more power, better equipment) and intrinsically (achieving higher levels of

complexity and accomplishing difficult tasks increase self-esteem through feelings of competence). Games reinforce the player's commitment so that they engage actively in the game.
- Video games have a good system of advancement with tutorials to learn how to play and increase difficult levels that require to master the previous ones. Games alternate teaching a skill (i.e. using shooting controls) with immediate practice, feedback, and adjustment to the player's preferences.
- The level of difficulty in the games is adaptable and they offer a good combination of massed and distributed practice. Every try in the game receives feedback (i.e. a score), and players can try repeatedly until they progress. This massed practice eventually produces diminishing returns as the player gets fatigued, but the mental and physical skills of the task began to develop (i.e. hand-eye coordination). Every time the player plays again he/she benefits from distributed practice, relearning anything that was forgotten.
- The video game skills and knowledge are practiced in different situations or problems, acquiring a better chance to be transferred to new contexts and generalized whereas if it is only practiced in one situation. Violent video games come in a variety of formats, some are realistic, some cartoonish, etc., and employ a variety of tools (weapons). Nevertheless they all share a common feature, violence *is* the solution.

Since videogames are very efficient learning tools, their content is indeed relevant, but not only because of the possibility of learning aggressive cognitions, emotional reactions and behaviors. Content is also relevant because of the kind of constrained interactions and the role taking opportunities that take place during the game, regardless of whether they contain violence or not. In this line, Huesmann (2007) suggests that the possible long-term effects of media on behavior is the result of observational learning behaviors and desensitization of emotional processes and in the case of video games, also enactive behavioral processes. This is coherent with the hypothesis that certain cognitive variables would mediate in the relation between media and antisocial behavior during adolescence. In particular, cognitions related to social perspective and empathy (i.e. motivational values or prosocial tendencies) should play a relevant role. In current research, little attention is paid to cognitive variables that relate to the social perspective of the adolescent, and most cognitive and personality variables studied on the analysis between media and aggression have been related to dispositional traits referred to anger and hostility, (Anderson & Bushman, 2001; Kiewitz & Weaver, 2001; Gentile, Lynch, Linder, & Walsh, 2004; Giumetti & Markey, 2007; Zillmann & Weaver, 2007). Huesmann's review (Huesmann, 2007) focuses on media violence, but its conclusions can also support the hypothesis that media, irrespective of content, has a general impact on antisocial behavior in the adolescent. In this sense, Ivory and Kalyanaraman (2007), in a study on the short-term effect of video games, found no difference between players who participated in violent and non-violent games. Although there was no comparison control group, these results support, to some extent, the hypothesis that the effects of videogames happen regardless of their content.

More evidence in this line comes from Clemente, Espinosa, and Vidal (2008), who obtained results linking the amount of media used in aggression, irrespective of its content. This might suggest that media effects is not the result of violent contents, "priming" violent behaviors and cognitions, modeling aggressive behavior patterns or increasing hostile attribution bias, and aggressive patterns of conflict resolution. It is possible that the effect of media on antisocial behavior is due to a general deficit in socialization, given that the quality of socialization that media offers is presumably very limited. Maybe, subjects who watch less television and spend less time with video games and the Internet, engage in other leisure activities such as reading or group play that enhance role taking opportunities or provide a wider social perspective (Espinosa, Clemente, & Vidal, 2002). It might also be that people with a broader social perspective (that is, at a higher stage of moral judgment) reject media as the sole means for entertainment and look for "something else". Additionally, children that watch an excessive amount of television may possibly suffer from social deprivation and do not learn the actual social perspectives from real life people, and only learn the simplified roles and characters portrayed in television. Using a similar argument from the perspective of neuroscience, Spitzer (2005) argues that television effects on aggression are best understood from the perspective of role learning in young people, in terms of neuroplasticity or the brain, generating new synaptic connections to absorb different examples or roles they are exposed to. Spitzer also argues that in children who are exposed to television, part of their experience will consist on degraded and impaired input in sensory terms, for instance, leading to attention disorders. From our perspective, we argue that lacking a proper social perspective leads to egocentric bias, which in turn increases the probability of violent or antisocial behavior.

Espinosa and Clemente (2008) provide additional evidence reporting that social perspective in adolescents, measured through their prosocial tendencies (Carlo & Randall, 2002), together with their motivational values (Schwartz, 1992) are mediating variables in the link between the raw amount of video game playing and aggressive antisocial behaviors. The strength of these mediators diminish the link between violent video game playing and aggressive antisocial behaviors. Both social perspective variables are related to an orientation towards others, either because they imply an external or internal social orientation. For instance, the egocentrism that defines the public social orientation (Carlo & Randall, 2002) is an example of the lack of an internal orientation, whereas personal transcendence (Schwartz, 1992) is an orientation defined by feeling accomplished through the welfare of others.

A plausible explanation for this mediation effect could be that the socialization offered by media lacks in the role taking opportunities. Social interaction and this kind of social deprivation is related to an underdevelopment in social perspective variables. Not being able to adopt other's perspective and the lack of opportunities for cognitive de-centering and reducing egocentric bias, implies a limited capacity to calculate the consequences of the adolescent own behaviors and to understand the needs, feelings, desires, purposes, intentions and worries of others. This can happen via the utilization of learned aggressive schemas wherein there is a lack of more complex social interaction schemas, or absence of the ability to calculate the effect of the aggressive behaviors the individual engages in. This inability to predict the consequences of his/her own behavior can mask the utilization of cognitive distortions (Bandura, Barbanelli, & Caprara, 1996) or provoke a shortsighted social perception caused by a deprived social perspective. Dwelling in his explanation, Espinosa and Clemente (2008) suggest that the kind of socialization provided by video games leads to a deprived social perspective and egocentrism. This effect is probably more extreme when other sources of socialization of the child and adolescent do not act as an effective counterbalance. Adolescents in this situation would be unable to understand anything beyond the most direct consequences of their behavior.

Thus, the mere exposure to video games has a general effect on aggression, which is explained by the social perspective of the child and adolescent, regardless of whether the contents of video games are violent or not. Violence in video games has its own specific effects on behavior, but there is evidence that the amount of video game playing, regardless of content, has also an important effect via the social perspective of the child and adolescent. The following figure shows the effect of the amount of video game playing on antisocial behavior and the mediating role of social perspective variables, even when controlling for violent content.

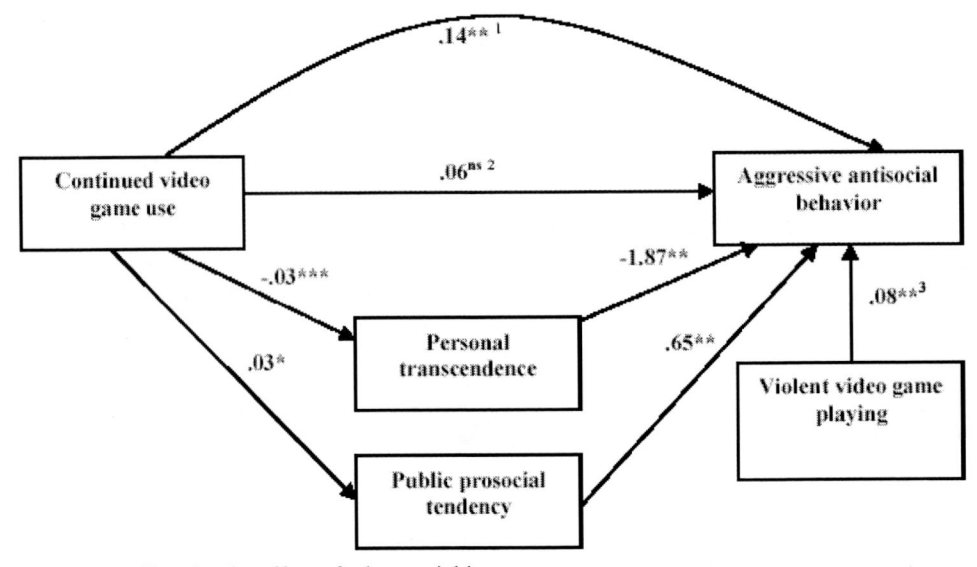

[1] without controlling for the effect of other variables;
[2] controlling for the effect of personal transcendent and public prosocial tendency;
[3] effects on aggressive behavior controlled for exposition to violent games.
^{ns}= not significant *= p<.05; **= p<.01; ***= p<.001 n= 529. Model's adjusted R^2= .170 (p<.001).
Figure 1. Multiple mediation of personal transcendent and public prosocial tendency on the relation between continued video game play and aggressive antisocial behavior (Espinosa & Clemente, 2008).

It appears that computer gaming reduces the chances for social interaction. Many children start playing computer games at a very early age, and if videogame playing or other media substitutes companionship time or other leisure activities involving groups, it becomes the main source for children's socialization. The interaction provided by computer games is very simplified, even in the most complex network games. The gamer just has to take into account the consequences for him or her or maybe for another gamer (computer controlled or not) in quite complex strategy games. Conflict resolution is harsh and swift in these games (often includes eliminating an opposed party), and long-term consequences are irrelevant. This depiction of the level of interaction in computer games matches the social perspective of Kohlberg's (1992) pre-conventional stages of moral development, characterized by an over-present egocentric bias. Thus a child or teen, whose main source of interaction is his or her computer, would not advance much in his/her social perspective and would only acquire limited problem solving patterns (Huessman et al., 2003). This child or teen would even prefer computer gaming to other activities over time, as it would be a comfortable environment where her or his social perspective is not stressed. Social situations would cause him frustration. Frustration is found to be related to aggression approval (Colwell & Payne, 2000) and it is pointed out as an important factor in the relationship between interactive game play and aggression (Brooks, 2000). Thus, frustration, and not knowing how to properly interact with people would likely result on antisocial behavior.

Conclusion

Research has repeatedly shown the direct effects of media violent content on children and adolescents' behavior, cognition and emotion. By contrast, the effects of raw media exposure irrespective of content have received much less attention. Since media has become one of the major sources of socialization, it is neccessary to determine its effects on behavior and cognition, especially when socialization through media prevails over other sources, such as parents, peers or school. Most problably, the different cognitive mechanisms involved in media violence exposure and socialization through media have a combined effect on antisocial violent behavior, although further research is needed to address this question.

The kind of leisure activities that child and adolescent engage in, particularly video games, is a powerful source of socialization and an effective learning model (Gentile & Gentile, 2008) which can lead to an underdeveloped social perspective, oriented towards oneself. Parents and educators must be aware of the risks of excessive media exposure to children and the need to provide alternatives of socialization. Today's adults have been socialized in a much richer environment, and their involvement with media (particularly computers and the Internet) started once they were already socialized. Modern children use media from a much earlier age and they grow up more isolated from other sources of socialization, with a potential greater risk of developing dysfunctional and antisocial cognitions and behaviors.

References

Anderson, C. A. (2004). An update on the effects of playing violent video games. *Journal of Adolescence, 27*(1), 113-122.

Anderson, C. A., & Bushman, B. J. (2001). Effects of violent video games on aggressive behavior, aggressive cognition, aggressive affect, physiological arousal and prosocial behavior: A meta-analytic review of the scientific literature. *Psychological Science, 12(5),* 353-359.

Anderson, C. A., & Bushman, B. J. (2002a). Human Aggression. *Annual Review of Psychology, 53,* 27-51.

Anderson, C. A., & Bushman, B. J. (2002b). The effects of media violence on society. *Science, 95*(5564), 2377-2378.

Anderson, C. A., & Dill, K. E. (2000). Video games and aggressive thoughts, feelings and behavior in the laboratory and life. *Journal of Personality and Social Psychology, 78*(4), 772-790.

Anderson, C. A., Carnagey, N. L., & Eubanks, J. (2003). Exposure to violent media: the effects of songs with violent lyrics on aggressive thoughts and feelings. *Journal of personality and social psychology, 84*(5), 960-971.

Anderson, C. A., Sakamoto, A., Gentile, D. A., Ihori, N., Shibuya, A., Yukawa, S., Naito, A., & Kobayashi, K. (2008). Longitudinal Effects of Violent Video Games on Aggression in Japan and the United States. *Pediatrics, 122*(5), 1067 – 1072.

Bandura, A. (1994). Social cognitive theory and mass communication. In J. Bryant, & D. Zillmann, (Eds.), *Media effects: Advances in theory and research* (pp 61-90). Hillsdale, NJ: Lawrence Erlbaum.

Bandura, A., Barbaranelli, C., & Caprara, G. V. (1996). Mechanisms of moral disengagement in the exercise of moral agency. *Journal of Personality and Social Psychology, 71*(2), 364-374.

Bandura, A., Barbaranelli, C., Caprara, G.V., Pastorelli, C., & Regalia, C. (2001). Sociocognitive self-regulatory mechanisms governing transgressive behaviour. *Journal of Personality and Social Psychology, 80,* 125– 135.

Barlett, C. P., & Rodeheffer, C. (2009). Effects of Realism on Extended Violent and Nonviolent Video Game Play on Aggressive Thoughts, Feelings, and Physiological Arousal. *Aggressive Behavior, 35*(3), 213-224.

Barlett, C., Branch, O., Rodeheffer, C., & Harris, R. (2009). How Long Do the Short-Term Violent Video Game Effects Last? *Aggressive Behavior, 35*(3), 225-236.

Barlett, C.P., Harris, R.J., & Bruey C. (2008). The effect of the amount of blood in a violent video game on aggression, hostility, and arousal. *Journal of Experimental Social Psychology, 44,* 539–546.

Berkowitz, L. (1990). On the formation and regulation of anger and aggression: A cognitive-neoassociationistic analysis. *American Psychologist*, 45, 494–503.

Brooks, M. C. (2000). Press start: Exploring the effects of violent video games on boys. *Dissertation Abstracts International (The Sciences and Engineering), 60*(12-B), 6419.

Browne, K. D., & Hamilton-Giachritsis, C. (2005). The Influence of violent media on children and adolescents: A public-health approach. *The Lancet, 365,* 702-710.

Buckley, K. E., & Anderson, C. A. (2006). A theoretical model of the effects and consequences of playing video games. In P. Vorderer & J. Bryant (Eds.), Playing video games: Motives, responses, and consequences (pp. 363–378). Mahwah NJ: Lawrence Erlbaum.

Buselle, R.W. (2003). Television Exposure, Parents' precautionary warnings, and young adults' perceptions of crime. *Communication Research, 30*(5), 530-566.

Bushman, B. J, & Anderson, C.A. (2001). Media violence and the American public, scientific facts versus media misinformation. *American Psychologist, 56*(6-7), 477-489.

Bushman, B. J. (1998). Priming effects of media violence on the accessibility of aggressive constructs in memory. *Personality and Social Psychology Bulletin, 24*(5), 537-545.

Bushman, B. J., & Anderson, C. A. (2009). Comfortably Numb: Desensitizing Effects of Violent Media on Helping Others. *Psychological Science, 20*(3), 273-277.

Carlo G., & Randall R. A. (2002) The Development of a Measure of Prosocial Behaviors for Late Adolescents. *Journal of Youth and Adolescence*, Vol. 31, No. 1, 31–44.

Chandra, A., Martino, S., Collins, R., Elliott, M., Berry, S., Kanouse, D., & Miu, A. (2008). Does Watching Sex on Television Predict Teen Pregnancy? Findings from a National Longitudinal Survey of Youth. *Pediatrics, 122*(5), 1047-1054.

Clemente M., Espinosa P., & Vidal, M. A. (2008). The media and violent behavior in young people. Effects of the media on antisocial aggressive behavior in a Spanish sample. *Journal of Applied Social Psychology, 38*(10), 2395-2409.

Clemente M., Espinosa P., & Vidal, M. A. (2009). Aggressive symbolic model identification in 13 year-old youths. *European Journal of Psychology Applied to Legal Context, 1*(1), 45-68.

Clemente, M., & Vidal, M. A. (1996). *Violencia y Televisión (Violence and Television)*. Madrid: Noesis.

Collins, R., Elliott, M., Berry, S., Kanouse, D., Kunkel, D., Hunter, S., & Miu, A. (2004). Watching Sex on Television Predicts Adolescent Initiation of Sexual Behavior, *Pediatrics, 114*(3), 280-289.

Colwell, J., & Payne, J. (2000). Negative Correlates of Computer Game Play in Adolescents. *British Journal of Psychology, 91,* 295-310.

Coyne, S. M., & Archer, J. (2004). Indirect, relational, and social aggression in the media: A content analysis of British television programs. *Aggressive Behavior, 30*, 254–271.

Coyne, S. M., & Whitehead, E. (2008). Indirect aggression in animated Disney films. *Journal of Communication, 58*(2), 382-395.

Coyne, S. M., Archer, J., & Eslea, M. (2004). Cruel intentions on television and in real life: Can viewing aggression increase viewer's subsequent indirect aggression?. *Journal of Experimental Child Psychology, 88,* 234-253.

Coyne, S. M., Nelson, D. A., Lawton, F., Haslam, S., Rooney, L., Titterington, L., Trainor, H., Remnant, J., & Ogunlaja, L. (2008). The effects of viewing physical and relational aggression in the media: Evidence for a cross-over effect. *Journal of Experimental Social Psychology, 44*(6), 1551-1554.

Crick, N. R. & Grotpeter, J. K. (1995). Relational aggression, gender, and social-psychological adjustment. *Child Development, 66,* 710–722.

Damasio, A. (1999). *The feeling of what happens.* London: Heineman.

Derksen, D. J., & Strasburger, V. C. (1996). Media and television violence: Effects on violence, aggression, and antisocial behaviors in children. In A. M. Hoffman (Ed.), *Schools violence and society* (pp 61-77). Westport: Praeger Publishers.

Dill, K. E., & Dill, J. C. (1998). Video game violence: A review of the empirical literature. *Aggression and Violent Behavior, 3*(4), 407-428.

Eron, L., Huesmann, L., Lefkowitz, M., & Walder, L. (1996). Does television violence cause aggression? In D. Greenberg (Ed.), *Criminal careers, Vol. 2. The international library of criminology, criminal justice and penology.* (pp 311-321). Brookfield: Dartmouth Publishing.

Espinosa, P., & Clemente, M. (2008). La estructura y el contenido de la perspectiva social del menor como mediadores entre el consumo de videojuegos y el comportamiento antisocial agresivo. (*Structure and content of social perspective in under-18s as mediators between video game playing and aggressive antisocial behavior*). Paper presented at the 7º Congreso Iberoamericano de Psicología. La Laguna, Tenerife (Spain). 13th –15th November.

Espinosa, P., Clemente, M., & Vidal, M.A. (2002). Conducta antisocial y desarrollo moral en el menor (Antisocial behavior and moral development in minors). *Psicothema, 14*(Supl.), 26-36.

Fanti, K. A., Vanman, E., Henrich, C. C., & Avraamides, M. N. (2009). Desensitization to Media Violence Over a Short Period of Time. *Aggressive Behavior, 35*(2), 179-187.

Felson, R. B. (1996). Mass media effects on violent behavior. *Annual Review of Sociology, 22,* 103-128.

Funk, J. B., Baldacci, H. B., Pasold, T., & Baumgardner, J. (2004). Violence exposure in real-life, video games, television, movies, and the internet: is there desensitization? *Journal of Adolescence, 27*(1), 23-39.

Funk, J. B., Hagan, J., Schimming, J., Bullock, W. A., Buchman. D. D., & Myers, M. (2002). Aggression and Psychopathology in adolescents with a preference for violent electronic games. *Aggressive Behavior, 28,* 134-144.

Gentile, D. (2009). Pathological Video-Game Use Among Youth Ages 8 to 18: A National Study. *Psychological Science, 20*(5), 594-602.

Gentile, D. A., & Gentile, J. R. (2008). Violent video games as exemplary teachers: A conceptual analysis. *Journal of Youth and Adolescence, 37*(2), 127-141.

Gentile, D. A., & Walsh, D. A. (2002). A normative study of family media habits. Journal of Applied Developmental Psychology, 23, 157–178.

Gentile, D. A., Lynch, P. J., Linder, J. R., & Walsh, D. A. (2004). The effects of violent video game habits on adolescent hostility, aggressive behaviors, and school performance. *Journal of Adolescence, 27,* 5-22.

Gentile, D. A., Lynch, P. J., Linder, J. R., & Walsh, D. A. (2004). The effects of violent video game habits on adolescent hostility, aggressive behaviors, and school performance. *Journal of Adolescence, 27*(1), 5-22.

Giumetti, G. W., & Markey, P. M. (2007). Violent video games and anger as predictors of aggression. *Journal of research on personality, 41,* 1234-1243.

Gracia-Blanco, M. de, Vigo-Anglada, M., Fernández-Pérez, M.J., & Marcó-Rabonés, M. (2002). Problemas conductuales relacionados con el uso de Internet: Un estudio exploratorio. (Internet related behavioral problems: an exploratory study). *Anales de Psicología, 18(2),* 273-792.

Greitemeyer, T. (2009). Effects of songs with prosocial lyrics on prosocial thoughts, affect, and behavior. *Journal of Experimental Social Psychology, 45*(1), 186-190.

Griffiths, M. (1999). Violent video games and aggression: A review of the literature. *Aggression and Violent Behavior, 4*(2), 203-212.

Grooves, B. M. (1997). Growing up in a violent world: the impact of family and community violence on young children and their families. *Topics in Early Childhood, especial edition, 17*(1), 74-102.

Haninger, K. H., & Thompson, K. M. (2004). Content and ratings of Teen-Rated Video Games. *Journal of the American Medical Association (JAMA), 291,* 856-865.

Huesmann, L. R. (2007). The impact of electronic media violence: Scientific Theory and research. *Journal of Adolescent Health, 41,* Sup., 6-13.

Huesmann, L. R., Moise-Titus, J., & Podolski, C. (2003). Longitudinal relations between children's exposure to TV violence and their aggressive and violent behavior in young adulthood: 1977 –1992. *Developmental Psychology, 39,* 201–221.

Ivory, J. D., & Kalyanaraman, S. (2007). The effects of technological advancement an d violent content in video games on players' feelings of presence, involvement, physiological arousal and aggression. *Journal of Communication, 57,* 532-555.

Johnson, J. G., Cohen, P., Smailes, E. M., Kasen, S., & Brook, J. S. (2002). Television viewing and aggressive behavior during adolescence and adulthood. *Science, 295*(5564), 2468-2471.

Johnson, R. N. (1996). Bad news revisited: The portrayal of violence, conflict, and suffering on television news. *Peace and Conflict: Journal of Peace Psychology, 2*(3), 201-216.

Jung, J-Y., Qiu, J. L., & Kim, Y-C. (2001). Internet connectedness and inequality: Beyond the "divide". *Communication Reseach, 28*(4), 509-537.

Kiewitz, C., & Weaver, J. B. III. (2001). Trait aggressiveness, media violence, and perceptions of interpersonal conflict. *Personality and individual differences, 31*, 821-835.

Kish, S. J. (1998). Seeing the world through Mortal Kombat-colored glasses: Violent video games and the development of a short-term hostile attribution bias. *Childhood: A global Journal of Child Research, 5*(2), 177-184.

Kohlberg, L. (1992). *Psicología del desarrollo moral (Moral Development Psychology).* Bilbao: Descleé de Brouwer.

Krahé, B., & Möller, I. (2004). Playing violent electronic games, hostile attributional style, and aggression-related norms in German adolescents. *Journal of Adolescence, 27*(1), 53-69.

Kronenberger, W. G., Mathews, V. P., Dunn, D. W., Wang, Y., Wood, E. A., Giauque, A. L., Larsen, J. L., Rembusch, M. E., Lowe, M. J., & Li, T-Q. (2005). Media violence exposure and executive functioning in aggressive and control adolescents. *Journal of Clinical Psychology, 6*(16), 725-737.

Loges, W. E., & Jung, J-Y. (2001). Exploring the digital divide. Internet connectedness and age. *Communication Reseach, 28*(4), 536-562.

Mathews, V. P., Kronenberger, W. G., Wang, Y., Lurito, J. T., Lowe, M. J., & Dunn, D. W. (2005). Media violence exposure and frontal lobe activation measured by functional magnetic resonance imaging in aggressive and nonaggressive adolescents. *Journal of Computer Assisted Tomography, 29*(3), 287–292.

Mitrofan, O., Paul, M., & Spencer, N. (2009). Is aggression in children with behavioural and emotional difficulties associated with television viewing and video game playing? A systematic review. *Child Care Health and Development, 35*(1), 5-15.

Moller, I., & Krahe, B. (2009). Exposure to Violent Video Games and Aggression in German Adolescents: A Longitudinal Analysis. *Aggressive Behavior, 35*(1), 75-89.

Morgan, S. E., Movius, L., & Cody, M. J. (2009). The Power of Narratives: The Effect of Entertainment Television Organ Donation Storylines on the Attitudes, Knowledge, and Behaviors of Donors and Nondonors. *Journal of Communication, 59*(1), 135-154.

Nie, N., & Erbring, L. (2000). *Internet and society: A preliminary report.* Stanford, CA: Stanford Institute for the Quantitative Study of Society.

Osofky, J. D., & Osofky, H. J. (1998). Children's exposure to violence: a critical lens for reporting violence. *Nieman Reports, Winter*, 22-40.

Ostrov, J. M., Gentile, D. A., & Crick, N. R. (2006). Media exposure, aggression and prosocial behavior during early childhood: A longitudinal study. *Social Development, 15*(4), 612-627.

Pennell, A. E., & Browne, K. D. (1999). Film violence and young offenders. *Aggression and Violent Behavior, 4*(1), 13-28.

Richmond, J., & Wilson, J. C. (2008). Are graphic media violence, aggression and moral disengagement related? *Psychiatry Psychology and Law, 15*(2), 350-357.

Roberts, D. F., Foehr, U. G., Rideout, V. J., & Brodie, M. (1999). *Kids and media @ the new millenium: A comprehensive national analysis of children's media use (November).* Menlo Park, CA: Kaiser Family Foundation Report.

Rubin, A. M., West, D. V., & Mitchell, W. S. (2001). Differences in aggression attitudes toward women and distrust as reflected in popular music preferences. *Media Psychology, 3,* 25–42.

Santisteban, C., Alvarado, J. M., & Recio, P. (2007). Evaluation of a Spanish version of the Buss and Perry aggression questionnaire: Some personal and situational factors related to the aggression scores of young subjects. *Personality and Individual Differences, 42,* 1453-1465.

Savage, J. (2004). Does viewing violent media really cause criminal violence? A methodological review. *Aggression and Violent Behavior, 10,* 99-128.

Schwartz, S. H. (1992). Universals in the content and structure of values: Theoretical advances and empirical tests in 20 countries. En M. Zanna (Ed.), Advances in experimental social psychology, Vol. 25, (pp. 1-65). Nueva York: Academic Press.

Slater, M. D., Henry, K. L., Swaim, R. C., & Anderson, L. L. (2003). Violent Media content and aggressiveness in adolescents. A downward spiral model. *Communication Research, 30*(6), 713-736.

Smith, S. L., & Boyson, A. R. (2002). Violence in music videos: Examining the prevalence and context of physical aggression. *Journal of Communication, 52,* 61–83.

Spitzer, M. (2005). Influence of violent media on children and adolescents. *The Lancet, 365,* 1387-1388.

Sweet, D., & Singh, R. (1994). *TV viewing and parental guidance. Education Consumer Guide.* Retrived on July, 2008, from: http://www.cwrl.utexas.edu.

Tejeiro Salguero, R. A., & Bersabé Morán, R. M. (2002). *Measuring problem video game playing in adolescents. Addiction, 97,* 1601– 1606.

Thompson, K. M., & Haninger, K. H. (2001). Violence in E-Rated video games. *Journal of the American Medical Association (JAMA,) 286,* 591-598.

Uhlmann, E., & Swanson, J. (2004). Exposure to violent video games increases automatic aggressiveness. *Journal of Adolescence, 27*(1), 41-52.

Urra, J., Clemente, M., & Vidal, M. A. (2000). *Televisión: Impacto en la infancia. (Television: its impact during childhood).* Madrid: Siglo XXI.

Valkenburg, P. M., & Soeters, K. (2001). Children's positive and negative experiences with the Internet. *Communication Research, 28*(5), 652-675.

Vandewater, E. A., Shim, M. S., & Caplovitz, A. G. (2004). Linking obesity and activity level with children's television and video game use. *Journal of Adolescence, 27*(1), 71-85.

Vidal, M. A., Clemente, M., & Espinosa, P. (2003). Types of media violence and degree of acceptance in under-18s. *Aggressive Behavior, 29*(5), 381-392.

Von Feilitzen, C. (1990). Tres tesis sobre los niños y los medios de comunicación (Three thesis on children and the media). *Infancia y Sociedad, 3,* 31-47.

Wallenius, M., & Punamaki, R. L. (2008). Digital game violence and direct aggression in adolescence: A longitudinal study of the roles of sex, age, and parent-child communication. *Journal of Applied Developmental Psychology, 29*(4), 286-294.

Wiegman, O., & van Schie, E. (1998). Video game playing and its relations with aggressive and prosocial behavior. *British Journal of Social Psychology, 37*(3), 367-378.

Wilson, B. J., Smith, S. L., Potter, W. J., Kunkel, D., Linz, D., Colvin, C. M., & Donnerstein, E. (2002). Violence in children's television programming: Assessing the risks. *Journal of Communication, 52*(1), 5-35.

Yanovitzky, I., & Stryker, J. (2001). Mass Media, social norms and health promotion efforts. A longitudinal study of media effects on youth binge drinking. *Communication Research, 28*(2), 208-239.

Yomota, F., & Thompson, K. M. (2000). Violence in G-Rated animated films. *Journal of the American Medical Association (JAMA), 283,* 2716-2720.

Zillmann, D., & Weaver, J. B. (1997). Psychoticism in the effect of prolonged exposure to gratuitous media violence on the acceptance of violence as a preferred means of conflict resolution. *Personality and Individual Differences, 22*(5), 613-627.

Zillmann, D., & Weaver, J. B. (2007). Aggressive personality traits in the effects of violent imagery in unprovoked impulsive aggression. *Journal of Research in Personality, 41,* 753-771.

Chapter 12

WITNESSES TO BULLYING: VOICES FOR PREVENTION AND INTERVENTION IN SCHOOLS

Marcela López[*], *María José Aguilar and Josefina Rubiales*
National University of Mar del Plata / CONICET, Argentina.

ABSTRACT

The student's ill-treatment or bullying is a systematic and consistent aggression from one student to another. It is a complex dynamics, which remains veiled and supported by the silence of those who suffer the aggression but also for those who observe it. Investigations in this field refer to the need of valuing the meaning that witnesses of these situations confer on bullying. The present research provides a description of the state of the bullying situation among schoolmates in Junior–Senior High School, exploring its impact and manifestations. The central objective is to assess the attitude shown by bystanders towards bullying, putting forward as a hypothesis that the attitude of bystanders favors bullying situations, and therefore does not benefit their report and intervention. To verify this, a Likert-type scale and a questionnaire were constructed, validated and administered to 764 students. The analysis of results allowed to confirm the hypothesis and the interpretation of the possible reasons impeding the denunciation and intervention of witnesses. The obtained information allowed elaborating a prevention and interventional program. This attempts to be a valid and innovative model of intervention, by considering the witnesses as a break point of the dynamics of bullying.

INTRODUCTION

"Every morning upon arriving to school, some students know that they will have to bother someone in order to hide their pain, in this way obtaining a strong image of power. Others know that they will have to face all kinds of mockery as soon as they enter school

---

[*] Correspondence: Marcela López, Faculty of Psychology, National University of Mar del Plata / CONICET. Mar del Plata, 7600. Buenos Aires. Argentina. e-mail: mclopez@mdp.edu.ar, Telephone/Fax : (54) 223-752266

grounds. The majority knows that when they enter school, they will, willingly or not, take part in a reality that does not seem to have a solution" *(Agustina, High School student)*.

Situations of violence in schools are becoming more and more frequent. Classrooms have turned into hidden battlefields, where harassment, derogatory language and aggression between peers are the main sources of violence that remain hidden behind the daily routine. Among peers, ill-treatment and constant aggression seem to form part of the school dynamics. These asymmetrical power relationships are embodied in imbalanced bonds of control and segregation from which, the consequences appear to be isolation and social exclusion (Aguilar, López, & Rubiales, 2008). What is ill-treatment or bullying among classmates? From a conceptual definition it is a systematic and an ongoing aggression from one student to another (Olweus, 1998). However, for many people, it is something that they experience daily, in or out of the classroom and from which, by their own means, they cannot escape. It is a complex dynamic that remains hidden and ongoing within the silence of not only those who suffer the aggression, but also of those who witness it and many times remain "passive accomplices" to the situation.

There have always been one or more students who have been targets for jokes, pranks or mockery. Sometimes, they are intimidated because of their weaknesses; and other times, because they show weakness in their own defense. In these situations, there is always a stage on which there are actors and spectators. The actors set the stage, and the spectators, as the term well defines, are those who "attentively watch."

Everybody is involved. Bullies who attack, victims who cannot defend themselves and bystanders who do not commit themselves; all form part of this suffering. Bullies attack for many reasons that lead them to show themselves as violent, hostile and intolerant. However, they also suffer. The victim, to a large extent, showing himself broken and unable to defend himself, putting up with what is intolerable while building up anger and rage, which, in the case of a breakdown, is prone to uncontrollable behavior, illogical impulses and reactions shaped by worn out bonds.

Spectators, who play the role of the observer, also suffer, becoming witnesses to a situation that needs intervention (Rubiales, Aguilar, & López, 2009). However, these situations tend to be played down to "children's games". This "naive" perception maintains the dynamics of the suffering, many times revealed in unfortunate episodes. An infamous case occurred in 1999 at the Columbine High School, in Colorado, USA (Gallardo, 2009). This was the first case that highlighted this issue, setting a before and after, not only regarding the structure of the educational system, but also the way of dealing with these incidents.

This problem, which is not unique, calls for society, which has begun to suffer the consequences of these actions; to reflect upon this issue Bullying behavior among peers is gaining in importance, not only because of the need to guarantee an adequate environment of coexistence in schools, but also because of the possibility of needed intervention.

In Argentina, although according to the Ministry of Education there are no official figures regarding this situation, it is estimated that around 15% of young people aged between 11 and 17 years have been either bullies or victims (Dragui, 2007). This research is based on the framework of violence and social clash. It describes the current situation of bullying in schools, focusing on witnesses as a tipping point and mediators in the dynamics of bullying. Our chapter aims to contribute to the awareness of the dynamics of bullying with the purpose of creating prevention and intervention workshops in the educational field in order to stimulate actions to diminish bullying behavior among classmates.

VIOLENCE: A CONDITION THAT PERMITS BULLYING

Violence is a timeless and spaceless phenomenon that has always existed. Nowadays however, the magnitude of violent acts that we as a society experience, have forced us to analyze, prevent and intervene against situations that can be called violent. The concept of violence has varied according to history, the social-cultural context and the theoretical focus on which it is being observed. Likewise, from a wide diversity of viewpoints, it has been theoretically and empirically defined (Baron & Richardson, 1994; Parke & Slaby, 1983).

From a psychoanalytical approach, Sigmund Freud (1930) argued that aggressiveness is manifested as an autonomous urge-driven-impulse that can be directed out or within oneself. These aggressive impulses must be expressed and need to find a way out, through allowed social rules. From an etiological point of view, Lorenz (1978) agrees with Freud in that aggressiveness is instinctive; it is internally generated and released by an appropriate stimulus. If it does not come out, it will provoke an accumulation of aggressive impulse-driven-urges that will in the end be released by an inappropriate stimulus. To prevent that uncontrolled aggressive expression, human beings need to vent their aggression in an accepted social manner. Eibl-Eibesfeldt (1993) contributes to Lorenz's Theory, by considering that the human being can solve his problems through verbal negotiations.

Additional theories exist that explain violence through the hypothesis of frustration–aggression. Dollard (1939) expressed that aggression is produced by the frustration of instincts, being frustration the result of a block in the pursuit of goals which provoke an aggressive behavior. Berkowitz (1974) explains that frustration does not directly provoke aggression, but it creates a disposition to aggression, with the violent response emerging only when the person is exposed to aggressive stimuli.

Furthermore, from Skinner's and Bandura's perspectives, aggressiveness is a learned behavior. Skinner (1953) points out that aggressiveness is learned, is kept and disappears through instrumental conditioning, which is considered a way of learning on which the consequence is contingent to the response emitted by the person; the association rises from the responses and the consequences derived from them. Hence, this behavior is gained early and easily if it leads to success (Palomero-Pescador & Fernández-Dominguez, 2001).

Bandura (1984) establishes that violence in human beings is not an individual but a social phenomenon, and thus, violence emerges originally from the system and not from the individual (Morales-Ruiz, García de la Cadena, & Grazioso de Rodríguez, 2006). He explains that violent behavior is learned from a model (i.e., the observation and imitation of other people who behave in a violent way). However, for aggressive behavior to remain over time depends on its consequences.

Adding to Bandura's contributions, Geen (1990) considers that when violent behavior is repeatedly reinforced in certain daily situations, it provokes the generalization of this behavior into other contexts. (Palomero-Pescador & Fernández-Dominguez, 2001). Galtung (1998) builds a social construct of violence, by considering that the human being is shaped by culture so that his/her behavior depends as much on the person as on society and the culture that surrounds her/him.

If currently there is no universal agreement on the concept of violence, the World Health Organization defines it as: "The intentional use of physical force or power, fact or threat, against oneself, another person, or against a group or community, that leads or would lead to injury, death, psychological damage, underdevelopment or deprivation" (Caballero-Gutiérrez & Ramos, 2004).These types of relationships are set on asymmetric bonds of power, wherein it does not flow but crystallizes and is detected by one who is part of the relationship and takes advantage of it to harm another.

Social relationships of power are a multitude of interactions between two or more persons or social groups in which one of the parts exerts power over the other (frequently, in a disciplinary or involuntary way) in a coercive way. According to Weber, power consists of one person managing to have others to do what (s)he wishes, even against their own will. Therefore, relationships of power are always inter-individual: only individuals act and they are the only ones that can act (Labourdette, 2007).

These relationships of power among individuals are found in all environments, family, society, and state, among others. School is not exempt from these relationships; according to Jiménez (2005) there is a strong relationship between prevailing social violence and school aggressiveness, the last considered as a particular case of general violence. School violence is a kind of violence occurring within school facilities or at their surroundings and within extra school activities (Serrano-Sarmiento & SerIborra-Marmolejo, 2005). Nowadays, within schools, there is a type of violence that is especially worrisome: Bullying.

BULLYING: A PROBLEM OF VIOLENCE IN SCHOOLS

Ill treatment among classmates is an old phenomenon; however, research on this issue has become more important since the seventies, thanks to the work done by Olweus. Bullying is characterized by the violent and systematized action of one student against another. Olweus (1998) defines it as a "physical or psychological behavior carried out by a student against another, who is chosen to be the victim of repeated attacks." This negative and deliberate deed puts the victims in such a position that it is very difficult for them to escape by their own means. The continuousness of these relationships provokes, on them, clearly negative effects, among these: lack of self-esteem, anxiety and even depressive episodes, which makes their integration into the school environment very difficult, together with normal learning development.

Bullying is not always differentiated from other events related to the coexistence that takes place simultaneously within the school context, which makes its process and treatment difficult. (Avilés-Martínez & Casares, 2005). According to Hoyos, Aparicio and Córdoba (2005), there are three criteria that enable one to distinguish this specific kind of ill-treatment from others: it is an aggressive and intentional behavior, repeated throughout time and one-sided with respect to power. Likewise, according to these authors, in order to consider the situation as "ill-treatment", one must also consider the victim's perception of the deed.

The new definition of bullying, which has been inserted in the updated version of Olweus Bully/Victim Questionnaire (Solberg & Olweus, 2003), takes into account that students are victims of their classmates when: they are being assaulted with words, or mocked, or completely ignored or excluded from their friends or projects, when they are hit, kicked or punched, when lies and false rumors about them are spread, or when they are sent hurtful messages or belittled in front of their classmates. With reference to this definition, the literature acknowledges different types of school harassment which often appears in a simultaneous way:

a. *physical harassment:* hitting, pushing, breaking or stealing classmates objects;
b. *verbal harassment:* mocking, insulting, speaking behind their backs, given nicknames, spreading false rumors about classmates;
c. *relational harassment:* excluding classmates from activities, hampering their participation, ignoring, preventing them from performing tasks with that classmate.

Three Protagonists: Just One Victim?

Three main characters can be distinguished in a bullying situation: the victim, the bully and bystanders. The first one refers to the student who suffers the consequences of his classmate's behavior and does not have the resources to prevent those acts from happening. Generally, victims are insecure, vulnerable and silently suffer the attack. Likewise, they show a lack of social skills and react to conflicts with their classmates in a negative way, by crying or being anxious; they frequently feel fear and loneliness, which in some cases, may lead them to failure, absenteeism and dropping out of school (Moreno, Vacas, & Roa, 2006).

In addition, the bully manifests an offensive and impulsive temperament, with a lack of social skills in order to communicate and get across his/her wishes. (S)he is assumed to have a lack of empathy and feelings of guilt (Olweus, 1998). The idea of hurting, showing himself stronger compared to the one he is bullying spaks his actions. According to Cerezo (2001), the bully has the feeling that his/her classmates cheer him/her on the aggression. They generally develop antisocial behavior and poor school adjustment with risk of failure, and also show difficulties in developing emotional bonds. Rigby (2004) and Mynard, Joseph and Alexande (2000) found certain personality variables associated to the patterns of behavior of the bully and the victims. In the first case, a high tendency to psychoticism, and in the case of the victims, a high tendency to introversion and low self-esteem.

A not unimportant piece of information is that, in a kind of vicious circle, the bully usually suffers that same situation in his private life, searching for an "escape" in school. Many times, he tends to minimize his actions, even claiming them as positive, as a way of setting social bonds (Cerezo, 2006). Finally, there are the bystanders, who at first would seem to have a secondary role; however, they play an important part, considering that the bully carries out his/her actions only at the presence of bystanders. This group constitutes the environment in which, from the group of peers, one can observe helpers and passive witnesses, who, in certain cases, tend to admit the bully's behavior and support him/her. These "neutral" spectators do not usually give away the bullying incident; this remains hidden. Sometimes the fear of being bullied, or becoming a victim, makes them keep silent. In Hoyos, Aparicio, and Córdoba's study (2005) it is reported that witnesses only intervene if the victim is a friend.

Current data indicate that a considerable number of students are involved in situations of bullying. A study conducted in Finland, in 2001, with children and teenagers aged between 8 and 16 years, reported that around 15% of males and 7% of females victimized their classmates, and around 12% and 13% were victims. Both, bullies and victims presented a wide range of psychological problems, deducing that bullying is associated to severe emotional and behavioral problems (Moreno, Vacas, & Roa, 2006).

In Spain, Avilés-Martínez (2006) report that one out of twenty students suffers from bullying actions and the same proportion of bullies intimidates their classmates in a continuous and systematic way. In Argentina, according to a survey conducted with 5,000 high school students in 21 provinces (Draghi, 2007), half experienced bullying in actions such as ignore a peer, ridicule him/her or insult her/him.

In addition to what has been reported, many adults do not know how to intervene in bullying situations. Only 25% of Spanish students report that their professors intervene in situations of mistreatment (Moreno, Vacas, & Roa, 2006). Furthermore, although not directly taking part in the bullying process, a number of classmates know, allow and confer bullying incidents. Victims and bullies act in the presence of witnesses, who, by and large, stay on the sidelines, although they acknowledge that bullying actions are part of their daily routine (Cerezo, 2001; Ortega, 1994).

BYSTANDERS AS A TIPPING POINT IN THE BULLYING DYNAMIC

When speaking about bullying situations, we generally focus on the analysis of the bully-victim relationship, leaving aside the role played by the witnesses as supporters of this dynamic. Nevertheless, nowadays, a number of studies refer to the need of considering how important witnesses are in bullying situations (Cerezo, 2006; Ferroni, Penecino, & Sánchez, 2005). Data contributed by Avilés Martínez demonstrate that bystanders in a bullying situation are capable of acknowledging the intentionality of the bully's behavior and assessing the damage produced on victims. The author proposes two assumptions by which bystanders are watching the intimidation and harassment without taking part: because they would rather be on the stronger student's side or for fear of being bullied.

What has been shown obliges bystanders to find difficult breaking such dynamics. It is worth considering that in order to select strategies that tend to decrease bullying actions it is necessary to take into account the bystanders' cognitive aspects in the comprehension of the bullying group phenomenon, as much as the assessment of the actions they should engage in in that particular situation. Finding out the possible causes that prevent them from their reporting and intervention in the face of bullying situations, would allow setting up spaces for reflection in order to promote actions aimed at diminishing bullying situations between schoolmates.

RESEARCH GOALS AND OBJECTIVES

The conducted research provides a description of the state of the bullying situation among schoolmates in Junior–Senior High School, exploring its impact and manifestations. The central objective was to assess the attitude shown by bystanders towards bullying, putting forward as a hypothesis that the attitude of bystanders favors bullying situations, and therefore does not benefit their report and intervention.

METHOD

Design

The research corresponds to a kind of explorative and descriptive study, empirically and analytically focused, with a non experimental, psychometric and transversal design.

Participants

The study was conducted with a deliberate sample of 764 private and public High School students (399 females and 365 males) in Mar del Plata, Argentina, aged between 15 and 18 years.

Instrument

A brief closed questionnaire was constructed, in a Likert scale. It was validated and administered in a self-managed way. The questions were based on age, sex, year of school, years of permanence at the educational institution, experience regarding bullying situations (victim, bully and bystander) and the kind of episode and the frequency they have witnessed those situations. Likewise, the inclusion of the students' personal opinions on the subject was considered of great importance. A Likert-type scale is the most used tool in psychology to assess attitudes. It was developed by Rensis Likert during the thirties. It is a kind of accumulatory scale that corresponds to ordinal measurement and consists of a series of items in the form of affirmations before which a person is asked to indicate the alternative that most suits his opinion, choosing from one of the offered options. The person has to express his agreement or disagreement with the affirmation by selecting an alternative to the answer. A numerical value is assigned to each of these alternatives. In this way, each participant obtains a score regarding each affirmation as well as a total grade obtained by adding the total scoring for all the affirmations, which is interpreted as the participant's position on the scale of attitudes that expresses a score regarding the object of study.

The Likert scale used for this research, was initially built with 26 items, each valued on a four point scale, that goes from one (never) up to four (always). The integration of these items was carried out based on authors such as Avilés-Martínez (2006), Cerezo (2006), Moreno, Vacas, and Roa, (2006), and Avilés-Martínez & Casares (2005). Research conducted by these authors presents as a focal point in the characterization of bullying situations, taking into consideration the incidence, the differences between causal reasons and the identification of strategies.

After assembling the questionnaire, it was checked by three expert judges (Psychologists from the Universidad Nacional de Mar del Plata, experts in the field). Some modifications were implemented to the test, such as reformulating items to assure its comprehension and modification to the writing. Then, the 26-item questionnaire was tested and a definitive questionnaire resulted including 23 items (See Annex 1).

Procedure

After selecting the schools, an informed consent was requested from those educational institutions, in which the characteristics of the research and also the method used were explained. It was clearly expressed that it would be an absolutely voluntary and anonymous collaboration, with a commitment to not provide any information to the school staff. Subsequently, it was explained to the participants that the objective of the research was to understand teenagers' view regarding bullying incidents between peers. It took approximately fifteen minutes to respond to the questionnaire.

DATA ANALYSIS

To validate the questionnaire, the data were processed using SPSS 11.5. The analysis included the following: 1) descriptive analysis; 2) exploratory factor analysis to evaluate the questionnaire's dimension through the method of principal components with varimax rotation; 3) reliability analysis through Cronbach's Alpha Correlation Coefficient.

The analysis of data obtained through the instrument's administration included the following: a) descriptive analysis of the incidence and manifestations of bullying incidents between peers; b) analysis of the total results in relation to the general assessment of bystanders' attitudes towards bullying situations; profound item analysis; d) qualitative analysis of the observations carried out by students through the content analysis method (Ander-Egg, 1987). This latter technique enabled the study of the contents expressed, classifying its different parts according to set categories, with the aim of systematizing the data.

RESULTS

In order to offer crystal clear information for the presentation of results, they have been divided into two sections. In the first one, the validity of the questionnaire is presented; in the second one, the analysis of the data obtained.

Descriptive Analysis of Items in the Pilot Test

From the descriptive analysis of the items in the pilot test (Table 1), *item 15* was deleted because it presented a mean higher than 3.5; *items 9 and 26*, although they presented high averages, were not deleted from the scale as they are considered important in regard to the concept that we intended to assess. *Item 12* was excluded as it seemed to be difficult to understand, and *item 18* was put aside because its content was more clearly evaluated by another item of the questionnaire. *Items 6, 8 and 21* were modified and clarified.

Table 1. Means and Standard Deviation of the 26 items in the pilot-study scale

	Mean	Std Dev
1. Bullying among classmates is a normal behavior in teenagers.	2.5490	.7529
2. I consider that it is wrong that a classmate bully another classmate.	3.3725	.8074
3. When there is a bullying situation between classmates I intervene in order to help.	2.1078	.7162
4. Bullying situations among classmates can be avoided.	2.8137	.9090
5. When a classmate harasses another I move away from the situation.	3.1176	.6019
6. I feel bad when I see a classmate bullying another.	2.8725	.8522
7. When I see a bullying situation between classmates I report it to someone in school.	1.4804	.7543
8. When there is a bullying situation between classmates I take part in the aggression.	3.5980	.5846
9. I enjoy bullying situations at school.	3.5000	.6563
10. When there is a bullying situation between classmates I talk to the bully.	1.9804	.6446
11. If the victim is not a friend I don't care.	2.8725	.7919
12. I don't like a classmate to be bullied.	3.0490	1.0472
13. Classmates who are bullied deserve the harassment.	3.4020	.6488
14. When a classmate bullies another one I stay looking.	2.8529	.7758
15. When I witness a bullying situation I feel scared.	3.5686	.6676
16. When there is a bullying situation among my classmates I talk it over with my family.	1.8725	.8863
17. It makes me sad when I see a classmate bullying another.	2.7745	.8777
18. I speak with the school authorities, about bullying situations among classmates.	1.4216	.6361
19. I don't intervene when a classmate bullies another.	2.7745	.7434
20. When I witness a bullying situation between classmates I speak with the victim.	2.2549	.7132
21. I consider it a betrayal to talk about a bullying situation out of my group of friends.	3.4608	.8637
22. Bullying situations among classmates upsets me.	2.4804	.8870
23. When a classmate bullies another one I don't intervene because I don't know what to do.	3.0294	.7766
24. We only talk about bullying problems among classmates.	2.6961	.8418
25. I don't care if a classmate bullies another.	3.3627	.6718
26. Bullying situations among classmates causes psychological problems.	2.6765	.8104

Statistics for the scale	Mean	Variance	Std Dev	N of Variables
	71.9412	54.1549	7.3590	26

Reliability Analysis, Pilot Test

The scale's total alpha was $\alpha=0.74$. This indicates good internal consistency as it exceeds the valid established minimum of 0.70.

Descriptive Analysis of Items, Modified Instrument

Table 2 shows means, standard deviations and maximum levels for the final instrument.

Table 2. Mean and standard deviation to the 23 items that compose the final scale

Items	Mean	Std Dev
1. Bullying among classmates is a normal behavior in teenagers.	2.3101	.82777
2. I consider that it is wrong that a classmate bully another classmate.	3.2810	.90088
3. When there is a bullying situation between classmates I intervene in order to help.	3.2810	.81740
4. Bullying situations among classmates can be avoided.	2.1367	.91085
5. When a classmate harasses another one I move away from the situation.	2.8853	.81641
6. I feel bad when I see a classmate bullying another one.	3.0569	.97078
7. When I see a bullying situation between classmates I report it to someone in school	2.4432	.79595
8. When there is a bullying situation between classmates I take part in the aggression.	1.5217	.72982
9. I enjoy bullying situations at school.	3.5493	.85602
10. When there is a bullying situation between classmates I talk to the bully.	3.3120	.76615
11. If the victim is not a friend I don't care.	2.0131	.95639
12. Classmates who are bullied deserve the harassment.	2.7563	.69175
13. When a classmate bullies another one I stay looking.	3.3342	.89846
14. When there is a bullying situation among my classmates I talk it over with my family.	2.6562	1.00431
15. It makes me sad when I see a classmate bullying another one.	1.8949	.94022
16. To intervene when a classmate is being bullied might worsen the situation	2.5000	.73320
17. When I witness a bullying situation between classmates I speak with the victim.	2.5035	.78341
18. I consider it a betrayal to tell on a friend who is bullying a classmate.	2.1130	1.03495
19. Bullying situations among classmates upsets me.	2.7373	1.00920
20. When a classmate bullies another one I don't intervene because I don't know what to do	2.4612	.91720
21. We only talk about bullying problems among classmates.	2.9264	.97561
22. I don't care if a classmate bullies another one.	2.6232	.83244
23. Bullying situations among classmates causes psychological problems.	3.2362	.92480

Analysis of Dimensionality

The sample adequacy measure by Kaiser-Meyer-Olkin (.840) and Bartlet's sphericity proof-test with values of 3004.773 (gl=253; $p<0.001$) suggest that it is possible to evaluate the dimensional scale through factor analysis of principal components. The exploratory factor analysis of the scale's items (Table 3) manifests the existence of three factors; however, as the group did not match any useful theoretical criteria, the scale was interpreted as one-dimensional, grouping the items according to a unique factor: *attitude*.

Table 3. Exploratory factor analysis of the scale's items

	Factor								
	1	2	3	4	5	6	7	8	9
Item26	0.740								
Item9	0.640								
Item11	0.604								
Item14	0.566								
Item25	0.555				0.353				
Item18		0.617							
Item16		0.616						0.399	
Item20		0.533						-0.343	
Item7		0.520							
Item15		-0.517							
Item13									
Item6			0.694						
Item12			0.588						
Item8	0.435		0.474						
Item21			0.337						
Item3				0.713					
Item5				0.540					
Item19				0.334					
Item17			0.406		0.558				
Item22					0.512				
Item1					-0.457				
Item2						0.956			
Item4							0.709		
Item10				0.334				-0.458	
Item24								0.430	
Item23									0.667

Reliability Analysis, Modified Instrument

In the instrument's final version, the Cronbach's alpha's value obtained was α=0.71, no item being deleted, because if this process was to be carried out, no variations in alpha's value would have been shown.

Perception of Blullying among Peers and Ways It Manifests out

94% of the polled students witnessed bullying situations. Likewise, 23% of these were sometimes a victim and the same proportion considered himself/herself a bully. Regarding participation in bullying situations, more male than female bullies were found (69% males and 31% females). In relation to the types of bullying, the most mentioned ones by students were verbal and social aggressions (81%). Nevertheless, physical aggressions were recognized by almost the total of those polled *(N= 763)*.

Evaluation of the Bystanders' Attitude

With reference to the bystanders' attitude (n= 704) towards bullying situations, the total data, obtained from the analysis of the final scale, showed that the scores flow from 23 to 92 points, the majority being close to the average. (57,5) (see Figure 1).

These results indicate that the bystanders' attitude is unfavorable towards bullying situations; however, its tendency is not strongly defined.

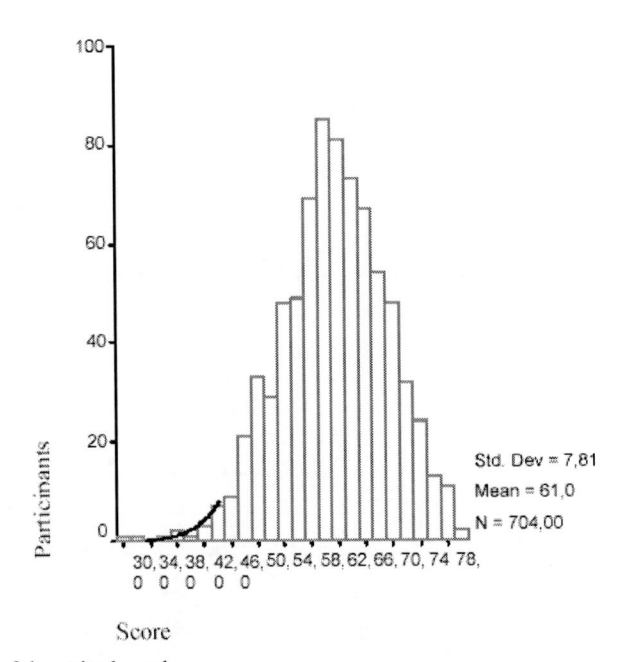

Figure 1. Total score of the attitude scale.

Profound Analysis of Items

The items were grouped according to theoretical criteria of interest for the research.
What do bystanders think?

A high percentage of bystanders (55%) admit that bullying between classmates is a normal behavior among teenagers. However, 92% of the total of the witnesses consider that victims do not deserve the ill-treatment and 75% consider bullying to be wrong between classmates. Also, 56% admit that bullying might cause psychological damage.

Do bystanders report bullying situations?

Although 61% of the students think that it is possible to prevent bullying, the majority (85%) does not report bullying situations; and if they do, they report it to friends.

Do they intervene when a bullying incident is taking place?

According to the tendency in the previous analysis, witnesses neither report nor take part in bullying situations. They rarely talk to the bully or the victim and 61% consider that taking part may worsen the situation. Likewise, 71% reported that they seldom intervene because they do not know what to do. However, the results indicate that 83% remain watching the situation, even though they do not enjoy it (51%), nor do they take part in it (66%). These kinds of situations are not unimportant to the majority of bystanders arousing uneasiness (44%), anger (41%) and sadness (44%). However, they only intervene when the victim is a friend.

Qualitative Analysis, Students' Opinions

Of all the students' opinions about bullying situations there are three categories that were identified from the analysis: 1) causes of mistreatment; 2) mistreatment assessment; 3) ways of prevention and intervention. Within the first category students identify three possible causes that might create bullying situations among classmates. The first one refers to bullying as a result of a violent society; in students' words: "I think that bullying among people is a social disease...", "...bullying in schools is the reflection of the society and system in which we live." As a second cause, polled students identify bullying as the result of dysfunctional families: "That parents should care more about their children, since the majority of kids are violent because of the lack of an adequate relationship with their family", "...in many occasions problems of violence in school are due to the fact that bullies have the same problems at their homes."

Finally, students refer to bullying as a way of gaining respect, "I don't agree with bullies, but you can't avoid defending yourself and not end up in physical aggression." To them bullying is not an option but the only way out of situations in which relationships with others are seen as controversial: "Sometimes there is a need for violence in order to be respected and gain respect by using your fists because if you suffer now, tomorrow you will feel better". "...many times in my neighborhood I must be violent to gain respect or to defend what's mine or many times we use it just for the sake of winning."

In the category of bullying assessment, ambiguous expressions rise among students. On the one hand, they tend to minimize bullying situations to the extent that they consider them as jokes; on the other hand, they admit the adverse impact that these situations cause on victims: "It all depends on the kind of bullying, if it goes beyond respect, it's obvious that I wouldn't like the situation but if it's a joke, and the other feels harassed, it's his problem, because the provoker just wanted to play..."Many bullying situations start as a joke and get out of hand." "It is far too common nowadays to observe acts of violence, which to some may appear as a joke, without being conscious of how much the other party is affected."

Within the third category, ways of prevention and intervention, teenagers identify three possible ways: dialogue, education in correct values and institutional intervention. Regarding dialogue, students say: "I think that first you must talk it out instead of attacking; otherwise, it will not get solved", "...maybe these kinds of situations would be avoided just by talking...", "...you can talk it out to avoid things getting out of hand..." Others consider that the solution would come up from each of the students, their personal and individual values and empathy and social capabilities, elements that would provide them to overcome the interpersonal obstacles and reach an agreement: "We should all learn that all of us are equal, that no differences are so great that they make us harass another person." "Daily bullying situations are very common in the school environment...I think that it's because of intolerance and lack of respect", "...as a suggestion it can be said that there should be more respect among people, as many don't realize the magnitude of the aggression and that they're really hurting someone; they should be more aware of the situation and put themselves in the other student's shoes." Others highlight the role of the educational institutions as mediators in bullying situations: "I think that the school should always mediate as long as it is acquainted with the problem between the peers. Workshops should also be carried out in order to deal with the subject and to make students aware of it, on top of preventing them from spending much time in the streets." "I think that some conscience-raising campaigns on this subject could be launched in schools and at the same time put students to work in order to realize the damage caused by these attitudes. On top of this, violence would be reduced." "School authorities and parents should pay more attention to students to prevent aggression, since they never turn to grown-ups." "...teachers could also do something..."

CONCLUSION

In this work, the students' vision about bullying reveals that the majority are aware that bullying is part of their daily routine and that aggression is frequent among teenagers. As they say: "Aggression is a teenager matter; sometimes, being attacked might help one to live in today's world," Regarding participation in bullying situations, gender is crucial when assessing intimidation but not victimization, finding more aggressors among males than among females. However, according to Moreno, Vacas, and Roa (2006), women more frequently use indirect harassment (false rumoring, social exclusion, etc.), being these more difficult to detect and quantify. In this context, the present research shows that the most frequent bullying methods are verbal and social: "It's very sad to see how schoolmates are bullied, and at the same time mocked by the rest of the students." However, it is important to point out that physical aggression has been admitted by almost the total of those polled. The effect shown is close to the results of other studies conducted in European and American contexts (Moreno, Vacas, & Roa, 2006; Hoyos, Aparicio, & Córdoba, 2005; Avilés-Martínez & *Casares,* 2005).

When analyzing the attitude of the witnesses, the results let us consider that it is unfavorable to bullying situations. The majority thinks that it is wrong to harass a classmate and also that bullying situations are avoidable. "I think that first it is necessary to talk because otherwise, nothing can be worked out. I will try to prevent bullying situations between classmates and I will try to intervene." Likewise, most of the students consider that victims do not deserve to be bullied, and they admit that it might cause psychological damage.

However, the statistical analysis shows that the attitude of witnesses is not strongly defined (Figure 1). A possible explanation arises from the data gathered by the group analysis of the items, in which ambiguity towards the witnesses might be related to the way bullying incidents are assessed. It can be observed that bystanders neither intervene nor report the incident.

With respect to the search for mediators, students do not report bullying situations and if they do so, most of them report it to friends. This situation has also been recognized in research carried out by Avilés-Martínez & *Casares* (2005) and Hoyos, Aparicio, Heilbron, & Schamun, (2004). Perhaps the answer is in Hoyos, Aparicio, and Córdoba, (2005) study, in which it was found that for all bullying situations among schoolmates, help comes from a friend. In the same sense, Cerezo (2001) sets out that teenagers do not consider that grownups contribute to a solution in bullying situations; otherwise, they think that the grownups' intervention is not convenient and that only peers could put an end to a bullying incident.

Nevertheless, in this work, students also consider that their own intervention could worsen the situation; also saying that they do not intervene because they do not know how to do it. "...many times I don't know how to intervene because I am afraid of being attacked; I think that many of my schoolmates feel the same way."

Contributions to the Discussion of Bullying Situations

The data here presented confirm that bystanders' attitude in bullying situations does not favor reporting or intervention. It can be considered that students understand what is going on but they cannot assess the impact of a bullying incident on the victim. The possibility of assuming an active role in the intervention in certain situations depends on the bond with the victim.

Bystanders distance towards bullying situations prevents them from committing themselves and assessing the damage to the victims, raising a fact that calls society to reflect on this matter. It is fundamental to consider that the school bullying dynamics is supported by the absence of voices that intervene not only in reporting these situations but also in committing to a change.

Letting these situations pass, encouraging them or not seeing them for what they are, is nothing more than a lack of commitment to other individuals. Everyone needs other people, in order to develop as a person as (s)he grows, interacts and identifies with his/her peers. However, every one is different from the rest and this difference is what enables us to understand and respect the other.

Extension Workshop Proposal

This reality in school, the outcome of multiple factors, allows for new ways of acting within educational institutions, considering supporting values, emotional intelligence, gender equity, tolerance and respect towards differences as areas to be worked on in school. However, it is a very hard task for the educational institution, as it must promote attitudes which tend to decrease aggressive behavior supported by society and, in some cases, family.

In these postmodern times, in which individualism prevails over community life, it is necessary to reconsider the values that lead us to live in a society in a decent way, by not tolerating episodes of violence that are witnessed but not responded. Sensitivity and empathy allow people to reflect on this through what they sense and act in favor of the other. Being a passive witness to a bullying episode is nothing more than being an observer. To get involved with the problem is to commit oneself as a person.

From this point on, prevention and interventional strategies must be elaborated in order to contribute to the strengthening and generating of new resources to decrease bullying situations and aggression between peers, reinforcing the idea expressed by Avilés-Martínez and Casares (2005), who consider that intervention must be directed to offering a variation in the position of the subjects who participate in bullying dynamics, starting with empathy, the management of feelings, and acknowledgment of the facts.

In relation to what has been exposed, the obtained data from the presented research has enabled the creation of an extensive proposal named *What goes on in the classrooms?* intended to open spaces for reflection which allows the promotion of initiatives to create actions to diminish bullying situations between classmates. Its main objectives are: to sensitize and involve high school students in the bullying dynamic between peers and to generate awareness on the role of each of the participants in the dynamic. The workshop method allows teenagers to put themselves "in the other's shoes", in order to understand through empathy what the other person feels as he/she is being the "target" of these situations, as well as the aggressor's reality which under certain circumstances, he ends up being the "victim" of his own story.

However, the focus is on the witness's role which accompanies and supports this dynamic from the silence, becoming an accomplice to a situation that needs to be revealed. Working and intervening in bullying situations between peers enables us to question how we consider these situations as regular, modifying a reality that can only be discerned when it is far too late. In this way, it is considered that witnesses are the key at the moment of breaking the dynamic of silence in the face of bullying situations. The attitude that they show is a fertile field in which the expression of concrete actions can be worked out, not only to face but also to prevent bullying situations between classmates. Trying to put an end to these situations will not bring an end to violence, but it is a good start to begin to coexist in peace, respecting and accepting what is different, and showing tolerance.

REFERENCES

Aguilar, M. J., López, M., & Rubiales, J. (2008). Bullying: a new perspective towards prevention V Psychiatrics Atlantic Congress. Mar del Plata. Argentina.

Ander-Egg E. (1987). *Social Investigation Techniques*. Humanitas: Argentina. (21st edition).

Avilés Martínez, J., & Casares, I. (2005). Study of the incidence of intimidation and bullying between peers in compulsory High School by means of the questionnaire CIMEI (Avilés, 1999)-questionnaire on intimidation and bullying between peers.- *Psychology Annals-Records, 21*, (1), 27-41.

Avilés Martínez, J. (2006).Differences in causal reasons in bullying among its protagonists. *Psycho-educational Research Electronic Magazine* 9, (4), 201-220.

Bandura, A. (1984). Representing personal determinants in causal structures. *Psychological Review, 91*, 508-511.

Baron, R., & Richardson, D. (1994). *Human aggression* (2nd ed.). New York: Plenum.

Berkowitz, L. (1974). Some determinants of impulsive aggression: The role of mediated associations with reinforcements for aggression. *Psychological Bulletin*. 81, 165-176.

Caballero Gutiérrez M., & Ramos L. (2004). Violence: a revision of the subject within the framework of the research in Instituto Nacional de Psiquiatría Lira. *Mental Health*, 27, (2).

Cerezo, F. (2001) Variables in personality associated to bullying dynamics (bullies *versus* victims). *Psychology Annals-Records* 17, (1), 37-43.

Cerezo, F (2001) Violence in classrooms. Madrid. Pirámide.

Cerezo, F (2006) Violence and victimization between students. Bullying: strategies for identification and elements for the intervention through Bull-S Test. *Psycho-educational Research Electronic Magazine* 2, (4), 333-352.

Dollard, J., Doob, L. W., Miller, N. E., Mowrer, O. H. & Sears, R. R. (1939). Frustration and aggression. New Haven, CT: Yale University Press.

Draghi, C (2007). *52% of students suffers from or exercises violence.* Retrived on August 9, 2007, from: http://www.lanacion.com

Eibl-Eibesfeldt, I. (1993). Biología del comportamiento humano: Manual de etología humana. España: Alianza Editorial.

Ferroni, M., Penecino, E., & Sánchez, A. (2005). Violence in school: visible situation in invisible settings (pp.79-85). *In violence, means and* fears: *the meaning of violence: danger, children at school.* Buenos Aires: Educational Novelties.

Freud, S. (1930). *El malestar en la cultura*. Buenos Aires: Amorrortu. Ed. 1986.

Gallardo, L. (2009). School harassment: domain and submission in the classroom. Retrived on March 4, 2009, from: http://www.aprendemas.com/Reportajes.

Galtung, J. (1998). After violence, 3R: reconstruction, reconciliation, resolution. Confronting the visible and invisible effects of the war and the violence. Bilbao: Bakeaz/Gernika Gogoratuz

Geen, R. G. (1990). Human Aggression. Pacific Glove, Brooks, Cole.

Jiménez, M. (2005). Socially constructed attitudes in response to violence. Bullying in High School students. *Annals of Psychology 1,* (36), 61-82.

Hoyos, O., Aparicio, J., Heilbron, K., & Schamun, V. (2004). Representations of bullying between peers in school of 9, 11 and 13 year old boys and girls from a high and low socio-economical level in Barranquilla City (Colombia) *Psychology From the Caribbean,* Universidad del Norte, 14, 150-172.

Hoyos, O., Aparicio, J., & Córdoba, P. (2005). Characterization of bullying between peers in Barranquilla (Columbia) schools' meeting. *Psychology From the Caribbean,* 16, 1-28.

Labourdette, S. (2007). Social and power relationships. *Society and Orientation*, 7, (1).

Lorenz, K. (1978). *Sobre la agresión: el pretendido mal.* 7ª Ed. México: Ed. Siglo XXI.

Morales Ruiz, M., García de la Cadena, C., & Grazioso de Rodríguez, M. (2006). Awareness of intimidation in Preschool Teacher training. *Interamerican Magazine of Psychology,* 40, (1), 69-76.

Moreno, M., Vacas, C., & Roa, J. (2006). School victimization and social-family environment. *Ibero-American Magazine of Education, 40,* (6), 1-20.

Mynard, H., Joseph, S., & Alexander, J. (2000). Peer-victimisation and posttraumatic stress in adolescents. *Personality and Individual Differences, 29,* (5):1, 815-821.

Olweus, D. (1998) *Bullying behavior and threat among students.* Madrid: Morata.

Ortega, R. (1994). Interpersonal violence in High School educational centers. A study on harassment and intimidation among classmates. *Magazine of Education,* 304, 253-280.

Parke, R., & Slaby, R. (1983). The development of aggression. *Handbook of child psychology, 4,* 547-641.

Palomero Pescador, J. M., & Fernández Dominguez, M. R. (2001). School violence: a global viewpoint. Interuniversity Teacher Training Magazine, 41, 19-38.

Rigby, K. (2004). Addressing Bullying in Schools. Theoretical Perspectives and their Implications. *School Psychology International, 25,* (3), 287-300.

Rubiales, J., Aguilar, M. J., & López, M., (2009). Bullying: voices for prevention and intervention. 1st International Congress on Psychology Research and Practice. 16th Research Conference 5th MERCOSUR'S Psychology Researchers Meeting. Buenos Aires Argentina.

Serrano Sarmiento, A., & Iborra Marmolejo, I. (2005). Violence among classmates in school. Reina Sofía Center Report for the study of violence.

Skinner, B.F. (1953). *Science and Human Behavior.* New York: Macmillan.

Solberg, M., & Olweus, D. (2003). Prevalence estimation of school bullying with the Olweus Bully/Victim Questionnaire. *Aggressive Behavior, 29,* (3), 239-268.

ANNEX 1. DIFFERENCES BETWEEN PILOT TESTS AND FINAL TEST ITEMS

Scale Pilot Test	Final Scale
1. Bullying among classmates is a normal behavior in teenagers.	1. Bullying among classmates is a normal behavior in teenagers..
2. I consider that it is wrong that a classmate bullies another classmate.	2. I consider that it is wrong that a classmate bully another classmate.
3. When there is a bullying situation between classmates I intervene in order to help.	3. When there is a bullying situation between classmates I intervene in order to help.
4. Bullying situations among classmates can be avoided.	4. Bullying situations among classmates can be avoided.
5. When a classmate harasses another I move away from the situation.	5. When a classmate harasses another I move away from the situation.
6. I feel bad when I see a classmate bullying another one.	6. I feel bad when I see a classmate bullying another.
7. When I see a bullying situation between classmates I report it to someone in school.	7. When I see a bullying situation between classmates I report it to someone in school.
8. When there is a bullying situation between classmates I take part in the aggression.	8. When there is a bullying situation between classmates I take part in the aggression..
9. I enjoy bullying situations at school.	9. I enjoy bullying situations at school.

Scale Pilot Test	Final Scale
10. When there is a bullying situation between classmates I talk to the bully.	10. When there is a bullying situation between classmates I talk to the bully.
11. If the victim is not a friend I don't care.	11. If the victim is not a friend I don't care.
12. I don't like a classmate to be bullied.	
13. Classmates who are bullied deserve the harassment.	12. Classmates who are bullied deserve the harassment.
14. When a classmate bullies another I stay looking.	13. When a classmate bullies another I stay looking.
15. When I witness a bullying situation I feel scared.	
16. When there is a bullying situation among my classmates I talk it over with my family.	14. When there is a bullying situation among my classmates I talk it over with my family.
17. It makes me sad when I see a classmate bullying another.	15. It makes me sad when I see a classmate bullying another.
18. I speak with the school authorities, about bullying situations among classmates.	
19. I don't intervene when a classmate bullies another.	16. To intervene when a classmate is being bullied might worsen the situation
20. When I witness a bullying situation between classmates I speak with the victim.	17. When I witness a bullying situation between classmates I speak with the victim.
21. I consider it a betrayal to talk about a bullying situation out of my group of friends.	18. I consider it a betrayal to tell on a friend who is bullying a classmate.
22. Bullying situations among classmates upsets me.	19. Bullying situations among classmates upset me.
23. When a classmate bullies another I don't intervene because I don't know what to do.	20. When a classmate bullies another I don't intervene because I don't know what to do.
24. We only talk about bullying problems among classmates.	21. We only talk about bullying problems among classmates.
25. I don't care if a classmate bullies another.	22. I don't care if a classmate bullies another.
26. Bullying situations among classmates causes psychological problems.	23. Bullying situations among classmates causes psychological problems.

PART THREE:
INTERVENTIONS, METHODS AND EVALUATION IN INTERPERSONAL VIOLENCE

In: Bio-Psycho-Social Perspectives on Interpersonal Violence   ISBN: 978-1-61668-159-3
Editors: M. Frías-Armenta et al., pp. 281-310   © 2010 Nova Science Publishers, Inc.

Chapter 13

METHODS IN PSYCHOLOGY & LAW AND CRIMINOLOGICAL RESEARCH. THE ASSESSMENT OF INTERVENTIONS FOR PREVENTION OF CRIME

Eugenio De Gregorio
Università Degli Studi Di Roma, Italy.

ABSTRACT

This chapter deals with the main themes of research in Psychology & Law and Criminology referring to evaluation of interventions for the prevention of crime. Classical methodological themes are described here, as well as the historical phases, epistemological issues and terms of debate between quantitative and qualitative approaches. Beyond differences, opportunities for methodological recomposition are prefigured. In the second section, the basic assumptions of evaluation research are described and some examples of wide and effective projects are provided. The treatment is completed with a review of criteria and indicators to be considered in evaluating the effectiveness of interventions.

INTRODUCTION: ISSUES AND METHODS IN EMPIRICAL RESEARCH IN CRIMINOLOGY AND IN PSYCHOLOGY AND LAW

Broadly speaking, criminological research adopts the forms and methods of social and psychological research, the former is an empirical-applicative adaptation of the latter two. So, beginning from a traditional direction, in criminology it will also be possible to cover research planning and information review phases, mainly using either of the two approaches: quantitative and qualitative. We will not dwell on a description of the different characterisations of the two approaches, since we are sure that the differences lie more in the options regarding the nature of awareness (Mannetti, 1998) and in the training of researchers rather than in actual diversities in the reality of the social objects (Kruglanski & Jost, 2000). In this sense, the directions of the research procedures become more or less customary, consolidated and traditional. In fact, the researcher is left with the discretion to select from epistemological paradigms, cultural currents or simply from previous research sources. In this chapter, we do not intend to claim *"empirical relativism"*; instead, we are keen to stress the importance of the first choices that can be made when deciding to study a complex social object, such as crime. As a matter of fact, the researcher is required to theoretically "place her/himself" in a context and make choices consistent with that position. We can use a classic issue in criminology as an example: through biographical methods Sutherland (1949) discovered the existence of the "obscure number", a percentage of crimes outside official statistics. But a similar result could be obtained – from the logical point of view – by analysing the same official statistics and crosschecking; for example, the figures relative to arrests with the figures relative to the total number of charges reported for all crimes. The result would most probably be a "discovery" of economic and financial crimes and crimes committed through the internet (fraud, credit card cloning, paedophilia), since the first group (the ones held in detention for common crimes) would include episodes of robberies, theft, drug dealing and trafficking, and because these are more frequent and more socially visible.

The problem of the choices begin with the options on the nature of the reality and awareness regarding the methods used for research rather than beginning from the quality of the information collected (statistics or narrations, indices and coefficients or conceptual and thematic frames), where we consider that addressing the arguments towards the paradigms of reference is profitable. The Researcher (in social and legal psychology as well as criminology) could decide to place their work on a point between two extremes that represent the realist approach and the constructionist approach.

In social sciences, the realist approach has had a long, consolidated history. Beginning from behaviourism, the advocates of a "realistic way of looking at things" claimed that there is a reality *out there* (outside the individual cognitive system) and that this reality can be recognised objectively, without any interference, using methods borrowed from natural sciences. This orientation (positivist and post-positivist) has produced considerable theoretical *corpora*, it suggested the research and survey techniques of data, emphasising the concepts of validity and reliability of the studies and of research tools (Guba & Lincoln, 1994). The constructionist (or "narrative") approach borrowed something from natural sciences, but in terms of W. Heisenberg's "uncertainty principle" (Berger & Luckmann, 1966): *there is no such thing as an objective reality out there, the knowledge of reality depends on the tools used to know it, including the researcher himself, whose activity changes the object of the knowledge, in the final analysis making it impossible to know.* In social sciences, and particularly in psychology, the "narrative turn" (Harré & Gillett, 1994; Bruner, 1990) – intended as a paradigmatic passage from a realist to a constructionist approach – represented a moment of development and proliferation of reflections, also referring to the nature of the subject area and to the epistemological identity of researchers; in this direction, their own criteria for evaluating the quality of empirical studies have been proposed (Silverman, 1993, 2000; Seale, 1999).

The *realistic* approach to qualitative data leads to an attempt for "objectivization" of the responses given in an interview or drawn from focus groups, diaries or film clips (Miller & Glassner, 1997), as if they described an external reality. Following this approach, it is appropriate to include several tools in the research design, to ensure the accuracy of interpretation. On the other hand, the second orientation, the *narrative* approach, is represented by those research orientations that consider narrative materials as an access to different stories that people use to describe their world (Holstein & Gubrium, 1997).

At this point, we can briefly sum up the key traits of the methodology of criminology research based on an objectivist approach[1]. The researcher will follow a direction that begins from choosing the problem and through structuring of hypotheses, data collection and data processing tools, arrives at verifying specific hypotheses. Each of these phases will include problems to solve and choices to make, but the common thread running through the process will come from the certainty that – irrespective of the research designs, of operationalisations, the variables and the data analysis techniques used – the external reality is factual and, given some forethought in the logical and methodological procedures, it can be objectively known. As represented in the experimental tradition, prediction and control are the main objectives of research and they can be achieved by standardising processes and techniques. Neopositivist criminological researchers will carefully select their sample, will formulate the questionnaire (or the content analysis plan, or the interaction observation plan) and keep the cognitive and relational *biases* (distortions) under control; their data analysis techniques will be oriented towards identifying clear and as far as possible the direct effects of variable X on variable Y.

As regards the other aspect, in methods usually defined as "qualitative", it is believed that the objective of the research is the in-depth understanding of phenomena without expecting too much generalisation. There is an awareness of the fact that knowledge is, by its nature, situational and also (but not above all) that it depends on the relationship that is set up between researcher and object/subject of the study. So, the researcher will work in a context where formalisation is relative, forecasting is absent and knowledge is subjective. According to these approaches, the tools used to study and analyse the information will be "open", biographical, and narrative (Charmaz, 1995; Strauss & Corbin, 1990; Silverman, 2000; Henwood & Pidgeon, 1992).

From the epistemological point of view, the use of one approach over the other has led to extensive debate on respective "usefulness" for scientific awareness of crime and on intervention policies. Kruglanski and Jost (2000) stated a number of considerations about the scientific and epistemological status of research from the constructivistic social psychological point of view. They also discussed the meaning of quantification in qualitative research as well as the criteria of its quality assessment (Silverman, 1993, 2000; Peräkylä, 1997).

In the last section of this paper, I will introduce some issues on the use of mixed methods in psychology-and-law and criminological research. According to this perspective, the quality criteria of qualitative research should be reviewed in terms of coherence and accuracy in the entire length of research (Seale, 1999; Silverman, 1993).

Psychology and criminology researchers have access to a number of research methods available to them, and evaluative research is particularly important in regards to the objectives of this section. This territory is usually not very popular among psychologists, who probably pay the price of a greater distance from the issues of assessing social action, but it is certainly relevant to those who deal with the assessment of crime prevention measures. Due to its interdisciplinary nature, it would be desirable for this sector to include the participation of psychologists, sociologists, social workers, experts in law and intervention policies. Indeed,

---

[1] In any case, it must be considered that in order to carry out research, criminologists must choose from an extensive and varied range of methodological tools, and their training and orientation, the kind of problem

the object of the evaluation (the deviance prevention measures), forces researchers-evaluators to be familiar not only with the research method but also with the issues of deviance, prevention, unease, and the effects that interventions of this type may have on the social actors involved.

So, what exactly is evaluation research? We selected what we consider two of the most complete definitions provided in literature, also due to the persons that refer to it. The first concept considers evaluation research as

> *the use of social science research procedure to systematically assess the effectiveness of social intervention programs.* More specifically, evaluation researchers (evaluators) use social research methods to study, appraise, and help to improve social programs in all their aspects, including the diagnosis of the social problems they address, their conceptualization and design, their implementation and administration, their outcomes, and their efficiency (Rossi, Freeman, & Lipsey, 1999, p. 4, emphasis in original).

The second one is taken from the first edition of the publication by Bezzi (2001, pgs 55-56), and according to this, evaluation

> is mainly (but not only) an applied social research activity, within a decision-making process, integrated with programming, planning and intervention phases, whose purpose is to reduce decision-making complexity through analysis of direct and indirect, expected and unexpected, desired and undesired, effects of the action, including those that cannot be ascribable to material aspects; in this context the evaluation takes on the special role as shared role of opinion of socially relevant actions, necessarily ascertaining the operative consequences as regards the relationship between decision makers, operators and beneficiaries of the action.

We can immediately see how each definition places an accent on different but complementary aspects: strongly research-oriented, in a broad sense (and to its techniques), the former and with a particular orientation to the context and to the "decision", as regards crucial and strategic choices, the second.

And these are the two precise areas (social research *for the purposes* of a decision on crucial choices) that will direct the rest of this section. We will therefore attempt to understand what tools are available (in terms of research techniques, concrete functioning) so as to be able to express an opinion for the purpose of the decision (third party, of the client) in the sector of deviant behaviour prevention: what are the appropriate techniques to evaluate success of the prevention interventions, in terms of effectiveness and efficiency? What are the differences between the adult sector and the sector of minors? Are there any differences between the use of quantitative and qualitative methods in terms of practical repercussions?

These are just some of the questions we will attempt to answer.

---

they intend to deal with, and the economic costs and deontological problems that every method has become particularly important when making these choices.

However, we must, first of all, briefly deal with two fundamental aspects[2]: the methodologies of evaluation research, on the one hand and the decision-making context of the research (and the intervention it addresses), on the other.

QUANTITATIVE METHODOLOGY

The definition proposed by Rossi, Freeman, and Lipsey (1999) seems to lead to the issue of the evaluation of research procedures that revolve around the experimental model. In this sense evaluation research would be social research to all intents and purposes and as such it would use some of those methods. Please note that all the methodological indications covered in this section apply to any area of empirical research in criminology, not just to evaluate projects aimed at preventing deviance. Following Bachman and Schutt (2008; 2007), we can clarify the difference between the common representations of phenomena with criminological relevance (domestic violence, for example) and scientific theory. According to "naïve theories" (Kruglanski, 1980), the awareness of given problems is based on representations of common sense, stereotyping processes, cognitive distortions ("*biases*") that favour the elicitation of opinions (in some way) deformed by the emotional and sentimental participation of people.

The starting point is always a good research question, the answer to which forms the objective of the study and it is used to produce hypotheses:

> Are children who are violent more likely than nonviolent children to use violence as adults? "Does the race of the victim who is killed influence whether someone is sentenced to death rather than life imprisonment?" "Why some kinds of neighborhoods have more crime than others?" […] "Does community policing reduce crime rate?" […]. So many research questions are possible in criminology that it is more a challenge to specify what does not qualify as a social research question than to specify what does (Bachman & Schutt, 2008, p. 282).

The sources of good research questions are usually daily experience (own and others) or the request of a client that promises handsome funds. However, the main source of inspiration comes from criminology theory: it gives the hypotheses of the causes, preceding or concurrent events, and conditions of the context of crime. Whatever the source for planning a research study, the next step consists of choosing deductive or inductive reasoning. Both involve a relationship between theory and data, but in a different way.

> Theory and data have a two-way, mutual reinforcement relationship. Research that begins with a theory implying that certain data should be found involves **deductive reasoning**, which moves from general ideas (theory) to specific reality (data). In contrast, **inductive reasoning** moves from the specific to the general.
> Both deductive and inductive reasoning are essential to criminologists. We cannot test an idea fairly unless we use deductive reasoning, starting our expectations in advance and setting up a test in which our idea could be shown as very tentative.

---

[2] In this case, the explanation (discussed below in note 8) of the "selection" of the issues we consider most relevant for the purposes of consistency and overall legibility of the work apply.

Yet theories, no matter how cherished, cannot make useful predictions for every social situation or research problem that we can seek to investigate (Bachman & Schutt, 2008, p. 34).

The "research circle" in figure 1 illustrates the two procedures. Research that uses deductive reasoning formulates one or more hypotheses (*theory-driven*) of relations between variables to move from theory to data. These hypotheses are then verified using an experimental research design aimed at clarifying whether there is a cause-and-effect relationship between the variables and if so, how statistically significant it is (Logio, Dowdall, Babbie, & Halley, 2008). More specifically, in regards to the evaluation of the effectiveness of interventions of deviance prevention, one valid and reliable evaluation could, therefore, be conducted by implementing an experimental research design that clarifies the relationship of the variables of "problem", "intervention", and "solution to the problem".

A variable is a characteristic or property that can vary; it takes on different values and attributes. An independent variable (for example, time spent watching television or number of crimes committed) is hypothesized to cause or it can lead to a variation in the dependent variable. A dependent variable is hypothesized to vary depending on or under the influence of the independent variable. A hypothesis is a tentative statement about empirical reality, involving a relationship between two or more variables (in other words, the amount of time children spend watching violent programmes on television *determines* the amount of bullying they commit at school and their peer relationships).

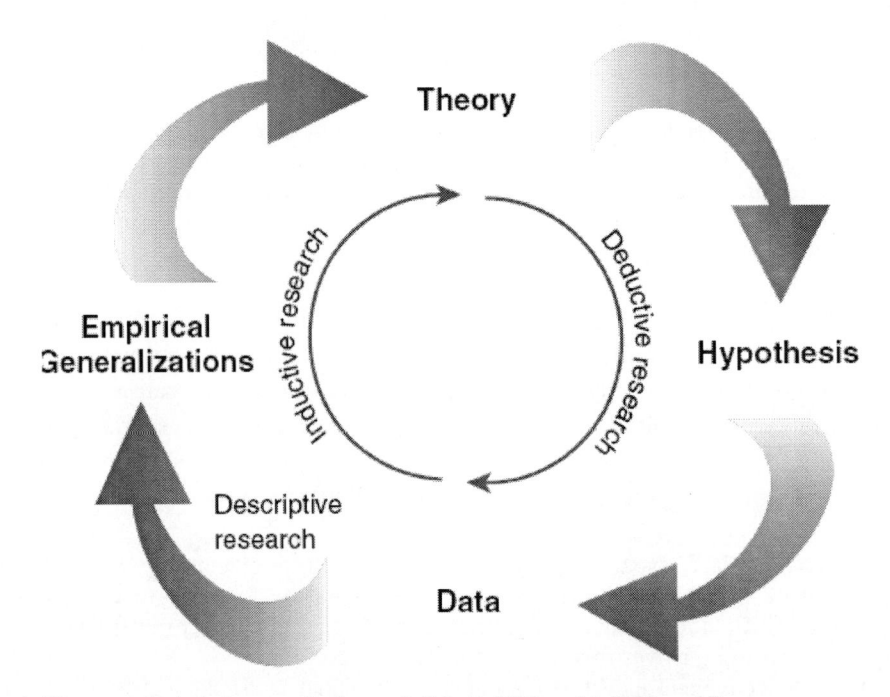

Figure 1. The research circle (*source*: Bachman & Schutt, 2008, p. 34; 2007, p. 44).

Indeed, the experimental method used in social and natural sciences makes possible to detect, ascertain and evaluate, in terms of "statistical significance", the influence of one or more independent variables on other ("dependent") variables. Those are the ones of interest in terms of the effect of the intervention. We imagine implementing an experiment to verify whether watching a video of an advert against alcohol abuse in public premises has an effect on people's inclination to drink.

> In our example of alcohol abuse, two groups of subjects are examined. To begin, each group is administered a questionnaire designed to measure their alcohol use in general and binge drinking in particular. Then, only one of the groups – the experimental group – is shown the video. Later, the researcher administers a posttest of alcohol use to both groups […]
> Using a control group allows the researcher to control for the effects of the experiment itself. If participation in the experiment leads the subjects to report less alcohol use, that should occur in both the experimental and the control group. If, on the one hand, the overall level of drinking exhibited by the control group decreases between the pretest and posttest as much as for the experimental group, then the apparent reduction in alcohol use must be function of the experiment or of some external factor, not a function of watching the video specifically. In this situation, we can conclude that the video did not cause any change in alcohol use.
> If, on the other hand, drinking decreases only in the experimental group, then we can be more confident in saying that the reduction is a consequence of exposure to the video (because that's the only difference between the two groups). Or, alternatively, if drinking decreases more in the experimental group than in the control group, then that, too, is grounds for assuming that watching the video reduced alcohol abuse (Maxfield & Babbie, 2008, pp. 179-180).

In the evaluation of prevention projects, information must first be collected (using questionnaires, statistics, observation techniques), at time_ 1, before implementing an intervention or a project/program[3] (on two groups: one using the intervention and the other acting as control group), and an evaluation, at time_ 2, to verify – through the differences between the two groups – the extent and significance of the effect of the intervention (or of the program).

This general model of the experimental method must be analysed in light of the specificities of the contexts of the evaluations. Specifically, it is not always possible to respect the criteria that characterise the experimental research designs that can be reproduced in a laboratory. For example, we can imagine having to evaluate the effect of the positioning of video-surveillance cameras in a delimited neighbourhood on the frequency of crime and sense of security perceived by the residents in that neighbourhood. Does video-surveillance have an effect on reducing crime? Do citizens feel safer if they know "Big Brother" is watching over them?

A research design that must necessarily take place in a natural context (a city neighbourhood) cannot use "golden rules" that assure absolute control of the experimental situation. We define research designs that cannot use a random selection of subjects and their assignment to experimental conditions as "quasi-experimental"[4]). There are possible variations on the theme: for example, increasing the number of groups and the variability of

---

[3] The distinction between interventions, projects and programs is intuitive and refers to the different space and time characterisation.

[4] Still, we must point out that many Anglo-Saxon sources specifically talk about the possibility of implementing "truly" experimental research designs and that these can discriminate the effect of treatments with precision. However, where it is not possible to randomise they suggest falling back on quasi-experimental research (Weisburd, Lum, & Petrosino, 2001; Farrington & Petrosino, 2001; Petrosino, Boruch, Soydan, Duggan, & Sanchez-Meca, 2001).

the programs, or simply doing a before and after surveys of a single group of beneficiaries[5]. Naturally, the premise will comprise hypotheses (formed from previous studies and/or from theory models) whose verification is the priority objective of the research. These hypotheses can refer to the positive or negative effect of an intervention, or to its impact[6], or to other long-term variables.

One of the main limits for the use of experimental or quasi-experimental designs to evaluate interventions in criminology is ethical. Speaking of evaluation projects of interventions for prevention of violence to women, Skinner, Hester, and Malos (2005, p. 7) state:

> The "purest" form of evaluation, the experimental approach, involving random controller trials (RCT), was deemed neither ethical nor possible in relation to the CRP domestic violence, rape and prostitution projects. In relation to the domestic violence and rape projects, it was inappropriate to withhold from half the women in contact with interventions the service that had been put in place to maximize safety or to provide other support. In relation to the projects concerning street prostitution it was not only difficult to gain access to the women who were involved with the project, but gaining access to a separate sample of women without project workers as gatekeepers would have been particularly difficult […] and may possibly have been dangerous for the evaluators.

In order to guarantee that the variables considered adequately represent constructions, the phenomena that occur in daily life, the variables of the evaluation must be suitably operationalized. What do we mean by operationalization of a variable? It is the logical procedure – analytically formulated by Lazarsfeld (1958) – whereby a concept with a high level of abstraction (for example, the complex concept of "prevention", or that of "deviance") is turned into a variable of the research design at a lesser level of abstraction/complexity (figure 1). In other words it is transposed into concrete research and measurement operations in the real world.

This passage is possible through a precise definition of the starting concept and of breaking this down into the dimensions that constitute it (in figure 2: from C1 to D_1, D_2 and D_3). Breaking it down can lead to conceptually simple dimensions – with a low level of abstraction – and therefore easy to transpose into indicators and into the relative operative definitions (e.g.: the questions in a questionnaire or the survey of "simple" behaviours), as in D_2 and D_3; or another passage of conceptual definition and breaking down into smaller dimensions may be necessary to specify the complexity and make it possible to identify empirical indicators (as in D_1, in figure 2).

In criminology and in the other social sciences, theory plays an important role as a basis for formulating research questions and later interpreting findings and projecting interventions. The criminological theory guides the entire process of identifying dimensions and indicators.

---

[5] At the risk of oversimplifying, we will restrict ourselves to giving the reader only some of the main coordinates for each aspect of evaluation research. This is so the treatment is not too heavy going, keeping the focus on the possibility of carrying out the evaluation of the deviance prevention interventions. For all details and descriptions of the experimental methods, amongst the many, we refer to Maxfield & Babbie (2008).

[6] The difference between "impacts" and "effects" is linked to the time dimension, being direct and immediate objectives of the event on the one part and (at times unplanned) long-term consequences on the other; but this dimension tends to disappear in an overlap, so that effects are one of the possible types of impact.

In other words, figure 3 represents the anchorage process of theory models to the reality of daily life in order to know this by means of the former.

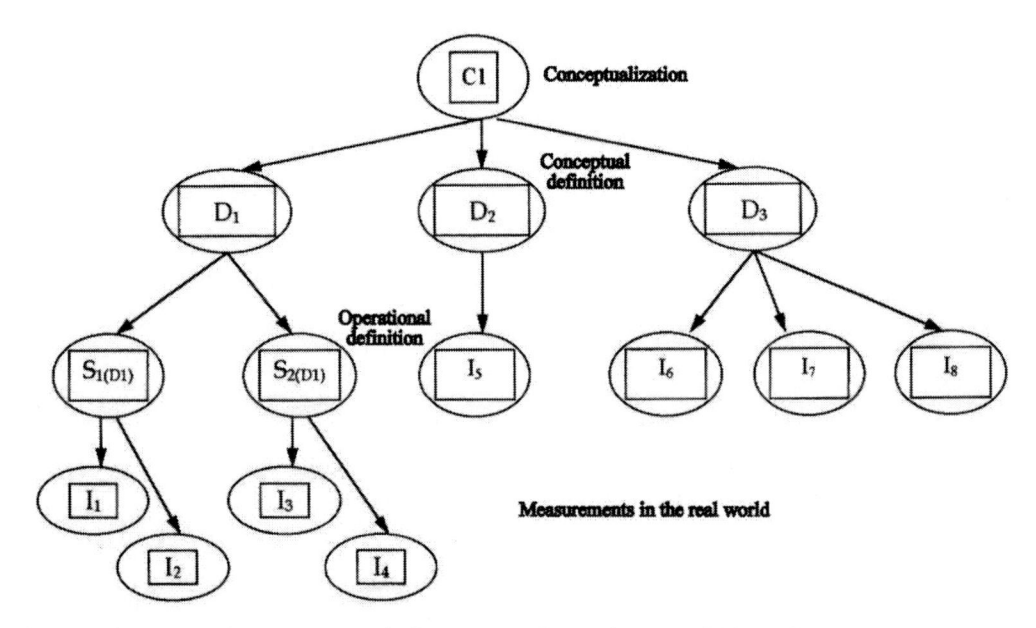

Figure 2. The passage from concepts to indicators according to the Lazarsfeld paradigm (*source*: Cannavò, 1999, p. 131).

In criminological research, the adoption of experimental designs has favoured the creation of evaluation committees of prevention and intervention projects (see further, as regards the *Campbell Collaboration Crime and Justice Group, as an example*) that – by taking advantage of the key features of this type of study – deal with them in the search for what works in preventive practice (Farrington & Petrosino, 2001; Petrosino, Boruch, Soydan, Duggan, & Sánchez-Meca, 2001; MacKenzie, 2000). Special emphasis is placed on the quality of the research and on the standards for inclusion in the commission databases. In particular, we wonder whether it is only the experimental method that allows the quality of the studies and if this may inevitably condition the conclusions in some way, restricting their interpretative keys (Weisburd, Lum, & Petrosino, 2001; Weisburd, 2000; Feder, Jolin, & Feyerherm, 2000).

Special attention must be paid to the ethical problems related to the experiments (Boruch, Victor, & Cecil, 2000; Weisburd, 2000). Another application of quantitative research concerns the verification of hypotheses explaining criminal behaviour and the association between the risk factors that predispose to commit crimes and the actual implementation of these behaviours.

If we follow the representations spread by the media or if we pay attention to the conversations of people on streets or in bars, it is possible to detect representations of common sense that they provide concerning explanations of reality and causes of human behaviour, including criminal behaviour.

> What are your perceptions of violence committed by youth, and how did you acquire such perceptions? What do you believe are the causes of youth violence? Many factors have been blamed for youth violence in American society, including the easy availability of guns, the use of weapons in movies and television, [...] poor parenting, rap and rock music, and the Goth culture [...] Each of you probably has your own ideas about what factors may be related to violence in general and youth violence in particular. However, the factors you believe are important in explaining a phenomenon may not always be the ones supported by empirical research (Bachman & Schutt, 2007, pp. 2-3).

Different processes contribute to form and consolidate this consciousness of common sense: the tendency to overestimate the presence of personal traits or the characteristics of the context that look as the ones we know and that are familiar to us. The distortions caused by selective and partial observation, resistance to change and other completely natural processes that characterise the "non-expert" knowledge of the world. The production of scientific consciousness works differently. Beginning from the reprocessing of classic philosophy (the Aristotle model in particular) and renewed by the current of positivism and post-positivism, the modern idea of scientific consciousness is based on the following assumptions (that we mentioned at the beginning of this chapter):

- The existence of a reality outside the individual;
- this reality can be objectively known through structured, neutral procedures;
- the aim of scientific consciousness and of researchers is to achieve consciousness of this reality.

> The social science approach to answering questions about the social world is designed to greatly reduce these potential sources of error in everyday reasoning. Science relies on logical and systematic methods to answer questions, and it does so in a way that allows others to inspect and evaluate its methods (Bachman & Schutt, 2007, p 7).

Contrary to consciousness of common sense, the production of scientific consciousness must be based on an adequate path that guarantees the possibility of generalising what is observed (in terms of association of variables). Apart from the operationalization process, just described and summarised in figure 1 and from the use of experimental research designs, it is necessary to consider the criteria of validity and reliability of the research procedures and of the results obtained.

Inductive research starts from the bottom of the research circle in figure 1 and the main objective is to explore sets of data.

> In strictly inductive research, researchers already know what they have found when theorizing, or attempting to explain what accounts for these findings. The result can be new insights and provocative questions. But the adequacy of an explanation formulated after the facts is necessarily less certain than an explanation presented prior to the collection of data. Every phenomenon can always be explained in some way. Inductive explanations are thus more trustworthy if they are tested subsequently with deductive research (Bachman & Schutt, 2008, p. 41).

It must be said that this vision is a representation of inductive reasoning as being ancillary, secondary or subordinate to deductive reasoning. Qualitative research is mainly based on this kind of reasoning and, as regards this, it is worth stressing how research and qualitative analysis techniques have acquired progressive autonomy and dignity of scientific consciousness in recent years (as we introduced at the start of this chapter).

QUALITATIVE METHODOLOGY

So, starting up a qualitative research project is dictated by a need to explore thorough understanding of a given area. In regards to domestic violence, Bennett, Goodman, and Dutton (1999) provide an example of research that uses qualitative interviews in order to explore the experiences, the processes of attributing sense of 49 victims, where their aims were to provide "voice to the victims", to see reality (crime) from their point of view, to understand their needs, requests, positions in terms of the experience they went through, in terms of their assailant, the justice system and its representatives.

> Explanations derived from qualitative research will be richer and more finely textured than those resulting from quantitative research, but they are likely to be based on fewer cases from a limited area. We cannot assume that the people studied in this setting are like others or that other researchers would develop explanations similar to ours to make sense of what was observed or heard (Bachman & Schutt, 2008, p. 41).

This is why even generalising results obtained must be intended as something specific. Seale (1999, p. 119) wrote that "the simplest way in which qualitative social research can be defined in negative terms is: the research that does not use numbers". But if it does happen to be the simplest way, it also is the shortest form (as the same Seale explains): a lot of research strategies exist and some of them consist of a *mixed use of quantification and interpretation*. From this standpoint, if the numeric information always refer to a totally interpretative process which comes before any quantification, then researchers can reconstruct ulterior interpretative pathways to give a meaning to the information obtained. Fielding and Fielding (1986) claimed that some interpretative process is embedded in more specifically quantitative analysis techniques. As stated, all techniques used to gather data are analysed "qualitatively", because the action of analysing is a selective action and therefore it is necessarily interpretative. It is proposed where the integration of quantification and qualitative orientation does not lie only on combining these two approaches. On the contrary, because they are integrated you cannot easily define boundaries: where does the interpretative analysis stop and where does quantification start?

Papers on qualitative research clearly indicate how the quality of qualitative studies is to be intended. Kruglanski and Jost (2000) recently upheld that the two approaches (qualitative and quantitative) are related in terms of a mutual continuity (historical, logical and methodological). These authors wrote an extensive historical-critical review on the relationship between social construction and experimental social psychology, and they claimed that "the question arises spontaneously […] if the division has ever really had reason to exist" (p. 53).

We discussed the importance of qualitative research in the history of criminology. Now, we would like to briefly look at the qualitative techniques specifically dedicated to evaluation. It is preferable to use them in the planning phase, as a kind of *ex ante* evaluation (or in any case during the *start-up phase of a wide-ranging program*) in particular when we want to increase the participation of the concerned actors (beneficiaries, operators, experts, local communities). Indeed, we are talking about techniques that favour a participatory approach consistent with a logic of *request to the protagonists of the event*.

The different qualitative research strategies share the same basic logic and some phrases summed up by Bachman and Schutt (2008):

- *Exploratory research questions, with a commitment to inductive reasoning.* Typically, a qualitative research project does not start from a pre-packaged hypothesis; on the contrary, the researcher approaches the field and the participants with the aim of discovering and valorising the new;
- *An orientation to social context, to the interconnections between social phenomena rather than to their discrete features.* Irrespective of the specific context of the research study, it will be necessary to look at the entirety and complexity of the phenomena and observed processes so as not to artificially separate aspects of social reality that acquire sense only in mutual interconnection;
- *A focus on human subjectivity.* People who work in qualitative research are more interested in discovering people and their inner worlds than quantifying phenomena removed from the reality of everyday life. "The language of variable and hypothesis appears only rarely in the qualitative literature" (Bachman & Schutt, 2008, p. 259).

Broadly speaking, it is possible to describe qualitative approaches as tools to access the complexity of the social reality. In this framework, the task of the researcher's is to bring order to this complexity, arranging it into a *theoretical model*. The classic concept of association between theory and reality is summarised by Legewie (2006): «the reality and the model are bound by a bilateral relationship of resemblance. The builder of the model, the researcher, is usually excluded from that relationship, which has some consequences on the concept. A more complex concept of formulating models is based on the fact that theories or models (we use these two concepts here as synonyms) are *constructions*, where it is also important to involve the person who drafted the model – the builder. The result of this is a *trilateral relationship between reality, builder of the model and model/theory*» (figure 3).

According to Legewie (2006), the researcher develops a model that represents reality, but since this is complex the model can only re-propose some elements, a summary mediated by the researcher. The question is: How are reality and model mutually connected?, when is a model true or pertinent?, when does a model correctly represent reality?

> The concept of model set out here can be intuitively explained using the example of the relationship between a city and the "model" of this city in the form of a map of the city. A city is complex, full of elements, chaotic – a map of the city on the other hand must be clear. The example shows the simplification taken through the construction of the model. The type of map of the city, the type of formulation of the model depends on what it is to be used for. A map for vehicles is considerably different from the schematic maps of public transport: so the construction of the model depends on the aim of the builder. If a map of the city were as complicated as the city itself it would be of no use in finding your way around the city. Users of the model or of the theory head in the opposite direction to that of the builder: they use the theory to logically draw the conclusions that allow them to find their way in the complex reality. Obviously, for this purpose they

always need to have some knowledge of the reality as well: for example, if they are using a map of the city they have to know where they are on that map.

Certain implications follow from these considerations, which have to do with the role (and with the responsibility of the researcher) and the truthfulness of the model as a representation of reality: the subjectivity of the builder (researcher), with his/her aims, interests and values is a component of the scientific model or theory. This cannot be ignored.

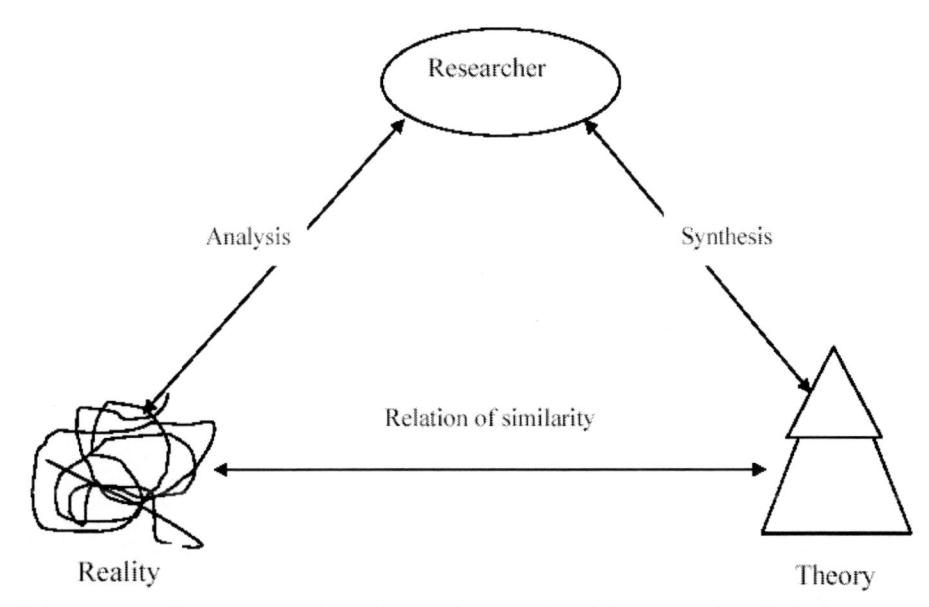

Figure 3. The relationship between social reality and theoretical models processed qualitatively.

In qualitative research the builder should rather reflect on their subjectivity and make it obvious so that the model user can take this into account. We must also point out that the exponential growth of "Computer-Assisted Qualitative Data Analysis Software" made the traditional analysis techniques even more complex, configuring a situation where the creator of the results described in research reports and academic articles is not only the researcher.

Today we can say that the most sophisticated techniques of quantitative data analysis succeed with difficulty in grasping the complexity of human action in everyday life. On the other hand, the drive towards increase emphasis on the interpretative aspects of the research process means we risk our not being able to grasp the "general laws" that govern human social processes.

Until now, the growth of software products, which support research in the social sciences, has proceeded in a parallel direction with the increasingly complex "ways of thinking" of those who carry out social and psychological research (Bazeley, 2006). In our opinion, those who create such software programs are inclined to reproduce the complexity of thought processes which are characteristic, both of the researchers who deal with the problem or specific set of problems and the people who participate in the research. In this way, the complexity of software programs (complexity understood as complexity of use and complexity in terms of coefficients, indices or networks of theoretical connections) reflect the "cognitive complexity" and "psychosocial complexity" of human activity, including the process of acquiring knowledge in human and social terms (De Gregorio & Arcidiacono, 2008).

> The researcher, like his informants, is a social animal. He has a role to play, and he has his own personality needs that must be met in some degree if he is to function successfully. Where the researcher operates out of a university, just going into the field for a few hours at a time, he can keep his personal social life separate from field activity. His problem of role is not quite so complicated. If, on the other hand, the researcher is living for an extended period in the community he is studying, his personal life is inextricably mixed with his research (Bachman & Schutt, 2007, p. 277).

Therefore, the choices researchers make, the values they bear and guide their action, the presence of a context that has its own rules and its own schemes-systems of interpreting reality (in one word its "positioning") cannot be separated from the same operation of consciousness they are conducting. Besides, the same key passages of qualitative research is to clarify how it is difficult, methodologically incorrect, to separate aspects of the process of awareness (figure 4).

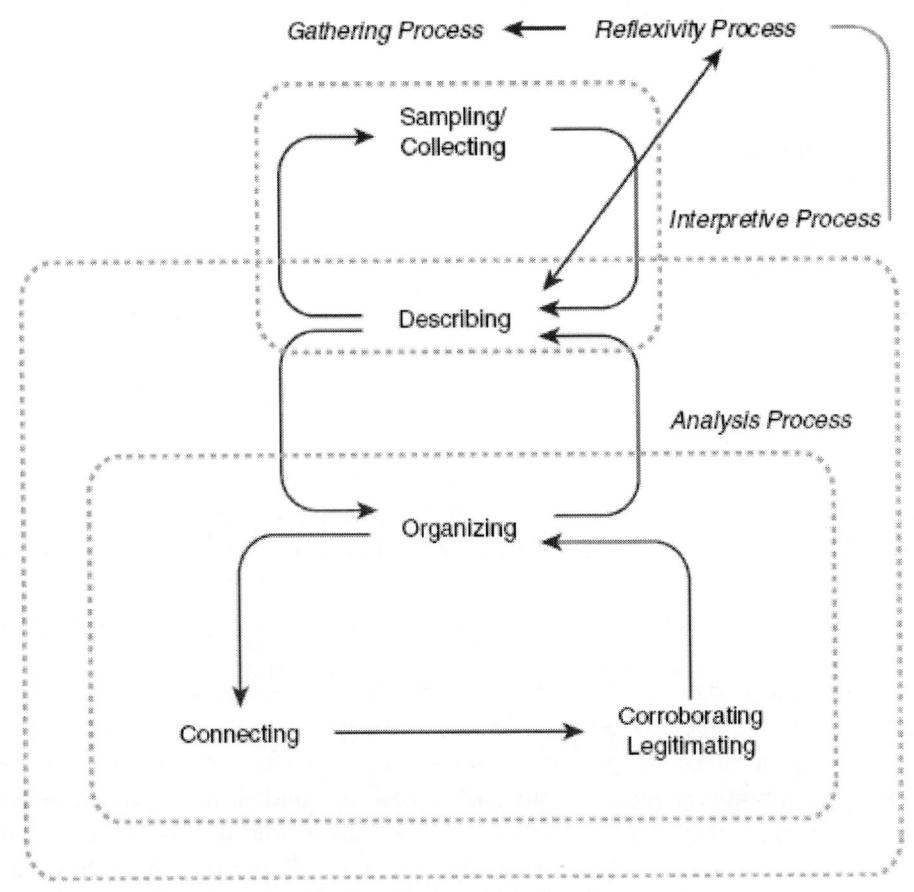

Figure 4. Qualitative research process (*source*: Bachman & Schutt, 2007, p. 260).

In this diagram, qualitative research begins with the qualitative research reflecting on the setting and its relation to and interpretations of it. The researcher then describes the goals and means for the research. This description is followed by *sampling* and *collecting* data, *describing* the data, and *organizing* those data. Thus, the *gathering process* and the *analysis* process proceed together, with repeated description and analysis of data as they are collected. As the data are organized, *connections* are identified between different data segments, and efforts are made to *corroborate* the credibility of those connections. This *interpretative process* begins to emerge in a written account that represents what has been done and how the data have been interpreted. Each of these steps in the research process informs the others and is repeated throughout the research process (Bachman & Schutt, 2007, p. 260).

The connection between the data gathering phase and the analysis phase is in the definition of the interpretation of the results, as a brief and exhaustive representation of the whole procedure and the positioning of the researcher inside the whole procedure, which support the idea of complexity of qualitative research, particularly in the context of criminality that is never neutral in terms of values, nor inoffensive in its implications (Järvinen, 2007).

If the objective of a good research project is quantitative, the *verification* of hypotheses and theories in the qualitative studies is to foreground the *discovery* of new phenomena and hypotheses, as well as the development and perfection of theories. It is still possible to verify hypothesis through the processes of deduction (that we discussed). *Qualitative studies* are more open in relation to the potential results: their greatest strength lies in discovering brand new connections, often unexpected, in developing new theories or in updating-revising existing theories. For this reason, in qualitative studies there is no formulation of hypotheses drawn from known theories and formulate a priori. In planning, realising and evaluating their studies, the qualitative researcher still relies to a great extent on their preliminary knowledge of the object of the research (Legewie, 2006).

The different techniques used to gather qualitative data can be framed in two main areas: "individual" techniques on the one hand, and, on the other, "group" techniques. Among the former, we will briefly dwell on intensive interviewing, specifically meant as *interviews with privileged testimonials*. These information collecting techniques are strongly characterised by the emphasis on the relationship between the person asking and the person providing the information (in this case, people whose position, responsibilities and competences represent a "privileged" observatory). Indeed, interviews can be used to build up and maintain a relationship of comparison and mutual exchange of meanings to arrive, particularly through consciousness of the topic studied, enhancing the value of an "inside" perspective from trade.

In the technical meaning of interview, through the free or guided evocation of content, conceptual and representational nuclei, it favours the in-depth understanding and interpretation of narrated content. The different interview techniques are used to favour a gradual, reasoned and contextualised elicitation of the purposes of the research to be implemented. In general, the use of narrative methods (Clandinin, 2007; Czarniawska, 2004) responds to needs for close examination, search for profound contents of representation. It also responds to the logic of participation in producing results of subjects that will use interventions. Intending the "participant" as protagonist of the "story" that the research summaries and tells, it also means attempting to approach their world, the experience and the meaning attributed to the "self in situation" and to relationships with others (Sarbin, 1986).

As far as the group techniques are concerned, the literature on evaluation research highlights some of these that by their nature are well suited to be used in criminology research:

a. *brainstorming*: very common in training, this tool is used preferentially in the initial phases of an evaluation research (or intervention). Indeed it makes possible to use the group as a creative resource so as to bring out concepts, dimensions, problems, criteria relative to the object of the evaluation (we are talking about groups of experts, or of individuals whose positions is important in the overall research design). After encouraging the group to freely express itself (without participants interfering or censuring each others), the researcher will then trace the material emerged back to general guidelines, in order to try and find its significance to the objectives;

b. *focus groups*: these are mainly used in market research. This technique stimulates the group to think about and discuss one or more issues proposed by the researcher. Like brainstorming, the objective is to bring out an implicit, hidden consciousness that is substantially shared by the participants. The researcher's grounding is fundamental and in this case, their competence is more as facilitator of an awareness process than as a researcher in the strictest sense (Bloor, Frankland, Thomas, & Robson, 2001);

c. the Delphi technique: in this case (more than in the other two) it is fundamental for the participants to be experts. Indeed, an evaluation from the specifically professional point of view is requested. Delphi can be conducted "remotely", in other words participants may not be in the same place at the same time, but may be IT-connected (also asynchronously). In this case the researcher-facilitator will ask questions, sort the answers and develop conceptual summaries in order to attain the most complete and consensual knowledge of the evaluation topics (Rowe & Wright, 1999).

Psychological, social and organisational research has produced and proposed other tools and techniques of different levels of complexity that it is not possible to cover further: diaries (Symon, 2004), *critical incident technique* (Flanagan, 1954), personal and group stories (Czarniawska, 2004; Gabriel & Griffith, 2004; Musson, 2004).

When it comes to analyze the obtained information, without a doubt the most well-known approach is *Grounded Theory* (Strauss & Corbin, 1990). This is rather a systematic and careful collection of heuristic passages (Legewie, 2006). Many authors have described the basic features of this approach, summarising, expanding, updating or criticising the work of Glaser and Strauss (1967) and of Strauss & Corbin (1990). This is an interpretation approach to qualitative research rather than an analysis technique. It was first proposed in the sociological area in the '60s to arrive without many revisions to the present day (Charmaz, 1995; Charmaz, 2006; Pandit, 1996). Grounded theory – or more promptly, *grounded theory methodology* (Strauss & Corbin, 1994; 1998) – whose tradition is widely consolidated in social sciences, but only in the early stages in psychology (Henwood & Pidgeon, 1992), favours generating a theory *emerging* from data rather than searching data constructions before the survey itself. So it is proposed as the most suitable method to "order" large quantities of information, identifying recurring themes and the relationships between them. Like the neo-positivist verification paradigm (which it is quite different in terms of the emphasis it places on "hypotheses", the objectives of control and prediction) Grounded theory developed own epistemological apparatus, areas of application and its own criteria of validity that also allow anyone carrying out qualitative research to conduct systematic studies

(Silverman, 2000; Onwuegbuzie & BurkeJohnson, 2006). According to Charmaz (1995), with *Grounded theory* it is possible to give qualitative research the same systematic and validity requirements that characterise studies using the neo-positivist paradigm.

According to the procedure initially proposed by Glaser and Strauss (1967) and then more systematically developed by Strauss and Corbin (1990), the researcher should approach the participants without any theoretical model to guide the interview, without any order of questions and of course without interpreting the interviews. Instead, the researcher should implement an interactive process of data, interpretation and theory emerging from their interaction, also with the aid of recent software created on the basis of the proposed model. This process, where the interpretation begins from the very first interview gathered (figure 5)[7], aims to construct the social reality from the participants' point of view, attempting to determine the symbolic meanings these have for groups of people as they interact with each other.

Still, the certainty of being able to "set aside" theoretical categories of references seems to be a naïve cognitive operation, because it does not take into account the fact that the researcher inevitably brings their own orientations and inclinations, and research interests, subjectivity to the whole research process (from formulating the questions for the interview to analysze the information), including the visual angle of their theoretical training and their group of reference (scientific community).

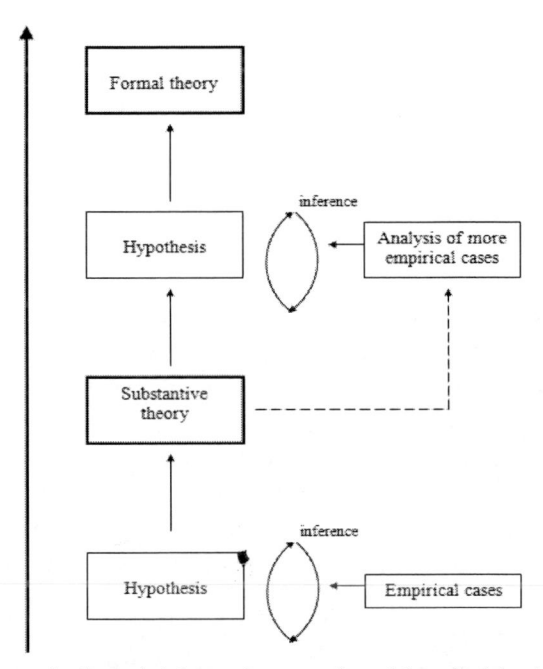

Figure 5. The research process in Grounded theory (*source*: adapted from Steinke, 1999, p. 26).

As regards this, we consider useful the notion of *"sensitizing concepts"* (Blumer, 1969) used to refer to the actual explicit or implicit starting points of the analysis. The theoretical premises the researcher evaluates (we repeat: *explicitly or implicitly*) fit the data that emerges

---

[7] In the figure, the terms "formal" and "substantive" refer to the level of generality/specificity of the theoretical explanation: the former limit themselves to the single social phenomenon, the latter take broader classes.

from the research situation (for example, the interview with the respondent). In other words, this is a "double meaning" process where the core of the qualitative analysis lies on the *interpretation the researcher gives to the interpretations of the actor*, intended as ways of conceptualising their own experience.

Therefore, the overall research process seems to be characterised by a basic divergence from the neo-positivist approach. Rather than a standardised sequence of phases, the qualitative method is usually described as a *circular* process, which is not developed through a linear sequence of sequential phases, but rather moves forward and backward between empirical data and evidence, always open to innovation and adjustment.

The procedure proposed by Grounded theory, inverts the terms of the model: it starts from data (at an abstraction level similar to that of the indicators) to arrive at the theoretical concepts, producing an explanation that takes into account the relationship between data and the processes that organise these relationships.

Overall, the approach is distinguished by an internal consistency described by a series of key concepts that, in some ways, aim to outline an ideal direction to conduct research according to the grounded perspective. We have already discussed the conditional matrix, the other concepts are:

- *theoretical sampling*: step-by-step formulation of the research sample according to the information that emerges during the analysis of the information required to construct the theory. This is guided by contingent theoretical interests. The aim is to collect events and situations that are indicative (not necessarily representative) of the categories, of their properties and dimensions, and of the relationships between them;
- *theoretical saturation*: this is the situation where there is no more relevant information that can be drawn from a relevant theoretical concept; the relationships between categories have stabilised and any new element adds nothing new to the obtained results.

This version of *Grounded theory* has been criticised since. As claimed by Silverman (2000) it demonstrates incapacity to acknowledge the role of the implicit theories that guide the work from the outset. Furthermore, it is clearer on the production of theories and less so on their control. If it is not used intelligently, it can also degenerate into a construction quite empty of theories or into a smokescreen used to legitimise purely empirical research.

As we said earlier, it would be naïve to consider that researchers can approach their research without any parameter (scientific, cultural, personal orientation) to direct them and that inevitably conditions the interpretation of the phenomenon. Obviously, as far as the psychological-legal and criminological area is concerned we are talking about a fundamental criticism.

In short, qualitative methods and quantitative methods have obvious advantages, but also limitations that must be evaluated before initiating an arduous path of evaluation and research in the criminological area, particularly for interventions such as those we are about to cover in the following sections, which involve considerable investments, complex management policies and decisions relating to people's lives.

ADVANTAGES, LIMITS AND PERSPECTIVES OF INTEGRATION

The decision the evaluation researcher makes as to the research methods and techniques (and to the subsequent analyses of the information) will depend, in the first place, on the specific objectives of the research and the object of the evaluation. We can say that it will be possible to choose from an experimental-quantitative approach (hard methods) when it is necessary to focus attention on the entity of the *changes that have transpired after a specific intervention* (where the highest number of variables have been controlled): the main implication of this kind of design (sometimes we are talking about a limit for studies) lies on the need to work on large amounts of data for the evaluation to be considered reliable; and even it may not be possible to explain which mechanisms of a given intervention worked, unless particularly complex design researches that are difficult to implement in the psychological and social area are used. Instead, researchers will favour a qualitative approach (soft methods) when interest is oriented towards the context-specific variables and to the evolutionary processes used as the basis to develop a given phenomenon (for example, an intervention or a social policy). In this case, the disadvantage lies on the excessive emphasis that may be placed implicitly on the specific phases on the passages, losing sight of the overall net result.

Without getting into detail of each possible methodological option, we will limit to show how a series of middle ground choices have been recently unravelling between the two ideal extremes of the continuum between qualitative and quantitative techniques and tools:

> Between the two extremes, intermediate paths are found as experiences of integration between quantitative and qualitative instruments, which are now being observed with increasing attention. [...] The mixed methods, whose attention is focusing more on right now, that integrate different sources, qualitative observations with quantitative surveys, seem to show promising directions between these different families of methods and techniques, particularly where they accompany participative paths (De Ambrogio, 2003, p. 232).

Apart from the technical choices and options of "simple" reciprocal joining and completion we can outline other solutions that refer to different models of integration to arrive at a real "contamination" between the numerical-statistical precision research and the tendency towards qualitative exploration. Several recent publications have dealt with mixed models and methodologies. We make a brief mention of the main proposals, summarising what is proposed by Arcidiacono and De Gregorio (2008).

Actually, new research field supports the mixed methods research. At any rate, during the last 50 years, different names have been used to locate studies that might relate to mixed methods (Bryman, 2008; Tashakkori & Teddlie, 2007). As suggested by Ivankova, Creswell and Stick (2006, p. 3), "mixed methods is a procedure for collecting, analysing, and 'mixing' or integrating both quantitative and qualitative data at some stage of the research process within a single study for the purpose of gaining a better understanding of the research problem".

When used in combination, qualitative and quantitative methods complement each other and allow a more robust analysis, taking advantage of the strengths of each. We can affirm that the primary goal of mixed research is not to replace either quantitative and qualitative research: the goal of this *third* type of research is to utilize the strengths of two or more approaches by combining them in one study, and attempting to minimize the weaknesses of approaches in mixed designs (Cresswell, Plano-Clark, Gutmann, & Hanson, 2007; Burke-Johnson, Onwuegbuzie, & Turner, 2007). As suggested by Tashakkori and Teddlie (2003), "mixed methods designs incorporate techniques from both the quantitative and qualitative research traditions yet combine them in unique ways to answer research questions that could not be answered in any other way" (p. 10, preface).

In basic concurrent mixed designs, the following three conditions sustain: both the quantitative and qualitative data are collected separately at approximately the same point in time; neither the quantitative nor qualitative data analysis builds on the other during the data analysis stage; and, the results from each type of analysis are not consolidated at the data interpretation stage, until both sets of data have been collected and analysed separately. After collection and interpretation of data from the quantitative and qualitative components, a meta-inference is drawn which integrates the inferences made from the separate quantitative and qualitative data and findings.

Despite its popularity and straightforwardness, mixed method designs are not easy to implement. Researchers have to consider the priority or weight given to the quantitative or qualitative data collection and analysis in the study, the sequence of data collection and analysis, and the stage in the research process at which the quantitative and qualitative phases are connected and the results integrated (Morgan, 1988; Cresswell & Plano-Clark, 2006).

If we consider the elements set out above, it is possible to recognize the need of the following questions: Is it misleading to triangulate, consolidate, or compare quantitative findings and inferences stemming from a large random sample on equal grounds with qualitative data arising from a small purposive sample? When findings conflict, what is the one to conclude?

As in any mixed method design, we had to deal with the issues of priority, implementation, and integration of the quantitative and qualitative approaches. Priority refers to which approach (quantitative, qualitative or both) a researcher gives more weight or attention to throughout the data collection and analysis in the study. Implementation refers to whether the quantitative and qualitative data collection and analysis follow each other in sequence, or are concurrent. Integration refers to the stage in the research process wherein the mixing or integrating of the quantitative and qualitative methods occurs.

We are talking about perspectives that are of sure interest in terms of our objectives: evaluation research on the effectiveness of prevention of deviance interventions could take advantage of the use of mixed methods. Against a study on the "extension" of effectiveness on a broad scale, it could be useful to evaluate single cases, based on experiences (gained using narrative or semi-structured methods) of "privileged testimonials" (Stake, 1994; 1998).

Furthermore, the use of these approaches is perfect in criminology and legal psychology, since these disciplines are the grounds where different areas of study, research and intervention converge:

> Criminology, as an academic subject, is held together by a substantive concern: crime [...]. Consequently, it is multi-disciplinary in character rather than being dominated by one discipline. For this reason, it is helpful to view criminology as a "meeting place" for a wide range of disciplines including sociology, social policy, psychology and law among others (Noaks & Wincup, 2004, p. 5).

ASSESSING THE EFFECTIVENESS OF CRIME PREVENTION PROJECTS

In the above section, we discussed what was meant by evaluation and evaluation research; in particular, the meaning of evaluation of prevention interventions. We need to make a short confrontational digression about the possibility of "evaluating prevention" and to do so we must follow the reflections of De Ambrogio (1996, p. 2): «one must wonder how it is possible to verify the results of an action that aims to avoid verification of a given behaviour. Indeed, the results of prevention, almost by definition, cannot be seen, in so much as prevention is an intervention that acts upstream. The ultimate result of prevention comes from something that is not seen». The apparent contradiction is resolved by considering evaluation not as ultimate and final phase of the intervention but as a «research process that accompanies interventions, whose aim is to 'construct by correcting.' This process observes and measures some partial results, considering the positive and verifiable objectives of a preventive intervention».

In legal contexts, in particular, the concept of prevention is expressed in such a way as to make the panorama even more complex. Indeed it is necessary to distinguish, at least, three levels:

- *primary prevention*, whose objective is to eliminate or reduce the causes (broadly speaking both in the social and/or environmental sense as well as in the physical and architectural sense) that deviance may develop. It may consist of programs that improve the general social wellbeing of given urban areas, educational campaigns, urban planning interventions that re-plan the city network taking into account the ecology of crime […], of interventions in socialising institutions;
- *secondary prevention*, based on the expectation of early recognition of subjects at potential risk of deviance and the implementing interventions aimed at reducing their involvement in delinquent activities or more broadly, in anti-social behaviour (Stattin & Magnusson, 1996; Farrington, 1995; Loeber & Farrington, 1997; 2000);
- *tertiary prevention*, implemented *a posteriori*, when the objective is to limit (or totally prevent) recidivism. In this case the attention is focused more on the experiment. In any case, this is a form of prevention that research has paid increasing importance to and various examples and reports are now available on this and will be described on the next pages.

Indeed, in this latter case, prevention strategies must be more concretely integrated with legislative solutions adopted in the specific context and with relative inspirational principles on the origins of deviant behaviour and on the significance of the punishment, as well as within the contexts of prevention.

In the case of adolescents, "effective prevention" means the level where the legal systems is profitably interconnected with the social area where the minor goes through the path of (re)socialising and the activities connected to it. In the Italian legal system, for example, regarding juvenile prosecution (Presidential Decree n° 448 of 22 September 1988), the article that governs "probation" for juvenile offenders (art. 28), provides that the juvenile criminal may undertake a non-detention course aimed at activate individual and social resources which protect the subject from the risk of recidivism. In this case, a strong emphasis on the contribution that the context outside prison may provide to succeed is connected to the objective of non-interference with the underway evolutionary processes. On the contrary, supporting them in the direction of a guided adaptation towards taking responsibility.

As regards the adult sector and more recent orientations towards restorative justice the question is more complex. The reasons for this complexity can be found still on one hand in the open debate on what must be meant by treatment of criminals (definition that naturally must take into account the entity of the crime itself) and on the other hand, the legislation that governs this type of intervention. In fact, in ordinary justice, it is possible to find normative ideas that favour non-penitentiary treatment[8] and similarly, more convinced trends in the theoretical and operating debate, but facts show that detention is still the prevailing and preferred measure (in spite of the decades of study highlighting the deleterious effects of incarceration and the need for active, empowering proposals, for a re-socialising path, in "natural" living contexts). On the other hand, the difficulty of preparing evaluation research that can confirm the operating hypotheses and theoretical reflections favouring external measures must also be represented. Research designs on evaluation of the results (in particular, of the effectiveness) of the prevention interventions must take into account a variety of factors, including: the period of imprisonment served, whether previous alternative measures have been used and their results, the presence and extent of the contribution of social agencies outside prison (including family and social services, just to mention two), the age and dimensions of the deviant career of the subject, and the gravity (comparative to different situations) of the crime committed.

Although it is not possible to include these issues (due to lack of space and centrality of the topic), we think it is useful to stress the explicitly preventive function of these interventions according to the already described meaning of "tertiary prevention." It is obvious how, given the elevated number of variables involved, the application of the experimental logic and the Lazarsfeld paradigm (figure 3) poses problems: the complexity of the object of study is such that a study of the effectiveness of treatment programs must, in our opinion, necessarily be oriented towards a mixed method.

According to Welsh and Farrington (2001), the effectiveness of the prevention projects can be evaluated with different methods: each one corresponds to a research instrument, thus reprising the distinction between *prevalently* quantitative methods and *prevalently* qualitative methods. Indeed, the Authors identify:

- the evaluation study of the single case, which normally uses experimental and quasi-experimental research designs in methodologically correct and quality information research on the crucial variables that influence the success/failure of a project;

---

[8] In this sense we find:
- the *penitentiary act and execution of freedom privation and limitation measures* (law n° 354 of 26 July 1975 et seq. in particular the "Gozzini reform", Legislative Decree n° 663 of 10 October 1986),
- the "Simeone-Saraceni law" (Legislative Decree n° 165 of May 1998),
- the law execution reform 354/75 (30 June 2000 n° 230).

For more in-depth information of the contribution that each reference makes in defining the non-penitentiary dimension of the treatment see De Leo and Patrizi (2002).

- the narrative report, which provides a discursive and all-inclusive summary of the main elements characterising a set of like studies. This method is preferable where the researcher cannot hypothesise the direction of the effect of the variables involved;
- the *vote-count method*, which is distinguished from the narrative report on account of the inclusion of studies that provide statistically significant results to confirm and not confirm the hypothesis: the decision on what research to include in the evaluation, therefore it depends on stringent methodological criteria;
- the meta-analysis, which by imposing greatest scientific severity makes it possible to summarise the results of different research on the same object in a single study using similar survey methods. This is the method for large-scale verification of the effectiveness of preventive treatment [Wilson, 2001].

Still, in our opinion these studies lack attention of the context the intervention lies on; the living environment of the beneficiary. The evaluation of the treatment program cannot ignore [...] adding a broader context of interventions involving all the control/support agencies to the specific incarceration activity, at the macro and micro-systemic levels (from the judge and the surveillance court to adult social services, the penitentiary, the public services and private social agencies to be found in the territory), constructing a targeted network of shared actions that are centred on the problem. A pathway of this kind that considers the relationship inside and outside the prison central, must also aim at planning and realising interventions inside and outside prison that jointly involve the perpetrators and their family system.

For these reasons, and also stressing the critical points and limits that literature provides on the application of experimental, quasi-experimental and longitudinal methods (Bernfeld, Farrington, & Leschied, 2001; Welsh & Farrington, 2001; Weisburd, 2000; Feder, Jolin, & Feyerherm, 2000; Boruch, Victor, & Cecil, 2000; Stouthamer-Loeber, Van Kammen, & Loeber, 1992; Loeber & Farrington, 1994), we have decided to describe "Communities that Care", as an example of a prevention intervention *that works*. It is an extensive project where the evaluation dimension is joined by prevention interventions planned so as to include the deviant subject and their living context.

THE "COMMUNITIES THAT CARE" PROJECT

We now propose an example of primary prevention aimed at eliminating or reducing criminogenic conditions present in a physical or social context before danger signs are manifested. Still, this division is not the only one present in the literature. Indeed, it is possible to describe deviance prevention interventions with reference to two axes, indicated by Bandini, Gatti, Gualco, Malfatti, Marugo, and Verde, (2003). The time sequence of the intervention (before or after committing a crime), and the context of the type of response adopted (penal or non-penal) and, on the basis of these, break down the realizable interventions into four types (Table 1):

"Communities that Care" is a primary prevention and non-penal intervention program before the commission of a crime (first section in Table I). Designed and conducted in the first half of the nineties at the University of Washington in Seattle, it is a community-based social program. *Communities that Care* mainly propose to identify the risk factors present in

certain locations and to implement carefully experimented community prevention strategies, aimed at eliminating or reducing these criminogenic factors by means of active citizen participation.

In particular, the program we are dealing with refers to a specific community prevention approach based on mobilisation of residents for the purposes of preventing and reconstructing informal social control, particularly youth deviance. For this purpose, *Communities that Care* comprised the involvement of the foremost leaders in the considered community. They formed a committee called the *Community Board*, which included the active participation of various stakeholders including school, police, social services, family, youth, local media and the legal apparatus. The *Community Board* was responsible for conducting detailed assessments of the examined community in order to identify the risk factors and the protective factors that need to be faced through a specific prevention plan selected by the actual board.

Table 1. Models of prevention (*source*: Bandini *et al.* 2003, p. 297)

		CONTEXT	
		Non-penal responses	Penal responses
TIME SEQUENCE	Actions before committing the crime	*Individual programs* *Social programs* *Situational programs*	*Penal law used for intimidation programs (deterrence)*
	Actions after committing the crime	*Mediation or "diversion" programs*	*Treatment programs*

Members of the *Community Board* received expert assistance from the trade to decide which of the various prevention strategies presented to them could be the most suitable to deal with the risk factors identified in the community. These factors include family problems (separations, lack of control, low social and economic status etc...). For each cause, the community had to find its own resources for intervention. The effectiveness of these prevention strategies were assessed with a series of experimental studies that were never realised due to its high costs. Still, Farrington (1997) proposed an experimental assessment design for the program, which involved comparison between experimental and control communities relative to three areas: delinquency, substance abuse and problematic adolescent behaviour. This comparison should be made in both conditions (experimental and control) before the intervention is carried out, during implementation of the prevention techniques and after their implementation, in order to limit the possible threats to internal validity of the experimental (or quasi-experimental) design adopted.

Basically, *Communities that Care* aim to modify the social conditions, considered as favour criminality, and the methods used to implement this type of prevention while entailing the organisation of appropriate strategies by the community, direct involvement of inhabitants, environmental modifications, and mobilisation of resources, increased formal and informal controls within the actual community. Farrington (1997) proposes two geographically similar, but not neighbouring communities, for the comparison, keeping the contact between the two communities to a minimum. The experimental communities should be selected considering criteria such as cooperativeness of local stakeholders, availability of intervention techniques and adequacy and accessibility of local documentations. Therefore, there was plenty of room for involving the various stakeholders, considering that in

Communities that Care prevention was based on the active involvement of the citizens themselves that we could define, in conclusion as the stakeholders and the beneficiaries of the intervention implemented[9].

THE EVALUATION LEVELS

To conclude this section on the applications and their evaluation, we would like to report a topic that in some way provides the framework for (and should accompany) the assessment procedures: the evaluation criteria. In a recent contribution, MacKenzie (2000) concentrated on the choices that work in the implementation of deviance prevention projects: The Author first describes the evaluation criteria of the empirical research and then goes on to give a brief explanation of the main results of those experiences. These evaluations can be applied to what we have called "tertiary prevention" (i.e. programs oriented towards reducing recidivism).

The first essential evaluation phase is determining scientific quality ("*scientific rigor*"), intended to verify univocal cause and effect relationships between intervention/treatment on a specific target of crime-perpetrators (Hollin, 2003; Skinner, Hester, & Malos, 2005) and the variation of a phenomenon (the deviant behaviour). This evaluation can be anchored to shared criteria by assigning a score of 1 to 5:

Level 1 studies. These studies indicated some correlation between the program and measures of recidivism. Usually there was no comparison group. Studies in this category were judged to be so low that they were not used to assess the effectiveness of the correctional programs.

Level 2 studies. The studies indicated some association between the program and recidivism but were severely limited because many alternative explanations could not be ruled out, given the research design […].

Level 3 studies. These studies compared two or more groups, one with the program and one without the program. The design of the study and the statistical analysis assured reasonable similarity between the treated group and the comparison(s).

Level 4 studies. These studies included comparison between a program group and one or more control groups controlling the other factors, or a nonequivalent comparison group that only slightly differed from the program group.

Level 5 studies. These studies included the "gold standard", random assignment, and analysis of comparable program and comparison groups, including control for attrition (MacKenzie, 2000, p. 460).

---

[9] Further information on specific projects and on assessment criteria can be found on the following websites:
http://www.colorado.edu/cspv/blueprints/ suggested by Prof. Rolf Loeber, (*personal communication*) whom we thank for his helpfulness;
http://www.ojjdp.ncjrs.org, website of the *Office of Juvenile Justice and Delinquency Prevention*;
http://www.csc-scc.gc.ca/text/prgrm/corr_e.shtml, website of the *Correctional Service of Canada – Programs and evaluation section suggested by Prof.* Patrizia Patrizi (*personal communication*);
www.homehoffice.gov.uk/crime/index.html and www.crimereduction.gov.uk, prevention and intervention sections of the UK Home Office website;
www.transcrime.unitn.it, the website of the inter-university centre of the University of Trento and the Cattolica University of Sacred Heart that carries out research on criminality and intervention policies and their evaluation.

The second phase is the evaluation of the actual effectiveness. It is obviously preferable to carry it out with studies that have at least passed level three, although most of the research is placed at level one or two. In this phase, each study can be categorized according to the nature of the results.

What works. These are programs that we are reasonably certain reduce recidivism in the kinds of contexts (and with the types of participants) in which they have been evaluated and for which the findings should be generalizable to similar settings in other places and times. Programs defined as *working* must have at least two Level 3 evaluations, with statistical significance tests showing effectiveness and the preponderance of all available evidence supporting the same conclusion.

What does not work. These are programs that we are reasonably fail to reduce recidivism in the kinds of contexts (and with the types of participants) in which they have been evaluated and for which the findings should be generalizable to similar settings in the other places and times. Programs classified as *not working* must have at least two Level 3 evaluations, with statistical tests showing ineffectiveness and the preponderance of all available evidence supporting the same conclusion.

What is promising. These are programs for which the level of certainty from available evidence is too low to support generalizable conclusions but for which there is some evidence predicting that further research could support such conclusions. Programs are defined as *promising* if they have at least one Level 3 evaluation, with significance tests showing their effectiveness in reducing recidivism and the preponderance of all available evidence supporting the same conclusions.

What is unknown. Any program not included in one of the above three categories is defined as *having unknown effects*. There is simply not enough research, or not enough research employing adequate scientific rigor, upon which to draw even tentative conclusion. Program areas with unknown effects should not be interpreted as ineffective (MacKenzie, 2000, p. 462).

REFERENCES

Arcidiacono, F., & De Gregorio, E. (2008). Methodological thinking in psychology: Starting from mixed methods. *International Journal of Multiple Reseacrh Approaches, 2* (1), 118-126.

Bachman, R., & Schutt, R. K. (2007), The practice of research in criminology and criminal justice (3rd edition). London: Sage.

Bachman, R., & Schutt, R. K. (2008), *Fundamentals of research in criminology and criminal justice*. London: Sage.

Bandini, T., Gatti, U., Gualco, B., Malfatti D., Marugo, M. I., & Verde, A. (2003). *Criminologia. Il contributo della ricerca alla conoscenza del crimine e della reazione sociale* (2nd edition), vol. I. Milano: Giuffrè.

Bazeley, P. (2006). The contribution of computer software to integrating qualitative and quantitative data and analyses. *Research in the schools, 13* (1), 64-74.

Bennett, L., Goodman, L., & Dutton, M. A. (1999). Systemic obstacles to the criminal prosecution of a battering partner: A victim perspective. *Journal of Interpersonal Violence, 14* (7), 761-772.

Bennett, L., Goodman, L., & Dutton, M. A. (1999). Systemic obstacles to the criminal prosecution of a battering partner: A victim perspective. *Journal of Interpersonal Violence*, *14* (7), 761-772.

Berger, P. L., & Luckmann, T. (1966). *The social construction of reality*. Garden City: Doubleday.

Bernfeld, G. A., Farrington, D. P., & Leschied, A. W. (2001) (Eds.), *Offender rehabilitation in practice: Implementing and evaluating effective programs*. New York: John Wiley & Sons.

Bezzi, C. (2001). *Il disegno della ricerca valutativa*. Milano. Franco Angeli.

Bloor, M., Frankland, J., Thomas, M., & Robson, K. (2001). *Focus group in social research*. London: Sage.

Blumer, H. (1969). *Symbolic interactionism: Perspective and method*. Englewood Cliffs: Prentice-Hall.

Boruch, R. F., Victor, T., & Cecil, J. S. (2000). Resolving ethical and legal problems in randomized experiments. *Crime and Delinquency*, *46* (3), 330-353.

Bruner, J. (1990). *Acts of meaning*. Cambridge: Harvard University Press.

Bryman, A. (2008). Why do researchers integrate/combine/mesh/blend/mix/merge/fuse quantitative and qualitative research?. In M. M. Bergman (Ed.), *Advances in mixed methods research* (pp.87-100), London: Sage.

Burke Johnson, R., & Onwuegbuzie, A. J. (2004). Mixed methods research: A research paradigm whose time has come. *Educational Research*, *33* (7), 14-26.

Burke Johnson, R., Onwuegbuzie, A. J., & Turner, L. A. (2007). Toward a definition of mixed methods research. *Journal of mixed methods research*, *1* (2), 112-133.

Cannavò, L. (*1999). Teoria e pratica degli indicatori nella ricerca sociale*. Milano: LED.

Charmaz, K. (1995). *Grounded theory*. In J. A. Smith, R. Harré & L. Van Langenhove (Eds.), *Rethinking methods in psychology (*pp. 27-49*)*, London: Sage.

Charmaz, K. (1995). *Grounded theory*. In J. A. Smith, R. Harré and L. Van Langenhove (Eds.), *Rethinking Methods in Psychology* (pp. 27-49). London: Sage..

Charmaz, K. (2006). *Constructing grounded theory*. London: Sage.

Clandinin, D.J. (2007) (Ed.). *Handbook of narrative inquiry*. Thousand Oaks: Sage.

Cresswell, J. W., & Plano Clark, V. L. (2006). *Designing and conducting mixed method research*. London: Sage.

Cresswell, J. W., Plano Clark, V. L., Gutmann, M. L., & Hanson, W. E. (2007). Advanced mixed methods research design. In V. L. Plano Clark & J. W. Cresswell (Eds.), *The mixed method reader* (pp. 161-196). London: Sage.

Czarniawska, B. (2004). *Narratives in social research*. London: Sage.

De Ambrogio, U. (1996). Valutare gli interventi di prevenzione. *Prospettive sociali e sanitarie*, *2*, 2-7.

De Ambrogio, U. (2003) (Ed.), *Valutare gli interventi e le politiche sociali*. Roma: Carocci.

De Gregorio, E., & Arcidiacono, F. (2008), Computer-assisted analysis in the social sciences: A unique strategy for mixed methods?. *International Journal of Multiple Reseacrh Approaches*, *2* (1), 31-35.

De Leo, G., & Patrizi, P. (2002). *Psicologia giuridica*. Bologna: Il Mulino.

Farrington, D. P. (1995). The development of offending and antisocial behaviour from childhood: Key findings from the Cambridge study in delinquent development. *Journal of Child Psychology and Psychiatry*, *36* (6), 929-964.

Farrington, D. P. (1997). Evaluating a community crime prevention program. *Evaluation, 3* (2), 157-173.

Farrington, D. P., & Petrosino, A. (2001). *The Campbell collaboration crime and justice group.* Annals of the American Academy of Political and Social Science, 578, 35-49.

Feder, L., Jolin, A., & Feyerherm, W. (2000). Lesson from Two Randomized Experiments in Criminal Justice Settings. *Crime and Delinquency*, 46 (3), pp. 380-400.

Fielding, N. G., & Fielding, J. (1986). *Linking data.* London: Sage.

Flanagan, J. C. (1954). The critical incident technique. *Psychological Bulletin, 51* (4), 327-358.

Gabriel, Y., & Griffith, D.S. (2004). Stories in organizational research. In C. Cassell & G. Symon (Eds.), *Essential guide to qualitative method in organizational research* (pp. 114-126). London: Sage.

Gabriel, Y., & Griffith, D.S. (2004). Stories in organizational research. In C. Cassell & G. Symon (Eds.), *Essential guide to qualitative method in organizational research* (pp. 114-126). London: Sage.

Glaser, B. G., & Strauss, A. L. (1967). *The discovery of grounded theory: Strategies for qualitative research.* New York: Aldine.

Guba, E. G., & Lincoln, Y. S. (1994). *Competing paradigms in qualitative research.* In N. K. Denzin & Y. S. Lincoln (Eds.) Handbook of Qualitative Research (pp. 105-117). Thousand Oaks: Sage,

Harré, R., & Gillett, G. (1994). *The discoursive mind.* London: Sage.

Henwood, K. L., & Pidgeon, N. F. (1992). *Qualitative research and psychological theorizing.* British Journal of Psychology, 83, 97-111.

Henwood, K. L., & Pidgeon, N. F. (1992). *Qualitative research and psychological theorizing.* British Journal of Psychology, 83, 97-111.

Hollin, C.R. (2003). To Treat or Not to Treat? An Historical Perspective. In Hollin, C.R. (ed) *The Essential Handbok of Offender Assessment and Treatment* (p1-10). John Wiley & Sons Ltd.

Holstein, J. A., & Gubrium, J. F. (1997). *Active interviewing.* In D. Silverman (Eds.) Qualitative Research: Theory, Method and Practice (pp. 113-129). London: Sage.

Ivankova, N. V., Creswell. J. W., & Stick S. L. (2006). Using mixed-methods sequential explanatory design: From theory to practice, *Field Methods, 18* (1), 3-20.

Järvinen, P. (2007). Action Research in similar to design science. *Quality and Quantity, 41*, 37-54.

Kruglanski, A. (1980). Lay epistemo-logic process and contents: Another look at attribution theory. *Psycological Review, 87*, (1), 70-87.

Kruglanski, A. W., & Jost, J. T. (2000). *Il costruzionismo sociale e la psicologia sociale sperimentale: Storia delle divergenze e prospettive di riconciliazione. Rassegna di Psicologia, 17* (3), 45-67.

Lazarsfeld, P. F. (1958). Evidence and inference in social research. *Daedalus, 4*, 99-109.

Legewie, H. (2006). *Vorlesungen zur Qualitativen Diagnostik und Forschung*; disponibileavailable suon . Retrived on August, 2008, from:
http://www.ztg.tu-berlin.de/download/legewie/Dokumente/downloads.htm.

Loeber, R., & Farrington, D. P. (1994). Problems and solutions in longitudinal and experimental treatment studies of child psychopathology and delinquency. *Journal of Consulting & Clinical Psychology*, 62, 887-900.

Loeber, R., & Farrington, D. P. (1997). Strategies and yields of longitudinal studies on antisocial behaviour. In D. M. Stoff, J. Breiling, & J. D. Maser (Eds.), *Handbook of antisocial behavior* (pp. 125-139), New York: John Wiley & Sons.

Loeber, R., & Farrington, D. P. (2000). Young children who committed crime: Epidemiology, developmental origins, risk factors, early interventions, and policy implications. *Development and Psychopathology*, 12, 737-762.

Logio, K., Dowdall, G., W., Babbie E. R., & Halley, F. (2008). *Adventures in Criminal criminal Justice justice Researchresearch* (IV edition). London: Sage.

MacKenzie, D. L. (2000). Evidence-based corrections: Identifying what works. *Crime and Delinquency*, 46 (4), 457-471.

Mannetti, L. (1998) (Ed.). *Strategie di ricerca in psicologia sociale*. Roma: Carocci.

Maxfield, M. G. & Babbie, E. (2008). *Research methods for criminal justice and criminology* (5th edition), Belmont: Thomson Wadsworth.

Miller, J., & Glassner, B. (1997). The "inside" and the "outside". Finding realities in interviews. In D. Silverman (Eds.), *Qualitative research: Theory, method and practice* (pp. 99-112), London: Sage.

Morgan, D. (1988). Practical strategies for combining qualitative and quantitative methods: Applications to health research. *Qualitative Health Research*, 8, 362-376.

Musson, G. (2004). Life histories. In C. Cassell & G. Symon (Eds.), *Essential guide to qualitative method in organizational research* (pp. 34-44). London: Sage.

Noaks, L. & Wincup, E. (2004). *Criminolgical research. Understanding qualitative methods*. London: Sage.

Onwuegbuzie, A. J. & Burke Johnson, R. B. (2006). The validity issue in mixed research. *Research in School*, 13 (1), 48-63.

Pandit, N. R. (1996). *The creation of theory: A recent application of the grounded theory method. Qualitative Report*, 2 (4), available on www.nova.edu/ssss/QR/QR2-4/pandit.html.

Peräkylä, A. (1997). Reliability and validity in research based on tapes and trascripts. In D. Silverman (Ed.), *Qualitative research: Theory, methods and practice* (pp. 201-220). Sage: London.

Petrosino, A., Boruch, R. F., Soydan, H., Duggan, L., & Sanchez-Meca, J. (2001). *Meeting the challenger of evidence-based policy: The Campbell collaboration. Annals of the American Academy of Political and Social Science*, 578, pp. 14-34.

Rossi, P. H., Freeman, H. E., & Lipsey, M. W. (1999). *Evaluation: A systematic approach*. Thousand Oaks, CA: Sage.

Rowe, G. & Wright, G. (1999). The Delphi technique as a forecasting tool: Issues and analysis. *International Journal of Forecasting*, 15, 353-375.

Sarbin, T. R. (1986) (Ed.). *Narrative psychology: The storied nature of human conduct*. New York: Praeger.

Seale. C. (1999). *The quality of qualitative research*. London, Sage.

Silverman, D. (1993). *Interpreting qualitative data: Methods for analyzing talk, text and interaction*. London: Sage.

Silverman, D. (2000). *Doing qualitative research. A practical guide*. London: Sage.

Skinner, T., Hester, M. & Malos, E. (2005). *Researching gender violence. Feminist methodology in action*. Cullompton: Willan Publishing.

Stake, R. E. (1994). *Case studies*. In N. K. Denzin & Y. S. Lincoln (Eds.), *Handbook of qualitative research* (pp. 236-247) Thousand Oaks: Sage.

Stake, R. E. (1998). *Case studies*. In N. K. Denzin e Y. S. Lincoln (Eds.), *Strategies of qualitative inquiring* (pp. 86-109). Thousand Oaks: Sage.Strauss, A. L. & Corbin, J. (1994). *Grounded theory methodology. An overview*. In N. K. Denzin & Y. S. Lincoln (Eds.), *Handbook of qualitative research (*pp. 273-285*)*, Thousand Oaks: Sage.

Stattin, H. & Magnusson, D. (1996). Antisocial development: An holistic approach. *Development and Psychopathology, 8*, 617-645.

Steinke, I. (1999). *Kriterien Qualitativer Forschung. Ansätze zur Bewertung qualitativ-empirischer Sozialforschung*, Munchen: Juventa Verlag.

Stiles, D. R. (2004). Pictorial representation. In C. Cassell & G. Symon (Eds.), *Essential guide to qualitative method in organizational research* (pp. 127-139). London: Sage.

Stouthamer-Loeber, M., Van Kammen, W., & Loeber, R. (1992). The nuts and bolts of implementing large-scale longitudinal studies. *Violence and Victims, 7* (1), 63-78.

Stouthamer-Loeber, M., Van Kammen, W., & Loeber, R. (1992). The nuts and bolts of implementing large-scale longitudinal studies. *Violence and Victims, 7* (1), 63-78.

Strauss, A. L., & Corbin, A. (1990). *Basics of qualitative research. Grounded theory procedures and techniques*. Newbury Park: Sage.

Strauss, A. L. & Corbin, J. (1994). *Grounded theory methodology. An overview*. In N. K. Denzin & Y. S. Lincoln (Eds.), *Handbook of qualitative research (*pp. 273-285*)*, Thousand Oaks: Sage.

Strauss, A. L. e Corbin, J. (1998). *Grounded theory methodology. An overview*. In N. K. Denzin & Y. S. Lincoln (Eds.), *Strategies of qualitative inquiring (*pp. 158-183*)*, Thousand Oaks: Sage.

Sutherland, E. H. (1949). *White collar crime*. New York: Holt, Rinehart and Winston.

Symon, G. (2004). Qualitative research diaries. In C. Cassell & G. Symon (Eds.), *Essential guide to qualitative method in organizational research* (pp. 98-113). London: Sage.

Tashakkori, A. & Teddlie, C. (2003) (Eds.). *Handbook of mixed methods in social and behavioral research*, Thousand Oaks: Sage.

Tashakkori, A & Teddlie, C. (2007). Introduction to mixed method and mixed model studies in the social and behavioural sciences. In V. L. Plano Clark & J. W. Cresswell (Eds.), *The mixed method reader* (pp. 7-26). London: Sage.

Weisburd, D. (2000). Randomized experiments in criminal policy: Prospects and problems. *Crime and Delinquency, 46* (2), 181-193.

Weisburd, D., Lum, C. M., & Petrosino, A. (2001). *Does research design affect study outcomes in criminal justice?* Annals of the American Academy of Political and Social Science, *578*, 50-70.

Welsh, B. C., & Farrington, D. P. (2001). Toward an evidence-based approach to preventing crime. *Annals of the American Academy of Political and Social Science, 578*, 158-173.

Wilson, D. B. (2001). Meta-analytic methods for criminology. *Annals of the American Academy of Political and Social Science, 578*, 71-89.

Chapter 14

THE IMPACT OF THE PPS-VCJ ON ATTITUDES AND BEHAVIOR OF JUVENILES PLACED IN CENTERS AS A RESULT OF JUDICIAL MEASURES

Ana M. Martín, Cristina Ruiz, Estefanía Hernández-Fernaud, José Luis Arregui and Bernardo Hernández
Universidad de La Laguna, Spain.

ABSTRACT

This study analyzes the impact of services provided by the *Programa de Tutorías Educativas* (PTE), or Educational Tutorials Program, on attitudes and behavior of juveniles in centers in the Canary Islands as a result of judicial measures, as well as the effect of psychological variables on this impact. The program under assessment focused on basic education, work skills training, training in cross-curricular contents and the implementation of the Spanish short version for juveniles of the R&R program (PPS-VCJ). Participants were 171 males, with ages ranging from 14 to 22 years, sentenced to custody in three centers as a result of judicial measures. The evaluation was conducted using questionnaires that assessed risk and protective factors, antisocial behavior inside and outside the center, time perspective, motivation toward six behaviors and PPS-VCJ implementation. Results show that attending to all or most sessions of the PPS-VCJ relates to changes in participants' attitudes and behavior within the institution. The staff in charge of delivering the PPS-VCJ was satisfied with the experience; however, they also identified several difficulties that might be solved if larger numbers of juveniles received all sessions in the program.

INTRODUCTION

The meta-analyses carried out in the 1980s and 1990s on the efficacy of programmes for offenders provided a relatively consolidated body of knowledge, collectively known as "What Works" (Hollin & Palmer, 2006). These works concur in concluding that intervention with offenders has a small but significant effect and is effective in terms of cost-benefit (Hollin,

2001). The mean effect size is 0.10, but there are considerable differences between forms of treatment (Lösel, 1995). Hence, it has been pointed out that traditional psychodynamic and nondirective therapy and counselling, low-structured milieu therapy and therapeutic communities, merely formal variations in punishment or diversion, deterrence, boot camps and other forms of punishment have little or no effect (Lösel, 2001; McGuire, 2002). On the contrary, multi-modal, cognitive-behavioral and skills-orientated programmes with a good theoretical and empirical base, which respond to offenders' levels of risk, needs and responsivity show higher effects than the mean (0.20). Clearly structured therapeutic communities, socio-therapeutic prisons and family-oriented programmes in the case of ambulatory treatment for serious delinquents have also shown promising results (Lösel, 2001).

Although the category of effective programmes is not homogeneous, since it includes forms of intervention that vary in advantages and limitations, structured, group-orientated, cognitive-behavioral programme, they have proven to be the most effective. Wilson, Bouffard, and Mackenzie (2005), for example, conclude from a meta-analysis of 20 cognitive-behavioral programmes that the mean effect size for high quality studies reaches 0.32.

THE REASONING AND REHABILITATION PROGRAM

The Reasoning and Rehabilitation Program (R & R; Ross & Fabiano, 1985) figures among the most used and evaluated cognitive-behavioral programmes. This program was developed as a result of reviewing the characteristics of effective rehabilitation programs reported by Gendrau and Ross (1979) and Ross and Fabiano (1985). Ross and Fabiano (1985) formally integrated the empirical findings on the topic, by formulating the *cognitive model of offender rehabilitation*, a variant of the *cognitive social learning theory* (Bandura, 1977, 2001) for criminal conduct with a particular focus on cognitive skills (McGuire, 2006). Ross and Fabiano (1985) reported differences between offenders and comparison groups in cognitive functioning that sustain cognitive training. Accordingly, R&R encourages users to be aware of thought process that led them to make or follow their decision to commit criminal acts (Wilson, Bouffard, & Mackenzie, 2005). Specific targets for change include interpersonal cognitive problem-solving skills, social skills, self-control, emotional management, creative thinking, critical reasoning, values enhancement and meta-cognition (McGuire, 2006).

In a work aimed at assessing the efficacy of the R & R programme, Tong and Farrington (2006) analyzed 16 evaluations of the programme, including 26 comparisons between experimental groups and control groups in Canada, the United States and the United Kingdom. In general terms, they confirmed a 14-point reduction in the percentage of recidivism in institutional and community interventions for high- and low-risk offenders who had been involved in the programme. The assessment of the efficacy of the R & R programme is clearly positive, although they propose conducting evaluations with larger samples and better measures of recidivism, including self-reports.

Positive effects of the R & R programme have also been confirmed in Sweden. Berman (2004) report results from applying the programme after a 3-year follow-up, highlighting the fact that completers showed a 25% reduction in the risk of recidivism, compared to a paired control group, while dropouts (juveniles and more criminally active) revealed a 38% increase in the risk of recidivism. The rate of recidivism was 73.4% for dropouts, 60% for the control groups and 48.1% for the intervention groups. The author also found a short-term increase in prosocial attitudes of completers, in relation to variables such as "sense of coherence, impulsiveness, venturesomeness, attitudes toward the law, courts and police, tolerance of law violation and criminal identification" (Berman, 2004, p.85).

Finally, data pertaining to the evaluation of the implementation of the R & R programme and the Enhanced Thinking Skills (ETS) programme by the Prison Service of England and Wales are available. The ETS is a cognitive skills programme which addresses similar targets to the R & R but with fewer sessions (Hollin & Palmer, 2006). Friendship, Blud, Erikson, Travers, and Thorton (2003) evaluated the implementation of these programmes (R& R and ETS) in the context of programme accreditation (HM Prison Service, 1998; Home Office Probation Unit, 1999). This evaluation refers to 667 users, of whom 66 dropped out, and a comparison group of 1801 prisoners, matched in offence, sentence duration, age at first sentence, age when released, age when sentenced, number of previous convictions and likelihood of reoffending. The results indicate that both programmes had significant effects on the percentage of recidivism but only for the medium-low and medium-high risk groups. The percentage of recidivism was reduced in high- and low-risk groups, but the differences were not statistically significant. Although the users' sentence duration, risk of reoffending and ethnic group was linked to recidivism, the impact of the treatment was sustained when the effect of these variables was controlled.

But conclusions about the lead position of the R & R programme among cognitive-behavioral programmes are not as unanimous as it might seem. A second evaluation of the R & R and ETS programmes by the Prison Service of England and Wales with 649 inmates and a comparison group of 1947, uncovered no significant differences in reoffending rates after 2 years, even when the user risk level was taken into account and were excluded the dropout cases from the analysis (Falshaw, Friendship, Travers, & Nugent, 2003; Falshaw, Friendship, Travers, & Nugent, 2004).

In the study run by Cann, Falshaw, Nuget, and Friendship (2003) (see also Cann, Falshaw, & Friendship, 2005) with a sample of 2195 adult offenders and 1534 juvenile offenders, eliminating dropouts from the analysis introduced changes in the statistical significance concerning reoffending in the first year, but not in the second. In any case, the positive effects after the first year on those completing treatment occurred in the ETS, but not in the R & R programme.

This difference between the ETS and R & R could bear more relation to the manner of implementation than to the nature of the programme itself, since the former might be considered as a reduced version of the latter. In this sense, in a meta-analysis of 58 studies with adult and juvenile offenders, Landenberger and Lipsey (2005) established that the factors associated with a greater reduction in recidivism in relation to cognitive-behavioral programmes dealt with high-risk offenders, high-quality implementation and using programmes that included anger control and interpersonal problem solving. When these factors were controlled, the differences between specific programmes disappeared.

Other authors are more categorical in their conclusions regarding the lack of efficacy of the R & R programme. For example, after an 18-month follow-up, Mitchell and Palmer (2004) compared a group of 31 offenders who completed the R & R programme with another group of 31 who did not. Both groups were matched according to the type of offence, sentence duration, age and number of previous convictions. The results showed that there were no significant differences between groups, although there was a reduction in re-offending and fewer new prison sentences for the intervention group. In the same vein, Wilkinson (2005) states that the efficacy of the R & R programme depends on which result variable is considered and that the effect of the programme has been overestimated because of methodological problems in its assessment. Friendship *et al.*, (2003) also considers that the positive effects on recidivism attributed to the R & R could due more to motivational factors than to social-cognitive skills. And that motivation to change may be the factor that differentiates groups trained with the R & R and comparison groups.

Finally, other authors make a very positive evaluation of the R & R programme, but consider that it fails to take into account the economic and social context of the individual (McGuire, 2001; Tong & Farrington, 2006). In spite of repeated confirmation that factors such as drug abuse, employment, finances and housing are important predictors of recidivism, even when criminal history has been controlled (May, 1999). In the same vein, Martín and Hernández (1995) and Martín, Hernández, & Hernández-Fernaud (2004) observed that facilitating access to employment is a factor that boosts the impact of the R & R programme, whereas acquiring specific work skills by vocational training makes no difference.

THE RISK-NEEDS-RESPONSIBILITY MODEL VS THE GOOD LIVES MODEL OF REHABILITATION

To make sense of these latter results, both the Risk-Needs-Responsivity Model (RNRM) (Andrews & Bonta, 2003) and the Good Lives Model (GLM) (Ward & Brown, 2004) are needed. Like the *cognitive model of offender rehabilitation* (Ross & Fabiano, 1985), both the RNRM and the GLM are based on Bandura's (1977, 2001) *cognitive learning theory,* which "represents a synthesis of ideas from traditional behavioral learning theory with others from cognitive and development psychology" (McGuire, 2006, p.70-71). Nevertheless, the RNR model focuses on risk and criminogenic need emphasizing offender's deficits; whereas the GLM points out offenders' strengths, according to the *positive psychology* approach (Seligman, 2002; Seligman & Csikszentmihalyi, 2000).

On the one hand, in terms of the RNRM, work skills are not criminogenic needs because it is the relation between offence and economic conditions what counts (Piehl, 1998), and arrest causes more employment problems than any deficit of working skills (Bushway, 1998). Therefore, there is no reason to expect that work programmes in general would reduce recidivism. The meta-analysis carried out by Wilson, Gallagher, and Mackenzie (2000) supports this assertion, showing that work programme efficacy varies considerably but it is always lower than for cognitive-behavioral programmes. These authors only analyzed vocational training interventions, correctional work and correctional industries. However, not even the delivery of employment programmes for ex-offenders in the community, alone, improve significantly reintegration (Visher, Winterfield, & Coggeshall, 2005). The explanation for this lack of significance in terms of methodological problems in the evaluation (Bouffard, Mackenzie, & Hickman, 2000) does not allow a different conclusion.

Methodological problems not only affect work programmes but are commonplace when evaluating programmes for offenders in general (Lösel, 2001).

On the other hand, results supporting the enhancement effect of helping offenders to access a job (and not vocational training) are coherent with the GLM. The GLM focuses on helping offenders to achieve satisfaction in a range of life areas rather than reduce the risk of offending. These life areas are considered "primary human goods" because they are essential ingredients of human well-being. Employment is one of the life areas in which most people aim for satisfaction (Cox & Klinger, 2004). Priestley, McGuire, Flegg, Welham, Hemsley, and Barnitt (1984) list employment as one of prisoners' main concerns on release. McMurran, Theodosi, Sweeney, and Sellen (2008) have also shown that finding and keeping a job, as a way to stop offending, is the second concern expressed by prisoners they interviewed. These authors consider that motivation to engage in treatment as a way of increasing programme efficacy may be enhanced by developing a more goal-focused approach. Therefore, monitoring ex-offenders to attain and maintain a job may increase the motivation to engage in the R & R programme and therefore its effects on recidivism.

Martín et al. (in press) assessed the extent to which social and employment integration enhances the efficacy of social-cognitive training carried out in prison through a Spanish adaptation of the Reasoning & Rehabilitation (R & R) programme (Ross, Fabiano, Garrido, & Gómez, 1996). The results obtained through a Kaplan-Meier survival analysis after a six-year follow up, indicate that both intervention groups are significantly different from the comparison group. The group that received social and employment integration had the highest level of delayed recidivism, but the difference with the group that only received social-cognitive training was not statistically significant. The results are discussed in relation to the Good Lives Model and to the Risk-Needs-Responsivity Model of offender rehabilitation, emphasizing the role of motivational variables in the efficacy of intervention programs.

This study aims to explore the role participants' motivations, risk/protective factors and cognition play in the effectiveness of a rehabilitation program for delinquents in custody. The evaluation of this program, the *Programa de Tutorías Educativas* (PTE), or Program of Educational Tutorials, is of interest for research as it includes a short version for juveniles of the R& R program outlined above as one of its main components.

THE PROGRAM OF EDUCATIONAL TUTORIALS

The Spanish Law for the Organization of the Educational System (Ley Orgánica General del Sistema Educativo, LOGSE)[1] provided a "program of social guarantee" for students with special difficulties in passing on to mandatory secondary education. This program of social guarantee was addressed by the regional Ministry of Education of the Canary Islands Government[2] through the *Programa de Tutorías Educativas* (PTE), or Educational Tutorials Program. The program was a result of state and regional government policies and it was characterized by contents and methodology adapted to the profile of students aged 15 to 18

---

[1] LEY ORGÁNICA 1/1990, de 3 de octubre, de Ordenación General del Sistema Educativo. BOE 238, 4-10-1990. Retrieved on october from http://www.boe.es/boe/dias/1990/10/04/pdfs/A28927-28942.pdf

[2] The Canary Islands is one of the 19 regions that integrate the Spanish state, very much along the lines of a federal system.

years with educational difficulties arising from social exclusion, continuous absenteeism from school, low academic achievement, problems in their interactions with teachers and peers, and low interest and motivation in the classroom. Teachers assigned to the PTE were selected by specific examination in which candidates' educational skills for dealing with programs users were assessed by considering their knowledge of the profile and the educational needs of problematic students. The PTE included basic educational content, work skills training and training in specific skills aimed at improving social integration (education in sexuality, health, road safety).

The PTE was implemented at the three centers in the Canaries in which juveniles serve custodial sentences, as a result of a collaboration between the regional Ministries of Education, Culture and Sports, and Employment and Social Services of the Canary Islands Government. Following the guidelines of the PTE, the two regional ministries agreed to set up five tutorials at the Valle Tabares Center, two at La Montañeta Center and 1 at the Gáldar Center. Each of the 8 tutorials included 15 students who were assigned a teacher for basic education, another for work skills training (gardening, electricity, car repairing, cook's assistance and carpentry), a social educator for cross-curricular contents (skills for social integration) and a support tutor. The regional Ministry of Education was responsible for hiring teachers for basic education and for the curriculum and accreditation, while the regional Ministry of Employment provided the equipment for classrooms and workshops at the centers, as well as the teachers for work skills training, social educators and support tutors.

The PTE was characterized by emphasizing curricular adaptations related to flexibility, dynamism and individualized attention, and the ability to motivate students to attend workshops and classrooms. Flexibility was especially important given that students may enter or leave the program at different times, depending on their entry to the center, final release or a change of judicial measure. Another innovative feature of the PTE was the inclusion of the Spanish adaptation of the short version for juveniles of the Reasoning and Rehabilitation Program (Garrido & López, 2005), as part of training in skills for social integration (cross-curricular contents).

THE SPANISH SHORT VERSION FOR JUVENILES OF THE R&R PROGRAM

The *Programa de Pensamiento pro-Social Versión Corta para Jóvenes* or PPS-VCJ (Prosocial Thinking Program Short Version for Juveniles) is a Spanish version of the R&R program (Ross & Fabiano, 1985) aimed at juveniles aged 14 to 18 years who are serving a custodial sentence as a result of judicial measures, according to the law regulating criminal responsibility for the underage[3] (Garrido & López, 2005). Intervention, according to this program, is adapted to the nature of the (usually short-term) measures as well as to the context of their application. The program aims to train juveniles in socio-cognitive skills and

---

[3] Ley Orgánica 5/2000, de 12 de enero, reguladora de la responsabilidad penal de los menores. BOE nº 11, 13-Enero-2000, pp.1422-1440. Retrieved on January from http://www.boe.es/boe/dias/2000/01/13/pdfs/A01422-01441.pdf. This law was modified by the Ley Orgánica 8/2006. BOE nº 290, 5-Dic-2006, pp.42700-42712 retrieved on December from http://www.boe.es/boe/dias/2006/12/05/pdfs/A42700-42712.pdf

in pro-social attitudes, and values by using effective psychological techniques. However, the main objective of the program is to make juveniles aware of the thinking process that led them to behave in a specific way in several problematic situations in their lives.

Intervention methodology is based on implementing highly participatory and motivating sessions, in which a qualified professional previously trained in the program uses modeling and role-playing techniques. Juveniles learn to use specific skills in each session, developing activities that are attractive and amusing for them (games, contests, etc.) and that resemble examples and cases from their daily lives (Garrido & López, 2005). The program is composed of 13 sessions including: program presentation and motivation to participate; skills for thinking, feeling and behaving; control of thinking, emotions and behaviors (2 sessions); seeking information; identification of thoughts and emotions; seeking alternatives; detection of one's thinking bias or that of others; choosing right alternatives/solutions; implementation of the chosen alternative; development and change of values; and conflict management. Each session lasts approximately one hour and its recommended frequency is three times a week (Garrido & López, 2005).

This chapter aims to analyze the impact of services provided by the *Programa de Tutorías Educativas* (PTE), on the attitudes and behavior of juveniles placed in centers as a result of judicial measures, as well as the effect of psychological variables on this impact. Special attention is given to the outcomes of the Spanish short version for juveniles of the R&R program (PPS-VCJ), included in the PTE as part of training in skills for social integration (cross-curricular contents). The evaluation described below was carried out by administering questionnaires measuring risk and protective factors, antisocial behavior inside and outside the center, temporal perspective, motivation toward six behaviors and PPS-VCJ implementation. According to the GLM, the protective factors, future orientation and motivation, were expected to have a more relevant role in program attendance and changes in attitudes and behavior than risk factors, as proposed by the RNRM.

METHOD

Participants

One hundred seventy one boys aged 14-22 years (M = 17.93 SD = 1.56) participated in this study[4]. They were serving sentences imposed by the juvenile court, according to the law regulating the criminal responsibility of the underage[5], at the three centers for juveniles in the Canary Islands (Spain): Valle Tabares (51%), La Montañeta (33%) and Galdar (16%). Fifty three of them were included in the PTE outlined above, whereas the remaining participants received some educational services outside the program. Fifty five percent of the sample was serving sentences under a semi-open regime and 45% were in a closed regime. Thirty point five percent of the sample had served three or more previous sentences as a result of judicial measures and only 15% had had three or more judicial measures imposed on them at the

---

[4] In Spain, the age of majority is eighteen and therefore some participants were underage and some were young. However, as all of them were under juvenile court supervision, we will use the term juveniles to refer to both, thereby simplifying the reading of the text.

[5] See footnote 3.

moment of data collection. Forty four point six percent had infringed judicial measures twice or more.

Instruments

Three types of measurement devices were used: check-lists and inventories for staff evaluation of juveniles' profile and behavior as well as the services provided by the program; self-report questionnaires for juveniles' beliefs and motivations in several life domains; and, check-lists for tutor evaluation of juveniles' attitudes and behavior in workshops and classrooms.

1) Check-lists and inventories included the following:

- Hoge, Andrews and Leschied's (2002) Youth Level of Service/Case Management Inventory (YLS/CMI), adapted to Spanish by Garrido, López and Silva do Rosario (cited in Garrido & López, 2005). Juveniles were rated in the YLS/CMI by psychologists working at the centers.
- Frick and Hare's (2001) Antisocial Process Screening Device (APSD), adapted to Spanish by Garrido, López and Silva do Rosario (cited in Garrido & López, 2005). Juveniles were rated in the APSD by teachers, tutors and social educators.
- The Questionnaire for Juveniles Institutional Behavior (QJIB) was an adaptation for juveniles serving sentences at centers of the Questionnaire for Institutional Behavior (QIB) devised by Hernández and Martín (2000) to measure the behavior of adults in prison. Juveniles were rated in the QJIB by teachers, tutors and social educators.
- The Questionnaire for the Delivery of the PPS-VCJ. The staff was also asked to rate sixteen variables related to the delivery of the PPS-VCJ on an 11-point scale. More specifically, they were asked about the perception of the results, difficulties, positive and negative points of the experience, and the changes needed for enhanced future delivery of the program (see Table 4 below).

2) Self-report questionnaires included the following:

- The Motivational Scale (MS) was used to assess the motivation and level of control that the juveniles perceived they have in relation to six behaviors, following Bandura's (1991) social cognitive theory of self-regulation. Three of these behaviors referred to future development (to not commit offences, to find and keep a job, and to continue their education after release). The other three behaviors were of present development (to make contact with non-delinquent persons, to attend educational activities at the center, and to avoid fights with peers inside the center). Juveniles rated each of these six behaviors on 6-point scales related to self-efficacy, difficulty level, future goals, past habits and results, past and future satisfaction, and perceived effort.
- Zimbardo and Boyd's (1999) Temporal Perspective Inventory (TPI), which measures six factors related to the ability to situate oneself at several temporal moments: negative past (to think negatively of what has happened in the past); hedonistic present (to focus on the here and now without planning the future); future (to

establish goals, deadlines, obligations and punctuality); positive past (to go back to the past, to take advantage of good experiences); and fatalistic present (to see the negative side of everything that happens). Juveniles rated each item on a 5-point scale depending on how often they think or behave in the described way. Díaz-Morales's (2006) Spanish adaptation of the inventory was used.

3) Check-lists for attitudes and behavior at workshops and classrooms, which included the following:

- Two check-lists were devised and used by the staff to evaluate each session of the PPS-VCJ. One check-list addressed staff's perception of their own performance and level of comfort during the session. Data from this check-list could not be included in the statistical analyses because of methodological problems. The other check list covered staff's perception of juveniles' achievement in terms of understanding, skill attainment and awareness of benefits, attitude toward peers during the session and the extent to which what was learned related to the content of the other sessions.
- Daily records of juveniles' attendance and attitude during programmed activities and routines at the center.

Procedure

First, the evaluation project was presented by the research team to management and staff in each of the three centers. Afterwards, the directors, the educational coordinators and the psychologists were asked to collaborate in supplying the questionnaires and check-lists to the professionals who completed them, as outlined in the instrument section. At the same time, each center was visited several times by a research team collaborator in order to collect successive measures of juveniles' attitudes and behavior in the classrooms and workshops.

Because one of the main objectives of this research project was to evaluate the effectiveness of the PPS-VCJ, were conducted several related measures during its implementation. The PPS-VCJ was administered at two of the three centers: Valle Tabares and La Montañeta. In both cases it was addressed to juveniles involved in the PTE and to juveniles at other center services outside of the PTE. For juveniles involved in the PTE, the staff in charge of PPS-VCJ delivery involved social educators, while psychologists worked with juveniles attending center services out of tutorials. At Valle Tabares, the PPS-VCJ was implemented twice a week for six weeks. At La Montañeta, juveniles in the PTE received training over three weeks and juveniles outside the PTE over four weeks.

Irrespective of the center, during the implementation of the PPS-VCJ, the research team collaborator contacted the professionals who implemented the program to gather information on each session regarding juveniles' performance, achievements and comfort. Teachers, educators and tutors also provided information on juveniles' attitude and behavior in the classrooms and workshops during this period of time.

RESULTS

Data collected by the instruments described above were analyzed using SPSS 15.0 software. The results obtained are preliminary until the program follow-up is completed, and data on relapse are included in the analyses. The available results are described in relation to: 1) risk and protective factors (YLS/CMI), 2) institutional and antisocial behavior (APSD, QJIB), 3) juveniles' motivation and time perspective, 4) PPS-VCJ implementation, and 5) staff's perception of PPS-VCJ implementation.

Risk and Protective Factors

Fifty percent of juveniles under evaluation presented no protective factors. The other 50% ranged from three to seven protective factors. Only two participants were rated by staff using the YLS/CMI as having seven protective factors.

The most common protective factors were having job training and the intention to find a job, while the least common (only 10 participants) was to have positive relationships.

Risk factors ranged from 3 to 38, the average being 16. This average corresponds to a moderate level of risk as suggested in the norms for correction. Psychologists who rated juveniles in the YLS/CMI considered that 44% of the participants had a high risk level and 22% had a very high risk level. However, the correlation between the estimated level of risk and the number of risk factors was .60, showing that, although qualitative estimation is more negative than quantitative estimation, the relationship between both estimations is acceptable in terms of internal consistency.

The highest level of risk relates not to have adequate leisure activities and positive relationships. Inadequate rearing patterns and drug abuse are also important risk factors for this sample. The number of risk factors is moderately related to the number of protective factors (-.37).

INSTITUTIONAL AND ANTISOCIAL BEHAVIOR AND ITS RELATIONSHIP WITH YLS/CMI

Teachers, social educators and tutors rated juveniles in the APSD and the QJIB. Each juvenile was rated by around 3 professionals to avoid individual bias. Ratings by all judges were averaged to obtain a single score for each juvenile. Cronbach's Alpha for APSD was 0.83 and for QJIB 0.88. The average of all items on each scale was calculated for further analyses. The correlation between both scores was 0.74. In addition, both scores correlated positively with the number of risk factors and negatively with the number of protective factors measured by the YLS/CMI. Risk factors correlated 0.46 with QJIB and 0.53 with APSD. Protective factors correlated -0.23 with QJIB and -0.37 with APSD. As expected, the worst institutional behavior and antisocial attitude is related to a higher number of risk factors and to a lower number of protective factors.

SELF-REPORT QUESTIONNAIRES AND THEIR RELATION TO RISK FACTORS, INSTITUTIONAL BEHAVIOR AND ANTISOCIAL BEHAVIOR

Juveniles had difficulties in filling out the self-report questionnaires because of their low academic ability and, in some cases, because Spanish was not their first language[6]. Psychologists and social educators helped those with more difficulties by reading the questions for them.

Cronbach's Alphas of five factors of the Temporal Perspective Inventory (TPI) ranged from 0.60 to 0.73. The only statistically significant correlation found between any of the factors of the TPI and the variables measured by the YLS/CMI, the APSD and the QJIB, were those of the factor future with the number of protective factors (0.28) and with QJIB (-0.25). Juveniles more future oriented behaved better inside the center and had more protective factors. The relationship between the TPI Subscales and the Motivational Scales (MS) is described below.

Cronbach's Alphas were calculated for each of the six behaviors included in the MS. The level of difficulty was not included in the analyses as it was just a control variable. The level of internal consistency was appropriate and scores were averaged for each behavior. Cronbach's alphas for the six behaviors ranged from 0.63 to 0.86. Since the Cronbach's alpha resulting from considering the six behaviors together was 0.85, an overall score on motivation was calculated by averaging all single scores.

Table 1. Correlation between juveniles' motivation toward specific behaviors (MS) and risk/protective factors (YLS/CMI), and institutional (QJIB) and antisocial behavior (APSD)

	Risk factors	Protective Factors	Institutional behavior	Antisocial behavior
New offence	-.32	.31	-.23	
Job	-.30	.29	-.28	
Education after release		.22		
Non-delinquent Peers	-.20			
Activities in the center	-.27		-.35	-.26
Fights		.24		
General motivation	-.28	.30	-.24	

Note: All correlations are significant at $p<.05$.

Table 1 shows the significant negative correlations between the number of risk factors and motivation to not commit an offence, to find a job, to make contact with non-delinquent peers, to participate in educational activities inside the center, and the level of general motivation. The number of protective factors was also related to motivation, not to commit an offence, to find a job, to continue education after release, to avoid fights, and the level of general motivation. A significant negative correlation was found between institutional behavior and motivation not to commit an offence, to find a job, to participate in educational

---

[6] Given the short distance that separates the Canaries from northwest Africa, the islands are the first step for many African immigrants to illegally enter Europe. Many of them are underage, traveling alone.

activities inside the center, and the level of general motivation. A significant negative correlation was also found between antisocial behavior and motivation to find a job and to participate in educational activities inside the center.

In relation to the TPI, Table 2 shows significant correlations found between motivational subscales and the different time orientations.

Table 2. Correlation between juveniles' motivation toward specific behaviors (MS) and temporal perspective (TPI)

	Future	Positive Past	Negative Past	Fatalistic Present
New offence	.46	.23	.31	
Job	.43		.22	
Education After release	.48	.25		.25
Non-delinquent Peers	.44	.27	.32	
Activities in the center	.52	.20	.28	
Fights	.56		.27	
General motivation	.63	.28	.34	.21

Note: All correlations are significant at $p<.05$.

Future orientation significantly correlates with all motivational subscales. The negative past correlates significantly with all the motivational subscales except with being motivated to continue education after release. The positive past correlates significantly with all the motivational scales except with motivation to find and keep a job and motivation to avoid fights. The fatalistic present only correlated with to continue education after release and with overall motivation. No significant correlation was found in relation to the hedonistic present. The highest correlation was between future orientation and general motivation.

In order to predict institutional behavior of juveniles, a step by step regression analysis was carried out using the variables described above as predictors, and the scores in QJIB as criteria. The results show that 56.7% of the variance is predicted by a model including antisocial behavior orientation ($\beta = .679$) and motivation to participate in the educational activities at the center ($\beta = -.186$).

A step-by-step regression analysis was also conducted by using the variables described above to predict the number of risk factors as measured by the YLS/CMI. The results show that a 36.4% of the variance is predicted by a model including antisocial behavior orientation ($\beta = .397$), protective factors ($\beta = -.213$), and motivation to not commit a new offence after release ($\beta = -.208$).

Attendance at the PTE and PPS-VCJ

Juveniles attending the PTE received basic education, work skills training and training in specific skills aimed at improving social integration (education in sexuality, health, road safety). Correlations between attendance at PTE actions and juveniles' psychological variables, risk and protective factors, and antisocial attitudes and behavior were not statistically significant. Juveniles who attended more frequently to these activities were not better evaluated in relation to their attitudes or behavior. Neither did they have a specific profile in relation to their motivation or time perspective. However, as already mentioned, these results are preliminary until program follow-up is completed and data on relapse are included in the analyses. Although attendance at PTE activities might not influence attitudes and behavior at the center, it could influence behavior after release.

A total of 67 juveniles attended at least one PPS-VCJ session. Some attended one of five tutorials at Valle Tabares, others one of two tutorials at La Montañeta, and others at La Montañeta were not included in any tutorial. Ages range from 15 to 22 years, with a mean of 18.12 ($SD = 1.72$). Table 3 shows the frequency of attendance at the PPV-VCJ sessions.

The group of 14 juveniles who left the program after receiving various sessions was considered as the withdrawal group. They were distributed similarly across the different tutorials. Although they scored more negatively in some of the variables under study, the differences were not statistically significant, except for the number of protective factors, which was considerably lower for the withdrawal group. The group that did not abandon was also divided into those who attended the sessions more intensively ($n = 26$) and those who did so intermittently ($n=28$).

Table 3. Number of juveniles who attended a specific number of PPV-VCJ sessions

Number of sessions	Number of juveniles
1	2
2	3
3	6
4	7
5	3
6	2
7	2
8	9
9	7
10	10
11	3
12	9
13	4
Total	67

Attendance at the PPS-VCJ did significantly influence several variables under study. The results available in relation to the delivery of the PPS-VCJ are presented in three separate sections: 1) The relationship between juveniles' level of program attendance and their scores in the instruments described above, 2) Juveniles' performance in the sessions and 3) Juveniles' changes in attitudes and institutional behavior in relation to the level of program attendance.

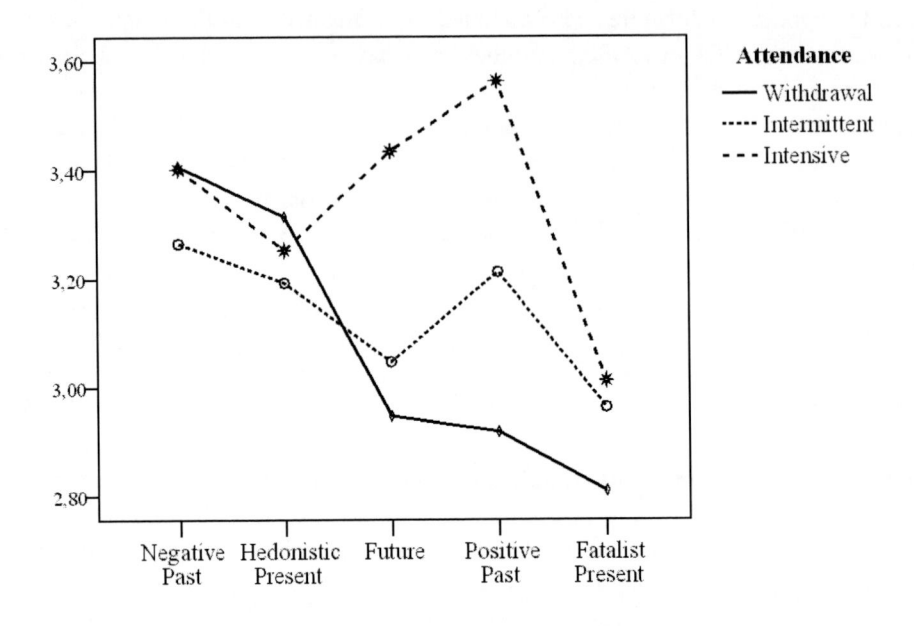

Figure 1. Temporal perspective (TPI) in relation to the level of PPS-SVJ attendance.

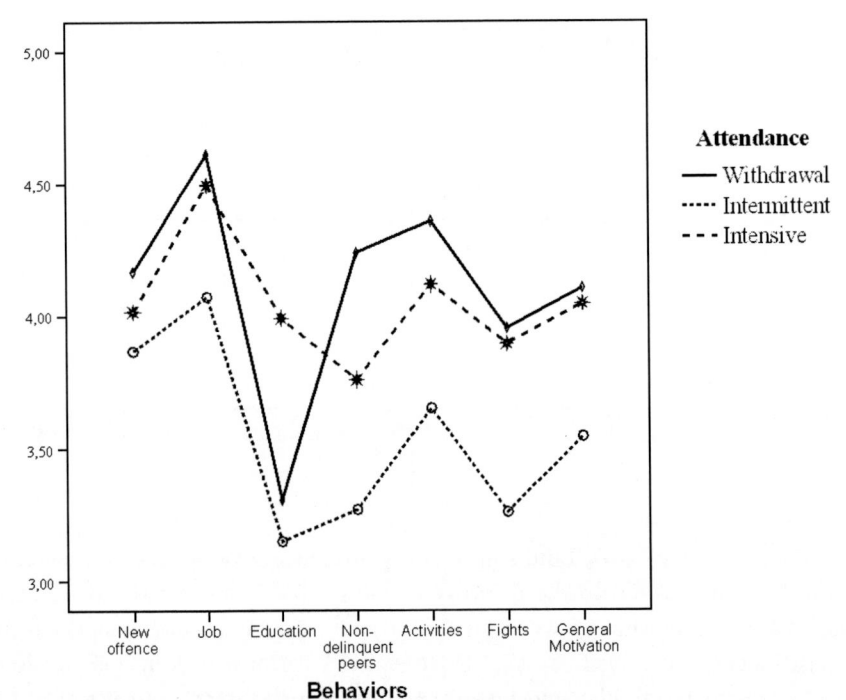

Figure 2. Motivation toward specific behaviors (MS) in relation to the level of PPS-VCJ attendance.

1) The Relationship between Juveniles' Level of Program Attendance and Psychological Variables

Comparisons between the three groups of attendance showed that, though the differences between groups were not statistically significant, there were some trends that could be highlighted for further research. The intensive attendance group scored higher than the other groups in the number of protective factors, and lower in institutional behaviors.

Figure 1 also displays higher scores in future orientation and in positive past for the intensive attendance group, whereas Figure 3 shows that scores in motivation toward education after release seem to be what differentiated this group from the others.

2) Juveniles' Performance During the Sessions

Professionals in charge of implementing the program completed one check-list related to each juvenile's comfort and achievement during the session. This achievement was evaluated by assessing the juvenile's level in terms of understanding, skill attainment and awareness of the benefits, attitude toward peers during the session and the extent to which what was learned related to the content of the other sessions. The Cronbach's alpha for the scale was 0.93. Therefore, a simple score was calculated by averaging all the items related to each session. There was a significant difference in performance between session 10 and session 1 ($t(26) = 4.4$, $p<.001$). Although the relationship was not statistically significant ($p = .06$), the performance tended to increase for the higher attendance groups.

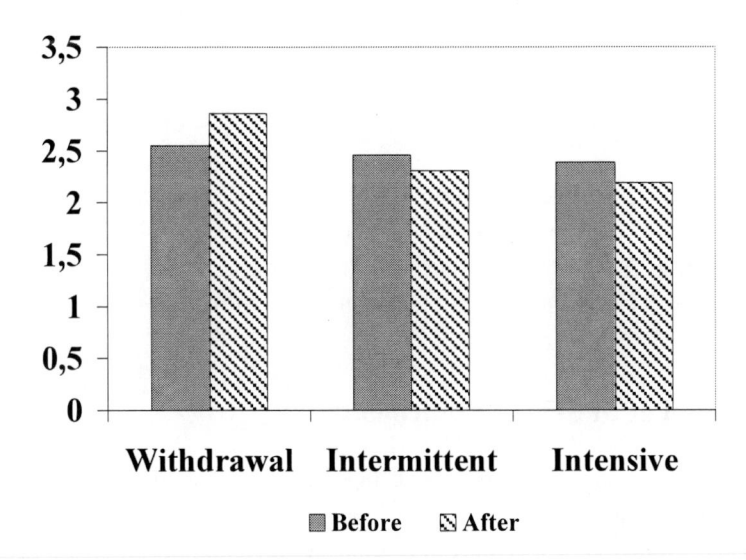

Figure 3. Means for institutional behavior (QJIB) before and after the program in relation to the level of PPS-VCJ attendance.

3) Juveniles' Changes in Attitudes and Institutional Behavior in Relation to the Level of Program Attendance

The difference between juveniles' attitude before and after program attendance was not statistically significant, although there is a tendency to obtain a better valuation when attendance was more intense. This evaluation was made by tutors not involved in implementing the program.

In relation to juveniles' behavior, there was a significant difference for institutional behavior ($t(39) = 2.35, p = .24$) but not for antisocial behavior, when comparing scores before and after program attendance. Figures 3 and 4 shows the means of each group before and after the program. Both figures register a slight decrease in problematic behaviors in the intensive attendance group and an increase in the withdrawal group. However, these differences are significant only for the intensive group and only in relation to institutional behavior.

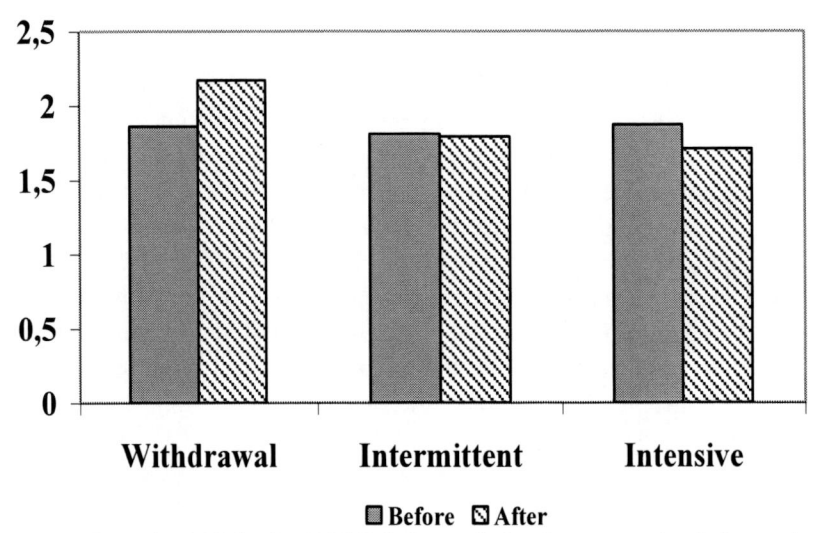

Figure 4. Means for antisocial behavior (APSD) before and after the program in relation to the level of PPS-VCJ attendance.

Looking only at scores after the program, the differences are significant for institutional ($F(2)= 8.71, p <.001$) and antisocial behavior ($F(2)= 8.06, p<.001$). Post hoc comparisons show that differences between the withdrawal group and the other two groups after program attendance are always significant but not between the intermittent and the intensive groups.

Staff Evaluation of PPS-VCJ Implementation

As soon as the program was finalized, the staff who had implemented it completed a questionnaire to evaluate their perception of implementation. They were asked to score 16 variables related to difficulties found in program implementation on an 11-point scale. They were also asked to rate their perception of the results, their satisfaction with the experience and to record the positive points of the experience and the changes required for futures implementations.

Table 4 shows that overlapping with other educational activities was rated as the main difficulty in implementing the program, followed by the lack of technical supplies needed to carry out sessions. The suitability of the materials for the juveniles and their level of understanding were pointed out in some cases. Contrary to researchers' expectations, the lack of staff training and the juveniles' rejection of the program were rated as unimportant.

Staff rated their perception of the results obtained by juveniles at around 5, whereas they rated their own satisfaction at 6.

The points they considered as positive are: the possibility of working in a team; juveniles' progressive acceptance of the program; repetition of the activities; the possibility of reflection; the increase in juveniles' awareness of their problems; and the adaptation of materials to juveniles' level of understanding, life experience, culture, and progressive increase of knowledge.

Table 4. Minimums, maximums, means and standard deviations for staff's perception of the integrity, difficulties, results and satisfaction with the delivery of the PPS-VCJ

		Mm.	Mx.	M	SD
Integrity		3	9	5.1	2.3
Difficulties	Technical supplies	3	9	7.6	1.9
	Overlapping	6	10	8.1	1.3
	Training	1	8	3.6	2.7
	Group variability	1	10	6.7	2.6
	Juveniles' rejection	0	10	4.7	3.4
	Timetables	1	10	6.5	2.9
	Planning	1	10	6.2	3.3
	Material suitability	3	10	7.5	2.4
	Juveniles' understanding	3	10	7.5	2.3
Results	Goals	4	7	5.5	1.0
	Situation interpretation	4	7	5.6	.91
	Behavior	1	7	5.5	2.0
	Problem interpretation	3	8	5.7	1.5
	Conflictive situations	1	7	5.1	1.8
	Knowledge	3	7	5.4	1.3
Satisfaction		5	7	6.2	.88

In order to improve future implementations of the PPS-SVJ, they suggested the following: 1) to use more realistic examples adapted to juveniles, 2) to adapt material to foreign juveniles, 3) to use more audiovisual material to overcome problems of illiteracy, 4) to create more homogeneous groups according to juveniles' educational levels, type of confinement and interests, 5) to increase practical exercises, 6) to respect timetables, 7) to motivate juveniles to participate in the program before starting, linking their participation to specific objectives and using simpler sessions at the beginning, and 8) to have more information and preparation for each session.

CONCLUSIONS

The results available from the follow-up enable us to reach some conclusions. In relation with the PTE and the PPS-VCJ and, indirectly, to the GLM and the RNRM. First, the protective factors measured by the YLS/CMI should be an intervention goal to improve juveniles' opportunities for social insertion, given their relationship with motivation, future orientation and behavior. Second, juveniles more motivated towards education are those who attend the PPS-VCJ longer, whereas those more oriented to looking for a job leave the program earlier; intermittent attendance is not related to a defined motivational profile. This suggests that the self-regulation mechanism toward specific behaviors requires improvement for future implementation.

The results summarized in the above paragraph indirectly support the GLM to the extent that juveniles' strengths (protective factors, motivation and future orientation) seem to relate to program attendance whereas risk factors do not. However, as risk factors, also, relate to antisocial and institutional behavior, it is not reasonable to ignore the RNRM. Also, in order to check the alternative fitness of these models. It would be needed a more complex research design than the one that describes it. Therefore, it seems more acceptable to integrate the postulate of both models in juveniles' intervention until more research on the topic is carried out.

Third, intensive attendance at PPS-VCJ produces effects on juveniles, whereas intermittent or poor attendance has no effect. Juveniles' involvement in training sessions also improves as the number of sessions increases. Fourth, staff in charge of PPS-VCJ implementation expresses satisfaction with the experience and willingness to continue. However, they also identify several problems to be rectified in order to improve future delivery. Most of these difficulties could be solved with higher institutional support, reflected in better planning to integrate the program into the routine activities of the center and to supply program staff in advance with the equipment and materials required.

REFERENCES

Andrews, D.A., & Bonta, J. (2003). *The psychology of criminal conduct.* Cincinnati, OH: Anderson.

Bandura, A. (1977) Social Learning Theory. New York: General Learning Press

Bandura, A. (1991). Social cognitive theory of self-regulation. *Organizational Behavior and Human Decision Processes, 50,* 248-287.

Berman, A. (2004). The reasoning and rehabilitation program: assessing short- and long-term outcomes among male Swedish prisoners. *Journal of Offender Rehabilitation, 40,* 85-103.

Bushway, S. (1998). The impact of an arrest on the job stability of young white American men. *Journal of Research in Crime and Delinquency, 35,* 459-479.

Bouffard, J., Mackenzie, D., & Hickman, L. (2000). Effectiveness of vocational education and employment programs for adult offenders: A methodology-based analysis of the literature. *Journal of Offender Rehabilitation, 31,* 1-41.

Cann, J., Falsaw, L., & Friendship, C. (2003). *Understanding 'What works': accredited cognitive skills programmes for adult men and young offenders.* Home Office Research Findings No. 226. London: Home Office.

Cann, J., Falsaw, L., & Friendship, C. (2005). Understanding 'What works': accredited cognitive skills programmes for young offenders. *Youth justice, 5,* 165-179.

Cox, W.M., & Klinger, E. (2004). A motivational model of alcohol use: Determinants of use and change. In W.M. Cox, & E. Klinger (Eds.), *Handbook of motivational counselling: Concepts, approaches, and assessment* (pp.121-138). Chichester, UK: Wiley.

Díaz-Morales, J.F. (2006). Estructura factorial y fiabilidad del Inventario de Perspectiva Temporal de Zimbardo [Factorial structure and reliability of Zimbardo's inventory of temporal perspective]. *Psicothema, 18*, 565-571.

Falshaw, L., Friendship, C., Travers, L., & Nugent, F. (2003). *Searching for "what works": An evaluation of cognitive skills programmes.* Home Office Research Findings No. 206. London: Home Office.

Falshaw, L., Friendship, C., Travers, L., and Nugent, F. (2004). Searching for "what works": HM Prison Service accredited cognitive skills programmes. *British Journal of Forensic Practice, 6*, 3–13.

Frick, P. J., & Hare, R. D. (2001). *The Antisocial Process Screening Device.* Toronto: Multi-Health Systems.

Friendship, C., Alud, L., Erikson, M., Travers, R., & Thorton, D. (2003). Cognitive-behavioral treatment for imprisoned offenders: an evaluation of HM Prison service's cognitive skills programmes. *Legal and Criminological Psychology, 8*, 103-114.

Garrido, V. & López, M. (2005a). *Manual de intervención educativa en readaptación social.* [Manual of educative intervention in social re-adaptation]*Vol. 1 and 2.* Valencia: Tirant Lo Blanch.

Gendreau, P., & Ross, R. R. (1979). Effective correctional treatment: Bibliotherapy for cynics. *Crime and Delinquency, 25*, 463-489.

Hirschi, T. (1969). *Causes of delinquency.* Berkeley, CA: University of California Press.

HM Prison Service (1998). *Criteria for accrediting Programmes 1998-99.* London: HM Prison Service, Offender Behaviour Programmes Unit.

Hoge, R., Andrews, D.A., & Leschied. A. (2002). *Youth Level of Service / Case Management Inventory: YLS/CMI Manual.* Toronto: MultiHealth Systems

Hollin, C. (Comp.)(2001). *Handbook of offender assessment and treatment.* Chichester: Wiley.

Hollin, C., & Palmer, E. (2006). *Offending behaviour programmes: Development, application and controversies.* Chichester: Wiley.

Home Office Probation Unit (1999). *What Works Initiative: Crime Reduction Programme. Joint Prison and Probation accreditation Criteria.* London: Home Office.

Tong, L.S.J., & Farringhton, D.P. (2006). How effective is the R&R program in reducing re-offending: A meta-analysis of evaluation in few countries. *Psychology, Crime and the Law, 12*, 3-24.

Landenberger, N.A., & Lipsey, M. (2005). The positive effects of cognitive-behavioral programs for offenders: A meta-analysis of factors associated with effective treatment. *Journal of Experimental Criminology, 1*, 451-476.

Lösel, F. (1995). The efficacy of correctional treatment: A review and synthesis of Meta-evaluations. In J. McGuire (Ed.), *What works: Reducing reoffending*, (pp. 79-111). Chichester: John Willey & Sons.

Lösel, F. (2001). Evaluating the effectiveness of correctional programs: Bridging the gap between research and practice. In G.A.Bernfeld, D.P. Farrington, and A.W. Leschied (Comps.), *Offender rehabilitation in practice* (Chap. 4, pp. 67-92). New York: John Wiley & Sons.

McMurran, M., Theodosi, E., Sweeney, A., & Sellen, J. (2008). What do prisoners want? Current concerns of adult male prisoners. *Psychology, Crime & Law, 14*, 267-274.

Martín, A.M., & Hernández, B. (1995). PEIRS: The efficacy of a multifaceted cognitive program for prison inmates. In R. R. Ross, and R. D. Ross (Eds.), *Thinking Straight* (pp. 389-409) Ottawa (Canada): Air Training and Publications.

Martín, A. & Hernández, B. (2000). *La evaluación de Programa HOPECAN*. Unpublished research report. La Laguna, Spain: Universidad de La Laguna.

Martín, A.M., Hernández, B., & Hernández-Fernaud, E. (2004). The assessment of a work program for high-risk offenders. En R. Abruhnosa-Goncalvez, (Eds.), *Victims and offenders* (pp. 83-93). Brussels: Politeia editors.

Martín, A.M., Hernández, B., Hernández-Fernaud, E., Arregui, J.L. y Hernández, J.A. (in press). The enhancement effect of social and employment integration on the delay of recidivism of released offenders trained with the R & R Programme. *Psychology, crime & law*.

May, C. (1999). *Explaining reconviction following a community sentence: the role of social factors*. London: Home Office Research Study 192

McGuire, J. (2001). What Works in correctional intervention? Evidence and practical implications. In G.A.Bernfeld, D.P. Farrington and A.W. Leschied (Eds.), Offender rehabilitation in practice (Chap. 2, pp. 25-43). New York: John Wiley & Sons.

McGuire, J. (2002). Criminal sanctions versus psychologically-based interventions with offenders: A comparative empirical analysis. *Psychology, Crime & Law, 8*, 183-208.

McGuire, J. (2004).Commentary: Promising Answer, and Next Generation of Questions. *Psychology, Crime & Law, 10*, 335-345.

McGuire, J. (2006). General offending behaviour programmes: Concept, theory, and practice. In C. Hollin and E. Palmer (Eds.), *Offending behaviour programmes: Development, application and controversies* (Chap.3, pp. 69-111). Chichester: Wiley.

Mitchell, J., & Palmer, E. (2004). Evaluating the 'Reasoning and Rehabilitation' program for young offenders. *Journal of Offender Rehabilitation, 39*, 31-45.

Piehl, A. (1998). Economic conditions, work, and crime. In M. Tonry (Ed.), *The handbook of crime and punishment* (pp. 302-319). New York: Oxford University Press.

Priestley, P., McGuire, J., Flegg, D., Welham, D., Hemsley, V., & Barnitt, R. (1984). *Social skills in prisons and the community: Problem-solving for offenders*. London: Routledge.

Ross, R., and Fabiano, E. (1985). *Time to think: A cognitive model of delinquency prevention and offender rehabilitation*. Johnson City, Canada: Institute of Social Sciences & Arts.

Ross, R., Fabiano, E., Garrido, V., & Gómez, A. (1996). *Programa "El pensamiento prosocial": Una guía de trabajo detallada para la prevención y el tratamiento de la delincuencia y la drogodependencia* ["The Prosocial thinking programme": A detailed work guide for the prevention and treatment of offending behavior and drug abuse]. Valencia: Cristóbal Serrano Villalba.

Seligman, M.(2002) *Authentic happiness: Using the new positive psychology to realize your potential for lasting fulfillment*.New York: Free Press.

Seligman, M. & Csikszentmihalyi, M.(2000) Positive psychology: An introduction. *American Psychologist, 55*,5-14

Visher, C., Winterfield, L., & Coggeshall, M. B. (2005). Ex-offender employment programs and recidivism: A meta-analysis. *Journal of Experimental Criminology, 1*, 295-315.

Ward, T., & Brown, M. (2004). The Good Lives Model and conceptual issues in offender rehabilitation. *Psychology, Crime & Law, 10*, 243-257.

Wilkinson, J. (2005). Evaluating evidence for the effectiveness of the Reasoning and Rehabilitation Programme. *The Howard Journal, 44*, 70-85.

Wilson, D.B., Gallagher, C.A., & Mackenzie, D.L. (2000). A meta-analysis of corrections-based education, vocation, and work programs for adult offenders. *Journal of Research in Crime and Delinquency, 37*, 347-368.

Wilson, D.B., Bouffard, L.A., & Mackenzie, D.L. (2005). A quantitative review of structured, group-oriented, cognitive-behavioral programs for offenders. *Criminal Justice and Behavior, 32*, 172-204.

Zimbardo, P. & Boyd, J.N. (1999). Putting time in perspective: A valid, reliable individual-differences metric. *Journal of Personality and Social Psychology, 66*, 742-752.

In: Bio-Psycho-Social Perspectives on Interpersonal Violence   ISBN: 978-1-61668-159-3
Editors: M. Frías-Armenta et al., pp. 333-353   © 2010 Nova Science Publishers, Inc.

Chapter 15

JUVENILE OFFENDERS' RECIDIVISM IN SPAIN: A QUANTITATIVE REVISION

Juan García-García[*], Elena Ortega-Campos and Leticia de la Fuente-Sánchez
University of Almería, Almeria, Spain.

ABSTRACT

The area of juvenile justice of the European Economic and Social Committee warns about the need to conduct quantitative studies in the field of juvenile offenders in order to collect and harmonize current information in the European Union, especially in the study of recidivism. Recidivism is the commission of a new crime when a previous offense or offenses have been committed. However, in our study, recidivism is understood as a sign of (lack of) success of the legal action in minors trailed by Juvenile Justice. The aim of our study was to conduct, through the use of quantitative-revision methodology, a meta-analysis showing the factors or variables that best explain and predict the risk of recidivism in Spanish juvenile offenders. The methodology used implied the collection of studies that have been conducted in Spain on juvenile offender's recidivism. During the bibliographic search process we selected a total of 22 papers which provided 26 independent studies covering data from 22,484 juveniles. In the meta-analysis, the general recidivism rate was taken to calculate the average recidivism rate. The average rate of recidivism, weighted by the sample size of the studies resulted to be 23.19% with a standard deviation of 14.14.

INTRODUCTION

Current criminological theories aim to distinguish juvenile delinquency from criminal career. Rechea and Fernández (2001) insist on the idea that many youths are involved in

---

[*] Correspondence concerning this chapter should be addressed to Juan García García. Faculty of Psychology, University of Almería. Cañada de San Urbano s/n.04120 Almería (Spain), e-mail: jgarciag@ual.es.

criminal behaviors during adolescence but only a few will persist in these behaviors after this stage. The persistence of criminal behavior is a decisive factor in the criminal career prediction that will go beyond their current age. In this sense, juvenile recidivism is important as a reinforcing factor of the criminal behavior, considering personal, social, cultural and other factors as modulating variables of the recidivism causes.

Therefore, recidivism rate is not only a statistical value of knowledge on the *criminogenic situation* in a specific geographical context and in a certain period of time but, even more importantly, it is a predictive value of later, possible behaviors in youths.

Recidivism in Juvenile Justice is known as a new offence when one or more offences have been previously committed. In the Juvenile Justice field, there is a consensus in using the concept of recidivism as a new entry of the youth into the Judicial System although, in a bibliographic review of studies conducted in Spain, we can find different definitions of juvenile recidivism (see Table 1). In this study, we will take the more extended concept of recidivism, this is to say, a new entry of the minor into the Juvenile Judicial System.

Table 1. Juvenile recidivism definition, according to different Spanish studies

Study	Recidivism Definition
Redondo, Funes & Luque (1993)	Being incarcerated when adults
Escofet & Pérez (1995)	Commiting a new crime
Rechea, Barberet, Montañés & Arroyo (1995)	Self-reported
Funes, Luque, Ruiz & Sanchez-Meca (1996)	Reentry into the Juvenile Justice System
Forcadell, Camps, Rivarola & Pérez (2004)	Receive a measure criminal or a technical advice report
Capdevila, Ferrer & Luque (2005)	Reentry into Juvenile Justice or be derived to Adult Justice

One of the purposes of the studies on recidivism risk prediction is to identify the persistent career of criminal behavior (Buelga & Lila, 1999; Olver, Stockdale, & Wormith, 2009; Schalwe, 2009; Unruh, Gan, & Waintrup, 2009), focusing on the study of youths who committed a criminal offence and searching the reduction of reoffending risk through intervention and treatment (Camps & Cano, 2006).

Authors who are working on this line, aim to discriminate those variables which would explain, in an empirical way, the presence or absence of risk or protective factors which lead some youths to commit criminal offences once, but without reoffending, while other youths consolidate dissocial behavior through criminal careers. *The Agency for Re-education and Reintegration of the Minor Offender* (ARRMI, Madrid) recently published a study reporting that one out of four minors, who were sentenced to a Juvenile Justice Reform Center in the autonomous region of Madrid, reoffended for the same offence he or she was previously sentenced for (Graña, Garrido, & González, 2008).

Regarding individual variables, there is a consensus in considering gender as a predicting variable, understanding that boys have a higher risk of reoffending than girls (Becedóniz, Rodríguez, Herrero, Menéndez, Bringas, Balaña, & Paíno, 2007; Capdevila, Marteache, & Ferrer, 2008; Cottle, Lee, & Heilbrun, 2001; García, Díez, Pérez, & García, 2008). Age is a well accepted factor, since there is a higher risk of reoffending if the minor had an early contact with the justice system, committed criminal offences or has been responsible for violent episodes at an early age (Capdevilla, Marteache, & Ferrer, 2008; Cottle, Lee, &

Heilbrun, 2001; Graña, Garrido, & González, 2008; Latimer, 2001; Katsiyannis, Zhang, Barrett, & Flaska, 2004).

There is not similar agreement on race, ethnic group or origin and geographic area. Although some authors identify, as relevant, being white (Sabol, Adams, Parthasarathy, & Yuan, 2000; Sánchez-Meca, 1996), black (Spohn & Holleran, 2002), gypsy (Forcadell, Camps, Rivarola, & Pérez, 2004) or belonging to a minority group (Cain, 2000), other authors warn against the fact that these differences disappear when other variables are controlled such as family support, unfavourable economical situation or personal or social resources within the reach of them (Benda, Flynn, & Toombs, 2001; Cottle, Lee, & Heilbrun 2001; Forcadell, Camps, Rivarola, & Pérez, 2004 Gendreau, Little, & Goggin, 1996; Winner, Lanza-Kaduce, Bishop, & Frazier, 1997).

In Spain, a research on immigrant youth offenders was conducted. All registered reports of sentences in the Minor Courts of the Basque Autonomous region from January 2001 to December 2003 were revised, where 168 minor immigrants were sanctioned. The purpose of the study was to show a descriptive analysis in order to identify the profile of the offender minor immigrant which was based on the prevalence of psychosocial patterns. The authors found that offending minor immigrants showed a general profile of social exclusion resulting the lack of parental control, family unit disruption and the alternative socialization based on the minor integration in a peer group aimed to law breaking, the most important risk factors (Ocáriz & San Juan, 2006).

Regarding psychological and individual health variables, the most reported measures are: behavior problems at an early age, impulsiveness, low control, limited skills to solve problems, and antisocial attitudes. Concerning health, substance use and abuse and its consumption initiation at an early age are the most influencing variables to understand recidivism (Capdevilla, Marteache, & Ferrer, 2008; Cottle, Lee, & Heilbrun, 2001; Katsiyannis, Zhang, Barrett, & Flaska, 2004; Schalwe, 2009).

Family and social environment variables are the most quoted in regard to the prediction of dissocial behaviors and recidivism. These variables are linked to improper educational guidelines from parents, since these rules moderate children problems, external problems expressed in problematic behavior and environmental stress regarding social adaptation in the local school and close context of the youth (Torrubia, 2004). Other risk factor is the existence of child maltreatment and family violence, and finally, when children reach adolescence, the lack of supervision regarding their activities and the places and company they frequent predict recidivism. Different studies give the group of peers a great importance regarding the presence or absence of recidivism. The loyalty towards the group members at certain age is superimposed against the personal interest of the youth (Camps & Cano, 2006; Capdevilla, Marteache, & Ferrer, 2008; Ocáriz & San Juan, 2006).

Regarding school and training variables, the most reported variables in the literature are a deficient academic performance and failure to adapt to school. These variables cause school drop-out of many youths who commit offences. The fact that they do not take up leisure time during adolescence causes a bad management of their spare time leading them to mix with dissocial peers and commit offences. Furthermore, in Spain, the fact that the job age starts at 16 years old does not enable a proper job opportunity as an alternative to formal education before this age (Cottle, Lee, & Heilbrun, 2001; Schalwe, 2009).

Regarding the spare time management, its bad usage is the most reported risk factor, since its deficient organization leads to substance use, dissocial peers partnership and absence of gratifying prosocial activities which promote and maintain self-esteem. In a study carried out by Martín, Martínez, López, Martínez and Martín (1997) with a discussion group of youths between 15 and 30 from the Autonomous Region of Madrid, the authors collected a list of motivations to practice violent behavior expressed by them. Among the most important variables they mention highlighting material wealth for obtaining objects, money, drugs, etc; to reach a personal satisfaction; to demonstrate superiority as an individual or as a group; to have fun; protecting their territory, people, and ideologies; to relieve stress or frustration; acknowledgment or social power; revenge; group cohesion; and conflict and problem resolution.

Regarding criminal and criminal record variables, being too young when they had their first contact with the Juvenile Justice System and having a previous criminal record are the most reported variables, as the best predictive factors of recidivism. Related to the type of offense and the way of its commission, criminal offenses against property are considered as the best predictive factor of recidivism (Capdevilla, Ferrer, & Luque, 2005; Forcadell *et al.*, 2004; Funes, Luque, Ruiz, & Sánchez-Meca, 1996). Youth who commit the offense in association with adults had a worse forecast as compared to those who offended alone or with other juveniles (Cain, 2000; Redondo, Funes, & Luque, 1993; Tournier, 1997). In addition, the time taken to reoffend is shorter when the minors show criminal careers (*Correctional Service of Canada* 1989, 1993a, 1993b, 1993c).

QUANTITATIVE REVIEWS

The International guidelines provide a high relevance to the necessity of investigating on issues related to juvenile offenses and juvenile justice. In the United Nation Standard Minimum Rules for the Administration of Juvenile Justice (*1985), the 30th rule,* defines investigation in Juvenile Justice as: *"The use of research as a basis of an informed Juvenile Justice policy [which] is widely acknowledged as an important mechanism for keeping practices abreast of advances in knowledge and the continuing development and improvement of the Juvenile Justice System. The mutual feedback between research and policy is especially important in Juvenile Justice. With a rapid and often drastic changes in the lifestyles of the young and in the forms and dimensions in juvenile crime, the societal and justice responses to juvenile crime and delinquency quickly become outmoded and inadequate"* (García, Díez, Pérez, & García, 2008).

The scientific development of knowledge is based on the contribution that researchers or specialists offer in different areas of research. However, investigations are more and more specialized, together with the exponential growth of scientific production, it is difficult, in practise, to access all studies conducted on any topic (Price, 1963). At this point, research reviews are developed in order to establish the starting point for new researches and facilitate the compilation and study of previous ones.

Research reviews are focused on studying the state of a due topic, enabling the integration of empirical outcomes from researches included in the review. Those results represent the first step for any researcher who tries to get in touch with an investigated issue. For this purpose, a methodology leading to systematize the development of any revision is needed. This methodology should guide researchers, step-by-step, in order to obtain a revision with suitable patterns required in a scientific research: rigour, objectivity, transparency and replicability (Marín, Sánchez-Meca, Huedo, & Fernández, 2007). Traditionally, researchers lack systematic guidelines to develop research reviews. Every researcher, after an exhaustive search of studies on the same topic has contributed with a particular point of view or synthesis of the matter influenced by those authors and/or studies which they consider more relevant or closer to their own theoretical position (Jackson, 1980). In that sense, Cooper (1989) considers that traditional reviews are excessively conservative in facing the possibility of reserving the reviser's previous beliefs, who is unlikely to abandon his/her prejudices and previous hypothesis. Without tools adapted to the statistical probabilistic nature of results in the primary research and without a systematization during the process, which leads to establish minimum standard guidelines, the research synthesis is limited to a mere value exercise, unlikely replicable, rather arbitrary, not necessarily right and conditioned to the reviewer's point of view (Marín & Sánchez-Meca, 1999).

In 1976, from the Psychology Field, Gene V. Glass formalized a methodological proposal to the systematic development of research reviews. He called the proposal "meta-analysis." According to Glass, meta-analysis can be defined as: *"the statistical analysis of a large collection of analysis' results from individual studies for the purpose of integrating the findings. It connotes a rigorous alternative to the casual, narrative discussions of research studies which typify our attempts to make sense of the rapidly expanding research literature"* (Glass, 1976, p.3).

Therefore, meta-analysis was born as an alternative to traditional research review, with the aim of offsetting their subjectivity. It can be defined as a researching methodology towards systematic and quantitative review of a group of empirical studies on the same topic (Botella & Gambara, 2002; Cooper & Hedges, 1994; Lipsey & Wilson, 2001; Sánchez-Meca & Ato, 1989).

Although meta-analysis (Glass, 1976) is the given name to these reviews, it is also common the use of other names such as *quantitative review* (Green & Hall, 1984), *research integration* (Walberg & Haertel, 1980) or *quantitative assessment of research domains* (Rosenthal, 1980). All these names have in common a basic principle: to put in practise quantitative methods in order to sum up the results of several studies and to check the interrelations among their features (Glass, McGaw, & Smith, 1981; Hattie & Hansford, 1984; Hunter, Schmidt, & Jackson, 1982).

Regarding the stages that a meta-analysis must cover, there is a wide consensus causing a great parallelism with the primary investigation process: the conceptualization of the problem, the statement of the hypothesis, definition of variables and measures, sampling and data treatment (Durlak & Lipsey, 1991). These stages will be followed in the present study.

OBJECT OF THE STUDY

This study has been set out in order to estimate the juvenile recidivism rate from empirical studies made on juvenile criminal recidivism in Spain. As mentioned before, a recidivism rate is not only a statistical value of a criminogenic situation but this rate provides us a predictive value of possible subsequent behavior in youths. The rate is known as a sign of the effect of legal actions. For this purpose, a collection of studies on juvenile recidivism was conducted and subsequently the results of those studies were quantitatively integrated through meta-analysis.

PROBLEM FORMULATION AND HYPOTHESIS

The definition of recidivism in the present chapter refers to a new entry of youths in the Juvenile Justice System after they have committed a previous offense. From this point of view, recidivism is understood as a sign of success of the legal action in minors implemented by the Juvenile Justice. In that way, a lower recidivism will imply a higher success of the legal actions imposed to minors and, on the contrary, a higher recidivism would imply a lower effectiveness of the actions imposed to them. The estimate of the recidivism rate, therefore, gives us a success or failure sign of the legal actions imposed.

BIBLIOGRAPHY SEARCH

An explicit set of criteria was established for the studies in order to be included in the meta-analysis:

a. The studies should have been published after 1993.
b. The studies should be based on real data of Spanish population.
c. The studies should give, at least, a general recidivism rate.

The bibliography search process was based on the following sources:

a. A search of electronic data was conducted (ISOC[1], COMPLUDOC[2], DIALNET[3], and PSICODOC[4]) using the keywords: younger, menores infractores, reincidencia, delincuencia juvenil, jóvenes delincuentes, offenders, recidivism, juvenile delinquency, juvenile delinquents. The search was conducted from January to September 2008.
b. Direct review of specialized journals.
c. To extend the search engine, an additional review was conducted in the Google search engine.
d. Contact with expert researchers in the area and revision of contributions in Legal Psychology and Criminology Congress.
e. In order to include all the studies on juvenile recidivism, the bibliographic references of every article included in each study were revised.

---

[1] ISOC: Spanish National Research Council. Social Sciences Data Base.
[2] COMPLUDOC: Database of the Complutense University of Madrid
[3] DIALNET: Hispanic Scientific Production Diffusion Portal
[4] PSICODOC: Bibliographic Database on Psychology

EFFECT SIZE

The effect size is the estimation of the effect of the legal action imposed, based on the offense. This estimation was obtained through the calculation of the *odds ratio* of proportion or quotient of complementary probabilities of recidivism, defined as the quotient between recidivism probability (p) and non-recidivism probability (*1-p*).

$OR= p/1\text{-}pOR= p/1\text{-}p$

To interpret the odds ratio, we must take into account that a value of 1 indicates the same probabilities in both groups (recidivism, non-recidivism). In this paper, an *odds ratio* higher than 1 indicates a higher probability of recidivism; on the contrary, an *odds ratio* lower than 1 indicates a lower probability of recidivism.

DESCRIPTIVE CHARACTERISTICS OF THE STUDIES

Once selected the studies to be included in the meta-analysis, their codification was conducted by two researchers who reached a consensus regarding their discrepancies.

Firstly, recidivism was codified, measured as the percentage of individuals' entry into the Juvenile Justice System again after the base offense and the *odds ratio* of that percentage was estimated.

Later, the modulating variables registered in the studies included in the meta-analysis corresponding to youth's family features, etc., were codified. The modulating variables are not common for all the included studies. Those modulating variables were grouped in three categories (Lipsey, 1994): extrinsic variables, substantive variables and methodological variables (see Table 2).

The extrinsic variables codified for every study were: (a) Authors of the study, (b) Date of report, (c) Publication source (journal, report, book, congress), (d) Date of data gathering, (e) Place of data gathering (Juvenile Justice reform center, county, Autonomous Region or national), (f) Type of offense (if indicated), (g) Judicial Measure imposed/sentenced, (h) Current law under which the younger was judged (Tutelary Courts of Minors, Organic Law 4/92 or Organic Law 5/2000).

The subject's variables codified for the samples were: (a) Average time rate of recidivism (months), (b) Violence in the base offense, (c) Substance use (younger), (d) Victim of Physical abuse, (e) Victim of Psychological abuse, (f) Family Criminal records, (g) Physical family problems, (h) Family Mental Health problems, (i) Family use of substances, (j) The younger studies, (k) The younger works, (l) Dissocial peer-group, (m) (S)has a couple.

The methodological variables codified for the samples were: (a) Sample size, (b) Percentage of men in the sample, (c) Average age in first contact with the law.

Table 2. Extrinsic, substantive (subject) and methodological characteristics included in the meta-analysis

Variables	
Extrinsic Variables	
Authors of the study	Law under the younger was judged
Publication source	Base offense committed
Place of gathering information	Judicial Measure imposed
Date of gathering information	Date of report
Substantive variables	
Average time of recidivism	Violence in the base offense
Substance use (younger)	Victim of Psychological abuse
Victim of Physical abuse	Family criminal records
Physical family problems	Family mental health problems
Family use substance	The younger studies
The younger works	Relationship with dissocial peer-group
Has a couple	
Methodological variables	
Sample size	
Male /Boys percentage in sample size	
Average age in first contact with law	

STATISTICAL ANALYSIS

As described above, the measures of the effect size used in the present chapter is the proportion and the *odds ratio* of proportion or quotient of complementary probabilities. We considered the neperian logarithm of the *odds ratio* for its addition in the analysis and weighted by the inverse of its variance.

To assess the possible homogeneity of the effect size the statistical Q Test (Hedges & Olkin, 1985) was used. Maintaining a null hypothesis of homogeneity will indicate the dispersion of the effect size; in regard to the mean, this is not higher than the expected from the sampling error.

To analyze the effect of the modulating variables on the effect sizes, two strategies were used on the fixed effects model: in the categorical variables, the analogous model to variance analysis for meta-analysis was applied (Hedges, 1982) and, when the quantitative or dichotomy variables were analyzed, we used the simple weighted regression (Hedges & Olkin, 1985).

The analysis was conducted with the statistical software SPSS 15.1 and the macros *MeanES, MetaF y MetaReg* for SPSS described in Lipsey and Wilson (2001). When required, a significance level of $\alpha = .01$ was considered.

RESULTS

Descriptive Analysis of the Studied Variables

The bibliographic search process and codification selected a total of 22 papers which provided 26 independent studies including data from 22,484 juveniles. The selected studies were published during the 1993-2008 period (5 studies were published before 2000, and 21 studies between 2000 and 2008). These studies were carried out under three different laws: Tutelary Courts of Minors 1948, Law 4/1992 and Law 5/2000. Specifically, the studies included in the meta analysis were divided for the law variable as it follows: 2 studies cover data of minor judged by the Tutelary Courts of Minors, 7 studies where minors were judged under Law 4/1992 and 17 studies show data of minors that were judged under Law 5/2000.

The participants included in each study were minors at the moment of the offense and the charging age according to each law was the following: In Tutelary Courts of Minors, 1948, the age was under 16 at the moment of the base offense; in Law 4/1992, the age was between 12 and 16 and, finally, in Law 5/2000 the age was between 14 and 18 years old. The average value of the age variable is 15.12 years with a standard deviation of 1.06, being the median value = 15.8 years old. The minimum value of the age average in the studies is 13 and the maximum value is 16.3 years old.

Regarding the gender of the minors studied, the male percentage in each study is the main reference. The average value for this variable is 89.33% males with a standard deviation of 6.25, taking a minimum value of 76.92% and a maximum of 100%, were the median obtains a value of 90.70% of males.

From each study included in meta-analysis the general recidivism rate was taken (graph 1) to calculate subsequently the average recidivism rate.

As seen in graph 1, the recidivism percentages found in the selected studies vary from 2.4% (Rechea & Fernández, 2000) to 77% (Forcadell, Camps, Rivarola, & Pérez, 2004). The average rate of recidivism percentage is 38.72% with a standard deviation of 18.76 and the median shows a value of 38.73%. The average rate of recidivism, weighted by the sample size of the studies is 23.19% with a standard deviation of 14.14. The recidivism median weighted by the sampling size is 21.11%, being the percentile 25 in 17.65% and the percentile 75 in 26.1%.

The average recidivism rate, according to the gender of the reoffenders, has been calculated in studies whenever possible. In graph 2, the recidivism percentage by gender is shown, with a recidivism percentage among girls between 8.8% (García, Díez, Pérez, & García, 2008) and 33.3% (Romero, Melero, Cánovas, & Antolín, 2005). Regarding boys, the recidivism percentage has a minimum rate of 15.2% (Romero, Melero, Cánovas, & Antolín, 2005) and a maximum of 86.2% (Menéndez, 2007). The percentages are always higher in boys than in girls, so this reinforces the general belief that gender is a risk factor in juvenile recidivism.

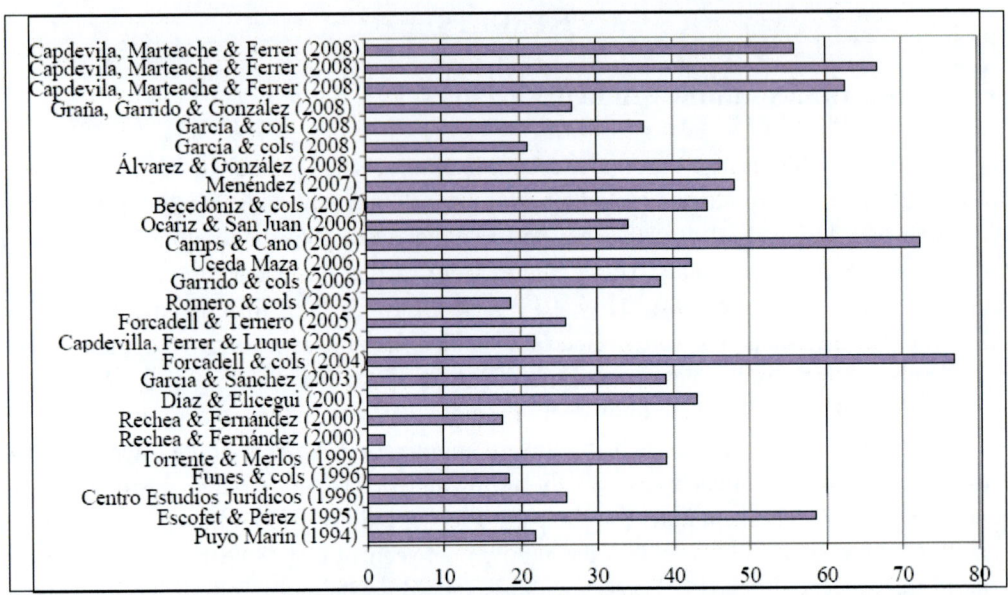

Graphic 1. Recidivism Percentage in every study included in the meta-analysis.

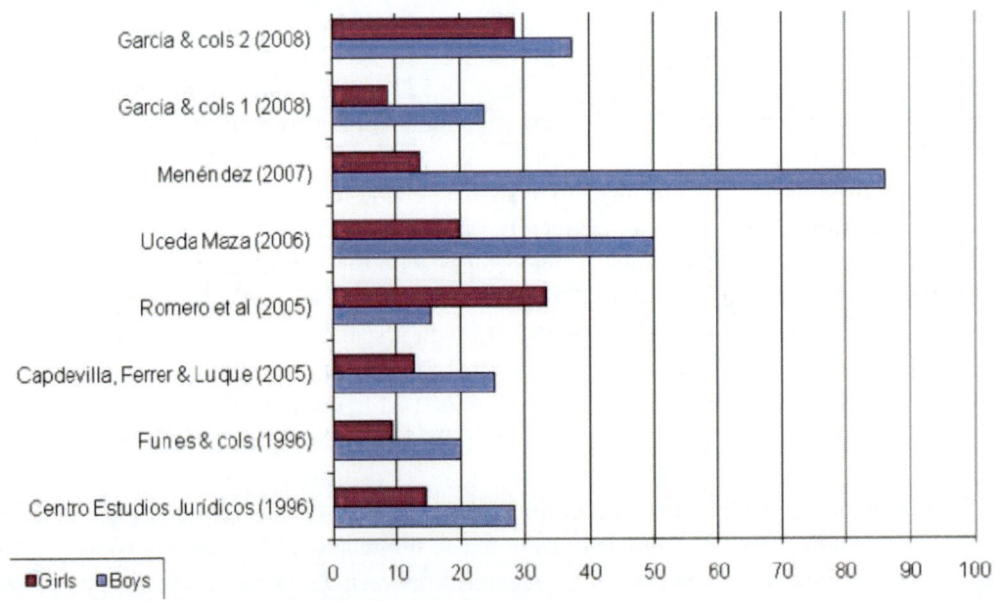

Note: the sample size considered 8 studies with a total of 12728 juveniles.
Graphic 2. Recidivism Percentage in every study by gender.

Table 3 exhibits a descriptive account of variables included in the meta-analysis. Categorical and dichotomic variables are shown with the number and percentage of studies included in each variable category, specifically for variables: *publication source, place of gathering information, judicial measure imposed ,base offense committed* and *Law under which the youth was judged.*

Table 3. Descriptive characteristics (sample size and percentage) of categorical and dichotomous variables included in the meta-analysis

Variable	K	%
Source Publication		
Journal	8	30.8
Report	8	30.8
Book	7	26.9
Congress	3	11.5
Place of collection data		
Juvenile justice reform center	3	11.5
County	4	15.4
Region	17	65.4
National	2	7.7
Judicial Measure imponed/sentenced		
Indicated in the study	22	84.6
Not indicated in the study	4	15.4
Offense/crime commited		
Indicated in the study	21	80.8
Not indicated in the study	5	19.2
Law under which the younger was judged		
Tutelary Courts of Minors	2	7.7
Law 4/92	7	26.9
Law 5/2000	17	65.4

k: number of studies; %: Percentage of studies for every variable.

In Table 4 a summary of all quantitative variables in the study is gathered with the corresponding information about its way of measurement, the number of studies where they appear in and the average value and standard deviation.

Table 4. Description of quantitative variables included in the meta-analysis

Variable	Variable Description	K	Mean (SD)
Average age	Youngers medium age in base offense	18	15,12 (1,06)
Male Percentage	% *Male Percentage* in each study	26	89,33 (6,25)
Family criminal records	% Family criminal records	9	7,19 (10,86)
Violence in the base offense	% juveniles with violence in base offense	7	66,00 (16,07)
Substance use/abuse (younger)	% Juvenile Consumption toxic	17	7,57 (28,49)
Average time of recidivism	Time to recidivism (months)	3	7,86 (1,35)
Victim of Physical abuse	% juveniles who are suffered physical abuse	7	20,16 (12,83)
Victim of Psychological abuse	% juveniles who are suffered psychological abuse	4	6,90 (20,85)
Physical family problems	% Physical family problems	4	19,76 (8,51)
Family mental health problems	% Family mental health problems	9	17,21 (9,93)
Family use substance	% Family Consumption toxic	9	27,43 (14,14)
The younger studies	% juveniles who are schooling	16	31,10 (13,92)
The younger works /is employed	% juveniles who are employed	12	20,05 (12,75)
Relationship with dissocial peer-group	% juveniles who have relationship with social-excluded peer group	11	49,65 (27,03)
Having couple	% juveniles who have a partner	7	19,40 (8,95)

k: number of studies; SD: Standar Deviation.

Effect Sizes Estimation

The weighted average effect size (OR) was 0.8711 (IC95%: 0.8497 − 0.8925), with a weighted standard deviation of 0.919, showing a minimum value of 0.025 and a maximum value of 3.348. The rate v, as a sign of the variance component of the model of randomized effects, obtained a value of 0.91, showing that the fixed effect model must be followed in order to perform the meta-analysis. The homogeneity test between the simulation conditions resulted significant ($Q_{(25)}$ = 7090.2001; p = .0000). In Table 5, the results of the analysis of variance for each categorical variable of the study are detailed. We must highlight that, from the statistical significance point of view, all variables included in the study are contributing in a certain percentage to the explanation of the effect size variability in the minor's recidivism rate: The variables *type of publication, place of data gathering* and the variable *Law under which the younger was judged*, might explain part of the heterogeneity showed by the recidivism rate in the different studies included.

Table 5. ANOVA estimates for the categorical moderator variables

Variable	k	ES	CI95% ES	Q_W	I^2
Source Publication		,8711		Q_B=1000,3437	
Journal	8	,9408	,8986-,9830	1007,886*	99,31
Report	8	1,2540	1,2173-1,2906	4993,679*	99,86
Book	7	,4092	,3713-,4471	87,7301*	93,16
Congress	3	,8587	,7845-9329	,5612	
Place of collection data		,8711		Q_B=5324,3921	
Juvenile justice reform center	3	3,1202	3,0551-3,1854	269,7346*	99,26
County	4	,3551	,2469-,4633	8,6989	65,51
Region	17	,7102	,6827-,7378	1444,927*	98,89
National	2	,3682	,3253-,4111	42,4473*	97,64
Lawunder was judged the minor		,8711		Q_B=43,7182	
Tutelary Courts of Minors	2	,5236	,4183-,6290	75,3416*	98,67
Organic Law 4/92	7	,8902	,8585-,9220	5594,487*	99,89
Organic Law 5/2000	17	,8824	,8522-,9125	1376,653*	98,84

k: number of studies; ES: effect size (odds ratio); CI95%ES: Confident Intervals for the effect size; Q_W: Within-category heterogeneity statistic with k − 1 degrees of freedom; Q_B: Between-category heterogeneity statistics Q statistic for testing the influence of the moderator variables on the score reliability estimates; I^2: I squared index; *p<.01.

Regarding the effect of quantitative and dichotomy variables, the results obtained after the weighted simple regression are shown in Table 6. In view of the results, we can state that all variables analyzed, excepting the variables *family mental health problems, Judicial Measure imposed and base offense committed* contribute significantly and to some extent to the explanation of minors' recidivism.

Table 6. Simple weighted-regression models for the continuous moderator variables

Variable	k	N	β	$Q_{M(gl)}$	$Q_{R(gl)}$	R^2	ES
Having couple	7	3682	-.2529	244,8408(1)*	3581,9537(5)*	,0640	1,7572
Family mental health problems	9	4648	-.0347	5,2069(1)	4323,9308(7)*	,0012	1,5366
Family use substance	9	4648	.2263	221,6455(1)*	4107,4922(7)*	,0512	1,5366
Family criminal records	9	4648	.1382	82,6863(1)*	4246,4514(7)*	,0191	1,5366
Relationship with dissocial peer group	11	5282	-.1718	136,3415(1)*	4483,3284(9)*	,0295	1,4447
Substance use (younger)	17	9264	.0767	28,9852(1)*	4903,3246(15)*	,0059	1,3776
Victim of Physical abuse	7	3689	.6616	525,7999(1)*	675,5016(5)*	,4377	1,0592
Victim of Psychological abuse	4	3401	.2905	79,2274(1)*	859,8008(2)*	,0844	1,0101
Physical family problems	4	3401	.6966	455,6251(1)*	483,4031(2)*	,4852	1,0101
The minor works /Be employed	12	4995	-.5692	406,9198(1)*	849,0408(10)*	,3240	,9761
Violence in the base offense	7	3887	.8059	647,6697(1)*	349,4992(5)*	,6495	,9487
Average age at the moment of the base offense	18	15504	-.2640	469,8641(1)*	6269,2503(16)*	,0697	,9285
Average time of recidivism	3	3253	.7521	454,4250(1)*	349,0389(1)*	,5656	,8893
Male Percentage	26	22484	.4102	1192,8899(1)*	5897,3102(24)*	,1682	,8711
Judicial Measure imposed/sentenced	26	22484	.0020	,0270(1)	7090,1731(24)*	,0000	,8711
Base offense committed	26	22484	.0109	,8474(1)	7089,3527(24)*	,0001	,8711
The younger studies	16	11653	-.2957	153,3808(1)*	1600,2282(14)*	,0875	,7141

Note: * p<.01; k: number of studies; N: number of younger; β: standardized regression coefficient; Q_M: Weighted error sum of squares with k - 2 degrees of freedom to assess the model misspecification; Q_R: Weighted regression sum of squares with 1 degree of freedom to assess the model fitting; R^2: Variance proportion explained by the moderator variables; ES: Effect size (Odds ratio).

If we pay attention to the R^2 rate -the proportion of variance associated to each variable- we can observe that variables with a higher explanatory power are: *violence in the base offense*, which explains a 64.95% of the variance; *average time of recidivism*, which account 56.56%; *physical family problems*, which justify a 48.52%; *victim of physical abuse*, which defend a 43.77%; and *the younger works*, which explains a 32.40% of the variance. According to the effect size rate obtained in the analysis of weighted simple regression, the continuous variables showing higher rates and, therefore, association to recidivism are: *having or not, family mental health problems, family use substance, family criminal records, relationship with dissocial peer-group, younger substance use, victim of physical abuse, victim of psychological abuse* and *physical family problems*.

CONCLUSION

This study was conducted in order to estimate the juvenile recidivism rate from empirical studies on this topic in Spain. This value, weighted by sampling size, has been estimated in 23.19%. The last official figures on this topic estimate minor criminal recidivism rate in Spain in 31.4% in 2007 (INE[31], 2007). As our study collects the historical record of fifteen years, we can state that the data obtained coincide with the trends of official data.

As mentioned before, recidivism is usually interpreted as a success or failure of legal actions imposed to minor judged by the juvenile justice. In this way, a lower recidivism should imply a higher success of those legal actions and vice versa. The meta-analysis study allowed us to estimate, regarding recidivism, an average rate of OR= 0.87, as an average effect rate in the efficiency of the legal action imposed. This estimation confirms, in general terms, that there is a positive effect from the actions imposed to minors.

Regarding the variables contribution to the explanation of this effect, from the homogeneity analysis we can infer that merely passing through juvenile justice does not explain the effect variability found, so that additional modulating variables are to be considered in order to explain it. Regarding the categorical variables, we found that the variable *Law* partially contributes to the variability's explanation, due to the lower recidivism estimated in the *Law of Tutelary Courts of Minors*, which is the opposite for more current laws. From the variable *publication source*, we obtained a higher effect size for the reports, showing a higher probability of recidivism, which results in a higher variability. This type of publications is issued by official institutions, whose data are collected from the Juvenile Justice Reform Center, which considers the commission of the highest serious offense committed, so that this can influence the recidivism probability. The same occurs in the variability provided by the variable *place of data gathering*, which includes the values Juvenile Justice Reform center, county, region and national. The effect size for the studies whose data have been collected in a *Juvenile Justice Reform center* resulted very high, influenced by the type and seriousness of the offenses committed by minors who are residents or by those who have concluded a legal action of internship (Graña, Garrido, & González, 2008).

---

[31] INE: Spanish National Institute of Statistics

Regarding the quantitative and dichotomy modulating variables, these are negatively related to the effect size found, and it would be associated to minors' nonrecidivism. The following variables were found: *the younger works, the younger studies, average age in first contact with law* and *having a couple*. These data coincide with the existing literature in our context, showing that a minor who makes a good use of time, working or studying, indicates that he/she has a normal life. This is a protecting factor, which prevents young people involvement in activities that might lead them to a criminal career (Cottle, Lee, & Heilbrun, 2001; Menéndez, 2007; Ocáriz & San Juan, 2006). A minor who has a couple, reduces the probability of a dissocial group relationship; having a couple helps the minor to have a normal life. Finally, a negative relation with the variable *average age in first contact with law* is consistent with former research pointing out that the commission of a criminal offense at an early age would aggravate criminal behaviour (Capdevilla, Marteache, & Ferrer., 2008; Cottle, Lee, & Heilbrun, 2001; Graña, Garrido, & González, 2008). At this point, we should clarify that the definition of recidivism assumed in this study may reduce the recidivism probability. If the minor commits a criminal offense at 16 and 17 years old, the time he or she has to reoffend within the juvenile justice is shorter, reducing subsequently the estimated probability of recidivism.

On the other hand, among the quantitative and dichotomic variables directly related to the found effect size and, therefore, associated to the variability found in the recidivism of the youth, we discovered the variables *family substance use, victim of physical abuse, victim of psychological abuse, physical family problems, violence in the base offense, average time to reoffend* and finally, *male percentage*. The data unveiled in our study coincide with the revised bibliography, because there is a consensus among researchers in agreeing that boys are more violent than girls. Boys commit more offenses and, consequently, reoffend more than girls (Becedóniz *et al.*, 2007, Capdevilla, Marteache, & Ferrer., 2008; García, Díez, Pérez, & García, 2008). Regarding family variables (*family substance use , victim of physical abuse, family physical problems*) it is a fact in the literature that a problematic family environment leads to this type of situations and family dysfunction starts to be demonstrated in adolescence with behavioral problems many times related to the juvenile justice area (Martín, Martínez, López, Martínez, & Martín, 1997; Torrubia, 2004).

In this chapter we presented variables studied in relation to juvenile recidivism in Spain. These variables explain part of the effects size of the variability of studies, with the purpose of identifying and working with them, in order to deal with research related to this study that might be found in the management and prediction of the minor recidivism risk, through tools designed and planned to highlight the clinical structured assessment model (*SAVRY*. Bartel, Forth, & Borum, 2003). The aim of these tools is to identify the risk and/or protective factors for minors. The risk factors are grouped into historical, contextual and personal factors. The results found in this meta analysis coincide with the results from former research validating the tool of recidivism risk prediction in minors (Dolan & Rennie, 2008; Gammelgård, Weitzman-Henelius, & Kaltiala-Heino, 2008; Lodewijks, Doreleijers, Ruiter, & Borum, 2008; Meyers & Schmidt, 2008; Vallés & Hilterman, 2007; Viljoen, Scalora, Ullman, Cuadra, Bader, Chavez, & Lawrence, 2008; Welsh, Schmidt, McKinnon, Chattha, & Meyers, 2008). This research has shown that the risk factors proposed by *SAVRY* are related to future recidivism of the offender. The historical risk factors are *History of violence, history of Nonviolent offending, Early initiation of violence, Past supervision/intervention failures, History of self-harm or suicide attempts, Exposure to violence at home, Childhood history of maltreatment, Parental/caregiver criminality, Early caregiver disruption, Poor school achievement*. In our meta analysis, we have found the variables *family use substance, victim of physical abuse, victim of psychological abuse, physical family problems, violence in the base offense, average time in reoffending* associated to the variability found in minors' recidivism, as well as the variable *the younger studies* is related to their non-recidivism; so they could be related to the historical risk factors of the *SAVRY*. As historical factors, they are considered as experimented by the youth; thus, a change in them is not possible. Therefore, the efforts focusing on this type of factors -to prevent juvenile recidivism- are *little productive* (Cottle *et al.*, 2001).

Among the *SAVRY* social and contextual risk factors, the variables P*eer delinquency, Peer rejection, Stress and poor coping, Poor parental management, Lack of personal/social support* and *Community disorganization* are mentioned In our study, we found that the variable *dissocial peer group relationship* is related to youth recidivism.

Finally, the individual risk factors proposed by *SAVRY* are *Negative attitudes, Risk taking/impulsivity, Substance-use difficulties, Anger management problems, Low empathy/remorse, Attention deficit/hyperactivity difficulties, Poor compliance,* and *Low interest/commitment to school or job*. In this study, we have found that the variable *youth substance use* is related to future recidivism of the minor. The variables *the youth studies and the youth works* are related to non-recidivism, coinciding, partly with the individual risk factors from *SAVRY*.

In this study, a meta-analytic study has been presented with the articles that have quantitatively studied juvenile recidivism in the Spanish Juvenile Justice. The information included may be useful for researchers working in the area of juvenile recidivism and for specialists who directly deal with problems in the juvenile justice sphere. The study includes a systematic and detailed analysis review of research conducted in Spain and can be used as a scheme in international studies.

We have also pointed out that this study has been conceived with the scope of having a general overview about the state-of-the-art in the Spanish investigation on juvenile recidivism, and to set up bases for a new investigation and planning of specific actions in this field.

REFERENCES

*Álvarez, A., & González, I. (2008). Relación entre el tiempo que transcurre entre que el menor comete el delito y se dicta sentencia, con la reincidencia. [Relationship between the time that elapses among the juvenile commits the crime and sentencing with recidivism]. IV Congreso de Psicología Jurídica y Forense. U*npublished document.*

Bartel, P., Forth, A., & Borum, R. (2003). Development and concurrent validation of the Structured Assessment for Violence Risk in Youth (SAVRY). *Manuscript under review.*

*Becedóniz, C., Rodríguez, F. J., Herrero, F. J., Menéndez, B., Bringas, C., Balaña, P., & Paíno, S. (2007). Reincidencia de menores infractores: Investigando factores de la problemática familiar. [Recidivism in Juvenile Offenders: Investigation on family factors] In F. J. Rodríguez, & C. Becedóniz. (Eds.), *El menor infractor. Posicionamientos* *y realidades* (pp. 105-121). Oviedo: Consejería de Justicia, Seguridad Pública y Relaciones Exteriores. Gobierno del Principado de Asturias.

Benda, B., Flynn, R., & Toombs, N.J. (2001). Recidivism among adolescent serious offenders. Prediction of entry into the correctional System for Adults. *Criminal Justice and Behavior,* 28(5), 588-613.

Botella, J., & Gambara, H. (2002). *¿Qué es el meta-análisis?* [What is a meta-analysis?] Madrid: Siglo XXI.

Buelga, S., & Lila, M. (1999). Adolescencia, familia y conducta antisocial. [Adolescence, family and antisocial behaviour] Valencia: C.S.V.

Cain, M. (2000). An Analysis of Juvenile Recidivism. Sidney NSW. Department of Juvenile Justice.

*Camps, J., & Cano, T. (2006). *Incidència de l'aplicació d'un programa de control de la conducta violenta en joves infractors.* [The incidence of the application of a programme to control the violent behaviour in young offenders] Barcelona: Centro de Estudios Jurídicos y Formación Especializada.

*Capdevila, M., Ferrer, M., & Luque, E. (2005). La reincidencia en el delito en la justicia de menores. [Recidivism in juvenile justice] *Colección Justicia y Sociedad.* Barcelona: Centro de Estudios Jurídicos y Formación Especializada.

*Capdevila, M., Marteache, N., & Ferrer. M. (2008). Evolució del perfil dels joves infractors ingressats en centres educatius y taxa de reincidencia. [Evolution of Juveniles sentenced with deprivation of liberty profile and recidivism rates] *Justidata,* 48.

*Centro de Estudios Jurídicos y Formación Especializada. (1996) Població que arriba a la justícia de menors. 1 de juny de 1994-31 de maig de 1995. [Juvenile Justice Population. 1/June/1994-31/May/1995] *Justidada,* 14. Departamento de Justicia. Generalitat de Cataluña.

Cooper, H.M. (1989). Integrating Research: A Guide for Literature Reviews (2ª ed.). Beverly Hills, CA: Sage.

Cooper, H., & Hedges, L.V. (Eds.) (1994). *The handbook of research synthesis.* New York: Russell Sage Foundaton.

Correctional Service of Canada (1989). The Statistical information for Recidivism Scale (SIR). Correctional Service Canada Web.

Correctional Service of Canada (1993a). So you want to know the recidivism rate. Correctional Service Canada Web.

Correctional Service of Canada (1993b). The Life Span of Criminal Behavior: What do we know?. Correctional Service Canada Web.

Correctional Service of Canada (1993c). Recidivism: How inmates see it. Correctional Service Canada Web.

Cottle, C., Lee, R., & Heilbrun, K. (2001). The Prediction of Criminal Recividism in Juveniles: A Meta-Analysis. *Criminal Justice and Behavior,* 28(3), 367-394.

*Díaz, O., & Elícegui, M (2001). Desarrollo moral en menores infractores: Una aproximación empírica a partir de Kohlberg. [Moral thinking in under-age transgressors: An empiric approach based on Kohlberg] Actas del IV Congreso Iberoamercano de Psicología Jurídica, pp. 139-164.

Dolan, M. C., & Rennie, C. E. (2008). The Structured Assessment of Violence Risk in Youth (SAVRY) as a predictor of recidivism in a UK cohort of adolescent offenders with conduct disorder. *Psychological Assessment, 20,* 35-46.

Durlak, J. A., & Lipsey, M. W. (1991). A practitioner's guide to meta-analysis. *American Journal of Community Psychology, 19*(3), 291–332.

*Escofet, J., y Pérez, A. (1995). Menors desinternats del Centre Oriol Badia. [Minors disinterned from the Oriol Badia Center] *Justiforum*, 3.

*Forcadell, A., Camps, C., Rivarola, P., & Pérez, J. (2004). Avaluació de la reincidència dels menors desinternats del Centre Educatiu L'Alzina. [Evaluation of the recidivism of the minors disinterned from the Educational Center "L'Alzina"] *Centre d'Estudis Juridics i Formació Especialitzada*

*Forcadell, A., & Ternero, R. (2005). Sistema motivacional y variables individuales en el proceso rehabilitador. [Motivational system and individual variables in the rehabilitation of minors] *Colección Justicia y Sociedad*. Barcelona: Centro de Estudios Jurídicos y Formación Especializada.

*Funes, J., Luque, E., Ruiz, A., & Sánchez-Meca, J. (1996). *Reincidència: en la justícia de menors. Avaluaciò internacional.* [Juvenile Justice Recidivism. Internacional Assessment] Colecció Justicia i Societat, nº 15. Barcelona: Centre d'Estudis Juridics i Formació Especialitzada. Generalitat de Catalunya.

Gammelgård, M., Weitzman-Henelius, G., & Kaltiala-Heino, R. (2008). The predictive validity of the Structured Assessment of Violence Risk in Youth (*SAVRY*) among institutionalised adolescents. *Journal of Forensic Psychiatry & Psychology, 19*, 352–370.

*García, M. L., & Sánchez, E. (2003). Perfiles de la delincuencia juvenil en la provincia de Cádiz. [Profiles of Youth delinquency in Cadiz] *Revista de Derecho Penal en la red Poenalis*. http://usuarios.lycos.es/icapda/crimi.htm

*García, O., Díez, J. L., Pérez, F., & García, S. (2008). *La delincuencia juvenil ante los Juzgados de Menores.* [Juvenil delinquency in Juvenil Justice System] Valencia: Tirant lo Blanch.

*Garrido, V., López, E., Silva, T., López, M. J., & Molina, P. (2006). *El modelo de la competencia social de la ley de menores. Cómo predecir y evaluar para la intervención educativa.* [The social competence model of juvenile law. How to predict and evaluate for the educational intervention] Valencia: Tirant lo Blanch.

Gendreau, P., Little, T., & Goggin, C. (1996). A Meta-Analysis of the predictors of adult offender recidivism: What Works!. *Criminology, 34*(4), 575-608.

Glass, G. V. (1976). Primary, secondary and meta-analysis of research. *Educational Research, 5,* 3-8.

Glass, G. V., McGaw, B., & Smith, M.L. (1981). *Meta-analysis in social research.* Newbury Park: Sage Publications.

*Graña, J. L., Garrido, V., y González, L. (2008). *Reincidencia delictiva en menores infractores de la Comunidad de Madrid: Evaluación, Características delictivas y Modelos de Predicción.* [Criminal recidivism of juvenile offenders in Madrid: Assessment, criminal characteristics and prediction models] Madrid: Agencia para la Reeducación y Reinserción del Menor Infractor.

Green, B. F., & Hall, J.A. (1984). Quantitative methods for literature reviews. Annual Review of Psychology. 35, 37-53.

Hattie, J. A., & Hansford, B.C. (1984). Meta-analysis: A reflection on problems. *Australian Journal of Psychology.* 36, 239-254.

Hedges, L. V. (1982). Estimation of effect size from a series of independent experiments. *Psychological Bulletin, 92,* 449-493.

Hedges, L. V., & Olkin, I. (1985). *Statistical methods for meta-analysis*. Orlando: Academic Press.

Hunter, J. E., Schmidt, F. L., & Jackson, G. B. (1982). *Meta-analysis: Cumulating Research Findings across Studies*. Beverly Hills, CA: Sage.

Jackson, G. B. (1980). Methods for integrative reviews. *Review of Educational Research, 50*, 438-460.

Katsiyannis, A., Zhang, D., Barrett, D.E., & Flaska, T. (2004). *Journal of Emotional and Behavioral Disorders, 12(1)*, 23-29.

Latimer, J., (2001). A meta-analytic examination of youth delinquency, family treatment, and recidivism. Canadian Journal of Criminology, 43(2), 237-253.

Lipsey, M. W. (1994). "Identifying potentially interesting variables and analysis opportunities", en H. Cooper y L. V. Hedges (eds.), *The Handbood of Research Synthesis,* Nueva York: Russell Sage Foundation.

Lipsey, M. W., & Wilson, D.B. (2001). *Practical meta-analysis*. Thousand Oaks, CA: Sage.

Lodewijks, H.P.B., Doreleijers, T.A.H., de Ruiter, C., & Borum, R. (2008). Predictive validity of the Structured Assessment of Violence Risk in Youth (SAVRY) during residential treatment. *International Journal of Law and Psychiatry, 31,* 263-271.

Marín, F., & Sánchez-Meca, J. (1999). Averaging dependent effect sizes in meta-analysis: A cautionary note about procedures. *Spanish Journal of Psychology, 2,* 32-38.

Martín, A., Martínez, J.M., López, J.S., Martínez, M.J., & Martín, J.M. (1997). Comportamientos de riesgo: violencia, prácticas sexuales de riesgo y consumo de drogas ilegales en la juventud. [Risk behaviors: violence, risky sexual behaviors and illegal drug use in youth] Madrid: Entinema.

Marín, F., Sánchez-Meca, J., Huedo, T., & Fernández, I. (2007). Meta-análisis: ¿Dónde estamos y hacia dónde vamos?. [Meta-analysis: where are we now and where are we going to?] In A. Borges Del Rosal, & P. Prieto Marañón, (Eds.), *Psicología y Ciencias Afines en los Albores del S. XXI*. La Laguna: Grupo Editorial Universitario (pp. 87-102).

*Menéndez, B. (2007). Menores y actividad delictiva en el Principado de Asturias: Análisis de las variables psicosociales diferenciales en el comportamiento reincidente. [Juvenile and criminal activity in Asturias: Analysis of psychosocial variables in recidivist behavior]. *Unpublished document.*

Meyers, J. & Schmidt, F. (2008). Predictive validity of the Structured Assessment for Violence Risk in Youth (SAVRY) with juvenile offenders. *Criminal Justice and Behavior, 35,* 344-355.

*Ocáriz, E., & San Juan, C. (2006). Perfil criminológico del menor infractor inmigrante: una investigación retrospectiva. [Immigrant Juvenile Criminological profile: a retrospective investigation] In C. San Juan, C., & J. L. De la Cuesta, (Eds.), *Menores extranjeros infractores en la Unión Europea*. Bilbao: Servicio Editorial de la Universidad del País Vasco (pp.57-68)

Olver, M.E., Stockdale, K.C., & Wormith, J.S. (2009). Risk Assessment With Young Offenders: A Meta-Analysis of Three Assessment Measures. Criminal Justice and Behavior, 36(4), 329-353.

Price (1963). *Little Science, Big Science*. NY: Columbia University Press.

*Puyó, M. C. (1994). Características psicosociológicas y tipología de los menores infractores en Ceuta y Melilla. [Psychosociological characteristics and typology of juvenile offenders from Ceuta and Melilla] *Anuario de Psicología Jurídica, 4,* 89-99.

Rechea, C., Barberet, R., Montañés, J. y Arroyo, L. (1995). La delincuencia juvenil en España: Autoinforme de los jóvenes. [Self Reported Juvenile Delinquency in Spain] Madrid: Ministerio de Justicia e Interior.

*Rechea, C., & Fernández, E. (2000). Impacto de la nueva ley penal juvenil en Castilla-La Mancha. [Impact of the new Juvenile Penal Law in Castilla la Mancha] *Centro de Investigación en Criminología*, informe nº 7.

Rechea, C., & Fernández, E. (2001). Panorama actual de la delincuencia juvenil. [Current overview of juvenile delinquency] En: Giménez-Salinas y Colomer, E. (ed.), *Justicia de menores: una justicia mayor. Comentarios a la rey reguladora de la responsabilidad penal de los menores* (pp. 345-367). Madrid: Consejo General del Poder Judicial.

Redondo, S., Funes, J., & Luque, E. (1993). *Justicia penal i reincidencia*. [Juvenile Penal Law and Recidivism] Justicia i Societat nº9. Barcelona: Centre d'Estudis Jurídics i Formació Especialitzada.

*Romero, F., Melero, A., Cánovas, C., & Antolín, M. (2005). La violencia de los jóvenes en la familia: una aproximación desde la justicia a los menores denunciados por sus padres. [The violence of the juveniles in the family: An approach to the minors denounced by their parents] *Colección Justicia y Sociedad*. Barcelona: Centro de Estudios Jurídicos y Formación Especializada.

Rosenthal, R. (1980). *Quantitative assessment of research domains* (New Directions for Methodology of Social and Behavioral Science No. 5). San Francisco: Jossey-Bass.

Sabol, W.J., Adams, W.P., Parthasarathy, B., & Yuan, Y. (2000). Offerders Returning to Federal Prison. 1986-97. Federal Justice Statistics Program. USA: Department of Justice.

Sánchez-Meca, J. (1996). *Avaluaciò internacional*. [Internacional Assessment] Colecció Justicia i Societat, nº 15. Barcelona: Centre d'Estudis Juridics i Formació Especialitzada. Generalitat de Catalunya.

Sánchez-Meca, J., & Ato, M. (1989). Meta-análisis: una alternativa metodológica a las revisiones tradicionales de la investigación. [Meta-analysis: a methodological alternative to traditional research reviews] In J. Arnau & H. Carpintero (Eds.), *Tratado de psicología general I: Historia, teoría y método* (pp.617-669): Madrid: Alhambra.

Schalwe, C.S., (2009). Risk Assessment Stability: A Revalidation Study of the Arizona Risk/Needs Assessment Instrument. *Research on Social Work Practice, 19(2),* 205-213.

Spohn, C., & Holleran, D. (2002). The Effect of Imprisonment on Recidivism Rates of Felony Offenders. A Focus on Drug Offenders. *Criminology,* 40(2), 329-358.

*Torrente, G., & Merlos, F. (1999). Aproximación a las características psicosociales de la delincuencia de menores en Murcia. [Approach to juvenile delinquency psychosocial characteristics in Murcia] *Anuario de Psicología Jurídica*, pp. 39-63.

Torrubia, R. (2004). Els estils educatius familiars com a factors de risc per a la inadaptación social i la conducta delictiva. [The educational family styles as risk factors for the social maladjustment and the criminal behaviour] Barcelona: Centre d'Estudis Jurídics i Formació Especialitzada.

Tournier, P. (1997). Nationatily, crime and criminal justice in France. *Crime and Justice: Ethnicity, Crime and Immigration: Comparative and Cross-National Perspectives, 21,* 523-551.

*Uceda Maza,F. X. (2006). Menores Infractores: Construyendo un perfil e investigando la aplicación de la Ley de Responsabilidad del Menor en el municipio de Burjassot. [Juvenile Offenders: Building up a profile and researching the application of the Juvenile

Responsibility Law in the Burjassot town] *Congress of Social Work in the European Twenty-First Century.* Zaragoza.

Unruh, D.K., Gau, J.M. & Waintrup, M.G. (2009). An Exploration of Factors Reducing Recidivism Rates of Formerly Incarcerated Youth with Disabilities Participating in a Re-Entry Intervention. *Journal of Child and Family Studies, 18(3),* 284–293.

Vallés, L. & Hilterman, E. (2007). SAVRY. *Manual para la valoración estructurada de riesgo de violencia en jóvenes.* [SAVRY Manual. Structured Assessment of Violence Risk in Youth]. Barcelona: CEJFE.

Viljoen, J. L., Scalora, M., Ullman, D., Cuadra, L., Bader, S., Chavez, V., & Lawrence, L. (2008). Assessing risk for violence in adolescents who have sexually offended: A comparison of the J-SOAP-II, SAVRY, and J-SORRAT-II. *Criminal Justice and Behavior, 35,* 5-23.

Walberg, H. J., & Haertel, E. H. (1980). Research integration: the state of the art. *Evaluation in Education, 4(1).*

Welsh J., Schmidt F, McKinnon L, Chattha H., Meyers J. (2008). A comparative study of adolescent risk assessment instruments: predictive and incremental validity. *Assessment, 15,* 104-15.

Winner, L., Lanza-Kaduce, L., Bishop, D., & Frazier, C. (1997). The Transfer of Juveniles to Criminal Court: Re-examining Recidivism over the Long Term. *Crime and Delinquency,* 43, 548-563.

* Studies included in the meta-analysis.

INDEX

A

AAS, 53
abnormalities, 48
abusive, 102, 126, 128, 133, 138, 140, 176, 193, 194, 199, 204, 209
academic, xiii, 12, 31, 34, 96, 105, 108, 116, 118, 143, 144, 148, 149, 150, 152, 154, 157, 159, 193, 215, 225, 237, 293, 300, 316, 321, 335
academic performance, 12, 105, 149, 152, 154, 159, 335
academic problems, 96
accessibility, 246, 252, 304
accomplices, 260
accreditation, 313, 316, 329
acculturation, 200
accuracy, 282, 283
achievement, 8, 10, 11, 30, 34, 108, 116, 118, 175, 178, 179, 182, 215, 237, 316, 319, 325
action research, 213
activation, 45, 146, 247, 255
activity level, 256
acts of aggression, 236
acute, 243
adaptation, 11, 32, 43, 86, 87, 103, 105, 106, 107, 109, 110, 115, 119, 146, 149, 151, 152, 153, 159, 221, 227, 231, 281, 302, 315, 316, 318, 319, 327, 329, 335
adaptive functioning, 80, 85
addiction, 236, 246
adequate housing, 129
ADHD, 16, 34, 35, 44, 46, 48, 49, 94
adjustment, 43, 54, 118, 120, 145, 148, 149, 152, 159, 160, 212, 227, 248, 253, 298
administration, 38, 74, 88, 143, 220, 221, 222, 223, 225, 299, 266, 284
adolescence, 24, 30, 31, 45, 46, 47, 48, 49, 57, 82, 94, 95, 96, 97, 116, 143, 144, 145, 146, 147, 148, 149, 155, 161, 162, 163, 164, 175, 182, 213, 214, 236, 247, 248, 255, 256, 334, 335, 347
adolescent behavior, 116
adolescent boys, 84
adolescent psychopathy, 99
adulthood, 24, 47, 48, 82, 87, 97, 104, 115, 128, 163, 176, 183, 195, 236, 247, 254, 255
adults, 24, 32, 34, 45, 46, 49, 54, 97, 98, 106, 119, 138, 140, 141, 145, 170, 204, 230, 231, 234, 251, 252, 264, 284, 285, 302, 303, 313, 318, 328, 330, 331, 334, 336, 350
affective meaning, 87
affective reactions, 87, 240
affective states, 86, 108
African American, 116
agent, 104, 146, 185
AGFI, 67
aggressive personality, 238
aggressiveness, 27, 55, 95, 146, 203, 219, 237, 241, 243, 255, 256, 261, 262
aging, 16
aid, 35, 74, 182, 187, 236, 246, 297
air, 91, 219
alcohol, 7, 8, 12, 24, 26, 27, 35, 48, 52, 85, 96, 127, 171, 195, 246, 287, 329
alcohol abuse, 287
alcohol consumption, 26, 96, 127
alcohol dependence, 48
alcohol use, 8, 85, 287, 329

alcoholics, 84
alcoholism, 34, 47, 151
alertness, 29, 33, 36, 38, 39, 43
alexithymia, xii, 51, 52, 53, 54, 55, 56, 57, 58, 60, 61, 67, 68, 69, 70, 71, 72, 73, 74, 75, 76, 77
alienation, 220
alpha, 53, 88, 111, 113, 135, 151, 152, 153, 267, 270, 321, 325
alternative, 4, 7, 8, 17, 18, 21, 43, 44, 58, 106, 117, 160, 218, 240, 242, 244, 251, 265, 302, 305, 317, 328, 335, 337, 352
alternative hypothesis, 21
alters, 198
altruism, 6, 194
ambiguity, 273
ambiguous stimuli, 241
American Psychiatric Association (APA), 52, 55, 71, 72
American Psychological Association, 76, 118, 211, 231
analysis of variance, 38, 344
anger, 84, 95, 146, 204, 248, 252, 254, 260, 271, 313
anger management, 204
Anglo-Saxon, 287
animals, 91
anomalous, 33
ANOVA, 29, 38, 344
antagonistic, 3, 19, 22, 23
antecedents, 126, 131, 142
anthropology, 164, 170, 171
antisocial acts, 16, 82
antisocial adolescents, 35, 145
antisocial personality, 25, 34, 45, 47, 52, 55, 56, 57, 69, 70, 95, 225, 227, 228
antisocial personality disorder, 25, 34, 45, 47, 52, 55, 56, 57, 69, 70, 95
anxiety, 12, 35, 56, 71, 77, 82, 94, 144, 195, 212, 213, 215, 223, 262
anxiety disorder, 12, 35, 195, 213
apathy, 169, 221
application, 74, 110, 200, 203, 209, 289, 296, 302, 303, 309, 316, 329, 330, 349, 352
argument, xi, 30, 228, 249
ariel, 76
arousal, xiv, 6, 8, 95, 233, 234, 236, 237, 239, 240, 243, 246, 252
arrest, 55, 80, 314, 328
asia, 218
assassination, 170

assault, 80, 89, 130, 179, 196, 224, 225, 227, 228, 229, 230
assertiveness, 203
assessment, 38, 46, 47, 49, 58, 108, 120, 141, 151, 264, 266, 271, 283, 304, 305, 311, 312, 314, 329, 330, 337, 347, 352
assessment procedures, 305
assignment, 287
assimilation, 244
assumptions, xiv, 7, 104, 146, 264, 281, 290
asynchronous, 11, 12
atmosphere, 86, 236
attachment, 20, 31, 70, 82, 83, 197
attacks, 196, 219, 222, 227, 262
attention problems, 35, 43, 46, 247
attitudes, xiii, xiv, 21, 27, 84, 101, 105, 145, 194, 197, 198, 200, 220, 222, 223, 225, 234, 235, 239, 240, 241, 242, 244, 256, 265, 266, 272, 274, 275, 311, 313, 317, 318, 319, 322, 323, 335, 348
attribution, xiv, 233, 235, 236, 241, 242, 243, 249, 255, 308
attribution bias, xiv, 233, 235, 236, 241, 242, 249, 255
attribution theory, 308
authoritative, 105, 120
authority, 59, 91, 175, 176, 221, 222, 223
automatic processes, 17
automatization, 243
autonomy, 145, 181, 291
availability, 86, 197, 290, 304
averaging, 72, 132, 133, 321, 325
aversion, 10
avoidance, 20, 25, 162
awareness, 85, 260, 274, 281, 282, 283, 285, 294, 296, 319, 325, 327

B

babies, 87
barriers, 128, 140, 181
basic needs, 177, 182
beating, 145
Beck Depression Inventory (BDI), 56, 69, 71, 73
behavioral aspects, 112
behavioral change, 43
behavioral difficulties, 149, 235
behavioral dimension, 84
behavioral disorders, 30
behavioral dispositions, 19, 22
behavioral effects, 245

behavioral problems, 43, 48, 127, 146, 147, 160, 254, 264, 347
behavioral sciences, 4
behaviorism, 27
behaviorists, 18
behaviours, 210, 220, 221, 222, 288, 289
beliefs, 83, 86, 127, 128, 140, 197, 199, 200, 220, 228, 235, 241, 242, 318, 337
benefits, 3, 10, 11, 12, 13, 83, 105, 202, 248, 319, 325
Best Practice, 47, 215
betrayal, 267, 268, 277
bias, 54, 57, 74, 160, 162, 233, 242, 249, 250, 317, 320
bilateral relations, 292
binding, 177
binge drinking, 257, 287
BIQ, 53
birth, 12, 86, 169, 177
birth control, 12
blame, 235, 244
blocks, 37, 220, 224
blood, 171, 231, 252
blood pressure, 231
bonds, 20, 70, 81, 82, 83, 215, 260, 262, 263
boot camps, 312
borderline, 95
boredom, 95
borrowing, 6
bottom-up, 18
bounds, 82
boys, 31, 45, 84, 94, 95, 97, 194, 200, 252, 275, 317, 334, 341, 347
brain, 14, 16, 17, 25, 30, 31, 32, 33, 36, 45, 46, 48, 49, 55, 98, 247, 249
brain activity, 36
brain damage, 16, 31, 36
brain development, 31, 33
brain structure, 49
brainstorming, 296
Brazilian, 212
breakdown, 230, 260
brothers, 182
buildings, 38, 217
bullies, 195, 196, 197, 198, 199, 202, 203, 204, 207, 209, 210, 260, 263, 264, 267, 268, 270, 271, 275, 276, 277

C

campaigns, 272, 301
candidates, 129, 316
cannabis, 163
card sorting test, 46
caregiver, 109, 197, 348
CAS, 35
cast, 161
categorization, 83, 94, 96
categorization theory, 83
catharsis, 6
catholic, xiii, 167, 182
cation, 156
causal interpretation, xiii, 167
causal model, 46
causality, 148
causation, 10
cell, 196, 219, 224
cell phones, 196
census, 127
Center for Epidemiologic Studies Depression Scale, 152
Central Asia, 218
cerebral hemisphere, 54
CES, 164
chaos, 221
cheating, 20
chemical energy, 6
child abuse, xiii, xiv, 52, 81, 101, 102, 106, 109, 110, 112, 113, 114, 115, 117, 120, 126, 130, 138, 142, 210, 223
child development, 127, 199
child maltreatment, 95, 102, 103, 105, 106, 107, 116, 117, 118, 119, 121, 126, 127, 130, 132, 133, 136, 137, 138, 140, 210, 335
childbearing, 20
childhood, 4, 12, 20, 44, 45, 48, 54, 74, 82, 87, 96, 106, 108, 109, 116, 117, 119, 128, 140, 141, 144, 146, 148, 162, 175, 176, 177, 181, 182, 215, 236, 242, 255, 256, 307
childrearing, 81, 93, 105
child-rearing practices, 81
cigarette smoking, 98
cigarettes, 222
citizens, xiii, 167, 169, 180, 194, 287, 305
classes, 4, 58, 297
classical, xi, xiv, 35, 44, 81
classification, 37, 44, 105, 170, 224, 227

classroom, 35, 111, 144, 147, 149, 150, 153, 155, 157, 159, 162, 205, 206, 207, 209, 213, 236, 246, 260, 274, 275, 316, 318, 319
clinical assessment, 98
clinical symptoms, 54
clinics, 70
cloning, 282
clusters, 13, 14, 15, 16
cocaine, 84
cocaine use, 84
codes, 24, 145, 173
coercion, 25, 196, 228, 231
cognition, xiv, 87, 93, 96, 107, 198, 213, 233, 234, 237, 239, 243, 246, 251, 312, 315
cognitive abilities, 32
cognitive capacity, 33
cognitive development, 30, 45
cognitive dysfunction, 47
cognitive flexibility, 32
cognitive function, 34, 48, 312
cognitive performance, 48
cognitive perspective, 121
cognitive process, 17, 32, 87
cognitive style, 197
cognitive system, 282
cognitive tasks, 32
cognitive variables, 248
coherence, 20, 283, 313
cohesion, 106, 159, 160, 162, 200, 336
cohort, 349
collaboration, 25, 104, 266, 289, 308, 309, 316
collateral, xii, 3, 4
colors, 37
combined effect, 251
commercials, 246
communication, xiii, 35, 57, 58, 86, 87, 98, 102, 105, 143, 148, 149, 150, 151, 153, 159, 160, 162, 185, 202, 238, 242, 252, 256, 305
comorbidity, 35
Comparative Fit Index (CFI), 21, 67, 89, 92, 112, 113, 114, 133, 137, 157, 206, 208
compatibility, 14
competence, 106, 107, 108, 115, 120, 142, 162, 248, 296
competition, 21, 178, 180
compilation, 336
complement, 299
complexity, 104, 105, 172, 209, 248, 284, 288, 292, 293, 295, 296, 302
compliance, 18, 109, 348

components, 13, 32, 33, 39, 41, 42, 43, 47, 84, 111, 129, 137, 151, 193, 196, 204, 211, 240, 241, 266, 269, 300, 315
comprehension, 103, 151, 264, 265
computer software, 306
computer use, 245
concentration, 38, 60, 131, 197, 200
conception, 103
conceptual model, 4
conceptualization, 3, 4, 108, 284, 337
concrete, 172, 176, 184, 220, 274, 284, 288
conditioning, 27, 261
conduct disorder, 34, 35, 43, 44, 46, 47, 48, 49, 97, 120, 349
conduct problems, 127, 198, 213
confinement, 36, 220, 221, 231, 327
confirmatory factor analysis, 54, 88, 112, 205, 211
conflict, 6, 8, 17, 19, 22, 26, 55, 75, 120, 130, 162, 203, 222, 236, 242, 243, 249, 255, 257, 300, 317, 336
conflict of interest, 19
conflict resolution, 203, 236, 242, 243, 249, 257
conformity, 83, 221, 224, 229
confounding variables, 239
confusion, 57, 69
congress, viii, 274, 276, 338, 339, 343, 344, 353
congruence, 58
connectivity, 32
consciousness, 290, 291, 294, 295, 296
consensus, 10, 17, 177, 334, 337, 339, 347
consent, 38, 88, 110, 111, 132, 266
consilience, 25
constitution, 98, 210
constraints, 120, 130, 140, 201
construct validity, 27, 88, 92, 118
construction, 56, 175, 228, 292, 298
constructionist, 282
consumers, 223, 239, 246
consumption, 26, 84, 96, 127, 144, 184, 186, 187, 247, 335
contamination, 299
content analysis, 253, 266, 283
contingency, 11, 12, 18
continuity, 104, 115, 195, 291
control group, xii, 29, 33, 34, 35, 36, 38, 39, 42, 43, 44, 56, 87, 88, 244, 248, 287, 305, 312, 313
convergence, 55
coping, 162, 197, 231
coping strategies, 85, 197
corporal punishment, 121

correlation, 15, 20, 21, 22, 34, 51, 52, 54, 56, 57, 59, 60, 61, 62, 64, 65, 68, 69, 70, 72, 132, 133, 136, 149, 157, 158, 237, 241, 305, 320, 321, 322
corridors, 134
cortex, 32, 33, 34, 247
cost-benefit analysis, 228
costs, xi, 3, 8, 10, 11, 12, 81, 83, 87, 148, 228, 284, 304
counseling, 39, 154, 213
counterbalance, 249
couples, 130
courts, 36, 93, 313
covering, 333
craving, 84, 94
creative thinking, 312
creativity, 247
credibility, 295
credit, 282
credit card, 282
criminal activity, 83, 351
criminal acts, xi, 81, 82, 83, 186, 312
criminal behavior, xi, 12, 16, 43, 45, 81, 82, 83, 92, 93, 138, 160, 181, 209, 236, 334
criminal justice, 141, 253, 306, 309, 310, 352
criminal violence, 167, 170, 171, 173, 176, 178, 180, 187, 256
criminals, 56, 81, 83, 95, 97, 162, 175, 177, 180, 183, 199, 218, 228, 295, 302, 304, 305, 348
criminology, xiv, 199, 201, 202, 209, 229, 231, 253, 281, 282, 283, 285, 288, 291, 296, 300, 306, 309, 310
critical points, 303
criticism, 58, 69, 298
cross-cultural, 58, 71, 118
cross-cultural comparison, 118
cross-sectional, 210
cross-validation, 72
CRP, 288
crying, 263
CTS2, 142
cues, 8, 10, 224, 241
cultural factors, 58, 209
cultural norms, 128
cultural values, 181
culture, 4, 12, 103, 107, 120, 128, 147, 148, 172, 173, 196, 198, 200, 206, 207, 215, 261, 290, 327
curriculum, 207, 316
cycles, 117, 222

D

daily living, 137
danger, 70, 82, 86, 167, 169, 170, 179, 180, 184, 185, 228, 275, 303
data analysis, 51, 283, 293, 300
data collection, 283, 300, 318
data gathering, 295, 339, 344, 346
data processing, 283
death, xi, 30, 102, 107, 168, 171, 179, 180, 184, 186, 262, 285
death sentence, 186
debts, 222, 223
decision makers, 284
decision making, 30, 32, 33, 43, 107, 145
decision-making process, 42, 71, 148, 200, 284
decisions, 32, 107, 144, 148, 151, 154, 219, 247, 298
deduction, 295
deductive reasoning, 285, 286, 290
defense, 93, 170, 174, 260
deficiency, 147, 170
deficits, 9, 15, 16, 22, 31, 33, 34, 35, 42, 43, 45, 46, 47, 48, 49, 53, 54, 56, 69, 79, 80, 98, 99, 181, 195, 249, 314, 348
definition, 14, 15, 32, 55, 86, 98, 106, 107, 194, 196, 217, 260, 262, 284, 285, 288, 295, 301, 302, 307, 334, 337, 338, 347
degenerate, 298
degradation, 218
degrees of freedom, 67, 344, 345
delinquent adolescents, 35
delinquent behavior, 79, 93, 95, 164
delinquent group, 29, 34, 36, 87
delinquents, xii, 29, 30, 34, 35, 36, 38, 39, 40, 41, 42, 43, 44, 46, 49, 56, 79, 87, 148, 172, 173, 174, 176, 178, 180, 181, 182, 183, 184, 185, 186, 187, 230, 312, 315, 338
delirium, 54
delivery, 314, 318, 319, 323, 327, 328
Delphi technique, 296, 309
demand characteristic, 109
dementia, 16
democracy, 149, 218
demographic characteristics, 38
demographic data, 89, 112, 155, 193, 205
demographics, 34, 39
denial, 173, 244
Department of Corrections, 224
Department of Justice, 45, 352
dependent variable, 159, 193, 205, 208, 224, 286

depression, xii, 51, 52, 54, 56, 57, 58, 60, 61, 63, 64, 65, 66, 67, 69, 70, 71, 72, 73, 74, 75, 76, 77, 82, 121, 148, 153, 154, 164, 195, 198, 212, 213
depressive disorder, 57, 74
depressive symptomatology, xiii, 143, 150, 152, 157, 159
depressive symptoms, 153
deprivation, xi, 230, 249, 262, 349
desensitization, xiv, 233, 234, 240, 241, 248, 254
destruction, 146, 174, 176, 225
detection, 44, 317
detention, 230, 282, 301, 302
determinism, 103
deterrence, 96, 304, 312
developing brain, 45
developing countries, 218
developmental change, 115
developmental delay, 42
developmental factors, 20
developmental origins, 309
developmental process, 102, 104, 105, 116, 139
developmental psychology, 107
developmental psychopathology, 76, 103, 104, 116, 120
deviant behaviour, 284, 301, 305
deviation, xii, 51, 52, 53, 55, 57, 58, 60, 61, 62, 63, 64, 65, 66, 67, 68, 69, 70, 72, 145, 157, 177, 341
diagnostic criteria, 55
dichotomy, 58, 60, 340, 344, 347
dictatorship, 169
dietary, 120
differential approach, 70
diffusion, 170, 180, 235
digital divide, 255
dignity, 102, 126, 181, 201, 291
dimensionality, 84
diminishing returns, 248
directionality, 239, 242
discipline, 38, 39, 82, 109, 149, 182, 199, 200, 215, 219, 242, 300
disclosure, 76
discounting, 11, 12, 14, 98
discrete variable, 111
discriminant analysis, 57
discrimination, 206, 207
diseases, 54, 58
dishonesty, 55, 59
disinhibition, 7, 8, 47, 48, 84, 234
disorder, xiii, 34, 35, 44, 47, 48, 49, 52, 55, 56, 57, 70, 76, 119, 143, 154, 157, 159, 200, 213

dispersion, 340
displacement, 234, 235
disposition, 19, 20, 177, 261
disputes, 141
distortions, 9, 47, 223, 235, 249, 283, 285, 290
distress, 85, 240, 241
distribution, 58, 59, 71, 155, 169, 171, 173, 226
divergence, 298
diversity, 26, 47, 103, 104, 261
division, 173, 291, 303
dizziness, 195
domestic violence, 8, 24, 125, 126, 127, 129, 130, 131, 137, 138, 285, 288, 291
dominance, 197
donors, 246
dopaminergic, 30
download, 308
drinking, 257, 287
dropouts, 313
drug abuse, 30, 59, 218, 225, 226, 227, 228, 314, 320, 330
drug abusers, 225, 226
drug consumption, 84, 144, 184, 187
drug dealing, 282
drug trafficking, 223
drug use, 195
drugs, 36, 44, 84, 171, 180, 185, 222, 223, 336
DSM, 52, 55, 56, 57, 69, 70, 72
DSM-II, 70, 72
DSM-III, 70, 72
DSM-IV, 52, 55, 56, 57, 69, 72
duration, 37, 86, 240, 313, 314
duties, 101
dysregulation, 54
dysthymia, 57

E

Eastern Europe, 218
eating, 54, 77, 118, 120, 195
eating behavior, 120
eating disorders, 54, 77, 195
ecological, 3, 7, 9, 10, 11, 12, 13, 14, 17, 23, 117, 128, 139, 140, 141, 147, 161, 198, 210, 215, 301
ecological models, 139
ecologists, 11
economic disadvantage, 200
economic status, 304
education, 98, 118, 162, 182, 193, 204, 210, 214, 215, 256, 276, 316, 321, 322, 353

Index 361

educational institutions, 150, 153, 266, 272, 274
educational services, 317
educational system, 260
educators, 210, 251, 316, 318, 319, 320, 321
EEG, 115
EEG activity, 115
ego, 109, 116
egocentrism, 249
elaboration, 172, 203
elderly, 141
electricity, 316
elementary school, 46, 48, 110, 111, 162, 182, 194, 195, 211, 212
email, 143
emission, 48
emotion regulation, 86, 98
emotional conflict, 70
emotional dispositions, 86
emotional experience, 85
emotional information, 54, 74
emotional intelligence, iii, 15, 75, 76, 274
emotional processes, 248
emotional reactions, 85, 86, 248
emotional stability, 93
emotional state, 85, 86, 87
emotions, 30, 34, 52, 53, 56, 57, 70, 79, 80, 85, 86, 87, 90, 93, 94, 95, 96, 97, 98, 108, 109, 152, 179, 234, 246, 251, 317
empathy, 15, 25, 55, 56, 57, 71, 85, 108, 111, 198, 204, 210, 241, 246, 248, 263, 272, 274, 348
employees, 112
employment, 314, 315, 328, 330
empowerment, 117
encoding, 96
energy, 5, 6, 7, 8, 146
engagement, 159
enterprise, 108
entertainment, 202, 249
environmental change, 33
environmental characteristics, 198
environmental conditions, 11, 13, 19
environmental context, 109, 129
environmental factors, 79, 83, 125, 127, 128, 137, 197
environmental influences, 31, 49
environmental stimuli, 18, 33, 43, 85
epidemiologic studies, 71
epigenetic, 11
epilepsy, 36
epistemological, xiv, 281, 282, 283, 296

equality, 60
equity, 209, 274
estimating, 52, 70
estimators, 157
ethnic groups, 218
ethnocentrism, 21
etiology, 12, 19, 53, 54, 55
European Union, 333
evidence-based policy, 309
evil, 217, 231, 243
evolution, 3, 4, 10, 11, 14, 22, 24, 170, 178, 219, 229, 230
evolutionary process, 299, 302
excitability, 235, 243
excitation, 5
exclusion, 15, 171, 181, 196, 198
excuse, 176, 200, 220
execution, 9, 32, 302
executive function, xii, 3, 14, 16, 17, 23, 26, 27, 29, 30, 31, 32, 33, 34, 35, 36, 37, 42, 44, 45, 46, 47, 235, 255
exercise, 172, 175, 176, 179, 186, 252, 337
exosystem, 128, 147, 198, 199
experimental condition, 287
experimental design, 288, 289
exploitation, 102, 126, 147
explosions, 169
exposure, 107, 127, 141, 195, 235, 236, 238, 239, 240, 241, 242, 245, 246, 247, 250, 251, 252, 254, 255, 256, 257, 287, 347
expressivity, 117
external constraints, 130
external environment, 5, 11
external locus of control, 20
externalization, 59, 162
externalizing behavior, 162
extrapolation, 242
extraversion, 84
extreme poverty, 204
extroversion, 59
eyes, 244

F

facial expression, 87, 96
factor analysis, 25, 54, 59, 74, 77, 88, 112, 118, 138, 205, 211, 217, 266, 269
factorial, xi, 152, 329
FAD, 163

failure, 8, 43, 55, 57, 145, 240, 263, 302, 335, 338, 346
fairness, 200, 203
familial, xiii, 9, 14, 49, 143, 145, 147, 148, 149, 150, 151, 152, 153, 157, 159, 160
family environment, 33, 54, 137, 199, 276, 347
family factors, xiv, 199, 348
family functioning, 120, 125, 139
family income, 82, 101, 110, 112, 131, 132
family interactions, 129, 138, 139
family members, 36, 126, 127, 128, 129, 136, 137, 138, 139, 151, 159
family relationships, 140, 238
family support, 335
family system, 106, 303
family violence, xii, xiii, 81, 102, 119, 125, 127, 128, 129, 130, 132, 135, 136, 137, 138, 139, 140, 141, 142, 177, 335
fatalistic, 319, 322
fatherhood, 13
fear, 83, 128, 174, 175, 184, 186, 195, 196, 202, 210, 219, 234, 263, 264, 275
Federal Bureau of Investigation (FBI), 45, 80
feedback, 37, 198, 247, 248, 336
feelings, 51, 52, 53, 54, 55, 56, 57, 58, 59, 60, 61, 62, 63, 64, 65, 66, 67, 68, 69, 85, 90, 148, 154, 182, 203, 219, 233, 236, 239, 240, 242, 244, 248, 249, 251, 252, 254, 263, 274
females, xii, 30, 36, 51, 52, 61, 67, 68, 71, 87, 234, 236, 244, 245, 246, 263, 265, 270, 272
feminist, 26
fidelity, 223
films, 234, 236, 237, 244, 253, 257, 282
filters, 242
fire, 6, 186
firearm, 6
first dimension, 13
first language, 321
fitness, 10, 11, 12, 13, 27, 86, 150, 328
fixation, 56
fixed effect model, 344
flexibility, xii, 11, 29, 31, 36, 42, 44, 85, 104, 107, 108, 111, 247, 316
flooding, 5
flow, 129, 183, 262, 270
fluctuations, 33, 144
fluid, 5, 148, 151, 159
FMRI, 48
focus groups, 282, 296
focusing, 31, 146, 219, 260, 299, 334, 348

forecasting, 283, 309
formal education, 148, 335
fraud, 282
freedom, 65, 67, 151, 176, 182, 302, 344, 345
Freudian theory, 6
friendship, 184, 204, 236, 246
frontal lobe, 17, 26, 27, 31, 32, 37, 45, 255
frontotemporal dementia, 16
frustration, 6, 109, 146, 219, 220, 236, 251, 261, 336
fulfillment, 330
functional magnetic resonance imaging, 255
functionalism, 151
funds, 101, 285
futures, 326

G

gambling, 16
games, 7, 210, 233, 234, 236, 237, 238, 239, 240, 241, 244, 245, 246, 247, 248, 249, 250, 251, 252, 254, 255, 256, 260, 317
gangs, 12, 173, 176, 223
gender, xii, 31, 36, 46, 51, 52, 53, 57, 58, 60, 69, 70, 71, 72, 75, 142, 170, 204, 207, 212, 244, 245, 253, 272, 274, 309, 334, 341, 342
gender differences, xii, 51, 58, 69, 142, 245
gender equity, 274
gender role, 75, 245
general intelligence, 16, 25, 27, 34
generalization, 170, 261
generation, 8, 13, 125
generators, 202
genes, xii, 13, 14, 20, 25, 103
genocide, 55
gestures, 8, 196
GFI, 67, 157
girls, 31, 194, 200, 213, 236, 245, 275, 334, 341, 347
glasses, 144, 154, 255
goal-directed, 32, 43
goal-directed behavior, 43
goals, 56, 85, 108, 117, 173, 175, 187, 238, 244, 261, 295, 318, 319
god, 182
gold, 305
gold standard, 305
goodness of fit, 52, 89, 92, 112, 133, 137, 157, 205
governance, xii, 3, 16, 18, 19
government, xiii, 102, 168, 169, 186, 218, 315
GPI, 67
grades, 31, 149, 154, 194, 201, 240

graph, 341
gratuitous violence, 243
gravity, 302
gray matter, 31
grey matter, 48
grounding, 296
group size, 61
grouping, 269
growth, 102, 151, 219, 228, 293, 336
guardian, 75
guerrilla, 169
guidance, 13, 182, 256
guidelines, 119, 223, 228, 296, 316, 335, 336, 337
guiding principles, 235
guilt, 59, 60, 176, 182, 183, 263
guilty, 179, 183, 221, 238
guns, 180, 186, 290

H

handling, 160
hands, 221
happiness, 330
harassment, 195, 196, 213, 260, 263, 264, 267, 268, 272, 275, 276, 277
harm, xi, xii, 3, 4, 19, 21, 22, 98, 102, 126, 178, 195, 196, 262, 347
harmony, 178
hate, 196
headache, 195
healing, 74, 218
health, 54, 76, 85, 102, 105, 107, 121, 126, 129, 140, 148, 161, 183, 210, 212, 213, 222, 228, 252, 257, 309, 316, 322, 335
health care, 120, 228
health problems, 102
health services, 24, 102, 148
heart, 34, 35, 239, 243
heart, 305
heart rate, 34, 35, 239, 243
heating, 218
heavy metal, 239
hedonic, 10, 12
helping behavior, 246
helplessness, 20, 195
hemisphere, 115
heterogeneity, 344
heterogeneous, 46
heuristic, 5, 9, 19, 148, 296

high school, 13, 88, 149, 150, 154, 155, 194, 195, 210, 211, 264, 274
high scores, 62, 63
higher education, 145
high-level, 17
high-risk, 12, 13, 14, 15, 16, 26, 27, 119, 223, 313, 320, 330
hip, 81, 199, 260, 275
hiring, 316
hispanic, 338
holistic, 310
holistic approach, 310
homelessness, 218, 228
homeostasis, 86
homework, 91, 154, 247
homicide, 30, 80, 170, 181, 225
homogeneity, 340, 344, 346
honesty, 194
hopelessness, 56
hormones, 146, 162
hospital, 56, 70, 76
hostility, 7, 19, 55, 84, 169, 240, 241, 242, 248, 252, 254
house, 135, 231
household, xiii, 98, 107, 125, 126, 128, 129, 130, 131, 132, 134, 138, 139
housing, xii, xiii, 35, 125, 127, 128, 129, 130, 131, 133, 134, 137, 138, 139, 140, 142, 219, 229, 231, 314
human activity, 293
human behavior, 4, 86, 147, 198
human brain, 17, 31, 115
human development, 102, 103, 104, 105, 115, 119, 120, 125, 128, 139, 148, 161, 199
human rights, 121
humanity, xi, 170, 181
humans, 18, 81, 83, 86
humidity, 219
hyperactivity, 34, 35, 45, 48, 49, 85, 99, 348
hypothesis, xiv, 6, 7, 8, 21, 42, 52, 56, 58, 60, 68, 69, 71, 83, 95, 110, 138, 225, 229, 235, 243, 244, 248, 259, 261, 264, 286, 292, 295, 303, 337, 340

I

identification, 83, 94, 170, 245, 253, 265, 275, 313, 317
identity, 83, 160, 175, 221, 223, 282
illegal drug use, 351
illiteracy, 327

illumination, xiii, 75, 125, 129, 131, 132, 133, 135, 136, 138, 139
imagery, 4, 171, 255, 257
imitation, 147, 236, 242, 261
immediate gratification, 13, 16, 84
immediate situation, 200
immersion, 176
immigrants, 321, 335
impairments, 42, 44
implementation, xiv, 93, 139, 284, 289, 300, 304, 305, 311, 313, 317, 319, 320, 326, 327, 328
impotence, 169
imprisonment, xii, xiii, 82, 97, 217, 218, 220, 227, 228, 229, 230, 231, 232, 285, 302
impulsiveness, 14, 16, 19, 20, 30, 34, 36, 43, 44, 47, 52, 55, 56, 71, 79, 80, 84, 85, 89, 90, 93, 94, 95, 97, 98, 99, 127, 146, 198, 257, 263, 275, 313, 335, 348
in situ, 22, 263, 264, 295
inattention, 84, 85
incarceration, 98, 218, 231, 302, 303
incentives, 12
incidence, 105, 128, 138, 144, 149, 170, 194, 195, 202, 265, 266, 275, 349
inclusion, 67, 265, 289, 303, 316
income, 36, 82, 101, 110, 112, 113, 130, 131, 132, 133, 138, 141
incompatibility, 14
increased access, 180
independence, 16, 70, 87, 145, 229
independent variable, 286
indication, 57
indicators, xiv, 10, 14, 15, 27, 29, 38, 42, 79, 89, 92, 112, 113, 115, 132, 135, 136, 137, 138, 200, 205, 213, 281, 288, 289, 298
indices, 46, 60, 65, 67, 282, 293
indirect effect, xiii, 89, 107, 143, 159, 197, 208
individual character, 9, 105, 110, 147, 198
individual characteristics, 9, 105, 110, 147, 198
individual development, 105, 107
individual differences, 3, 4, 14, 18, 19, 74, 255
individualism, 274
inducer, 125
induction, 177
industrial, 7
ineffectiveness, 306
inequality, 71, 198, 255
inert, 5
infancy, 31, 96, 104, 109, 115
inferences, 300

informed consent, 110, 132, 266
inheritance, 218
inhibition, xii, 5, 7, 8, 17, 18, 19, 22, 29, 30, 31, 32, 33, 34, 35, 36, 42, 44, 45, 46, 49, 60, 81, 99, 111, 112, 114, 235
inhuman, 218
initiation, 6, 32, 236, 335, 347
injury, viii, xi, 47, 80, 96, 102, 121, 126, 170, 196, 240, 262
injustice, 171
inmates, xii, xiii, 34, 48, 70, 217, 219, 220, 221, 222, 223, 224, 225, 226, 227, 228, 230, 231, 313, 330, 349
innovation, 143, 298
inoculation, 108
insecurity, 219
insertion, 183, 328
insight, 23
inspection, 223
inspiration, 7, 285
instability, 199
instinct, 26, 180
institutions, xiii, xiv, 82, 93, 129, 150, 153, 167, 168, 169, 170, 185, 186, 187, 199, 200, 221, 229, 230, 266, 272, 274, 301, 346
instruments, 38, 88, 110, 133, 135, 150, 174, 299, 320, 323, 353
insults, 145, 196
intangible, 175
integration, xiii, 9, 103, 104, 114, 115, 143, 150, 152, 154, 156, 158, 159, 171, 173, 262, 265, 291, 299, 300, 315, 316, 317, 322, 330, 335, 336, 337, 353
integrity, 138, 327
intellectual development, 147
intelligence, 15, 16, 27, 32, 44, 49, 57, 76, 179, 185
intelligence tests, 32
intentional behavior, 262
intentionality, 264
intentions, 195, 249, 253
interdisciplinary, 283
interface, 215
interference, 6, 8, 22, 282, 302
intergenerational, xiii, 13, 101, 102, 109, 119, 120
internal consistency, 53, 54, 59, 89, 132, 135, 151, 153, 267, 298, 320, 321
internal validity, 304
internal working models, 20, 27
internalization, 82, 83, 108, 162, 195
International Classification of Diseases (ICD), 55

Internet, 233, 238, 239, 245, 249, 251, 254, 255, 256, 282
internship, 346
interpersonal conflict, 169, 245, 255
interpersonal empathy, 246
interpersonal interactions, xii
interpersonal relations, 70, 106, 147, 149, 197
interpersonal relationships, 70, 106
interrelations, 125, 129, 132, 136, 138, 205, 337
interrogations, 55
interview, 38, 53, 88, 111, 205, 282, 291, 295, 297, 298, 309
intimacy, 134
intimidation, 127, 196, 222, 264, 272, 275, 276, 304
intrinsic, 169, 173
introspection, 71
introversion, 70, 263
inventories, 318
Investigations, 129, 167, 168, 259
investment, 13, 210, 228
IRES, 111, 118
iron, 25
irritability, 34, 55
island, 183
isolation, 12, 15, 104, 107, 118, 131, 139, 145, 180, 219, 236, 246, 260

J

jails, 186, 231
JAMA, 254, 256, 257
job training, 320
jobs, 103, 186
joints, 236, 246
judges, 176, 186, 235, 265, 303, 320
judgment, 8
justice, 128, 141, 214, 218, 253, 291, 302, 306, 308, 309, 310, 328, 333, 334, 336, 343, 344, 346, 347, 348, 349, 352
justification, 55, 169, 174, 179, 235
juvenile crime, 336
juvenile delinquency, xii, xiv, 24, 27, 30, 44, 46, 80, 81, 82, 83, 333, 338, 352
juvenile delinquents, xii, 29, 34, 35, 36, 39, 42, 43, 44, 79, 87, 338
juvenile justice, 333, 336, 346, 347, 348, 349
juveniles, xi, xii, xiv, 29, 30, 31, 34, 36, 38, 42, 43, 44, 80, 83, 88, 311, 313, 315, 316, 317, 318, 319, 320, 321, 322, 323, 325, 326, 327, 328, 333, 336, 340, 342, 343, 352

K

killing, 169, 171, 181, 218

L

labor, 152
lack of control, 54, 304
lack of opportunities, 233, 249
land, 169, 202
land use, 202
language, 183, 235, 236, 246, 260, 292, 321
large-scale, 224, 303, 310
latency, 6
later life, 176
lateral eye movements, 76
Latin America, 30, 102, 167, 171, 218
Latin American countries, 218
law, xiv, 180, 184, 186, 219, 283, 293, 300, 302, 304, 313, 316, 317, 330, 335, 339, 340, 341, 346, 347, 350
leadership, 221, 222
learning, xiv, 5, 6, 7, 18, 30, 31, 109, 117, 146, 147, 149, 159, 160, 195, 220, 233, 234, 236, 237, 241, 245, 246, 247, 248, 249, 251, 261, 262, 314
learning difficulties, 30
learning environment, 195
learning process, 146, 149
LED, 307
legal systems, 301
legality, 186
legislation, 302
leisure, 83, 234, 247, 249, 250, 251, 320, 335
leisure time, 83, 234, 335
lens, 255
lesions, 32, 33, 37
Levant, 75
liberty, 349
libido, 146
life changes, 144
life course, 47, 231
life span, 46, 87, 93, 102, 103, 149, 197
life style, 17, 18, 56, 82, 173, 200, 201, 336
lifetime, 126
likelihood, xi, 9, 14, 30, 34, 35, 47, 82, 83, 86, 97, 101, 130, 145, 147, 160, 199, 201, 241, 313
Likert scale, 265
limitations, 71, 112, 115, 173, 174, 298, 302, 312
linear, 51, 60, 64, 229, 298

linear regression, 51, 60, 64
linguistic, 173
links, 115, 136, 177
listening, 148, 239, 246
living environment, 303
local government, 102
location, 197, 224, 227
logarithmic functions, 71
loneliness, 162, 195, 202, 263
long period, 5, 33
longitudinal study, 48, 81, 84, 97, 163, 195, 241, 245, 255, 256, 257, 309, 310
losses, 10, 11, 12, 14
love, 151
loyalty, 223, 335
lying, 55

M

macrosystem, 125, 147, 198, 200
magnetic resonance, 255
magnetic resonance imaging, 255
maintenance, 12, 83, 127, 128, 200
major depressive disorder, 74
maladaptive, 8, 12, 18, 20, 23, 27, 103, 105, 197
male bias, 72
males, xii, 19, 30, 36, 47, 51, 52, 61, 62, 68, 87, 215, 223, 234, 236, 237, 242, 243, 244, 245, 246, 263, 265, 270, 272, 311, 341
malicious, 8
maltreatment, 96, 102, 106, 107, 117, 121, 126, 127, 133, 135, 136, 138, 140, 141, 142, 348
management, 7, 8, 204, 211, 218, 224, 230, 274, 298, 312, 317, 319, 335, 347, 348
mania, 54
manipulation, 196
marginalization, 147
marijuana, 35, 98
marital status, 101, 110, 111, 112
market, 185, 296
marriage, 130, 225
masculinity, 222, 223
mass communication, 242, 252
mass media, 171, 186, 199, 208
material resources, 13
maternal, 55, 109, 141
matrices, 15
matrix, 60, 136, 298
maturation, 30, 32, 33, 46, 48, 76
maximum likelihood, 51, 60, 67

meals, 130
meanings, 172, 173, 295, 297
measurement, 14, 53, 57, 58, 72, 73, 77, 97, 111, 205, 265, 288, 318, 343
measures, xii, xiv, 15, 16, 34, 35, 44, 47, 56, 71, 84, 85, 92, 95, 97, 98, 109, 112, 115, 130, 132, 149, 160, 218, 222, 238, 283, 301, 302, 305, 311, 312, 316, 317, 318, 319, 335, 337, 340
meat, 17
media, xii, xiv, 71, 93, 171, 186, 199, 204, 208, 233, 234, 235, 237, 238, 239, 240, 241, 242, 243, 244, 245, 246, 247, 248, 249, 250, 251, 252, 253, 254, 255, 256, 257, 289, 304, 341
mediation, 15, 53, 57, 87, 130, 157, 159, 249, 250
mediators, 120, 249, 253, 260, 272, 273
memory, 16, 32, 33, 34, 35, 46, 197, 247, 252
men, 8, 16, 26, 30, 56, 57, 58, 59, 64, 67, 68, 69, 70, 71, 72, 75, 132, 135, 136, 155, 172, 178, 186, 218, 231, 236, 242, 328, 339
mental ability, 15, 21
mental disorder, 213
mental health, 7, 24, 162, 163, 195, 219, 221, 231, 340, 343, 344, 345, 346
mental illness, 218, 220, 227, 228
mental image, 5
mental processes, 215
merchandise, 185
mesosystem, 128, 147
messages, 196, 220, 262
meta-analysis, xii, xiv, 26, 35, 97, 118, 215, 303, 312, 313, 314, 329, 330, 331, 333, 337, 338, 339, 340, 341, 342, 343, 344, 346, 347, 349, 350, 351, 353
metabolism, 5, 33
metaphors, 4, 5, 7, 8
methamphetamine, 26
methodological procedures, 283
methylphenidate, 16
metric, 331
Mexican, x, xii, xiii, xiv, 29, 59, 60, 61, 68, 69, 79, 87, 98, 110, 113, 117, 126, 131, 138, 140, 193, 210
microsystem, 125, 128, 137, 139, 147, 148, 198
middle class, 58, 204, 223
middle schools, 150
military, 5, 56, 76, 186
Ministry of Education, 260, 315, 316
minority, 118, 145, 218, 228, 229, 335
minors, xii, 29, 30, 38, 42, 87, 88, 93, 101, 253, 284, 333, 334, 336, 338, 341, 344, 346, 347, 350, 352
misconceptions, 108
misleading, 300

misunderstanding, 169
MMS, 57
mobility, 197, 200
model fitting, 345
moderators, 26, 198
modulation, 8, 69, 79, 85, 86, 107, 114, 245
money, 24, 83, 91, 106, 151, 187, 196, 218, 222, 336
mood, 12, 35, 57, 74, 144, 154, 219
mood change, 219
mood disorder, 35, 74
mood states, 57
moral development, 250, 253
moral judgment, 249
moral standards, 55, 235
morality, 247
mortality, 13
motherhood, 13
mothers, xiii, 101, 102, 110, 111, 116, 120, 130, 131, 148, 164, 183, 184, 228
motivation, 3, 4, 25, 26, 76, 86, 96, 109, 171, 311, 314, 315, 316, 317, 318, 320, 321, 322, 323, 325, 328
motives, 179, 201
motor control, 35
movement, 5, 169, 239
multicultural, 203
multidimensional, 33, 150
multidisciplinary, 103, 170
multiple factors, 30, 93, 274
multiplicity, 174
multivariate, 13, 14, 15, 105, 108, 211
multivariate statistics, 211
murder, 80, 169, 179
music, 168, 233, 234, 239, 256, 290

N

narcissism, 59
narcissistic, 70, 243
narrative inquiry, 307
nation, 99, 210
National Academy of Sciences, 116, 119
National Research Council, 119, 338
natural, 7, 12, 23, 81, 83, 86, 94, 128, 282, 286, 287, 290, 302
natural science, 282, 286
natural selection, 86
negative affectivity, 127
negative attitudes, 240

negative consequences, 12, 101, 104, 107, 126, 149, 244, 247
negative emotions, 57, 85, 93
negative experiences, 108, 256
negative outcomes, 9, 222, 227
negative relation, xiii, 81, 101, 114, 347
neglect, 22, 43, 46, 102, 117, 126, 127, 130, 142
negligence, 177
negotiation, 107, 185
nervous system, 36
network, 48, 186, 204, 242, 244, 250, 301, 303
neural function, 24
neurobiological, 95, 115
neuroimaging, 33, 58
neurological deficit, 35
neuromotor, 33
neuronal density, 33
neuroplasticity, 249
neuropsychiatry, 44
neuropsychological assessment, 38
neuropsychological tests, 14, 34
neuropsychology, 25, 45, 47, 48
neuroscience, 48, 247, 249
neuroticism, 84
next generation, 13
NFI, 67, 92
NNFI, 67, 89, 92, 112, 113, 133, 137, 157, 206, 208
noise, xiii, 125, 129, 131, 132, 133, 135, 136, 138, 139, 168, 244
nongovernmental, 187
non-institutionalized, 42
Non-Normed Fit Index, 89
non-random, 12
non-reductionist, 103
nonverbal, 170
non-violent, 237, 246, 248
noradrenaline, 146
noradrenergic systems, 162
normal, 4, 6, 7, 8, 24, 54, 59, 71, 76, 81, 82, 83, 103, 105, 120, 125, 128, 149, 167, 169, 173, 178, 181, 184, 185, 193, 198, 200, 202, 241, 242, 255, 257, 262, 267, 268, 271, 276, 320, 347
normal curve, 71
normal development, 103, 193
normal distribution, 71
North America, 194
Northeast, 150
novelty, 32
nucleus, 173, 295
null hypothesis, 60, 71, 340

O

obedience, 221
obesity, 236, 256
objective reality, 282
objectivity, 337
obligations, 55, 83, 319
observational learning, 242, 248
observations, 16, 53, 77, 150, 266, 299
odds ratio, 339, 340, 344
offenders, xiv, 24, 30, 34, 35, 38, 42, 43, 44, 46, 52, 57, 74, 80, 194, 201, 209, 219, 223, 225, 226, 229, 230, 255, 301, 311, 312, 313, 314, 315, 328, 329, 330, 331, 333, 335, 338, 349, 350, 351
Office of Juvenile Justice and Delinquency Prevention, 305
omission, 126
online, 119, 238
open space, 274
openness, 57
opposition, 220
oppression, 171
optimism, 108, 111, 112
oral, 53, 134, 149, 172
organ, 185, 246
organic, 146, 174
organism, 5, 7, 9, 10, 11, 13, 14, 33, 86, 146
orientation, 16, 20, 108, 111, 149, 249, 282, 283, 284, 291, 292, 298, 317, 322, 325, 328
overload, 219
oxytocin, 30

P

Pacific, 275
paedophilia, 282
pain, xii, 10, 81, 177, 259
panic disorder, 54
parallelism, 337
parameter, 60, 66, 67, 112, 298
parameter estimates, 66
parental control, 335
parental involvement, 118
parental relationships, 12
parental support, 116
parent-child, 20, 81, 82, 86, 197, 242, 256
parenting, xiii, 12, 13, 31, 35, 81, 86, 101, 102, 104, 105, 106, 108, 109, 110, 111, 112, 113, 114, 115, 116, 118, 120, 139, 140, 161, 164, 199, 290

parenting styles, 101, 102, 105, 111, 115, 120
partnership, 126, 151, 335
passive, 105, 111, 112, 113, 197, 237, 260, 263, 274
paternal, 161, 176
paternity, 24
path analysis, 51, 60, 64
path model, 69
pathological gambling, 16
pathology, 9, 56, 84, 103, 232
pathways, 19, 21, 30, 104, 105, 107, 113, 117, 140, 291
patients, 16, 33, 37, 53, 60, 70, 73, 74, 75, 76, 77, 84
PCL-R, 56, 71
peer, xiv, 15, 35, 98, 160, 161, 162, 196, 202, 210, 211, 212, 213, 214, 215, 244, 247, 264, 286, 335, 339, 340, 343, 345, 346, 348
peer group, 161, 162, 196, 335, 343, 345, 348
peer influence, 15, 98
peer relationship, 161, 247, 286
peers, xii, 103, 106, 145, 147, 154, 160, 161, 164, 194, 197, 198, 199, 200, 202, 203, 234, 242, 247, 251, 260, 263, 266, 272, 273, 274, 275, 316, 318, 319, 321, 325, 335
penology, 219, 253
Perceived Stress Scale (PSS), 153, 164
percentile, 61, 69, 236, 341
permissive, 199
perseverance, 84, 108, 111, 112
personal benefit, 55
personal communication, 102, 305
personal history, 167, 174
personal identity, 83
personal life, 294
personal norms, 83
personal responsibility, 240
personality, 4, 15, 24, 26, 35, 52, 55, 56, 57, 58, 70, 72, 73, 76, 84, 94, 95, 99, 109, 117, 119, 146, 177, 221, 222, 248, 252, 254, 257, 263, 275, 294
personality dimensions, 94
personality disorder, 35, 52, 55, 58, 70, 72, 73
personality factors, 146
personality traits, 4, 84, 257
pessimism, 60, 73
phenotypic, 22
philosophical, 171
philosophy, 290
phosphate, 33
physical abuse, 97, 117, 133, 140, 141, 343, 346, 347, 348

physical aggression, 94, 145, 222, 223, 242, 247, 256, 270, 271, 272
physical environment, 129, 139, 200, 208
physical factors, 138
physical force, xi, 8, 261
physiological, 5, 8, 34, 35, 45, 47, 86, 94, 144, 229, 240, 251, 254
physiological arousal, 8, 251, 254
physiological correlates, 45, 94
physiological factors, 34
physiology, 164
pilot study, 88
plague, 229
planning, 11, 18, 31, 32, 35, 88, 90, 116, 220, 281, 284, 285, 291, 295, 301, 303, 318, 328, 348
plasticity, 11, 24, 103
play, xii, 17, 32, 81, 129, 143, 146, 182, 183, 196, 199, 211, 224, 234, 239, 240, 247, 248, 249, 250, 251, 260, 263, 272, 294, 315
pleasure, 10, 55, 81, 93
police, 80, 82, 169, 179, 180, 185, 186, 304, 313
political leaders, 71
politicians, 170
politics, 77
pollution, 219, 231
poor, xiii, 12, 30, 34, 53, 57, 59, 60, 107, 126, 130, 138, 147, 149, 159, 167, 177, 195, 199, 220, 224, 242, 263, 290, 328, 348
population, 24, 26, 29, 36, 52, 54, 57, 59, 73, 74, 87, 145, 150, 153, 155, 164, 167, 168, 169, 170, 175, 186, 213, 223, 227, 231, 338
pornography, 26
positive attitudes, xiv, 201, 233, 241, 243
positive behaviors, 106, 204, 247
positive correlation, 136
positive emotions, 57, 85
positive feedback, 198
positive interactions, 145, 148
positive relation, 184, 320
positivism, 290
positivist, 282, 296, 298
positron, 48
positron emission tomography, 48
post-traumatic stress, 54, 276
post-traumatic stress disorder (PTSD), 54, 121
posture, 244
poverty, 13, 147, 171, 174, 176, 177, 197, 200, 204, 218, 228
powder, 7

power, xi, 26, 61, 72, 92, 102, 126, 150, 151, 173, 175, 176, 178, 179, 180, 187, 195, 196, 197, 199, 202, 221, 223, 232, 247, 259, 260, 261, 262, 275, 336, 346
power relations, 197, 199, 260, 275
PPS, x, xiv, 311, 316, 317, 318, 319, 320, 322, 323, 324, 325, 326, 327, 328
pre-adolescents, 31, 94
prediction, xiii, 10, 14, 43, 59, 79, 95, 99, 160, 198, 208, 283, 296, 334, 335, 347, 350
predictive model, 150, 350
predictive validity, 350
predictors, xii, 23, 35, 64, 69, 79, 80, 87, 94, 117, 121, 127, 200, 213, 254, 314, 322, 350
preference, 11, 15, 206, 211, 245, 254
prefrontal cortex, 24, 26, 31, 32, 33, 34, 46, 76, 247
pregnancy, 12, 20, 82, 134, 236
preparedness, 11, 24
preschool, 35, 49, 109, 115, 212
preschool children, 35, 49
preschoolers, 98, 245
president, 38, 88, 168
pressure, 83, 145, 180, 184, 209, 219, 231
prestige, 4, 187
preventive, 10, 105, 213, 289, 301, 302, 303
primacy, 96, 99
primary school, 195, 215
priming, 235, 243, 248
prior knowledge, 247
prison environment, 219, 220, 230
prisoners, xiii, 56, 186, 217, 218, 219, 220, 221, 222, 223, 224, 225, 227, 228, 313, 315, 328, 330
prisons, xii, xiii, 217, 218, 219, 220, 221, 222, 223, 224, 227, 228, 229, 230, 231, 312, 330
private, xiii, 93, 125, 128, 129, 130, 131, 132, 133, 134, 135, 136, 138, 139, 145, 167, 187, 194, 196, 218, 219, 263, 265, 303
privatization, 228, 229, 230, 302
probability, 18, 67, 98, 103, 106, 147, 150, 240, 242, 249, 339, 346, 347
probation, 301
problem behavior, 24, 46, 164, 215
problem-solving, 32, 109, 197, 199, 203, 204, 242, 247, 250, 312, 313
problem-solving skills, 199, 203, 204, 312
problem-solving strategies, 109
processing deficits, 53
production, 13, 290, 298, 336
productivity, 148
profit, 186, 223

program, xii, xiv, 60, 111, 117, 153, 161, 203, 204, 213, 214, 257, 259, 284, 287, 292, 303, 304, 305, 306, 308, 311, 312, 315, 316, 317, 318, 319, 320, 323, 325, 326, 327, 328, 329, 330
proliferation, 180, 186, 282
promoter, xiii, 126
property, viii, 30, 81, 88, 89, 148, 225, 226, 286, 336
property crimes, 81, 89
prophylactic, 7
propriety, 16
prosocial behavior, 8, 237, 238, 245, 246, 251, 255, 256
prostitution, 288
protection, 107, 129, 180, 182
protective factors, 102, 103, 104, 106, 107, 108, 112, 113, 114, 115, 304, 311, 315, 317, 320, 321, 322, 323, 325, 328, 334, 347
protective role, 106
prototype, 70
provocation, 6
PSD, 326
psychiatric illness, 54, 77
psychiatrist, 54
psychic energy, 6
psychoanalysis, 75, 76
psychological development, 33, 103, 107, 108
psychological distress, 161
psychological problems, 102, 195, 264, 267, 268, 277
psychological variables, 149, 311, 317, 322
psychological well-being, 148
psychologist, 93, 96, 99, 140, 201
psychology, xi, xii, xiv, 10, 11, 24, 27, 33, 46, 51, 56, 59, 70, 75, 96, 103, 116, 117, 119, 139, 141, 164, 214, 231, 232, 265, 276, 282, 283, 296, 300, 306, 307, 309, 314, 328, 330
psychometric properties, 54, 71, 152
psychopathology, 34, 55, 57, 73, 82, 103, 116, 119, 308
psychopathy, xii, 26, 27, 31, 34, 51, 52, 55, 56, 57, 58, 60, 61, 64, 65, 66, 67, 68, 69, 70, 71, 72, 74, 76, 184, 224, 227, 230
psychopharmacology, 48
psychophysiology, 98
psychosocial variables, 150, 160, 351
psychosomatic, 53, 55, 58, 72, 73, 74, 75, 77, 195
psychotherapy, 53, 74, 77
psychoticism, 25, 84, 263
puberty, 30

public, 48, 88, 91, 118, 128, 141, 145, 150, 168, 186, 194, 204, 246, 249, 250, 252, 265, 287, 292, 303
public health, 48, 246
public opinion, 168
public policy, 118, 141
public schools, 150, 194, 204
public service, 303
publishers, 96
punishment, 35, 82, 105, 117, 121, 127, 129, 184, 199, 217, 222, 301, 312, 330
punitive, 106, 109, 128

Q

qualitative research, 283, 291, 292, 293, 294, 295, 296, 300, 307, 308, 309, 310
quality of life, 125, 128, 129
quantitative estimation, 320
quantitative research, 289, 291
quantitative technique, 299
questioning, 148
questionnaire, 24, 27, 36, 74, 111, 150, 151, 153, 224, 256, 259, 265, 266, 275, 283, 287, 288, 311, 317, 318, 319, 321, 326

R

race, 26, 35, 83, 207, 224, 285, 335
radio, 131, 135
rain, 32, 36
random, 150, 194, 224, 287, 288, 300, 305
random assignment, 305
range, xi, 13, 59, 70, 71, 72, 90, 91, 128, 133, 151, 152, 170, 234, 236, 246, 264, 283, 300, 315, 323
rape, 19, 288
rating scale, 26
ratings, 94, 254
Rational Choice Theory, 201, 209
rationality, 10, 169, 173, 186
rats, 223
reaction time, 36, 39, 41, 42
reactivity, 79, 81, 85
reading, 46, 98, 247, 249, 317, 321
reality, 75, 167, 171, 180, 186, 196, 198, 210, 243, 260, 274, 281, 282, 283, 285, 286, 289, 290, 291, 292, 293, 294, 297, 307
reasoning, 173, 285, 286, 290, 292, 312, 328
rebel, 175
recall, 213

receptors, 30
recidivism, xiv, 229, 301, 302, 305, 306, 312, 313, 314, 315, 330, 333, 334, 335, 336, 337, 338, 339, 340, 341, 343, 344, 345, 346, 347, 348, 349, 350, 351
recidivism rate, 333, 334, 337, 338, 341, 344, 346, 349
recognition, 81, 82, 174, 175, 178, 301
reconciliation, 275
reconstruction, 275
reconviction, 330
recovery, 119
recreational, 83, 199
recycling, 98
reflection, 170, 171, 182, 264, 271, 274, 327, 350
reforms, 218
refuge, 185
regeneration, 183
regional, 315, 316
regression, 51, 60, 64, 65, 69, 208, 322, 340, 344, 345, 346
regression analysis, 322
regular, 36, 70, 85, 228, 235, 238, 274
rehabilitation, 48, 70, 187, 228, 307, 312, 314, 315, 328, 329, 330, 331, 350
rehabilitation program, 70, 312, 315, 328
rehearsing, 243
reinforcement, xiv, 18, 128, 233, 241, 285
reinforcers, 198
rejection, 54, 55, 59, 145, 147, 162, 175, 177, 326, 327, 348
relapse, 320, 323
relatives, 13, 102, 106, 167, 183, 184, 223
relevance, 73, 127, 178, 217, 221, 229, 285, 336
reliability, 54, 59, 71, 76, 77, 121, 132, 150, 151, 152, 153, 164, 193, 205, 266, 267, 270, 282, 290, 309, 329, 344
religion, 164, 206, 207
religiosity, 108, 111, 112
religious groups, 154
remodeling, 30
rent, 130, 186
repair, 76
replicability, 337
replication, 27
reprocessing, 290
reproduction, xii, 3, 4, 13, 86, 174
reputation, 83, 143, 196
research design, xii, 282, 283, 286, 287, 288, 290, 296, 302, 305, 307, 310, 328

research reviews, 336, 337, 352
residential, 125, 129, 197, 351
residuals, 60
resilience, xiii, 101, 104, 105, 107, 108, 109, 110, 111, 112, 113, 114, 115, 116, 117, 119, 120, 121
resistance, 6, 35, 107, 151, 290
resolution, 203, 236, 242, 243, 249, 250, 257, 275, 336
resources, 13, 106, 109, 151, 160, 197, 207, 263, 274, 301, 304, 335
responsibilities, 105, 151, 183, 295
responsiveness, 85
retaliation, 22, 222
retention, 101
retribution, 185
returns, 186
rewards, 83, 86, 87, 201, 237
rhythm, 167, 198
rigidity, 219
risk assessment, 353
risk behaviors, 15, 85, 246
risk factors, xi, 35, 52, 104, 106, 107, 128, 148, 198, 228, 289, 303, 304, 309, 317, 320, 321, 322, 328, 335, 347, 348, 352
risk-taking, 3, 4, 9, 10, 11, 12, 14, 16, 20, 23, 30, 32, 48, 81, 89, 91, 164
RMSEA, 21, 89, 92, 112, 114, 133, 137, 157, 206, 208
road safety, 316, 322
robbery, 80, 176, 179, 181, 185, 225, 282
role playing, 204, 317
rolling, 244
romantic involvements, 215
Root Mean Square Residual, 67
roundtrip, 207
routines, 202, 319
Rule G, 17
rule-breaking, 225
runaway, 35, 82
rural, 169
Russian, 218

S

sadness, 60, 271
safety, 7, 55, 120, 288, 316, 322
sampling error, 340
sanctions, 82, 330
satisfaction, 81, 129, 151, 183, 315, 318, 326, 327, 328, 336
saturation, 298

schemas, 18, 20, 21, 23, 27, 197, 210, 245, 249
schizoid personality disorder, 70
schizophrenia, 59
Scholastic Aptitude Test, 15
school achievement, 159, 199, 348
school activities, 208, 262
school adjustment, xiii, 143, 149, 152, 154, 263
school authority, 175
school climate, 197, 200, 203, 213, 215
school failure, 26
school performance, 247, 254
school work, 195
schooling, 29, 36, 57, 113, 131, 132, 133, 138, 343
scientific community, 297
scientific theory, 285
scores, 46, 60, 62, 63, 64, 67, 68, 70, 71, 72, 84, 133, 151, 256, 270, 320, 321, 322, 323, 325, 326
scripts, 241
SCS, 31, 37
search, xiv, 5, 27, 81, 93, 98, 129, 144, 145, 160, 165, 175, 177, 225, 263, 273, 296, 289, 295, 333, 334, 337, 338, 340
search engine, 338
secondary education, 315
secondary schools, 202, 215
secret, 168, 244
security, 128, 168, 182, 185, 186, 200, 218, 227, 229, 287
sedentary, 236
segregation, 223, 260
seizure, 169
selecting, 31, 150, 265, 266
selective attention, 31, 33, 34, 36, 38, 39, 42, 43, 45, 46
self, ix, xi, 21, 22, 23, 44, 48, 79, 80, 83, 85, 88, 91, 92, 93, 96, 97, 101, 104, 108, 109, 111, 113, 117, 118, 152, 163, 174, 214, 229, 244, 318, 321, 334, 352
self esteem, 236
self-concept, 148, 152, 164, 197
self-consciousness, 144
self-control, xi, xii, 14, 15, 17, 18, 26, 32, 33, 34, 45, 46, 48, 79, 80, 81, 82, 83, 84, 87, 89, 92, 93, 94, 95, 97, 99, 109, 146, 162, 235, 312
self-efficacy, 108, 111, 181, 197, 318
self-esteem, xiii, 60, 116, 143, 148, 149, 150, 152, 154, 157, 158, 159, 160, 195, 202, 220, 243, 246, 248, 262, 263, 336
self-image, 149
self-monitoring, 111, 112, 113, 115

self-organizing, 104
self-regulation, xii, xiii, 19, 22, 31, 45, 79, 80, 85, 87, 89, 90, 92, 93, 95, 98, 101, 104, 108, 109, 112, 113, 114, 115, 117, 121, 318, 328
self-report, 15, 76, 77, 97, 115, 131, 138, 160, 164, 194, 224, 312, 318, 321
self-understanding, 71, 117
SEM, 89, 111, 205
semantic, 173
sensation, 20, 30, 34, 79, 84, 85, 89, 95, 99, 243
sensation seeking, 34, 79, 84, 85, 89, 95, 99, 243
sentences, 218, 224, 226, 227, 314, 316, 317, 318, 335, 348
separation, 81, 82, 181, 182, 221, 223, 227
sequelae, 102, 121
series, xii, 33, 39, 43, 130, 138, 144, 145, 146, 148, 231, 265, 298, 299, 304, 350
services, viii, xiv, 102, 148, 162, 171, 185, 227, 302, 303, 304, 311, 317, 318, 319
SES, 133, 137
severity, 35, 77, 93, 303
sex, 19, 29, 31, 36, 75, 76, 134, 164, 207, 211, 224, 236, 242, 256, 265
sex differences, 211
sexual abuse, 96, 97, 102, 126, 127, 141
sexual activity, 20
sexual assault, 223, 229
sexual behavior, 12, 20, 196, 351
sexual harassment, 145
sexual intercourse, 12, 236
sexual violence, 8
sexuality, 316, 322
sexually transmitted diseases, 12
shade, 168
shape, 4, 37, 115, 198, 199, 201, 225
shares, 185, 186
shelter, 130, 228
short period, 104, 181, 240
short-term, 11, 13, 23, 104, 239, 240, 248, 255, 313, 316
siblings, 126, 182
sign, 43, 146, 179, 183, 225, 303, 333, 337, 338, 344
signals, 8, 54, 56, 87
significance level, 60, 206, 340
similarity, 56, 305
simulation, 344
SIR, 349
skills, xiii, xiv, 22, 57, 70, 85, 86, 101, 108, 109, 197, 199, 202, 203, 204, 223, 237, 247, 248, 263, 311, 312, 313, 314, 316, 317, 322, 328, 329, 330, 335

skills training, xiv, 311, 316, 322
skin, 35
skin conductance, 35
slavery, 176
sleep, 181, 195
slums, 168, 180
smoke, 88
smoking, 84, 85, 96, 98
smuggling, 220, 223
sobriety, 185
social acceptance, 178
social adjustment, 108, 202
social anxiety, 162, 202
social assistance, 148
social attitudes, 220, 317
social behavior, 4, 14, 27, 87, 139, 161, 199, 242, 301
social categorization, 164
social class, 57, 58, 220
social cognition, 45
Social cognitive theory (SCT), 83, 252, 328
social cohesion, 106, 200
social competence, 117, 145, 202, 203, 350
social conflicts, 22
social construct, 261, 291, 307
social context, 102, 107, 117, 147, 292, 303, 314
social control, 82, 83, 106, 179, 304
social costs, 8
social desirability, 73
social development, 119, 200
social deviance, xii, 3, 4, 14, 15, 16, 17, 18, 19, 22, 23
social environment, xii, 14, 30, 86, 140, 147, 160, 196, 335
social events, 238
social exclusion, 145, 196, 260, 272, 316, 335
social factors, 150, 330
social group, 70, 87, 160, 262
social identity, 83
social influence, 94, 98, 142
social institutions, 234
social integration, 316, 317, 322
social isolation, 107, 236, 246
social learning, 147, 312
social learning theory, 312
social life, 93, 173, 294
social maladjustment, 352
social norms, 4, 59, 81, 82, 83, 125, 200, 257
social organization, 9, 200
social perception, 238, 246, 249
social phenomena, 292

social policy, 26, 105, 299, 300
social problems, 218, 227, 284
social psychology, 161, 171, 252, 256, 291
social relations, 20, 55, 149, 152, 197, 200
social resources, 301, 335
social rules, 261
social sciences, 10, 11, 14, 17, 282, 288, 293, 296, 307
social services, 302, 303, 304, 316
social situations, 21, 243
social skills, 70, 199, 202, 263, 312
social status, 16, 83, 242
social structure, 171
social support, xiii, 101, 106, 109, 110, 115, 117, 121, 152, 154, 197, 214, 348
social work, 93, 105, 283
social workers, 93, 283
socialization, 23, 24, 57, 86, 147, 149, 229, 233, 234, 235, 238, 239, 245, 249, 250, 251, 335
socially acceptable behavior, 146
socially responsible, 106
socioeconomic, 12, 126, 130, 204, 205
socioeconomic status, 12, 126, 130
socio-emotional, 30
sociological, 147, 161, 164, 170, 171, 296, 300
sociologists, 93, 224, 283
software, 77, 293, 297, 320, 340
solidarity, 174
somatization, 54
sorting, 42
sounds, 127
spatial, 201
spawning, 201
special education, 198
species, 8, 13, 18, 83, 86, 146
specificity, 297
speech, 175, 179
spheres, 145
sponsor, 236
sports, 187
spouse, 136
SPSS, 60, 266, 320, 340
stability, 53, 54, 59, 60, 72, 93, 101, 107, 151, 160, 239, 241, 328
stages, 30, 44, 144, 177, 250, 296, 337
STAI, 56
stakeholders, 304
standard deviation, 38, 59, 89, 91, 135, 205, 268, 327, 333, 341, 343, 344

standards, 35, 55, 59, 60, 71, 82, 105, 108, 111, 145, 149, 153, 229, 235, 289
starvation, 176
statistical analysis, 273, 305, 337
statistics, 67, 89, 90, 91, 111, 131, 132, 133, 134, 156, 170, 193, 206, 211, 282, 287, 344
statutory, xii, 29, 42
stereotyping, 285
stigma, 82
stimulus, 5, 10, 33, 37, 86, 87, 88, 219, 261
stimulus cards, 37
stimulus information, 219
stochastic, 7, 11
stomach, 195
storms, 144
strategies, 3, 4, 9, 13, 14, 15, 16, 19, 20, 21, 22, 23, 24, 31, 85, 105, 106, 109, 114, 115, 128, 197, 199, 203, 209, 218, 223, 227, 237, 244, 264, 265, 274, 275, 291, 292, 301, 304, 309, 340
strength, 195, 249, 295
stress, xiii, 35, 82, 106, 109, 121, 125, 127, 128, 129, 130, 138, 143, 148, 150, 151, 154, 157, 158, 159, 195, 217, 219, 220, 229, 236, 276, 282, 302, 335, 336
stress level, 138
stressors, xiii, 118, 127, 130, 138, 217
strikes, 22
structural equation model, 77, 79, 89, 94, 101, 105, 111, 118, 132, 135, 153, 193, 205
structuring, 172, 283
subgroups, 43
subjective experience, 10
subjectivity, 10, 57, 107, 129, 283, 292, 293, 297, 337
substance abuse, 12, 14, 15, 34, 35, 52, 84, 85, 95, 102, 304
substance use, 31, 47, 48, 118, 195, 335, 346, 347, 348
substances, xiv, 339
substitutes, 250
substrates, 44, 48
suburban, 223
suffering, 53, 74, 77, 81, 107, 167, 183, 255, 260
sugar, 187
suicidal, xi, 34, 48, 184, 195, 213
suicidal behavior, 34
suicidal ideation, 213
suicide, 12, 134, 195, 219, 227, 230, 347
suicide attempts, 12, 219, 227, 347
summaries, 295, 296

superimpose, 179
superiority, 14, 174, 175, 197, 336
supermax, 217, 224, 228, 230
supervision, 7, 35, 81, 82, 83, 93, 94, 105, 197, 199, 200, 202, 203, 206, 207, 210, 317, 335, 347
supply, 328
surgery, 36
surprise, 6, 168
surveillance, 128, 227, 287, 303
survival, xii, 3, 4, 13, 70, 86, 102, 126, 146, 223, 230, 315
susceptibility, 102
suspects, 6
symbolic, 53, 73, 128, 172, 253, 297
symbolic meanings, 297
symbols, 177
sympathetic, 162
sympathy, 236, 240
symptoms, 34, 44, 54, 121, 148, 153, 195, 212, 227, 236, 246
synchronous, 11
syndrome, 36, 46, 102
synthesis, 105, 172, 314, 329, 337, 349
systems, 26, 31, 103, 104, 106, 115, 128, 152, 162, 198, 199, 200, 204, 209, 228, 294, 301

T

tactics, 17, 18, 20, 110, 245
target behavior, 242
target variables, 115
targets, 108, 139, 201, 224, 260, 312, 313
task performance, 36
taxa, 349
taxonomy, 47, 163
teachers, xiii, 93, 111, 144, 149, 153, 154, 160, 161, 193, 197, 200, 202, 203, 204, 205, 209, 240, 254, 272, 316, 318
teaching, 94, 145, 148, 149, 182, 236, 243, 246, 248
teaching process, 149
teaching/learning process, 148
technological advancement, 254
teenagers, 29, 144, 147, 211, 263, 266, 267, 268, 271, 272, 273, 274, 276
teens, 12, 234, 236
television, 233, 234, 235, 236, 237, 238, 241, 245, 249, 253, 254, 255, 256, 257, 286, 290
television viewing, 255
temperament, 25, 263
temperature, 125, 129, 131, 133, 219, 229

temporal, 45, 53, 54, 59, 60, 69, 72, 160, 201, 317, 318, 322, 329
tension, 222, 227
term plans, 87
territory, 128, 283, 303, 336
terrorists, 184
test scores, 44
theft, 94, 196, 225, 282
theoretical biology, 116
therapeutic communities, 312
therapists, 140
therapy, 236, 246, 312
thinking, xii, 4, 5, 10, 11, 21, 51, 53, 54, 55, 56, 57, 58, 59, 61, 62, 63, 64, 67, 68, 69, 72, 84, 88, 90, 293, 306, 317, 330, 349
third party, 284
threat, xi, 130, 133, 134, 139, 145, 151, 169, 184, 194, 196, 197, 219, 220, 222, 224, 261, 276, 304
threshold, 5
time preferences, 23
timing, 11
tobacco, 35
tolerance, 16, 109, 170, 185, 203, 214, 221, 274, 313
tonic, 29, 33, 38, 39, 41, 43
top-down, 17
toxic, 117, 343
TPI, 318, 321, 322, 324
trade, 11, 13, 238, 295, 304
trade-off, 11, 13, 238
tradition, 108, 181, 283, 296
training, xiv, 94, 193, 203, 204, 205, 276, 281, 283, 296, 297, 311, 312, 314, 315, 316, 317, 319, 320, 322, 326, 328, 335
Trait Meta-Mood Scale (TMMS), 57, 76
traits, 4, 13, 14, 16, 21, 52, 56, 57, 60, 70, 74, 84, 221, 225, 227, 228, 240, 242, 244, 248, 283, 290
trajectory, 103, 160, 184
transcendence, 249
transfer, 120
transference, 235
transformations, 71, 145
transgression, 153
transition, 119, 144, 145, 230
transition to adulthood, 119
translation, 74, 76, 110, 175, 205
transmission, xiii, 5, 13, 101, 102, 109, 116, 119, 120, 140, 149, 199
transparency, 337
transport, 292
transpose, 288
trauma, 74
travel, 170
treatment programs, 302
trial, 18
tribunals, 93
triggers, 6
truancy, 35, 42
trust, 20, 102, 126, 182
tuberculosis, 218
twins, 54, 74
two-way, 285
type II error, 60
typology, 351

U

uncertainty, 10, 20, 282
underemployment, 13
undergraduate, 51, 84, 85
underlying mechanisms, 7
unemployment, 13, 36, 128
unemployment rate, 36
UNESCO, 102, 121
UNICEF, 102, 121, 212
uniform, 221
Uniform Crime Reports (UCR), 45, 80
univariate, 89, 90, 91, 111, 132, 133
university students, 72
unpredictability, 14, 20, 22, 27
updating, 17, 18, 295, 296
urban areas, 301
urban population, 169

V

vacation, 205
valence, 86
validity, 10, 11, 12, 27, 71, 73, 75, 76, 88, 92, 112, 118, 121, 150, 210, 266, 282, 290, 296, 304, 309, 248, 350, 351, 353
values, 12, 17, 59, 60, 61, 83, 89, 92, 107, 112, 113, 128, 135, 145, 147, 149, 157, 181, 199, 203, 205, 228, 239, 242, 243, 248, 249, 256, 269, 272, 274, 286, 293, 294, 295, 312, 317, 346
vandalism, 94, 144, 235
variance, 9, 10, 14, 38, 53, 59, 66, 71, 92, 93, 103, 104, 112, 113, 115, 138, 150, 152, 157, 274, 286, 287, 305, 322, 327, 340, 344, 346, 347
varimax rotation, 266

vehicles, 13, 292
vein, 129, 314
verbal abuse, 206
victimization, 126, 127, 141, 142, 153, 155, 156, 161, 162, 194, 197, 199, 202, 211, 212, 213, 214, 215, 222, 223, 231, 272, 275, 276
victims, xi, 7, 8, 30, 70, 82, 101, 103, 115, 149, 169, 170, 182, 183, 194, 195, 196, 199, 201, 202, 203, 204, 207, 218, 222, 223, 224, 229, 236, 240, 260, 262, 263, 264, 271, 273, 275, 291
video games, 233, 234, 236, 237, 238, 239, 241, 244, 245, 246, 247, 248, 249, 250, 251, 252, 254, 255, 256
violent behavior, xii, xiii, 6, 7, 33, 34, 35, 79, 128, 133, 143, 144, 145, 146, 147, 148, 149, 150, 153, 154, 156, 157, 159, 160, 161, 195, 198, 200, 221, 225, 235, 240, 241, 246, 248, 251, 253, 254, 261, 336, 349
violent crime, 7, 30, 34, 56, 80, 171, 219, 229, 231
violent offenders, 33, 34, 43, 45, 74, 172
visible, 275, 282
vision, 103, 105, 272, 290
visual attention, 24
visual memory, 35
vocational, 314, 315, 328
vocational education, 328
vocational training, 314, 315
voice, 291
volatility, 79, 88, 89
vulnerability, 105, 116, 120, 205, 227

W

walking, 178
war, 275
water, 185
WCST, 31, 34, 37, 39, 40
weakness, 81, 260
wealth, 171, 336
weapons, 221, 248, 290

web pages, 196
websites, 305
welfare, 13, 249
wellbeing, 106, 140, 148, 193, 194, 214, 219, 301, 315
wellness, 107
western culture, 12, 17
Western Europe, 218
wetting, 195
WHO classification, 170
windows, 128, 135, 154
winning, 271
winter, 131, 132, 133, 135, 138, 205, 219
withdrawal, 323, 326
witnesses, xiv, 172, 259, 260, 263, 264, 271, 273, 274
women, 8, 52, 56, 57, 58, 59, 67, 68, 69, 70, 71, 72, 117, 126, 129, 130, 132, 133, 134, 135, 136, 138, 155, 177, 183, 184, 228, 236, 242, 256, 272, 288
workers, 59, 288
working memory, 16, 32, 33
workplace, 128
World Health Organization (WHO), xi, 47, 55, 75, 96, 102, 119, 121, 126, 142, 170, 194, 261
worry, 144, 180, 223
writing, 144, 265
wrongdoing, 243

Y

yield, 173, 186, 246
young adults, 34, 45, 230, 252
young men, 56, 57, 178, 186
youth studies, 348

Z

zinc, 134